Pakistan Armed Forces

Gallantry Awards

The awards include those awarded
to their Colonial Predecessors

Muslim Soldiers of the Raj

Narindar Singh Dhesi

Published by

The Naval & Military Press Ltd
Unit 10 Ridgewood Industrial Park,
Uckfield, East Sussex,
TN22 5QE England
Tel: + 44 (0) 1825 749494
Fax: + 44 (0) 1825 765701
www.Naval – military- press.com

Copyright: Narindar Singh Dhesi

Pakistani Soldiers

Introduction

The art of appreciating the brave and gallant is not new. They form one of the most important constituents of a nation's stability. History defines gallantry as commanded respect and appreciation. Whether being the appointed head of a clan, raised memorials in honour of the martyrs-brave souls or granted titles, robe of honour, cash awards or medals etc. The recognition of bravery has always been a very prestigious affair, since ancient times soldiers have been honoured for gallantry in battle. Over the years and in different societies such honours have taken many forms, but since the 1850s specific acts of bravery 'in the face of the enemy' by British and Imperial forces have been recognised by the award of a range of wearable decorations. These provide a visible indication both of the bravery of the recipient and of its recognition by the government and nation. All the members of the Indian Defence Force were eligible for, and granted, the British Empire's decorations for gallantry. The Indian Order of Merit (I.O.M.) was the highest gallantry award available to Indian soldiers between 1837 and 1911, when the eligibility for the Victoria Cross was extended to Indian officers and men. Consequently the highest decorations an Indian could get were the Victoria Cross, followed by the Indian Order of Merit, the Military Cross, Indian Distinguished Service Medal, Military Medal, George Cross, etc. The Indian Order of Merit ranks high among the oldest and most venerable of decorations for bravery, pre-dating the Victoria Cross by nineteen years and the United State's Medal of Honour by twenty-four years. The order was removed when Pakistan became independent in 1947. Pakistan instituted its own gallantry awards when it turned Republic. Foremost in precedence were the wartime gallantry awards: Nishan-i-Haider, Hilal-i-Jurat, Sitara-i-Jurat and Tamgha-i-Jurat etc. They can be awarded to soldiers in their lives, as well as, after their death as a result of their bravery and courage fighting for the honour of Pakistan.

During the British times the gallantry awards include the ones which would be against the present sentiments of the Pakistan. They are included; the bravery of the soldiers involved cannot be denied. The colossal amount of the gallantry awards of the Muslim soldier needs to be recorded. In conclusion, let me add that if this brief survey inspires someone to take up an exhaustive treatment of the subject, I shall consider the effort well rewarded.

N.S. Dhesi

Dedication
Clara Rosalind Kaur Dhesi

Contents

Introduction	3
Dedication	4
Contents	5
India and Pakistan Wars	6
Nishan -i- Haider	8
Hilal–i–Jurat	20
Sitara-i-Jurat	74
Tamgha-i-Jurat	118
Indian Order of Merit	126
The India Distinguished Service Medal	227
Victoria Cross	327
George Cross	337
The Distinguished Conduct Medal	342
George Medal	343
Distinguished Service Order	344
Military Cross	352
Military Medal	483
Burma Gallantry Medal	489
Order of the British Empire	491
MBE	494
The Empire Gallantry Medal	498
British Empire Medal	499
Order of the Nile	500
MacGregor Medal	501
The Knights	502
The Distinguished Service Cross	526
Bronze Star	527
The Legion of Merit	530
The Legion of Honour	532
National Order of Merit (France)	534
Croix de Guerre (France)	535
Croix de Guerre (Belgium)	536
Cross of St. George (Russian)	536
St George Medal for Bravery (Russian)	538
Bibliography	540
Index	541

India and Pakistan Wars

The Partition of British India came about in the aftermath of World War II, when both Great Britain and British India were dealing with the economic stresses caused by the war and its demobilisation. It was the intention of those who wished for a Muslim state to come from British India to have a clean partition between independent and equal "Pakistan" and "Hindustan" once independence came. The partition itself, according to leading politicians such as Mohammed Ali Jinnah, leader of the All India Muslim League, and Jawaharlal Nehru, leader of the Indian National Congress, should have resulted in peaceful relations. As the Hindu and Muslim populations were scattered unevenly in the whole country, the partition of British India into India and Pakistan in 1947 was not possible along religious lines. Nearly one third of the Muslim population of British India remained in India. Inter-communal violence between Hindus, Sikhs and Muslims resulted in between 500,000 and 1 million casualties. Princely-ruled territories, such as Kashmir and Hyderabad, were also involved in the Partition. Rulers of these territories had the choice of joining India or Pakistan. Both India and Pakistan laid claim on Kashmir and thus it became the main point of conflict. The ruler of Kashmir, which had a Muslim majority population, joined India by signing the Instrument of Accession.

War of 1947

The war started in October 1947 when Pakistan feared that the Maharaja of the princely state of Kashmir and Jammu would accede to India. Following partition, states were left to choose whether to join India or Pakistan or to remain independent. Jammu and Kashmir, the largest of the princely states, had a predominantly Muslim population ruled by the Hindu Maharaja Hari Singh. Tribal forces with support from the army of Pakistan attacked and occupied parts of the princely state forcing the Maharaja to sign the Instrument of Accession of the princely state to the Dominion of India to receive Indian military aid. The UN Security Council passed Resolution 47 on 22ND April 1948. The fronts solidified gradually along what came to be known as the Line of Control. A formal cease-fire was declared at 23:59 on the night of 1ST January 1949. India gained control of about two-thirds of the state including (Kashmir valley, Jammu and Ladakh) whereas Pakistan gained roughly a third of Kashmir (Azad Kashmir and Gilgit–Baltistan),

India and Pakistan Wars

War of 1965

This war started following Pakistan's Operation Gibraltar, which was designed to infiltrate forces into Jammu and Kashmir to precipitate an insurgency against rule by India. India retaliated by launching a full-scale military attack on West Pakistan. The seventeen-day war caused thousands of casualties on both sides and witnessed the largest engagement of armoured vehicles and the largest tank battle since World War II. The hostilities between the two countries ended after a ceasefire was declared following diplomatic intervention by the Soviet Union and USA and the subsequent issuance of the Tashkent Declaration. Both India and Pakistan claimed victory.

War of 1971

This war was unique in the way that it did not involve the issue of Kashmir, but was rather precipitated by the crisis created by the political battle brewing in erstwhile East Pakistan between Sheikh Mujibur Rahman, Leader of East Pakistan, and Yahya Khan and Zulfikar Ali Bhutto, leaders of West Pakistan. This would culminate in the declaration of Independence of Bangladesh from the state system of Pakistan. Following Operation Searchlight and the 1971 Bangladesh atrocities, about 10 million Bengalis in East Pakistan took refuge in neighbouring India. India intervened in the ongoing Bangladesh liberation movement. After a large scale pre-emptive strike by Pakistan, full-scale hostilities between the two countries commenced.

Pakistan attacked at several places along India's western border with Pakistan, but the Indian Army successfully held their positions. The Indian Army quickly responded to the Pakistan Army's movements in the west and made some initial gains, including capturing around 5,795 square miles (15,010 km) of Pakistan territory (land gained by India in Pakistani Kashmir, Pakistani Punjab and Sindh sectors but gifted it back to Pakistan in the Simla Agreement of 1972, as a gesture of goodwill). Within two weeks of intense fighting, Pakistani forces in East Pakistan surrendered to the joint command of Indian and Bangladeshi forces following which the People's Republic of Bangladesh was created. This war saw the highest number of casualties in any of the India-Pakistan conflicts, as well as the largest number of prisoners of war since the Second World War after the surrender of more than 90,000 Pakistani military and civilians. In the words of one Pakistani author, 'Pakistan lost half its navy, a quarter of its air force and a third of its army'.

India and Pakistan Wars

Kargil War, 1999

Commonly known as the Kargil War, this conflict between the two countries was mostly limited. During early 1999, Pakistani troops infiltrated across the Line of Control (Loc) and occupied Indian Territory mostly in the Kargil district. India responded by launching a major military and diplomatic offensive to drive out the Pakistani infiltrators. Two months into the conflict, Indian troops had slowly retaken most of the ridges that were encroached by the infiltrators. According to official count, an estimated 75%–80% of the intruded area and nearly all high ground were back under Indian control. Fearing large-scale escalation in military conflict, the international community, led by the United States, increased diplomatic pressure on Pakistan to withdraw forces from remaining Indian Territory. Faced with the possibility of international isolation, the already fragile Pakistani economy was weakened further. The morale of Pakistani forces after the withdrawal declined as many units of the Northern Light Infantry suffered heavy casualties. The government refused to accept the dead bodies of many officers, an issue that provoked outrage and protests in the Northern Areas. Pakistan initially did not acknowledge many of its casualties, but Primenister Nawaz Sharif later said that over 4,000 Pakistani troops were killed in the operation and that Pakistan had lost the conflict. By the end of July 1999, organized hostilities in the Kargil district had ceased.

Nishan -i- Haider

Nishan -i- Haider is the highest military award in Pakistan. That gallantry award can only be awarded to the brave men of Armed forces for their extra-ordinary courage and bravery. Nishan-i- Haider is Urdu language word which literary means 'Mark of Lion', Haider is the name of legendary Muslim Caliph Hazrat Ali who is known for his bravery.

Captain Raja Muhammad Sarwar Shaheed

Captain Raja Muhammad Sarwar holds the distinction of being awarded with the Nishan -i- Haider, Pakistan's highest military award, for the first time in the country's history, owing to the tremendous valour that he displayed in the battlefield during the war in Kashmir and achieving martyrdom in the process. Raja Muhammad Sarwar was born in Singhori village in Gujar Khan Tehsil on November 10TH, 1910. His father, Raja Muhammad Hayat Khan, served in the British Army as a Sepoy. Raja Sarwar obtained his early education from Islamia High School in Faisalabad. He had three brothers and one sister. He was married in 1936 and became father to a son and a daughter. He entered into the army as a Sepoy in April 1929 and served in the Baloch regiment till 1941. He was commissioned in the Punjab regiment in 1944 and also got promoted to the rank of Second Lieutenant that very year. In 1946 and achieved the rank of Captain, months before the creation of Pakistan. Once the country emerged on the map of the world in 1947, Raja Muhammad Sarwar volunteered to be a part of the battalion formed to regain Kashmir. He was given the rank of Company Commander of the Second Battalion of the Punjab Regiment. Under his leadership, the regiment was able to force the Indian forces to retreat out of certain regions of Gilgit-Baltistan. However, his battalion faced heavy resistance from the opposing forces present in the Uri sector as the soldiers pushed forward to take over a well-guarded enemy position. As he along with his battalion continued moving forward, the intensity of gun-fire, grenade attacks and mortar fire increased. He received martyrdom on July 27TH, 1948, after receiving multiple shots on his chest as he attempted to cut a barbed wire barrier while making an effort to progress further into enemy lines.

In recognition of his courage, Captain Sarwar was posthumously awarded the Nishan-i-Haider, Pakistan's highest military decoration by the Pakistan Army. In addition Sarwar Shaheed College was named after his honour.

Major Tufail Muhammad Shaheed

Tufail Mohammad was born in 1914 in Hoshiarpur, Punjab. He was commissioned into the 1ST Battalion, 16TH Punjab Regiment in 1943. Tufail Mohammad was posthumously awarded the Nishan -i- Haider, Pakistan's highest military award and is the only person to win the award for an action outside the Indo-Pakistan Wars.

In 1958, Major Tufail Muhammed was posted to East Pakistan as company commander of a battalion of East Pakistan Rifles (a paramilitary force for border security). During his command, Indian troops violating international borders captured a village in the area of Laskhmipur of East Pakistan. On 7TH August 1958 Major Tufail launched an assault, to force withdrawal of Indian troops from the village. He divided his men into three groups and attacked the Indian troops during the hours of darkness. The groups were able to reach the enemy without being detected but as the fire fight started, the group came under heavy fire and Major Tufail received three bullets in his stomach. Despite being shot in stomach, he kept moving and was able to silence the incoming fire from machine gun. By tactically using grenades, Major Tufail was able to destroy key enemy posts. When he saw an enemy commander inflicting heavy casualties to his men he crawled towards enemy post and engaged the enemy in hand-to-hand battle which resulted in the killing of a commander of the Indian Army. He killed him by hitting him with his steel helmet on the face. He continued the operation with his men which resulted in the withdrawal of Indian forces. Despite being heavily injured, he called his junior officer 'I have completed my duty; the enemy is on the run.' He was rushed to hospital but he succumbed to the injuries on 8TH August. Mohammad was buried with full military honours in his native city Burewala Punjab. In recognition of his courage, Major Tufail Muhammad was posthumously awarded the Nishan-i-Haider, Pakistan's highest military decoration by the Pakistan Army. His native village has been named after him and is now known as Tufailabad or Tufail Abad.

Major Raja Aziz Bhatti Shaheed

Major Raja Abdul-Aziz Bhatti usually known as Aziz Bhatti was a Staff officer in the Pakistan Army who received Pakistan's highest award for valour. He was born in Hong Kong to a Punjabi Muslim Rajput family in 1928. He moved to Pakistan before it became independent in 1947, living in the village of Ladian, Kharian, Gujrat. There he enlisted with the newly formed Pakistani Army and was commissioned to the Punjab Regiment in 1950. His father's name was Abdullah Bhatti, and his mother's name was Bibi Amana. He had initially joined the Pakistan Air Force as Airman and later applied for commission in the Pakistan Army. Throughout his career, he was a brilliant officer and stood out among his peers. He did very well at the Academy and was awarded the Sword of Honour for being best in his batch of 300 officers, and the Norman Medal. Major Raja Aziz Bhatti was posted in the Burki area of Lahore sector during the Indo-Pakistani War of 1965. As the company commander, Major Bhatti chose to move his platoon forward under constant firing from Indian tanks and artillery. For three or more days he went without rest. He resisted for five days and nights defending a Pakistani outpost on the strategic BRB canal. On 6TH September 1965, as a Company Commander in the Burki area of the Lahore sector and he chose to stay with his forward platoon under incessant artillery and tank attacks for five days and nights in the defence of the strategic BRB Canal. Throughout the action, undaunted by constant fire from enemy small arms, tanks and artillery, he was reorganising his company and directing the gunners to shell the enemy positions. To watch every move of the enemy, he had to place himself in an elevated position, where he was exposed to Indian fury. He led his men from the front under constant attack from Indian Artillery batteries. Although he tried to counter every Indian offensive in his area, he was hit by an enemy tank shell in the chest while watching the enemy's moves, and embraced martyrdom on 11TH September 1965, and was buried in his native village. In recognition of his courage, Major Raja Aziz Bhatti was posthumously awarded the Nishan-i-Haider, Pakistan's highest military decoration by the Pakistan Army.

Nishan -i- Haider

Pilot Officer Rashid Minhas Shaheed

Rashid Minhas was born on February 17TH, 1951, at Karachi to a Muslim Rajput family of the Minhas clan. Rashid Minhas spent his early childhood in Karachi. Later, the family shifted to Rawalpindi. Minhas had his early education from St. Mary's Cambridge School Rawalpindi. Later his family shifted back to Karachi. Minhas was fascinated with aviation history and technology. He used to collect different models of aircraft and jets. He also attended St. Patrick's High School, Karachi. Minhas was commissioned on March 13TH, 1971. He began training to become a pilot. On August 20TH of that year, in the hour before noon, he was getting ready to take off in a T-33 jet trainer in Karachi, Pakistan. Minhas was taxiing toward the runway when a Bengali instructor pilot, Flight Lieutenant Rahman, signalled him to stop and then climbed into the instructor's seat. The jet took off and turned toward India. Minhas soon realized that the plane was being high jacked by Matiur Rahman, who intended to defect to India to join his compatriots in the Bangladesh Liberation War. Minhas struggled physically to wrest control from Matiur Rahman; each man tried to overpower the other through the mechanically linked flight controls. Some 32 miles (51 km) from the Indian border, the jet crashed near Thatta. Both men were killed. Minhas's Pakistan military citation for the Nishan -i- Haider states that he 'forced the aircraft to crash' in order to prevent Matiur Rahman from taking the jet to India.

Minhas was posthumously awarded Pakistan's top military honour, the Nishan -i- Haider, and became the youngest man and the only member of the Pakistan Air Force to win the award. After his death, Minhas was honoured as a national hero. In his memory the Pakistan Air Force base at Kamra was renamed PAF Base Minhas, often called Minhas-Kamra. In Karachi he was honoured by the naming of a main road, Rashid Minhas Road.

Nishan -i- Haider

Major Rana Shabbir Sharif Shaheed

He was born on 28TH April 1943 in a Rajput family at Kunjah, Gujrat District to Major Rana Muhammad Sharif. Sharif Completed his Matric from St. Anthony's High School, Lahore. While he was at Lahore he joins Pakistan Military Academy. He was commissioned in Pakistan Army on 19TH April. After successfully completing his training he was awarded the Sword of Honour, and was posted to the 6TH Battalion, Frontier Force Regiment. In the Indo-Pakistani War of 1971, the Pakistan Army launched an offensive on the Western front against the enemy. Shabbir, as commander of a company of 6TH Battalion, Frontier Force Regiment, was ordered to capture high ground overlooking Grumukhi Khera and Beri, a village in the Sulemanki Sector. On 3RD December 1971, in a well-organised action, he fought valiantly alongside his men and held Indian attacks at bay. He cleared the Jhangar post with utmost courage by fearlessly passing through the minefield laid by enemy and swimming across a water obstacle, the 'Sabuna distributaries', whilst under intense enemy fire and led his company to capture the objective. During the day, his troops repelled over 15 Indian attempts to recapture the high ground and furthermore, he and his men destroyed four enemy tanks and held two Indian battalions at bay by killing 43 soldiers. During an attack on the night of 5TH December, Shabbir jumped out of his trench on the call of an Indian Company Commander who dared him for a hand-to-hand combat. Shabbir soon snatched the Sten gun out of the Indian major's hand and mortally wounded him. The gallant act demoralized the Indian troops allowing Shabbir's men to consolidate their hard earned gains in the captured area. On the afternoon of 6TH December, the enemy launched another counter attack preceded by air strikes and heavy artillery shelling. After casualties amongst the crew, Shabbir Sharif took over as a gunner on an anti-tank gun and started firing on the enemy tanks. While this fight was on, one of the enemy tanks fired at him causing fatal injuries which resulted in his death at the age of 28. His last words were quoted as: 'Don't lose the bridge.' It was the same bridge he died defending from the enemy's attack. Major Shabbir Sharif was awarded the Nishan-i-Haider for his bravery.

Nishan -i- Haider

Sowar Muhammad Hussain Shaheed

Muhammad Hussain Shaheed was born in Gujar Khan in Dhok Pir Bakhsh village on June 18TH, 1949. On September 3RD, 1966 at a very young age he joined Pakistan Army as a Driver. When the 1971 war broke between India and Pakistan, Sowar Muhammad Hussain was serving in 20TH Lancers armoured regiment of Pakistan Army. Though the 1971 Indo-Pak war started in East Pakistan its flames soon spread to the West Pakistan's border. The battlefield spread from Sialkot to Sulemanki. The 20TH Lancers of Sowar Muhammad Hussain Shaheed was defending the frontline area of Zafarwal a town in the Narowal District. During pitched battles Sowar Muhammad Hussain Shaheed never missed any opportunity to kill enemy aggressor by firing through machine gun without taking care of any life threat. Sowar Muhammad Hussain knew like every other Pakistani Army Soldier the true meaning of Shahadat (Martyrdom). It was December 5TH, 1971 when Indians were on the offense with extreme shelling and tanks firing, Sowar Muhammad Hussain was delivering arms and ammunition to the brave soldiers of Pakistani Army from trench to trench. It is documented by witnesses belong from Pakistani armed forces that Sowar Muhammad Hussain not only patrolled but also participated in most dangerous skirmishes with Indian enemies. On December 10TH, 1971 that Sowar Muhammad Hussain spotted the enemy units near a village Harar Khurd where Pakistani Army laid mines to prevent aggressors from playing with lives of innocent Pakistanis. Instantly Sowar Muhammad Hussain Shaheed informed his second-in-command of 20TH Lancers unit about enemy moves. Sowar Muhammad Hussain took things onto his own and directed accurate firing enemy tanks through his crew. At afternoon the precious time of his life had arrived. Sowar Muhammad Hussain while defending the land of pure was hit by on the chest by a burst of machine-gun fire from an enemy tank leaving an exemplary legacy behind him. Sowar Muhammad Hussain left the prominence of being first Jawan e.g. lower rank soldier of Pakistan Army awarded with Nishan e Haider.

Nishan -i- Haider

Major Muhammad Akram Shaheed

Major Muhammad Akram, was a Pakistan Army officer who was posthumously awarded Pakistan military's highest decoration, the Nishan -i- Haider, for his actions during the 1971 Indo-Pak War. Akram was sent on several missions in the India-Pakistan War, and was in 1971 at the Battle of Hilli.

Ethnically Pothohari Punjabi, he belonged to the Awan cast of Pakistan. In 1959, Akram was accepted by the Pakistan Military Academy and eventually graduated in 1963. He gained a commission in 1963 as part of the 4TH Battalion, Frontier Force Regiment. Mohammad Akram participated in 1965 Indo-Pak September War as a Captain where he led several successful military operations against the Indian Army. While stationed in Lahore, Akram commanded a small company which led several decisive operations against the Indian Armed Forces. In 1969, Akram was promoted to Major of the Pakistan Army. In 1971, Major Akram fought in the war against Bangladesh. In the Battle of Hilli, his leadership, bravery and skilful strategising kept enemies at bay for five days and nights, resulting in the ultimate sacrifice (his death). Major Akram was posthumously awarded the Nishan -i- Haider, Pakistan's highest military honour, for his heroic efforts. During the East Pakistan War of 1971, the 4TH Battalion, Frontier Force Regiment, was at that time was commanded by then Colonel Muhammad Mumtaz Malik. The Battalion was placed in the forward area of the Hilli Municipality (under Hakimpur Upozila, Dinajpur District), in what was then East Pakistan. The regiment came under continuous and heavy air, artillery and armour attacks from the Indian Army. Despite enemy superiority in both numbers and firepower, Major Mohammad Akram and his men repulsed many attacks, inflicting heavy casualties on the enemy. Major Muhammad Akram embraced Shahadat during the action, and was posthumously awarded the Nishan-i-Haidar for his bravery. Called the hero of Hilli, Major Muhammad Akram was buried in the village of Boaldar, Thana/Upozila-Hakimpur (Banglahilly), District-Dinajpur. There is a monument, Major Akram Shaheed Memorial, in the midst of Jhelum city.

Nishan -i- Haider

Lance Naik Muhammad Mahfuz Shaheed

Muhammad Mahfuz was born on 25TH October 1944 in Pind Malikan (now Mahfuzabad), Rawalpindi District. He was enlisted in the Army on 25TH October 1962 and joined the 15TH Punjab Regiment. During the Pakistan India war of 1971, 15TH Punjab Regiment was deployed at Wagah Atari sector. On night 17-18TH December 1971, Alpha Company was ordered to attack and capture 'Pul Kanjri' village in enemy area. The attack was launched on 18TH December, and Lance Naik Mahfouz engaged the enemy through effective fire of Light Machine Gun. A shell that burst near him not only injured him, but also neutralized his Light Machine Gun. The injured Mahfouz crawled to a dead comrade, took his weapon and started effective fire onto enemy position. Lance Naik Mahfouz dashed towards the enemy trench 10 yards away without any covering fire. With a battle cry of 'Naara e Takbeer Allah O Akbar', Mahfouz jumped inside the enemy trench and strangulated the enemy fire using enormous force of his hands. The other two enemy soldiers inside the trench attacked Mahfouz with rifle bayonets critically wounding him. Mahfouz did not let his grip loose and was killed by the automatics firer and embraced martyrdom. The grip of Mahfouz's hand was so fierce that even after his death the enemy soldiers could not free the neck of their doomed accomplice. The sight of Mahfouz himself dead yet clinching the dead body of enemy soldier was a feat of courage and steadfastness in itself. Lieutenant Colonel Puri was commanding 3 Sikh Light Infantry Battalion (opposing force) and witnessed the gallantry action of Lance Naik Muhammad Mahfouz from the forward enemy trenches. After cease fire, enemy soldiers themselves carried the body of Mahfouz and handed it over to, 15TH Punjab Regiment. Lieutenant Colonel Mohinder Singh Puri (Later Lt. General, Indian Army) accompanied the body and remarked, 'During my entire service, I have not seen such a courageous being. Had he been in force, I would have recommended him for the highest gallantry award in the Indian Army'. On 23RD March 1972, Lance Naik Mahfouz was posthumously awarded the highest Gallantry Award of Pakistan, the Nishan -i- Haider

Nishan -i- Haider

Captain Karnal Sher Khan Shaheed

Karnal Sher Khan was born on 1ST January 1970. He was commissioned in the Pakistan Army on 14TH October 1994, and joined the 27TH Sind Regiment. During the Kargil conflict with India, he took up position on top of a feature that was around 18,400 feet high. Starting on the 25TH of June 1999, Indian artillery and the Indian Air Force pounded him and his men for 3 days and 3 nights with unrelenting bombardment. On the 27TH of June 1999, the Indian infantry attacked and Sher Khan's men and repulsed wave after wave of advancing Indian forces. But around midnight they lost part of the feature to the enemy. Captain Karnal Sher Khan successfully reclaimed the lost ground. On 28TH of June 1999, Captain Karnal Sher Khan was informed him that around sixty to seventy Indian soldiers of the 8 Sikh Regiment were taking position between his post and another post and he had to break the enemy 'Forming Up Position' (FUP). Captain Karnal Sher Khan took some of his soldiers and attacked the enemy position. The attack was so powerful that the Indians retreated leaving dozens of dead bodies. Captain Karnal Sher Khan followed the retreating enemy soldiers and entered their base camp where he was surrounded by Indian soldiers. One Indian soldier ordered Captain Sher Khan to surrender as he was surrounded. Sher promptly refused and replied that it is against a Muslim's honour to surrender, and instantly fired on that soldier and destined him to hell, and then he started firing on rest of the soldiers and embraced Shahadat after getting hit by several bullets from all sides. The CO of the Indian unit had been so impressed with the valour of Captain Sher Khan and his men, that he ordered his body to be brought back as he wanted to take a look at what kind of a soldier he was. That was why his mortal remains ended up on the wrong side. The enemy was inclined to cite to Government of Pakistan to award him with the highest award of gallantry. Captain Karnal Sher Khan was posthumously awarded the highest Gallantry Award of Pakistan, the Nishan -i- Haider.

Nishan -i- Haider

Havildar Lalak Jan Shaheed

Lalak Jan was born on 1ST April 1967. He was enlisted in the Army on 10TH December 1984. He was serving in Northern Light Infantry Regiment when skirmishes broke out in Kargil against Indian forces, in 1999. On 1ST July 1999, Indians launched a fierce attack on Tiger Hill, occupied by the Pakistani Army, under cover of heavy artillery shelling around the bunkers. Subedar Sikandar sneaked across the Line of Control and placed his men in well-entrenched positions, and managed to repulse the attack without any loss of life on their own part. On the morning of 2ND July 1999 the Indians launched another intense attack on Tiger Hills. Realizing the great difficulty in holding their previous positions that had been spotted and zeroed-in by the Indian artillery deployed below, Subedar Sikandar ordered his men to retreat to secondary positions around a secret bunker. Once the men were secure, Havildar Lalak Jan descended on Tiger Hill and, amidst the Indian Artillery shelling, plants the landmines in the area in front of the Indian forces. Havildar Lalak Jan put a bag of explosives on his back, and while shouldering an AK-47 descended Tiger Hills for the second time, again amidst heavy Indian shelling. He located the secret bunker and threw the explosives inside the bunker. The bunker blew up in a very big blast. Havildar Lalak Jan managed to take cover, and the Indian Army lost 16 men inside and nearby the bunker. The other Indian soldiers saw Havildar Lalak Jan and opened fire on him. Surrounded from all sides by Indian fire, Havildar Lalak Jan made a valiant effort to resist and returned fire and expired of his wounds. On 15TH September 1999, the commanding officer of 12TH NLI sent two Special Service Group Commando groups to Tiger Hills to recover the body of Havildar Lalak Jan. When his body was found, Havildar Lalak Jan had his AK-47 firmly clenched to his chest. Pakistan awarded him the Nishan -i- Haider, Pakistan's highest military award, for extraordinary gallantry. Havildar Lalak Jan was the first person from the Northern Areas of Pakistan to receive the award.

Nishan -i- Haider

Naik Saif Ali Janjua Shaheed

Naik Saif Ali Janjua of Pakistan Army Azad Kashmir Regiment (Haider Dil Battalion) was a platoon commander during the Indo-Pakistani War of 1947. He received the Hilal-e-Kashmir from the government of Azad Kashmir, which is equal to Nishan -i- Haider, the highest military award given by Pakistan. He fought in the Kashmir sector during the 1948 War and sacrificed his life after displaying extraordinary bravery and heroism during the siege of Budha Khanna. Naik Saif Ali Khan was born to Janjua Rajput family on 25TH April 1922 in Khandbaz (Khandhar) Tehsil Fateh pur thakyala (Azad Jammu and Kashmir). He enlisted in the Royal Corps of Engineers in British Indian Army on 18TH March 1941. After completing his service in the British Indian Army in 1947, he came back to his native town and started establishing Haidri Force. On 1ST January 1948, Haidri Force was raised under the command of Lieutenant Colonel Muhammad Sher Khan. Due to his unflinching devotion and undaunted courage, on the recognition of his dedication and commitment to the cause, Saif Ali Janjua was promoted to the rank of Naik and was made platoon commander. He set personal examples of gallantry and inflicted heavy losses on the enemy at Bhudha Khanna, where his platoon was given the responsibility to defend Budha Khanna, where he faced never-ending frontal and crossfire from machine guns. He defended the post with chivalry, which he established with his few jawans and repulsed many aggressive ventures by the enemy and imposed colossal losses on them. The enemy used every mean to capture the post with two companies attack and heavy shelling but still managed to hold onto that post with just a handful of men. During the course of action, despite being hit on his chest by artillery fire, he retained his position and frustrated the Indian assault. He succumbed to his injuries on 26TH October 1948. On 14TH March 1949, the Defence Council of Azad Jammu & Kashmir adorned him with Hilal-e-Kashmir (posthumous) and on 30TH November 1995 Government of Pakistan initiated the gazette notification to declare his Hilal-e-Kashmir equivalent to Nishan -i- Haider and it was declared as Nishan -i- Haider.

Hilal–i–Jurat

Crescent of Courage, spelled as Hilal-e-Jurat, is the second-highest military award of Pakistan. It was created and declared for official use on 16TH March 1957 by the President of Pakistan. The Hilal-i-Jurat is considered to be the equivalent of the Conspicuous Gallantry Cross and the Distinguished Service Cross. The medal is only conferrable to those who are ranked at an Officer level only and it is only allowed to be given to the Army, Navy and Air-force.

Major General Mian Hayauddin, HJ, MC, MBE.
Citation for Hilal–i–Jurat:
Major General Mian Hayauddin was an army officer of the Indian Army and later of the Pakistan Army. He saw active service in several campaigns and was an eminent soldier and government official in the early years of the new state of Pakistan. Mian Hayauddin was born in Peshawar, the capital of the North-West Frontier Province. His father, Mian Wasiuddin, belonging to the Mian Kakakhel family, was resident of a small village in Mardan, Baghicha Dheri, and served in the Archaeological Survey of India, and was awarded the title of Khan Bahadur for his service in excavating and cataloguing the Gandhara and Ashoka sites at Swat, Takht-e-Bahi, Sudher and ancient Taxila, among others.
Mian Hayauddin studied at the Edwards Mission School and then Islamia College, Peshawar. He was selected in an All-India competition to be a cadet at the Royal Military College, Sandhurst. At the time, most troops in the Indian Army were Indians and were commanded by British officers. At Sandhurst, he was the first non-European cadet to be promoted to Corporal of the Corps of Cadets. He was commissioned a King's Commissioned Indian Officer from Sandhurst on the Unattached List, Indian Army as of 28TH January 1932. He was then posted for one year regimental attachment to the 2ND battalion Royal Scots Regiment. He was the first non-British Officer to be so attached.

Hilal–i–Jurat

Major General Mian Hayauddin, (Cont)

His service commenced in Quetta, Baluchistan, where he met Ahmad Yar Khan, the Khan of Kalat, who was also attached to the same Regiment and they became close friends. During the 1930s he also formed another of his closest friendships with Khan Abdul Ghani Khan, the leading poet of the Pashtuns and eldest son of Khan Abdul Ghafur Khan, the Frontier Gandhi. In March 1933 he joined the 4TH battalion, 12TH Frontier Force Regiment. He was particularly effective in command of Sikh troops, as he was one of the few Muslim Officers in the British Indian Army certified as fluent in speaking, reading and writing Grumukhi, the Panjabi language of the Sikhs. He served on the North West Frontier in the 1930s and was posted to the 11TH battalion, 12TH Frontier Force Regiment on 20TH September 1938 at Nowshera near Peshawar. Appointed Local Captain 16TH November 1938 to 8TH March 1939, then received substantive promotion to Captain 27TH August 1939. He was appointed Adjutant 4TH September 1939. The battalion was embodied 4TH September 1939 as part of the Nowshera Brigade, which was completed by 20TH September, at Nowshera. It moved at the end of September 1939 to Dacca in East Bengal to relieve the 2ND battalion, 14TH Punjab Regiment. The battalion trained at Dacca as part of the Eastern Bengal Brigade Area and performed internal security duties for one year. It moved to Quetta on 16TH November 1940. It performed internal security duties at Quetta under the command of Baluchistan District. It was converted to an active battalion as the 14TH (Suba Sarhad) Battalion, 12TH Frontier Force Regiment at Quetta on 15TH September 1941. He was made a Member in Military Division of The Most Excellent Order of the British Empire (MBE) for service as adjutant with 11TH Battalion, 12TH Frontier Force Regiment in the London Gazette 1ST July 1941. He attended the Staff College, Quetta 21ST July to 4TH December 1941. His classmates included, among others, Major Muhammad Ayub Khan, later to become President of Pakistan. With Hitler's attack on Stalingrad it was thought a possible breakthrough to the Middle-Eastern oilfields may occur, so Indian Army units were transferred to Iraq. For his meritorious services on the staff as a General Staff Officer 2ND grade in Iraq and Persia with the Persia and Iraq Force he was mentioned in dispatches in the London Gazette on 5TH August 1943.

Posted to Burma in September 1944 he was appointed second in command of the 9TH battalion, 12TH Frontier Force Regiment. After two previous battalion commanders were wounded, in February 1945 he was promoted to battalion commander and later decorated with the Military Cross for gallantry.

Hilal–i–Jurat

Major General Mian Hayauddin (Cont)

Lieutenant Colonel Hayauddin then served with 80TH Brigade still commanding 9TH battalion 12TH Frontier Force Regiment as part of Allied Land Forces French Indochina in South East Asia. He was selected to receive the sword of surrender from the Commander in Chief of Japanese forces in that theatre of operations. For his distinguished conduct and gallantry in assisting French forces, Mian Hayauddin was later awarded the Cross of Commandeur of the Légion d'Honneur, by the French Government. Promoted to temporary Colonel he was selected to attend the first post-war course at the Joint Services Staff College, Latimer, England. He was the senior Indian Army officer on the course. In early 1946 he served as the President of the Indian Army Selection Board in Pune. He was then selected as the Deputy Commander of the Indian Army Mission to the Allied Peace Commission in Berlin from late 1946 to late 1947. Colonel Mian Hayauddin opted for Pakistan, and was 18TH on the officer seniority list of the newly formed Pakistan Army. Promoted to command the Banu Brigade in December 1947, he oversaw Operation Curzon, the name given to the withdrawal of troops from the Tribal Areas in Waziristan, bordering South Eastern Afghanistan. He met with tribal elders and informed them that while he and his soldiers were fellow Muslims and largely Pashtuns, as were the tribesmen, any firing on the withdrawing troops would be countered with a crushing response, in keeping with tribal customs of revenge. The tribes offered no resistance and the entire withdrawal were completed peacefully. He commanded the brigade, renamed 102 Brigade, until January 1948. During the 1947-1948 Kashmir war with India, Brigadier Hayauddin fought in the Poonch sector. He led a small group of volunteers, with mobile artillery transported by mules, shelling the airfield at Poonch from the surrounding hills to the point of rendering it unusable. Indian Army garrison forces in the town were preparing to surrender to him when a general cease-fire in all of Kashmir came into effect. For his bravery and successful command of operations, he was recommended by General Sir Douglas Gracey for the equivalent of the British Distinguished Service Order, its 2ND highest gallantry award after the Victoria Cross. As a result, he was awarded the Hilal-i-Jurat, Pakistan's second highest gallantry award. He was then posted to London in late 1948 as the first military advisor to the Pakistan High Commission in the United Kingdom. In early 1950, on promotion to major general, he returned to general headquarters and was appointed as the first non-British officer to command 7TH (Golden Arrow) Division as its General Officer Commanding at Rawalpindi.

Hilal–i–Jurat

Major General Mian Hayauddin (Cont)

In 1952 he attended the Imperial Defence College, London, and on the successful completion of this course, Major General Mian Hayauddin was appointed the Chief of General Staff of the Pakistan Army. In July 1955 Major General Mian Hayauddin was posted to Washington DC as Chief of the Pakistan Military Mission. Upon his departure from Washington in September 1960 as Dean of the Corps of Military Attaches, he was awarded the Legion of Merit by the Eisenhower Administration. This is the highest decoration that can be bestowed by the US Government upon a foreign military officer. His gallantry/service decorations, plus three Mentions in Despatches, made him the most highly decorated officer of the Pakistan Army. He was the only Officer ever to have been decorated by the Governments of Britain; France; Pakistan and the USA. He ended active service in the Pakistan Army upon completing 28 years of service, in the rank of Major General, and retired in December 1960.

Upon retirement from the Pakistan Army, he was appointed in a civilian capacity as Director General (Bureau of Mineral Resources) in the Ministry of Fuel, Power and Natural Resources. The Minister handling this portfolio was Zulfikar Ali Bhutto, a future Foreign Minister, President, Civilian Martial Law Administrator and Prime Minister of Pakistan. In October 1961, he visited the Sui Gas Fields to visit an Indian Army colleague, with whom he had served in Burma during WW II, who was an executive there. His Indian Army colleague's wife, Sylvia Matheson, was an archaeologist, who inscribed and gave him a copy of her book Time off to dig. During her time in Sui she later met and befriended Nawab Akbar Khan Bugti, who featured prominently in her next book - Tigers of Baluchistan. She dedicated this book to General 'Gunga' Hayaud Din, as he was known to his closest friends, including Sylvia Matheson and her husband. Under his leadership a very large gas deposit was found off the coast of East Pakistan, now Bangladesh. Ms. Viqar-un-Nisa Quadri's article 'OGDC Memories' published in the Dawn Magazine issue of Sunday, January 11TH, 1998 attests to his leadership and start-up of an organization in which Russians and Pakistanis worked side by side. He was leading a delegation of Pakistani journalists and tourism/travel executives to Cairo on Pakistan International Airlines' inaugural flight PK 705 when the aircraft crashed while landing at Cairo in the pre-dawn darkness on May 20TH, 1965. Of the 119 passengers and crew, only 6 survived. The remains of nearly all the crash victims, including those of Major General Mian Hayaud Din, were buried in a special graveyard at Cairo.

Hilal–i–Jurat

Brigadier Muhammad Aslam Khan, HJ, MC, FK, SJ

Muhammad Aslam Khan belonged to the Afridi clan in Tirah valley. He was brought up in Jammu Kashmir, and his primary education was at Srinagar. He came from a military family with the inherited bravery of his predecessors. He joined the British Indian Army and saw action in Burma against the Japanese, for which he was awarded the Military Cross which was presented to him by the British Royal family. The Americans owe him gratitude at the capture of the famous Kennedy peak in October 1944 in Yidium road operations which they themselves had failed to conquer. After partition of the subcontinent he was transferred to Pakistan Army in 6TH Battalion, 8TH Punjab regiment.

At that time governorship of Gilgit was given to Sardar Alam Khan, a political agent. Gilgit was a princely state which acceded to Pakistan but Skardu was under the tyrannical rule of Hari Singh. This mountainous area of Baltistan was not a part of Pakistan in 1947 until a strong, stoutly built man with rich experience of local geography was given the task of acquiring as much area as he can with mere resources. In the short span of time, he had to raise an effective organized force from within the civilian population that could counter the veteran soldiers of India. His mission was to defend the area so far acquired and liberate as much territory as possible on his own responsibility with merger resources and was ready to sacrifice his life for this objective. It was seen as a failed mission planning by the opponents who deemed it as impossible. But Major Aslam was determined to command men of unbreakable steadfastness, like the lofty mountains. He resumed his command in January, 1948 bringing with him his younger brother, Major Anwar khan who was appointed as brigade major for administering the logistics. Aslam Khan was a military genius, where he ordered his forces to occupy as much military blank territory as plausible in winter to make a rock solid ground till next summer on the South East, and South West pass. In this strategic victory, it was not possible for the enemy to retake possession of the ground so, conquered, and finally, to neutralize strength of army at Skardu integrating further into Baltistan. Major Aslam formulated, and gave rise to two new forces namely, the Tiger force, and Ibex the duty of the tiger force was to advance up to Tragbal, Gurez, and continue striking on Bandipur till the Indian army retreated from the borders. The task of Ibex force was to pave along River Indus; meeting Indian encroachment at Rondu, and move ahead occupying Skardu, onwards to Kargil, drass, and Ladakh. In this way, the enemy could not reinvigorate itself in any direction

Hilal–i–Jurat

Brigadier Muhammad Aslam Khan (Cont)

Extreme weather conditions were undoubtedly a huge hurdle but the commander was a man of steel, Major Aslam Khan who was ready to change strategies in lieu of transforming circumstances. When the Ibex force failed at Skardu, and got difficult to advance forward, Aslam Khan established his headquarters at the Chillum valley. He began to train another force in the mountains around Burzil. He trained the soldiers hailing from Yasin, and Hunza to wrap their legs in rugs, and they began to move towards Kargil through Deosai plains. They had to wade through fifteen inch snow in severe winter with the commander Major Aslam, and reached Kargil in three days. A junior of Major Aslam raised an icy-proof Eskimo force which had a challenging laborious task of crossing the 12000 feet high mountain sheets of Deosai plateau .They had to sleep on the snow as well as hammer the enemy logistics by surprise assaults. The scheme of this mission succeeded as these resolute soldiers were led by an inexhaustible commander. The personality of Aslam Khan was such that he never took absolute authority into his power, by suppressing his juniors rather he always gave them autonomy. He had given them the opportunity to transform the intelligence strategy as they liked to adopt, and carry out persistent attacks confusing him to keep the Maharaja's army away. Major Aslam had a geographical acquaintance with the area so he knew inch-by-inch of this land. Therefore, he was always successful in sending supplies, diverting troops, battalions, and platoons from one sector to another. Major Aslam moved men into Jammu Kashmir that began raiding Hirmal Pradesh, and sent a wireless message to his commandant at Rawalpindi. The Commander-in-chief General Douglas Gracey was bewildered, and ordered him to report back at his office. He was called back, and COAS appointed him as his private secretary. Colonel Aslam had keen passion to expand the frontiers to Srinagar from where the Maharaja had already fled away in apprehension. Leadership did not permit him to do so, and awarded him the Hilal-e-Jurat by Government of Pakistan. He was promoted to the rank of Brigadier at the age of 36 years ranking him as the youngest brigadier in the history of the world. Brigadier Aslam was struck off, and retired in 1963.He decided to eschew from politics, and work for the evolution of tourism in trans-isolated Himalayan zone for which he founded Shangri-La Resorts at Skardu. He died in 1994.

Hilal–i–Jurat

Major General Sher Ali Khan, HJ

Sher Ali Khan of Pataudi, was born 13TH May 1913, the second son of Nawab Ibrahim Ali Khan of Pataudi. He was educated at Aitchison College, Lahore, the Prince of Wales Royal Indian Military College (RIMC), Dehradun and the Royal Military Academy Sandhurst. He was commissioned into the 7TH Light Cavalry of the British Indian Army in 1933. He subsequently commanded the 1ST Battalion, 1ST Punjab Regiment during the Second World War. After the war, he served as the Defence Attaché of the Indian Armed Forces in Washington, D.C.. Having moved to Pakistan at independence, he commanded Pakistan's 14 (Parachute) Brigade during the 1947 Kashmir war in which action he was awarded the Hilal-i-Jurat. He was appointed Adjutant General of the Pakistan Army and later served as the Chief of General Staff. He was superseded along with the former Commandant Command and Staff College Major General M.A. Latif Khan when Major General Muhammad Musa and Major General Habibullah Khan Khattak were made C-in-C and COS respectively in October 1958. In 1958, on retirement from active service, he was appointed Pakistan's High Commissioner to Malaysia and in 1963 as Ambassador to Yugoslavia with concurrent accreditation to Bulgaria and Greece. He served in the cabinet of General Yahya Khan as Federal Minister for Information, Broadcasting & and National Affairs 1969 - 71. He was a member of Pakistan's Polo team for many years, Captain of the All Malaysia Polo team for six years and President of the Malayan Polo Association 1959/1963. He also established the Djakarta Riding/Saddle club and was its first elected President. He taught briefly at Aitchison College and was also Vice Chairman of its Board of Governors. He was the Co-founder and Chairman of the governing body of Viqar-un-Nisa Women's College at Rawalpindi.

He was the Author of several books and the recipient of the highest civil awards from governments in Malaysia, Yugoslavia and Indonesia, and was a Dato of the State of Pahang in Malaysia. He married Silvat Mueenuddin younger daughter of Mian Ghulam Mueenudin of Lahore, and had four sons and a daughter. He died 29TH May 2002 at Sher Manzil, Lahore. His son Major General Isfandiyar Ali Khan Pataudi is the commander of the 25TH Mechanized Division of Pakistan Army.

Hilal-i-Jurat

Field Marshal Mohd. Ayub Khan, HJ, HPk, MBE

Field Marshal Mohammad Ayub Khan was a military ruler and President of Pakistan. Ayub Khan was born at Abottabad in the Northwest Frontier Province in 1908. He was educated at Aligarh Muslim University and at Royal Military College, Sandhurst, UK. In World War II he was second-in-command of a regiment in Burma (Myanmar) and commanded a battalion in India. After the 1947 partition of British India he was rapidly promoted in the army of the new Muslim state of Pakistan. He was promoted to the rank of Major General in December 1948 and was then appointed the General Officer Commanding (GOC) in the province of East Bengal. He discharged the responsibility of Defence Minister of Pakistan between 1954 and 1956. In collusion with the then President Iskandar Mirza, army chief Ayub Khan imposed martial law in Pakistan on 7TH October 1958, and abrogated the Constitution. Ayub Khan was appointed the Chief Martial Law Administrator by President Mirza on 8TH October. But after a few days, he ousted Iskandar Mirza from power (27TH October) and declared himself the President of Pakistan. Ayub Khan's regime was a form of representational dictatorship, and he introduced a new political system in 1959 as basic democracies. The Basic democracies system set up five tiers of institutions. The lowest tier was composed of union councils and the members were designated as basic democrats. The urban areas had a similar arrangement, under which the smaller union councils were grouped together into municipal committees to perform similar duties. In 1960, the elected members of the union councils voted to confirm Ayub Khan's presidency, and under the 1962 Constitution they formed an electoral college to elect the President, the National Assembly, and the provincial assemblies. The system of Basic democracies did not have time to take root or to fulfil Ayub Khan's intentions before he and the system fell. By 1958 Ayub Khan and his fellow officers decided to turn out the politicians, a task easily accomplished without bloodshed. He then took some fiscal measure especially in land holding. The landholding ceiling was raised from thirty-three hectares to forty-eight hectares. Landholders retained their dominant positions in the social hierarchy. Some 4 million hectares of land in West Pakistan, much of it in Sindh, was released for public acquisition between 1959 and 1969 and sold mainly to civil and military officers, thus creating a new class of farmers having medium-sized holdings. These farms became immensely important for future agricultural development, but the peasants were scarcely benefited. In 1958, a legal commission was set up to suggest reforms of the family and marriage laws.

Hilal–i–Jurat

Field Marshal Mohd. Ayub Khan (Cont)

Ayub Khan examined its report and in 1961 issued the Family Laws Ordinance. Among other things, it restricted polygamy and 'regulated' marriage and divorce; giving women more equal treatment under the law than they had before. Ayub Khan adopted an energetic approach toward economic development that soon bore fruit in a rising rate of economic growth. The Export Bonus Vouchers Scheme (1959) and tax incentives stimulated new industrial entrepreneurs and exporters. These measures had important consequences in the development of industry and gave rise to a new class of small industrialists. On 1ST March 1962, Ayub Khan introduced a Constitution based on the presidential system and thereby became all-powerful in the country. In November 1964, election of basic democrats was held in both the wings of Pakistan. On 2ND January 1965, election for the presidency of Pakistan was held through an indirect system of voting. Ayub Khan was elected President by defeating the opposition candidate Fatema Jinnah. Ayub Khan articulated his foreign policy on several occasions. His objectives were the security and development of Pakistan and the preservation of its ideology as he saw it. Toward these ends, he sought to improve or normalise relations with Pakistan's immediate and looming neighbours, India, China, and the Soviet Union. While retaining and renewing the alliance with the United States, Ayub Khan emphasised his preference for friendship, not subordination. Other than ideology and Kashmir, the main source of friction between Pakistan and India was the distribution of the waters of the Indus River system. A compromise that appeared to meet the needs of both countries was reached during the 1950s. It was not until 1960 that a solution finally found favour with Ayub Khan and Jawaharlal Nehru. Broadly speaking, the agreement allocated use of the three western Indus Rivers (the Indus itself and its tributaries, the Jhelum and the Chenab) to Pakistan, and the three eastern Indus tributaries (the Ravi, Beas, and Sutlej) to India. Pakistan's tentative approaches to China intensified in 1959 when China's occupation of Tibet and the flight of Dalai Lama to India ended five years of Chinese-Indian friendship. An entente between Pakistan and China evolved in inverse ratio to Sino-Indian hostility, which climaxed in a border war in 1962. This informal alliance became a keystone of Pakistan's foreign policy and grew to include a border agreement in March 1963, highway construction connecting the two countries at the Karakoram Pass, agreements on trade, and Chinese economic assistance and grants of military equipment, which was later thought to have included exchanges in nuclear technology.

Hilal-i-Jurat

Field Marshal Mohd. Ayub Khan (Cont

China's diplomatic support and transfer of military equipment was important to Pakistan during the 1965 Indo-Pakistan War over Kashmir. The Soviet Union strongly disapproved of Pakistan's alliance with the United States, but Moscow was interested in keeping doors open to both Pakistan and India. Ayub Khan was able to secure Soviet neutrality during the 1965 Indo-Pakistan war. Ayub Khan was the architect of Pakistan's policy of close alignment with the United States, and his first major foreign policy act was to sign bilateral economic and military agreements with the United States in 1959. Nevertheless, Ayub Khan expected more from these agreements than the United States was willing to offer and thus remained critical of the role the United States played in South Asia. Especially troublesome to Pakistan was United States' neutrality during the 1965 Indo-Pakistan war. Pakistan did not extend the ten-year agreement signed in 1959. The 1965 war began as a series of border flare-ups along undemarcated territory at the Rann of Kutch in the southeast in April and soon after along the cease-fire line in Kashmir. The Rann of Kutch conflict was resolved by mutual consent and British sponsorship and arbitration, but the Kashmir conflict proved more dangerous and widespread. Each country had limited objectives, and neither was economically capable of sustaining a long war because military supplies were cut to both countries by the United States and Britain. On September 23RD, a cease-fire was arranged through the UN Security Council. In January 1966, Ayub Khan and India's Prime Minister, Lal Bahadur Shastri, signed the Tashkent Declaration which formally ended hostilities and called for a mutual withdrawal of forces. When war broke out between Pakistan and India on 6TH September 1965, Ayub Khan promoted himself to the rank of Field Marshal. Then in 1966, he chose the path of repression of his political opponents when the Six-point demand for autonomy of East Pakistan was raised by the awami league. The leaders of the Awami League including party Chief Bangabandhu Sheikh Mujibur Rahman were arrested. In the backdrop of an intense anti-Ayub movement during the period of 1966-68, Ayub Khan convened a round table conference of opposition political leaders at Rawalpindi on 26TH February 1969. But when the conference failed to resolve the crisis, Ayub Khan handed over power to the army chief General Aga Mohammad Yahya khan on 24TH March 1969, and retired from politics. He had been awarded the Hilal-i-Jurat by the Pakistan Army and BME by the British Government. He died on 20TH April 1974.

Hilal–i–Jurat

General Muhammad Musa Khan Hazara, HPk, HQA, HI, HJ, MBE

General Muhammad Musa Khan Hazara, was a four-star rank army general, politician, and the Commander in Chief of Pakistan Army, serving under President Ayub Khan from 1958 until 1966. Muhammad Musa Khan was born on 20TH October 1908 in Quetta, Baluchistan, British India, into a tribal Hazara family. He was of the Persian-speaking of Hazara tribal tradition. His family roots have been said to be descendants of Genghis Khan. His family was *Sardar* (lit. Chief) of Hazara Tribe and was the eldest son of Sardar Yazdan Khan who the local Tribal chief. After his schooling, he was recruited to the British Indian Army as a *Jawan* in 1926 and eventually joined the 4TH Hazara Pioneers after being promoted as the Naik– a non-commissioned officer in the British Indian Army. He was selected to join the Indian Military Academy at Dehra Dun as a cadet in October 1932. In 1935, he graduated from the Indian Military Academy and was commissioned as a Second Lieutenant in 1935. In 1936, he was posted to the 6TH Royal Battalion of the 13TH Frontier Force Rifles as a Platoon Commander and saw actions in the Waziristan campaign in 1936 till 1938. He participated in the World War II, and served well in the Burma Campaign and North African theatre as part of the Norfolk Regiment of the British Indian Army. In Middle East, he led the company and was listed in mentioned in despatches for "distinguished services in the Middle East during the period February to July 1941" and in the London Gazette 30 December 1941 as a Lieutenant and acting Major. In 1942, his heroic action for valour won him the praise and was appointed as Member of the Order of the British Empire for gallant and distinguished services in the Middle East. In 1945, he was promoted as army captain and major in 1946 and was serving with the Machine Gun battalion, 13TH Frontier Force Rifles by October 1942. After the partition of British India that followed the establishment of Pakistan in 1947, he opted for Pakistan and joined the Pakistan Army as a staff officer. In 1947, as Brigadier, commanded the 103RD Infantry Brigade based in Sialkot brigade in Kashmir and served as commander of military units in the first war with India. In 1948, he went on to command the 52ND Infantry Brigade positioned in Quetta. After the war in 1948, General Musa studied and graduated from the Command and Staff College in Quetta and proceeded to attend the Imperial Defence College in United Kingdom prior to his graduation. In 1950s, Musa Khan earned reputation as being respected in the officer corps for professional competence, commanding the military formations throughout the country.

Hilal–i–Jurat

General Muhammad Musa Khan Hazara, (Cont)

His commanding assignments included his role as the Chief of Staff of the East-Pakistan Army, and also having served as GOC of 14TH Infantry Division in Dhaka, East Pakistan, in 1951. In 1952, his field assignment included his role as commander of 8TH Infantry Division positioned in Quetta before stationed at the GHQ. In 1957, he served as the Deputy Chief of Staff and later Chief of Staff at the Army GHQ. His career progressed well in the army and was ascended as Commander-in-Chief by President Ayub Khan in 1958, when the latter disposed President Iskander Mirza who imposed martial law in 1958. Major-General Musa Khan never achieved the three-star appointment nor promotion as Lieutenant-General was approved at the time of his nomination towards appointed as the army chief of staff. His promotion to the four-star appointment came with controversy in the country as many saw that his appointment was based on 'dependability rather than merit.' There were three staff officers in line who were senior to Major-General Musa Khan that included: Major General Sher Ali Pataudi, Major General Latif Khan and Major General Adam Khan– all Sandhurst graduates of 1933. In October 1958, Musa Khan elevated as four-star general and appointed as Commander in Chief with Ayub Khan promoting himself as Field Marshal. President Ayub delegated the military affairs to General Musa Khan when heading the civic government. In 1964, he became aware of covert operation studied by the Foreign ministry led by Foreign Minister Zulfikar Ali Bhutto, and presented views against the operation due to no linkage between the covert actions and the conventional backup. General Musa Khan also had the support from President Ayub Khan on his views; however, the war began in 1965. General Musa Khan did not order the Pakistan Army without the confirmation by President Ayub Khan despite Foreign Minister Bhutto's urging. After the Indian Army moved to the Rann of Kutch, General Musa Khan ordered Army GHQ to responds back to Indian Army by moving the 12TH Division. After reviewing the aerial view of the area and getting directions from President Ayub to make way for Maj General Yahya, General Musa controversially relieved GOC Akhtar Hussain Malik and handed over the command of the 12TH Division to Major-General Yahya Khan, which was a big blunder that resulted in critical time delays of troop movements and eventual failure of the operation. About the failure due to command change, General Musa Khan justified his actions that he had not had time to select a commander or staff despite the authority was given to him. He led and commanded the Pakistan Army in the largest tank battle, which earned him the public fame and nobility.

Hilal–i–Jurat

General Muhammad Musa Khan Hazara, (Cont)

His strategy based on classical trench method supported by armoury, artillery and airpower was tactically powerful and successful due it had stopped the advancing Indian Army but politically unsuccessful due to the country being party of peace treaty brokered by the USSR in 1965. General Musa's military service is unique due to the fact that he had received two extensions as a Commander-in-chief from the period of 1958 till 1966, and had award of Hilal-i- Jurat conferred on him by the Pakistan Army. Upon his retirement, General Musa did not recommend Yahya Khan's nomination as Commander-in-chief and Yahiya's name was not included in the list of nomination sent to President Ayub Khan; nonetheless, General Musa was succeeded by General Yahya Khan as Commander in Chief. About the war with India in 1965, General Musa provided his views and testimonies in two books written on military history of Pakistan Army: first being the 'My Version' and the second being the 'Jawan to General'.

At the time of his retirement in 1966, General Musa Khan was a famed and popular military figure which led President Ayub Khan appointed him as the Governor of West Pakistan. Such news of appointment was met with great triumph and enthusiasm by the West Pakistani people. In 1967, he became Governor of West Pakistan until submitting his resignation on 2ND March 1969 when General Yahya Khan imposed martial law to take over the presidency. From 1969–84, he remained quiet and settled in Karachi while receiving military pension. In 1985, he became active in national politics on Pakistan Muslim League platform led by Prime Minister M. K. Junejo. He was appointed as Governor of Baluchistan by the President Zia-ul-Haq after the general elections held in 1985. After the general elections held in 1988, Governor Musa Khan controversially dissolved the provincial assembly on the then-Chief Minister Zafarullah Khan Jamali's advice.

However, the Baluchistan High Court restored the provincial assembly amid public condemnation of Governor's move. The step towards dissolving the assembly was believed to have been taken with the consent of the President and Prime Minister. On 12TH March 1991, General Musa Khan died while in office and per accordance to his wishes, he was buried in buried in Mashhad, Razavi Khorasan, Iran. In his honour, the provincial Baluchistan government established a vocational school, the General Muhammad Musa Inter-College (GMMIC), in Quetta, Pakistan in 1987.

Hilal–i–Jurat

Lieutenant General Akhtar Hussain Malik, HJ

Lieutenant General Akhtar Hussain Malik was a distinguished General, a war hero of Pakistan Army in the Indo-Pakistan war of 1965. He was born to an old farming Ahmadi family in a small village named Pindori, located in Punjab. He was the son of Malik Ghulam Nabi, a Headmaster at a local school. Despite the unavailability of schools in his village, his father made an effort to send him to school miles away, where he and his friends had to walk for hours every day. After graduating from college, he enlisted as a Sepoy in the British Indian Army. His personal qualities and education were soon noticed and he was sent to the Indian Military Academy, Dehra Dun for officer training and was commissioned a Second Lieutenant on the Special List on 1ST June 1941. He was admitted to the Indian Army and posted to the 16TH Punjab Regiment, specifically the newly raised 7TH battalion. He was promoted war substantive Lieutenant. He was appointed acting Captain 1ST January 1942 then promoted temporary Captain on 1ST April 1942. He was appointed the Brigade Intelligence Officer for the 114TH Indian Infantry Brigade on 1ST January 1942. He would later serve with his battalion in Burma and Malaya and in September 1945 as a temporary Major was commanding 'A' company, 7TH Battalion, 16TH Punjab Regiment in Malaya. On the partition of India in August 1947 Malik opted to join the Pakistani Army. Major General Akhtar Hussain Malik was known for his towering presence, unsullied boldness in strategy, quick thinking, and his love for his country. Although he was highly admired and respected by his subordinates, he was very outspoken. As a brilliant tactician he is also given for planning Operation Gibraltar and Operation Grand Slam with finalization from Ayub Khan. As GOC 12TH Division, he was the overall commander for Operation Grand Slam in the Indo-Pakistan war of 1965. For his successful handling of the initial phase of the operation, he was awarded the Hilal-i-Jurat, the second highest gallantry award of the Pakistan Army. Controversially, the command was handed over to General Yahya Khan in mid operation, resulting in delay and eventual failure of the operation. The cause for this midway switch over is an object of speculation to this day. Malik was posted to CENTO in Ankara, Turkey where he died in a road accident. His body was brought back to Pakistan and was buried in Rabwah.

Hilal–i–Jurat

Major General Abrar Hussain, HJ, MBE

Major General Abrar Hussain was a Pakistani military officer who served in World War II and the Indo-Pakistani War of 1965. Abrar Hussain was born on 2ND September 1918 in a Taluqdar family of Oudh. He was educated at La Martinere School and Colvin Taluqdars' College, Lucknow, where he excelled in both academics and sports. His excellent personal conduct and exemplary character led the College Principal to declare him as *"the best boy that has passed through my hands in 10 years."* These qualities would continue to be the hallmark of Abrar Hussain for the rest of his eventful life. In 1939, he graduated in History, Political Science and English Literature from Allahabad University. On the outbreak of World War II, he joined the Indian Military Academy at Dehradun and was commissioned into the British Indian Army on 31ST July 1940 and posted to 2ND Battalion of 10TH Baluch Regiment (now 7 Baloch). His brother (later Brigadier) Noor Ahmad Hussain, served as an aide-de-camp (ADC) to Quaid-i-Azam Muhammad Ali Jinnah. In October 1940, $2/10^{TH}$ Baluch was dispatched to Malaya in anticipation of the impending war with Japan. On 8TH December 1941, Japan invaded Malaya and rapidly overran the British forces, who surrendered on Singapore Island on 15TH February 1942. Among the Allied Prisoners of War was 2ND Battalion, 10TH Baluch, who had given an excellent account of themselves despite the Allied defeat. The Japanese separated Indian officers and men from the British and subjected them to intense propaganda and pressure to join the Japanese-sponsored 'Indian National Army' (INA). The Baluchis mostly stood firm. Prominent among them was Lieutenant Abrar Hussain, who refused to betray his Honour. The Japanese sent him along with 150 recalcitrant Gurkhas for use as coastal mine-breaching suicide troops on successive island landings. After three such landings, the group arrived on the island of New Britain in the South Pacific, where they were used for building airstrips. Led by their gallant commander, the group remained defiant despite severe privations and cruelty of their Japanese captors. By 1945, the Allies had severely disrupted Japanese communications in the South Pacific resulting in starvation among the Japanese, who reportedly had turned to cannibalism. Lieutenant Abrar not only managed to survive, but also demanded and received the surrender of the thousand-strong Japanese garrison. For his exemplary conduct, personal bravery and strength of character, Lieutenant Abrar Hussain was appointed Member of the Order of the British Empire (MBE). On the independence of Pakistan in 1947, Abrar Hussain opted for Pakistan.

Hilal–i–Jurat

Major General Abrar Hussain, (Cont)

In 1947 at the time of Independence Abrar Hussain joined the newly formed Pakistan Army. In 1949, he graduated from the Command and Staff College, Quetta. His varied appointments in Pakistan Army included Command of 17 Baluch (now 19 Baloch), instructor at Staff College and staff appointments at General Headquarters, Rawalpindi as Deputy Director Military Operations, Deputy Director and then Director Staff Duties. Here, he was directly involved from 1955 to 1958 in the induction of US military equipment for modernization of four infantry and one and a half armoured divisions. He was promoted Brigadier in 1956. As Military Secretary from 1958 to 1964, he was also president of the Army Reforms Committee. Promoted Major General in 1964, he was given the task of converting 100 (Independent) Armoured Brigade Group into 6 Armoured Division. The fact that he was an infantry officer and yet had been entrusted with the raising of an armoured formation, speaks volumes of the esteem in which he was held by the Army High Command. He would soon vindicate that confidence in the coming war with India. His task was far from complete, when India invaded Pakistan on 6TH September 1965. The 6 Armoured Divisions was still a paper formation without a division's normal complement of fighting or supporting elements. There were only two armoured regiments and one infantry battalion, while there were no integral brigade headquarters in the division. The main thrust of the Indian offensive was in the Sialkot Sector, where they attacked with three infantry and one armoured divisions. Facing them was the overstretched 15 Infantry Division. The 24 Infantry Brigade was provided to General Abrar, and with these meagre resources, he was ordered stop the enemy. Some of the fiercest tank battles since World War II were fought on the Battlefield of Chawinda but every attempt by the Indians to breakthrough was foiled by 22ND September, the Indians had shot their bolt and asked for a ceasefire. Major General Abrar Hussain and his 'Men of Steel' had saved the day for Pakistan. For his inspiring leadership and skilful conduct of operations, he was awarded the Hilal-i-Jurat. He remains one of Pakistan's most successful field commanders. In 1968, General Abrar was commanding the Command and Staff College, Quetta, when he asked for early retirement. On 16TH April 1975, in retirement, General Abrar suffered a stroke which paralyzed the right side of his body and impeded his speech. He battled against the affliction for seventeen long years with the same quiet dignity and fortitude with which he had lived his life. On 15TH March 1992, the grand old soldier and gentleman, one of Pakistan's greatest military heroes, faded away from this world.

Hilal–i–Jurat

General Akhtar Abdur Rahman Khan, HJ, TB, HI

Akhtar Abdur Rahman Khan, was an influential four-star rank general officer who tenured as the Chairman of the Joint Chiefs of Staff Committee of Pakistan from 1987–1988 and as 4TH Director-General Inter-Services Intelligence (ISI) from 1979-1987. As director of the ISI, Akhtar holds a world prestige for masterminding the resistance network against the Soviet Union in their war to protect the fragile regime of Communist Afghanistan. Close to General Zia-ul-Haq, Akhtar consolidated political power and was widely regarded as country's most powerful statesman to have an influence on country's covert and overt public policies. Being regarded as the consistent United States ally, he was a close friend of counterpart William Casey of Central Intelligence Agency (CIA). Abdur Rehman was born on 11TH June 1924 in Rampur, UP, British India in an Urdu speaking family of Pathan origin. After passing the university entrance exam, Abdur Rehman enrolled in the Imperial College London in London in 1941, and subsequently earned Bachelor of Science in Statistics in 1945, followed by Master of Science in Economics at Yale University. Akhtar joined the British Indian Army in 1946, before becoming Captain in Pakistan Army in 1949. Akhtar was appointed as an instructor at the Artillery School in Nowshera. Later, he was selected for an infantry training course with the British Army and was sent on deputation to complete a course in the United Kingdom. Upon returning to Pakistan, he secured the promotion as Major and posted as a military adviser to East-Pakistan Army from April 1954 to October 1954. He was later transferred back to General combatant headquarters (GHQ) as a staff officer whom he holds from April 1956 to February 1957. He actively participated in the Indo-Pakistani War of 1965 and appointed at IV Corps as an operational field officer. He fought well in Lahore sector that led to his promotion as lieutenant-colonel and remained second-in-command of the infantry regiment in Lahore. After the war, he was promoted as Colonel while being stationed with the IV Corps. Later, he was promoted as Brigadier and given transferred to northern parts of the country, and commanded an infantry brigadier as its brigadier commander, in Azad Kashmir. In 1971, he was promoted to two-star rank, Major-General, and served as General Officer Commanding (GOC) of the 12TH Infantry Division stationed in Murree. Akhtar was generally close to Bhutto and personally greeted Bhutto when he visited to command office of the 12TH Division. He privately opposed the martial law to remove Prime Minister Zulfikar Ali Bhutto.

Hilal–i–Jurat

General Akhtar Abdur Rahman Khan, (Cont)

In mere six months, he was appointed as adjutant general at GHQ for next two years. In June 1979, President General Zia-ul-Haq called Akhtar and awarded him a promotion while offering him the coveted position of the directorate of the Inter-Services Intelligence (ISI). After being promoted to three-star rank, lieutenant-general, General Rehman directed the ISI's operation that would make the ISI to become one of the major organs of Pakistan's fast expanding organisational machinery of military. His influence on atomic weapons program grew and worked tirelessly and collected around him colleagues who were equally dynamic and determined to make the ISI an organisation that would have great impact on the domestic and external policies of the country. During his eight-year tenure, the ISI became one of the most powerful spy agencies of the world. In 1987 at the principle of his career, General Akhtar was elevated to the four-star rank and secured the appointment as the Chairman of the Joint Chiefs of Staff Committee, the highest and most prestigious four-star assignment in the Pakistan Armed Forces. When the Soviet Union deployed its 40TH Army in Afghanistan, many of General Zia's leading generals believed that Pakistan would be the Soviet Union's next target. They felt that because of Pakistan's strategic location and given the fact that it has warm water ports in the Arabian Sea, it was a prime target for future invasion. Since the top military brass believed that the Soviet invasion of Afghanistan threatened Pakistan's national security, Pakistan's premier intelligence agency the ISI headed by General Akhtar started providing financial, military, and strategic assistance to the Afghan mujahidin. The ISI received billions of dollars in military assistance from the CIA and Saudi Arabia to train and command the Afghan rebels in a bid to defeat the Soviets. This covert operation would ultimately lead to the Soviet withdrawal from Afghanistan. In 1988, the C-130 carrying General Ziaul Haq, General Akhtar Abdul Rehman and many other Generals fell to the ground due to technical reasons. Akhtar laid to rest on 19TH August 1988.

Akhtar Abdur Rahman, who was known as the second most powerful man in Pakistan during the 1980s, known for being the head of the Inter-Services Intelligence Agency (ISI) during Zia-ul-Huq's presidency

Hilal–i–Jurat

Lt. General Amir Abdullah Khan Niazi, HJ, SPK, SK, MC

Amir Abdullah Khan Niazi, was a former three-star rank army general in the Pakistan Army and the last Governor of East Pakistan known for commanding the Eastern Command of Pakistani military in East Pakistan during the third war with India until surrendering on 16TH December 1971 to Lieutenant General Jagjit Singh of the Indian Army.

Amir Abdullah Niazi was born in 1915 in a small village, Balo Khel, located on the east bank of the Indus River in Mianwali, Punjab, British India After educating from a local school in Mianwali, he joined the British Indian Army as a 'Y cadet' in 1937 and was selected for an emergency commission, as he had passed out from the Officers Training School in Bangalore. He gained commission on 8TH March, 1942 and joined the 4TH Battalion, 7TH Rajput Regiment. On 11TH June 1942, Lieutenant Niazi was stationed in the Kekrim Hills located in regions of Assam-Manipur to participate in the Burma front. He was involved in bitterly fought battles along the Burma front and commended for his judgment of the best course of action. Lieutenant Niazi's gallantry had impressed his British commanders in the GHQ India and they wanted to award him the Distinguished Service Order, but his rank was not high enough for such a decoration. During the campaign Niazi was given the soubriquet *'Tiger'* for his part in a ferocious fight with the Japanese. After the conflict, the British Government Lieutenant Niazi with the Military Cross for leadership, judgement, quick thinking and calmness under pressure in action along the border with Burma. After World War II, in 1945, he was promoted as army captain and sent to attend the Command and Staff College in Quetta which he graduated with a staff course degree under then Lieutenant Colonel Yahya Khan. In 1947, after the creation of Pakistan in August 1947, Major Niazi decided to opt for Pakistan and joined the newly established Pakistan Army. In 1960–64, he was promoted as Brigadier and went on to participate in the second war with India in 1965 as he went commanding the paratrooper brigade stationed in Sialkot. *Initially, he commanded the 5TH AK Brigade directing military operations in Indian-held Kashmir but later assumed the command of 14TH (Para) Brigade in Zafarwal sector where he was decorated with the Hilal-e-Jurat by the President of Pakistan.*

(Brigadier (Retd) M.M. Mahmood, who was privy to the actions of 1965 war, stated that the 14TH (Para) Brigade stayed inactive during the action in which General Niazi was awarded Hilal-i-Jurat. And that Brigadier (Retd) M.M. Mahmood protested vehemently to the award, to no avail).

Hilal–i–Jurat

Lt. General Amir Abdullah Khan Niazi (Cont)

His leadership credentials led him to be appointed martial law administrator of both Karachi and Lahore to maintain control of law in the cities of West Pakistan in 1966–67. In 1968, he was promoted as Major-General and made GOC of the 8TH Infantry Division, stationed in Sialkot, Punjab, Pakistan. In 1969, Major-General Niazi was made GOC of 10TH Infantry Division, stationed in Lahore, Punjab, Pakistan. In 1971, he was promoted to three-star assignment and promoted as Lieutenant-General, initially appointed Commander of the IV Corps in Lahore. Lieutenant-General Niazi volunteered for the transfer to East Pakistan when Lieutenant-General Bahadur Sher Khan declined to the post despite being appointed. There were two more generals who had also refused their postings in East and General Niazi said 'yes' without necessarily realizing the risks involved and how to counter them. After General Tikka Khan had initiated the military crackdown on March 1971, many general officers had declined to be stationed in East Pakistan despite being appointed. Lieutenant-General Niazi arrived in Dhaka on 4TH April 1971 to assume the Eastern Command from Lieutenant-General Tikka Khan. The violent crackdown at the Dhaka University against the intellectuals had turned the East Pakistani people hostile towards the Pakistani military, which made it too tough for General Niazi to overcome the situation. From May through August 1971, the Indian Army trained Mukti Bahini led series of counter guerrilla campaigns against the Eastern Command stationed, and General Niazi began taking countermeasures against the Bengali rebellions. By June 1971, he sent the reports on the rebellion and noted that 30,000 insurgents were hurriedly trained by India at the India-East Pakistan border. On August 1971, General Niazi formulated a plan to defend the borders from the advancing Indian Army based on a 'fortress concept' which meant converting the border towns and villages into strongholds. The Government of East Pakistan appointed General Niazi as GOC-in-C of the Eastern Command, and Major-General Rao Farman Ali as their military adviser for East Pakistan Rifles and East Pakistan Coast Guard. On October 1971, Niazi lost contacts with the Army GHQ and was virtually independent of controlling the Eastern Command from the central government in Islamabad. On November 1971, General Abdul Hamid Khan, the Chief of Staff, warned him of an eminent Indian attack on East advised him to redeploy the Eastern Command on a tactical and political base ground but this was not need implemented due to shortage of time.

Hilal–i–Jurat

Lt. General Amir Abdullah Khan Niazi (Cont)

On 3RD December 1971, the Pakistan Air Force launched the pre-emptive strikes on Indian Air Force bases that officially led to start of the third war with India. When Indian Army soldiers crossed the borders and charged towards the Dacca, General Niazi panicked when he came to realise the real nature of Indian strategy. He became frantically nervous when Indian Army successfully penetrated the defence of the East Pakistan. On 9TH December, the Indian government accepted the sovereignty of Bangladesh and extended its diplomatic mission to Bangladesh. During this time, the Special Branch of East Pakistan Police notified Governor Niazi of the joint Indo-Bengali siege of Dhaka as the Eastern Command led by Lieutenant-General Jagjit Singh Aurora began encircling Dhaka. Governor Niazi appealed for a conditional ceasefire to Lieutenant-General Jagjit Singh Aurora which called for transferring power to elected government but without the surrender of the Eastern Command led by General Niazi. This offer was rejected by Indian Army's Chief of Army Staff General Sam Manekshaw but Manekshaw set a deadline for surrender, and President Yahya Khan considered it as 'illegitimate'. Niazi appealed for a cease-fire, but Manekshaw set a deadline for surrender, failing which Dhaka would come under siege. Subsequently, the Indian Army began encircling the Dacca and Lieutenant-General Jagjit Singh Aurora sent a message that issued an ultimatum to surrender in '30-minutes' time. On 16TH December 1971 Lieutenant-General Niazi agreed to surrender and sent a message to General Manekshaw despite many army officers declined to obey although they were legally bound. The Indian Army commanders, Lieutenant General Sagat Singh, Lieutenant General J.S. Aurora, and Major-General Rafael Farj Jacob arrived on Dhaka via helicopter with the surrender documents. The meeting took place at Ramna Race Course in Dhaka at 16:31 Hrs PST on 16TH December 1971, and General Niazi signed the Instrument of Surrender with the J.S. Aurora in the presence of Pakistani military and Indian army commanders that nearly surrendered ~95,000 personnel of the Eastern Command to Indian Army. Niazi was repatriated to Pakistan was handed over to Lieutenant-General Abdul Hamid, then-GOC-in-C of IV Corps, by Indian Army from the Wagah checkpoint in Lahore District, Punjab, in April 1975, in a symbolic gesture of last war prisoner held by India. Upon arriving in Lahore, he was immediately refrained from speaking to news media correspondents and immediately taken under the custody of the Pakistan Army's Military Police (MP)

Hilal–i–Jurat

Lt. General Amir Abdullah Khan Niazi (Cont)

He was shifted via helicopter to the Lahore Cantonment where he was detained despite his strong protests. He was immediately dismissed from his military commission and war honours were withdrawn from him. His three-star rank was eventually reduced to Major-General, a two-star rank, but was dismissed from the service in July 1975. He was also denied his military pension and medical benefits; though he lodged a strong complain against revoking of his pension. In 1980s, the Ministry of Defence quietly changed the status of 'dismissal' to 'retirement' but did not restore his rank. The change of order allowed Niazi to seek pension and medical assistance benefits enjoyed by the retired military personnel. Niazi remained active in the national politics in 1970s and supported the ultraconservative agenda on a conservative platform against Pakistan People's Party. In 1977, he was again detained by the police when the martial law was enforced and sought retirement from politics. In 1972, Niazi was summoned and confessed at the War Enquiry Commission led by Chief Justice Hamoodur Rahman and the Supreme Court of Pakistan on the events involving the secession of East Pakistan on April 1975. The War Commission indicted him of corrupt and moral turpitude while noting his bullying of junior officers who would resists his orders. Though he showed no regrets, Niazi refused to accept the responsibility of Breakup of East Pakistan and squarely blamed President Yahya. The War Commission endorsed his claims that President Yahya was to blame but noted that Niazi was the Commander who lost East Pakistan. The War Commission recommended court martial to be held by the Judge Advocate General that would induct Niazi of serious breaches of military disciplines and military code. However, no such court-martial took place but, nonetheless, he was politically maligned and inducted with the war crimes taken place in East Pakistan. Niazi did not accept the War Commission's inquiries and fact-findings, believing that the War Commission had no understanding of the military matters. Niazi claimed that a court-martial would have besmeared the names of those who later rose to great heights, and that he was being used as a scapegoat. After giving interview to ARY News, Niazi died on 1ST February 2004 in Lahore, Punjab, Pakistan. He was buried in Military Graveyard in Lahore.

(After the debacle in East Pakistan, Niazi was immediately dismissed from his military commission, and as mentioned before, his war honours and awards were withdrawn from him).

Hilal–i–Jurat

Lieutenant General Abdul Ali Malik, HJ

Lieutenant General Abdul Ali Malik was a Pakistan Army engineer officer and a high-ranking military general. He is a well-known figure from the Chawinda tank battle during the 1965 Indo-Pakistani war and was a member of the Ahamdiyya community.

He belonged to a small village called Pindori which is about 65 Kilometers away from Rawalpindi. He joined Pakistan Army as a cadet-officer and later inducted in Pakistan Army Corps of Engineers. He completed his B.Sc. in electrical engineering from the Pakistan Military Academy, and served in the civil projects of the Pakistan Army. He is known to present at the constructions of the dam and had supervised the various projects in Punjab. His brother Lieutenant General Akhtar Hussain Malik was also an Army general and was himself a hero of 1965 war too. He retired from the Army after commanding the I Corps at Mangla. During the Indo-Pakistan War of 1965, Brigadier Abdul Ali Malik was commander of the 24TH infantry brigade in the Sialkot-Phillurah-Chamb sector. At the start of the war, his brigade was ordered by the senior 15 division to defend the imaginary Indian attack at Jasser Bridge. Even though, he was reluctant to move forward (because of the Indian comprehensive orders were caught on the Indian side of border) he was forced to take his command to Jasser sector. However, it later turned out that those orders were indeed true, and he was ordered to move back into the same position. It was at this time, that Pakistan Army tanks caught the Indian armoured brigade by surprise, and hence was commenced the largest tank battle after the World War II. Later in the 1965 War, he was awarded the gallantry award, Hilal-i-Jurat, for leading an infantry brigade as part of the 6TH Armoured Division that fought the famous tank battle with the Indian Army at Chawinda in Sialkot and halted the advance of the invading Indian troops in Pakistan's territory. The war ended the following day. Pakistan had suffered attrition to its military might and serious reverses in the battle at Khemkaran and Chawinda which made way for the acceptance the UN Resolution.

Now promoted Major General Abdul Ali Malik commanded the 8TH Infantry Division in the western sector of 1971 Indo-Pakistani War. His troops were stationed in the Sialkot sector, and apart from some skirmishes, a major all-out war didn't happen.

Major General Abdul Ali Malik passed away in July 2015. It was military function; the army played its part with style. A smartly turned-out detachment of 19 Punjab Regiment presented arms and then fired its farewell salvo and a bugler played the "last post".

Hilal–i–Jurat

Brigadier Amjad Ali Khan Chaudhry, HJ

Brigadier Amjad Ali Khan Chaudhry HJ a Pakistani officer who distinguished himself in the 1965 Indo-Pakistan war. Brigadier Amjad was born in Poonch, Kashmir on 9 January 1917, where his father, Sher Ali Khan was on tour with his family. He was an outstanding student and scholarship holder throughout his school and college career. He did his BA (Honours) in English from the prestigious Government College, Lahore. He was commissioned in the then British Indian Army in 1942 in the 25 Mountain regiment. He served as second-in- command of the 2 Field Regiment, Royal Pakistan Artillery 1949-50. He was Brigade Major (BM) 7 Division Artillery during the Kashmir Operations 1947-49. He commanded the 4 Field Regiment Pakistan Artillery from 1956–57 and raised the 26 Field Regiment Artillery in 1957-59. He was Instructor (1954–55) and then Chief Instructor (1966–67) at the prestigious Command and Staff College, Quetta earning him the nickname 'thinking General'. He also served as Director Weapons and Equipment (DWE) at the General Headquarters (GHQ) 1959-61 of the Pakistan Army in Rawalpindi. He was Commander 7 Division Artillery 1961-64 and Commander 4 Corps Artillery 1964-66. Almost all subsequent accounts of the 1965 War have acknowledged the decisive role and outstanding performance of 4 Corps Artillery which was commanded by Brigadier Amjad Chaudhry in the Kashmir Operations preceding this war and in the battles of Chamb and Jaurain during Pakistan's thrust into Indian held Kashmir and in the battle of Chawinda in the Sialkot sector - the decisive battle of the 1965 War. Field Marshal Mohammad Ayub Khan, President of Pakistan during the 1965 War wrote the following tribute (in his own handwriting) on the performance of 4 Corps Artillery commanded by Brigadier Amjad Chaudhry as follows:

"*By all accounts the part played by the 4 Corps Artillery can only be termed as magnificent. The results they achieved are miraculous for which they deserve congratulations and gratitude of us all*". (Signed) Field Marshal Mohammad Ayub Khan President of Pakistan 13TH November 1965. According to Shuja Nawaz in his history of the Pakistan Army, "A bold and meticulous artillery plan for the attack (on Chamb) was devised by the energetic leader of the corps artillery Brig. Amjad Ali Khan Chaudhry and his staff to dominate the battlefield"

Hilal–i–Jurat

Brigadier Amjad Ali Khan Chaudhry (Cont)

"The enemy's attack on Chawinda ... broke up mostly under Artillery fire. Artillery was used most aggressively ... .In no other theatre of the Indo-Pak War of 1965 did the guns come so close to being overrun by Indian tanks so many times, nor were the Pakistani gunners more brilliant in their hour of crisis" (Ahmed, 2006, History of the Indo-Pak War-1965, Oxford University Press, p. 518). Writing also on the battle of Chawinda the armour corps officer and historian Major (Retd.) Agha Humayun Amin wrote, "4 Corps Artillery Brigade, led by Brigadier Amjad Chaudhry, described by many contemporaries as one of the finest artillery officers that the sub-continent produced played a crucial role in the Battle of Chawinda" (Amin, Agha Humayun, Maj. (Retd,), March 2001, "Battle of Chawinda", Defence Journal, Karachi.

His citation captures his and the role of 4 Corps Artillery which he commanded in support of 6 Armoured Division in the battle of Chawinda admirably:

During the Divisional operation in Chawinda sector the Corps of Artillery did a magnificent job in effectively supporting his formation. It was mainly due to the effective artillery support that determined attacks by superior enemy forces were beaten off with heavy losses to the enemy. It was purely due to the personal example, fine leadership qualities and devotion to duty of Brigadier Amjad Ali Khan Chaudhry that not only the enemy attacks were beaten off but the whole formation got inspiration for a fight to the bitter end.

For this conspicuous act to duty and gallantry he has been awarded the highly deserved gallantry decoration of Hilal-i-Jurat during course of the battle of Chawinda in the September 1965 India-Pakistan war. Brigadier Amjad Ali Khan Chaudhry passed away at Lahore on 5TH December 1990.

Hilal–i–Jurat

Brigadier Ahsan Rashid Shami, HJ

Brigadier Shami was close to retirement in 1965 when the country called upon him. He was the Commander Artillery for one of the divisions focused in the Lahore sector.....during the early days of the war while on inspection of the vast areas under his command he was moving in his command jeep with a few other senior officers....he wanted to take exact note of the situation and be aware of how far and deep his forces were into the Indian area, how much area was occupied by Pakistani soldiers under his command and how much still was left...... during his observation tour he went a bit too close to the disgruntled enemy who took the golden opportunity and attacked the commander and his jeep with heavy weapons....he came under direct fire of enemy's machine gun...Brig Shami received number of bullets on his chest and he embraced Shahadat.... His dead body was taken by the Indians and he was buried beyond the border inside India.....after the war his body was brought back to be buried on home ground. For his courage, brave act of going into the enemy's mouth to grab important information and leading his men from the front, Brigadier Shami was awarded Hilal-i- Jurat.

Major-General Naseerullah Khan Babar HJ, SJ and (Bar)

Major-General Naseerullah Khan Babar was Minister of Internal Security of Pakistan. Babar was born in Pirpiai, North-West Frontier Province, and British Indian Empire. His family is from the Babar tribe of Pashtuns and hails from the village of Pirpiai in district Nowshera. Babar's early education was from Presentation Convent School, Peshawar, North West Frontier Province, British India, between 1935 and 1939. From 1939 to 1941 he attended Burn Hall School then located at Srinagar. The school was subsequently shifted to Abottabad after the Partition of India in 1947. He then attended Prince of Wales Royal Indian Military College from 1941-1947 in Dehradun and joined the Pakistan Army in 1948. He was part of the first PMA long course which graduated in 1950. In his long career in the Army, Babar served in the Artillery Corps and pioneered the Army Aviation Corps. During the 1965 war with India, Babar single handily captured an entire Indian company of soldiers (over 70 POWs) and was awarded Sitara-i-Jurat for this action. In the 1971 war, he commanded an artillery brigade supporting 23 Division and later commanded an infantry brigade until he was wounded and evacuated from the battlefield. He also had the distinction of having been awarded SJ & Bar.

Hilal–i–Jurat

Major General Naseerullah Khan Babar, (Cont)

In 1972, he was appointed Inspector General Frontier Corps. Babar rose to become a Major General and led the Frontier Corps as its Commandant in 1974. During 1974, Babar was tasked to fund and train Afghan mujahidin, by the order of Bhutto, to suppress the government of Davood Khan, and disbandment of Pashtunistan policies. This operation was a complete and ultimate success after which Babar proceeded to retire from the army, in order to start his career in politics. However, the operation took a new direction when he became Governor of the Khyber-Pakhtunkhwa from 1975 to 1977 under Zulfikar Ali Bhutto's government until the term was cut short due to *Operation Fair Play*— a clandestine operation undertaken to remove Bhutto. In 1988, Babar was the "Special Advisor/Assistant on Internal Affairs" in Benazir Bhutto's government and between 1993 and 1996, Babar was appointed and tenured as the Interior Minister and supervised and successfully contended *Operation Blue Fox*. He resigned from the Army in 1974 while commanding an infantry division and was appointed as Governor of Khyber-Pakhtunkhwa. Babar joined the Pakistan People's Party (the PPP) in 1977 after the arrest of Zulfikar Ali Bhutto. He famously threw away his Hilal- i -Jurat (with bar) and other army medals at the presiding officer of a military tribunal, when Zulfikar Ali Bhutto was hanged by the military regime of General Muhammad Zia-ul-Haq in 1979. In 1988, Babar was a Special Assistant to the Prime Minister, Benazir Bhutto and successfully ran the election for Begum Nusrat Bhutto from Chitral during the preceding elections. Elected in the 1993 general election on a People's Party Ticket from Nowshera, he defeated Awami National Party President Ajmal Khattak, with the PPP's victory in the election and was appointed Federal Minister for the Interior by Benazir Bhutto. General Naseerullah Babar was one of the major proponents of backing what eventually became the Taliban. In October 2007, he left the Pakistan People's Party due to his disagreement with Benazir Bhutto over her support for General Pervez Musharraf. This action was considered as a major blow for the Pakistan People's Party because he was their major political leader in the Khyber-Pakhtunkhwa. On 19TH August 2008, Naseerullah Babar suffered a mild stroke and was admitted to a hospital. He recovered and returned home in November 2008. Naseerullah Babar died on 10TH January 2011.

Hilal–i–Jurat

Major General Aboobaker Osman Mitha, HJ, SPk, SQA

Major-General Aboobaker Osman Mitha popularize as A.O. Mitha, , was a two-star rank army general who is considered a legend in the Pakistan Army, and a conceptual founder of Special Services Group (SSG). With the help from the United States' Special Forces, he created the special forces unit in Cherat, Khyber Pakhtunkhwa in 1956. Aboobaker Osman Mitha was born 1ST June 1923 to an affluent and politically influential Memon family in Bombay. Mitha grew up in Bombay, spending his childhood and early years under the influence of a joint-family system presided over by an imperious grandfather and an omnipresent, all-powerful grandmother. As a young man, he rejected both a career in business, and the bride chosen for him by his grandfather, and deciding instead to embark upon a career in the army. After finishing high school he joined a pre-cadet academy, and was selected for a commission in the British Indian Army. He passed out of the Indian military academy, Dehradun, on 21ST June 1942 and was granted an emergency commission in the Indian Army and appointed to the 2ND Battalion, 4TH Bombay Grenadiers. After volunteering for the Indian Parachute Regiment, he served in Burma during World War II and was dropped behind Japanese lines for high-risk operations. He was promoted war substantive Lieutenant 21ST December 1942. He was granted a regular Indian Army commission on 25TH May 1946 with an initial commission date of 1ST June 1944 and to rank as a Lieutenant from 1ST December 1945. Mitha refers to the blatant racism that British officers practised against their Indian colleagues in his posthumously published book, *Unlikely Beginnings*. He wrote, 'If there were ten officers in a mess, two of them British, they would see to it that they had little, if anything, to do with their Indian counterparts'. When India divided into the Republic of India and the Dominion of Pakistan in August 1947, Mitha opted for Pakistan. He qualified for the Staff College, Quetta and served as GSO 1 in GHQ Pakistan. He fell in love with Indu Chatterji, daughter of Prof. Gyanesh C. Chatterji of Lahore Government College, who had grown up in Lahore but had since moved to Delhi. That it was not just puppy love but something more lasting was proved by Mitha's perseverance, and four years after the young lovers' separation, Indu, against the wishes of her family, came over to Karachi and they were married. The couple had three daughters, two of whom turned out to be very talented classical dancers.

Hilal-i-Jurat

Major General Aboobaker Osman Mitha, (Cont)

Aboobaker Osman Mitha describes the GHQ in Rawalpindi of the early days of Pakistan in graphic detail, with junior officers using wooden packing cases for desks and chairs and bringing their own pencils to work. Toilet paper, called 'bog paper' by the British, was used to write on, as ordinary paper was just not available. In 1954, Mitha was selected to raise an elite commando unit for Pakistan Army. Cherat, a hill station near Peshawar was chosen as the highly restricted site where the commandos were to be trained and based. Mitha's sole instruction to his handpicked Pakistani officers was, 'Be proud of your poverty.' He remained head of the SSG for 6 years. Mitha was particularly active in East Pakistan in the days preceding the military action of 25TH March 1971. Other generals were present in Dhaka along with Yahya Khan, and secretly departed on the evening of 25TH March 1971, that fateful day after fixing the deadline for the military action. Major General Mitha is said to have remained behind. Lieutenant General Tikka Khan, Major General Rao Farman Ali Major and General Khadim Hussain Raja were associated with the planning of the military action. Eventually their action bloodied the capital city Dhaka with the blood of thousands of residents including students, military and police personnel, politician and the general mass. Later documents regarding their action on the early hours of 26TH March 1971 known as Operation Searchlight was revealed to the world. Major General Mitha was Quartermaster General at GHQ when prematurely retired by the civilian Chief Martial Law Administrator, Zulfikar Ali Bhutto, in December 1971. He was just over 48 years old. Lieutenant General Gul Hasan added his name to a list of officers whose retirements were announced by Zulfikar Ali Bhutto in his first Major General Mitha had no hand in the *Officer's Revolt* at Gujranwala and the shooting down of General Abdul Hamid Khan (Chief of Staff) at a GHQ meeting. According to Major General Mitha, it was Gul Hasan who also saved then-Brigadier Muhammad Zia-ul-Haq from being sacked. Brigadier Zia was in Jordan. The year was 1971. Gen Yahya Khan received a signal from Major General Nawazish, the head of the Pakistan military mission in Amman, asking that Zia be court martial led for disobeying GHQ orders by commanding a Jordanian armoured division against the Palestinians, as part of actions in which thousands were killed. That ignominious event is known as Operation Black September. It was Gul Hasan who interceded for Zia and Yahya Khan let Zia off the hook.

Hilal–i–Jurat

Major-General Aboobaker Osman Mitha, (Cont)
In the course of his military career, he was awarded the Hilal-i-Jurat, Sitara-i-Pakistan, and Sitara-i-Quaid-i-Azam. After retirement he was stripped of his medals and pensions without due cause and that was quite a surprise to the public as he was never court-martial. But Major General Mitha gained more popularity by this due to which he was kept under surveillance by the Bhutto Administration as he was also a hero for his juniors in the SSG. He remained under surveillance through the Bhutto years. He had a hard time finding any kind of employment. Had it not been for the generosity of a friend living in Britain, who asked Mitha to manage his farm for him, he would have been on the street. Major General AO Mitha died in December 1999. After he died, one of his friends wrote to his wife, "At the end of a tumultuous life, all he wanted was a room to sleep in and one to write and eat in – a space to walk, reflect and gaze across the fields to the distant hills."

'Major General Aboobaker Osman Mitha came to prominence, when appointed to raise the Special Service Group (SSG). He became a legend within the SSG, a fact attested to by SSG officers who came after he had moved on from the SSG. He was extremely hands on and leading from the front type of an officer. This made him a legend not only in the Army, but also with the Navy and Air Force. He left his mark on hundreds of young cadets when he commanded the Pakistan Military Academy from 1966–1968. In 1965 he commanded an Infantry Brigade in East Pakistan and was also active there in early 1971 as Deputy Corps Commander. He also commanded the 1 Armoured Division from 1968–1970'.

Brigadier Abdul Qayum Sher, HJ
Abdul Qayum Sher was born into the prominent Shinwari tribe of Pathans and his father Khan Mohammed Azam Khan was engineer with the Indian Civil Service. At an early age Abdul Qayum Sher was sent first to Switzerland and then onto Durham in England, where he attended Durham High School and then Durham College. He participated in sports and was active in the rowing and rugby teams at school level. At the outbreak of World War II he was on a visit to India and he enrolled into the British Indian Army attending Dera Dun Military Academy. He served with distinction in the Burma campaign during the war. After the war in 1945 he met Amita, who was teaching in Lahore, and the same year proposed and married her even though she was from a different religion.

Hilal–i–Jurat

Brigadier Abdul Qayum Sher (Cont)

Amita Sher, a social worker, author of many books and a role model for many women in Pakistan. They had five children, three of whom survive them. Brigadier Abdul Qayum Sher was a legend of the Pakistani Army. He volunteered for the Indian Army pre partition and fought in Burma during World War II. At partition he opted for Pakistan and achieved fame for the capture of Pandu (in Kashmir) during hostilities in 1948 with India. He commanded various battalions including his parent 11 Baluch Regiment. He attended Pakistan Command and Staff College in Quetta and in the Indo-Pakistani War of 1965 was Brigade Commander 22 Brigade on the Lahore front. He led the counterattack force which repelled the Indian attack on Lahore, and captured Indian General N. Prasad's command headquarters (15TH Indian Division) and personally led the attack with his Brigadier insignia and flag on his command jeep. He was awarded the Hilal-i Jurat for outstanding bravery. After retirement he involved himself with voluntary work with the Pakistan Society for the Rehabilitation of the Disabled (PSRD) and worked there till weeks before his death in 2013.

Lieutenant Colonel Ghulam Hussain Shaheed, HJ

Lieutenant Colonel Ghulam Hussain Chaudry or Ghulam Hussain Chaudry Shaheed, HJ, born in 1926, was a Pakistan Army officer who received the Hilal-i-Jurat for his service in the Indo-Pakistani War of 1971. He graduated from the Pakistan Military Academy as part of the 6TH PMA, barely 3 years after the formation of Pakistan as an independent state. He was awarded the second most honourable and prestigious award in Pakistan, the HJ, which is awarded to officers for 'acts of valour, courage or devotion to duty performed on land, at sea or in air.' He was fatally wounded in the Indo-Pakistan war of 1971. The Indo-Pakistan border near Kasur, Pakistan is named in his honour. Lieutenant Colonel Ghulam Hussain Chaudry defended the Kasur border to his last breath; he was fatally wounded while holding up the Pakistani flag, when he was ambushed by soldiers from the Indian army. The outcome of this skirmish is unknown; however, this region still remains within Pakistani soil, and the border near where this skirmish took place is named in Chuddy's honour.

Hilal–i–Jurat

Lt. Colonel Muhammad Akram Raja, HJ

In 1971, following a divisive election result, civil war broke out in the former East Pakistan (now Bangladesh) between the West Pakistani administrative authorities and the majority local population. India, to where many of East Pakistan's exiled political leaders and refugees from the fighting had fled, provided support for the dissidents including arming and training a Bangladeshi irregular force (the Mukti Bahini) To relieve pressure on their forces in the east, in December 1971 Pakistani forces launched a pre-emptive attack on India from the west, which was only partially successful and met with massive retaliation. Fighting on two fronts, Pakistan agreed to a ceasefire after the surrender of her forces in the east and territorial losses in the west (later ceded back to Pakistan following the 1972 Simla Agreement). Frontier Force units fought in both east and west. The 31ST Frontier Force was raised in November 1971, as Pakistan's first national service battalion. It was deployed at Lahore and in the Khemkaran Sector. In East Pakistan, the 4TH Frontier Force was present at the Battle of Hilli, where it held its position until ordered out. Major Muhammad Akram of the 4TH Frontier Force was posthumously awarded Pakistan's highest award for gallantry, the Nishan -i- Haider Other ten units which operated from East Pakistan became prisoners of war once Dhaka fell in December 1971. In West Pakistan, the 11TH Cavalry saw heavy fighting in the Chamb sector. Five Frontier Force untis operated in the Kashmir sector, and in the Sialkot sector, and six Frontier Force untis took part in fighting. An Indian commander, Lieutenant-Colonel V P Airy, of the 3RD Grenadier Guards said of the 35TH Frontier Force: '35 Frontier Force's attack won their commanding officer, Lieutenant-Colonel Akram Raja, a posthumous Hilal-e-Jurat, with the highest compliment a gallant soldier could receive'. In this action Lieutenant-Colonel Akram Raja displayed courage, determination and personal bravery of the highest order with the tradition of the soldiers. The 8TH and 18TH Frontier Force fought on the Lahore front. In the Sulemanki sector, the 6TH Frontier Force gained fame when it captured the Gurmukh Khera Bridge on Sabuna Drain. Major Shabbir Sharif, a holder of the Sitara-i-Jurat from the 1965 conflict, was awarded a posthumous Nishan -i- Haider. The 36TH Frontier Force also fought in the Sulemanki sector, and three Frontier Force units saw action in the Rajhisthan sector.

Hilal–i–Jurat

Captain Muhammad Iqbal Khan Shaheed, HJ

Captain Muhammad Iqbal Khan from Pakistan Special Forces, SSG (3RD Commando Powindah Battalion) was born, on the 15TH of November, 1960 in a small village called Pushtoon Garhi, in the District Nowshera, Khyber Pakhtunkhwa of Pakistan. He joined the Pakistan army in 1982. On September, 1987 he was sent to Siachen, which is the world's highest battlefield. He led a company consisting of twelve soldiers. He always wanted to embrace Martyrdom. While fighting the enemy, he was severely wounded, but he kept moving forward. He kept climbing the steep mountains of Siachen with a gun in one hand and holding himself with the other. The enemy kept shooting at him, and he kept calling out 'Allah-O-Akbar'. He destroyed many pickets on his way till he reached the highest picket on the Siachen Glacier, held by the enemy where he waged the fiercest battle and in the process embraced martyrdom on the 25TH of September, 1987. Captain Muhammad Iqbal Khan was awarded the second highest military award, Hilal-e-Jurat by the government of Pakistan.

Lieutenant General Ziaur Rahman, HJ, BU

Ziau Rahman was born in the village of Bagbari in the Bogra District of the northwest Bangladesh. Ziaur's childhood was divided between living in the village and the city. He was later enrolled into the Hare School in Kolkata. With the partition of the British-India in 1947, Mansur Rahman with his family returned to East Bengal, which became part of the new state of Pakistan. Ziaur was enrolled in the Academy School in Karachi. Zia spent his adolescent years in Karachi and enrolled in the D.J. College there in 1953. In the same year, he entered the Pakistan Military Academy in Kakul as an officer cadet. He was commissioned as a second lieutenant in the Pakistan Army in 1955. After serving for two years in Karachi, he was transferred to the East Bengal Regiment in 1957. Ziaur Rahman himself won the distinguished and prestigious Hilal-i-Jurat medal, and his unit won 2 Sitara-i-Jurat medals and 9 Tamgha-i-Jurat medals from the Army for their brave roles in the 1965 War with India. In 1966, Ziaur was appointed military instructor at the Pakistan Military Academy, later going on to attend the prestigious Command and Staff College in Quetta, where he completed a course in command and tactical warfare. Although sectarian tensions between East and West Pakistan were intensifying, Ziaur travelled to West Germany to receive advanced military and command training with the German Army.

Hilal–i–Jurat

Lt General Ziaur Rahman, (Cont)

Ziau returned to Pakistan the following year, and witnessed political turmoil and regional division. East Pakistan had been devastated by the 1970 Bhola cyclone, and the population had been embittered by the slow response of the central government. The political conflict, between Sheikh Mujibur Rahman's Awami League, which had won a majority in the 1970 elections, and the President Yahya Khan and West Pakistani politician Zulfikar Ali Bhutto had brought sectarian tensions to a climax. Sheikh Mujib laid claim to form a government, but Yahya Khan postponed the convening of the legislature under pressure from West Pakistani politicians. Upon his return, Ziau attained the rank of Major and was transferred to the 8TH East Bengal regiment stationed in Chittagong to serve as its second-in-command. Ziau was appointed Sector Commander of Sector 1 of Bangladesh Forces in the Chittagong and Hill Tracts area, under General M. A. G. Osmani, the Chief General appointed by the Revolution ally Government of Bangladesh. He led the regular guerrilla force and coordinate attacks against the West Pakistani army in his Sector. Within three weeks, Zia travelled across the border into India to receive military resources and training for his troops, which was arranged by the revolutionary government in exile. On June 1ST, 1971 Ziau was appointed the commander of the first conventional brigade of the Bangladesh Forces. His brigade consisted of 1ST, 3RD and 8TH East Bengali regiments, enabling Ziau to launch major attacks on Pakistani forces. On August 15TH, 1975 Sheikh Mujibur Rahman and his family were killed by a group of military officers. One of Sheikh Mujibur Rahman's cabinet ministers Khondaker Mostaq Ahmad was appointed the president and, subsequently, Major General Ziaur Rahman was appointed as the army chief after removal of Major General K M Shafiullah. However, the coup of 15TH August caused a period of instability and unrest in Bangladesh and more so across the ranks and files of the army. Brigadier Khalid Musharraf and the Dhaka Brigade under Colonel Shafat Jamil made a counter-coup on November 3, 1975, and Ziaur Rahman was forced to resign and was put under house arrest. A third coup was staged under Colonel Abu Taher and a group of socialist military officers and supporters of the left-wing Jatiyo Samajtantrik Dal on November 7TH. Brigadier Khalid Musharraf was killed and Colonel Jamil arrested, while Colonel Taher freed Ziaur Rahman and re-appointed him as army chief. Following a major meeting at the army headquarters, an interim government was formed with Justice Abu Sadat Mohammad Sayem as chief martial law administrator.

Hilal–i–Jurat

Lt General Ziaur Rahman, (Cont)

Major General Ziaur Rahman became the 7th President of Bangladesh on April 21st, 1977 following Justice Sayem's resignation on grounds of "ill health", which many believed was simply a pretext for Zia's rise to power with army's backing. Although Sayem had held the title of president, historians believe it was Zia who exercised real power from the cantonment. Sayem had promised early elections, but Zia postponed the plans. The years of disorder had left most of Bangladesh's state institutions in disarray, with constant threats of military coups amidst strikes and protests. Assuming full control of the state, Zia banned political parties, censored the media, re-imposed martial law and ordered the army to arrest dissidents. Martial law restored order across the country to a large measure and as Zia crushed several attempted uprisings with ruthless measures, discipline was finally restored in the army. When Ziaur Rahman assumed the presidency after legalizing military coups and the revival of the multiparty system was seen again he appointed Hussain Muhammad Ershad as the new Chief of Army Staff, promoting him to the rank of Lieutenant General. Zia had taken charge of a nation suffering from severe poverty, chronic unemployment, shortages and economic stagnation. Muting the state's commitment to socialism, Zia announced a '19-point programme' which emphasised self-reliance, rural development, decentralisation and population control. Zia worked energetically and spent much of his time travelling throughout the country, preaching the 'politics of hope' by continually urging all Bangladeshis to work harder and to produce more. Zia focused on boosting agricultural and industrial production, especially in food and grains, and to integrate rural development through a variety of programs, of which population planning was the most important. Working with the proposals of international lending agencies, he launched an ambitious rural development program in 1977, which included a highly visible and popular food-for-work program. Zia began reorienting Bangladesh's foreign policy, addressing the concerns of nationalists who believed that Bangladesh was reliant on Indian economic and military aid. During his term of power, Zia was criticised for ruthless treatment of his army opposition. Although he enjoyed overall popularity and public confidence, h aroused fierce opposition from the supporters of veterans of the Mukti Bahini. In the early hours of the morning of May 30th, he was assassinated by a group of army officers along with six bodyguards and two aides.

Hilal–i–Jurat

Air Marshal Nur Khan, HJ,HS,HQA,SPK

Malik Nur Khan was born on 22ND February, 1923, at Tamman, District Attock. He hails from a family with military traditions, whose elders belonged to the Malik Awan tribe of ancient repute. His father, Malik Mehr Khan was a captain in the Indian Army and served in 20TH Lancers. Maternally, the family is related to Malik Ameer Muhammad Khan, the Nawab of Kalabagh. Nur Khan got his primary education from government middle school Tamman. When he was in fifth class, joined Prince of Wales Royal Indian Military College Dehra Dun. The principal remarked on his forms that it was 'An excellent military family from a very military centre. The boy has been well educated and is more advanced than many Awans of his age. He is physically fit and should make an officer anyhow, he is the right type'. To satiate his flying urge, Malik Nur Khan learnt flying at Lahore Flying Club Walton at the family expense. On successful completion of flying training, he got his pilot's A-license on Tiger Moth biplane. He was inducted as an Indian Air Force volunteer reserve. In December 1940 he went for air crew training. He was commissioned on 6TH January, 1941 as a fighter pilot in the Royal Indian Air Force, at the age of seventeen years ten months only. After initial training, he flew with RAF instructors on the more powerful Hawker Hart and Audax biplanes. On completion of the course, he earned the honour to be the only student of his course to have achieved 'Above Average' assessments from the RAF in armament, gunnery and bombing. His first operational posting was to No.3 Squadron of the original IAF at Peshawar, where he flew Addaxes and Hawker Harts. In 1942, he underwent instructors' course on Harvards at Ambala, where he while converting on Vultee Vengeance dive-bombers, again proved to be the best gunner. During the following years, he served on the Burma front and also rendered services in Japan with the Commonwealth countries occupying forces. On partition in 1947, he and Asghar Khan both opted for Pakistan. He was given the command of Air Base Chaklala. In January, 1948, he was sent to London to serve as a Liaison Officer in the Pakistan High Commission. After a brief stay there, he returned to Pakistan and was posted as Commandant of PAF College, Risalpur in September, 1948. He served as Director of Organization in Air Headquarters from January, 1950 to March, 1951.

Hilal–i–Jurat

Air Marshal Nur Khan (Cont)

His efforts for induction of F-86s instead of F-84s, despite opposition by many and commotion during meetings, he maintained his stance and pursued the procurement of F-86s. During the indo-Pak conflict in 1965, the world witnessed the stunning performance of the aircrew and the aircraft. He commanded Peshawar Station in 1955-56. Having commanded PAF Station Haripur from 1956 to 1957 and accomplishing the task of converting PAF from piston to Jet- served at Air Headquarters before he was appointed as Air Officer Commanding of the first re-organized Operation Group. In February, 1964, he was also appointed Chief Administrator of Civil Aviation and Tourism. He is the one known for his temper for flying and has not only flown fighter aircraft but also tried his hands on civil airliners. On 23RD July 1965, Nur Khan was back to Pakistan Air Force as Commander-in-Chief. He took quick briefs and underwent a conversion on advance jet fighters on the PAF inventory. Being away from fighter cockpit for about six years, he did quick check-outs on T-33, before converting on F-104 the Star fighter. As PAF Chief, it was his leadership that in 1965 war, he led a small but courageous and well trained air force faced and knocked out three time bigger air force. Each one gave his best during the war. The world saw him, his war strategy and his force that gained air superiority in the first 24 hours. The war ended with lot of success and glory. While expressing his feelings about airman and war, he said, 'It was good fortune to have assessed the situation correctly and to have commanded an organization of 100% dedicated pilots, ground crew and technicians', the performance of men was far beyond the expectations'. After retirement in July 1969, Air Marshal Nur Khan held various senior administrative posts in the government. He earned lot of military and civil honours. His decorations include Sitara-i-Pakistan, Sitara-i-Quaid-i-Azam, Hilal-e-Jurat and Hilal-e-Shujat. The King of Jordan awarded him the Order of Istiqlal (2ND Class) and was decorated as Commander of the National Order of the Cedars by the President of Lebanon, besides the award of Grand Officer in the order of Range Nassau with Swords by the Dutch Government. Air Marshal Nur Khan passed away in 2011. In commemoration of his services rendered to Pakistan Air Force, PAF Base Chaklala was renamed as PAF Base Nur Khan in 2012.

Hilal–i–Jurat

Air Commodore Mohammad Zafar Masud, HJ

Air Commodore Muhammad Zafar Masud, was a one star rank air force officer in the Pakistan Air Force and a military strategist who is known his role as commander of the Eastern Air Command of the Eastern Command. Masud had the area responsibility of defending the airspace border of East-Pakistan but resigned from his commission after the military operation took place on 26TH March 1971, and left the command to Air Commodore Inamul Haq on 30TH March 1971.

Muhammad Masud Zafar was born in Gujranwala, Punjab in British India into a Punjabi family in 1927. His father, Zafar Hussain, was an alumnus of Punjab University and was a civil officer in the Indian Railways who later headed the Railway Board in Delhi when the family was moved before the partition. In 1942, he did his matriculation from Model High School and joined the Royal Indian Air Force with a dream of becoming fighter pilot. In 1946, he gained commissioned in the RIAF as Pilot Officer (2ND Lieutenant) and joined the Pakistan Air Force after the independence of Pakistan as a result of the partition of India on 14TH August of 1947. He did not participate in the first war with India in 1947 as he joined the air force faculty. In 1948, Pilot Officer Masud joined the faculty of Air Force Academy in Risalpur where he began flight instructions to young air force cadets. In 1952, he did further training on flight management and qualified as a fighter pilot when he completed a Fighter Leader Course at the RAF. In 1957-58, Masud was tasked by Air Cdr-in-C, Air Marshal Asghar Khan, to organize, train, and lead an aerobatics team, the PAF Sherdils, of 16 F-86 Sabre jets that would set a world record, validating the PAF's place among the well-regarded air arms of the world. Group Captain Masud's first command assignment was included as base commander Sargodha Air Force Base, which would emerge him as the top hero of the 1965 war. In 1965, he actively participated in second war with India when he led a team of fighter pilots, including Fl. Lt. Mervyn Middlecoat, Sq. Ldr. Cecil Chaudhry, and Sq. Ldr. MM Allam, against the Indian Air Force.[1] Group Captain Masud flew against the Indian Air Force in Sargodha Sector with great courage and was regarded as an ace fighter for his ability in dogfight against the Indian pilots. It was clear that Masud's courage, tactical planning, guidance and training of the pilots had helped tremendously in achieving superiority over the much larger IAF. Masud was awarded the Hilal-i-Jurat and many of his pilots were also given military awards. And September 7TH was declared Yaum-e-Fazia (Pakistan Air Force Day). It continues to be celebrated annually in Pakistan.

Hilal–i–Jurat

Air Commodore Mohammad Zafar Masud (Cont)

From 1966–69, Group Captain Masud continued his role as a flight instructor with the Air Force and was appointed in the Air AHQ as Director-General of Air Operations. In 1969, Group Captain Masud was promoted to one star rank, Air Commodore (Brigadier), and was being speculated as a probable future air force chief once the retirement of Air Marshal Abdul Rahim Khan. In 1970, Air Commodore Masud was appointed as an AOC of the Eastern Air Command, and was assigned in Dhaka as top air commander by Yahya administration. He was also the honour of receiving Hilal-i-Jurat for his leadership. Masud established the presence of the air force with higher measure of courage and, since spending a year in East, Masud reached to the conclusion that, with increasing distress, the rapidly mounting military-political threat that none of the power wielders seemed able or interested to resolve. In April 1971, Masud relayed his concern to then-Governor East Vice-Admiral Syed Mohammad Ahsan and his Chief of Staff Lieutenant-General Yakub Ali Khan. Upon their retirement, Masud took the command of the Eastern Command but he suffered with high-level of local defections in his own staff when Air Commodore Masud's chief of staff Group Capt A. K. Khandker defected to India in an official plane in May 1971. This was followed by the defection of Wing Commander Muhammad Hamidullah and Squadron Leader M.G. Tawab who joined the Indian Air Force against the PAF in East. Air Commodore Masud refused to send and dispatch the No. 14 Squadron Tail Choppers under Squadron Leader PQ Mehdi for aerial support for searchlight. During this time, Air Commodore Masud made many contacts with President Yahya Khan but was unable to reach to him, eventually deciding to visit in Army GHQ in Rawalpindi. Masud handed over the air command to Air Commodore Inamul Haque and arrived in Pakistan but was unable to hold the meeting with President Yahya which eventually led Masud disheartened and frustrated. Despite urging against the early and premature retirement, Masud tendered his resignation from the Pakistan Air Force, which attracted the news media correspondents who tried getting his opinion but he declined to comment. After seeking retirement on July 1971, Masud worked as civilian flight instructor for the Pakistan International Airlines which he remained associated his entire life. Masud died due to a cardiac arrest in PAF Hospital in Islamabad and is buried in PAF cemetery in Islamabad, where his wife was also laid to rest next to him in 2003.

Hilal–i–Jurat

Squadron Leader Sarfaraz Ahmed Rafiqui Shaheed, HJ, SJ
Squadron Leader 18TH July 1935 Sarfaraz Ahmed Rafiqui was a fighter pilot in the Pakistan Air Force. He is known for bravery and courage in two of the aerial combats Indo-Pakistani War of 1965, and is a recipient of both the Hilal-e-Jurat (Crescent of Courage) and the Sitara-i-Jurat (Star of Courage).

Sarfraz Ahmed Rafiqui was born in Rajshahi (then East Pakistan, present Bangladesh) on 18TH July 1935. He started his education from St. Anthony's High School (Lahore), matriculating from Government High School, Multan in 1948. With the transfer of his father to Karachi, he joined DJ Singh Science College. Inspired by his elder brother Ijaz Rafiqui (of 4th GDP Course), he later joined RPAF with 13 GD (P) course, graduating in 1953 from RPAF College Risalpur, winning the Best Pilot Trophy. After graduation he was deployed to Miranshah, flying Hawker Sea Fury. Later he was selected for Advanced Flying Course as well as the Fighter Weapons Instructors- Course, in USA. Later after qualifying from Fighter Leaders School of PAF in 1960, he went as an exchange pilot with No 19 Sqn of RAF, flying Hawker Hunters. On return from UK in 1962, he was appointed OC of No 14 Squadron in Dhaka. After a year there, he was transferred to No 5 Squadron as OC, which he commanded during the war of 1965. On the evening of 1ST September 1965, IAF intervened at Chamb Sector to stop the Pak Army's XII Division offensive against Akhnoor, with three strike formations of de Havilland Vampires of No 45 Sqn of IAF flying in for Close Air Support. Rafiqui along with Flight Lieutenant Imtiaz Bhatti (of No 15 Sqn) while patrolling at 20,000 ft. near Chamb, was directed to the attacking aircraft. A total of four attacking aircraft (three from one formation only) were shot down, two by Rafiqui. He was awarded with Sitara-e-Jurrat for this mission. On 6 Sep 1965, he was tasked to lead four aircraft of No 5 Sqn to strike IAF Halwara Air Base along with Flight Lieutenant Younus Hussain as his number 2, Flight Lieutenant Cecil Chaudhry as number 3, and Flight Lieutenant Saleem as No 4, reaching there by at 1705 hours. However, due to the missions flown earlier in defence of Lahore, the aircraft were made ready for flights at given time, critically delaying the raid. Later on while taxiing, the generator of F/L Saleem malfunctioned and hence a 3 ship formation finally took off for Halwara. Halwara had two Hunter Squadrons (No 7 and No 27 Sqn, the former moving in from Ambala in August 65) stationed there. The formation pulled up for attack on target at 1753 hrs, immediately intercepting the CAP formation of Flying Officer A. R. Gandhi and Flying Officer P.S. Pingale of No 7 Squadron.

Hilal–i–Jurat

Squadron Leader Sarfaraz Ahmed Rafiqui (Cont)

After scoring one kill onto Pingale's Hunter, Rafiqui's guns jammed. He ordered Chaudhry to take lead carry on the attack and providing cover to his tail. While doing so, his plane was hit by Flying Officer A. R. Gandhi (who was shot down by Cecil, moments later). The wreckage of Rafiqui's Sabre #52-5248 is still held in IAF Museum at Palam. For his bold leadership displayed over Halwara, Rafiqui was awarded Hilal-i-Jurat. His citation read:

"On 6TH September 1965, Squadron Leader Sarfaraz Ahmad Rafiqui led a formation of 3 F-86 aircraft on a strike against Halwara airfield. The formation was intercepted by about 10 Hunter aircraft out of which Squadron Leader Rafiqui accounted for one in the first few seconds. But then his guns jammed due to a defect and stopped firing. However, Rafiqui refused to leave the battle area which he would have been perfectly justified to do; instead he ordered his No. 2 to take over as leader and continue the engagement while he tried to give the formation as much protection as was possible with an unarmed aircraft. This called on the part of Squadron Leader Rafiqui. The end for him was never in doubt but he chose to disregard it and, in the process, his aircraft was shot down and he was killed but not before enabling his formation to shoot down 3 more Hunter aircraft. Rafiqui's conduct was clearly beyond the call of duty and conformed to the highest traditions of leadership and bravery in battle against overwhelming odds. For this and his earlier exploits, he is awarded Hilal-i-Jurat and Sitara-i-Jurat"

'In this epic encounter, Rafiqui was at his leadership best. Of course he had scored a confirmed kill a third time. He had also not lost sight of the significance of the mission and, despite heavy odds, did his best to get the formation to put in the attack. But when the ultimate test came after his guns jammed during the dogfight, he stayed on. Though he got shot before long, it was the spirit of solidarity, that very brave gesture to stay with the team, which is remembered to this day. As a Squadron Commander, his act demonstrably inspired other Squadron Commanders and pilots to lead fearlessly. This may well have been Rafiqui-s greatest contribution to the 1965 air war'.

Pakistan's third biggest air base, Rafiqui Airbase (Shorkot Cantonment) is named after him. One of the largest roads of the Lahore Cantonment is named Sarfaraz Rafiqui Road in his honour. Rafiqui Shaheed Road in Karachi is also named after him. In Peshawar, the Rear Air Headquarters and PAF School and Degree College, are located on Rafiqui Road.

Hilal–i–Jurat

Air Marshal Abdur Rahim Khan, HJ, HQA, SPk, SBt

Air Marshal Abdur Rahim Khan, was a three-star rank air marshal who served as the last Commander-in-Chief of the Pakistan Air Force from 1969 until 1972.

Abdul Rahim Khan was born in Rawalpindi, Punjab, and British India on 25TH July 1925. He hailed from a Punjabi-Pathan family. He joined the Royal Indian Air Force and gained commissioned as Flight Officer in 1943. He participated in the RIAF's bombing missions against Japan in the Burma theatre in World War II. After the independence of Pakistan as a result of partition of India on 14TH August 1947, he opted for Pakistan and joined the newly established Pakistan Air Force while taking up the instructor position in the Air Force Academy. In 1950s, he was sent to United Kingdom where he attended the Imperial Defence College where he graduated with a staff course degree. He later went to the United States to attend the staff college and underwent to complete a pilot's training on the jet aircraft. In 1952, he earned distinction and notability when he broke the sound barrier; thus becoming the first Pakistani pilot to fly at a speed faster than sound. Upon returning to Pakistan, he was given the command of No. 11 Squadron Arrows, the only squadrons composed with jet fighters. In addition he also commanded the No. 9 Squadron Griffins. His command assignment included his role as commandant of the Air War College and AOC of Masroor Air Force Base in Karachi, Sindh, Pakistan. In 1965, Air Cdre Khan was appointed as Assistant Chief of the Air Staff of Air Operations (ACAS(Ops)) and participated in detailing the air operations during in the second war with India. On 1ST September 1 1969, Air Cdre Khan was promoted to three-star rank, Air Marshal, was appointed Commander in Chief of Pakistan Air Force, serving under President Yahya Khan. During this time, he paid a visit to China to strengthened military relations between two nations. In 1971, AM Khan led the PAF during the third war with India, and is noted for making leading the air force in making minimum aerial contact with the Indian Air Force. About the aerial missions, Khan reportedly marked: "Well, I suppose we did not commit any major blunders." He issued directives of banning the Bengali pilots flying for the bombing missions after a one pilot attempted to defect to India, but the attempt was made unsuccessful by the second pilot. After the Indian Navy's second attack on Karachi, AM Khan refused to make further retaliation against the Indian Navy and reportedly told the Pakistan Navy's Commander in Chief Vice-Admiral Muzaffar Hassan: "Well, old boy, this happens in war. I am sorry your ships have been sunk. We shall try to do something in the future."

Hilal–i–Jurat

Air Marshal Abdur Rahim Khan (Cont)

Air Marshal Khan played a critical and pivotal role in turning over the President Yahya Khan's administration and helped Zulfikar Ali Bhutto assuming the presidency on 20TH December 1971. Air Marshal Khan became to known and gained reputation as the strongest military influence in the country. On 2ND March 1972, President Bhutto dismissed Air Marshal Khan and Lieutenant General Gul Hassan Khan from their respective commands in an allegations of obstructing the hearings of the Hamoodur Rahman Commission. President Bhutto levelled charges on him of "Bonaparte" actions, and replaced with him Air Marshal Zafar Chaudhry who was appointed as first chief of air staff– thus making him the last commander in chief of the air force. On 11TH March 1972, President Bhutto, instead, posted him in the Ministry of Foreign Affairs and appointed him as the designated Pakistan Ambassador to Spain, alongside with Lieutenant General Gul Hassan Khan who was sent as Ambassador to Austria. He presented his diplomatic credentials to Juan Carlos I in Barcelona but his tenure ship remained until 13TH April 1977 when he resigned in protest against the allegations of riggings during the general elections held in 1977. He immediately appealed and called for Pakistani military to forcefully removed Prime Minister Bhutto. After the military takeover of civilian government by General Zia-ul-Haq, the Chief of Army Staff, Abdul Rahim left the Ministry of Foreign Affairs and moved to United States. He bought a house in Potomac, Maryland and lived until his death due to Kidney failure on 28TH February 1990. Abdul Rahim Khan was married to Princess Mehrunissa Khan, the only child of the beloved but unofficial third queen of the Nawab of Rampur. They got married in London when Rahim Khan was a group captain.

Abdul Rahim Khan was described as "soft-spoken" and was fond of golf and polo, and avoided making slighting remarks about his Indian adversaries.

Hilal-i-Jurat

Air Marshal Inamul Haque Khan, HI (M), SI (M), HJ

Air Marshal Inamul Haque Khan was a three-star rank air force general in the Pakistan Air Force who is known for his role as AOC of the Eastern Air Command of the Pakistan Air Force. Inamul Haque Khan was born in Delhi in India, on 23RD January 1921. He was educated at the Aligarh Muslim University. In 1948, he opted to Pakistan, following the partition of India, and joined the Pakistan Air Force. He participated in the second war with India in 1965 as Group-Captain, earning distinction as an ace fighter. In 1969, he was promoted to one star rank, Air Commodore in the Pakistan Air Force and was stationed in East Pakistan. In June 1971 as the Indo-Pak war progressed, Air Cdre. Haque was instrumental in getting almost all PAF pilots and their aircraft out of Dacca after the Dhaka Airport was permanently damaged by the Indian Air Force. Though, initially thought that the army aviation's evacuation by air was not possible due to the air superiority enjoyed by the IAF, he also provided his expertise to army aviation pilots to take fly out the army helicopters with remaining PAF pilots. He himself, however, stuck to his post till the end of the war and then was taken as war prisoner by Indian Army in 1971. In 1974, Air Cdre Inamul Haque was repatriated to Pakistan under the agreement signed with India and Bangladesh, and was allowed to continue his service, eventually attaining the three-star rank in the Air Force. Air Vice Marshal (Major-General) Haq had been appointed as the ACAS (Operations) at the Air AHQ, and later commanded as Air Defence Command as its AOC-in-C with a three-star rank, Air Marshal (Lieutenant-General).His command assignment also included as Director General Joint Staff at JS HQ. Air Mshl Haque was appointed as Interior Minister in Zia administration until 5TH July 1978. From 1978-82, he served as Minister of Housing and Works In 1980-81, he also led the Ministry of Water and Power In 1981, he was posted on a diplomatic assignment and envoy to Croatia until 1985.

From 1997–99, he remained part of the cabinet of Prime Minister Nawaz Sharif but eventually retired. Air Marshal Inamul Haque died of an old age, 90, as he was ailing for quite some time, and is funeral prayers was held at PAF Base Noor Khan on August 11TH with complete military honour. In 1971, Inamul Haque Khan, as Air Commodore , was one of the highest ranking officer who was taken war prisoner by India after Eastern Command's Commander Lieutenant-General A.A.K. Niazi signed an instrument of surrender with Indian Army's Eastern Command GOC-in-C, Lieutenant-General Jagjit Singh Aurora. He was repatriated in 1973, and continued to serve in the Air Force with distinction.

Hilal–i–Jurat

Vice-Admiral Afzal Akram Rahman Khan, HQA, HPk, HJ

Vice-Admiral Afzal Akram Rahman Khan was a three-star rank admiral, politician, and the Commander in Chief of Pakistan Navy, serving from 1959 until 1966. Afzal Akram Rahman Khan was born in 1921, and very little is known of his early life. He was educated at the Rashtriya Indian Military College at Dehradun, and gained commission as a Midshipman in the Royal Indian Navy in 1938. He was also trained as naval artillery specialist from Britannia Royal Naval College in United Kingdom and participated in World War II on behalf of Great Britain.

After World War II, he studied at the Command and Staff College in 1945 and graduated with a staff course degree in 1946 He provided his gunnery services to *HMS Duke of York* at the time of the partition of British India and decided to opted for Pakistan in 1947. He did not actively participated in first war with India in 1947, instead he commanded a destroyer from Karachi to Mumbai to oversee the evacuation of Indian emigrants to Pakistan. He was among the first twenty naval officers who joined the Royal Pakistan Navy (RPN) as a Lieutenant .He was the third most senior Lieutenant in the navy in terms of seniority list provided by the Royal Indian Navy to the Ministry of Defence in 1947.In 1949, he was promoted as Lieutenant-Commander and served as commanding officer of PNS Tariq, the first destroyer, when it was commissioned from the Royal Navy on 30TH September 1949. In 1950, he was promoted as Commander and commanded the *Tippu Sultan* and sailed on a goodwill mission to Middle East and Eastern Europe; he visited Jeddah, Malta, Venice, Athens, Istanbul, Izmir and Crete. In 1951, he participated in Task Force 91 that was held in Trincomalee Sri Lanka with the Royal Navy. At Trincomalee, they had a rendezvous with a large force (9 ships) of the Royal Navy, the Indian Navy and the Royal Ceylon Navy. It led to 14 days of strenuous exercises in harbour and at sea. The officers and men from these ships also took part in various Inter Services Tournaments. His career progressed well in the navy and helped establish the Naval Intelligence (NI) and helped establish the Karachi Naval Dockyard. In 1958–59, the Naval NHQ staff had been in a brief conflict with the Ministry of Defence over the rearmament issues which eventually led the resignation of Vice-Admiral HMS Choudrie. Afzal Rahman Khan was never appointed to four-star admiral rank but nonetheless was appointed as Commander in Chief of Pakistan Navy after his nomination papers were approved by then-President Iskander Mirza in 1959.

Hilal–i–Jurat

Vice-Admiral Afzal Akram Rahman Khan, (Cont)

Prior to his appointment as commander in chief of navy, his command responsibilities included as his role as Commander Pakistan Fleet (COMPAK) and Commander Logistics (COMLOG) commands headquartered in Karachi, Sindh with being promoted to the two-star rank of Rear-Admiral.[1] After promoting as Vice-Admiral, he oversaw the induction of submarines in the navy in 1960s; for this, he is viewed as the "father of submarines force" of Pakistan Navy. He earned public notability when he acted as a leader during the war with India in 1965 despite having prior no knowledge on covert operation in Indian Kashmir. He oversaw the planning of and execution of the naval operation to attack the Indian Navy which earned him the prestige in the country. After the war, he was publicly honoured and was decorated with Hilal-i-Jurat by President Ayub Khan. He is noted for his multiple extensions in the navy that made him noted as the longest serving chief of staff of navy. He was known to be closer to President Ayub Khan who appointed him as the Defence and Interior Minister in 1966 while serving as an active-duty admiral.:104[8] About the uprising and riots in East-Pakistan in 1969, Vice-Admiral Rahman told the journalists that the "country was under the Mob rule and that Police were not strong enough to tackle the situation." He served in ministerial post until 1969 when President Ayub Khan resigned and handed over the presidency to his Army Commander-in-Chief General Yahya Khan who suspended the Constitution. In protest to the martial law, Vice-Admiral A.R. Khan resigned from his portfolio on 25TH March 1969. Khan resigned from the ministries as a protest when General Yahya Khan, instituted another martial law on 25TH March 1969. After his resignation, Khan retired from national politics and moved to Islamabad in 1969 where he lived a very quiet and private life. He did not comment on war with India in 1971 as he diminished his role from the politics in 1970s. In 1987, the Pakistan Navy honoured him after establishing a naval base under his name. The PNS Akram now serves as a forward operating base for the Navy and acts as a depot for all naval personnel stationed west of Ormara. He avoided the media and lived on a military pensions; he died at an old age in Islamabad in 2005. His death went unnoticed in the media and was quietly buried in Islamabad with close family members attending his funeral.

Hilal–i–Jurat

Admiral Mohammad Shariff, NI (M), HI (M), SI (M), LM, HJ, SJ, SK

Admiral Mohammad Shariff is a retired four-star naval officer and a career war veteran. Admiral Mohammad Shariff took over the command of Pakistan Navy on 21ST March, 1979. He was the first four-star naval admiral who was appointed for the Chairmanship of Joints Chiefs of Staff Committee; hence, he became the principal and supreme commandant of the Pakistan Defence Forces.

Shariff joined Royal Navy in 1936 at age of 16 as a sailor in the Communication Branch and witnessed battle actions on the high seas in the Atlantic during World War-II. After the Partition and Independence of State of Pakistan, Lieutenant Shariff opted for the Pakistani citizenship, and joined the Pakistan Navy. In 1953, he was promoted to Lieutenant Commander in the navy, and in 1956, he was promoted to Commander where he was shifted as Staff officer at Karachi Naval Base (COMKAR). In 1961, Shariff was promoted to Captain, and commanded the PNS Tariq till 1964. In 1965, before the Indo-Pak War of 1965, Shariff was promoted to one-star rank, Commodore. Shariff, as one-star Commodore actively participated in Indo-Pakistani War of 1965, and was one of the key planners of Operation Somnath of 1965. While, he was presented at the meeting to commenced the mission and, was the first one to raise his voice for the operation. Commodore Shariff was put Second-in-Command of the Operation, while the Pakistan Navy's Flotilla was commanded by another one-star naval officer Commodore S.M. Anwar. In 1969, he was promoted to two-star rank, and as Rear-Admiral, he was given the command of Eastern Naval Command of the Navy. A Naval Commanding officer of Pakistan Navy's Eastern Naval Command, Rear-Admiral Shariff commanded the Pakistan Naval operations in the East-Pakistan. A commander of Eastern Naval Command, Rear-Admiral Shariff was the most senior commander, and second in command of Pakistan Defence Forces in East-Pakistan. As the war progressed, the pressure on Pakistan Navy was mounted and heightened by the Indian Navy. Shariff then launched the Marines and special naval operations near at the shore. A heavy deployment of Pakistan Marines and Special Service Group Navy (SSG (N)) were undertaken at Cox's Bazar and other strategic naval shore. Soon after the deployment of Marines and SSG (N), the bloody battle between Pakistan Navy and Indian Navy was insued, and the SSG (N) units and Marines had beaten assaults after assaults. Overall, the Pakistan Navy performed its mission task well and diligently by providing support to the army till the end.

Hilal–i–Jurat

Admiral Mohammad Shariff Khan (Cont)

However, while Navy was successful by performing its task, Pakistan Army's Eastern Military Commands were unsuccessful to achieve their objectives. After the securing the East-Pakistan's strategic shores, Shariff gained prominence, and for his actions, he was made Second-in-Command of Pakistan Defence Forces in Eastern-Pakistan led by Lieutenant-General Amir Niazi. As second-in-command, Shariff was then placed in important positions where he was presented in every coordination meeting led by General Niazi. After the success of East-Pakistan Air Operations of Indian Air Force (IAF), Rear-Admiral Shariff strongly urged that the Eastern Command to be permitted to evacuate all the serviceable aircraft that night to Akyab in Burma. However, Eastern Air Command's commander Air Commodore (Brigadier-General) Inamul Haq objected the plan as he felt that on view of total air superiority enjoyed by the IAF that it would not be possible. General Niazi agreed with Rear-Admiral Shariff and ordered to launch an evacuation operation immediately. As Indian Military intervened in East Pakistan, the Eastern Air Command and Eastern Military Command fell apart, forcing Lieutenant-General A. A. K. Niazi to surrender the Pakistan Eastern Command Forces to his counterpart Jagjit Singh Arora. As Indian Armed Forces entered in East-Pakistan, Shariff planned an immediate evacuation operation. He commanded and oversaw the maximum evacuation of Pakistan Naval assets from East Pakistan to Burma in a limited time. However, the night Pakistan Military Command were surrendered, Shariff with small number of military officers were planned to leave as the Pakistan naval vessel, with holding of other officers and civilian, was waiting for their evacuation. As the East-Pakistan fell, all the naval routes were successfully closed by Indian Navy, forcing Shariff to remain in East-Pakistan. Later, he joined General Niazi where he was presented at the time when the Instrument of Surrender was signed. After the surrender of East-Pakistan Forces, Shariff was taken as Prisoner of War (POW) and was taken to adjacent Camp No. 77A, where many of the senior military officials were held. He was released by Indian Government and handed over to Pakistan Government on March 1972. Following his return, he began his active service in the Navy; despite the fact other senior officers were subsequently retired or fired from their services. In 1972, He then testified in the absolute failure of Pakistan Eastern Military Command at the Hamoodur Rahman Commission, a stand-up civilian commission headed by then-Chief Justice of Supreme Court of Pakistan Justice Hamoodur Rahman.

Hilal–i–Jurat

Admiral Mohammad Shariff Khan (Cont)

As Chief of Naval Staff, Shariff also played an important role in the establishment of Pakistan Naval Air Arm in the Pakistan Navy. At first, with the help of PAF, Pakistan Navy raised its first squadron on March 1976. After the death of Chief of Naval Staff Vice-Admiral Hasan Hafeez Ahmed, Prime minister Zulfikar Ali Bhutto appointed him as Chief of Naval Staff As vice-admiral, Shariff assumed the command of Pakistan Navy on 23 March 1975. In January 1976, Bhutto later upgraded his rank from three-star vice-admiral Shariff to four-star admiral, hence, made him the first full four-star admiral in the Navy. He played an integral role in the establishment of Pakistan Naval Air Arm, and sought to improvise the navy as well. On 15TH December 1977, Admiral Shariff established the Naval air station, PNS Mehran, where PAF's No. 25 Squadron Night Strike Eagles, an Aggressor squadron of PAF, Admiral M. Shariff presented the Squadron Colour to the No. 25 Squadron Night Strike Eagles.[8] Admiral Mohammad Shariff commanded Pakistan Navy from 23RD March 1975 to 21ST March 1979, and was the first military officer belonging to the Navy Branch to become a Chairman of Joint Chiefs of Staff Committee (JCSC). In 1978, he was appointed by the Pakistan Military Promotion Regulatory Authority (PMPRA), in the absence of Prime minister and civil institutions. After his four-star assignment, Admiral Shariff was the Supreme Commandant of the Pakistan Defence Forces from 1978 to 1980. He is a recipient of Hilal-i-Jurat, which was awarded to him after the 1971 war when he commanded all the naval assets in the erstwhile East Pakistan as a rear admiral during the Bangladesh Liberation War. After his retirement from Pakistan Defence Forces, he was personally appointed Chairman of the Federal Public Service Commission, a civil administrative institution responsible for the recruitment of civil bureaucrats, by General Zia-ul-Haq. After his retirement, he lived a quiet life in Islamabad for more than a decade, and served as President of *Elaf Club of Pakistan*, a political and military think tank based in Islamabad. On September 23RD, 2010, Admiral Shariff wrote and launched his first autobiography "Admiral's Diary", in English. The ceremony was held at the Bahria University Auditorium. Chief of Naval Staff Admiral Noman Bashir was chief guest on the occasion. The book launching was attended by seasoned retired military officer and serving bureaucrats, senior retired and serving officers of the three services, family members and friends of the author, notable literary personalities, press and media. Admiral Shariff passed away in Lahore on 6TH August 1999.

Hilal-i-Jurat

Admiral Shahid Karimullah, LH, LM, NI(M), HI(M), HI(M), TI(M), SJ.
Shahid Karimullah was born in Karachi, Sindh, Pakistan on 14TH February 1948. After graduating from a local high school in 1963, he was admitted and studied at the D. J. Science College before joining the Pakistan Navy in October 1965. He trained at the Pakistan Military Academy but later sent to United Kingdom to attend the Royal Navy's HMS Mercury where he graduated with a communication courses and gained military commission as a Midshipman in the Navy in October 1965, and later promoted as Sub-Lieutenant in the Navy in 1971. In 1971, he was stationed in East Pakistan and took participation in violent civil war, followed by the war with India in East. He was promoted as Lieutenant and served as commanding officer of gunboat, participating in various operations against the Indian Army and Mukti Bahini. After the surrender of Eastern Command was announced, he was subsequently taken war prisoner and was seriously wounded. His gallantry actions won him the Sitara-e-Jurat which was given to him in 1972, following his repatriation. After the war, he became engage with his studies and went to the Newport in Rhode Island, United States to attend the Naval War College. He graduated from the Naval War College in master's degree in War studies and later attended the National Defence University where he graduated with another master's degree in the international relations degree.

In the 1980s, he served as an aide-de-camp to Chairman Joint chiefs Admiral Mohammad Shariff and former Chief of Naval Staff Admiral Karamat Rahman Niazi. In 1995–96, he was promoted as Commodore and took over the command of the 25TH Destroyer Squadron as its Flag Officer Commanding (FOC). He also served as Directing Staff in the War studies faculty at the National Defence University in Islamabad. In 1997, Commodore Karimullah was posted as Director Signals but later posted for a one-star staff assignment at the Navy NHQ in Islamabad. Commodore Karimullah was appointed as ACNS (Personnel) but later posted as DCNS (Operations) under Admiral Fasih Bokhari– the Chief of Naval Staff. After Admiral Bokhari resigned, he was promoted as Rear-Admiral and continued to serve as DCNS (Operations) in 1999. In 2000–01, he was promoted as Vice-Admiral and took over the command of Pakistan Fleet as its fleet commander. In 2002, Vice-Admiral Karimullah was appointed Chief of Naval Staff and was promoted to four-star admiral in the Navy before taking the post. During this time, he engaged in talks with the Chinese Navy for a technology transfer of building the modern warships in Karachi.

Hilal–i–Jurat

Admiral Shahid Karimullah (Cont)

In 2003, Admiral Karimullah pushed for the second strike capability in the government but publicly reiterated on the issue of nuclear weapons and announced that while no such immediate plans really existed, but he did stressed on the fact Pakistan would not hesitate to take such steps if it felt so compelled. In 2004, he successfully negotiated with the U.S. Navy to induct the Navy in the combined maritime force to provide cooperation in regional maritime and security affair. Admiral Shahid Karimullah was notably bypassed by President Pervez Musharraf for the chairmanship for the Joint Chiefs of Staff Committee in October 2004. Admiral Karimullah was the most senior-most four-star rank officer in the Pakistani military and was controversially superseded by the junior-most army general, Lieutenant-General Ehsan ul Haq. Admiral Karimullah retired from the Navy in 2005 and handed over the command of the Navy to Admiral Afzal Tahir who also superseded Vice-Admiral Mohammad Haroon by President Musharraf. Having by-passed as Chairman joint chiefs post, President Musharraf announced to appoint Admiral Karimullah for a diplomatic post and appointed him as Pakistan Ambassador to Saudi Arabia.[16] In 2009, he left the post once completing his tenure and returned to Karachi, Sindh, Pakistan. Admiral Karimullah is a recipient of Nishan-e-Imtiaz (military), Sitara-i-Imtiaz (military), and Hilal-i-Imtiaz (military) that were decorated to him during his military service. He was also decorated with the Legion of Merit by the United States, presented to him by US Navy's CNO Admiral Vern Clark in 2004. In 2005, he was conferred with French Legion d'Honneur for promoting Pakistan-Franco naval collaboration in various fields at different posts he held during his service career, including induction of French submarines and aircraft in Pakistan Navy. On 21ST September 2005, Admiral Karimullah was awarded with the Honorary Malaysian Armed Forces Order for Valour award as a Gallant Commander in acknowledgment of his long meritorious services. After retiring from the Foreign Service, he apparently joined the 'Progress', a public service think tank, and serves on its advisory board. He also remained chairman of Karachi Council on Foreign Relations for some time.

About the 'Fall of Dhaka' in 1971, Admiral Karimullah reportedly was of the view that: 'History is there to earn lessons from but unfortunately this did not happening in Pakistan.

He also remained Associate with the Bahria University in Karachi and reportedly maintained in favour of CPEC developmental projects in the country.

Hilal–i–Jurat

Major General Amir Hamza Khan Qaisrani Baloch, HJ, SJ and Bar

As a Lieutenant Colonel commanding 10 Punjab Regiment Baloch had participated in the Battle of Sulaimanke in 1965. (For India this sector was called Fazilka sector, for Pakistan it was called Sulaimanke sector) Baloch had already brilliantly commanded 10 Punjab for which he was honoured with the gallantry award of Sitara-i-Jurat. In 1971 Indo-Pak war, he was back in the same sector as OC 105TH Brigade and was awarded a bar to the SJ. Pakistan's 105 Brigade carried out a small scale but highly aggressive operation in Sulaimanke area opposite Indian town of Fazilka. The strength here was in Indian favour but Indian brigade commander S.S Chowdry was highly incompetent in placing his forward battalion 10 kilometres ahead of his other two battalions. This enabled Pakistan's 105 Brigade to capture the Bund ahead of Sabuna Distributary thus ensuring the safety of Pakistan's most crucial Sulaimanke Canal Headwork which was just 1,500 metres from the border. 105 Brigade's determined counter attack severely depressed Indian Higher Commanders and 11 Corps Commander expressed a desire to abandon the area and withdraw to Fazilka Fortress and to replace 67 Brigade which was defending the area. Such was the state of Indian demoralisation that Western Command Army Commander finally sacked 67 Brigade Commander on 11TH December. S.S Chowdhry was replaced by Brigadier Piara Singh. At this stage the Indian brigade commander was so demoralised that he overestimated the Pakistani strength opposite him to be two infantry brigades supported by an armoured regiment 24 while in reality the Pakistani strength on east bank of Sabuna was only an infantry battalion (6 FF) supported by a depleted tank squadron of WW Two vintage tanks. The Indians suffered heavy casualties at Sulaimanke. Some 190 Killed, 196 missing most of whom were killed or prisoners and 425 wounded. The key to Pakistani success here was the unique personality of Major General Ameer Hamza Khan Qaisrani Baloch. Sulaimanke was above all a show of a brilliant and extremely resolute Brigade Commander. Although he was super ceded for promotion by lesser beings, for his gallant performance he was awarded the Hilal–i–Jurat. Major General Amir Hamza Khan Qaisrani Baloch passed away on 15TH July 2000.

Hilal–i–Jurat

Major General Iftikhar Khan Janjua Shaheed, HJ & Bar, SPk, SQA

Major General Iftikhar Khan Janjua Shaheed of the Pakistan Army is the most senior Pakistani officer to have been killed in action. He is known in Pakistan as the hero of Rann of Kutch, as he was a brigadier in command of 6 Brigade, during the fighting in April 1965 prior to the Indo-Pakistani War of 1965. He was killed in a helicopter crash, in Kashmir, during the Battle of Chamb while in command of 23 Infantry Division during the Indo-Pakistan War of 1971.

In April 1965, as part of a tri-service exercise (Arrow Head), the Indians brought in 31 and 67 Infantry Brigades in area Karim Shahi - Kavda. The IAF and the Indian aircraft carrier INS Vikrant, supported by other naval vessels, also moved into the gulf. On 8/9TH April, in a series of events not entirely clear, clashes broke out between the Indians and the Pakistanis at a post near Ding, Rann of Kutch. On 23RD April Brigadier Iftikhar Janjua ordered the 4 Punjab to capture point 84 by first activity around Chad Bet. Since the progress of 6 Punjab was slow 2 Frontier Force (FF) was directed to join them. By first light, the battalion reached its objective without suffering too many casualties. 2 FF later attacked Biar Bet along with a squadron of 12 Cavalry. Biar Bet was captured by 0600 hours on 26TH April.

The outcome of the Rann of Kutch was considered as a positive for the Pakistan Army. As described by Lieutenant General Gul Hassan Khan, then Director of Military Operations, in his later memoirs - "the set back in Kutch proved immeasurably disconcerting to the Indian army. As a result the Government of India was in a quandary. On the other hand, ours was in a state of euphoria. The high command of our army was intoxicated by our showing and our morale could not possibly have been higher. We were ready for any task that may be assigned to us without any question." The restraint shown by India would later convince Field Marshal Ayub Khan that the Indian Government was in no mood to fight. This encouraged them into launching the Kashmir offensive, which led to the War in September 1965. After the 65 War, Janjua was the divisional commander of 6 Armoured Division even though he himself was an infantry officer - no mean feat. He spared himself the time to learn about the nuances of armoured fighting vehicles and their operations. Soon after, Janjua would command 23 Division based at Jhelum.

Hilal–i–Jurat

Major General Iftikhar Khan Janjua (Cont)

In the 1971 War, Janjua was divisional commander of 23 Infantry Division. He was assigned the task of capturing Chamb, a strategically important town in Kashmir, which would turn out to be the only decisive victory for Pakistan on the Kashmir front of 1971. The fighting around Chamb was intensely fierce and took toll on both the advancing Pakistani troops and the fiercely resisting Indian regiments. Although Janjua was advised by high command to try to take Chamb from the south, Janjua said it was a better to take Mandiala Bridge his troops would outflank the Indians eventually forcing them out of Chamb and all the area west of Tawa. After intense fighting Mandiawala was captured, then Pallanwala and Chak Pandit, and on 9TH December 1971, the first Pakistani troops entered the surrounding area around Chamb under the personal supervision of Janjua. In the middle of fighting around Chamb proper, on 9TH December 1971, Janjua was killed when his OH-13S (Sioux) light helicopter, in which he was travelling on to coordinate and position his troops, was attacked. He was badly burned and was evacuated to Combined Military Hospital Kharian. Iftikhar Khan Janjua Road is named after him in Rawalpindi.

Iftikhar Janjua was a brilliant and charismatic leader who inspired his troops to continue to fight. It was leading from the front for which General Iftikhar Janjua is remembered even today by the troops who served in 23 Division during the Battle of Chamb. It was this quality which enabled him to arrive at a realistic appraisal of the actual situation without undue reliance on exaggerated reports from lower echelons and successfully take Chamb. He was known for his boldness and for the confidence he inspired among his men by being in the front lines during the heat of the battle. He was a Janjua Rajput, a tribe known for its Martial Reputation and royal ancestry. His father Raja Mehmood Amjad was a barrister and the family was settled in Sargodha District. He is brother of Major General Ijaz Amjad, another outstanding general.

Sitara-i-Jurat

Sitara-i-Jurat (Star of Courage) is the third highest military award of Pakistan. It was established in 1957 after Pakistan became a Republic; however, it was instituted retrospectively back to 1947. It is awarded for gallantry or distinguished service in combat; and can be bestowed upon officers, junior commissioned officers and warrant officers and their equivalents in the Pakistan Army, Navy, Air Force, and various paramilitary forces under federal control such as the Frontier Corps, the Frontier Constabulary and the Pakistan Rangers. It may be considered to be roughly equivalent to the Military Cross and the Silver Star.

The Army 1948

Bibi Sahiba Shaheed, SJ

Bibi Sahiba came from a Muslim Rajput family and joined the Pakistan Army, registering as a soldier in the 5TH Battalion of the Azad Kashmir Regular Force, commanded by Captain Sher Khan in the Himalayan foothills. Bibi Sahiba was a part of the charging group (5 AKRF) during fighting around the Chirikot-Degear defile. She fought bravely, supplying ammunition to Pakistani soldiers fighting in the region. While undertaking this duty, she received a bullet wound and subsequently died on October 7TH, 1947. Mujahida Hussain Bibi was awarded Pakistan's third highest military award Sitara-i-Jurat for her exemplary courage and bravery.

Brigadier Sher Muhammad Khan, SJ

Brigadier Sher Muhammad Khan was awarded the first Sitara-i-Jurat as Sector Commander during Kashmir Operation of 1948. (First Sitara-i-Jurat-Kashmir Operation 1948)

Captain Sher Badshah Mahsud, SJ

Captain Sher Badshah Mahsud was awarded the Sitara-i-Jurat during Kashmir Operation of 1948.

Sitara-i-Jurat

The Army 1948

Lieutenant Colonel Ihsan Ali Khan, SJ

Lieutenant Colonel Ihsan Ali Khan was awarded the Sitara-i-Jurat as an Area Commander during Kashmir Operation of 1948.

Major General Muhammad Jamshed, MC, SJ

Major General Muhammad Jamshed was commissioned on November 8TH 1942 and joined the First Punjab Regiment. He rose to the rank of Major and was decorated twice with the Military Cross during the Second World War in Burma. After the war, he joined the Pakistan Army in 1947 and as a Colonel participated in the war against India in 1948, and was honoured with the award of Sitara-i-Jurat.

Lieutenant Colonel Ghulam Rasul Raja, MC, SJ

During the Indo-Pakistan war of 1948, Lieutenant Colonel Ghulam Rasul Raja was able to devise a strategically timed offensive. His men prepared for the offensive, waiting for the Indian defence to weaken; they attacked with aid of the artillery that had been repositioned. The Indians were stunned at the scale of the attack and fell immediately under the pretence that a large Pakistani force had arrived. They surrendered and subsequently the peak had been liberated and held by Pakistani forces. For his exemplary bravery Raja was awarded the honour of Sitara-e-Jurrat.

Brigadier M. Aslam Khan, SJ

Brigadier M. Aslam Khan was a Pakistan war hero and was awarded the Hilal-i-Jurat and Sitara-i-Jurat for the Liberation and holding of Gilgit-Baltistan in 1948. *His volunteers had to face terrible conditions; they had to wade through fifteen inch snow in severe winter with the commander, and reached Kargil in three days. They had to sleep on the snow as well as hammer the enemy logistics by surprise assaults. The scheme of this mission succeeded as these resolute soldiers were led by an inexhaustible commander.*

Major Mohammad Din, SJ

Major Mohammad Din was of The Azad Kashmir Regular Force, which was permanently stationed in Azad Kashmir. It took part in the Indo-Pakistan war in 1948 and Major Mohammad Din of the regiment was awarded Sitara-i-Jurat for his bravery. He was given the title of Hill Panther.

Sitara-i-Jurat

Air Force 1948

Air Commodore Mukhtar Ahmad Dogar, SJ

Air Commodore Mukhtar Ahmad Dogar was the Pakistan Air Force bomber pilot and aerial warfare specialist who was the first military person to receive the Pakistani military award Sitara-i-Jurat. Dogar gained a commission in Royal Air Force, and was accepted into the Royal Air Force Academy in Cranwell. After he graduated from the Academy, he gained his B.S. in Aerospace studies.

After his education he was stationed in Gilgit-Baltistan, and actively participated in Indo-Pakistani War of 1947. On 4TH November 1948, Flying officer Dogar, a fighter pilot of Hawker Tempest, was operating a defenceless Hawker Tempest, nickname Dakota, in the valleys of Kashmir was attacked by two Indian Air Force (IAF) Tempest fighter aircraft and ordered to surrender and land at Srinagar. Though unarmed and unable to retaliate, the undaunted pilot refused to capitulate. The government of Pakistan had given orders to Pakistan Air Force (PAF) to stay away from the conflict. Pakistan, faced with limited aircraft and the hazardous weather, issued specific orders to PAF to not be involved in the conflict while the ground operations were undertaken by the Army. In the early morning of 4 November 1948, Dogar, along with Flying Officer Jagjivan, took off to Skardu to drop the military load to Pakistan Army. While returning to base, the pilots had spotted the IAF's Hawker Tempests, in a covert operation. After 15 minutes, the IAF pilots ordered Dogar and Jagjivan to go to the nearest Indian airfield but Dogar and Jagjivan did not response and continued flying to Risalpur Airbase.

The order was repeated three times but the PAF pilots did not respond. Aggravated, the IAF pilots fired a free burst to show that they were armed. Dogar and Jagjivan tried to avoid responding as they had given orders by the Government of Pakistan. At this time, one of the IAF pilots broke off, gained a little height and came in to attack. He fired a full burst of 20 mm at the PAF pilots, fatally wounding Naik Mohammad Din and knocking Jagjivan unconscious with a profusely bleeding arm. The encounter had lasted twenty to twenty-five minutes. Flying Officer Dogar began to retaliate and wounded PAF pilot Alfred Jagjivan came to his rescue. The PAF pilots had shot down the IAF pilots, killing all the IAF pilots in action. Air Commodore Dogar and Air Commodore Alfred Jagjivan were awarded the Sitara-i-Jurat for his daring handling of the belligerent Indian Air Force fighters on 4TH November 1948. His Sitara-i-Jurat is the first for Pakistan Air Force.

Sitara-i-Jurat

Pakistan Navy 1948

During the first war with India in 1947–48, the Navy saw no action as all fighting was restricted to land and air combat missions. On operational planning, Captain HMS Choudri engaged on commanding a destroyer from Karachi to Mumbai to oversee the evacuation of Indian emigrants to Pakistan. In 1948, Pakistan Navy engaged in humanitarian missions to evacuate Indian immigrants trapped in disputed and hostile areas, with its frigates operating continuously. In 1948, the directorate-general for Naval Intelligence (DGNI), a staff corps, was established under Lieutenant Syed Mohammad Ahsan, who served as its first Director-General, in Karachi. When the first war came to an end in 1948, the Navy temporarily established its Navy NHQ in Karachi and acquired its first O Class destroyer from the Royal Navy.

The Army 1965
Subedar Muhammad Israel Khan, SJ and Bar
Subedar Muhammad Israel Khan of 39TH AK Regt was then part of Ghazi Battalion. He was awarded second Sitara-i- Jurat for his bravery. He had previously won an SJ in 1948 during the Battle of Paran Hill at the foothills of Pir Badesar in 1948.

General Shamim Alam Khan, SJ
General Shamim Alam Khan was commissioned in 20TH Lancers of the Armoured Corps in 1956 in the 14TH PMA Long Course. Later in his career, he commanded a SSG company in the Indo-Pakistani War of 1965, for which he awarded the Sitara-i-Jurat

Brigadier Nisar Ahmed Khan, SJ
Nisar Ahmed Khan moved to Pakistan and was commissioned in the Pakistani Army in August 1948. He raised the 25 Cavalry on 9TH June 1962 and was its first Commanding Officer. He took it into action during the 1965 war. For this courage and exemplary command of his regiment and his skill in handling his tanks, Lieutenant Colonel Nisar Ahmed Khan was awarded the Sitara-i-Jurat.

Lieutenant General Shah Rafi Alam, SJ
He was commissioned in 1951 in 5TH Probyn's Horse. In 1955, he was transferred to the 12TH Sam Brown Cavalry. In 1965 war, 12TH Cavalry fought on different fronts under the command of Lieutenant Colonel Bashir Ullah Khan Babar. Shah Rafi commanded B Squadron of his own regiment and won gallantry award of Sitara-i-Jurat.

Sitara-i-Jurat

The Army 1965

Brigadier Nisar Ahmed Khan, SJ

Nisar Ahmed Khan was commissioned in the Pakistani Army in August 1948. He raised the 25 Cavalry on 9TH June 1962 and was its first Commanding Officer. He took it into action during the 1965 war. For this courage and exemplary command of his regiment and his skill in handling his tanks, Lieutenant Colonel Nisar Ahmed Khan was awarded the Sitara-i-Jurat.

Major Mohammad Din, SJ

Major Mohammad Din of Azad Kashmir Regiment was awarded the Sitara-i-Jurat during the Indo-Pakistan war of 1965.

General Tariq Mehmood, SJ

As a Captain, Tariq Mehmood was awarded Sitara-i-Jurat for his acts of bravery during the Indo-Pak war of 1965. (See 1971 of his bar to the SJ)

Major Malik Aftab Khan, SJ

During the Indo-Pak war of 1965, for blowing the Bridge on the Canal at Batapur, and the Indian dreams of reaching Lahore were shattered. In recognition of his bravery and heroic work, Major Malik Aftab Khan was awarded the Sitara-i-Jurat.

Major Khadim Hussain Bangash, SJ

During the Indo-Pak war of 1965, Major Khadim Hussain, took part in operations across Rohi Nullah in Kasur Sector. In this operation by significant personal gallantry, Major Khadim Hussain destroyed three enemy tanks with an abandoned recoilless rifle at Khem Kiran and was awarded the Sitara-i-Jurat.

Major Malik Munawar Khan Awan, SJ

Major Malik Munawar Khan Awan was awarded the Sitara-i-Jurat for his actions in the Rajouri valley, during the Indo-Pak war of 1965. The Operation Gibraltar was launched in July 1965, with the aim of Pakistani infiltration of Jammu & Kashmir. Awan, who now held the rank of major, was involved in this, leading troops in heavy fighting at a pass near to Rajouri. He controlled an area of around 500 square miles for a period of three months. However, after the Tashkent Agreement between India and Pakistan, he was ordered to withdraw his forces and return to Rawalpindi. He was also referred to as the "King of Rajouri" by Field Marshal Ayub Khan.

Sitara-i-Jurat

The Army 1965

General Jilani Khan Ghulam Jilani Khan, SJ
As a Colonel Ghulam Jilani Khan in 1965 was the Military Intelligence Field Officer attached with the 6TH Armoured Division at Chawinda, during the 1965 Indo-Pakistan war. He was awarded with the Sitara-i-Jurat for his combat support service during the war.

Lieutenant Colonel Naseerullah Khan Babar, SJ
During the 1965 Pakistan war with India, Babar single handedly captured an entire Indian company of soldiers (over 70 POWs) and was awarded Sitara-i-Jurat for this action.

Captain Farooq Nawaz Janjua, SJ
Farooq Nawaz Janjua of Chakri Rajgan is a sword of honour. He joined the 4TH Punjab Regiment. He was awarded Sitara-i-Jurat during the 1965 Indo-Pakistan war of 1965, for his brave action in operation at Sulemanki Sector.

Lieutenant Colonel Rasheed Kayani, SJ
Lieutenant Colonel Rasheed Kayani of Medium Regiment Artillery was awarded Sitara-i-Jurat, at the Battle of Phillurah and Chawinda during the 1965 war with India.

Lieutenant Colonel Haq Nawaz Kayani, SJ
Lieutenant Colonel Haq Nawaz Kayani won the Sitara-i-Jurat in 1965 during the Indo-Pakistan war in Kashmir. (See 1971 to his Bar)

Honorary Captain Raja Sultan Sikandar, SJ
Honorary Captain Raja Sultan Sikandar of 2ND Punjab Regiment was awarded the Sitara-i-Jurat during the Indo-Pakistan war of 1965.

Major Mohammad Aslam Janjua, SJ
Major Mohammad Aslam Janjua was awarded the Sitara-i-Jurat during the Indo-Pakistan war of 1965, for the defence, and consolidation of military in Baltistan

Posthumous awards for Army 1965

Major Abdul Jalil Orakzai Shaheed, SJ
Major Abdul Jalil Orakzai was killed in action on 7TH September 1965, near the west bank of the Icchogil Canal, which was a de facto border of India and Pakistan, for which he was awarded a posthumous Sitara-i-Jurat.

Sitara-i-Jurat

Posthumous awards for Army 1965

Major Mohammad Zia Ud Din Uppal Shaheed, SJ
Major Mohammad Zia Ud Din Uppal of the Artillery Regiment was awarded a posthumous Sitara-i-Jurat, during the 1965 Pakistan war with India.

Major Mian Raza Shah Shaheed, SJ
Captain Mian Raza Shah, at the young age of 28 and was the first officer to have embraced Shahadat on 1ST September 1965, while leading the 11TH Cavalry Regiment during the Indo-Pakistan war. He was a Captain in September 1965 and was promoted to the Major rank after embracing Shahadat. On 23RD March 1966, President Mohammad Ayub Khan delivered Raza Shah's richly deserved gallantry award of Sitara-i-Jurat to his father Mian Firdos Shah.

Lieutenant Colonel Sahibzada Gul Shaheed, SJ
Lieutenant Colonel Sahibzada Gul of 6TH Lancers was killed in action at Chawinda on 9TH September 1965, for which he was awarded a posthumous Sitara-i-Jurat.

Lieutenant Colonel Abdur Rehman Shaheed, SJ
Lieutenant Colonel Abdur Rehman was killed in action at the 'Battle of Asal Uttar' on 11TH September 1965, for which he was awarded a posthumous Sitara-i-Jurat.

Major Saiyed Naseem Haider Rizvi Shaheed, SJ
Major Saiyed Naseem Haider Rizvi was killed in action on the Lahore Front on 22ND September 1965, for which he was awarded a posthumous Sitara-i-Jurat.

Major Kadhim Hussain Bangash Shaheed, SJ and Bar
Major Kadhim Hussain Bangash was a squadron commander in the 24 Cavalry. The unit took part in the operations across Rohi Nullah in the Kasur Sector in Indo-Pakistan war of 1965. For his gallantry during the war and supreme sacrifice Major Bangash was recommended for the posthumous award of Nishan-i-Haider but eventually was awarded Sitara-i-Jurat.

Captain Zahoor Afridi Shaheed, SJ
Captain Zahoor Afridi was killed in action on the Lahore Front on 22ND September 1965, for which he was awarded a posthumous Sitara-i-Jurat.

Sitara-i-Jurat

Posthumous awards for Army 1965

Major Zia ud Din Ahmed Abbasi Shaheed, SJ
Major Zia ud Din Ahmed Abbasi to embraced Shahadat in the 1965 Indo-Pak war at Chawinda for which he was posthumously awarded the Sitara-i-Jurat.

Major Mian Raza Shah Shaheed, SJ
Major Mian Raza Shah was the first Pakistani officer to embrace Shahadat in the 1965 Indo-Pak war. He was initially recommended for Nishan e Haider, the highest military award, but was subsequently awarded Sitara-i-Jurat.

Major Shah Nawaz Shaheed, SJ
Major Shah Nawaz of 8 Baloch Regiment was a part of the force which launched a counter offensive across the Cease-fire line against Chamb, Jourian and Akhnoor, during the 1965 Indo-Pak war in which Major Shah Nawaz embraced Shahadat. He was posthumously awarded the Sitara-i-Jurat.

Lieutenant Colonel Sahib Zad Gul Shaheed, SJ
During the 1965 Indo-Pakistan war 6 Lancers the operated in the Khem Karan Sector under command 11 Division. It was 6 Lancers that stepped first into Indian Territory and under its brave Commanding Officer, Lt Col Sahib Zad Gul, captured Khem Karan, amongst the first Indian towns to be captured by Pakistan. During this war, Lt. Col. Sahib Zad Gul embraced Shahadat, and posthumously awarded the Sitara-i-Jurat.

Major Abdul Jalil Orakzai Shaheed, SJ
Major Abdul Jalil Orakzai embraced Shahadat, during the 1965 Indo-Pakistan war and was posthumously awarded the Sitara-i-Jurat.

Lieutenant Colonel Abdur Rehman Shaheed, SJ
Lieutenant Colonel Abdur Rehman of Medium Artillery embraced Shahadat, during the 1965 Indo-Pakistan war and was posthumously awarded the Sitara-i-Jurat.

Captain Nisar Ahmed Shaheed, SJ
During his employment in 1965 Indo Pak War in Ranger Unit, Special Services Group (5 Azad Kashmir Brigade) Captain Nisar Ahmed embraced martyrdom during action on 13TH August 1965. He was awarded Sitara-i-Jurat posthumously.

Sitara-i-Jurat

Posthumous awards for Army 1965

Captain Muhammad Sadiq (Shaheed, SJ)
Captain Muhammad Sadiq of Field Artillery was killed in action during the Indo-Pakistan war of 1965. He was awarded Sitara-i-Jurat posthumously.

2ND Lieutenant Farooq Abdul Aziz Shaheed, SJ
2ND Lieutenant Farooq Abdul Aziz was killed in action during the Indo-Pakistan war of 1965. He was awarded Sitara-i-Jurat posthumously.

2ND Lieutenant Mohammad Sabir Beg Shaheed, SJ
2ND Lieutenant Mohammad Sabir Beg of Guides Cavalry was killed in action during the Indo-Pakistan war of 1965. He was awarded Sitara-i-Jurat posthumously.

Lieutenant Hussain Shah Shaheed, SJ
Lieutenant Hussain Shah of Guides Cavalry was killed in action during the Indo-Pakistan war of 1965. He was awarded Sitara-i-Jurat posthumously.

Lieutenant Ahmed Faruk Khatlani Shaheed, SJ
Lieutenant Ahmed Faruk Khatlani of 18 Punjab Regiment embraced Shahadat on 9TH April 1965, while successfully re-capturing Sardar post in area of Rann of Kutch. He was awarded Sitara-i-Jurat posthumously.

Lieutenant Kaleem Mahmud Shaheed, SJ
Lieutenant Kaleem Mahmud 3 Punjab Regiment was initially declared Missing in Action on 7 Sept 1965 while defending the Jasser Bridge over River Ravi where the Indian troops had launched a Brigade size attack to eliminate a small Pakistani enclave across the bridge. A couple of days before the ceasefire took effect, 6 FF which had arrived in this sector after successful operation in Chamb and Jourian, relieved 3 Punjab Regiment at Jasser Bridge. During patrolling of the area beyond the bridge 2ND Lieutenant Shabir Sharif SJ found out that the Indians had buried the dead body of Lieutenant Kaleem Mahmud just close to the bridge with his name written on a chit that was put in a glass bottle.

Captain Zaghir Hussain Shaheed, SJ
Captain Zaghir Hussain embraced Shahadat during the Indo-Pakistan war of 1965. He was posthumously awarded the Sitara-i-Jurat for gallantry.

Sitara-i-Jurat

Posthumous awards for Army 1965

Captain Abdul Jalil Shaheed, SJ
Captain Abdul Jalil of 12 Frontier Force Regiment embraced Shahadat in action during the Indo-Pakistan war of 1965. He was posthumously awarded the Sitara-i-Jurat for gallantry.

Major Sheikh Mobaruk Ali Shaheed, SJ
During the 1965 Indo Pak War, Major Mobaruk Sheikh under took the task of ejecting the enemy from Dial village and led his Company of 150 men into the attack. The enemy after a tough battle left the village and ran towards the border leaving behind 16 dead, 21 injured (taken POWs) and 3 destroyed tanks. Major Mobaruk kept on chasing the retreating enemy and in the process was hit by machine gunfire and embraced Shahadat. Havildar Durre Aman and Lance Naik Haider Ali got severely wounded while successfully retrieving the dead body of Major Mobaruk Shaheed.

Lieutenant Ahmed Munir Shaheed, SJ
10 FF Infantry Battalion was grouped with 4 Armoured Brigade which was leading a counter offensive in Khem Karan area. The battalion advance was led by C Company and Lieutenant Ahmad Munir commanded the leading platoon. When this platoon had reached Lakhna it came under heavy artillery- and small arms fires. Lieutenant Ahmad Munir manoeuvred his platoon to the west of Lakhna, and while doing so was hit by a burst of enemy automatic fire and embraced Shahadat Lieutenant Ahmad Munir was awarded a posthumous Sitara-i-Jurat for this action.

Sitara-i-Jurat

The Air Force 1965

Group Captain Eric Hall, SJ

Group Captain Eric Hall's finest hour came in 1965 when he was commanding the air transport Base at Chaklala. Group Captain volunteered to lead the first bombing mission that happened to be over Kathua Bridge, on 11TH September 1965. The mission was not only fraught with danger but the totally unarmed C-130 was also highly vulnerable to enemy action. But the success of this mission that was unique in the history of flying prompted the higher command to authorize thirteen more bombing missions on the C-130 including the precision bombing of Indian heavy guns at Atari. The success of all these missions proved that the Air Vice Marshal had hit the bull's eye it his innovative idea. For his valour and vision, Group Captain Eric G Hall was awarded Sitara-i-Jurat in 1965.

Wing Commander M. G. Tawab, SJ

Tawab joined the Pakistan Air Force in 1951. During the Indo-Pak war of 1965, he was awarded Sitara-i-Jurat, the citation reads: 'Wing Commander Mohammad Ghulam Tawab started taking part in operations from the very first day the hostilities began. He provided top cover for the first strike against Pathankot. During the war he flew sixteen air defence missions and eight close support sorties. He took part in the bombing of Srinagar airfield and Jammu radar. He was responsible for the destruction of ten enemy tanks and twenty vehicles. Wing Commander Mohammad Ghulam Tawab is therefore awarded Sitara-i-Jurat'.

Wing Commander Anwar Shamim, SJ

During the Indo-Pak war of 1965, he was awarded Sitara-i-Jurat, the citation reads: 'In his capacity as Officer Commanding, fighter-bombers wing, made significant contribution to the high morale and aggressive attitude of the pilots who flew from this station. He efficiently managed the changing air defence and other requirements and ensured, while fully meeting these requirements that the pilots got sufficient rest and other comforts to enable them to fly intelligently and confidently. During the operation, he led 14 air defence/escort missions and 5 ground attack missions. His leadership during these operational missions was aggressive and confident and served as a very good example for his pilots to follow. He accepted long hours of duty, including operational sorties at odd hours of the day, with enthusiasm. Wing Commander Muhammad Anwar Shamim was, therefore, awarded Sitara-i-Jurat.'

Sitara-i-Jurat

The Air Force 1965

Wing Commander M A Sikandar, SJ

During the Indo-Pak war of 1965, he was awarded Sitara-i-Jurat, the citation reads: 'Wing Commander Masood Ahmed Sikandar, in the capacity as Wing Leader, proved to be an excellent operational commander. He flew with zeal and enthusiasm and completed seventeen close support sorties and three air defence missions during these operations. Whilst attacking enemy armour, he was wounded when his aircraft was hit by ground fire. For his valour, courage and excellent leadership Wing Commander Masood Ahmed Sikandar was awarded Sitara-i-Jurat'.

Wing Commander Nazir Latif, SJ

During the Indo-Pak war of 1965, he was awarded Sitara-i-Jurat, the citation reads: 'During the nights of 6TH, 7TH and 8TH September, 1965, Wing Commander Nazir Latif led a flight of bombers on high and low level bombing of enemy airfields. Against intense enemy anti-aircraft fire and fighter opposition, he pressed home his attacks with great determination, courage and a high degree of accuracy. On two occasions, his aircraft was hit by anti aircraft guns but he flew back his aircraft and led the flights back to the base. For exceptional flying skill and valour displayed by him in the bombing operations against the enemy, the officer was awarded Sitara-i-Jurat'.

Wing Commander Salahuddin Zahid Butt, SJ

During the Indo-Pak war of 1965, he was awarded Sitara-i-Jurat, the citation reads: 'Wing Commander Salahuddin Zahid Butt is an exceptional transport pilot who applied his ability to the fullest limits in carrying out operational missions against the enemy. He flew a total of 8 sorties which included supply dropping and paratroopers over enemy territory. The hazardous operations were carried out with great skills and determination. Throughout the period of operations, he was a source of inspiration to all the other aircrew of the Wing. The success of all transport operations and its impact on the enemy reflected great credit to the ability and leadership of this officer. In recognition of his personal example, achievements and his contribution to the overall success of all transport operations, the officer was awarded Sitara-i-Jurat'.

Sitara-i-Jurat

The Air Force 1965

Squadron Leader Syed Manzoor Ul Hassan, SJ

During the Indo-Pak war of 1965, he was awarded Sitara-i-Jurat, the citation reads: 'Flight Lieutenant Syed Manzoor Ul Hassan flew 20 strike and 2 Air Defence missions against the enemy. His strikes were directed against enemy concentrations on Jammu, Sialkot, Wagha-Kasur sectors. He led his mission in a most competent manner and achieved considerable success against heavily defended enemy areas. His own aircraft was hit on six occasions by Ack Ack and small arms fire but, undaunted, he pursued his attacks on the enemy. His formation achieved notable success on 21st September, 1965, in which he destroyed many heavy guns of the enemy which were shelling Lahore and earned him deep appreciation on own army's Area Commander. His cool, courageous and operational leadership in complete disregard to his own safety in the face of heavy enemy fire and devotion to duty are commendable. Flight Lieutenant Syed Manzoor Ul Hassan is awarded Sitara-i-Jurat'.

Squadron Leader Mervyn Middlecoat, SJ and Bar

During the Indo-Pak war of 1965, he was awarded Sitara-i-Jurat, the citation reads: 'He was commanding No 9 Squadron during the 1965 War and believed in leading from the front. He kept the morale of the Squadron very high and guided his pilots in a highly professional manner. For his leadership and devotion to duty, Squadron Leader Middlecoat was awarded the Sitara-i-Jurat in 1965'.

Squadron Leader Azim Daudpota, SJ

During the Indo-Pak war of 1965, he was awarded Sitara-i-Jurat, the citation reads: 'Squadron Leader Azim Daudpota flew 15 strike and 5 Air Defence missions. He controlled and conducted his missions very ably and was always looked up to by his subordinates. He gave precise and clear-cut instructions in the air and was responsible for wrecking many tanks, guns, vehicles, etc, in the face of heavy enemy ground fire. His great moments came on 21ST September, 1965, when his formation destroyed many enemy medium guns at Wagha-Attari Sector. For his leadership, devotion to duty and complete disregard for personal safety, Squadron Leader Azim Daudpota was awarded Sitara-i-Jurat'.

Sitara-i-Jurat

The Air Force 1965

Squadron Leader Jamal A. Khan, SJ
During the Indo-Pak war of 1965, he was awarded Sitara-i-Jurat, the citation reads: 'Squadron Leader Jamal Ahmed Khan flew 29 Air Defence missions and one Photo Mission. He took part mainly in night operations. He was one of two pilots who were credited with the shooting down of a Canberra aircraft. His contribution to deterring the weight and accuracy of enemy night bomber's attacks was commendable. He carried out all his missions with aggressiveness. For his exceptional devotion to duty and courage, Squadron Leader Jamal Ahmed Khan was awarded Sitara-i-Jurat'.

Squadron Leader Rais A Rafi, SJ
During the Indo-Pak war of 1965, he was awarded Sitara-i-Jurat, the citation reads: 'Squadron Leader Rais Ahmad Rafi flew a total of 14 operational missions during the Indo-Pakistan War. The officer led his Squadron on most of the hazardous missions to Ambala, Adampur, Jamnagar and Jodhpur. He completed all the missions assigned to him in a highly professional manner and in complete disregard of his personal safety. The officer was a source of inspiration for other pilots in the Squadron and has set a fine example of courage, valour and determination. He invariably delivered his attacks with great accuracy and precision causing maximum damage to the enemy. For his courage and gallantry performance, Squadron Leader Rais Ahmed Rafi was awarded Sitara-i-Jurat'.

Squadron Leader Syed Sajjad Haider, SJ
During the Indo-Pak war of 1965, he was awarded Sitara-i-Jurat, the citation reads: 'He displayed exceptional leadership, courage and flying skill in the operations against the enemy during the Indo-Pakistan War. He destroyed with four enemy aircraft, eleven enemy tanks and damaged three tanks. Throughout the operations, his attitude both on the ground and in the air was exemplary. He infused his pilots with aggressiveness. The strike mission, which he led on 6TH September, 1965, against Pathankot airfield, where his formation destroyed 13 enemy aircraft including nine MIG-21's, was conducted in the best traditions of the Pakistan Air Force. The formation carried out repeated attacks in the face of heavy Ack Ack. For the determination, courage and exceptional flying skill with which he flew and led his Squadron during operations against the enemy, Squadron Leader Sayed Sajjad Haider was awarded Sitara-i-Jurat'.

Sitara-i-Jurat

The Air Force 1965

Squadron Leader Muhammad Mahmood Alam, SJ and Bar
During the Indo-Pak war of 1965, he was awarded Sitara-i-Jurat, the citation reads: 'On 6TH September, 1965, during an aerial combat over enemy territory, Squadron Leader Mohammad Mahmood Alam flying as pilot of an F-86 Sabre Jet, shoot down two enemies Hunter aircraft and damaged three others. For the exceptional flying skill and valour displayed by Squadron Leader Mohammad Mahmood Alam in operations, he was awarded Sitara-i-Jurat. On 7TH September, 1965, in a number of interception missions flown by Squadron Leader Mohammad Mahmood Alam against the enemy aircraft attacking Pakistan Air Force Station, Sargodha, and Squadron Leader Alam destroyed five more enemy Hunter aircrafts. In less than a minute, this remains a record till today. Overall he had nine kills and two damagers to his credit. For the exceptional flying skill and valour shown by him in pressing home his attacks in aerial combats with the enemy, Squadron Leader Mohammad Mahmood Alam is awarded a bar to his Sitara-i-Jurat'.

Squadron Leader Shabbir H Syed, SJ
During the Indo-Pak war of 1965, he was awarded Sitara-i-Jurat, the citation reads: 'On 7TH September, 1965, Squadron Leader Shabbir Hussain Syed led a flight of F-86 Sabre Jets on two separate strike missions on a well-defended enemy airfield at Kalaikunda. During these strikes, he and his flight destroyed on the ground 10 Canberra Light Bombers and two unidentified enemy aircrafts, and damaged two more. In an aerial combat following the strike, Squadron Leader Shabbir destroyed one enemy Hunter aircraft. For exceptional flying skill and outstanding valour in pressing home the attacks on enemy aircraft, Squadron Leader Shabbir Hussain Syed was awarded Sitara-i-Jurat'.

Squadron Leader Abdul Masood Khan, SJ
During the Indo-Pak war of 1965, he was awarded Sitara-i-Jurat, the citation reads: 'Squadron Leader Abdul Masood Khan flew many special missions in a transport aircraft over an important enemy airfield where he dropped paratroops. He succeeded in penetrating the enemy's concentrated radar defence to accomplish the mission. In doing so, he displayed great skill, determination, professional ability and courage. Squadron Leader Abdul Masood Khan was, therefore, awarded Sitara-i-Jurat'.

Sitara-i-Jurat

The Air Force 1965

Squadron Leader Najeeb A Khan, SJ
During the Indo-Pak war of 1965, he was awarded Sitara-i-Jurat, the citation reads: 'Squadron Leader Najeeb Ahmed Khan was commanding a Bomber Squadron during the Indo-Pakistan War. He flew 17 bombing missions against various Indian Air Force operational bases and led his Squadron with courage during the most hazardous raids on Ambala, Adampur, Jamnagar and Jodhpur. He carried out the raid on the well-defended airfield of Ambala deep in enemy territory at great personal risk. The attack was conducted with great accuracy and outstanding professional skills. By his example, he inspired confidence, determination and aggressiveness amongst personnel of his Squadron. For his outstanding courage, inspiring leadership and dedication to duty, he is awarded Sitara-i-Jurat'.

Squadron Leader Mir Abdul Rashid, SJ
During the Indo-Pak war of 1965, he was awarded Sitara-i-Jurat, the citation reads: 'Squadron Leader Mir Abdul Rashid made a valuable contribution to the operational effectiveness of the Pakistan Air Force by carrying out extensive surveillance of radar stations in India and by carrying out aerial photography of vital areas in enemy territory. He always responded most enthusiastically and courageously to all calls made on him in this regard and invariably set an inspiring example for his colleagues. In one particular sortie, after the aircraft was severely disabled, he showed tremendous coolness, courage and piloting skill to bring the aircraft back safely to his base. Squadron Leader Mir Abdul Rashid was, therefore, awarded Sitara-i-Jurat'.

Squadron Leader Shuaib Alam Khan, SJ
During the Indo-Pak war of 1965, he was awarded Sitara-i-Jurat, the citation reads: 'He flew fourteen operational missions very successfully. On all these missions, he displayed exceptional professional skill and navigated his aircraft with unerring accuracy to targets both by day and night. The confidence and enthusiasm, with which he undertook missions to the most heavily, defended targets deep in the enemy territory. His disregard for personal safety and comfort throughout the period of operations was in the highest traditions of the Pakistan Air Force. Squadron Leader Shuaib Alam Khan was, therefore, awarded Sitara-i-Jurat'.

Sitara-i-Jurat

The Air Force 1965

Flight Lieutenant Yousaf Ali Khan, SJ
During the Indo-Pak war of 1965, he was awarded Sitara-i-Jurat, the citation reads: 'While leading the fighter formation of two aircraft's over Chamb Sector, Flight Lieutenant Yousaf Ali Khan was attacked by 4 Hunters. During the engagement, when he had got behind the enemy, two more Gnats attacked him. His left elevator was shot away but he continued fighting them till the enemy aircraft broke off. He showed great courage and determination in engaging overwhelming odds and bringing home the damaged aircraft. On 13TH September, 1965, he shot down another Gnat. For his consistent determination, courage and aggressiveness, the officer is awarded Sitara-i-Jurat'.

Flight Lieutenant Amjad Hussain Khan, SJ
During the Indo-Pak war of 1965, he was awarded Sitara-i-Jurat, the citation reads: 'On the morning of September 7TH, 1965, Flight Lieutenant Amjad Hussain Khan engaged two Mysteres at low level, attacking Sargodha airfield. He fired at one aircraft but as his target was flying at a very low altitude it was ineffective. The two aircraft detected him and took evasive action. Flight Lieutenant Amjad Hussain Khan out manoeuvred the Indian pilots and destroyed both aircraft. The second, aircraft blew up in the air and the debris struck his aircraft and froze its flight controls. Flight Lieutenant Amjad Hussain Khan ejected at 50 feet above ground level. This narrow escape from death had no ill effects on the pilot and within a day he was available and more than willing to continue his duties. For his dedication to duty and courage, Flight Lieutenant Amjad Hussain Khan was awarded Sitara-i-Jurat'.

Flight Lieutenant Syed Saad Akhtar Hatmi, SJ
During the Indo-Pak war of 1965, he was awarded Sitara-i-Jurat, the citation reads: 'Flight Lieutenant Syed Saad Akhtar Hatmi as Flight Commander of a Fighter Squadron, led his formation in 30 Air Defence and 2 Strike missions and is personally credited with the destruction of one enemy Hunter and one Gnat in the air and two Tanks and Four vehicles. The Officer carried out all his missions during the operations with high professional skill, determination, courage and exceptional aggressiveness in the best traditions of the Pakistan Air Force. By his example, he infused his formation with confidence and aggressiveness. For his professional ability, devotion to duty and courage, the officer is awarded Sitara-i-Jurat'.

Sitara-i-Jurat

The Air Force 1965

Flight Lieutenant Cecil Chaudhry, SJ
During the Indo-Pak war of 1965, he was awarded Sitara-i-Jurat, the citation reads: 'On 6TH September, 1965, Flight Lieutenant Cecil Chaudhry was No. 2 in a flight of 3 F-86 aircraft led by Squadron Leader Rafiqui. Their target was Halwara airfield of the Indian Air Force. This formation of 3 F-86s was intercepted by 10 Hunter aircraft of the Indian Air Force. During the engagement, the leader's guns stopped firing and he handed over the lead to Flight Lieutenant Cecil Chaudhry, who very ably and aggressively continued the fight against heavy odds. About 60 miles inside enemy territory, he destroyed two enemies Hunter aircraft with his gun attack. His courage and professional ability in such adverse circumstances was outstanding and he successfully managed to return to base after having lost contact with other members of the formation. On 15th September, 1965, in spite of insufficient information from Ground Radar, Flight Lieutenant Cecil Chaudhry pursued his attack aggressively on enemy bombers and chased them 150 miles from his base. During the engagement, he destroyed one enemy Canberra bomber. For these acts of courage, dedication and professional ability, Flight Lieutenant Cecil Chaudhry was awarded Sitara-i-Jurat'.

Flight Lieutenant Amanullah Khan, SJ
During the Indo-Pak war of 1965, he was awarded Sitara-i-Jurat, the citation reads: 'Flight Lieutenant Amanullah Khan carried out 26 strike missions and one Air Defence mission against the enemy. He flew in a most aggressive and alert manner and was responsible for inspiring great confidence in his formation members. His leadership left nothing more to be desired. He participated in attacks on Amritsar and Firozepur Radar, Gurdaspur Railway Station, Ammunition Train at Dhaliwal and many other close support missions and invariably achieved most convincing results against heavy, enemy ground fire. On 21st September 1965, his formation achieved great successes in the destruction of enemy's heavy guns which were shelling Lahore. For his aggressive, and determined leadership and display of unbeatable courage in the face of heavy enemy ground fire, Flight Lieutenant Amanullah Khan was awarded Sitara-i-Jurat'.

Sitara-i-Jurat

The Air Force 1965

Flight Lieutenant Sikandar Mahmood Khan, SJ

During the Indo-Pak war of 1965, he was awarded Sitara-i-Jurat, the citation reads: 'Flight Lieutenant Sikandar Mahmood Khan has flown 15 bomber missions during the Indo-Pakistan War. He undertook some of the most hazardous missions and completed every one of them successfully causing maximum damage to the enemy in complete disregard of his own safety. On many occasions, he was chased by enemy fighters and in spite of warnings by own radar controllers, he pressed home his attack and completed the mission most successfully. By this performance he has shown great courage and determination, and his coolness under such difficult circumstances has been of the highest order. For his courage and gallant performance, Flight Lieutenant Sikandar Mahmood Khan is awarded Sitara-i-Jurat'.

Flight Lieutenant Syed Shamsuddin, SJ

During the Indo-Pak war of 1965, he was awarded Sitara-i-Jurat, the citation reads: 'He has completed a total of 14 successful bombing missions against enemy airfields at Ambala, Halwara, Adampur, Pathankot, Jamnagar and Jodhpur. Every one of the attacks undertaken by Flight Lieutenant Shamsuddin was delivered with great accuracy, causing maximum damage to the enemy in spite of very stiff enemy opposition. His coolness under difficult circumstances has been inspiring and he has set an example of great courage, determination and valour for his associates. For his outstanding courage and bravery, Flight Lieutenant Syed Shamsuddin Ahmed is awarded Sitara-i-Jurat'.

Flight Lieutenant Yousaf Hasan Alvi, SJ

During the Indo-Pak war of 1965, he was awarded Sitara-i-Jurat, the citation reads: 'Lieutenant Yousaf Hasan Alvi completed a total of 13 missions against Indian Airfields. His professional ability was of the highest order and he has displayed coolness, courage and determination in every one of his attacks which has resulted in the destruction of many Indian installations and airfields. He has conducted bombing attacks on Adampur, Halwara, Pathankot, Jamnagar and Jodhpur with such precise accuracy that he was always selected for the most difficult tasks. He showed determination, courage and singleness of purpose, in execution of every mission he undertook. For his outstanding bravery and devotion to duty, Flight Lieutenant Yousaf Hasan Alvi is awarded Sitara-i-Jurat'.

Sitara-i-Jurat

The Air Force 1965

Flight Lieutenant Arshad Sami Khan, SJ
During the Indo-Pak war of 1965, he was awarded Sitara-i-Jurat, the citation reads: 'Flight Lieutenant Arshad Sami Khan flew the maximum combat missions during the war with India. His enthusiasm and aggressive spirit was of the highest order and was responsible to ignite the spirit of competition amongst other pilots in its most effective form. He led formations in the battle area with exemplary determination and brought back excellent results. He has been credited with one aircraft, 15 tanks and 22 vehicles destroyed and 8 tanks and 19 vehicles damaged and 2 heavy guns destroyed. He never looked tired or apprehensive in the face of heavy odds but kept on inflicting maximum damage to the enemy as his only objective. For his outstanding devotion to duty and bravery, Flight Lieutenant Arshad Sami Khan was awarded Sitara-i-Jurat'.

Flight Lieutenant Dilawar Hussain, SJ
During the Indo-Pak war of 1965, he was awarded Sitara-i-Jurat, the citation reads: 'His personal score of enemy tanks and aircraft on the ground was three aircraft and eight tanks destroyed one aircraft and four tanks damaged, one armoured vehicle and thirteen others destroyed nine vehicles and one gun damaged. He flew a total of ten Air Defence sorties and 17 Strike/Close support missions. On one occasion, he continued his mission without being in the least bit apprehensive after having been hit by ground fire. For his courage and high spirits in the performance of his duty, Flight Lieutenant Dilawar Hussain is awarded Sitara-i-Jurat'.

Flight Lieutenant Mohammad Akbar, SJ
During the Indo-Pak war of 1965, he was awarded Sitara-i-Jurat, the citation reads: 'Flight Lieutenant Mohammad Akbar was responsible for programming of pilots for various duties. He was under extreme pressure of work but was able to exercise complete control over the Squadron and attached pilots and ensured adequate rest for everybody. In addition, he flew as much as was possible and completed every mission in highly professional manner. His personal conduct was a true reflection of his determined efforts. He flew 13 strike and 10 air defence missions. During the strike missions he was credited with two aircraft destroyed, one aircraft damaged on the ground, two tanks destroyed and 3 damaged; 5 vehicles destroyed and 3 damaged and 4 guns damaged. Flight Lieutenant Mohammad Akbar was, therefore, awarded Sitara-i-Jurat'.

Sitara-i-Jurat

The Air Force 1965

Flight Lieutenant Ghani Akbar, SJ

During the Indo-Pak war of 1965, he was awarded Sitara-i-Jurat, the citation reads: 'Flight Lieutenant Ghani Akbar flew 13 ground attack and 12 air defence missions during the Indo-Pakistan War. He destroyed one aircraft in a ground strike mission and was credited with 5 tanks destroyed and 5 damaged during close support missions. Throughout he flew aggressively, fearlessly and in a most professional manner. For his flying ability, determination and courage he was awarded Sitara-i-Jurat'.

Flight Lieutenant Imtiaz Ahmad Bhatti, SJ

During the Indo-Pak war of 1965, he was awarded Sitara-i-Jurat, the citation reads: 'Flight Lieutenant Imtiaz Ahmad Bhatti was one of the two pilots who were on an air patrol when they were directed to intercept enemy aircraft attacking our ground forces in Chamb area. This was the first air encounter of the Indo-Pakistan War. Though heavily outnumbered, Flight Lieutenant Bhatti fought with exceptional courage and professional skill and shot down two Vampire aircraft in this engagement. This set an inspiring example for others to emulate. For his gallantry, determination and dedication to the Service he was awarded Sitara-i-Jurat'.

Flight Lieutenant M. Tariq Habib Khan, SJ

During the Indo-Pak war of 1965, he was awarded Sitara-i-Jurat, the citation reads: 'Flight Lieutenant M. Tariq Habib Khan was one of the pilots who struck the enemy airfield at Kalai Kunda in the first strike mission against the enemy from East Pakistan. He flew three operational sorties and many other Air Defence missions and carried out these missions most courageously with success against heavy odds at great risk and in complete disregard for his personal safety. In one of these sorties, he engaged 4 Indian Air Force Hunters thus diverting their attention from other Pakistan Air Force aircraft that were attacking the enemy airfield. Later, he himself managed to evade the Indian Force aircraft and returned to base safely in a crippled aircraft. During all these operations, he destroyed three Canberra's and one C-119 on the ground and one Hunter in the air. Flight Lieutenant Tariq carried out all his missions with determination, courage and at great personal risk. For his act of bravery and devotion to duty, Flight Lieutenant Mohammad Tariq Habib Khan was awarded Sitara-i-Jurat'.

Sitara-i-Jurat

The Air Force 1965

Flight Lieutenant Saadat Mohammad Akhtar Khan, SJ
During the Indo-Pak war of 1965, he was awarded Sitara-i-Jurat, the citation reads: 'During the Indo-Pakistan War, Flight Lieutenant Saadat Mohammad Akhtar Khan completed a total of 15 operational missions against the enemy airfields. He undertook the most hazardous missions to Ambala, Adampur, Jodhpur, Halwara and Pathankot. In all these missions he displayed great courage and valour, Flight Lieutenant Saadat Mohammad Akhtar Khan was, therefore, awarded Sitara-i-Jurat'.

Flight Lieutenant William D. Harney, SJ
During the Indo-Pak war of 1965, he was awarded Sitara-i-Jurat, the citation reads: 'His performance and professional ability during the current opera he undertook all available bombing missions and especially the most hazardous ones to Ambala, Pathankot, Adampur, Halwara and Jodhpur. His mission planning and execution of the missions has been of the highest order in spite of very heavy odds. He has always reached his targets and made very significant contribution to accurate attacks. The officer has during the Indo-Pakistan War completed a total of 14 operational missions and every one of them has been of significant importance to the overall superiority of the Pakistan Air Force. For his courage dedication to duty, Flight Lieutenant William D. Harney is awarded Sitara-i-Jurat'.

Flight Lieutenant Iftikhar Ahmad Khan Ghauri, SJ
During the Indo-Pak war of 1965, he was awarded Sitara-i-Jurat, the citation reads: 'Flight Lieutenant Iftikhar Ahmad Khan Ghauri in the Indo-Pakistan War flew a total of 13 operational missions to Pathankot, Adampur, Halwara, Jodhpur and Jamnagar. The officer displayed great courage and determination in reaching his targets in spite of very heavy odds and against tough enemy opposition. His accurate and aggressive mission-planning has contributed significantly towards the success of our bomber raids against the enemy airfields. In all these missions he displayed great, courage, determination and complete devotion to duty. In spite of his serious stomach ailment, the officer remained fit throughout the period of operations and voluntarily offered his services for every mission much beyond the call of duty. For his outstanding devotion to duty, courage and velour, Flight Lieutenant Iftikhar Ahmad Khan Ghauri was awarded Sitara-i-Jurat'.

Sitara-i-Jurat

The Air Force 1965

Lieutenant Saadat Mohammad Akhtar Khan, SJ
During the Indo-Pak war of 1965, he was awarded Sitara-i-Jurat, the citation reads: 'During the Indo-Pakistan War, Flight Lieutenant Saadat Mohammad Akhtar Khan completed a total of 15 operational missions against the enemy airfields. He undertook the most hazardous missions to Ambala, Adampur, Jodhpur, Halwara and Pathankot. In all these missions he displayed great courage and valour, Flight Lieutenant Saadat Mohammad Akhtar Khan was, therefore, awarded Sitara-i-Jurat'.

Flight Lieutenant Chaudhry Rizwan Ahmed, SJ
During the Indo-Pak war of 1965, he was awarded Sitara-i-Jurat, the citation reads: 'Flight Lieutenant Chaudhry Rizwan Ahmed undertook a total of seven operational missions in enemy territory. By his objective thinking and sound ideas on the use of airborne radar equipment, a very high degree of accuracy in aerial delivery missions under blind flying conditions was achieved. In addition to this contribution, he was always available for strenuous flying duties even after long tiring hours of planning, and consistently displayed a great deal of zeal and stamina. His achievements made him stand out as a navigator who combines professional skill with a rare sense of objectivity. Flight Lieutenant Ch. Rizwan Ahmed was, therefore, awarded Sitara-i-Jurat'.

Flight Lieutenant Syed Khalid Hasan Wasti, SJ
During the Indo-Pak war of 1965, he was awarded Sitara-i-Jurat, the citation reads: 'Flight Lieutenant Syed Khalid Hasan Wasti took part in 5 operational missions during the War with India. These missions were by night into enemy territory. Some of these missions involved flying over mountainous terrain under adverse weather conditions, while the other was flown at 300 feet above ground level. Such operations, therefore, called for skill and courage. He repeatedly pushed himself forward to take part in these difficult missions and always conducted them with great skill and determination. By so doing, he displayed the highest degree of enthusiasm and determination. In addition, his sense of humour and his usual cheerfulness were apparent at all times. For cool courage and devotion to duty, Flight Lieutenant Khalid Hasan Wasti is awarded Sitara-i-Jurat'.

Sitara-i-Jurat

The Air Force 1965

Flight Lieutenant Syed Manzoorul Hasan Hashmi, SJ
During the Indo-Pak war of 1965, he was awarded Sitara-i-Jurat, the citation reads: 'Flight Lieutenant Syed Manzoorul Hasan Hashmi flew 20 strike and 2 Air Defence missions against the enemy. His strikes were directed against enemy concentrations on Jammu, Sialkot, Wagha-Kasur sectors. He led his mission in a most competent manner and achieved considerable success against heavily defended enemy areas. His own aircraft was hit on six occasions by Ack Ack and small arms fire but, undaunted, he pursued his attacks on the enemy. His formation achieved notable success on 21st September, 1965, in which he destroyed many heavy guns of the enemy which were shelling Lahore and earned him deep appreciation on own army's Area Commander. His cool, courageous and operational leadership in complete disregard to his own safety in the face of heavy enemy fire and devotion to duty are commendable. Flight Lieutenant Syed Manzoorul Hasan Hashmi is awarded Sitara-i-Jurat'.

Flight Lieutenant Saif-ul-Azam, SJ
During the Indo-Pak war of 1965, he was awarded Sitara-i-Jurat, the citation reads: 'Flight Lieutenant Saif-ul-Azam flew 12 ground-attack missions against the enemy in Sialkot, Wagha and Kasur Sector. His spotting of the enemy's dug-in and well dispersed armour was most commendable and invariably resulted in success of missions. His own attacks were very well executed and were a source of inspiration to other members of the flights. On 19th September, 1965, in spite of bad radio-communication and having been separated from his formation, his qualities of aggressiveness and alertness earned him and Indian Gnat Fighter. For his exceptional flying, courage, alertness and devotion to duty, Flight Lieutenant Saif-ul-Azam is awarded Sitara-i-Jurat'.

Flight Lieutenant Nazir Ahmed Khan, SJ
During the Indo-Pak war of 1965, he was awarded Sitara-i-Jurat, the citation reads: 'Flight Lieutenant Nazir Ahmed Khan took an active part in the air operation during the war with India. These operations involved flying over hazardous terrain in adverse weather condition by night as well as flying at extremely low levels. Such operations called for outstanding flying ability and great courage. He carried out these missions with great skill and determination, and his achievements are a tribute to his ability. Flight Lieutenant Nazir Ahmed Khan was, therefore was awarded Sitara-i-Jurat'.

Sitara-i-Jurat

The Air Force 1965

Flying Officer Ziauddin Hasan, SJ
During the Indo-Pak war of 1965, he was awarded Sitara-i-Jurat, the citation reads: 'In the nights of the 6TH, 7TH and 8TH September, 1965, Flying Officer Ziauddin Hasan flew as navigator of the leading aircraft of bombers which attacked the enemy airfields. Despite intense enemy anti-aircraft fire and some fighter opposition, Flying Officer Hasan navigated the bomber fights with cool, courage and accuracy and thus contributed to the success of bombing mission. For the high degree of professional skill, courage and determination shown by Flying Officer Ziauddin Hasan in the air operations against enemy airfields, he is awarded Sitara-i-Jurat'.

Flight Lieutenant Viqar Ahmed Abdi, SJ
During the Indo-Pak war of 1965, he was awarded Sitara-i-Jurat, the citation reads: 'On 7TH September, 1965, Flight Lieutenant Viqar Ahmed Abdi was the navigator on an operational mission flying at low level by night where precise navigation was no easy task. He succeeded in accomplishing the mission with the desired accuracy. In so doing so he, as a navigator, displayed great skill and determination. In addition to this special mission, he undertook many more successful night bombing missions. For his excellent performance, Flight Lieutenant Viqar Ahmed Abdi was awarded Sitara-i-Jurat'.

Squadron Leader Alauddin Ahmed Shaheed, SJ
During the Indo-Pak war of 1965, he was awarded a posthumous Sitara-i-Jurat, the citation reads: 'Squadron Leader Alauddin Ahmed led his squadron in twenty combat missions against the Indian ground and air forces. His leadership throughout the operations was cool, courageous and most determined which inspired the greatest confidence amongst pilots of his formation and resulted in destruction of many Indian tanks and vehicles. In his last sortie, he attached and blew up and important ammunition train at Gurdaspur rail-head in complete disregard to his personal safety. During this attack on September 13, his aircraft was damaged and was reported missing over enemy territory. Subsequently, it was confirmed that the officer died in this action. For his exemplary leadership, courage and valour, Squadron Leader Alauddin Ahmed was awarded Sitara-i-Jurat'.

Sitara-i-Jurat

The Air Force 1965

Squadron Leader Muhammad Iqbal Shaheed, SJ
During the Indo-Pak war of 1965, he was awarded a posthumous Sitara-i-Jurat, the citation reads: 'Squadron Leader Muhammad Iqbal flew many operational missions which played a vital part in the success of the Pakistan Air Force during the India-Pakistan war. He carried out these missions with determination, enthusiasm, and outstanding ability and at great personal risk. His performance, throughout, was exemplary and highly inspiring for the personnel under his command. For his outstanding leadership, valour, loyalty and invaluable services to the Pakistan Air Force and the country, he was awarded Sitara-i-Jurat'.

Squadron Leader Muniruddin Ahmed Shaheed, SJ
During the Indo-Pak war of 1965, he was awarded a posthumous Sitara-i-Jurat, the citation reads: 'During the war, a high-powered, heavily defended radar station in Amritsar, was eventually rendered infective after several determined missions by PAF fighters. In all these missions Squadron Leader Muniruddin Ahmed unhesitatingly volunteered to fly and without regard for his personal safety exposed himself within the firing zone of enemy guns for long periods in attempts to locate and destroy the targets. Squadron Leader Munir flew eight combat missions by persistently appealing to his colleagues to temporarily relieve him of his ground duties as Wing Operations Officer In the final successful attack on September 11TH he made the supreme sacrifice when his aircraft was fatally hit by the heavy concentration of ack-ack gums. For his outstanding leadership, valour, loyalty and invaluable services to the Pakistan Air Force and the country, he was awarded Sitara-i-Jurat'.

Flight Lieutenant Saifullah Khan Lodhi Shaheed, SJ
During the Indo-Pak war of 1965, he was awarded a posthumous Sitara-i-Jurat, the citation reads: 'Flight Lieutenant Saifullah Khan Lodhi was a navigator of exceptional ability and a complete dedicated officer. He possessed unusual skill, enthusiasm and drive, which enabled him to make a valuable contribution towards operations. He undertook several operational missions most cheerful and enthusiastically, invariable attaining outstanding results. It was on one such mission on 11TH September 65 that he lost his life. For his extreme dedication to duty Flight Lieutenant Saifullah Khan Lodhi was awarded Sitara'.

Sitara-i-Jurat

The Air Force 1965

Flight Lieutenant Yunus Hussain Shaheed, SJ
During the Indo-Pak war of 1965, he was awarded a posthumous Sitara-i-Jurat, the citation reads: 'Yunus fought in air battle over enemy territory aggressively, fearlessly and with great professional skill. On 6th September, while attacking Halwara airfield, his small formation was intercepted by a large number of enemy aircraft. He fought them with exceptional gallantry exceeding all limits and in the process shot down two Hunters. Although his aircraft was hit, he refused to break off engagement in complete disregard to his personal safety. He became a symbol of courage and professional ability for the other pilots. For his, valour, professional skill and devotion to duty he is awarded Sitara-i-Jurat'.

Squadron Leader Sarfaraz Ahmad Rafique Shaheed, SJ
During the Indo-Pak war of 1965, he was awarded a posthumous Sitara-i-Jurat, the citation reads: 'On 6TH September, 1965, Squadron Leader Sarfaraz Ahmad Rafiqui led a formation of 3 F-86 aircraft on a strike against Halwara airfield. The formation was intercepted by about 10 Hunter aircraft out of which Squadron Leader Rafiqui accounted for one in the first few seconds. But then his guns jammed due to a defect and stopped firing. However, Rafiqui refused to leave the battle area which he would have been perfectly justified to do; instead he ordered his No. 2 to take over as leader and continue the engagement while he tried to give the formation as much protection as was possible with an unarmed aircraft. This called on the part of Squadron Leader Rafiqui. The end for him was never in doubt but he chose to disregard it and, in the process, his aircraft was shot down and he was killed but not before enabling his formation to shoot down 3 more Hunter aircraft. Rafiqui's conduct was clearly beyond the call of duty and conformed to the highest traditions of leadership and bravery in battle against overwhelming odds. For this and his earlier exploits, he is awarded Hilal-i-Jurat and Sitara-i-Jurat'.

Army Aviation Corps
Pakistan Army Aviation gained autonomy from Pakistan Air Force in 1958, and gained full corps status in 1977. It is a most decorated Corps of Pakistan Army.

Sitara-i-Jurat

Army Aviation Corps

Lt. Col. Ullah Babar, HI, SJ and Bar

Babar was born in Pirpiai, North-West Frontier Province, and British Indian Empire. His family is from the Babar tribe of Pashtuns and hails from the village of Pirpiai in district Nowshera. Babar's early education was from Presentation Convent School, Peshawar, North West Frontier Province, British India, between 1935 and 1939. From 1939 to 1941 he attended Burn Hall School then located at Srinagar. The school was subsequently shifted to Abottabad after the Partition of India in 1947. He then attended Prince of Wales Royal Indian Military College from 1941-1947 in Dehradun and joined the Pakistan Army in 1948. In his long career in the Army, Babar served in the Artillery Corps and pioneered the Army Aviation Corps. (He was the First Commanding Officer of First Rotary Squadron of Pakistan Army). He was decorated with Sitara-i-Jurat in 1965. During the 1965 war with India, Babar single-handedly captured an entire Indian company of soldiers (over 70 POWs) and was awarded Sitara-e-Jurat for this action. In the 1971 war, he commanded an artillery brigade supporting 23 Division and later commanded an infantry brigade until he was wounded and evacuated from the battlefield. He also had the distinction of having been awarded SJ & Bar. In 1972, he was appointed Inspector General Frontier Corps. He resigned from the Army in 1974 while commanding an infantry division and was appointed as Governor of Khyber-Pakhtunkhwa. Naseerullah Babar died on 10TH January 2011.

Major Sarfraz Rabbani, SJ

Major Rabbani was the first flight commander who operated in Indian Held Kashmir during 'Operation Gibraltar' and later during 'Operation Grand Slam' as well. On 1ST September 1965, during the Battle of Chamb, enemy guns were hindering the advance of the Pakistani forces. Major Rabbani tasked to locate these guns. He located the guns and called the artillery fire and while flying the L-19 in a pattern to avoid the enemy ground fire directed at him. In the bargain some vehicles exploded and apparently heavy casualties were inflicted on the enemy. Then necessary fire correction was given, soon guns and the entire area became a scene of destruction and confusion. Major Rabbani was later decorated with Sitara-i-Jurat for this action.

Sitara-i-Jurat

Army Aviation Corps

Major Mohammad Akhtar, SJ

On 13TH September 1965, Major Akhtar, was second-in-command of 2 Army Aviation Squadron which flew in the Pasrur area for aerial observation. He spotted enemy infantry pausing under cover, due to communication problem he gained height and was easily picked up by the enemy fighter. Despite enemy fighter, Major Akhtar brought own artillery fire on enemy and completed the shoot successfully that resulted in stalling the enemy advance. His courageous and timely action inflicted heavy casualties on the enemy and earned him the Sitara-i-Jurat.

Captain HUK Niazi, SJ

September 1965 Captain HUK Niazi was sent for a surveillance mission around Zafarwal. He crossed the International Boundary, west of Deg Nadi, when he saw a huge concentration of enemy vehicles estimated of 2000-3000 vehicles, some 4 miles west of Samba. He informed his commanding officer requesting for Air Force strike. Lieutenant Colonel Mahmud immediately flew to Headquarters 1 Corps. He conveyed the information personally to Lieutenant General Rana, the corps commander. The Air Headquarters sent two fighter reconnaissance aircraft to the area, and they confirmed that news. They requested for all available aircraft to be sent for strike in that area. Soon four F-86 of 18 Squadron, led by Squadron Leader Alau Din 'Butch' arrived. They kept pounding them with all the weapons available, including the napalm bombs, used for the first time in war. For the destruction the Indian 14 Mountain Davisson earned Captain HUK Niazi the Sitara-i-Jurat.

Captain Muazzam Ali Shah, SJ

On 18TH September 1965 the Battle of Chawinda was in the final phase. Captain Shah took off with Captain Jamil as co-pilot to act as Forward Airborne Air Controller; target was enemy heavy guns, 6 miles inside enemy territory close to Nawan Shehr. Visibility was poor and observation difficult. As they flew forward for better observation they came under enemy anti aircraft fire but Captain Shah boldly and skilfully directed the fighters amidst this panoramic fire. He flew up till 500 yards of enemy guns, 3 out of 6 guns were destroyed and they were silenced forever. Captain Muazzam Ali Shah was honoured with the gallantry award of Sitara-i-Jurat.

Sitara-i-Jurat

The Navy 1965
When the Indo-Pak war broke out on 6TH September 1965, the 'Ghazi' was assigned to keep a vigil off the Bombay harbour which at that time was packed tight with Indian warships including the aircraft carrier Vikrant. The Ghazi was told not to tinker with smaller vessels, but focus on the heavier units. So effective was its blockade that no Indian warships dared run the gauntlet. It was the bottling-up of the Indian fleet by the Ghazi which enabled the Pakistan flotilla to move in and blast the Indian naval fortress of Dwarka. The Pakistani operation was successful and its warships harboured in Bombay, making the Indian Navy unable to sortie. Throughout the war Indian Navy's aircraft-carrier was besieged in Bombay.

Admiral Karamat Rahman Niazi, NI (M), SJ, HI (M)
Niazi was the first commanding officer of nation's first submarine, the Ghazi. On 2ND September in 1965, Ghazi was deployed off to Bombay coast covertly patrolling the Rann of Kutch coastal areas. However, Commander Niazi's mission was to remain off the Bombay coast and engage with only major warships of Indian Navy who were close to Karachi coast. After the naval shelling by Pakistan Navy in Dwarka, India, Ghazi again returned to patrol off the Rann of Kutch areas. Commander Niazi was public decorated with Sitara-i-Jurat for his actions of valour.

Lieutenant Commander Ahmad Tasnim, HI (M), SJ
In 1965, Lieutenant-Commander Tasnim was the executive officer and Second-in-Command of the Ghazi, and participated in second war with India in 1965. Ghazi, under command of Cdr KR Niazi, escorted the combined task group under Cdre S.M. Anwar, the OTC, to successfully raid a radar facility in Dwarka, India. Lt. Cdr. Tasnim was honoured with Sitara-i-Jurat, alongside with the Ghazi in 1966.

Commander Zafar Muhammad Khan, SJ, HJ
He briefly served in PNS Ghazi as an Electrical Engineer Officer (EEO), and actively participated in Indo-Pakistani War of 1965 and served as a Torpedo officer (TO) in Operation Dwarka on 7TH September 1965. "Though the submarine did not score any hits, it was a significant threat to any ships that came out of harbour (with that being its mission); but none came out. For his participation in this action won him the award of Sitara-i-Jurat.
No response from the naval authorities regarding the comprehensive list of gallantry winners!

Sitara-i-Jurat

The Army 1971

Major General Amir Hamza Khan HJ, SJ and Bar
In the battle of Sulaimanke, during the Indo-Pakistan war of 1965, Lieutenant Colonel Amir Hamza was awarded a Sitara-i-Jurat for this battle. In 1971 he was back in the same sector as OC 105TH Brigade and for his gallant performance was awarded a bar to the Sitara-i-Jurat.

Brigadier Muhammad Taj, SJ and Bar
During the Indo-Pakistan war of 1965, Major Muhammad Taj and his unit were directed to get to the Khokhars Par border in Tharparkar district. Major Taj attacked with a mobile force and captured the Post. Soon after, a rapid advance was made on the post by two Indian tanks accompanied by two rifle companies Taj engaged the advancing Indians with mortar and machine-gun fire, forcing them to withdraw, leaving behind a number of dead and two wrecked tanks. For this action, Taj was awarded Sitara-i-Jurat. Lieutenant Colonel Muhammad Taj won his second SJ in 1971, in recognition of his performance in Dhaka during military action and the subsequent march to Rajshahi, fighting a number of battles en route.

General Tariq Mehmood, SJ and Bar
As a Captain, Tariq Mehmood was awarded Sitara-i-Jurat for his acts of bravery during the Indo-Pak war of 1965. In 1971, as a Colonel Mehmood, volunteered to go East Pakistan to participate in the War of 1971. In this conflict, Mehmood was sent to Shahjalal International Airport (Dhaka Airport). The airport was heavily guarded. Mehmood commanded the Shaheen Company. His company saw heavy fighting in the airport. After 34 hours, the Shaheen Company gained control of the airport and its surrounding areas. For his gallant leadership Colonel Mehmood was awarded the Bar to his Sitara-i-Jurat. *Brigadier Tariq Mehmood took over the Command of Special Service Group on 3RD January 1982 and remained Commander of Special Service Group till his Shahadat on 9TH May 1989. One of the most decorated soldiers of Pakistan Army who fought in two Indo-Pakistan wars.*

Brigadier Syed Hazoor Hasnain, SJ and Bar
He was and commissioned in 15 Baluch Regiment and joined SSG. He was dropped in India in 1965 War and was the only one who ex-filtrated back to Pakistan for which he was awarded the Sitara-i-Jurat. During the Indo-Pakistan war of 1971, for his gallant leadership he was awarded the Bar to his Sitara-i-Jurat.

Sitara-i-Jurat

The Army 1971

Major Raja Nadir Pervez Khan, SJ and Bar

Major Raja Nadir Pervez Khan had been awarded the Sitara-i-Jurat for his services in the 1965 war. In 1971 he was posted to East Pakistan and was the Company Commander of the 6 Punjab Regiment troops which had boarded PNS Rajshah, a Pakistan Navy vessel. However, his team had gotten off the vessel and took the position in designated areas. Major Pervez was inducted in Pakistan Marines Battalion as a weapon specialist. During the conflict, the Maj Raja Nadir Pervez was informed of the attack on PNS Rajshah, he immediately directed an MI-8 helicopter in the vicinity to evacuate the wounded. His efforts in the 1971 war, which included leading an escape from the Indian prison in Fateh Garh, along with four other officers, gained him a second Sitara-i-Jurat and promotion to the rank of Lieutenant-Colonel.

Brigadier Jamal Mohammad, SJ

Brigadier Jamal Mohammad of 18 Baloch Regiment was awarded the Sitara-i-Jurat for his actions in the Fazilka – Sulaimanke Sector during the Indo-Pakistan war of 1971.

Colonel Sher Ur Rehman, SJ

Colonel Sher Ur Rehman of 29 Cavalry fought in the Indo-Pakistan war of 1971 in East Pakistan and called by the name of "the Desert Fox" at that time. He was taken prisoner of war and spent at Agra jail in India for a year facing several death sentences at that time, but he came to Pakistan during the P.O.W. exchange treaty. For his staunch resistance he was awarded the Sitara-i-Jurat.

Major Shabbir Sharif, Shaheed, SJ, NH

Major Shabbir Sharif was awarded the Sitara-i-Jurat for actions in Chamb-Jaurian Sector as 2ND Lieutenant in 1965. During the Indo-Pakistani War of 1971 he was killed while firing on the enemy tanks for which he was awarded the highest gallantry award of Nishan-i-Haider. He is the only person of Pakistan army to ever receive both the Nishan -i- Haider and Sitara-i-Jurat for his bravery. He is regarded as the most decorated officer of Pakistan Army

Sitara-i-Jurat

The Army 1971

Lieutenant Colonel Haq Nawaz Kayani Shaheed, SJ and Bar
During the Indo-Pakistan war of 1971 in Leepa Valley, Lieutenant Colonel Haq Nawaz Kayani counter-attacked a position and recaptured it and embraced Shahadat during the operation. The locals have named the ridge as 'Kayani Ridge' after his name. Lieutenant Colonel Haq Nawaz Kayani was awarded posthumous Bar to Sitara-i-Jurat he had won in 1965.

Captain Nawazish Ali Khan Shaheed, SJ
Captain Nawazish Ali Khan embraced martyrdom while serving in Headquarters East Pakistan Logistic Area during action on 16TH December 1971. He was awarded Sitara-i-Jurat posthumously.

Naik Sultan Ahmed Shaheed, SJ
During 1971 Naik Sultan was serving in 27 Field Company (173 Engineer Battalion) of 212 (Independent) Infantry Brigade Group in Chamb Sector. On 15TH December 1971, while attacking on enemy post in infantry role he displayed extra ordinary bravery and embraced martyrdom. He was awarded Sitara-i-Jurat posthumously.

Major Sabir Kamal Meyer Shaheed, SJ and Bar
Major Sabir Kamal Meyer fought The Battle of Hilli or the Battle of Bogra which was a major battle fought in the Indo-Pakistani War of 1971. During the battle Major Sabir Kamal Meyer refused to surrender and ordered his men to fight till last man and last bullet and told his men that Indians would take over Hilli and enter here only over his dead body and the very same happened. During the furious battle Major Sabir Kamal Meyer embraced Shahadat. He was awarded Sitara e Jurat and Bar.

Major Shabbir Sharif Shaheed, SJ, NH
Major Shabbir Sharif was a Pakistani Army officer who was killed in Indo-Pakistani War of 1971 and was awarded Nishan -i- Haider for his actions. He is the only person to have been awarded both the Sitara-e-Jurrat and Nishan -i- Haider, although they were given on separate occasions. He is regarded as the most decorated officer of Pakistan Army.

Captain Mujeeb Faqrullah Khan Shaheed, SJ
Captain Mujeeb Faqrullah Khan of 25TH Frontier Force Rifles, during the Indo-Pakistan war of 1971, in the Chamb-Jorian Sector took a Picquet of 1 Masud Battalion and defended it to death on December 4TH, 1971. He was posthumously awarded the Sitara-i-Jurat.

Sitara-i-Jurat

The Air Force 1971

Wing Commander Hakimullah, SJ
'Wing Commander Hakimullah was commanding a fighter bomber squadron during the Indo-Pakistan War, 1971. He led five strike missions against heavily defended enemy airfields. Every mission, led by him, including the first strike against Amritsar, was flown with tremendous courage and exceptional professional skill. He flew with nerve and cool composure, which was a source of inspiration to his team in particular and everyone else connected with operational activity in general. During some of these strikes his formation was intercepted by enemy fighters over Indian airfields. Wing Commander Hakimullah lived upto the highest traditions of leadership during these critical moments and accomplished the primary mission. Throughout the war, his unit inspired by him, flew boldly and without any losses in aircraft or pilot. For his gallant and professional performance, He has been awarded Sitara-i-Jurat'.

Squadron Leader Farooq Omer, SJ
'Squadron Leader Farooq Omer was employed on day and night air defence and reconnaissance duties during the Indo-Pakistan war of 1971. He flew reconnaissance mission against heavily defended enemy airfields and forward army positions. He always flew with immense courage and determination. On an air defence mission, Squadron Leader Farooq Omer successfully intercepted an enemy formation of Hunter aircraft and shot down / damaged four of them. The immense courage and determination displayed by Squadron Leader Farooq Omer during the war was always a source of inspiration to other pilots of squadron. He has been awarded Sitara-i-Jurat'.

Squadron Leader Farooq Omer, SJ
'Squadron Leader Ghulam Ahmed Khan was detailed along with Squadron Leader A. Basit on a counter air mission against the I.A.F. Base at Halwara on the night of $10/11^{TH}$ December, 1971. He flew the mission as planned. While a few minutes short of the target 4 SAMs were fired at his B-57 aircraft. He displayed great courage, skill and devotion to duty, assisted his pilot in evading these missiles, continuing the mission and successfully attacking the target even though there was all the likelihood of the enemy firing more SAMs. For his courage, determination and devotion to duty Squadron Leader Ghulam Ahmed Khan has been awarded Sitara-i-Jurat'.

Sitara-i-Jurat

The Air Force 1971

Squadron Leader Javed Afzal Ahmed, SJ
'On 4TH December, 1971 while flying on an air defence mission, Squadron Leader Javed Afzal Ahmed intercepted a formation of four Hunters approaching Dhaka airfield. During the combat he shot down two Hunters and chased away the others, thus preventing them from attacking any target. In the same mission, he engaged a formation of two SU-7 aircraft's which were attacking a Pakistan Army helicopter and chased them away. Throughout the war he fought valiantly. For his courage and excellent performance in the face of heavy odds, Squadron Leader Afzal has been awarded Sitara-i-Jurat'.

Flight Lieutenant Abdul Wajid Saleem, SJ
'Flight Lieutenant Abdul Wajid Saleem was the navigator of an aircraft detailed on a mission against a P.A.F. base on the night of 6/7th December, 1971. He planned the mission with great care. During the flight, Flight Lieutenant Abdul Wajid displayed a high degree of professionalism and courage which were a source of inspiration to all other crew members. As the aircraft approached the target it encountered heavy anti-aircraft fire. His accurate tactical navigation ensured a successful mission against heavy odds. In recognition of his devotion to duty and courage, Flight Lieutenant Abdul Wajid Saleem has been awarded Sitara-i-Jurat'.

Flight Lieutenant Israr Ahmad, SJ
On 4TH December, 1971, Flight Lieutenant Israr Ahmad was detailed to fly a mission over the Chamb-Akhnur sector. While over the battle area, his aircraft was hit by enemy ground fire and the pilot was seriously injured. In spite of his injuries, the pilot climbed to height, flew the aircraft and landed at a base during an air raid warning. When he was removed from the cockpit it was found that his right upper arm bone was shattered and he was suffering from serious loss of blood. Flight Lieutenant Israr showed tremendous courage and determination in flying the aircraft back and landing at his base with his left arm in spite of his injuries. In doing this, he displayed sterling qualities of devotion to duty and courage and determination. In recognition of his performance, he has been awarded Sitara-i-Jurat'.

Sitara-i-Jurat

The Air Force 1971

Flight lieutenant Javed Ahmed, SJ
'On 4TH December, 1971 Flight Lieutenant Javed was detailed to fly as No.2 on an air defence mission. As he was scrambled for take-off, the airfield was subjected to a surprise attack by two enemies Hunter aircraft. Flight Lieutenant Javed was about to take off when the enemy aircraft spotted the aircraft on the runway and commenced a straffing attack forcing the leader to abort. With total disregard to his personal safety this pilot continued his take-off with the enemy bullets landing just to the left of his aircraft. After successfully getting airborne, Flight Lieutenant Javed intercepted the raiders and shot down one of the Hunters. In continuing his take-off in the face of grave danger to his life and subsequently shooting down the enemy aircraft. For his display of the highest standard of initiatives, courage and professional skill beyond the call of duty, Flight Lieutenant Javed Ahmed has been awarded Sitara-i-Jurat'.

Flight Lieutenant Mir Alam Khan, SJ
'Flight Lieutenant Mir Alam Khan was detailed on a mission against an I.A.F. base on 6th December, 1971. At the time of his take-off, the airfield came under enemy raid. Undaunted by the danger, he took off during the raid and proceeded on his mission. Despite heavy anti-aircraft fire he successfully completed his mission. During this mission, his aircraft also received a hit from anti-aircraft fire. However, he successfully exited leaving behind his target in flames. The fire was also seen by another friendly aircraft flying thirty miles away. Flight Lieutenant Mir Alam Khan's action in the execution of his mission bears testimony to his undaunted courage and devotion to duty in keeping with the highest traditions of the service. He has been awarded Sitara-i-Jurat'.

Flying Officer Mohammad Shamsul Haq, SJ
'On 4TH December, 1971 he was ordered to scramble and intercept a formation of four SU-7 aircraft's attacking Dhaka airfield. As he got airborne, the SU-7s attacked his formation with missiles. He very coolly broke into the attacking aircraft at very low speed and asked his wingman to do the same and in the ensuing battle shot down on SU-7. Meanwhile four Hunters joined the battle. He engaged these Hunters and shot down two of them. There-after he was attacked by 4 MIG-21's. He put off their attack by quick planning and superior handling of aircraft. Against such heavy odds he displayed exemplary courage and leadership. Flying Officer Shamsul Haq has been awarded Sitara-i-Jurat'.

Sitara-i-Jurat

The Air Force 1971

Flying Officer Riffat Jamil, SJ
'Flying Officer Riffat Jamil flew as a co-pilot on a bombing mission to Jaisalmir on 6TH December, 1971. He made a significant contribution to the success of the mission as result of which the enemy suffered heavy losses. In recognition of his courage and determination, he has been awarded Sitara-i-Jurat'.

Flying Officer Syed Shamshad Ahmed, SJ
'On 4TH December, 1971 Flying Officer Syed Shamshad Ahmed was scrambled to intercept a formation of four SU-7s attacking Dhaka airfield. As he got airborne he was attacked by the SU-7s with missiles. He put off their attack by superior handling of his aircraft. In the same mission he intercepted a formation of four Hunters. In the subsequent air battle he shot down one Hunter. On another mission he spotted one Hunter attacking our troop positions. Fearlessly he engaged that aircraft and shot it down. Though very young and having very little experience of fighter flying he kept his spirits high and displayed great courage throughout the war. For his courage, skill and performance, Flying Officer Syed Shamshad Ahmed has been awarded Sitara-i-Jurat'.

Wing Commander Mervyn L Middlecoat Shaheed, SJ and Bar
'On the outbreak of war on 3RD December 1971, Wing Commander Mervyn L Middlecoat joined operations against India. He was detailed on a strike mission to the heavily defended Jamnagar airfield. While returning after the successful mission he was engaged by 2 enemy Mig-21s. In the encounter his aircraft was hit by an enemy missile. He was heard to be ejecting in Indian Territory and was officially declared missing in action. For his devotion to duty, determination and courage he was awarded a Bar to the Sitara-i-Jurat'

Wing Commander Muhammad Ahmed Shaheed, SJ
'On 4TH December, 1971 one of our combat air patrols over Dhaka was engaged by an enemy formation. With the arrival of more enemy aircraft the patrol was heavily out-numbered and the leader gave a call for help. Wing Commander Muhammad Ahmed was immediately airborne and his timely intervention enabled the patrol to return safely to base. In the encounter Wing Commander Ahmed's aircraft was hit by an enemy aircraft and he was heard to be ejecting in territory occupied by rebels. For his personal example, courage and devotion to duty, he was awarded the Sitara-i-Jurat'.

Sitara-i-Jurat

The Air Force 1971

Squadron Leader Aslam Choudhry Shaheed, SJ

'Squadron Leader Aslam Choudhry flew a total of fifteen missions since the outbreak of war. As he had spent most of his service in training establishments, he had to start with a disadvantage in a fighter squadron. But he was a keen pilot and managed to polish up his fighter flying in a comparatively short time. He was always keen to fly operational missions. On 10 December 71, while flying in leading a section of two F-86s in Chamb Sector on a Close Air Support mission, his flight was engaged by six Hunters. Being heavily out-numbered, he was presumed to have been shot down by the enemy. He was officially declared missing in action. For his valour, courage, determination and devotion to duty, he was awarded Sitara-i-Jurat'.

Squadron Leader Ishfaq Hameed Shaheed, SJ

'Squadron Leader Ishfaq Hameed was recalled from PIA for operational flying, with a B-57 Squadron. From the onset of the hostilities he displayed distinct qualities of patriotism and aggressiveness to achieve positive results. This was a source of inspiration to other aircrew. Unfortunately, he was unable to return from his second mission of the war on 5TH December 1971. Squadron Leader Ishfaq displayed exceptional determination and tenacity under adverse conditions that existed at his base from 4th morning of December till the night he went for his last mission. For his dedication, courage and display of excellent fighting spirit he was awarded Sitara-i-Jurat'.

Squadron Leader Peter Christie Shaheed, SJ

'Squadron Leader Peter Christie was on deputation to PIAC when recalled for war duties. He showed great keenness to fly, and in spite of overwhelming family responsibilities, he was ever willing to take on any mission at any odd hour of the day or night. He was completely devoted to the task in hand. His sense of humour under war conditions, his dedication to the cause of the country and his personal courage contributed immensely to the Squadron's morale. On 6TH December 1971, he was detailed as navigator for a bombing mission to Jamnagar. He failed to return from the mission and was officially declared missing in action. For his personal example and complete devotion to duty, he was awarded Sitara-i-Jurat'.

Sitara-i-Jurat

The Air Force 1971

Squadron Leader Khusro Shaheed, SJ
'Squadron Leader Khusro had retired from the PAF but was recalled for the war. In spite of many personal problems, he showed great keenness, courage, determination and fighting spirit. On 6TH December 1971, he volunteered for bombing mission to Jamnagar airfield regardless of the consequences. He failed to return from the mission and was officially declared missing in action. His fighting spirit, determination and devotion were an example to all aircrew of the unit. For his outstanding courage and devotion to duty, Squadron Leader Khusro was awarded the Sitara-i-Jurat'.

Flight Lieutenant Fazal Elahi Shaheed, SJ
'Flight Lieutenant Fazal Elahi was a young and energetic pilot. He flew the first two missions to Srinagar airfield and subsequent Close Air Support missions every day till 7TH December 1971. On 8th December, his aircraft was hit by ground fire in Chamb-Jaurian sector; the ground fire presumably hit a bomb fuse, causing the aircraft to explode. Flight Lieutenant Fazal always volunteered to fly irrespective of the danger of the mission. He displayed exemplary courage and determination at his young age in spite of limited experience. He was awarded the Sitara-i-Jurat'.

Flight Lieutenant Saeed Afzal Khan Shaheed, SJ
'On 4TH December 1971, Flight Lieutenant Saeed Afzal Khan was flying as No. 2 in a formation of two F-86 aircraft, when he engaged four Indian Hunters and immediately shot one down. Meanwhile another formation of four Hunters joined the aerial battle. In the subsequent combat, although facing great odds, he was not deterred from attacking them. He put up a gallant fight with complete disregard to his own safety. Due to his determination and flying skill, he prevented every one of them from attacking their target i.e. Dhaka airfield. While being heavily outnumbered by superior performance aircraft, he continued the fight but was later shot down by a Hunter. He bailed out safely but was captured by the rebels and has been missing since then. For his courage, determination and devotion to duty, he was awarded the Sitara-i-Jurat'.

Sitara-i-Jurat

The Air Force 1971

Flight Lieutenant Syed Safi Mustafa Shaheed, SJ
'Flight Lieutenant Syed Safi Mustafa was Flight Commander of No. 246 Squadron PAF. Towards the end of February 71, orders were issued for MOUs to regroup and take shelter with the nearest army garrison due to the insecure conditions created by civil agitation. Flight Lieutenant Safi Mustafa along with 37 airmen thereupon took refuge with the East Pakistan Rifles' Headquarters at Mymensingh. Throughout the period of civil strife and agitation, he continued to look after his men with great courage and dedication. On 16th March he came to Dhaka for a day where he was advised by friends and relatives not to go back to his unit because of the prevailing danger to non locals. He was, however, determined to return to his post and was in contact with the Base till 27th March. The evidence available indicates that in all probability, he was executed by the rebels on 17th April 1971. For his gallantry and dedication, Flight Lieutenant Syed Safi Mustafa was awarded the Sitara-i-Jurat'.

Flight Lieutenant Abdul Samad Changezi Shaheed, SJ
'Flight Lieutenant Abdul Samad Changezi flew eleven missions on F-104 during the war. Despite his limited experience, he was very keen and aggressive. He was responsible for the destruction of an enemy radar station and damage to one of their aircraft. In the last mission, disregarding the danger to his life, he pursued his attack on an enemy aircraft till he was shot down by an enemy missile. For his act of valour and for sacrificing his life for the cause of the country, he was awarded the Sitara-i-Jurat'.

Flight Lieutenant Zulfiqar Ahmed Shaheed, SJ
'Flight Lieutenant Zulfiqar Ahmed was employed as a navigator on a B-57 aircraft. Although he could not return from his second mission of the war, he displayed outstanding qualities of courage and keenness to undertake the most arduous missions from the very onset of operations. This was a source of inspiration to others since he was one of the youngest crew members in the bomber organization. On the first day of operations, when only experienced and mature aircrew were being selected for the first strikes, Zulfiqar insisted on being included. He was eventually detailed for a mission to Jodhpur which was very successful. For his determination, courage and tenacity, he was awarded the Sitara-i-Jurat'.

Sitara-i-Jurat

Army Aviation Corps

Major Qasim Shaheed, SJ

Major Qasim was assassinated by Lieutenant Muhammad Humayun Raza, a Bengali officer of 24 Signal Battalion. Major Qasim in his usual helpful attitude and politeness picked up Lieutenant Muhammad Humayun Raza at Satrah airport. Lieutenant Muhammad Humayun Raza probably had threatened Major Qasim to turn towards India soon after takeoff, but on refusal and seeing him attempting to land back, fire the first round. This round was not fatal and Major Qasim still attempted to land back. This is also validated by the accounts of eye witnesses on ground, who described the aircraft banking and then straightening up. It is at this stage that Humayun fired the second fatal round. After shooting Major Qasim this officer knowing a bit of flying, flew towards India. Major Qasim's body was received from India on 7TH January 1972 i.e. after four days of his Shahadat. Major Qasim was posthumously awarded Sitara-i-Jurat for the act of bravery and supreme sacrifice in an effort to uphold the honour of his motherland. Later, Army Aviation Base Dhamial was named after Major Muhammad Qasim. It is to be known as Qasim Army Aviation Base.

Major Fayaz Ibrahim Shaheed, SJ

During the second day of Indo-Pakistan war of 1971, as Major Fayaz Ibrahim flew inside the Indian Territory and to locate the Indian Armour, his aircraft was shot down by the Indian aircraft. He was still alive, but died on 15TH December at Naval Hospital Karachi. Major Fayaz Ibrahim was awarded a posthumous Sitara-i-Jurat by the Pakistan Army.

Major Saeed Asmat, SJ

General Iftikhar Janjua's helicopter piloted by Major Sajid Islam crashed on 9TH December 1971 at Padhar. Flight Commander Major Asmat learnt about the accident and he rushed to the scene and landed there. He learnt that both - General and Major Sajid had been evacuated by road to Padhar. General was in precarious condition and Major Asmat volunteered flying him to Rawalpindi; a stretcher was improvised and fitted in L-19. At 2000hour from Padhar, Major Asmat got airborne with injured Major General Janjua on a pitch-dark night. Pilot had an awful journey and after 50 minutes of flying he landed in Kharian. Major General Iftikhar Janjua was rushed to Combined Military Hospital (CMH) Kharian. The General later expired in CMH Kharian on 10TH December 1971. For the night rescue Major Saeed Asmat was awarded the Sitara-i-Jurat by the Pakistan Army.

Sitara-i-Jurat

Army Aviation Corps

Captain Raheel Hafeez Sehgal, SJ
Captain Sehgal was the captain in command of the operation to support the ground parties which were sent to capture the saddle of Chumik Glacier. The Indians had established new posts and had attained the predominant position with deep observation of glacier. The flying became extremely suicidal due to the fact that Lama Helicopters were in the range of Indian missile. All the Pakistani posts in the region which were supported by the aviation were now looking desperate. Due to extreme bad weather and razor edged sharp climb, little progress was made by the troops. Time was running short, it was extremely important that enemy should not be allowed to strengthen at the top and contact should be made as early as possible. The contact was made and the Indians thwarted by the Lama Helicopters. Captain Raheel Hafeez Sehgal was one of the Lama pilots who awarded the Sitara-i-Jurat for his heroic act.

Major Hanif Shaheed, SJ
Major Hanif arrived at Skardu on 4TH June 1999 and took over the command of MI-17 Flight. On 9TH June 1999, a mission for carrying of artillery ammunition to Gultri Post was passed and Major Hanif not only accepted the mission but keeping in view the hazards decided to go himself along with Captain Uzair. They landed at Gultri after dumping and sling operations. Before taking off for Skardu Major Hanif checked the weather conditions. Soon after taking off they crashed. When weather became absolutely clear, the ground parties, located the wreckage, all souls on board had perished. Major Hanif, the legendary 'Daud 19' was posthumously awarded Sitara-i- Jurat for his commitment and dedication.

Brigadier Masood Naveed Shaheed, SJ
Major Khalid Sohail Sultan Shaheed, SJ
Major Babar Ramzan Shaheed, SJ
In August 1992, Major Babar Ramzan along with Major Khalid Sohail Sultan and Brigadier Masood Naveed got airborne in a helicopter from the highest elevation battlefield of Siachen area. They were carrying out reconnaissance on a Lama Helicopter. The Helicopter was hit by a missile fired by the Indian Army, killing all its occupants. Major Ramzan and both other officers' embraced martyrdom were awarded the Sitara-i-Jurat.

Sitara-i-Jurat

Kargil Conflict 1999

For the first time in nearly 30 years, in May 1999, India launched air strikes against Pakistani-backed forces that had infiltrated into the mountains in Indian-administered Kashmir, north of Kargil. Pakistan responded by putting its troops on high alert as the fighting built up towards a direct conflict between the two states. India repeatedly claimed that Pakistani forces belonging to the northern light infantry, based in the Pakistani-administered Northern Areas, were engaged in the operations - a claim Pakistan consistently denied. Pakistan insisted instead that the forces were "freedom fighters" fighting for the liberation of Indian-administered Jammu and Kashmir. At the height of the conflict, thousands of shells were fired daily, and India launched hundreds of airstrikes. The Red Cross reported that at least 30,000 people had been forced to flee their homes on the Pakistani side of the Line of Control. Correspondents reported that about 20,000 people became refugees on the Indian side. Both sides claimed victory in the conflict, which ended when, under pressure from the United States, Prime Minister Nawaz Sharif called upon the infiltrating forces to withdraw. 11 years after the Kargil war in 1999, the Pakistan Army has included the names of 453 soldiers and officers who were killed during the conflict on its website, according to The Hindu. The 453 Pakistani soldiers are shown as killed in the Batalik-Kargil sector in Jammu and Kashmir. The names of those who died in Kargil are tucked away in a list of thousands of personnel killed while on duty posted in the Shuhada's Corner (Martyrs Corner) of the website. Several causes are cited for those who died in Kargil — "killed in action", "enemy action", "enemy firing", "and enemy artillery shelling "and even" road accident". The list gives the name, rank, unit and location of death of each casualty. A majority of those who died in Kargil were soldiers from the Northern Light Infantry, a formation that was made a regular regiment of the Pakistan Army because of its performance in the 1999 conflict. It was earlier a paramilitary force formed by the amalgamation of several militias from the Northern Areas or Gilgit-Baltistan. During the Kargil conflict and in subsequent years, the Pakistan Army insisted that none of its regular soldiers were involved in the hostilities. This stance continued despite the Indian Army capturing several serving soldiers. The Pakistan Army never issued an official list of its casualties. The first admission of the Pakistan Army's involvement in the conflict came from the former Army Chief and President Pervez Musharraf, who revealed in his 2006 memoir In The Line of Fire that regular soldiers had fought in Kargil.

Sitara-i-Jurat

Kargil Conflict 1999

The opposition Pakistan Muslim League-Nawaz put the death toll at 3,000 and nearly 200 Pakistani casualties were buried on the Indian side. Whatever the hidden intent, most of us do believe that nothing is higher than a soldier (no matter what country) who dies for his country. Whether they were Pakistanis or Indians, they fought for what they believed in and put their lives on the line. The following Kargil Heroes who fought for Pakistan and the Shaheeds who died for their country and won the Sitara-i-Jurat.

Lieutenant General Masood Aslam, SJ, HI	(Kargil 1999)
Lieutenant Colonel Khalid Nazir, SJ	(Kargil 1999)
Lieutenant Colonel Tanveer Ahmed Khan, SJ	(Kargil 1999)
Major Muhammad Hanig SJ	(Kargil 1999)
Major Tariq Mahmood, SJ	(Kargil 1999)
Captain Kashif Khalil, SJ	(Kargil 1999)
Captain Zafar, SJ	(Kargil1999)
Captain Rommel Akram, SJ	(Kargil 1999)
Captain Hussain Ahmed, SJ	(Kargil 1999)
Captain Adil Bahadur, SJ	(Kargil 1999)
Subedar Qalbi Ali, SJ	(Kargil 1999)
Naib Subedar Nadil Karim, SJ	(Kargil1999)
Naib Subedar Aleem Zar, SJ	(Kargil 1999)
Major Muhammad Arshad Hashim Shaheed, SJ	(Kargil 1999)
Major Abdul Wahab Shaheed, SJ	(Kargil 1999)
Captain Ahsan Wasim Sadiq Shaheed, SJ	(Kargil 1999)
Captain Farhat Haseeb Haider Shaheed, SJ	(Kargil 1999)
Captain Muhammad Ammar Hussain Shaheed, SJ	(Kargil 1999)
Captain Sardar Izhar Haider Baloch Shaheed, SJ	(Kargil 1999)
Captain Kashif Khaleel, Shaheed, SJ	(Kargil 1999)
Captain Israr Haider Shaheed, SJ	(Kargil 1999)
Captain Umair Iftikhar Ahmed Shaheed, SJ	(Kargil 1999)
Lieutenant Faisal Zia Ghumman Shaheed, SJ	(Kargil 1999)
Subedar Syed Muhammad Shah Shaheed, SJ	(Kargil 1999)
Naib Subedar Aqeel Hussain Shaheed, SJ	(Kargil 1999)
Naib Subedar Muhammad Khaqan Shaheed, SJ	(Kargil 1999)
Naib Subedar Muhammad Rashid Shaheed, SJ	(Kargil 1999)
Naib Subedar Sher Dullah Khan Shaheed, SJ	(Kargil 1999)
Sepoy Irfanullah Shaheed, SJ	(Kargil 1999)
Sepoy Bakhmal Jan Shaheed, SJ	(Kargil 1999)

Tamgha-i-Jurat

Tamgha-i-Jurat (Medal of Courage) is the fourth highest military award of Pakistan. It was established in 1957 after Pakistan became a Republic, however, it was instituted retrospectively back to 1947. It is awarded for gallantry or distinguished service in combat and can be bestowed upon non commissioned officers and other ranks in the Pakistan Army, Navy, Air Force, and various paramilitary forces under federal control such as the Frontier Corps, the Frontier Constabulary and the Pakistan Rangers. It may be considered equivalent to the Military Medal under the old Commonwealth honours system and the Silver Star in the United States.

The Army 1948

Colonel Mirza Hassan Khan, TJ

Mirza Hassan Khan was a Captain of the 6TH Infantry of the Jammu and Kashmir State Forces based at Bunji in the Gilgit wazarat. On 2ND November 1947, Mirza Hassan Khan and other officers announced a provisional government for Baltistan. The Gilgit Agency was absorbed into Pakistan. Mirza Hassan Khan was appointed the military governor for the Bunji sector. On 19TH January 1948, Pakistan appointed Major Mohammad Aslam as the commander of Gilgit Scouts. Major Aslam organised all the forces in Gilgit into three wings of 400 men each. The three forces were ordered to advance along three directions into the state of Jammu Kashmir. Mirza Hassan Khan was put in charge of the Tiger Force, which advanced on the Gilgit-Bunji-Kamri-Gurais-Bandipora axis. The force reached Bandipora on 28TH April, but had to withdraw to Tragbal. When Gurais was recaptured in June by the Indian forces, the Tiger Force withdrew to Minimarg. For his participation Khan was awarded the title of Fakhr-e-Kashmir by the Azad Kashmir Government and Tamgha-i-Jurat by the Pakistani government.

Tamgha-i-Jurat

The Army 1948

Naib Subedar Ibarat Shah, TJ

Naib Subedar Ibarat Shah was an inhabitant of Hussainabad, a village of Hunza, Gilgit-Baltistan. He joined Northern Scout in 1938. During the Indo-Pakistan war in 1948, he was serving as Platoon Commander in Kashmir's Khel-to-Ladakh Division. Under his command, a small-scaled group of N.A scouts Jawans evicted the Dogra forces from the said division. During the fight, he was wounded and had three bullets in his thigh. He refused to stay long in the bed and returned to the war field within a week of the severe injury, and led his group, while setting extraordinary example of gallantry in the face of enemy. He was awarded with the fourth Military decoration of Pakistan Tamgha-i-Jurat later by president of Pakistan General Ayub Khan for his valour and extraordinary gallantry in the Gilgit Independence War against Dogra Raj of Kashmir.

The Army 1965

Lance Naik Khushi Muhammad, TJ

On September 6TH 1965, as Indo-Pak war broke out, Lance Naik Khushi Muhammad's unit was directed to reach the border of Khokhars Par in Tharparkar district. The Lance Naik was given the assignment to recapture ranger post Shakarbu about sixteen miles from Khokhars Par. His force included a rifle company and a section of mortar guns. His company reached the outskirts of Shakarbu by first light on the attacking day and carried out the operation successfully. The Indian fled away, leaving some dead, and the post was recaptured. It was soon noticed some activity at Kharin Post on the Indian side of the border, which was captured without any opposition. Soon thereof, it was sighted two enemy tanks advancing rapidly towards the post with two rifle companies. They immediately opened fire with machine guns. Lance Naik Khushi Muhammad, Commander RR, knocked out one tank and rendered the other dysfunctional. The advancing Indian elements were engaged with mortar and machine gun fire, which forced it to withdraw leaving behind a number of dead bodies and the wreckage of two tanks. Lance Naik Khushi Muhammad was awarded Tamgha-i-Jurat for his gallant performance.

Tamgha-i-Jurat

The Air Force 1971

Flight Lieutenant Ghulam Murtaza Malik, TJ
Flight Lieutenant Ghulam Murtaza Malik was an able and experienced navigator. He was a very active member of the squadron and always showed great enthusiasm and determination. He flew two missions against the most heavily defended Indian airfields and showed great bravery and courage in the execution of these missions in complete disregard of personal safety. On 5th December, 1971, he was detailed as navigator on a bombing mission to Amritsar airfield. He failed to return from the mission, and was officially declared missing in action. For his courage, determination and devotion to duty he has been awarded the Tamgha-i-Jurat.

Flight Lieutenant Syed Shahid Raza, TJ
Flight Lieutenant Syed Shahid Raza flew a total of eleven operational missions during the war. Throughout this period, the officer displayed an extremely high standard of professional skill, aggressiveness and determination. On 5TH December 1971, during an aerial engagement Flight Lieutenant Raza was credited with one enemy Hunter aircraft shot down. On the evening of 17th December, while off duty, he requested to be detailed for a close support mission. His aircraft was hit by enemy ground fire during that mission, and he was heard to be ejecting in enemy territory. He was officially declared missing in action. For his courage, determination and devotion to duty he has been awarded the Tamgha-i-Jurat.

Flying Officer Nasim Nisar Ali Baig, TJ
Flying Officer Nasim Nisar Ali Baig flew a total of eight successful operational missions during the 1971 war. During all those missions he displayed exemplary courage, dedication and professionalism in spite of his limited experience. On 13th December, '71, he was ordered to get airborne from a forward base to intercept intruding enemy aircraft. Immediately after take-off he was intercepted by 3 enemy fighters. Placed in a very vulnerable situation, Flying Officer Baig manoeuvred his aircraft with determination and aggressiveness but was unable to gain an advantageous position because he was outnumbered during a critical stage of flight. He was subsequently shot down and fatally injured. For his valour, courage and undaunted spirit he has been awarded the Tamgha-i-Jurat.

Tamgha-i-Jurat

The Air Force 1971

Corporal Technician Syed Shaukat Ali, TJ
While a POW in India he twice tried to escape from the POW camp. In the second attempt he received serious bullet injuries; even then he pounced upon the armed guard in a bid to prevent him from firing at his colleague Corporal Technician Nawab. For his outstanding and excellent performance he has been awarded the Tamgha-i-Jurat.

Junior Technician Muhammad Latif, TJ
During an enemy air raid, realising that the pilots strapped in air defence alert aircraft were exposed to grave danger, he disregarded his personal safety, ran up to each aircraft and helped the pilots to unstrapped and take cover. In this process he was fatally wounded by enemy fire and died soon after. For his outstanding courage and devotion to duty he has been awarded the Tamgha-i-Jurat.

Leading Aircraftman Muhammad Azam Nasir, TJ
During an enemy air raid at PAF Chander, instead of taking shelter, he proudly faced the Indian bomber with G-3 rifle and kept on firing at the attacking aircraft. A bomb fell about 6 yards from his trench and buried him along with other occupants of the trench. All except him were dug out alive. For his outstanding courage and devotion to duty he has been awarded the Tamgha-i-Jurat.

Corporal Technician Ghulam Abbas, TJ
Corporal Technician Ghulam Abbas was I/c of a unit during the war. He was ordered to deploy his unit in the Kasur sector. When he reached there, he was advised by the Army personnel that the area was not safe but he told them that this was his place of duty and he would execute the orders given by his superiors. On 10th September, 1965, the enemy artillery shells started falling within about 200 feet of his post but he continued carrying out his job without any fear. His personal example of devotions to duty and courage was a source of inspiration to his fairly inexperienced subordinates and the Unit kept on functioning perfectly. On 11th September, 1965, the shells started falling within a few yards of his post but even this did not deter him from carrying out his duties. He told three of his men to sit in the trench and the remaining two, including himself, kept on manning the observation post and the operator's seat. Thus, his team continued functioning efficiently in spite of heavy shelling by the enemy. For his gallantry he was awarded the Tamgha-i-Jurat by the Pakistan Army.

Tamgha-i-Jurat

The Air Force 1971

Corporal Omar Ali, TJ

During the War, Corporal Omar Ali was NCO I/C of a unit attached to a forward Brigade. In spite of frequent strafing bombing and shelling by the enemy, Corporal Ali performed his duties most efficiently. His unit was one of the first to report the four enemy Vampire aircraft which were shot down on 1ST September, 1965. On 5TH September, 1965, his unit was strafed by four enemy Hunters and it was noticed that Cpl. Ali continued to work along with his operator when everyone else had taken cover. He remained unconcerned about his personal safety and went on performing his duties even under enemy fire. His outstanding courage and devotion to duty earned him the Tamgha-i-Jurat.

Corporal Sher Mohammad, TJ

During the War, Corporal Sher Mohammad was manning a Light Ack. Ack. gun at P.A.F. Station, Sargodha. On 6TH September, 1965, while Indian aircraft were strafing the base, Corporal Sher Mohammad courageously performed his duty by keeping up an accurate fire against the invaders and damaged one enemy aircraft. His determined fire greatly enhanced the morale and fighting spirit of the P.A.F. gun-crew. For his gallantry he was awarded the Tamgha-i-Jurat.

Master Warrant Officer Mohammad Ashfaq, TJ

Master Aircrew Mohammad Ashfaq while performing the duties of an aircrew during the war, and undertook the maximum number of missions against the enemy. In addition to flying several missions, he personally supervised the ground handling of the a/c. He most conscientiously devoted himself to the work assigned to him with utmost enthusiasm without any regard for personal comfort or the dangers involved. In spite of long hours of work on the ground as well as in the air, his cheerfulness and willing co-operations earned him the Tamgha-i-Jurat.

Master Warrant Officer Mohammad Hafeez, TJ

During the War, Aircrew 1 Mohammad Hafeez undertook a large number of missions against the enemy. As an aircrew, he displayed great keenness and extreme dedication to his duties with least regard for his personal comfort or the hazardous nature of these operations. In addition to flying operations, he personally supervised the loading of aircraft before undertaking the missions. In spite of long hours of work on the ground and in the air, he remained cheerful and showed remarkable co-operation at all times, for which he was awarded the Tamgha-i-Jurat.

Tamgha-i-Jurat

The Air Force 1971

Flight Lieutenant Javed Latif, TJ

During the war, Flight Lieutenant Javed Latif flew twenty operational missions in Air Defence role and displayed professional excellence, cool courage and aggressive spirit of a very high order. Throughout the war, he remained undeterred by hazards posed to his personal safety and undertook tasks assigned to him even though their execution was fraught with many risks. On 4TH December, 1971 at 0920 hours he was ordered to scramble for combat air patrol. When he was still in the process of starting up his aircraft, the airfield was attacked by two enemy SU-7s. His aircraft pen received a direct rocket hit but luckily no damage was caused to his aircraft. Under the circumstances he was fully justified to abandon his aircraft and take cover but he decided to continue his mission and successfully destroyed one enemy SU-7 aircraft which attacked the airfield ten minutes later. For his professional excellence, cool courage and a high degree of aggressive spirit when in contact with the enemy, Flight Lieutenant Javed Latif has been awarded Tamgha-i-Jurat.

Flight Lieutenant Abdul Karim Bhatti, TJ

On 7th December, 1971, Flight Lieutenant Abdul Karim Bhatti sighted two Hunters during a close support mission. On leader's instructions he engaged one of the Hunters, pursued it for about 15 miles over enemy territory and finally shot it down. In the process he lost contact with his leader. Flight Lieutenant Bhatti, alone and without any cover, pursued the attack, disregarding his personal safety and achieved a kill. For his devotion to duty and courageous performance, he has been awarded Tamgha-i-Jurat.

Flight Lieutenant Maqsood Amir, TJ

Flight Lieutenant Maqsood Amir was detailed to carry out a close support mission in an F-86 aircraft on 17th December, 1971. During the mission his formation was engaged by four MIG-21s. Although the F-86 was in a vulnerable position, Flight Lieutenant Maqsood took aggressive evasive action and swiftly manoeuvred to gain offensive on the enemy. In the ensuing combat, he handled his aircraft against a much superior adversary in a professional and skilful manner and shot down one of the MIG-21s. The sequence of shooting recorded by his aircraft camera film reflects a very high professional standard. For his courage and high professional skill, he has been awarded Tamgha-i-Jurat.

Tamgha-i-Jurat

The Air Force 1971

Lance Naik Khushi Muhammad, TJ

On September 6TH as Indo-Pak war broke out, his unit was directed to reach the border of Khokhars Par in Tharparkar district.

He was given the assignment to recapture ranger post Shakarbu about sixteen miles from Khokhars Par, which had earlier been occupied by the Indian army. His force included a rifle company and a section of mortar guns. The company reached the outskirts of Shakarbu by first light on the attacking day and carried out the operation successfully. The Indian fled away, leaving some dead, and the post was recaptured. On reaching the post, he noticed some activity at Kharin Post on the Indian side of the border, and immediately planned an attack with mobile force consisting of about sixteen men with MGs and RRs. The post was captured without any opposition. Soon thereof, he sighted two enemy tanks advancing rapidly towards the post with two rifle companies. They immediately opened fire with machine guns. Lance Naik Khushi Muhammad, Commander RR, knocked out one tank and rendered the other dysfunctional. The advancing Indian elements were engaged by him with mortar and machine gun fire, which forced it to withdraw leaving behind a number of dead bodies and the wreckage of two tanks. Lance Naik Khushi Muhammad was awarded Tamgha-i-Jurat for his performance.

2ND Lieutenant Imran Ahmed Khan Shaheed, TJ

When 2ND Lieutenant Imran Ahmed Khan embraced Shahadat, he was posthumously awarded the Tamgha-i-Jurat. Ahmed Ali Khan, father of 2ND Lieutenant Imran Ahmad Khan (Shaheed) received Tamgha-i-Jurrat from the Chief of Army Staff, General Ashfaq Parvez Kayani.

Flight Lieutenant Taloot Mirza, TJ

Flight Lieutenant Taloot Mirza flew a total of fifteen operational missions and was engaged in aerial combat thrice. He demonstrated a high degree of cool courage in both ground attack and aerial combat. On 10th December, 1971, when on a close support mission, his formation of two aircrafts was engaged by six enemy SU-7 aircrafts. Flight Lieutenant Taloot accepted the challenge coolly and successfully destroyed one SU-7 in the face of heavy odds. For his courage and dedication to service he has been awarded Tamgha-i-Jurat.

Tamgha-i-Jurat

Army Aviation Corps

Major Zafar, TJ

During the Indo-Pakistan war of 1971, Major Zaffar got orders for surveillance across the border to assess the enemy dispositions. He was Successful in his intelligence gathering but a burst of ground fire from the hostile troops ruptured the aircraft and he made a forced safe landing. Major Zafar was awarded Tamgha-i-Jurat for his part in 1971 War. On promotion he commanded an Azad Kashmir Regiment. He later returned to aviation, started the Tactical Courses in Aviation School. He retired as a Colonel and settled in England.

Captain Iftikhar, TJ

On 7TH December 1971, Captain Iftikhar and Major Fayaz Ibrahim took off at dawn and flew inside the Indian Territory and to locate the Indian Armour. After an uneventful sortie, when Captain Iftikhar landed back he found that Major Fayaz Ibrahim had been shot down by the Indian aircraft and that he was alive and being transported back to Main Dressing Station on a railway engine. Captain Iftikhar got hold of the ambulance and rushed towards the railway station by the time I reached there, he had already arrived. His head was swollen and he was unable to talk, and the doctor told him that he should be moved to Hyderabad. So he put Major Fayaz Ibrahim in the rear of L-19 in lying position and took off for Hyderabad. Because of the adverse weather conditions he was unable to land on the first two occasions. He landed on the third occasion and was told by the doctors about severe head injuries sustained by him and that he needed to be immediately evacuated to Karachi so he called Mauripur Base Commander who was helpful and promised that helicopter would take off at dawn for evacuation which it did. Major Fayaz Ibrahim died on 15TH December at Naval Hospital Karachi. For his bold efforts Captain Iftikhar, was awarded Tamgha-i-Jurat

Major Sohail Sadiq, TJ
Major Umar Faroq Rana, TJ
Captain Nadeem Raza, TJ

During March 2006 'Operation Noor Payo Khan' was conducted at Saidgi, to eliminate the terrorists. In recognition of their heroic efforts, Major Sohail Sadiq, Major Umar Faroq Rana, and Captain Nadeem Raza, were all awarded the Tamgha-i-Jurat.

Indian Order of Merit

The East India Company first introduced this medal in 1837 and it was proposed for "conspicuous gallantry in the field". The Indian Order of Merit was the highest gallantry award available to Indian soldiers between 1837 and 1911, when the eligibility for the Victoria Cross was extended to Indian officers and men. The Indian Order of Merit ranks high among the oldest and most venerable of decorations for bravery, pre-dating the Victoria Cross by nineteen years and the United State's, Medal of Honour by twenty-four years. The order was removed when the continent of India became independent in 1947.

The medal was originally introduced with three classes (first, second and third classes), until others medals were made available to Indian soldiers, at which point it was reduced to two classes (the Victoria Cross replacing the first class), and reduced to one class in 1944. A recipient technically needed to be in possession of the lower class before being awarded a higher class, although recipients were sometimes awarded the higher class if they performed more than one act of gallantry, then they may have been awarded the higher class, without receiving the lower one. The recipients of the order received increased pay and pension allowances and were very highly regarded.

First Anglo-Afghan War

In 1838, the governor-general of India Lord Auckland declared war on Afghanistan, triggering the first Anglo-Afghan War. The East India Company, in tandem with the ruler of Punjab, Maharaja Ranjit Singh, launched a two-pronged invasion of Afghanistan—through the Khyber and Bolan Passes. The objective was to unseat the Afghan ruler, Amir Dost Mohammad Khan, whom the British accused of collusion with the Russians, and replace him with Shah Shuja ul-Mulk. The invasion was executed swiftly. The following soldiers were awarded the Indian Order of Merit for their conscious gallantry in action during the First Afghan War.

Indian Order of Merit

First Anglo-Afghan War

Ahmed Khan, IOM
Trooper Ahmed Khan of Poona Auxiliary Horse was awarded the 2ND Class IOM, for he displayed a great gallantry and devotion on 31ST August 1840, in defending and bringing off his Commanding Officer, Lieutenant Lokh, when that officer was wounded in action against a Baluch tribe at the Pass of Nufook, in Upper Sind.

Mohammad Hussain Khan, IOM
Naib Risaldar Mohammad Hussain Khan of 1ST Irregular Cavalry was awarded 3RD Class IOM on 29TH October 1840 in consideration of his gallant conduct on that date, on the occasion of defeat and dispersion a large body of Brahooees by a small detachment of the regiment at Dadur in Cutch Gundava.

Gholam Muhammad Khan, IOM
Meer Kurramut Ullee, IOM
Daffadars Gholam Muhammad Khan and Meer Kurramut Ullee of 1ST Bengal Irregular Cavalry were awarded the 3RD Class IOM. During the attack on the garrison at Dadur on the afternoon of 1ST November 1840, the enemy's fire having very much increased, the order was given to charge. The two Ressallahs gallantly led by Daffadars Gholam Muhammad Khan and Meer Kurramut Ullee closed with the enemy and with the most determined bravery routed them. Both Daffadars were severely wounded.

Allee Buccus, IOM
Jemadar Allee Buccus of 44TH Bengal Native Infantry was admitted to the 3RD Class IOM for his conspicuous gallantry in the defence of Khelat, when that town was attacked by a body of rebels in August 1840. Lieutenant Loveday was Assistant Political Agent at Khelat. On hearing that the enemy had gained the walls in considerable force, he turned to Allee Buccus, Havildar of his escort, and him if he could do anything with his party of twelve men. The Havildar replied that he was most willing to try, and having told his men to follow him. Allee Buccus led the way to the walls in possession of the enemy, and after a hard fight drove them back. For his conspicuous gallantry and leadership Havildar Allee Buccus was admitted to the 3RD Class IOM. Other soldiers present in the action were Sepoys Narun Khan, Meer Khan and Sirdar Khan.

Indian Order of Merit

First Anglo-Afghan War

Dullee Khan, IOM

Sowar Dullee Khan of Christie's Horse, was admitted to 3RD Class IOM. He also behaved with great gallantry as Ressaidar Wuzier Khan in action near Khelat-i-Ghilzai on 29TH May 1941, killing three or four of the enemy. Though severely wounded, he could only with utmost difficulty prevailed upon to go to the rear to have his wounds dressed, and even then returned immediately to the field where he remained actively engaged till the close of the skirmish.

Wherwan Khan, IOM
Shaik Hyat Mahmod, IOM

Troopers Wherwan Khan and Shaik Hyat Mahmod of 5TH Bengal Light Cavalry were admitted to 3RD Class IOM. They were ordered under the command of the Quartermaster-Sergeant to attack a small part of the enemy at Kuratoo on 5TH August 1841. They had hand to hand fight in which the Quartermaster-Sergeant was knocked off his horse. The Troopers immediately rallied round him and told him to retire on the main body and that they would protect him. At this moment, about hundred and fifty of the enemy's horse made a dashing charge down the hill, but Captain Oldfield of the same regiment, who was a short distance away, came forward with his troop and drove the enemy back. Had it not been of the gallantry of these Troopers, the Quartermaster-Sergeant would have lost his life.

Bahadoor Ally, IOM
Illahi Bux, IOM

Jemadar Bahadoor Ally and Sowar Illahi Bux of Christie's Horse were admitted to 3RD Class IOM. They behaved with great gallantry in the action with the mutinous Janbax near Chuplanie on 27TH December 1941, and were means of saving life of Lieutenant Wilson, who had been deserted by his own men of the 2ND Janbax Regiment. Jemadar and Sowar dashed forward to Lieutenant Wilson's assistance when he was surrounded by the enemy, and fought with utmost bravery by his side until the assailants were drive off. Kullunder Khan Janbax, the murder of Lieutenant Gosling, was cut down by Sowar Illahi Bux.

Indian Order of Merit

First Anglo-Afghan War

Moolive Azim Ally, IOM
Risaldar Moolive Azim Ally Christie's Horse was admitted to 3RD Class IOM for behaving in the most gallant manner on the same occasions as Bahadoor Ally and Illahi Bux. He killed several of the Janbax and saved the life of Ensign Chamberlain, the acting Adjutant, by cutting down the horseman who was in the act of spearing Ensign Chamberlain.

Akhtar Khan, IOM
Sowar Akhtar Khan also of Christie's Horse was admitted to 3RD Class IOM. He was one of the assailants of Kullunder Khan, the murderer of Lieutenant Gosling. After killing Kullunder Khan he cut down another man and his gallantry throughout the skirmish was most conspicuous.

Nutteh Khan, IOM
Nishanburder Nutteh Khan also of Christie's Horse was admitted to 3RD Class IOM. He was with Ensign Neville Chamberlain in the charge against the enemy at Baba Wully on 25TH March 1942, and displayed utmost coolness and bravery. He was the first amongst the ranks of the Ghazis, and although encumbered with the standard, he cut down several of the enemy; and being driven back by overwhelming numbers; he was last in the retreat and defended his standard in the most gallant manner. The standard undoubtedly would have been captured had it been entrusted to a less courageous man. On the attack being renewed, Nutteh Khan called out to his troops to 'rally round the standard and fight for victory' and by his noble behaviour instilled courage into all near him.

Shaik Sooliman, IOM
Private Shaik Sooliman of 20TH Bombay Native Infantry was admitted to 3RD Class IOM, for conspicuous gallantry on the occasion of the first assault on the Afghan post of Hykulzee in Shawl by the troops under the command of Major-General Sir Richard England on the 28TH March 1842.

Goolshah, IOM
Havildar Goolshah of Broadfoot's Sappers was admitted to 3RD Class IOM as a reward for his conspicuous gallantry in the field during 1942.

Alum Shah, IOM
Sepoy Alum Shah of Broadfoot's Sappers was admitted to 3RD Class IOM for displaying extraordinary coolness and precision in firing when forcing the Khurd Kabul Pass under heavy fire in October 1841.

Indian Order of Merit

First Anglo-Afghan War

Nihal Khan, IOM

Sepoy Nihal Khan of Broadfoot's Sappers was admitted to 3RD Class IOM. He was one of the very few men who were employed with Sergeant Major Kelly to hold a hill in the Jugdulluk Pass from which the troops had just before been driven, and they gallantly held it although the enemy carried all the other hills on that side of the Pass. Sepoy Nihal Khan showed distinguish courage, and was shot through the hand while closely engaged with the enemy.

Mahub Ally, IOM
Meer Yad Ally, IOM

Trumpeters Mahub Ally and Meer Yad Ally of 5TH Bengal Light Cavalry were admitted to 3RD Class IOM. A sally was made by the garrison of Jalalabad on the 14TH November 1841. The men were employed in cutting up the enemy's infantry, when the body of the enemy's horse threatened the right flank. Captain Oldfield immediately collected his men to meet the attack of the horsemen who advanced, and two of them crossed swords with this British officer, on the right and the other on the left. Mahub Ally and Meer Yad Ally seeing the perilous situation of their commandant dashed forward to Captain Oldfield's assistance and killed both the Afghan horsemen. Apart from the trumpeters, troopers Shaik Yar Mohammad and Moortazah of the regiment were recommended for the IOM. The awards were not approved.

Salloo Khan, IOM

Sowar Salloo Khan of 1ST Bengal Irregular Cavalry was admitted to 3RD Class IOM, as a reward for his conspicuous gallantry in the field during the defence of Jalalabad.

Mohammad Hayat Khan, IOM
Noor Khan, IOM

Daffadar Mohammad Hayat Khan and Jemadar Noor Khan of 2ND Cavalry, Shah Shuja's Force were admitted to 3RD Class IOM as a reward for their conspicuous gallantry in the field.

The regiment was stationed in Kabul in 1841 before the storm broke out. One of the Ressallahs under Lieutenant William Mayne was saved from the destruction that befell the Kabul garrison. It was disbanded in October 1842, along with most other units of the late Shah Shuja's Force.

Indian Order of Merit

First Anglo-Afghan War

Boorhan Khan, IOM
Naik Boorhan Khan of Broadfoot's Sappers was admitted to 3RD Class IOM. He was one of the covering parties that drove the enemy from the ruins of Jalalabad on 24TH March 1842, and was the first among the enemy and bayoneted one of them. Later on the same day, in the endeavour made by the Afghans to enter the Gate of Jalalabad along with other troops, Naik Boorhan Khan was part of the party under Lieutenant Orr that attacked the Afghans. He bayoneted the Afghan leader who had succeeded in entering the works, and threw him down the riverbank.

Bahadur Khan, IOM
Sepoy Bahadur Khan of Broadfoot's Sappers was admitted to 3RD Class IOM. With another Sepoy at Jalalabad on 24TH March 1842, he rushed in between Major Broadfoot and some Afghans who made a desperate charge at that officer, and bayoneted one of the assailants. Sepoy Bahadur Khan's conduct was very conspicuous and he had to be recalled from the pursuit. He would have been promoted but the Shah's service was abolished immediately after the relief of Jalalabad.

Shaik Ahmud, IOM
Sepoy Shaik Ahmud of 60TH Bengal Native Infantry was admitted to 3RD Class IOM. He was on duty with Lieutenant Christie, when this officer was killed on the march from Peshawar on 23RD August 1842. The convey was attacked in the Khyber Pass, Shaik Ahmud behaved in a very gallant manner , being one of the three men who stood round Lieutenant Christie and did their duty against an overwhelming number of the enemy.

Sirdar Khan, IOM
Sepoy Sirdar Khan of 3RD Bengal Irregular Cavalry was admitted to 3RD Class IOM. On 12TH September 1842, twenty camels and as many bullocks strayed from the Piquet in the Tenzin Valley and had got within reach of the enemy, about three hundred in number, who were prevented by the position of the cavalry Piquet from coming to seize them. No inducement could prevail upon the owners of the cattle to try to get them back, owing to the heavy fire which was kept up by the enemy. Sepoy Sirdar Khan, in spite of the danger, went forward and brought in whole of the cattle, with the exception of two or three which the enemy had driven behind the Sangars. His gallant example induced two or three of his comrades to go forward and meet him on his return.

Indian Order of Merit

First Anglo-Afghan War

Golaum Mohammed Khan, IOM
Risaldar Golaum Mohammed Khan of 3RD Bengal Irregular Cavalry was admitted to 3RD Class IOM. He was in the charge made against the enemy's cavalry in the Tenzin Valley on 13TH September 1842. He gallantly led a long way ahead of his men. By leaping his horse over a nullah, he got in the middle a large *ghol* of the enemy's cavalry, about seventy or eighty in number, and although alone, was seen cutting to the right and left and killed one of the Afghan chiefs.

Aslam Khan, IOM
Subedar Aslam Khan of Broadfoot's Sappers was admitted to 3RD Class IOM. He was awarded the IOM for gallantry on at least five separate occasions in 1941.

Azeez Khan, IOM
Havildar Azeez Khan of Broadfoot's Sappers was admitted to 3RD Class IOM. He was awarded the IOM for gallantry on at least three separate occasions in 1941.

Mata Deen, IOM
Havildar Mata Deen of Broadfoot's Sappers was admitted to 3RD Class IOM. He was awarded the IOM for gallantry on at least three separate occasions in 1941.

Baz Gool, IOM
Sepoy Baz Gool of Broadfoot's Sappers was admitted to 3RD Class IOM. He was awarded the IOM for gallantry on at least three separate occasions in 1941.

Azum Gool, IOM
Bugler Azum Gool of Broadfoot's Sappers was admitted to 3RD Class IOM. He was awarded the IOM for gallantry on at least three separate occasions in 1941.

Shaik Soubrette, IOM
Bugler Shaik Soubrette of Broadfoot's Sappers was admitted to 3RD Class IOM. He was awarded the IOM for gallantry on at least three separate occasions in 1941.

Indian Order of Merit

First Anglo-Afghan War

Mohammad Hussain Khan, IOM
Daffadar Mohammad Hussain Khan of 3RD Bengal Irregular Cavalry was admitted to 3RD Class IOM. Lieutenant Liptrott was covering the retreat of Brigadier Wilde's rear guard on the evening of 3RD November 1842 when, during the charge, a Risaldar of the rissalah was wounded. His horse being killed and fell over him. Daffadar Mohammad Hussain Khan on noticing this immediately dismounted under heavy fire and rescued the Risaldar from under the dead horse, and then assisted in bringing him to camp on another horse, his own horse having been lost while he was engaged in releasing his comrade.

Insurgents and Bandits

During the period 1840 to 1842, the Army had been largely preoccupied with the war in Afghanistan. There were nevertheless some serious disturbances erupting at the same time Bundelkhand and in the Saugor and Narmada territories which would eventually lead to a significant military intervention.

Hyder Ali Khan, IOM
Private Hyder Ali Khan of 16TH Madras Native Infantry was admitted to 3RD Class IOM for conspicuous gallantry in the operations in the Kolapoor and Sawunt Waree district in 1844 to 1845.

Mohammad Buksh Khan, IOM
Naib-Risaldar Mohammad Buksh Khan of 9TH Bengal Irregular Cavalry was Infantry was admitted to 3RD Class IOM and later to 1ST Class IOM. During the night attack of a large force at Ooch on 15TH January 1945, he acted in most daring manner, killing one of the Baluch chiefs with his own hand and giving great encouragement to his men. For this exemplary gallantry, he was presented by Sir Charles Napier with dead chieftain's sword and with a turban which Sir Charles Napier tied on the Risaldar's head with his own hands. Naib-Risaldar Mohammad Buksh Khan advanced directly to 1ST Class IOM in 1857. He later transferred to the 12TH Bengal Irregular Cavalry, and was one of the grandest horsemen that the Indian Cavalry possessed.

Risaldar Shaik Ali, Naib Risaldar Azeem Khan, and Sowars Bujjoo Khan, Kurreem Khan, Nahar Khan, Bahadoor Khan, Kaller Khan and Suller Khan of 1ST Scinde Irregular Horse were admitted to 3RD Class IOM for their gallant conduct in the action with Boogtees on 1ST October 1847.

Indian Order of Merit

Insurgents and Bandits

Risaldar Sheik Kurreem, Daffadar Sheik Golam Nubbee, Daffadar Kallie Khan, Jemadar Hafeezola Khan and Sowar Sheik Ismail of 2ND Scinde Irregular Horse were admitted to 3RD Class IOM for gallant conduct in an affair with a band of Mtani robbers on 3RD April 1853 near Kusmore.

Meer Dilawar Hussain, IOM
Risaldar Meer Dilawar Hussain of 2ND Cavalry, Hyderabad Contingent was admitted to 3RD Class IOM. In the action at Sailoor against Rohilla on the night of 21ST September 1854, Risaldar Meer Dilawar Hussain charged the enemy with Captain Macintyre, his commanding officer, and as many men of the regiment as could be hastily collected on the spot. During the fight, Captain Macintyre was unhorsed by a blow from a spear and while of ground, was surrounded by seven or eight Rohilla, who were all cut down and killed by Risaldar Meer Dilawar Hussain and two others. Captain Macintyre attributed his escape to the devotion and bravery of the Risaldar and his comrades.

Ressaidar Meer Mohammad Shah, Daffadar Sheik Hyder, Daffadar Mohammad Noor Khan, Troopers Meer Ahsan Ali, Sheik Chand and Eman Ali Khan of 2ND Cavalry, Hyderabad Contingent. Daffadar Syed Goolam Ghouse, Daffadar Ghoolam Dustagheer, Sillidar Nuttay Khan, Troopers Mohammad Khan, Alla Dawd Khan, Mehboob Khan and Ali Sher Khan of 3RD Cavalry, Hyderabad Contingent, were admitted 3RD Class IOM for conspicuous gallantry in the action on 7TH January 1859 at Camp Chichumba.

Townkul Khan, IOM
Sowar Townkul Khan of 4TH Cavalry, Hyderabad Contingent, was admitted to 3RD Class IOM. With two others, he went after a party of six or seven Rohilla. They first took on man prisoner who had laid down his arms. Then they went against the rest, when Townkul Khan speared an Arab and disabling him, gave him over as prisoner. He then returned in the charge of the remaining Rohilla but was severely wounded by two sword cuts, one on his left shoulder and the other on his arm.

Myboob Khan, IOM
Sowar Myboob Khan of 4TH Cavalry, Hyderabad Contingent, was admitted to 3RD Class IOM. While proceeding through a jungle in pursuit of the Arabs, he charged them, when a shot shattered his leg.

Indian Order of Merit

Insurgents and Bandits

Peer Khan, IOM
Subedar Peer Khan of 14TH Bombay Native Infantry was admitted to 3RD Class IOM, in consideration of the great bravery and coolness he displayed in the repulse of the Wagheers in their night attacks on the picquets during the operations in Kathiawar and Okamundel on the 26TH, 30TH, and 31ST October 1859.

China
The First China War originated in the attempt by the Chinese Government to put an end to Britain's highly profitable opium trade in China. In January 1839 the Chinese managed to destroy a vast amount of opium stocks and other British property in Canton and elsewhere in China. Several attacks were made on British ships, and in December 1839 the Chinese Government officially banned all trade with Britain. As a result a military force was assembled and set sail from Calcutta in April 1940 with the objective of forcing the Chinese to reopen the trade. The British Force was provided almost entirely by the Madras Army. Following the storming and capture of Chin-Kiang-Foo on 21ST July 1842, the Chinese finally sued for peace and the hostilities ended on 17TH August 1842. Shortly afterwards the Treaty of Nankin was signed, under the terms which the Chinese agreed to cede Hong Kong to Great Britain and pay a substantial cash indemnity. The seven Madras regiments had made good account of themselves during the course of the lengthy China expedition. For conspicuous gallantry in action against the Chinese the following soldiers were admitted to the 3RD Class IOM:

Subedar Shaik Homed
Havildar Shaik Hyder
Havildar Savoo Deen
Naik Alla Khan
Naik Laul Homed
Private Shaik Deenah
Private Shaik Modeenah
Private Shaik Burray
Private Sana Homed
Private Shaik Homed
Private Shaik Sillar
Private Syed Cassin
Private Mohammad Hussain

Private Hoosain Surwar
Private Ramiah
Private Shaik Meeran
Private Mohammad Cassim
Private Shaik Ally
Naik Dawood Khan
Private Ramiah
Private Shaik Secunder
Private Lateef Khan
Private Shaik Homed
Private Syed Silliman
Private Shaik Emam
Privat Bootcheah

Indian Order of Merit

Burma

In 1852, Commodore Lambert was dispatched to Burma by Lord Dalhousie over a number of minor issues related to the previous treaty. The Burmese immediately made concessions including the removal of a governor whom the British had made their *casus belli*. Lambert eventually provoked a naval confrontation in extremely questionable circumstances and thus started the Second Anglo-Burmese War in 1852, which ended in the British annexation of Pegu province, renamed Lower Burma. The war resulted in a palace revolution in Burma, with King Pagan Min (1846–1852) being replaced by his half brother, Mindon Min (1853–1878).

Shaik Sillar, IOM

Subedar Shaik Sillar of 19TH Madras Native Infantry was admitted to 3RD Class IOM on 14TH November 1854. He was in charge of the guard at the river piquet at Pegu, between 4TH and 8TH January 1853. He was superintended of the digging of the trenches, while under fire of the enemy. Shaik Sillar gallantly stood in the trenches in which the men were digging and putting up stockades. Seeing him exposed to a heavy fire, his officer called out to him to get out of the trenches, but his reply was, 'If I leave, the Sepoys who are working will wish to go too', and he remained in the bold and exposed position from daybreak till noon.

Abdool Hoosain, IOM

Subedar Abdool Hoosain of 19TH Madras Native Infantry was admitted to 3RD Class IOM on 3RD April 1855, for conspicuous gallantry in the field in February 1854, when in action with the enemy at Lai Groung in the Bassien District.

For one of his for conspicuous gallantry an extract from the Testimony of Havildar Ram Kishnama:

We were advancing with Major Fytche was in the centre, Subedar Abdool Hoosain myself and others on the left. We were in extended order and firing on the enemy who was firing on us and retreating. A Burmese with a musket in his hand had crouched under some bushes, and after the Commissioner had passed he levelled at him when Subedar Abdool Hoosain dashed at him and seized his musket with his left hand, and the Burmese with his right. The Burmese freed himself and ran off, when the Subedar called out to Sepoy Padsha Meean to shoot him, which he did.

Indian Order of Merit

Persia

In 1856 the Shah of Persia invaded Afghanistan country to treaty arrangements with Britain, captured Heart, and refused to withdraw his army. As a result war was declared and within the year an Expeditionary Force set sail from India. The Expeditionary Force systemically destroyed the Persian Army. Further operations of the Expeditionary Force in South Persia involved very little fighting. The Persian Army crumbled and fled before the assault on Mohumra, and would not again make a token stand. The war formally ended on 4TH April 1857 when a treaty was signed in Paris, allowing the bulk of the Expeditionary Force to return to India.

Ghoolam Hussein Khan, IOM
Sowar Ghoolam Hussein Khan of Poona Irregular Horse was admitted to 3RD Class IOM in 1859. He killed the standard bearer, and captured the standard of the Kashkai Regiment.

Shumshoodeen, IOM
Sowar Shumshoodeen of Poona Irregular Horse was admitted to 3RD Class IOM in 1859. He spiked the gun with a horse-shoe nail, driving it in with the butt of his carbine, and performed most efficient service.

Shaik Hussein Bux, IOM
Risaldar Shaik Hussein Bux of Poona Irregular Horse was admitted to 3RD Class IOM in 19TH March 1860, for conspicuous gallantry displayed at the battle of Khooshab in Persia on 8TH February 1857. On this occasion he charged the enemy in front of the leading troops by the side of his Commanding Officer, Colonel Tapp, and was of great assistance to that officer.

Sind

Shaik Baker Ally, IOM
Subedar Shaik Baker Ally of 9TH Bengal Light Cavalry was admitted to 3RD Class IOM on 8TH September 1843, for displaying great gallantry. He killed two men on one occasion and had his horse badly wounded under him. Captain Tucker, who fell in the fight severely wounded, witnessed the Subedar cheering and leading his men in a most gallant manner, and he was of essential service in assisting Major Story in reforming the regiment after the charge. In every respect Shaik Baker Ally proved himself to be a good soldier and an excellent Indian officer.

Indian Order of Merit

Sind

Emam Bux, Bhurmadeen, Goolam Rasool
Subedar Emam Bux, Troopers Bhurmadeen and Goolam Rasool of 9TH Bengal Light Cavalry were admitted to 3RD Class IOM on 8TH September 1843. They were with party engaged with body of the enemy in the bed of nullah, and after a smart engagement captured a standard planted near some guns. The enemy were very numerous and defended the standard stoutly, but they took to flight as soon as it was taken.

Shaik Emam Bux, IOM
Havildar Shaik Emam Bux of 9TH Bengal Light Cavalry was admitted to 3RD Class IOM on 8TH September 1843. On moving into the nullah, Havildar Shaik Emam Bux wounded a Baluchi, who advanced and cut the Subedar down for the timely interference of Havildar Shaik Emam Bux who charged and killed the man. The Havildar's conduct was conspicuous throughout the battle. He killed three of the enemy on one instance, and shot one, and cut down another near the guns.

Fyzullah Khan, IOM
Trooper Fyzullah Khan of 9TH Bengal Light Cavalry was admitted to 3RD Class IOM on 8TH September 1843. He was engaged in single combat with a Baluchi in the bed of the nullah, and after a hard fight succeeded in cutting down his antagonist.

Nussoor Ally, IOM
Trooper Nussoor Ally of 9TH Bengal Light Cavalry was admitted to 3RD Class IOM on 8TH September 1843. He behaved with great gallantry during a charge against the tribesmen.

Ahmed Khan, IOM
Ressaidar Ahmed Khan of Scinde Irregular Horse for his gallantry was admitted to 3RD Class IOM in 1841. However, he was advanced to 2ND Class on 11TH March 1856 in consideration for the conspicuous and devotion displayed by him on the 24TH March 1843 in action against Omeer Shere Mohammad Talpoor at Hyderabad in Sind.

The advancement of Ressaidar Ahmed Khan was the result of a second petition submitted by the tenacious officer; seven years after the first petition had been refused.

Indian Order of Merit

Gwalior

The death of the Maharajah of Gwalior in 1843, and the disturbances to the succession, was a cause of concern for the British. Breakdown of law and order might conceivably endanger the security of the British governed districts bordering the Gwalior state. This prediction became the pretext for a British military intervention.

Meer Hyat Mohammad, IOM
Jemadar Meer Hyat Mohammad of 4TH Bengal Light Cavalry was admitted to 3RD Class IOM in 1ST March 1844. At the battle of Maharapore, Captain Nash was attacked by several of the enemy's foot-soldiers. He parried their spears when another of them attacked him from behind. Jemadar Meer Hyat Mohammad rushed in at the moment, interposed between the enemy and his officer, and parried the sabre cut aimed at the British officer.

Ghassy Khan, IOM
Trooper Ghassy Khan of 4TH Bengal Light Cavalry was admitted to 3RD Class IOM in 1ST March 1844. He was in the charge against the enemy's infantry, when the Indian officer was killed, and he showed great gallantry while engaged with the enemy after the Subedar-Major had fallen.

Aman Khan, IOM
Trooper Aman Khan of 4TH Bengal Light Cavalry was admitted to 3RD Class IOM in 1ST March 1844. He went forward alone during the action at Maharapore and attacked a man who was carrying a standard in the rear of the retiring enemy. Aman Khan shot the standard-bearer and carried off the standard. The Trooper was sick in hospital on the day of the battle of Maharapore, but he quitted it of his own accord to join his comrades in the battle.

Usman Khan, IOM
Trooper Usman Khan of 4TH Bengal Light Cavalry was admitted to 3RD Class IOM in 1ST March 1844. Trooper Usman Khan and his horse were disabled by a cannon ball during the battle of Maharapore. He immediately mounted on another horse and joined in the general charge which followed. On seeing one of his comrades dismounted Trooper Usman Khan made over his horse to the man, and remounted on another which he had seized from one of the enemy whom he had killed.

Indian Order of Merit

Gwalior

Meer Heidat Ali, IOM
Woody-Major Meer Heidat Ali of 4TH Bengal Irregular Cavalry was admitted to 3RD Class IOM in 1ST March 1844. During the battle of Maharapore, he gallantly charged through a body of the enemy's infantry. Within ten yards of the enemy, he was obliged to bend his head and body on his horse's neck, in order to pass under trees and to get to them. He was one of the very few men, under the immediate command of Major Oldfield, who made their way through the enemy and made good the charge. The men who joined Woody-Major Meer Heidat Ali in the charge were all members of his family.

Inayat Ali Shah Khan, IOM
Daffadar Inayat Ali Shah Khan of 4TH Bengal Irregular Cavalry was admitted to 3RD Class IOM in 1ST March 1844. He captured one of the enemy's standard during a charge at the battle of Maharapore by shooting and bayoneting the standard-bearer, and took possession of the standard.

Askur Ali, IOM
Daffadar Askur Ali of 4TH Bengal Irregular Cavalry was admitted to 3RD Class IOM in 1ST March 1844. Early on the day of the battle of Maharapore, Major Oldfield ordered Askur Ali with one of the enemy's tumbrils to the rear to carry off the wounded. Shortly after this the British officer was directed by the Commander-in-Chief to charge the enemy. This was done in a brilliant style and some guns were captured near the village. The delay in taking away the guns enabled Daffadar Askur Ali to rejoin his troop in time to take part with Woody-Major Meer Heidat Ali in the gallant charge against the enemy's infantry under the trees. He was one of those who cut his way through the enemy and was most severely wounded.

Jaffer Ali, IOM
Nishanburder Jaffer Ali of 4TH Bengal Irregular Cavalry was admitted to 3RD Class IOM in 1ST March 1844. He cut his way through the enemy's infantry in the charge under the trees in which he was severely wounded and lost his left eye.

Mohammad Shah, IOM
Sowar Mohammad Shah of 4TH Bengal Irregular Cavalry was admitted to 3RD Class IOM in 1ST March 1844. On observing a foot-soldier of the enemy carrying a standard, charged the standard bearer and took possession of the standard.

Indian Order of Merit

Sikh Wars

Sikh Wars, (1845–46; 1848–49), two campaigns fought between the Sikhs and the British. They resulted in the conquest and annexation by the British of the Punjab in north-western India.

Hussan Khan, IOM
Drummer Hussan Khan of 48TH Bengal Native Infantry was admitted to the 3RD Class IOM on 3RD July 1846. Almost immediately after the 48TH Infantry came under fire of the enemy's infantry in the battle of Moodkee on the evening of 18TH December 1845, Captain Palmer was directed by a General Staff Officer to prepare to receive the charge of cavalry which was about to take place from the left flank. The regiment was then in line, and the fire from the enemy's guns and musketry had been so heavy that the left section of one of the companies had been swept away by a discharge of grape. On to forming up into 'square', their place left was left vacant, and Captain Palmer had difficulty in persuading any of his men to go into it. He was still endeavouring to get it filled up, when Drummer Hussan Khan took up a musket from the ground and placed himself in the front rank of the vacant space. His brilliant example immediately caused the space to be filled up when there was no prospect of getting this done.

Aseem Khan, IOM
Subedar Aseem Khan of 16TH Bengal Native Infantry was admitted to the 3RD Class IOM on 14TH August 1846. He displayed a great gallantry in cheering on the men, of several companies, when they came across the enemy's horse artillery guns at the battle of Moodkee on the 18TH December. Subedar also pluckily cheered and urged the men on his own regiment at the battle of Ferozeshah on the 21ST December, when they came under heavy fire of grape, and was in this action severely wounded in the left arm.

Chand Khan, IOM
Subedar Chand Khan of 47TH Bengal Native Infantry was admitted to the 3RD Class IOM on 17TH February 1847, for his gallant conduct in the action at Moodkee on the 18TH December 1845. Although most of his men fell and killed and the remainder wounded, Subedar Chand Khan behaved in the most exemplary manner. Four guns were taken and spiked.

Indian Order of Merit

Sikh Wars

Azim Khan, IOM
Azim Khan of Bengal Horse Artillery Infantry was admitted to the 3RD Class IOM on 31ST July 1846. He commanded one of the guns during the action at Ferozeshah on 21ST and 22ND December 1845. He laid his guns during the heaviest fire as calmly as if he were on parade and performed personally manual labour in moving the trail of the gun into position etc. One after another eleven horses of his gun were killed, but for his exertion in bringing up the spare horses to replace those killed, the gun would have become unserviceable.

Shekh Khoda Bux, IOM
Sepoy Shekh Khoda Bux of 30TH Bengal Native Infantry was admitted to the 3RD Class IOM on 3RD July 1846. During the battle of Aliwal the 30TH Infantry was down in the nullah behind the village of Bhoondrie, when a Sikh soldier rushed out of the crevice in the bank and charged Subedar Ghunsam Sing of the 5TH company of this regiment. He got to within three paces of the Indian officer when Sepoy Shekh Khoda Bux stepped out of the ranks and struck the Sikh with the butt end of his musket and bayoneted him.

Nizam Ullee Khan, IOM
Sepoy Nizam Ullee Khan of 30TH Bengal Native Infantry was admitted to the 3RD Class IOM on 3RD July 1846. He was in the third file from the right flank of his Company during the action at Aliwal, and observed two Sikhs advancing with drawn swords on the colours of his regiment. He left the ranks at once and went to meet them, and shot one of them. He had not the time to reload when he attacked the second man with his bayonet, and bayoneted him. The Sikh simultaneously struck the Sepoy with his tulwar, inflicting a severe wound on his left leg, on the lower part of the calf. The tulwar then fell out of his hand and while doing so inflicted another severe wound between the thumb and the forefinger of the Sepoy's left hand. Sepoy Nizam Ullee Khan then took up the tulwar and decapitated his opponent.

Roshun Khan, IOM
Sepoy Roshun Khan of 41ST Bengal Native Infantry was admitted to the 3RD Class IOM on 30TH April 1847, for gallant conduct in the battle of Sabraon on 10TH February 1846.

Indian Order of Merit

Sikh Wars

Sheikh Rujub Ullee Shaheed, IOM
Havildar Sheikh Rujub Ullee of 41ST Bengal Native Infantry was admitted to the 3RD Class IOM on 30TH April 1847, for gallant conduct in the battle of Sabraon on 10TH February 1846, in which he was killed.

Shaikh Koodrut Ali, IOM
Sepoy Shaikh Koodrut Ali of Bengal Sappers and Miners was admitted to the 3RD Class IOM on 13TH January 1849 for gallant conduct on the 13TH September 1848 before Multan.

Alif Khan, IOM
Trooper Alif Khan of 5TH Bengal Light Cavalry Miners was admitted to the 3RD Class IOM on 31ST March 1849 for conspicuous gallantry during the skirmish at Ramnagar on 22ND November 1848.

Khooshud Allie, IOM
Jemadar Khooshud Allie of 3RD Bengal Irregular Cavalry Miners was admitted to the 3RD Class IOM on 31ST March 1849 for conspicuous gallantry when leading a party of skirmishers of the 1ST Troop at Sadoolawalla on the 3RD December 1848.

Sahadut Khan, IOM
Sepoy Sahadut Khan of Bengal Sappers and Miners was admitted to the 3RD Class IOM on 14TH April 1849, for gallant action at Multan on 11TH January 1849. Sepoy Sahadut Khan was orderly to Lieutenant Maxwell, and accompanied that officer into the trenches on the night of 11TH January, when sortie was made by the enemy. The Sikhs were at the ditch and a noise having been heard, Lieutenant Maxwell told Sahadut Khan to go up to the edge of the ditch and see what was going on. The Sepoy said, 'Give me your sword, sir, and I will go and look.' He then took his officer's sword and walked straight up the ditch, and although challenged and fired upon by the enemy, succeeded by his coolness and courage in obtaining the information required. Sepoy Sahadut Khan also accompanied Lieutenant Maxwell on 7TH January, when the officer crept up to the crest of the glacis and measured the depth of the ditch opposite the Daulat Gate. On this occasion also, Sepoy Sahadut Khan behaved with steadiness and coolness.

Meera Ahmed Allie Beg, IOM
Ressaidar Meera Ahmed Allie Beg of Scinde Irregular Horse was admitted to the 3RD Class IOM in 9TH June 1849, for distinguished conduct in action at Gujarat on the 21ST February 1849.

Indian Order of Merit

Sikh Wars

Khurattee Khan, IOM
Jemadar Khurattee Khan of Scinde Irregular Horse was admitted to the 3RD Class IOM in 1850. He is fine dashing soldier, who did excellent service throughout the actions at Multan and Gujarat. When the enemy as broken up after the charge at Gujarat, some of them retreated slowly and stood at times in small bodies of from six to fifteen. Jemadar Khurattee Khan collected sowars wherever he could, and made several spirited and successful charges on these bands. He also saved the life of a Sowar whose horse had been killed by the enemy; and cut down five Sikhs and captured a standard.

Sonawar Khan, IOM
Naib Risaldar Sonawar Khan of 14TH Bengal Irregular Cavalry was admitted to the 3RD Class IOM on 14TH February 1851, for daring manner in which he captured Sant Nihal Singh, alias Guru Maharaj Singh in December 1849. Maharaj Singh was a man considered sacred among the Sikhs and other Punjabis, who had engaged with most daring characters in the country in a large conspiracy, essentially Sikh one, against the British at Jullundur.

The capture of this holy man, who had firmly convinced the people that he could work miracles and was tirelessly working to organize the people of the Punjab to raise in a general insurrection, was considered necessary, and a reward of Rs. 5000 offered for his arrest. On 28TH December 1849, it was learnt that Maharaj Singh was concealed in one of the surrounding villages, fourteen miles from Jullundur. A party of twelve men moving with great speed came up the fugitives just as they had taken shelter in an enclosed building. When they came to the enclosure Naib Risaldar Sonawar Khan, with his son and nephew, volunteered to enter. A desperate resistance was expected from the concealed party and Sonawar Khan, before entering called on his companions to stand firm on their ground and to do their duty and the Deity alone knew who would return. The compartments in the enclosure were quite dark and the men had to grope about inside the huts in search of the refugees. But this being fruitless, Sonawar Khan lit some maize, and with the aid of the light thus thrown into the dark rooms, he soon discovered Maharaj Singh and his men. Making a bold rush on them, and unexpectedly them unarmed, he took them prisoners without much resistance. Maharaj Singh was exiled to Singapore, without trial, where he died in captivity on 5TH July 1856.

Indian Order of Merit

North West Frontier

Hoolas Khan and Buctour Khan, IOM
Naik Hoolas Khan and Sepoy Buctour Khan of Bengal Native infantry were admitted to the 3RD Class IOM on 15TH March 1850, for valour and self-devotion exhibited by them in the expedition against Afridis in the mountain range between Peshawar and Kohat on 12TH February 1850.

Meer Jaffir, IOM
Subedar Meer Jaffir of Punjab Infantry was admitted to the 3RD Class IOM on 20TH January 1854, for conspicuous gallantry in various actions in Afghanistan and elsewhere. He was present during the operations under Sir Charles Napier in the Kohat Pass in February 1850, and in the attack on Kohat Kotal in March of the same year under Captain Coke on which occasion thirty men of the 1ST Punjab Infantry were killed and wounded.
(Subedar Meer Jaffir was later advanced to 2ND and 1ST Class, IOM)

Mirza Ellahie Beg, IOM
Ressaidar Mirza Ellahie Beg of Bengal Irregular Cavalry was admitted to the 3RD Class IOM on 27TH April 1855. In an action in the Peshawar Valley on the 3RD January 1852, he attacked and defeated a body of maurdars with the utmost gallantry, leading his men to the charge with unflinching courage and killing two men with his own hand.

Nawab Khan, IOM
Daffadar Nawab Khan of Punjab Irregular Force was admitted to the 3RD Class IOM on 9TH September 1853, for brave and gallant conduct very conspicuously displayed near Vehowah during an attack made by the Kasrani hill tribe against the town of Dera Futteh Khan on 17TH March 1852. After charging through the enemy and back again, he assisted to carry off his dismounted officer, Naib-Risaldar Nusseer Khan.

Hubeeb Khan, IOM
Subedar Hubeeb Khan of Punjab Irregular Force was admitted to the 3RD Class IOM on 13TH October 1854. He was present on the Kotal on 12TH November 1853 when the Afridis attack the hill and with three orderlies, he stopped the first rush of the Afridis, killing their man in a hand-to-hand fight.
(Subedar Hubeeb Khan was later advanced to 2ND and 1ST Class, IOM)

Indian Order of Merit

North West Frontier

Fyz Mohammad Khan, IOM
Subedar Fyz Mohammad Khan of Punjab Irregular Force was admitted to the 3RD Class IOM on 20TH November 1855, for conspicuous gallantry on the occasion of the assault and capture of the Orakzai strongholds of Sungar and Nasseem Meylah on 2ND September 1855.
(Subedar Fyz Mohammad Khan was later advanced to 2ND Class IOM).

Shazadah, Meer Afzul Khan and Shere Ali, IOM
Havildar Shazadah, Naik Shere Ali and Sepoy Meer Afzul Khan of Punjab Infantry were admitted to the 3RD Class IOM in 1857, for conspicuous gallantry in action against the Bozdars on 7TH March 1857. On this occasion the enmity which had for many years estranged the Sikhs and the Pathans was put aside, and these two races in the above regiments fought most gallantly, shoulder to shoulder, in the same cause.

Mohammad Khan, Mohammad Bux and Jahangeer Khan, IOM
Havildar Mohammad Khan, Sepoy Mohammad Bux and Sepoy Jahangeer Khan of Punjab Irregular Force were admitted to the 3RD Class IOM in 1857. They displayed conspicuous gallantry in an action against the village of Narinji on the Yusafzais border on 21ST July 1857.

Abdoola Khan and Shah Gool, IOM
Subedar Abdoola Khan and Havildar Shah Gool of Punjab Infantry were admitted to the 3RD Class IOM on 13TH July 1858, for the conspicuous gallantry in action on the heights above Sitana on the 4TH May 1858.

Daffadar Wullee Mohammad and Sowar Shahdul Khan of Punjab Irregular Force were admitted to the 3RD Class IOM in 1860.

Daffadar Wullee Mohammad saved the life of Risaldar Sing by cutting down a Waziri who had attacked the Risaldar. He also assisted Sowar Heeera Sing in saving the life of a wounded and a dismounted comrade, killing one of the Waziris who was advancing upon him.

Sowar Shahdul Khan he attacked single handed three Waziris, he killed one before his horse fell, and then he fought on foot and killed another of the three. The third man was killed by another Sowar who came to his help.

Indian Order of Merit

Sepoy Mutiny

Shaik Phultoo, IOM
Sepoy Shaik Phultoo of Bengal Native Infantry was admitted to the 3RD Class IOM in 1857, for fidelity and bravery in defending the life of his officer against the murderous attack of the mutineer Mangal Pandy.

Mahaboolah Khan, IOM
Bugler Mahaboolah Khan of Sylhet Light Infantry was admitted to the 3RD Class IOM in 1858. Bugler Mahaboolah Khan was orderly bugler to Captain Stevens during these actions, and set an exemplary example to the men by remaining in an advanced position under heavy fire and by waving his cap and calling on the men to follow him.

Shaik Alla Deen, IOM
Naik Shaik Alla Deen of Bengal Native Infantry was admitted to the 3RD Class IOM on 5TH March 1858, he remained loyal to the British Government when the troops mutinied at Meerut on 10TH May 1857; Shaik Alla Deen saved the lives of the wife and three children of Sergeant-Major Rawson. He protected them for several days, until he was called away to join the Police Corps; and did excellent service afterwards.

Syud Alli and Soobhan Alli, IOM
Sowar Syud Alli and Sowar Soobhan Alli of Bengal Irregular Cavalry were admitted to the 3RD Class IOM on 20TH January 1858. In addition to the exceptional admission to higher classes of the Order of Merit, the two Sowars were promoted to Jemadar. The two Sowars were further rewarded with land grants to the value of Rs. 400 per annum. For his loyal services Naib Risaldar Shaik Bahadur Ali was rewarded with the admission to the 1ST Class the Order of British India, and received a land grant assessed at Rs. 2,000 per annum.

Hyat Khan, IOM
Deputy Inspector Hyat Khan of Seetapore Police and late of Bengal Irregular Cavalry was admitted to the 3RD Class IOM in 1864 for loyalty and good service during the Sepoy Mutiny.

Munowar Khan, Mohammad Buksh Khan, and Meer Futteh Khan, IOM
Risaldar Munowar Khan and Risaldar Mohammad Buksh Khan of Bengal Irregular Cavalry were directly admitted from 3RD Class to 1ST Class IOM in 1857. Risaldar Meer Futteh Khan was promoted to 2ND Class IOM, for their conspicuous gallantry during the Sepoy Mutiny.

Indian Order of Merit

Sepoy Mutiny

Sheik Mokeem, IOM
Havildar Sheik Mokeem of Bengal Native Infantry was admitted to the 3RD Class IOM in 1859, in recognition of the eminent loyalty displayed by him during the Sepoy rebellion.

Emam Bux Khan, IOM
Jemadar Emam Bux Khan of Multan Regiment of Cavalry was admitted to the 3RD Class IOM on 2ND July 1858 and promoted to the rank of Risaldar for distinguished gallantry and faithful service to the state.

Mohammad Akbar and Mohammad Alli, IOM
Trooper Mohammad Akbar and Trooper Mohammad Alli of Madras Light Cavalry were admitted to the 3RD Class IOM, for conspicuous gallantry in action at Debreheeah in the Goruckpore District on 23RD July 1858.

Shaik Daood, IOM
Subedar Shaik Daood of Shekhawttee Battalion was admitted to the 3RD Class IOM in 1857, for gallant and loyal service during the outbreak of Midnapore on 4TH June 1857. *He was later promoted to 2ND Class IOM.*

Dabee Deen and Hossien Allee, IOM
Subedar Dabee Deen and Jemadar Hossien Allee of Shekhawttee Battalion were directly admitted 2ND Class IOM in 1859, in consideration of their loyalty to the State during the Sepoy Mutiny.

Shaik Amanut, IOM
Subedar Shaik Amanut of Ramghur Light Infantry Cavalry was admitted to the 3RD Class IOM, in 1857, for exemplary loyalty on the occasion of the disaffection of the Infantry of the Corps when sent out to operate against the rebels. On the mutineers at Ramghur waylaying him and trying to force him to return with them to Dorundah, the gallant Subedar Shaik Amanut steadfastly refused to do so, telling the men, when they threatened his life, that they might shoot him if they liked, but that go with them he would not.

Shaik Panchcouree, IOM
Subedar Shaik Panchcouree of Ramghur Light Infantry was admitted to the 3RD Class IOM, in 1857. He was in command of the detachment of his battalion at Sumbalpore during the Mutiny, and not only remained loyal, but withstood the exposed attempts of his comrades to mutiny. By his influence and authority he succeeded in keeping his men together and averting an outbreak.

Indian Order of Merit

Sepoy Mutiny

Sultan Bux, IOM
Havildar Sultan Bux of Bengal Military Police Battalion was admitted to the 3RD Class IOM, in 1857. He went out and brought in tools with which some of the rebels were endeavouring to dig under the walls. In doing so he ran a considerable risk.

Havildar Shaik Abdool Cawdar, Havildar Moodookistnah, Lance Naik Mohammad Ghalib, Lance Naik Mohammad Kassim, Private Iyanah, Private Syed Imam and Private Mohammad Ally of Madras Native Infantry were admitted to the 3RD Class IOM, in 1861, in consideration of their conspicuous gallantry in the field against the mutineers near Azimgarh.

Shadil Khan, IOM
Naib Risaldar Shadil Khan of Sikh Irregular Cavalry was directly promoted to 1ST Class IOM in 1858, for his conduct was pre-eminently good and loyal on various occasions, particularly in saving the life of Captain Evans in Oudh.

Muddut Ali, IOM
Jemadar Muddut Ali of Sikh Irregular Cavalry was admitted to 3RD Class IOM in 1858, for he behaved with great gallantry on the occasion when Lieutenant Hamilton, adjutant of the Regiment was mortally wounded.

Sungur Khan, IOM
Sowar Sungur Khan of Sikh Irregular Cavalry was admitted to 3RD Class IOM in 1858, he exhibited great bravery against the mutineers.

Fuqroodeen, IOM
Private Fuqroodeen of The Madras Rifles was admitted to 3RD Class IOM, with effect from 20TH April 1858, for his conspicuous gallantry in the field when in pursuit of the rebel force under Koer Kanwar Singh from Azimgarh to the Ganges.

Sheik Ibrahim, IOM
Naik Sheik Ibrahim of Bengal Military Police Battalion was admitted to 3RD Class IOM with effect from 20TH July 1858, in consideration of the gallant service rendered by him in assisting in the capture of the rebel chief Sirnam Sing

Indian Order of Merit

Sepoy Mutiny

Daffadar Akbar Khan, Lance Daffadar Kala Khan, Trooper Shabaz Khan, were admitted to 3RD Class IOM, for their gallant conduct in action against the rebels at Suhujnee near Peroo on 27TH September 1858

Fyzoollah Khan, IOM
Risaldar Fyzoollah Khan of Sikh Irregular Cavalry was admitted to 3RD Class IOM, in the same action as above.

Mahboob Khan, IOM
Jemadar Mahboob Khan of Sikh Irregular Cavalry was admitted to 3RD Class IOM and later to 2ND Class IOM, for conspicuous gallantry in the field.
Jemadar Mahboob Khan rightly claims further mention. He was one of the finest specimens of the Indian soldier, and his daring pluck and the high opinions expressed of him by British officers, showed that a true soldier in was then hard to find in the Indian Army.

Nawab Khan, IOM
Naib-Risaldar Nawab Khan of Sikh Irregular Cavalry was admitted to 3RD Class IOM and later to 2ND Class IOM in 14TH February 1859. He displayed conspicuous gallantry in attacking a large body of rebels at Ramgarh in December 1858, when at distance from all support. He had been posted in charge of the Ramgarh thanna with twenty troopers of his regiment when a large body of mutineers had halted in the neighbourhood. He attacked them in a most gallant manner, killing the rebel leader, with his own hand and securing his tulwar, pistols, horse and Enfield rifle.

Ellei Bux Khan, IOM
Jemadar Ellei Bux Khan of Bengal Military Police Battalion was admitted to 3RD Class IOM in 1859. He displayed conspicuous gallantry by a determine manner in which he followed the enemy in their retreat into the hills at the midnight action.

Ameer Ally Khan, IOM
Naib-Risaldar Ameer Ally Khan of Bengal Irregular Cavalry was admitted to 3RD Class IOM in 1857. He evinced a great zeal and loyalty, on 20TH May 1857, when employed with Colonel Chute's Column against the mutineers of the 55TH Bengal Native Infantry in the neighbourhood of the Hoti Mardan. He aided in capturing several rebels and shot one with his own hand.

Indian Order of Merit

Sepoy Mutiny

Meer Bunda Allee and Munsabdar Khan, IOM
Risaldar Meer Bunda Allee and Woodie Major Munsabdar Khan Bengal Irregular Cavalry were admitted to 3RD Class IOM in 1857. They were presented with a reward of Rs. 500 each and admitted to the Order of Merit, for the zeal and fidelity evinced by them in having, without hesitation, reported to their commanding officer the disaffection of some of the Indian troops stationed at Multan, and thus averting serious mischief.

Sheikh Inayut Huck, Munsabdar Khan, and Soobhan Khan, IOM
Kot Daffadar Sheikh Inayut Huck, Sowar Munsabdar Khan, and Daffadar Soobhan Khan of Bengal Irregular Cavalry were admitted to 3RD Class IOM in 1858, for their distinguished conduct at Multan on the outbreak of mutiny of the 62ND and 69TH Regiments Native Infantry at that station.

Sher Khan, IOM
Subedar Sher Khan of Punjab Irregular Force was admitted to 3RD Class IOM. At Multan in May 1857 efforts were made by rebel agents to gain over the battalion, with no better result than the sentence on a Pay Havildar, a Hindustani, of nine years imprisonment with hard labour for endeavouring to incite the men of his battalion to mutiny. Subedar Sher Khan, Native Adjutant, rewarded for his loyalty on this occasion with the Khilat worth Rs, 200 and admission to the Order of Merit. The regimental Munshi was also rewarded for his loyalty by a present of Rs. 100 from the Government.

Neamut Allie, Baichoo Khan, Gungadeen, and Sooklal Dooby, IOM
Subedar Neamut Allie, Havildar Baichoo Khan, Jemadar Gungadeen, and Naik Sooklal Dooby of Bengal Artillery were admitted to 3RD Class IOM on 9TH December 1858, for exemplary conduct and loyalty to the State.

Kullunder Buksh, IOM
Havildar Kullunder Buksh of Punjab Irregular Force was admitted to 3RD Class IOM on 16TH December 1858, in consideration of the gallantry and soldier-like conduct displayed by him on the 8TH June 1857, in the encounter with the Jullundur Mutineers at Ludhiana.

Sheikh Khoda Buksh, IOM
Havildar Sheikh Khoda Buksh of Bengal Native Infantry was admitted to 3RD Class IOM on 11TH March 1858. He served throughout the attack upon the troops at Cawnpore, in the entrenchments and displayed conspicuous gallantry and fidelity to the State.

Indian Order of Merit

Sepoy Mutiny

Mohammad Khan, IOM

Risaldar Mohammad Khan of the Corps of Guides was advanced to 1ST Class IOM on 26TH March 1858. He was always forward in a fight and always marked by gallantry. On 20TH August 1857, he was detached with twenty-five Sowars to cut out camels grazing near the Ajmir Gate. With this small body Mohammad Khan surprised and drove in a strong piquet of the rebels, and from the midst of their camp brought away seventy camels and baggage animals. Again, when reconnoitring near Najafgarh on 25TH August, the Risaldar slew the leader of the rebel cavalry who came out and met him in single combat. He is already on possession of 2ND Class, now recommended for advancement to the 1ST Class IOM.

Abdool Rahman, IOM

Sowar Abdool Rahman of the Corps of Guides was admitted to the 3RD Class IOM on 26TH March 1858. He dismounted in the thick of a fight on 16TH June on observing his Sillidar on the ground with his horse killed and, resigning from his own horse, cut his way out on foot, killing and wounding two or three of the rebels.

Fuzul Khan, IOM

Daffadar Fuzul Khan of the Corps of Guides was admitted to the 3RD Class IOM in 1857, for distinguished conduct in the field.

On 10TH September 1857, the rebel cavalry attacked the Azadpore piquet in force and drove it in. Captain Sanford Guides Cavalry, went to the rescue, supported the piquet and repelled the attack with considerable slaughter. The following men of the Corps of Guides were conspicuous in the personal combats which ensued.

Mookhtyar Ali, IOM

Kot Daffadar Mookhtyar Ali was admitted 3RD Class IOM. He went on most gallantly and cut down a dismounted Sowar who had already beaten back two of his men.

Ghazee, IOM

Sowars Ghazee was admitted 3RD Class IOM. They gallantly charged a group of dismounted rebels.

Kassim Alli, IOM

Sowar Kassim Alli was admitted 3RD Class IOM. After snapping his carbine at a footman and standing his fire, he closed and killed him with the butt-end of his carbine.

Indian Order of Merit

Sepoy Mutiny

Ushruff Khan, IOM
Ressaidar Ushruff Khan of the Guides Cavalry was admitted to 3RD Class IOM on 6TH April 1858. He distinguished himself in the action fought at the village of Narnool on 16TH November 1857, against a body of mutineers of the Jodhpore Legion. Ressaidar Ushruff Khan was conspicuously forward, sword deep in blood, in the thick of the fight.

There was a delay in the bestowal of gallantry awards to several officers and other ranks of Corps of Guides for their gallantry at Delhi. It exemplifies the supply problem arising from the entirely unexpected increase in demand for Order of Merit badges.

The following Guides Infantry and Cavalry were awarded the 3RD Class IOM: Risaldar Khurman Khan, Daffadars Yakoob Khan, Mirza Abdul Beg, Mahammad Hosein Khan, Sowar Mirza Fuzal Beg, Sowar Kummur Deen, and Sowar Mirza Hossain Beg, Subedars Ahmed Khan. Peer Buksh, Kudrat Shah, and Jemadar Allah Dad.

The following Multani Horse were awarded the 3RD Class IOM, for distinguished loyalty and good service performed during the period of disturbances: Risaldar Attah Mohammad Khan, Risaldar Wulleeedad Khan, Naib Daffadar Assud Khan, Jemadar Mullick Surfraz Khan, and Sowar Nutty Khan.

Mohammad Bux Khan, IOM
Daffadar Mohammad Bux Khan of Punjab Irregular Force was directly admitted to the 2ND Class IOM. On 3RD July 1857, the mutineers in considerable numbers attacked two troops of the 5TH Punjab Cavalry when encamped at Alleepore, near Delhi. The Hindustani Mussulmans from both troops joined the rebels, Daffadar Mohammad Bux Khan, although he a Hindustani and resident of Rewari in the district of Delhi remained firm and loyal.

Mohammad Akram and Abdoola Khan, IOM
Jemadar Mohammad Akram and Sowar Abdoola Khan of Punjab Irregular Force were admitted to the 3RD Class IOM on 19TH March 1858, in consideration of their gallant conduct and faithful services to the State.

Indian Order of Merit

Sepoy Mutiny

For their conspicuous loyalty and gallantry in several engagements with the mutineers in 1857 and 1858 the following soldiers of the Punjab Irregular Force were awarded the various grades of IOM:

Subedar Hubbeeb Khan advanced to 2ND Class and later to 1ST Class. Havildar Gholam Mohammad Khan, Havildar Meean Gool, Naik Ahmed Khan, and Sepoys Darren Shah, Noor Hussen, Munsoor and Kurruma, admitted to 3RD Class in 1857.

Naik Mowland 3RD Class and later to 1ST Class, Jemadar Syud Mohammad 3RD Class and later to 2ND Class, Sepoy Neaz Mohammad 3RD Class and later to 2ND Class, and Subedar Mohammad Shah, Subedar Shumush Khan, Havildar Peer Bux, Naik Poyudah Khan, admitted to 3RD Class in 1858.

Sepoys Hummeed, Lall Khan, Bkukkha Khan, Bostan, Syud Mohammad, and Sahib Gool, were admitted to 3RD Class IOM for distinguished conduct in action, and for faithful service to the State.

For their conspicuous loyalty and gallantry in several engagements with the mutineers in 1857 and 1858 the following soldiers of the Bengal Horse Artillery awarded the various grades of IOM:

Havildar Wuzeer Khan direct to the 1ST Class, Trooper Ullee Khan to the 2ND Class. Jemadar Nadir Shah, Havildar Hyder Shah, Naiks Khadim Khan, Quadir Buksh, Khooshial, Wuzeer Beg, Ishar Ullee, Trumpeter Azim Khan, Ferriers Mudar Bux, Sirdar Khan, and Troopers Ullee Khan, Nubbee Buksh, Busharat Khan, Ullee Husn, Bechee Khan, Quadir Dad Khan, Shumsheer Khan, Ukbar Khan, Mobaruk Allee, Suffder Ullee, Syud Mohammad Khan, Muddath Khan, Yar Ullee Beg, Abar, Khairat Ullee, Yurseen Khan, Sirdar Ullee, Noor Khan, Peer Buksh, Nisar Ullee, Mudar Buksh, Fazil Khan, Muckdoom Buksh, Ullee Mohammad and Bahadur Allee. Privates Khoda Buksh, Muckdoom Buksh, Husn Buksh, Noor Khan, Sirdar Khan, and Shaik Umar, were admitted to 3RD Class IOM for distinguished conduct in action, and for faithful service to the State.

The Bengal Artillery saw further active service after the fall of Delhi, notably in North West Provinces.

Suffer Ally, IOM
Jemadar Suffer Ally of Bengal Artillery was admitted to 3RD Class IOM on 7TH June 1859, for his conspicuous gallantry in supervising the gun against the enemy.

Indian Order of Merit

Sepoy Mutiny

For their faithful services and loyalty to the State the following men of the Bengal Artillery were admitted to the 3RD Class IOM:
Jemadar Shaick Khoda Bux, Jemadar Baboo Khan, Havildar Mungal Khan, Havildar Shaick Qomaid, Privates Taig Allee, Shaick Juan Mahmmad, Russool Bux, Kullunder, Lall Mohammad, Khodur Bux, Gungadeen, Gomain, Shaick Ismail, Kurreem Bux, Ramzaun Khan, Shaick Elie Bux, and Matta Deen.

Peer Bux, IOM
Subedar Peer Bux of Belooch Battalion was admitted to the 3RD Class IOM in 1860. On 14TH September 1857, fifteen European soldiers and twelve Sepoys, the latter under Subedar Peer Bux, were ordered to advance to Kashmir Gate at Delhi. The party got into the town and took a small battery which the General told the men to hold in case the enemy got to the rear. A short while after, a party of the enemy's cavalry came up to the battery and killed two of Subedar Peer Bux's men. The Subedar immediately took up a musket and fired at the standard-bearer of the enemy's cavalry, who fell across his horse wounded, whereon Peer Bux rushed out with his sword and killed the man and captured the standard and the horse. Peer Bux presented the standard and horse to General Nicholson who was much pleased with his gallantry.

Sew Churrun Misser, IOM
Subedar Sew Churrun Misser of Belooch Battalion was admitted to the 3RD Class IOM in 1858, with effect from 27TH November 1857, for his conspicuous gallantry in the field and exemplary loyalty to the State. During the operations at the siege and the capture of Delhi from 7TH to 20TH September 1857, Sew Churrun Misser was the Indian adjutant of the battalion and his uniformly good conduct, his devotion to Government, and his zeal and anxiety for credit of his men was most conspicuous. During the hard struggle before Delhi, he showed himself a gallant and intelligent officer, rendering every aid in his power to all the European officers and to the Battalion generally. Later he was advanced to 2ND Class, on 18TH

Zurreef Khan, IOM
Subedar Zurreef Khan of Belooch Battalion was admitted to the 3RD Class IOM in 1859. His gallantry was conspicuous at Delhi. He commanded his company at Doondia Kevia on 24TH November 1858 and led his men with a rush upon one of the enemy's guns.

Indian Order of Merit

Sepoy Mutiny

Pyand Khan, IOM
Subedar Pyand Khan of Belooch Battalion was admitted to the 3RD Class IOM in 1859. He was senior Indian officer in command of the four companies of the Belooch Battalion before Delhi, and behaved extremely well. He also showed great coolness and gallantry in a close encounter with the enemy at Rampore Kusseeah on 3RD November 1858, where he acquitted himself admirably.

Mohammad Ukbar Khan, IOM
Lance Naik Mohammad Ukbar Khan of Belooch Battalion was admitted to the 3RD Class IOM in 1858. He was promoted to the rank of Havildar for signal gallantry and devotion to the State during the siege of Delhi, and also in action at Rampore Kusseeah on 3RD November 1858.

Shaick Abdool and Nehal Khan, Bitind Khan, Shiekh Sobhan, Emam Bux and Hubeeb Khan.
Naik Shaick Abdool and Naik Nehal Khan, Havildar Bitind Khan, Jemadar Shiekh Sobhan, Jemadar Emam Bux and Havildar Hubeeb Khan, of Corps of Sappers and Miners were admitted to the 3RD Class IOM in 1858, in special recognition of conspicuous gallantry displayed by them in the demolition of the Kashmir Gate of the Fort of Delhi on the 14TH September 1857, as well as for good service and gallantry on other occasions.

Deen Mohammad, IOM
Subedar Major Deen Mohammad of Bengal Artillery was directly promoted to the 1ST Class IOM, for his conspicuous gallantry at Lucknow.

Kalley Khan, IOM
Jemadar Kalley Khan of Bengal Native Infantry was admitted to the 3RD Class IOM in 1859, in recognition of his services during the Mutiny campaign.

Kurreem Khan, IOM
Subedar Kurreem Khan of Oudh Irregular Force was promoted to 1ST Class IOM in 1860, as a reward for his distinguished loyalty and devotion during the mutiny at Lucknow during 1857.

Fayez Mohammad Khan, IOM
Sowar Fayez Mohammad Khan of Lucknow Cavalry Levy was admitted to the 3RD Class IOM in 1859, for faithful service in the garrison of Lucknow during its siege.

Indian Order of Merit

Sepoy Mutiny

Nubbee Buksh Khan, IOM
Naib-Risaldar Nubbee Buksh Khan of Bengal Irregular Cavalry was admitted to 3RD Class IOM on 26TH March 1858, in consideration of loyal and gallant conduct with detachment of the 12TH Irregular Cavalry.

Rahmut Ally Khan, IOM
Jemadar Rahmut Ally Khan of Bengal Irregular Cavalry was admitted to 3RD Class IOM on 11TH March 1864, for gallant and meritious services during the relief of Lucknow.

Ghunnee Khan, IOM
Kot- Daffadar Ghunnee Khan of Bengal Irregular Cavalry was admitted to 3RD Class IOM on 27TH April 1877, with effect from 12TH July 1859, for loyalty and good services during the Sepoy Mutiny.

Jewra Khan, IOM
Havildar Jewra Khan of Bengal Artillery was admitted to 3RD Class IOM on 15TH November 1859, for conspicuous loyalty and distinguished service in the relief and defence of Lucknow.

Subedar Moossum Allee, Havildar Meer Hyder Allee, Havildar Buccus Khan, Havildar Shaick Loll Mohammad, Lance Naik Hussain Buksh and Privates Shaik Lall Mohammad, Shaik Budhoo, Baj Khan, Aliff Khan, and Shaik Alleebux of Bengal Artillery were admitted to 3RD Class IOM on 27TH February 1858 in consideration of their loyal and gallant conduct during the many severe actions they has been engaged in especially since the force left Cawnpore.

Secunder Khan and Gohur Shah, IOM
Subedar Secunder Khan and Havildar Gohur Shah of The Regiment of Ferozepore was promoted directly to 1ST Class IOM on 6TH April 1858, for their gallant conduct during the many severe actions in which they have been engaged.

Peer Buccus Khan, IOM
Subedar Peer Buccus Khan of Oudh Irregular Force was admitted to 2ND Class IOM in consideration of his loyal and good conduct to the State when his regiment mutinied.

Indian Order of Merit

Sepoy Mutiny

Risaldar Mohammad Reza Khan was promoted directly to the 1ST Class IOM, Risaldar Futteh Alli Shah 3RD Class and later to 2ND Class IOM. Sowar Bagh Khan was admitted to 3RD Class IOM.

Shere Mohammad Khan, IOM
Risaldar Shere Mohammad Khan of Hodson's Horse was admitted to 3RD Class IOM. He was present with his regiment throughout the siege of Delhi, and when Delhi was captured, he accompanied Major Hodson to seize the King of Delhi and three princes. In the action at Gungairee Shere Mohammad Khan in the presence of his officers and men most pluckily attacked a rebel Subedar and slew him. At Mynpoorie he again distinguished himself. Some ten rebels had taken refuge in a house, and Major Hodson desired his Sowars to go in and seize them. When the Sowars hesitated, Shere Mohammad Khan immediately dismounted his horse and entered the building alone and took them all prisoner together with their arms.

Feroze Khan, Saleem Khan, Mohammad Afzul, IOM
Naib-Risaldar Feroze Khan, Daffadar Saleem Khan, and Sowar Mohammad Afzul of Punjab Irregular Force were admitted to 3RD Class IOM, for conspicuous and in many cases repeated acts of gallantry in action.

Subedar Shaick Goolam Ghose, Subedar Mukurrum Khan, Naik Roshun Khan, Naik Peer Bux, Sepoy Sirdar Khan, Sepoy Goolab, Sepoy Hyat, Sepoy Ghose Beg, Sepoy Hullum Khan, Sepoy Kukhoo Khan, Sepoy Omeer Khan, Sepoy Bahadoor Khan, Sepoy Ameer Khan and Sepoy Fuzil Khan of Punjab Irregular Force were admitted to 3RD Class IOM, for conspicuous and in many cases repeated acts of gallantry in action.

Subedar Shere Khan, Jemadar Peer Khan, Havildar Nitoolla Khan, Jemadar Kallee Khan, Havildar Futteh Deen, Naik Ibrahim, Naik Shahzada, Sepoy Golab of Punjab Irregular Force were admitted to 3RD Class IOM, for conspicuous and in many cases repeated acts of gallantry in action during the past campaign,

Ibrahim Khan, IOM
Kot-Daffadar Ibrahim Khan of Hodson's Horse was admitted to 3RD Class IOM in 1859. He had two horses badly wounded under him, and was highly conspicuous for gallantry in an action on 18TH February 1858.

Indian Order of Merit

Sepoy Mutiny

Morad Khan, IOM
Daffadar Morad Khan of Hodson's Horse was admitted to 3RD Class IOM in 1859, for he was very conspicuous in charging the guns at Jalalabad on 25TH February 1858, on which occasion he was badly wounded.

Ibrahim Beg, IOM
Gun Lascar Ibrahim Beg of Madras Artillery was admitted to 3RD Class IOM in 1859. He carried the powder for blowing up a gate of the keep. While engaged at this gateway, among other casualties a soldier of Her Majesty's 20TH Regiment was shot dead. Ibrahim Beg took up his rifle and loaded and fired it with great coolness, telling the sergeant of the dead man's company, that he would take care and bring up the rifle to them afterwards. The cool and collected manner, in which the gun lascar behaved on this occasion, while under a close fire of matchlocks from the loopholes of the keep, was admired by all. He assisted subsequently in dragging away under heavy fire, two captured guns from under the very walls of the fort.

Futteh Alli Shah, IOM
Risaldar Futteh Alli Shah of Hodson's Horse was advanced to 2ND Class IOM. He was an excellent officer. On 13TH June 1858, he showed a gallant example by dashing into the middle of a body of desperate fanatics.

Hoosain Alli Khan, IOM
Jemadar Hoosain Alli Khan of Hodson's Horse was admitted to 3RD Class IOM in 1858. He dismounted from his horse and threw himself on a gunner who had attacked Lieutenant Baker on 13TH June 1858.

Jhuadah Shah, IOM
Sowar Jhuadah Shah of Hodson's Horse was admitted to 3RD Class IOM in 1858. A gallant soldier, he was desperately wounded in charging a body of footmen on 13TH June 1858.

Zearut Khan and Mohammad Bux, IOM
Jemadar Zearut Khan and Sepoy Mohammad Bux of Punjab Irregular Force were admitted to 3RD Class IOM in 1859, for conspicuous gallantry in action against the rebels.

Kumuroo Din Khan, IOM
Naib-Risaldar Kumuroo Din Khan of Bengal Cavalry was admitted to 3RD Class IOM with effect from 12TH July 1859, for his loyal and gallant services during the Sepoy Mutiny

Indian Order of Merit

Sepoy Mutiny

Shumshodeen, IOM
Naib-Risaldar Shumshodeen of Mahratta Irregular Horse Cavalry was admitted to 3RD Class IOM in 1857. He displayed conspicuous gallantry and exemplary loyalty to the State on 10TH August 1857, near Kolhapore, Bombay Presidency, during the engagement with and victory over a party of the 27TH Bombay Native Infantry, which was fought by a combined detachment of the Southern Mahratta Horse and volunteers of the 27TH Infantry, under Lieutenant Kerr. Shumshodeen displayed great activity, tact and bravery throughout the affair. He volunteered to lead a ladder party, carried messaged under heavy fire, and by his daring bravery inspired confidence in all present.

Sirdar Khan, IOM
Risaldar Sirdar Khan of Mahratta Irregular Horse was admitted to 3RD Class IOM in 1858. He displayed conspicuous gallantry in the cavalry action near Nuggoond on 1ST June 1858. He gallantly led his troops into body of the enemy, who numbered between eight hundred and thousand, and beat them back.

Shaick Hossain, IOM
Daffadar Shaick Hossain of Mahratta Irregular Horse was admitted to 3RD Class IOM in 1858. He was foremost in the pursuit at Nurgoond on 1ST June 1858. He was surrounded by the enemy, Sabring right and left upto within four hundred yards of the gate of the town, and with two Sowars brought back three armed prisoners. His gallant and fearless conduct in the dashing after the flying enemy had the best possible effect on the whole regiment. He also behaved most gallantly at Hulyullee on 30TH November 1857 in leading dismounted men into the town.

Shaick Abdoola, IOM
Sowar Shaick Abdoola of Mahratta Irregular Horse was admitted to 3RD Class IOM in 1858. He was one of the parties to the capture of the fortress of Nurgoond on 2ND June 1858. He climbed the wall, eighteen feet high, to open the Gate and thus affected the entrance of his part. The second Gate was similarly opened by Shaick Abdoola. They found the guardrooms were deserted.

Shaick Dyanut Allie, IOM
Havildar- Major Shaick Dyanut Allie of Bengal Native Infantry was admitted to 3RD Class IOM in 1858. He was promoted to Subedar in consideration of his conspicuous gallantry/

Indian Order of Merit

Sepoy Mutiny

Cassim Sahib, IOM
Jemadar Cassim Sahib of Nagpore Irregular Force was admitted to 3RD Class IOM in 1857. A trooper named Dildar Khan stationed at Seetabuldee, entered the courtyard of Lance Naik Sheik Rahim Buksh, and apprised him of the murderous project of the rissalah to mutiny. Two recruits Nuree Buksh and Shaik Hissamudeen were present, and when the rebellious trooper attempted to draw his sword and escape from the courtyard, these two youths threw themselves on the mutineer, wrested his sword and secured him. Then they took him to Jemadar Cassim Sahib, who closely examined the prisoner and those who accompanied him, and feeling satisfied that a massacre had been decided on by the city Mussulmans and the rissalah. He promptly confined the rebel and hastened to his commanding officer's house and disclosed the matters. Within the short space the whole regiment was under arms and prepared to oppose any party acting offensively towards the Government. Jemadar Cassim's fidelity on the occasion was most marked, and the promptness and energy evinced by him at so critical a time was most praiseworthy. For his devotion Cassim Sahib was admitted to the Order of Merit.

The following Indian officers and other ranks of Bengal Artillery were admitted to the 3RD Class IOM, for having acted as artillerymen since the commencement of the Sepoy Mutiny, and for having distinguished themselves by their gallantry in action, as well for their devoted loyalty to the State:
Naik Shaick Madar Bux, Private Shaick Bhoomead, Private Shaick Imamee, Private Khoda Bux, Private Shaick Jahaun, Private Shaick Bulakee, Private Shaick Abdool, Private Meerra Hyder Beg, Private Soobhan Khan, and Private Mattadeen.

Havildar Jaffer Ally Khan, Jemadar Shaick Jaffer, Sepoy Edoo Khan, Sepoy Toraub Khan, and Sepoy Hussoo Khan of Bengal Native Infantry were admitted to the 3RD Class IOM for distinguished conduct in action and for the faithful service to the State.

Mohammad Wuzzeer Ally Khan, IOM
Jemadar Mohammad Wuzzeer Ally Khan of Hyderabad Contingent was admitted to the 3RD Class IOM in 1857, for conspicuous gallantry in the field in an action with a body if insurgents at Rawal and his exemplary loyalty to the State.

Indian Order of Merit

Sepoy Mutiny

The following officers and other ranks of Bengal Irregular Cavalry were admitted to the 3RD Class IOM in 1864, for distinguished conduct in action and for the faithful service to the State.
Risaldar Rahim Khan, Naib-Ressaidar Sahib Zuma Khan, Jemadar Dad Shere Khan, Daffadar Nubbee Hussein, Daffadar Abdool Rehman Khan, Daffadar Yad Hussein, Ressaidar Amanut Khan, Naib-Ressaidar Zoolfeeker Ally, Jemadar Summund Khan, Daffadar Wullee Mohammad Khan, Daffadar Golam Huzrut Khan and Trumpeter Meah Khan.

Meer Furzand Ally, IOM

Risaldar Meer Furzand Ally of the Bhopal Contingent was admitted to the 3RD Class IOM in 1860. The cavalry portion of the Contingent was generally loyal, but there was one Indian officer, Risaldar Meer Furzand Ally, afterwards in command of the Residency Escort Indore, whose conduct was conspicuous. Throughout the mutiny, Risaldar Meer Furzand Ally's loyal conduct was most prominent. He exerted himself honestly and earnestly to restrain the most violent, and maintain order. His life was threatened by the disaffected, yet he invariably declared his determination of remaining true to the regiment.

The following officers and other ranks of Gwalior Contingent were admitted to the 3RD Class IOM in 1858, for distinguished conduct in action and for the faithful service to the State.
Risaldar Mir Umjid Ali, Jemadar Mir Koorshaid Ali, Jemadar Sheikh Hidayut Ali, Jemadar Sheikh Nujjuf Ali, Jemadar Khudiyar Khan, Daffadar Zubberdust Khan, Daffadar Azim Khan, Daffadar Inayut Ali, Daffadar Meer Nasir Ali, Daffadar Sheikh Husirudin, Daffadar Kurrum Elahi Khan, Daffadar Meer Ali Rasul, Sowar Meer Ijut Ali, Sowar Golab Khan, Sowar Kurrum Khan, Sowar Sheikh Kaim Ali, Sowar Ghazi Khan, Sowar Gohur Khan, Sowar Mohammad Umami Khan, Sowar Sheikh Subsati, Sowar Wazir Khan, Sowar Sheik Rahim-ud-Din, Sowar Inyut Khan and Sheik Dowlut.

Babur Khan, IOM

Risaldar Babur Khan of Central India Horse was admitted to the 3RD Class IOM in 1861, in consideration of his distinguished services at Mundisore on the night of 23RD November 1857.

Indian Order of Merit

Sepoy Mutiny

Goolam Hoosein Khan, IOM
Jemadar Goolam Hoosein Khan of Hyderabad Contingent was admitted to the 3RD Class IOM in 1858, in consideration of his conspicuous gallantry in action with a large body of the enemy at Ratghur.

Soojut Khan, IOM
Subedar Soojut Khan of Bombay Light Cavalry was first admitted to the 3RD Class Order of Merit for gallantry during the capture of Gwalior on 21ST June 1858. Although his gallantry at Barodia on 30TH January 1858 had been noticed, advancement to the 2ND Class appears to have been based on a broader perspective of his services throughout his campaign in Central India. The Subedar was also mentioned in despatches for gallantry on attack on the rebels near Mhow on the Pohooj River on 4TH September 1858.

The following Indian officers and non-commissioned officers of Hyderabad Contingent were admitted to the 3RD Class Order of Merit. They displayed conspicuous gallantry during the investment of the Fort at Jhansi which lasted for twenty days, requiring incessant vigilance and duty of a harassing nature.
Ressaidar Allah Oodeen, Jemadar Mohammad Deen Khan, Jemadar Meer Kurrum Ali, Jemadar Meer Noor Ali, Daffadar Himmat Khan, and Jemadar Mattadeen.

Vilayut Ali Beg, IOM
Jemadar Vilayut Ali Beg of Hyderabad Contingent was admitted to the 3RD Class Order of Merit. He was promoted to the rank of Ressaidar with effect from 30TH April 1858, in consideration of his gallant and meritorious conduct during the campaign in Central India.
In addition to his reward for gallantry in defending the Lohari outpost on 30TH April 1858, Vilayut Ali Beg was brought to notice for gallantry at Berar on 15TH January 1859. He also served for some time as Sir Hugh Rose's orderly, and on the conclusion of the Central India campaign the General presented him with a sword of honour.

Shaik Ali and Abdoola, IOM
Subedar Shaik Ali and Sepoy Abdoola of Hyderabad Contingent were admitted to the 3RD Class Order of Merit in 1858 and promoted to Subedar- Major and Havildar respectively for their conspicuous gallantry in the action at Belowah. In the same action at Belowah Trooper Koodrut Khan Ali was awarded the 3RD Class IOM.

Indian Order of Merit

Sepoy Mutiny

The following Indian officers and non-commissioned officers of Hyderabad Contingent were admitted to the 3RD Class Order of Merit, for gallantry and good service in the field in Central India especially the capture of Calpee on 24TH May 1858.

Ressaidar- Major Mohammad Hossein Khan, Ressaidar- Major Ahmed Buksh Khan, Ressaidar- Major Mustijab Khan, Trooper Shere Ali and Trooper Mohammad Khan.

Soojub Khan, IOM

Subedar Soojub Khan of Bombay Light Cavalry was admitted to the 3RD Class Order of Merit in 1858. Dr. Mackenzie of the Hyderabad Cavalry being interrupted in his attendance on the wounded, by the fire of party of the enemy from behind a wall and ditch, called on Subedar Soojub Khan to dislodge them. Their position was difficult one, but the Subedar, with one half of his party with slung carbines, and the other with drawn swords, gallantly led the charge and succeeded in dislodging them and killing every man.

The following Indian officers and non-commissioned officers of Hyderabad Contingent were admitted to the 3RD Class Order of Merit, in consideration of their gallant conduct at the capture of Gwalior.

Daffadar Nahar Khan, Jemadar Alluf Khan, Troopers Mukarram Khan, Nutteh Khan, Sadoola Khan, Mohammad Khan, Jaffer Khan, Mytab Khan, Suadut Khan, Sheikh Goolam Nubbi, Sheikh Mohammad, Budroodeen Khan, Abdul Kurreem Khan, Shaick Kubeerodeen, Lalloo Khan, Noor Khan, Shaick Meeran, Shaick Omar, Jaffer Ali Beg, Syud Osman, and Nutteh Khan.

Ressaidar Bukshi Ali, Jemadar Beg Mohammad Khan and Jemadar Meer Akbur Ali of Hyderabad Contingent were admitted to the 3RD Class Order of Merit on 10TH June 1858, for their conspicuous gallantry in action at Banda.

Ahmed Shah and Wuzeer Shah, IOM

Daffadar Ahmed Shah and Daffadar Wuzeer Shah of Sikh Mounted Police were admitted to the 3RD Class Order of Merit on 10TH June 1858, in consideration of their conspicuous gallantry in action with rebels in the Jaloun District.

Indian Order of Merit

Sepoy Mutiny

Alyar Khan and Mohammad Khan, IOM
Jemadar Alyar Khan and Daffadar Mohammad Khan of Sikh Irregular Cavalry were admitted to the 3RD Class Order of Merit in 1859. They specially distinguished themselves in a gallant charge against rebels at Kentee in Bundelkhand on 4TH March 1859.

Meer Mohammad, IOM
Risaldar Meer Mohammad of Guzerat Irregular Horse was admitted to 3RD Class IOM on 16TH November 1858, in consideration of his excellent services against the Rebels.

Abdool Azees, IOM
Subedar Abdool Azees of Bombay Native Infantry was directly admitted to 2ND Class IOM, for distinguished service in the field during the late campaign in Central India.

Roostum Ally Khan, IOM
Risaldar Roostum Ally Khan of Beatson's Horse was admitted to 3RD Class IOM, in consideration of his distinguished conduct in action against a body of rebels in the Narsinghur District.

Bhurmadeen, IOM
Daffadar Bhurmadeen of Central India Horse was advanced to 2ND Class and later to 1ST Class IOM, for his gallant conduct on the night of 29TH December 1859 in an attack upon a band if rebels near Sindhora.

Sheikh Rahimudin and Rahim Khan, IOM
Jemadar Sheikh Rahimudin and Daffadar Rahim Khan were admitted to 3RD Class IOM, on 10TH May 1858, for conspicuous gallantry at Hurra on 5TH April 1858 during an action against rebel forces led by Latah S ing.

Kurreemooolah, IOM
Sowar Kurreemooolah of Hodson's Horse was admitted to 3RD Class IOM in 1859. He made a dashing charge on the rebels on 18TH September 1858, and was the first to reach their guns.

Jehangir Khan, IOM
Naib-Risaldar Jehangir Khan of Hodson's Horse was admitted to 3RD Class IOM in 1859. Jehangir Khan sprang from his saddle and closed in a death grapple with a rebel Sepoy whom he killed, but was wounded in the struggle. Lieutenant Palliser had fallen from his horse and was at the mercy of the rebel, but for the Naib-Risaldar Jehangir Khan's timely aid would have been killed.

Indian Order of Merit

Sepoy Mutiny

Khroolla Khan, IOM
Subedar Khroolla Khan of Baluch Battalion was admitted to 3RD Class IOM in 1859. When Lieutenant Beville was in command of Jalalabad in August 1858, he received intelligence of a few rebels being concealed in a village about twenty-five miles distant, and situated in the Province of Oudh. Among them was a man, Mamoor Khan, formerly a Daffadar of the 8TH Bengal Cavalry, and was supposed to have been concerned in the murder of Brigadier Sibbard at Bareilly on 31ST May 1857. The capture of this murderer was considered most important and Lieutenant Beville detached a party of one Daffadar and ten Sowars of De Kantozow's Horse with three volunteers of the Bengal Irregular Cavalry, in command of Subedar Khroolla Khan to capture the ruffian. The Subedar performed the duty in a most satisfactory manner. He not only succeeded in capturing the rebel Daffadar Mamoor Khan, but in the encounter killed Dad Khan, the brother in law of the Nawab of Shajahanpore, who was present at the time. Dad Khan was proclaimed rebel of some influence in the district, and his death was a great gain to the Government. Lieutenant Beville was so pleased with the manner, in which Subedar Khroolla Khan performed this duty, that he again detached him in command of a party to capture a Sowar of Gwalior Contingent, who had fought against the British at Delhi and was then concealed in a village close to Jalalabad. Subedar Khroolla Khan was again successful. He captured and brought in the rebel Sowar, who was tried and hanged by the Magistrate.

Mohammad Ayaz Khan, IOM
Risaldar Mohammad Ayaz Khan of Punjab Irregular Force Battalion was admitted to 3RD Class IOM in 1859, for conspicuous gallantry in the pursuit of rebels at Rampore Kussiah on 3RD November 1858, and again at the passage of the Gogra at Fyzabad on 25TH November 1858.

Nizamoodeen Khan and Aumzoolah Khan, IOM
Ressaidar Nizamoodeen Khan and Daffadar Aumzoolah Khan of Sikh Irregular Cavalry were admitted to 3RD Class IOM in 1859. Ressaidar Nizamoodeen Khan proved himself a first rate soldier. He led his troop in a dashing manner in eight different engagements with the rebels, and distinguished himself at Besan when the three squadrons of the regiment charged and captured two of the enemy's guns. Daffadar Aumzoolah Khan was always to the front and was severely wounded during the encounter with the rebels

Indian Order of Merit

Sepoy Mutiny

Ally Hoosain, IOM
Havildar Ally Hoosain of Madras Artillery was admitted to 3RD Class IOM in 1859. He was thirty times, more or less, engaged with rebels and being mounted was always to the front looking for good places for gun crossings, impediments, taking up points and all other duties when going into action and in pursuit. At Toolsepore, on 23RD December 1858, some rebel Sepoys who had been shot down by canister at short range persisted in firing into the battery, although its fire had been diverted from them into larger masses of the enemy. As there was no other troop closer at hand to do the business, Havildar Ally Hoosain, to gallop forward among them and stop their firing. This was done most willingly and smartly, and service of no ordinary danger, as each rebel calmly reserved his fire till he was close to them.

Hadjee Khan, IOM
Subedar Hadjee Khan of Baluch Battalion was admitted to 3RD Class IOM in 1859. He was one of the best Indian officers in the regiment. He behaved will on all occasions. He commanded his company with great distinction when it was detached as skirmishers against the Fort of Majouda and displayed conspicuous gallantry in action.

The following officers of Bengal Horse Artillery were advances to 2ND Class IOM on 18TH March 1859 in consideration of their conspicuous gallantry and distinguished conduct in action at Maylah ghat on that date. Havildar Azeem Beg, Ressaidar Huckdad Khan and Trooper Allie Khan.

Hidayutullah and Moosddee Khan, IOM
Jemadar Hidayutullah and Havildar Moosddee Khan of Punjab Irregular Force were admitted to 3RD Class IOM in 1859, in consideration of their excellent conduct in action with a body of rebels in the neighbourhood of Toolsepore when they particularly distinguished themselves on the occasion of the action at Jarwah on 30TH March 1859.

Mohammad Buksh, IOM
Daffadar Mohammad Buksh of Hodson's Horse was admitted to 3RD Class IOM in 1859. He displayed gallantry at Jarwah in dismounting and closing in with a fanatic who had kept several Sowars at bay. Daffadar Mohammad Buksh rushed on the man and cut him down, though severely wounded by sabre cut to the head during the struggle.

Indian Order of Merit

Sepoy Mutiny

Abdool Ruhman Khan, IOM
Ressaidar Abdool Ruhman Khan of Punjab Irregular Force was advanced directly to 2ND Class IOM, for conspicuous gallantry in the action on the Kowrialllee River on 25TH April 1859. He was at one time engaged in single-handed with three rebel Sowars, two of them he killed. After this he was most active in collecting the men of his troop, broken by the pursuit, and leading them against scattered parties of rebels.

Hubeeboolah Khan and Fakeer Shah, IOM
Naik Hubeeboolah Khan and Sepoy Fakeer Shah of Punjab Irregular Force were admitted to 3RD Class IOM in 1859, in consideration of their conspicuous gallantry in the action at Kurwania Sota, on which occasion Bukht Khan, the rebel leader during the siege of Delhi, and many of his followers were slain.

Hubeeb Khan, IOM
Subedar Hubeeb Khan of Punjab Irregular Force was admitted to 3RD Class IOM in 1859, for gallant conduct in action during operations to drive out a party of rebels who had established themselves at Khungra-ka-Naka near Musha in the Trans-Raptee District.

Abdool Razak Khan, IOM
Trooper Abdool Razak Khan of Bengal Light Cavalry was admitted to 3RD Class IOM in 1858, and promoted to Jemadar the 2ND Punjab Cavalry with effect from 13TH October 1857, for meritorious conduct during the late mutinies.

Allee Woodee Khan and Goolam Allee Khan, IOM
Risaldar Allee Woodee Khan and Kot-Daffadar Goolam Allee Khan of Bengal Irregular Cavalry were admitted to 3RD Class IOM in 1857, in consideration of their conspicuous gallantry in the field.

The following officers and other ranks were admitted to 3RD Class IOM in 1858, for gallantry and good service rendered to the State.
Naib Ressaidar Sheik Ahmed Buksh, Sowar Nujjo Khan, Sowar Meer Zoolficar Ally, Risaldar Alum Khan, Jemadar Dulel Khan, Jemadar Sheik Abdoola Kha, Subedar Shaick Ibrahim, Naib-Risaldar Mirza Shadee Beg, Havildar Fukeeria, Daffadar Kullunder Beg, Ressaidar Fazil Khan, Jemadar Deedar Buksh Khan, Naib-Risaldar Meer Shamshad Allee and Bargheer Synd Shureef.

Indian Order of Merit

Sepoy Mutiny

Fyz Mohammad Khan, IOM
Risaldar Fyz Mohammad Khan of Sikh Irregular Cavalry was directly advanced to 2ND Class IOM in 1859 in consideration of his conspicuous acts of loyalty to the State and distinguished service in the field,

Meer Modood Buksh, IOM
Risaldar Meer Modood Buksh of Guzerat Irregular Horse was admitted to 3RD Class IOM in 1859, for valuable services rendered by him to the State in effecting the surrender of his relative, rebel leader Captain Fiddeh Hossein, and as recognition of the gallantry and loyalty of his troops.

Shaick Hossein and Jemaun, IOM
Havildar Shaick Hossein and Havildar Jemaun of Madras Horse Artillery were admitted to 3RD Class IOM in 1859. They were always well to the front in action and ready and hard working on all occasions to clear away any difficulty of ground for the passage of the guns. They invariably showed an excellent example to the men of their department during the trying period of service.

The following officers and other ranks were admitted to the 3RD Class IOM, for gallantry and good services rendered by them during the Sepoy Mutiny.
Subedar Syud Mohammad Khan, Subedar Mohammad Raheem Khan, Subedar Sudderooddeen, Havildar Peer Bux, Havildar Sherauz, Havildar Oomer, Naik Hashim Allee, Naik Haous Khan, Naik Goolam Allee, Sepoy Fuzl Khan, Sepoy Khumeed, Sepoy Khaista Khan, Sepoy Shukker Khan, Sepoy Syud Mohammad, Sepoy Sahibadeen, Sepoy Shahzada, Sepoy Peer Bux, Sepoy Mohammad Goal, Sepoy Ghunee, Sepoy Abdul Munaf, Sepoy Hussun, Sepoy Russool, Sheikh Allah Buksh, and Sepoy Ukhter.

Shaick Futteh Mohammad, IOM
Naik Shaick Futteh Mohammad of Bengal Foot Artillery was admitted to the 3RD Class IOM in 1859, in recognition of the loyalty displayed during the early stages of the Mutiny, at a time when desertion or misconduct would possibly have paralysed the efforts of the first force that the enemy met in the field; also for his excellent service in the Azimgarh district.

Ghulam Hussan Khan, IOM
Indian Commandant Ghulam Hussan Khan of Multani Regiment of Cavalry was admitted to the 3RD Class IOM in 1859, in consideration of the admirable services rendered by the Multani Regiment of Cavalry during the Sepoy Mutiny.

Indian Order of Merit

Sepoy Mutiny

Eman Khan, IOM

Subedar Eman Khan of Bombay Light Cavalry was admitted to the 3RD Class IOM in 1859, for faithful and gallant service, especially in the campaign in Malwa and Rajputana against the rebels.

Nasrut Jung Khan, IOM

Woordie-Major Nasrut Jung Khan of Hodson's Horse was admitted to the 3RD Class IOM in 1859. He was present with his corps throughout his service and was always conspicuous by his zeal and gallantry.

Meerza Jewon Beg, IOM

Naib-Risaldar Meerza Jewon Beg of Hodson's Horse was admitted to the 3RD Class IOM in 1859. He was a gallant soldier and has served with great distinction in many fights.

Ahmed Syud Khan and Goolam Nabee Khan, IOM

Risaldar Ahmed Syud Khan and Risaldar Goolam Nabee Khan of Hodson's Horse were admitted to the 3RD Class IOM in 1859, for conspicuous acts of loyalty and gallantry during the Sepoy Mutiny.

Sahadut Ally, IOM

Trooper Sahadut Ally of Bengal Irregular Cavalry was admitted to the 3RD Class IOM in 1859, for conspicuous acts of loyalty and good services rendered by him throughout the Sepoy Mutiny.

The following officers and other ranks of Hyderabad Contingent were admitted to the 3RD Class IOM in 1859, for gallantry and good services in Central India.

Daffadar Meer Kurramut Ali, Daffadar Sultan Khan, Daffadar Mirza Ahmed Ali Beg, Troopers Mohammad Uzgur, Hussun Khan, Meer Hossain Ali, Alluf Khan, Salar Buksh Khan, Fyzoollah Khan, Ruza Beg, Sheik Mohammad Ali, Inayat Ali Beg, Goolam Gouse Khan, Ameer Khan, Nujmodeen Khan, and Sheik Kurramut Khan.

Nawab Khan and Mahboob Khan, IOM

Naib-Risaldar Nawab Khan and Jemadar Mahboob Khan of Sikh Irregular Cavalry were advanced to 2ND Class IOM, for repeated acts of gallantry during the Mutiny.

Shaik Mohammad Khan and Mahmood Khan Bahar, IOM

Risaldar Shaik Mohammad Khan and Risaldar Mahmood Khan Bahar of Mooltani Division Mounted Police were admitted to the 3RD Class IOM in 1859, for gallant services during the Mutiny.

Indian Order of Merit

Sepoy Mutiny

Mirza Hatim Ali Beg, IOM
Jemadar Mirza Hatim Beg of Mooltani Division Mounted Police was admitted to the 3RD Class IOM in 1860, for gallantry in action during the Sepoy Mutiny.

Seweblurn Misser and Ellahee Bux, IOM
Subedar Seweblurn Misser and Jemadar Ellahee Bux of Belooch Battalion were admitted to the 3RD Class IOM in 1860, in consideration of their gallant service and exemplary loyalty to the State.

The following officers of Multani Regiment of Cavalry were admitted to the 3RD Class IOM in 1860, for gallantry and good services during the Sepoy Mutiny. Adjutant Kaleh Khan, Daffadar Shere Mohammad Khan, Daffadar Azeem Beg Khan, and Daffadar Jehan Khan.

The following officers of Nagpore Irregular Force were admitted to the 3RD Class IOM in 1860 as a reward for conspicuous gallantry on various occasions during the Sepoy Mutiny, Jemadar Futteh Mohammad, Havildar Shaik Raheem Buksh, and Jemadar Shaik Ismail.

Dad Mahammad Khan, IOM
Risaldar Dad Mohammad Khan of Belooch Levy was admitted to the 3RD Class IOM in 1860 as a reward for his admirable conduct and exertions in the field during the long and arduous pursuit of the Gwalior rebels in 1858.

The following officers of Madras Native Infantry were admitted to the 3RD Class IOM in 1860, as a reward for conspicuous gallantry on various occasions during the Sepoy Mutiny, Havildar Mohammad Yacoob, Havildar Abdool Kadir, Naik Sheik Abdoola, Naik Abdoola Khan, Privates Uzeem Ooddeen, Mohammad Ali, Mulluq Ahmed, Mahammad Yacoob and Sheik Mohdeen.

The following officers of Punjab Irregular Force were admitted to the 3RD Class IOM in 1860, for gallantry in action with the enemy during the Sepoy Mutiny, Risaldar Huckdad Khan, Kot-Daffadar Meer Ahmed Khan, and Risaldar Abbas Khan.

Noor Khan, IOM
Havildar Noor Khan of Bengal Native Infantry was admitted to 3RD Class IOM, for conspicuous gallantry against the mutineers in 1858.

Indian Order of Merit

Second Afghan War

British Government in 1878 was anxious to counter Russian Influence in Afghanistan and demanded the Afghans to receive a British military mission to Kabul. When the Afghan ruler Sher Ali refused, Britain mounted an expedition mainly composed of Indian soldiers to compel his submission.

The following soldiers were awarded the Indian Order of Merit for their conscious gallantry in action during the Second Afghan War.

Gour Khan, IOM
Sepoy Gour Khan of 14TH Bengal Native Infantry was awarded the 3RD Class IOM for conspicuous gallantry in action on the 21ST November 1878 in the attack on Ali Masjid.

Hassan Khan, IOM
Sepoy Hussan Khan of 24TH (Punjab) Bengal Native Infantry was awarded the 3RD Class IOM for conspicuous gallantry on the 27TH January 1879 in the Bazaar Valley, in coming to the assistance of a British officer, when suddenly attacked by a party of the tribesmen.

Salim Khan, IOM
Ressaidar Salim Khan of 1ST Punjab Cavalry (PFF) was awarded the 2ND Class IOM for conspicuous gallantry in attacking an Afghan fanatic single-handed at Camp Kandahar on the 6TH February 1879.

Fyztulub Khan, IOM
Subedar Fyztulub Khan of 1ST Punjab Infantry (PFF) was awarded the 1ST Class IOM, in consideration of the excellent arrangements made by him when in command of a detachment of his regiment at Fort Abdoola (near Gulistan Karez, Afghanistan), by which two determined attacks by Kakozai and Atchakazai raiders were successfully repulsed on the night of the 9TH January 1879.

He was also chosen to receive a sword offered by Mir Imdad Ali, CSI, for presentation to the native officer or soldier who had distinguished himself most in the 'late' Afghan War.

Jemadar Mir Butt, Naik Peer Mahmud, and Sepoy Gool Mahmud of the Mhairwara Battalion were awarded the 3RD Class IOM for conspicuous gallantry in action with the enemy at Baghao on the 24TH March 1879.

Syed Noor Khan, IOM
Syed Noor Khan Hospital Assistant was awarded the 3RD Class IOM for conspicuous gallantry in action at Kam Dakka on the 22ND April 1879.

Indian Order of Merit

Second Afghan War

Ahmed Khan, IOM
Havildar Ahmed Khan 24TH (Punjab) Bengal Native Infantry was awarded the 3RD Class IOM for conspicuous gallantry in action in the Choora Valley on the 31ST January 1879.

Hakim, IOM
Naik Hakim of 45TH (Rattray's Sikhs) Bengal Native Infantry was awarded the 3RD Class IOM for conspicuous gallantry in action in the Choora Valley on the 31ST January 1879.

Fuzl Achmud Ali, IOM
Jemadar Fuzl Achmud Ali of 29TH (Punjab) Bengal Native Infantry was awarded the 3RD Class IOM for conspicuous gallantry in charging the enemy single-handed during the assault of Zawa in the Zaimukht Country, on the 13TH December 1879.

Zeadeh Khan, IOM
Sowar Zeadeh Khan of 18TH Bengal Cavalry was awarded the 3RD Class IOM for conspicuous gallantry in attacking single-handed a party of marauders between Mandoria and Chapri in the Kurram Valley on the 20TH November 1879, and compelling them to abandon their plunder and disperse.

Bahawaklin Khan, IOM
Ressaidar Bahawaklin Khan of 11TH Bengal Lancers was admitted to 3RD Class IOM for conspicuous gallantry at the storming of a fortified 'Sarai' near Kabul on the 13TH December 1879.

Sher Khan, IOM
Recruit Sher Khan of 21ST (Punjab) Bengal Native Infantry was awarded the 3RD Class IOM for conspicuous gallantry in action at the Sarkai Kotal on the 14TH October 1879.

Fateh Khan, IOM
Recruit Fateh Khan, 21ST (Punjab) Bengal Native Infantry was awarded the 3RD Class IOM for their conspicuous gallantry in action at the Sarkai Kotal on the 14TH October 1879.

Mir Alam Khan, IOM
Risaldar Mir Alam Khan of 1ST Punjab Cavalry (PFF) was awarded the 2ND Class IOM for conspicuous gallantry in the action fought at Saiad-But in Shorewak on the 27TH March 1879.

Indian Order of Merit

Second Afghan War

Zaidulla, IOM
Sowar Zaidulla of Guides Cavalry (PFF) was awarded the 3RD Class IOM for conspicuous gallantry in action at Kabul on the 13TH December 1879.

Shadil Khan, IOM
Kot – Daffadar Shadil Khan of 5TH Punjab Cavalry (PFF) was awarded the 2ND Class IOM for conspicuous gallantry in action at Kabul on the 14TH December 1879.

Juma Khan, IOM
Subedar Juma Khan 5TH Punjab Infantry (PFF) was awarded the 3RD Class IOM for their conspicuous gallantry in action at Kabul on the 23RD December 1879.

Shahgood Khan, IOM
Havildar Shahgood Khan, of 28TH (Punjab) Bengal Native Infantry was awarded the 3RD Class IOM for conspicuous gallantry on the 19TH December 1879 in carrying, at great personal risk, important despatches from Latabad to Jagdalak, through a country at the time wholly in possession of the enemy.

Akbar Khan, IOM
Sepoy Akbar Khan of 28TH (Punjab) Bengal Native Infantry was awarded the 3RD Class IOM for conspicuous gallantry on the 19TH December 1879 in carrying, at great personal risk, important despatches from Latabad to Jagdalak, through a country at the time wholly in possession of the enemy.

The following soldiers of No. 2 (Derajat) Mountain Battery (PFF) were awarded the 3RD Class IOM for conspicuous gallantry in action at Kabul and in the vicinity between the 10TH and the 23RD December 1879, Subedar Nuzzur Khan, Havildar Kootub Deep, Naik Alam Shere and Driver-Naik Fuzl.

Hazrat Shah, IOM
Jemadar Hazrat Shah of 2ND Punjab Cavalry (PFF) was awarded the 3RD Class IOM for conspicuous gallantry in action fought at Shahjui on the 24TH October 1879, during the charge, he cut down one of the leaders of the enemy and was chiefly instrumental in killing their Chief, Sahibjan, whom he was the first to attack.

Indian Order of Merit

Second Afghan War

The following soldiers of 5TH Punjab Cavalry (PFF) were awarded the 3RD Class IOM for conspicuous gallantry in action at Kabul and in the vicinity between the 10TH and the 23RD December 1879, Risaldar Amir Ali Shah, Trumpeter Shah Alum, Sowar Hidayutullah, and Sowar Zeeaoodeen.

Rahim Khan, IOM
Sepoy Rahim Khan of 28TH (Punjab) Bengal Native Infantry was awarded the 3RD Class IOM for conspicuous gallantry in action at Kabul and in the vicinity between the 10TH and the 23RD December 1879.

The following soldiers of Guides Infantry, (PFF) were awarded the 3RD Class IOM for conspicuous gallantry in action at Kabul and in the vicinity between the 10TH and the 23RD December 1879, Naik Hazir, Sepoy Mohammad Shuffi, and Sepoy Gul Shere.

The following soldiers of 5TH Punjab Infantry, (PFF) were all awarded the 3RD Class IOM for conspicuous gallantry in action at Kabul and in the vicinity between the 10TH and the 23RD December 1879, Subedar Baz Gul and Sepoy Akram.

Mansur Khan, IOM
Ressaidar Mansur Khan of 2ND Punjab Cavalry (PFF) was awarded the 3RD Class IOM for conspicuous gallantry in action at Shahjui on the 24TH October 1879, in rescuing Sowar Omar Buksh of the same regiment, whose horse had fallen on him, and one of the assailants he killed and also for gallant conduct in the subsequent charge of the regiment on the same occasion.

Izzat, IOM
Sepoy Izzat of Corps of Guides (PFF) was awarded the 3RD Class IOM for conspicuous gallantry in action near Charasia on the 25TH April 1880.

Mohammad Yunus, IOM
Daffadar Mohammad Yunus Izzat of Corps of Guides (PFF) was awarded the 3RD Class IOM for conspicuous gallantry in action near Charasia on the 25TH April 1880.

Lall Mir Khan, IOM
Private Lall Mir Khan of 29TH Bombay Native Infantry was awarded the 3RD Class IOM for conspicuous gallantry in action at Kaj-Boz near Kelat-i-Ghilzai on the 2ND May 1880, on which occasion he was very forward in the storming of the position taken by the enemy, several of whom were killed.

Indian Order of Merit

Second Afghan War

Saiad Gul, IOM
Havildar Saiad Gul of 3RD Sikh Infantry, (PFF) was awarded the 2ND Class IOM for conspicuous gallantry in action at Mir Kerez on the 10TH December 1879 when with Jemadar Ganesha Singh and Naik Sam Singh, he was very forward in the attack on the enemy's position, setting the men a brilliant example and receiving a severe wound in hand-to-hand conflict with the Afghans.

Haider Khan, IOM
Hospital assistance Haider Khan, attach to Corps of Guides was awarded the 3RD Class IOM for conspicuous gallantry in action at Charasia. On the 25TH April 1880, on which occasion he continued, under a heavy fire, passing across the open from group to group of the skirmishers so as to ensure no wounded man remaining long without assistance. In the performance of this duty he himself fell severally wounded.

Ghulam Jelani, IOM
Daffadar Ghulam Jelani of 1ST Punjab Cavalry (PFF) was awarded the 3RD Class IOM for conspicuous gallantry in action at Patkao Shana on the 1ST July 1880, in singly engaging and killing two of the enemy, armed with swords and rifles, receiving a severe wound in the encounter.

Mowaz Khan, IOM
Lance Daffadar Mowaz Khan 1ST Punjab Cavalry (PFF) was awarded the 3RD Class IOM for conspicuous gallantry in action at Ahmed Khel on the 19TH April 1880, on which occasion, observing two Ghazis, armed with guns and swords, had taken post in a nullah, he dismounted and holding his horse with one hand, engaged both of them, killing one and capturing the other.

Fazal Khan, IOM
Sowar Fazal Khan was 1ST Punjab Cavalry (PFF) awarded the 3RD Class IOM for conspicuous gallantry in action at Patkao Shana on the 1ST July 1880, on which occasion he attacked and killed in succession three of the enemy, himself receiving two wounds in the encounter.

Mohammad Khan, IOM
Jemadar Mohammad Khan of 19TH Bengal Lancers was awarded the 3RD Class IOM for conspicuous gallantry in action at Ahmed Khel on the 19TH April 1880, in defending his commanding officer, from the attacks of the Ghazis by whom he was assailed; also for conspicuous gallantry in action at Patkao Shana on the 1ST July 1880.

Indian Order of Merit

Second Afghan War

Alum Ali Shah, IOM
Daffadar Alum Ali Shah of 19TH Bengal Lancers was awarded the 3RD Class IOM for conspicuous gallantry in action at Ahmed Khel on the 19TH April 1880, in rescuing Daffadar Hookum Singh, who was badly wounded and surrounded by Ghazis.

Mohammad Ishak, IOM
Daffadar Mohammad Ishak of 19TH Bengal Lancers was awarded the 3RD Class IOM for conspicuous gallantry in action at Ahmed Khel on the 19TH April 1880, in charging of the enemy who were attacking Sowar Saidal, killing the two of them and saving the Sowar's life; also in the action at Patkao Shana on the 1ST July 1880, on which occasion he dismounted and singly attacked seven or eight of the enemy, who had taken post behind some rocks, and killed four or five of them.

Kan Jan Khan, IOM
Sowar Kan Jan Khan of 19TH Bengal Lancers was awarded the 3RD Class IOM for conspicuous gallantry in action at Ahmed Khel on the 19TH April 1880, in dismounting and attacking a number of the enemy posted in a deep ditch, jumping into the ditch among them, cutting down of them and saving the life of Gulab Singh, himself receiving a wound in the conflict.

Burkut Ali, IOM
Daffadar Burkut Ali of 3RD Punjab Cavalry (PFF) was awarded the 3RD Class IOM for conspicuous gallantry in charging, during the pursuit of the enemy, three Ghazis, armed with rifles and fixed bayonets, who were attacking Lance-Daffadar Maiboob Ally Khan of the same regiment, killing one of them and saving the Lance- Daffadar's life.

Maroof Shah, IOM
Sepoy Maroof Shah of Bengal Native Infantry was awarded the 3RD Class IOM for conspicuous gallantry in descending from a dandi in which, being wounded, he was being conveyed from the field, and killing two out of four Ghazis who had rushed on him and the kahars who were carrying him.

Hakim, IOM
Sepoy Hakim of 2ND Sikh Infantry (PFF) was awarded the 3RD Class IOM for conspicuous gallantry in joining Naik Davie Singh in a charge on a strong band of Ghazis, one of whom he killed.

Indian Order of Merit

Second Afghan War

Syud Imam Ali Shaheed, IOM
Sowar Syud Imam Ali of 3RD Sind Horse was killed in the defence of the post of Dabrai on the 16TH April 1880, would, if they had lived, have been awarded the 3RD Class IOM.

Elahi Bux, IOM
Private Elahi Bux of 19TH Bombay NI was killed in the defence of the post of Dabrai on the 16TH April 1880, would, if they had lived, have been awarded the 3RD Class IOM.

Rahim Khan, IOM
Naik Rahim Khan of 29TH Bombay Native Infantry was awarded the 3RD Class IOM for conspicuous gallantry in endeavouring, at great personal risk, in August 1880, to convey a message from Kelat-i-Ghilzai to garrison of Kandahar, and then closely besieged by Sardar Mohammad Ayub Khan. In carrying out this duty he was taken prisoner by the enemy.

Lall Mohammad, IOM
Private Lall Mohammad of 29TH Bombay Native Infantry was awarded the 3RD Class IOM for conspicuous gallantry in August 1880 in conveying at great personal risk, a letter from General Primrose at Kandahar to the officer commanding at Chaman, then intervening county being entirely in the hands of the enemy, who had intercepted and put to death several messengers previously despatched on the same errand.

Russul Khan, IOM
Lance Naik Russul Khan of Poona Horse was awarded the 3RD Class IOM for conspicuous gallantry in action at Deh Khojan near Kandahar on the 16TH August 1880, on which occasion he charged down a street of the village in order to clear the way for the late Brigadier General Brooke and a small part of the 7TH Fusiliers, who were at the time surrounded by the enemy.

Mohammad Seedick Khan, IOM
Lance Naik Mohammad Seedick Khan Horse was awarded the 3RD Class IOM for conspicuous gallantry in action at Deh Khojan near Kandahar on the 16TH August 1880, on which occasion he charged down a street of the village in order to clear the way for the late Brigadier General Brooke and a small part of the 7TH Fusiliers, who were at the time surrounded by the enemy.

Indian Order of Merit

Second Afghan War

The following cavalrymen of Poona Horse were awarded the 3RD Class IOM for conspicuous gallantry in action near the banks of the Argandab on the 28TH July 1880, when serving with the detachment sent out to help in Kandahar the remnants of Brigadier General Burrow's force, then retreating from Maiwand, Daffadar Hamudoollah Khan, Daffadar Akbar Nowaz Khan, Naik Mohammad Esack Khan, Lance Naik Goolshair Khan, Sowar Ameer Khan and Sowar Shaik Hoossain.

The following cavalrymen of Sind Horse were awarded the 3RD Class IOM for conspicuous gallantry during the retreat from Maiwand on the 27TH July 1880, in keeping off then parties of the enemy's cavalry who were in pursuit, and saving the lives of many wounded and exhausted men, Ressaidar Shaik Jamal, Kot Daffadar Abdoola Khan, and Daffadar Sarfaraz Khan.

The following miners of 2 Co. Bombay Sappers & Miners were awarded the 3RD Class IOM for conspicuous gallantry in the attack on Deh Khojah near Kandahar on the 16TH August 1880, Lance Naik Shaik Abdoola, Private Abdoola Khan, and Private Said Mohammad.

Sirbuland Khan, IOM
Sowar Sirbuland Khan of 1ST Punjab Cavalry (PFF) was awarded the 3RD Class IOM for conspicuous gallantry in at Patkao Shana in the Logar Valley on the 1ST July 1880, on which occasion he singly charged three of the enemy, armed with guns, killing two of them and himself receiving a severe gun-shot wound from the third.

Burma Deen, IOM
Sowar Burma Deen of 3RD Bombay Light Cavalry was awarded the 3RD Class IOM for conspicuous gallantry in at Maiwand on the 27TH July 1880.

Shaik Amir Ali, IOM
Woodie-Major Shaik Amir Ali of 3RD Sind Horse was awarded the 3RD Class IOM for conspicuous gallantry for exhibiting great coolness and presence of mind before the enemy during the retreat from Maiwand on the 27TH July 1880, and for his energy and gallantry at the attack on Deh Khoja near Kandahar on the 16TH August 1880; and for gallantry displayed on the battle of Mazra, Kandahar, on the 1ST September 1880.

Indian Order of Merit

Second Afghan War

Hyder Khan, IOM
Subedar Major Hyder Khan of 30TH Bombay Native Infantry was awarded the 3RD Class IOM for conspicuous gallantry for exhibiting great coolness during the retreat from Maiwand on the 27TH July 1880.

Chuddo Beg, IOM
Bugler Chuddo Beg of 30TH Bombay Native Infantry was awarded the 3RD Class IOM for conspicuous gallantry for exhibiting great coolness during the retreat from Maiwand on the 27TH July 1880

Goolam Mahammad Shaheed, IOM
Private Goolam Mahammad was killed in that action would if he had lived, have been awarded the 3RD Class IOM: The widow of Goolam Mohammad will be allowed to draw the Order of Merit pension.

Mazr Ali, IOM
Kot Daffadar Mazr Ali of 1ST Bengal Cavalry was awarded the 3RD Class IOM for conspicuous gallantry in action at Bhagwana in the Chardeh Valley, near Kabul, on then 11TH December 1879, at great personal risk, after his horse had been shot under him, seized the Malik of Bhagwana, who had treacherously attempted the life of the Lieutenant-General.

Bahadur Khan, IOM
Jemadar Bahadur Khan was awarded the IOM in 1892 for service in the Northern Chin Hills during the Siyin-Nwengal uprising when the Chins rose up in rebellion against the British proposals to disarm the tribes.

1ST World War
Aden

On the outbreak of war with Turkey on October 31ST 1914, reports were received that the Turks were gathering in some strength in the Sheik Saad peninsula, and were contemplating against the Aden Protectorate. The 29TH Indian Infantry Brigade, on their way to Suez, Egypt, was diverted to capture Sheikh Saad peninsula. A landing was affected on November 10TH and the enemy was driven inland, abandoning their field guns. Next day, Turbah Fort and other enemy works in the neighbourhood were demolished.

Indian Order of Merit

1ST World War

Aden

Shah Nawaz Khan, IOM
Havildar Shah Nawaz Khan of 109TH Infantry was awarded the 2ND Class IOM for gallantry on the 4TH and 5TH July 1915, while in charge of a machine-gun section. It was mainly to his exertion that the guns were got up to Lahej. He handled his men well throughout the action and showed much discretion in checking one or two rushes.

Gul Baz, IOM
Lance Naik Gul Baz of 126TH Baluchis was awarded the 2ND Class IOM. This non-commissioned officer, while wounded, was of the greatest assistance in steadying the men during the action on the 4TH and 5TH July 1915.

Bahadur Shah and Allah Khan, IOM
Naik Bahadur Shah, Sepoy Allah Khan, were awarded 53RD Sikhs the 2ND Class IOM for conspicuous gallantry on 28TH August 1915, during operations in the vicinity of Aden. After three other signallers had been shot down, these two men, in spite of a heavy fire directed at them, succeeded in correctly transmitting a message to their commanding officer.

Faiz Talab, IOM
Jemadar Faiz Talab of 53RD Sikhs was awarded the 2ND Class IOM for conspicuous gallantry on 28TH August 1915.

Mohammad Khan, IOM
Jemadar Mohammad Khan was awarded the 2ND Class IOM for conspicuous gallantry and courage in a skirmish near As-sela in the vicinity of Aden on the 7TH October 1915. He showed great dash and gallantry in leading an attack on the enemy of Arabs armed with rifles. He killed three and wounded another but was shot by a fifth.

Zaman Khan, IOM
Risaldar Zaman Khan of 26TH Cavalry was awarded the 2ND Class IOM for conspicuous gallantry in the field. He recovered the body of a wounded non-commissioned officer under heavy fire at about 20 yards range. Throughout the campaign he has shown great coolness and courage under fire on several occasions, and has set a splendid example to his men.

Indian Order of Merit

1ST World War

Aden

Mohammad Amin, IOM
Ressaidar Mohammad Amin of 26TH Cavalry was awarded the 2ND Class IOM for conspicuous gallantry in action on the 6TH July 1917, in rescuing a trumpeter of his troop who was lying stunned from a fall from his horse. Under heavy fire from the enemy at 150 yards range, Mohammad Amin dismounted, placed the trumpeter on a horse and carried him to safety.

Fazl Ahmed, IOM
Naik Fazl Ahmed of 69TH Punjabis was awarded the 2ND Class IOM for gallantry in action on the 11TH September 1917. He was conspicuous in his brilliant inspiring courage. He was killed in an attempt to carry a wounded British officer out of action.

Sher Mohammad, IOM
Lance Naik Sher Mohammad of 69TH Punjabis was awarded the 2ND Class IOM for gallantry in action on the 11TH September 1917, in trying to rescue an officer, till he himself was wounded in many places.

East Africa

The East African Campaign was a series of battles and guerrilla actions, which started in German East Africa and spread to portions of Mozambique, Northern Rhodesia, British East Africa, Uganda and the Belgian Congo. The campaign all but ended in November 1917, when the Germans entered Portuguese East Africa and continued the campaign living off Portuguese supplies.

The largest concentration of German troops in the continent in East Africa was unable to fight an aggressive war. The main objective for the German forces in East Africa was to force Allied governments to keep military forces and supplies in Africa, rather than sending them to fight in Europe.

The German Commander Lettow-Vorbeck was cut off and could entertain no hope of a decisive victory. His aim was purely to keep as many British forces diverted to his pursuit for as long as possible and to make the British expend the largest amount of resources in men, shipping and supplies to his pursuit. Although succeeding in diverting in excess of 200,000 Indian and South African troops to pursue his forces and garrison German East Africa in his wake, he failed to divert additional Allied manpower from the European Theatre after 1916.

Indian Order of Merit

1ˢᵀ World War

East Africa

Gul Mohammad, IOM
Naik Gul Mohammad of 29TH Punjabis was awarded the 2ND Class IOM for the conspicuous resourcefulness and pluck displayed by him during the action at Tsavo River, on the 6TH September 1914, in bringing up reinforcements, in the course which he was twice wounded.

Sher Baz Shaheed, IOM
Subedar Sher Baz of 29TH Punjabis was awarded the 2ND Class IOM for the conspicuous courage and gallantry during the action at Tsavo River, in attempting, though wounded himself, to drag under cover Naik Gul Mohammad of the same regiment who was severally wounded. During this brave attempt to save a comrade, Subedar Sher Baz lost his own life.

Fazal Khan, IOM
Sepoy Fazal Khan of 101ST Grenadiers was awarded the 2ND Class IOM for an action at Tanga on 3RD November 1914. He remained with Lt. Hughes, the Adjutant of his regiment, and two other men until they were all killed. He refused to leave Lt. Hughes until he was assured that the officer was dead and then brought away the latter's sword with him.

Sewaz Khan Shaheed, IOM
Sepoy Sewaz Khan of 101ST Grenadiers was awarded the 2ND Class IOM posthumously in action at Mito Andi, on the 15TH May 1915. He was with a party of men clearing jungle when he discovered and enemy patrol. He at once led his men against them and pursued them. Being somewhat in advance of his comrades, he was wounded. He would allow no-one to attend him but insisted on their following the enemy, saying 'Leave me alone; your business to catch the enemy'. On their return they found that he had bled to death.

Ghulam Haidar, IOM
Subedar Ghulam Haidar of 130TH Baluchis was awarded the 2ND Class IOM, posthumously, for the conspicuous courage and gallantry on 5TH May 1915 at Mbuyuni. Whilst in charge of a patrol of 15 men he boldly led them to attack a party of the enemy who were 100 strong with three machine-guns. The conduct of Subedar Ghulam Haidar was most prompt and gallant. He was wounded and died of his wounds the next day.

Indian Order of Merit

1ST World War

East Africa

Alim Khan, IOM
Lance Naik Alim Khan of 127TH Baluchis was awarded the 3RD Class IOM, who discovered the location of the enemy position covering the Ruwa River on 20TH March 1916. Walking round a thicket, he ran into a picquet, so he knelt down and shot four; the fifth escaped.

Wazir Khan, IOM
Ressaidar Wazir Khan of 17TH Cavalry was awarded the 2ND Class IOM for conspicuous gallantry in action with the enemy on the 16TH February 1916. Ressaidar Wazir Khan was left in charge of the main body while an advanced party engaged the enemy. The advance party had to retire and in a general action which ensued Jemadar Wazir Khan, to whom the command of the party devolved, displayed courage and ability.

Sher Baz, IOM
Subedar Major Sher Baz of 27TH Mountain Battery was awarded the 2ND Class IOM for gallantry and devotion to duty in the field, and eventually awarded the OBI.

Khoda Baksh, IOM
Havildar Khoda Baksh of 55TH Rifles was awarded the 2ND Class IOM during the fighting near Newala on 21ST November 1916, in the attempt to cut off Von Lettow-Vorbeck's column as it neared that village.

Saif Ali, IOM
Lance Naik Saif Ali of Burma Military Police was awarded the 3RD Class IOM, for gallantry and devotion to duty in the field on 10TH August 1916.

They following soldiers of 2ND Kashmir Rifle were awarded the 3RD Class IOM, for gallantry and devotion to duty in the field on 21ST November 1916, Sepoy Rahim Ali, Havildar Atta Ullah, and Sepoy Hafiz Ali.

Jan Gul, IOM
Subedar Jan Gul of 26TH Punjabis was awarded the 2ND Class IOM on 27TH September 1916, for conspicuous gallantry and courageous example in leading his men across the open up to 300 yards from the enemy's position at Lindi and maintaining them for three hours under very heavy fire.

Indian Order of Merit

1ST World War

East Africa

Puma Khan, IOM
Naik Puma Khan of 40TH Pathans was awarded the 3RD Class IOM, for gallantry in action on 27TH September 1916. He maintained his machine-gun for three hours under heavy frontal machine-gun and rifle fire 300 yards from the enemy's position. During this time, the enemy brought up another machine-gun on his right flank in order to enfilade the line, but Naik Puma Khan silenced this machine-gun every time it opened fire, until he was wounded.

Munsib Dar, IOM
Sepoy Munsib Dar 129TH Baluchis was awarded the 2ND Class IOM for conspicuous gallantry in action on the 7TH December 1916. At Kibata, he was continually with his guns which were situated in the open under heavy shell and machine-gun fire. He kept down the fire of two hostile guns and stopped their being employed against a redoubt. He has since died of his wounds.

Allah Ditta Shaheed, IOM
Jemadar Allah Ditta of 30TH Punjabis was awarded the 2ND Class IOM for the action on Rufiji River on 7TH January 1917. The Punjabis crossed the Rufiji at night and single handily engaged a superior force of Germans and drove them back securing a bridgehead on the other side of the river. During this action Jemadar Allah Ditta the commander of the Punjabi Muslim Platoon dropped dead.

Mohammad Afzal, IOM
Subedar Mohammad Afzal of 124TH Baluchis was awarded the 2ND Class IOM. He commanded the party of Mahsuds of the 124 Baluchis and earned the award of IOM for fighting at Kibata on the 15TH December 1916, in which he was wounded during a bombing attack.

Ayub Khan, IOM
Jemadar Ayub Khan of 124TH Baluchis was awarded the 2ND Class IOM. He was badly wounded in the fighting at the Lodgement, Kibata, on 15TH December 1916, when he acted with great gallantry in a bomb attack.

Ghulam Khan, IOM
Lance Naik Ghulam Khan of 124TH Baluchis was awarded the 3RD Class IOM, for gallantry in action at Kibata, on 15TH December 1916. The attack was a success.

Indian Order of Merit

1ST World War

East Africa

The following soldiers of 127TH Baluchis were awarded the 2ND Class IOM for conspicuous gallantry while serving with the East African Expeditionary Force during in the Great War, Havildar Ghulam Mohammad, Havildar Sarfaraz, and Sepoy Karam Ilahi.

Jabar Khan and Abdulla Kha, IOM
Havildar Jabar Khan and Sepoy Abdulla Khan of 127TH Infantry were awarded the 3RD Class IOM, for gallantry in action at Kibata, on 15TH December 1916, when they acted in great gallantry in the bombing party.

Sarbuland, IOM
Subedar Sarbuland of 127TH Infantry was awarded the 2ND Class IOM for gallantry in action at Kibata, on 15TH December 1916. He was promoted to 1ST Class IOM for gallantry in East Africa.

Mirjan, IOM
Sepoy Mirjan of 129TH Baluchis was awarded the 3RD Class IOM, for gallantry in action fought on the night of the 15TH -16TH near Kibata, when he formed one of a bombing party.

Mirza Khan, IOM
Havildar Mirza Khan of 129TH Baluchis was awarded the 2ND Class IOM for gallantry in action fought on the night of the 15TH -16TH near Kibata, when he formed one of a bombing party. He led his men with great gallantry and the attack was a success.

Fazal Ali, IOM
Lance Naik Fazal Ali of 130TH Baluchis were awarded the 3RD Class IOM for serving with the East African Expeditionary Force during in the Great War.

Malik Aman, IOM
Jemadar Malik Aman of 130TH Baluchis were awarded the 3RD Class IOM for serving with the East African Expeditionary Force during in the Great War.

Sher Akhmed, IOM
Jemadar Sher Akhmed was awarded the 3RD Class IOM for the action at Rumbo on the 18TH April 1917, when the regiment finally had to retire and was closely pressed, Sher Akhmed commanding the escort of the guns, though wounded, refused to leave the near bank of Ngaura and stood by Captain Foley till the last porter had crossed.

Indian Order of Merit

1ST World War

East Africa

Salim Khan and Sher Baz, IOM
Havildar Salim Khan, Naik Sher Baz of 57TH Rifles was awarded the 3RD Class IOM, for serving with the East African Expeditionary Force during in the Great War.

Wahid Ali Khan, IOM
Subedar Wahid Ali Khan of 5TH Infantry was awarded the 2ND Class IOM for conspicuous gallantry in action on the 30TH June 1917. He commanded his platoon with great gallantry and skill against a superior enemy force at close range. Though exposed to very heavy rifle and machine-gun fire, he beat off numerous enemy attacks and counter-charged them. Throughout the action, though wounded, he displayed great courage and devotion to duty.

Mohammad Suleiman Khan, IOM
Acting Subedar Major Mohammad Suleiman Khan of 17TH Infantry was awarded the 2ND Class IOM, for conspicuous gallantry in action on the 5TH August 1917. He defeated an enemy post capturing two Askaris (African Soldiers) and four rifles. Acting Subedar Major Mohammad Suleiman Khan was acting independently and was twice wounded during the action.

Shah Nawaz, IOM
Lance Naik Shah Nawaz of 21ST Punjabis was awarded the 3RD Class IOM for conspicuous gallantry in action on the 5TH August 1917. When all the remainder of his machine-gun detachment had become casualties, he worked his gun with perfect coolness for about two hours, within sixty yards of the enemy.

Gul Zaman, IOM
Subedar Gul Zaman of 40TH Pathans was awarded the 2ND Class IOM for conspicuous gallantry and energy under fire on the 19TH July 1917 at Narungombe. When all the British officers had become casualties, he rallied his men and took them out of action. He is an excellent hard-working officer and has done good work throughout the war.
(Gul Zaman was one of those who represented the regiment in the Victory Parade through London in August 1919)

Indian Order of Merit

1ˢᵀ World War

East Africa

Sarbuland, IOM
Subedar Major Sarbuland of 127ᵀᴴ Infantry was awarded the 2ᴺᴰ Class IOM for conspicuous gallantry in action on the 5ᵀᴴ August 1917, when he led his platoon in a most gallant manner, showing fine example to his men under trying circumstances with complete indifference to personal danger. When all his British officers were missing or wounded, he continued to handle his men with judgement and coolness till the retirement was affected. (He won the 1ˢᵀ Class IOM award at Nanuati in East Africa).

Munshi Khan, IOM
Jemadar Munshi Khan of 18ᵀᴴ Infantry was awarded the 3ᴿᴰ Class IOM for conspicuous gallantry while serving with the East African Expeditionary Force.

Sardar Khan, IOM
Gunner Sardar Khan of 27ᵀᴴ Mountain Battery was awarded the 2ᴺᴰ Class IOM for conspicuous gallantry on the 18ᵀᴴ October 1917 in carrying out of action a wounded British officer under heavy fire. He was wounded but returned to the firing line, bringing away telephone equipment though all the time exposed to very heavy fire from the advancing enemy.

Karam Ilahi, IOM
Havildar Karam Ilahi of 33ᴿᴰ Punjabis was awarded the 2ᴺᴰ Class IOM for conspicuous gallantry in bringing his machine-gun into action under heavy fire and defending it until seriously wounded.

Abdul Khan, IOM
Havildar Abdul Khan of 5ᵀᴴ Bhopal Infantry was awarded the 2ᴺᴰ Class IOM for conspicuous gallantry in an encounter with an enemy patrol on the 19ᵀᴴ August 1917. After the non-commissioned in charge had been wounded, he took command of his patrol and successfully charged and drove off the enemy.

Indian Order of Merit

1ST World War

Egypt & Palestine

The history of Egypt under the British lasts from 1882, when it was occupied by British forces during the Anglo-Egyptian War, until 1956, when the last British forces withdrew in accordance with the Anglo-Egyptian agreement of 1954. On the outbreak of war with Turkey on October 31ST 1914, the Indian troops were despatched for the defence of Egypt and the protection of the Suez Canal. The Egyptian Expeditionary Force formed on 10TH March 1916 under the command of General Archibald Murray from the Mediterranean Expeditionary Force and the Force in Egypt (1914–15), at the beginning of the Sinai and Palestine Campaign of the First World War. Serving alongside were the 'Imperial Service Troops'.

Ali Khan, IOM
Sepoy Ali Khan of Bikaner Camel Corps was awarded the 3RD Class IOM for conspicuous gallantry throughout the engagement at Bir-el-Nuss, Egypt on the 20TH November 1914, during which he displayed self-reliance and power of command of a very high order and by his example encouraged his comrades, all of whom were young soldiers.

Safdar Ali Shaheed and Sher Khan, IOM
Naik Safdar Ali and Sepoy Sher Khan of 62ND Punjabis were awarded the 2ND Class IOM for conspicuous bravery in the action near Tussum in the Suez Canal operations on 3RD February 1915. These two men led their comrades down a steep sandy bank practically to the water level, under a practically hot fire, to charge the enemy who were landing from a boat. Sepoy Sher Khan was severally wounded six yards from the boat. In the final advance to the boat, Naik Safdar Ali was again in advance of his comrades and was hit one yard from the water's edge. He died few minutes later.

Mohammad Arbi, IOM
Subedar Mohammad Arbi occupied a post on a hill with a small detachment in action on the 19TH November 1917. The party was heavily shelled and was attacked three times. The position was an important one and it was due to the courage, skill and initiative of Subedar Mohammad Arbi that it was held.

Indian Order of Merit

1ST World War

Egypt & Palestine

Mohammad Afzin, IOM

Havildar Mohammad Afzin of 92ND Punjabis was awarded the 3RD Class IOM for conspicuous gallantry near Serapeum in operations on the Suez Canal on the 4TH February 1915. He was wounded in the side when close to trench of the enemy, who had made signs of surrender and apparently treacherously fired on the company he was with. He remained with his section though wounded and when his company took up a position to engage the enemy he kept his men steady under hot fire and directed their fire with coolness and pluck. He was present at the final surrender of the enemy and marched back with the prisoners to camp, refusing any attention to his wound until he arrived there.

Niamat Ali Khan, IOM

Captain Niamat Ali Khan of Jind Infantry was awarded the 3RD Class IOM for conspicuous gallantry and devotion to duty while serving with Egyptian Expeditionary Force. On 15TH December 1916, an ambuscade patrol of the 57TH Rifles having discovered the enemy at Hui in very superior numbers, had retired. The officer was ordered to take 50 rifles, Jind, with him and proceed in that direction. At a point about four miles from camp, this party came in touch with the enemy. The latter opened very heavy fire from front and flank. The enemy being in superior numbers, this small party (including 25 rifles of the 57TH who had met them) was forced to retire, which they steadily and in good order for about two miles and then took up position covering camp and holding it until relieved. This party fought the whole day and checked the enemy's advance. It was due to this officer's skilful and able holding of his force that the enemy's advance was checked.

Khan Mohammad Khan

Subedar Khan Mohammad Khan of Khairpur Escort was awarded the 3RD Class IOM, for devotion to duty in the field on the night of the 4TH -5TH November 1917, when in command of patrol which was attacked by superior enemy forces with machine guns, when his skilful handling of his men he prevented the enemy from rounding up his patrol and eventually drove them off after an action lasting two hours. (Subedar Khan Mohammad Khan was attached to the Alwar State Infantry; he is the only IOM to the Alwar Infantry or to the Khairpur Escort).

Indian Order of Merit

1ST World War

Egypt & Palestine

Lal Khan, IOM
Subedar Lal Khan of 58TH Rifles was associated with Subedar Mohammad Arbi in the action on the 17TH November 1917, described above, and shared with him the success in seizing and retaining the position mentioned for which he was awarded the 3RD Class IOM.

Shahzad Khan, IOM
Sowar Shahzad Khan of 2ND Lancers was awarded the 2ND Class IOM for gallantry and devotion to duty on the 17TH June 1918. During the attack by two troops under Ressaidar Imdad Khan on a party of the enemy, Ressaidar Imdad Khan's horse was shot. Sowar Shahzad Khan dismounted and gave up his horse to the Ressaidar. Having done so, he went on foot to the assistance of Jemadar Mohammad Yusuf Khan, whose horse had been shot and the Jemadar himself wounded in the thigh, extricated him from the dead horse, carried him on his back into thick scrub, caught a loose horse, placed the wounded Jemadar on it and brought him back to the support squadron. This occurred under continues machine-gun fire at about 150 yards from the enemy.

Rahim Khan, IOM
Subedar Rahim Khan of 101 Grenadiers was awarded the 3RD Class IOM. On the night of the 30TH -31ST May 1918, he displayed much skill and initiative in leading his patrol forward to surround an enemy post. At the head of his men, he personally sprang upon the enemy sentry, silenced and disarmed him without raising an alarm, with the result that the total enemy post of four was brought in, although the neighbouring occupied enemy posts were within 150 and 200 yards of either flank. He set a splendid example of dash and plucks to his men.

Atta Ullah Khan, IOM
Jemadar Atta Ullah Khan of 36TH Jacob's Horse was awarded the 3RD Class IOM. Jemadar Atta Ullah Khan with seven other ranks on the 26TH August, on patrol duty, encountered about twenty of the enemy in thick scrub. Khan immediately galloped at them killed two and captured one. Meanwhile, one of the patrol horses which had pinned its rider under it. Three of the enemy were standing over this rider with levelled rifles. Jemadar Atta Ullah Khan galloped up, dispersed the enemy and released his man.

Indian Order of Merit

1ST World War

Egypt & Palestine

Abdul Rahim, IOM

Assistant Surgeon Abdul Rahim was awarded the 3RD Class IOM, for conspicuous bravery and devotion to duty. On the 19TH April 1918, during an attack, he frequently exposed himself to heavy shell fire in search of wounded men. When stretcher-bearers failed to find an officer who was severely wounded, he went into the firing line and brought him in himself.

Dur Khan Rahim, IOM

Jemadar Dur Khan Rahim of Scinde Horse was awarded the 3RD Class IOM. On the 28TH May 1918, he was ordered to lie up with a fighting patrol, with the object of destroying enemy parties who had been continuously firing into the piquet. When he captured three of the enemy, he was fired on at close range by a party of the enemy. He promptly gave the order to charge the enemy, which fled in all directions. The promptness and determination with which he closed on the enemy was only a fine example of courage and good leadership, but also an incentive to his men to attack with the bayonet whenever possible.

Malik Khan Mohammad Khan, IOM

Risaldar Malik Khan Mohammad Khan of 36TH Jacob's Horse was awarded the 3RD Class IOM. On the 28TH May 1918, when on outpost duty, he was in command of the right picquet. While on his way with an orderly to visit a picquet on his right, he observed through his glasses three men in the bushes about 800 yards away and thinking they belonged to a neighbouring regiment, he rode towards them. These men then disappeared, but he came in sight of them again about seventy to eighty yards distant and saw that they were the enemy. He immediately drew his revolver and rode straight at them. They raised their rifles to fire and then dropped and surrendered. All were well-armed and equipped.

Maida Khan, IOM

Havildar Maida Khan of 54TH Sikhs was awarded the 3RD Class IOM. On the night of the 12TH-13TH August 1918, Maida Khan though wounded at the enemy's wire, showed great courage and determination. He took charge of the remainder of his platoon when half were killed or wounded and his platoon commander had been killed. He himself was first through the wire and he continued to lead his platoon until the arrival at the concentration point.

Indian Order of Merit

1ST World War

Egypt & Palestine

Ahmed Din, IOM
Subedar Ahmed Din of 101ST Grenadiers was awarded the 3RD Class IOM. On the night of the 12TH-13TH August, he commanded a platoon in an attack on the enemy's position. After cutting the wire under machine gun fire he charged and captured the right hand work and got behind the centre work. He then led a charge the work from the rear, capturing an officer and 13 men. Throughout the operation he showed gallant leadership and utter personal disregard for danger.

Amir Hussein, IOM
Naik Amir Hussein of 123RD Rifles was awarded the 3RD Class IOM, for conspicuous gallantry during the raid on the enemy trenches on the morning of the 13TH August 1918. Naik Amir Hussein formed a part of a screen of scouts who proceeded in front of the attacking party. When within a hundred yards of the enemy trenches, he pushed forward right up to within a few yards of the enemy to reconnoitre a small wadi which ran into the enemy line. In spite of heavy machine-gun and rifle fire, Naik Amir Hussein made thorough reconnaissance of the wadi and enemy works behind, bringing back most valuable information which greatly assisted the launching of the attack. (The only IOM to the battalion for the Great War)

Mir Muhiyddin, IOM
Regimentdar Mir Muhiyddin of Mysore Lancers was awarded the 3RD Class IOM, for conspicuous gallantry, during the action on the 26TH October 1918. Mir Muhiyddin showed great coolness and devotion to duty under very heavy fire, during a charge against a strongly held enemy position. Though wounded he continued to perform his duties.

Ghulam Shah, IOM
Jemadar Ghulam Shah of 51ST Sikhs was awarded the 3RD Class IOM. On the night of the 20TH-21ST September 1918, he was sent with two sections in support of a small picquet up the hill. The enemy opened a heavy fire and the Jamadar's party was greatly out-numbered. He decided, and instructed the party to shout continuously at the top of their voices so as to convey an impression of strength, charged up the hill. The ruse was entirely successful and the enemy fled, 1 officer and 14 men being captured, with 2 machine-guns and 3 automatic rifles. Jemadar Ghulam Shah's action with his very small force was extremely outstanding.

Indian Order of Merit

1ST World War

Egypt & Palestine

Sher Mohammad Khan, IOM
Subedar Sher Mohammad Khan of 2ND Patiala Infantry was awarded the 3RD Class IOM, for gallant and meritorious service. During recent operations he was badly shot through the wrist on the first day the regiment went into action. Though suffering considerable pain he refused to be evacuated and remained on duty throughout the operations another five days.

Mirzaman Khan Shaheed, IOM
Jemadar Mirzaman Khan of 38TH Central India Horse was awarded the 3RD Class IOM. On the 6TH September 1918, Jemadar Mirzaman Khan was in command of the leading half squadron when they charged the enemy, routed them and inflicted considerable casualties. When the squadron leader was subsequently disabled, he took command of the squadron which he handled with marked skill. (Mirzaman Khan had already been brought to notice for an action on 7TH June 1918, near Ghoranuye bridge-head after a Turkish patrol met and killed a small reconnoitring party. Mirzaman Khan heard the firing and galloped to some high ground, from where he saw the party being surrounded and wounded. He immediately called up the rest of his platoon and attacked the Turks. Though the Turks rallied and fought off the attack, Mirzaman led his men back and brought in the wounded men, who subsequently died.

Ghulam Mohammad, IOM
Lance Naik Ghulam Mohammad of 72ND Punjabis was awarded the 3RD Class IOM, for conspicuous bravery and devotion to duty. During the advance on 19TH September 1918, after his commander had been killed, Lance Naik Ghulam Mohammad rushed forward with Colour Havildar Saif Ali and forced a strong enemy post to surrender, capturing 20 prisoners. His prompt action saved the lives of many of his comrades.

Saif Ali, IOM
Havildar Saif Ali of 72ND Punjabis was awarded the 3RD Class IOM, for conspicuous bravery and devotion to duty. During the advance on 19TH September 1918, after his commander had been killed, Colour Havildar Saif Ali rushed forward with Lance Naik Ghulam Mohammad, and forced a strong enemy post to surrender, capturing 20 prisoners. His prompt action saved the lives of many of his comrades.

Indian Order of Merit

1ST World War

Egypt & Palestine

Ashraf Khan, IOM
Havildar Ashraf Khan of 92ND Punjabis was awarded the 2ND Class IOM, for gallantry and dash on the 19TH September 1918, during the advance on the foothills. Havildar Ashraf Khan, with two sections, was sent to work round a hill on the enemy's flank, fire from which was delaying the main attack. Under heavy enfilade fire he advanced up the hill, on approaching the crest, ordered rifle-grenade overhead fire and at the same moment charged, capturing the hill and taking several prisoners. During the charge he was seriously wounded. His gallant action was mainly responsible for the success of the main attack.

Zaman Khan, IOM
Subedar Zaman Khan of 92ND Punjabis was awarded the 2ND Class IOM, for conspicuous gallantry on the 19TH September 1918. During the attack and after first objective had been taken, the enemy opened fire from a hill on the right. Subedar Zaman Khan on his own initiative immediately disposed his platoon and attacked under heavy fire, driving the enemy from the hill, thus securing the flank of the advance. His coolness and ability throughout were of the highest order.

Mian Khan, IOM
Sepoy Mian Khan of 101ST Grenadier was awarded the 3RD Class IOM, for conspicuous gallantry and devotion to duty during an attack on the 20TH September 1918. When the first attack had reached within 500 yards of a village, the gun which Colour Havildar Shah Mohammad had, up to then been operating ceased firing and Sepoy Mian Khan on seeing the Havildar was lying senseless across the gun, dashed across the open ground swept by heavy cross and frontal machine-gun and rifle fire, and pulled the wounded man aside. Finding all the ammunition was expended, he coolly proceeded to collect ammunition from the dead and wounded nearby. He remained at the gun until the village was captured.

Buta Khan Ali, IOM
Naik Buta Khan Ali of 92ND Punjabis was awarded the 3RD Class IOM, for conspicuous bravery and initiative on the 19TH September 1918 in an attack in which he was wounded.

Indian Order of Merit

1ST World War

Egypt & Palestine

Buta Khan Ali, IOM
Havildar Mohammad Sawar of 93RD Burma Infantry was awarded the 3RD Class IOM. On the 19TH September 1918, Colour Havildar Mohammad Sawar showed conspicuous gallantry during the passage through the enemy's barrage, one complete section his platoon was wiped out. He, however, collected and organised his platoon under intense fire with the greatest coolness and thereby set a fine example to him men.

Shah Mohammad, IOM
Havildar Shah Mohammad of 101ST Grenadiers was awarded the 3RD Class IOM, for conspicuous gallantry during an attack on the 20TH September 1918. When his officer was wounded, Colour Havildar Shah Mohammad command and proceeded with the advance, exhibiting splendid leadership and initiative. Owing to heavy casualties, his Lewis gun section would have remained out of action had he not taken it on himself until he was brought down with a broken leg. Even then he continued to fire his gun until he had expended all his ammunition, when he fainted from loss of blood.

Rahim Ali, IOM
Havildar Rahim Ali of 125TH Rifles was awarded the 3RD Class IOM, for conspicuous gallantry and devotion to duty during the attack on 19TH September 1918. Colour Havildar Rahim Ali collected parties from various companies, re-organised them and continued to advance over the enemy trenches, although out of touch with his supports. His boldness and initiative undoubtedly contributed to the capture by handful of the men of a battery of howitzers, one field gun and the battery personnel including its officers.

Abdul Karim, IOM
Lance Daffadar Abdul Karim of 34TH Poona Horse was awarded the 3RD Class IOM, for conspicuous gallantry and devotion to duty when in command of a patrol of three other ranks on then 20TH September 1918. He advanced under heavy machine-gun fire although twice wounded and one of his men had been killed. He did not withdraw until he had gained his objective and subsequently rejoined his squadron bringing in useful information.

Indian Order of Merit

1ST World War

Egypt & Palestine

Suleman Khan, IOM
Jemadar Suleman Khan of 5TH Cavalry was awarded the 2ND Class IOM for gallantry and d initiative on the 20TH September 1918, when in command of the vanguard troop. He led his troop, charging the enemy five times and captured 300 prisoners, 7 Lorries and a motor car. His utter disregard of danger greatly inspired his men and his action materially assisted the operations.

Dost Mohammad, IOM
Risaldar Dost Mohammad of 9TH Hodson's Horse was awarded the 2ND Class IOM for on the 30TH September 1918; he acted with dash and gallantry, charging columns of retiring infantry and securing some prisoners. On another column being seen and an attack being attempted to them, he handled his troop with skill and bravery. On being order to retire, he withdrew his troop in an orderly manner under very heavy machine-gun fire.

Nawab Ali Khan, IOM
Jemadar Nawab Ali Khan of 9TH Hodson's Horse was promoted to 2ND Class IOM for on the 19TH September 1918, a troop of enemy cavalry were holding some trenches on a hill near his position. Jemadar Nawab Ali Khan at once charged their position with his troop, causing the enemy, who had kept fire on him until the last moment, to surrender. This incident occurred near Markhalid.

Dhuman Khan, IOM
Risaldar Dhuman Khan of 18TH Lancers was awarded the 3RD Class IOM, for on the night of the 21ST-22ND September 1918, when the squadron was being heavily attacked by the enemy infantry, Risaldar Dhuman Khan led the right flank of the counter attack in the face of heavy rifle and machine-gun fire. With his own hands he captured an enemy machine-gun which was in action directly before his unit. His courage and coolness throughout the action was an example to his men.

Ahmed Beg Khan, IOM
Kot-Daffadar Mirza Ahmed Beg Khan 20TH Deccan Horse was awarded the 3RD Class IOM, in spite of automatic rifle fire from motor cars and considerable rifle fire; he managed to get a footing in the station buildings with his troop, enabling the station to be captured on the 20TH September 1918. This incident occurred at Afule station.

Indian Order of Merit

1ST World War

Egypt & Palestine

Khan Mohammad Khan, IOM
Sowar Khan Mohammad Khan of 18TH Lancers was awarded the 3RD Class IOM for on the 20TH September 1918, about 100 of the enemy with three machine-guns approached in motor lorries and commenced an attack on a village, garrisoned at the time by 3 Hotchkiss guns and 12 rifles. The enemy tried to work his machine-guns around the left flank. Sowar Khan Mohammad Khan asked permission to advance his Hotchkiss gun and crept forward 600 yards in advance of the main position. From this position he maintained such an accurate fire, and in spite of heavy machine-gun fire that the enemy abandoned the attack. He then concentrated his fire on the Lorries, the last of which was disabled and captured. Sowar Khan Mohammad Khan bold action undoubtedly saved a critical as the garrison of the village was very small.

Khuda Baksh Khan, IOM
Risaldar Khuda Baksh Khan of 19TH Lancers was awarded the 2ND Class IOM. On the night of the 21ST-22ND September 1918, after a counter attack, Risaldar Khuda Baksh Khan attempted with only three men to cut off the enemy retreat. He succeeded in turning a considerable number of the enemy and nearly succeeded in turning the whole party. His bold action with only three men resulted in the capture of a large number of prisoners and three machine-guns. He set a fine example of courage and coolness to his men.

Mohammad Wazir Khan, IOM
Risaldar Mohammad Wazir Khan of 36TH Jacob's Horse was awarded the 2ND Class IOM. On the 23RD September 1918, when attacking then rearguard of the Turkish Army Headquarters, Risaldar Mohammad Wazir Khan in command of his troops with 3 Hotchkiss rifles occupied a position from which he so harassed the enemy fire with that the enemy organized and attack in three lines against him. He resolutely held out until he saw the enemy in large numbers were enveloping him on his flanks. He then withdrew section by section. The skill and determination with which he handled his men was most marked and his coolness was a fine example to all ranks.
(Mohammad Wazir Khan, Honorary Lieutenant, Bahadur)

Indian Order of Merit

1ST World War

Egypt & Palestine

Mohammad Ramzan Khan Shaheed, IOM
Havildar Mohammad Ramzan Khan of 152ND Punjabis was awarded the 2ND Class IOM for conspicuous gallantry on the 19TH September 1918. After his platoon commander had been incapacitated, he took command of the platoon and although wounded, led three separate attempts to enter the enemy trenches. He was killed in the third attempt. His great personal courage and devotion to duty were a fine example to all.

Mohammad Alam, IOM
Subedar Mohammad Alam of 153RD Rifles was awarded the 2ND Class IOM. On the night of the 18TH-19TH September 1918, Subedar Mohammad Alam was left in command of his company in very difficult circumstances after his company commander had been wounded. On arrival of reinforcements, his left flank was almost surrounded and he was holding off the enemy with great coolness and energy. He rallied his men in the charge which followed on the enemy's main positions, through bursting bombs and heavy rifle and machine-gun fire. His personal gallantry, enthusiasm, and devotion to duty were invaluable and the effect was immediately visible among his Sepoys, many of whom were under fire for the first time.

Mir Turab Ali, IOM
Jemadar Mir Turab Ali of Mysore Lancers was awarded the 2ND Class IOM, for gallantry and initiative on the 23RD September 1918. He brought his machine-gun sub-section across the open under heavy fire and galloped up stony ground to a position which the enemy was just evacuating. He himself was on ahead with his range-taker and killed a Turkish officer with his sword on his way to the position. (He was attached to 15TH Cavalry Brigade).

Nasser Khan, IOM
Jemadar Nasser Khan 1ST Sappers & Miners was awarded the 3RD Class IOM for conspicuous gallantry and leadership on the 19TH September 1918, during the attack on the enemy's trenches. He was in command of his section of sappers making a gun road across No Man's Land and the enemy trench system and carried out his work so efficiently that the road kept pace with the advancing infantry and the artillery were able to advance immediately the infantry reached their objective. He displayed ability and power of command on other occasions.

Indian Order of Merit

1ST World War

Egypt & Palestine

Abdul Guffar Khan, IOM
Jemadar Abdul Guffar Khan of Mysore Lancers was awarded the 3RD Class IOM. On the 3RD October 1918, Jemadar Abdul Guffar Khan showed great gallantry under heavy fire while leading his squadron in a charge against strongly held enemy position. He rallied the squadron after his British officer had been killed and continued in action though the squadron had suffered heavy casualties.

Makhmad Ali Shaheed, IOM
Sepoy Makhmad Ali of 20TH Punjabis was awarded the 3RD Class IOM for conspicuous gallantry on the 19TH September 1918, in pushing forward his Lewis gun under heavy machine-gun fire and opening fire on an enemy machine-gun with the result that it was silenced and the forward advance greatly helped. Sepoy Makhmad Ali in charge of the gun was killed during the action. (His wife was awarded the pension of IOM).

Mohammad, IOM
Jemadar Mohammad of 53RD Sikhs was awarded the 3RD Class IOM for conspicuous gallantry and devotion to duty throughout the period of recent operations. He also did particularly well while in command of two sections during a raid on the enemy's trenches on the night of 27TH-28TH July 1918, when after penetrating the enemy's wire, he rushed to the front and captured five of the enemy. Subsequently, he displayed great coolness and initiative in assembling prisoners and wounded and conducting them through the enemy's position regardless of the fire.

Ali Shah Ali, IOM
Sepoy Ali Shah Ali of 53RD Sikhs was awarded the 3RD Class IOM for conspicuous gallantry on the 19TH September 1918. His platoon had advanced to reinforce the advance guard and came under heavy fire and close fire of machine-guns from a concealed position, all men of the leading wave being hit, except himself and one non-commissioned officer. He could have easily withdrawn to cover, but remained and continued to fire steadily with a Lewis gun until his drums were expended and then waited until reinforcements of another platoon came up and went forward with them. Sepoy Ali Shah Ali has always done consistently well.

Indian Order of Merit

1ST World War

Egypt & Palestine

Gul Amir, IOM
Havildar Gul Amir of 56TH Punjabis was awarded the 3RD Class IOM for conspicuous gallantry and devotion to duty, especially during the fighting on the 19TH-20TH September 1918. During the attack on 19TH September, he showed resource and initiative in the way he handled his platoon, pushing forward with great determination in spite of heavy hostile machine-gun and rifle fire.

Karam Dad, IOM
Subedar Karam Dad of 151ST Infantry was awarded the 3RD Class IOM for conspicuous gallantry on the 20TH September 1918, when being the only Indian officer left unwounded with his company, he personally led forward his own and other platoon to two positions, under heavy machine-gun and rifle fire, notwithstanding the very heavy casualties, which included his brother who was killed. His fearless leading gave a splendid example to the company.

Najib Ullah Khan, IOM
Subedar Najib Ullah Khan 46TH Punjabis were awarded the 3RD Class IOM for conspicuous gallantry and devotion to duty on several occasions throughout a long period of service in France, East Africa and Egypt. He set a splendid example by his untiring energy, coolness and exceptional ability.
(This award was made while serving in the Egyptian Expeditionary Force)

Western Front

In August 1914, as the German Army advanced through France and Belgium, more Allied troops were desperately needed for the Western Front. The Indian Army, 161,000 strong, seemed an obvious source of trained men. At the time when the Indians landed, the resistant power of the British army, cruelly outnumbered, and exhausted by constant fighting against superior and a more numerous equipment of machine-guns, was almost overcome. And except the Indian Army there were no other trained regular soldiers in the Empire available at that moment for service.
'Of the Indians on the western front it may be said that as much was asked of them as has been asked of any troops at any period or in any theatre of this war. They were asked to do much, and they tried to do everything they were asked, and through their efforts did save the Empire'.

Indian Order of Merit

1ST World War

Western Front

Usman Khan, IOM
Sepoy Usman Khan of 55th Rifles was awarded the 2nd Class IOM for conspicuous gallantry in the trenches east of Wytschaete on 24th October 1914. Although twice wounded he refused to leave his position and continued to fire at the enemy until wounded a third time.

Havildar Yakub Khan, Lance Naik Said Akbar, and Sepoy Daulat Khan of 57th Rifles were awarded the 3rd Class IOM for conspicuous gallantry on the 23rd and 24th November 1914. They accompanied Captain Acworth along the enemy trenches throwing bombs over the traverses as they proceeded, and thus forcing the enemy to evacuate.

Biaz Gul and Zarif Khan, IOM
Lance Naik Biaz Gul and Sepoy Zarif Khan of 59th Rifles were awarded the 3rd Class IOM on December 12th, 1914. The two men went out to rescue Sepoy Abdullah Khan, who was wounded in three places and lying in the open after taking part in a patrol which had been seen and fired upon. He died soon after being brought in. Both rescuers were recommended for VC but received the IOM.

Sar Amir and Ghulam Mohammad, IOM
Naik Sar Amir and Colour Havildar Ghulam Mohammad of 129th Baluchis were awarded the 2nd Class IOM for conspicuous gallantry on the 31st October 1914. At Hollenbeck fighting, their machine-gun section was put out of action by a shell and the whole detachment of the other gun had been killed. (This award of the IOM was for the famous incident in which Khudadad Khan of the 129th won the first VC to be given to an Indian Soldier. The entire gun team with the exception of Khudadad Khan were killed, received posthumous awards for gallantry. Apart from the VC and Sar Amir and Ghulam Mohammad's IOM, four men received posthumous IDSM's)

Hayat Ali Beg, IOM
Jemadar Hayat Ali Beg of 29th Lancers was awarded the 3rd Class IOM, for gallantry while serving with the Indian Army Corps, British Expeditionary Force on the Western Front.

Indian Order of Merit

1ST World War

Western Front

Redi Gul, IOM
Sepoy Redi Gul of 129TH Baluchis was awarded the 3RD Class IOM for gallantry while serving with the Indian Army Corps, British Expeditionary Force on the Western Front.

Habib Gul, IOM
Lance Naik Habib Gul of 129TH Baluchis was awarded the 3RD Class IOM for gallantry while serving with the Indian Army Corps, British Expeditionary Force on the Western Front.

Mohammad Khan, IOM
Havildar Mohammad Khan of 3RD Sappers & Miners was awarded the 2ND Class IOM. The award was given for conspicuous gallantry during the fighting in the centre of the village of Neuve Chapelle on 28TH October 1914.

The following soldiers of 58TH Rifles were awarded the 3RD Class IOM for gallantry on the night of 30TH October 1914 when they delivered a successful counter attack and held their ground in spite of heavy casualties, Lance Naik Lal Badshah, Lance Naik Sher Khan, Havildar Saidak, and Havildar Roshan Khan.

The following soldiers of 59TH Rifles were awarded the 2ND Class IOM for gallantry and devotion to duty at Givenchy on the 20TH December 1914, whilst serving with the Indian Army Corps, British Expeditionary Force on the Western Front, Havildar Muzaffar Khan, Havildar Mohammad Jan, Havildar Dost Mohammad, Havildar Abdul Wahab.

Zaman Khan, IOM
Subedar Zaman Khan of 107TH Pioneers was awarded the 2ND Class IOM for gallantry. He took command of the Pathan company of the 107TH when its British officers were wounded and skilfully led them in the remainder of the fight; this was at Festubert on the 24TH November 1914.

Mir Badshah and Sahib Jan, IOM
Jemadar Mir Badshah and Sepoy Sahib Jan of 129TH Baluchis were awarded the 2ND Class IOM for gallantry while serving with the Indian Army Corps, British Expeditionary Force on the Western Front.

Indian Order of Merit

1ST World War

Western Front

Makhmand Azam and Nek Amal, IOM 1
Subedar Makhmand Azam and Lance Naik Nek Amal of 129TH Baluchis, were awarded the 2ND Class IOM for gallantry while serving with the Indian Army Corps, British Expeditionary Force on the Western Front. Lance Naik Nek Amal, for his action near Hollenbeck on 26TH October 1914, was recommended for the VC but received the 2ND Class IOM.

Saiday Khan Shaheed, IOM
Sepoy Saiday Khan of 129TH Baluchis joined Nek Amal in the attempt to rescue Captain Vincent after the action near Hollenbeck on 26TH October 1914. He was rewarded with the 2ND Class IOM for his gallantry, but was killed very soon afterwards.

Sayyid Abdulla, IOM
Driver Sayyid Abdulla of 31ST Mule Corps was awarded the 3RD Class IOM for gallantry and devotion to duty while serving with the Indian Army Corps, British Expeditionary Force on the Western Front.

Sheik Abdul Rahman, IOM
Sapper Sheik Abdul Rahman of 1ST Sappers & Miners was awarded the 3RD Class IOM for the fighting at Neuve Chapelle on 10TH-12TH March 1915. In particular, for his gallantry on the 10TH March when he went back two others to bring up supplies of bombs, all the while under heavy fire. This enabled the Leicesters to continue their attacks along German trenches before a general retirement was ordered.

Mohammad Arabi, IOM
Jemadar Mohammad Arabi of 58TH Rifles was awarded the 2ND Class IOM for gallantry on October 1914 near Neuve Chapelle when the 58TH Rifles delivered a successful counter attack and held their ground in spite of heavy casualties. He was wounded in France on 18TH May 1915 and again on 19TH September in Egypt and awarded the 1ST Class IOM for Egypt.

Zarif Khan Shaheed, IOM
Sepoy Zarif Khan of 59TH Rifles was awarded the 2ND Class IOM for gallantry in action France on 29.1.15. In an action January 1915 near Neuve Chapelle he was awarded the 1ST Class IOM. He was killed while performing his duty and awarded the posthumous IOM.

Indian Order of Merit

1ST World War

Western Front

Maula Baksh, IOM
Assistant Surgeon Maula Baksh was awarded the 2ND Class IOM for gallantry and devotion to duty while serving with the Indian Army Corps, British Expeditionary Force on the Western Front.

Jiwan Khan Baksh, IOM
Sapper Jiwan Khan Baksh of 1ST Sappers & Miners was awarded the 2ND Class IOM for gallantry and devotion to duty while serving with the Indian Army Corps, British Expeditionary Force on the Western Front.

Rajiv Khan, IOM
Sepoy Rajiv Khan of 129TH Baluchis was awarded the 2ND Class IOM for bravery during the second battle of Ypres on 26TH April 1915, in carrying an urgent message under heavy shell and rifle fire. A shell burst about three yards from him during his progress, wounding and almost putting him out of action, but he managed to struggle on and delivered the message.

Suleiman Khan, IOM
Sepoy Suleiman Khan of 89TH Punjabis was awarded the 3RD Class IOM for gallantry and devotion to duty while serving with the Indian Army Corps, British Expeditionary Force on the Western Front.

Ayub Khan, IOM
Jemadar Ayub Khan of 124TH Baluchis was attached to 129TH Baluchis and was awarded the 1ST Class IOM for East Africa in 1917. On the Western Front in Yypres on 26TH April 1914 he was in command of a party sent out at night to recover the wounded. According to the officer in charge of search parties, he was the moving spirit of the lot and full of pluck. By brilliant reconnaissance work from trenches near Neuve Chapelle on 23RD June, and running great risks to obtain the required information, he was always to the fore in scouting work, repeatedly bringing in useful information. One of the noteworthy adventures was to pretend to surrender to the Germans near the Bois du Biez on 22ND June 1915. Accepted as a genuine Muslim deserter, he spent some days with the Germans, picking up as much information as he could, before being allowed to return to British lines on the understanding that he would bring over many more disaffected Muslim troops.

Indian Order of Merit

1ST World War

Western Front

Abas Khan, IOM
Havildar Abas Khan of 40TH Pathans was awarded the 3RD Class IOM for gallantry and devotion to duty while serving with the Indian Army Corps, British Expeditionary Force on the Western Front.

Jehandad Khan Shaheed, IOM
Subedar Jehandad Khan of 40TH Pathans was awarded the 2ND Class IOM for distinguished service in the field on 26TH April 1915 near Wieltje, during the second Ypres battle, in re-organising and leading until killed.

Malik Mehr Khan, IOM
Jemadar Malik Mehr Khan of 15TH Lancers was awarded the 3RD Class IOM for gallantry and devotion to duty while serving with the Indian Army Corps, British Expeditionary Force on the Western Front.

Allah Rakka Khan, IOM
Jemadar Allah Rakka Khan of Signal Company was awarded the 3RD Class IOM for gallantry and devotion to duty while serving with the Indian Army Corps, British Expeditionary Force on the Western Front.

Likayat Ali and Mohammad Baksh, IOM
Jemadar Likayat Ali and Havildar Mohammad Baksh of 3RD Sappers & Miners were awarded the 2ND Class IOM for gallantry and devotion to duty while serving with the Indian Army Corps, British Expeditionary Force on the Western Front.

Fateh Haider, IOM
Havildar Fateh Haider of 129TH Baluchis was awarded the 2ND Class IOM for gallantry on 20TH December 1914 at Givenchy when he fought his machine-gun until his sap-head was literally surrounded by Germans and for helping Captain Vincent when wounded on the same day. Fateh Haider then a Jemadar was killed at Plain Hill near Kibata in East Africa on 8TH December 1916. His death was recorded as a great loss to the regiment.

Bahadur Khan, IOM
Subedar Major Bahadur Khan of 33RD Punjabis was awarded the 2ND Class IOM for gallantry on the Battle of Loos 25TH September 1915. He was killed under heavy fire against German line near Manquiossart.

Indian Order of Merit

1ST World War

Western Front

Mohammad Khan, IOM
Subedar Major Mohammad Khan of 69TH Punjabis was awarded the 2ND Class IOM for the withdrawal of the 69TH from captured German trenches on the first day of the Battle of Loos, 25TH September 1915, when Subedar Mohammad Khan and Jemadar Sardar Khan took up a position in the centre communication trench and created a block from the cover of which they prevented the enemy from following too closely on the heels of their comrades.

Sardar Khan, IOM
Jemadar Sardar Khan of 69TH Punjabis was awarded the 2ND Class IOM for the withdrawal of the 69TH from captured German trenches on the first day of the Battle of Loos, 25TH September 1915, when Subedar Mohammad Khan and Jemadar Sardar Khan took up a position in the centre communication trench and created a block from the cover of which they prevented the enemy from following too closely on the heels of their comrades.

Dost Mohammad, IOM
Subedar Dost Mohammad of 74TH Punjabis was awarded the 2ND Class IOM for gallantry and devotion to duty, while serving with the Indian Army Corps, British Expeditionary Force on the Western Front.

Zergun Khan, IOM
Subedar Zergun Khan of 127TH Baluchis was awarded the 2ND Class IOM for gallantry. He was wounded in the fighting north of Ypres near Hilltop Ridge on the 26TH April 1915, when the regiment suffered severe casualties.

Abdullah Khan, IOM
Sowar Abdullah Khan of 9TH Hodson's Horse was awarded the 2ND Class IOM for services in June-July 1916 when the regiment supplied working parties to dig trenches round Mometz Wood, Longueval, Becourt Chateau and Contalmaison.

Hayat Mohammad, IOM
Sowar Hayat Mohammad of 10TH Lancers was awarded the 2ND Class IOM for services while serving with the Indian Army Corps, British Expeditionary Force on the Western Front.

Indian Order of Merit

1ST World War

Western Front

The following soldiers of 19TH Lancers were awarded the 2ND Class IOM for services while serving with the Indian Army Corps, British Expeditionary Force on the Western Front, Kot-Daffadar Hashim Khan, Sowar Muhaman Hussein, and Daffadar Sarbulan Khan.

Mohammad Nur Khan, IOM
Risaldar Mohammad Nur Khan of 36TH Jacob's Horse was awarded the 3RD Class IOM for gallantry and distinguished service in the field. Risaldar Mohammad Nur Khan was one of a party of men of the 36TH employed on mining fatigues near Neville St. Vaast. On one occasion, Risaldar Mohammad Nur Khan led seven men to rescue some miners who had been overcome by carbonic gas, a very dangerous service for which the Risaldar was deservedly rewarded.

Hajee Ahmed, IOM
Daffadar Hajee Ahmed of 36TH Jacob's Horse was awarded the 3RD Class IOM for services while serving with the Indian Army Corps, British Expeditionary Force on the Western Front.

Fateh Jang, IOM
Driver Fateh Jang of Royal Horse Artillery was awarded the 3RD Class IOM for gallantry and devotion to duty while serving with the Indian Army Corps, British Expeditionary Force on the Western Front.

Zari Gul Khan, IOM
Jemadar Zari Gul Khan of 12TH Cavalry was awarded the 3RD Class IOM for gallantry and devotion to duty while serving with the Indian Army Corps, British Expeditionary Force on the Western Front.

Abdul Rahman Khan, IOM
Jemadar Abdul Rahman Khan of 29TH Lancers was awarded the 3RD Class IOM for gallantry with the machine-gun squadron which served in the fighting at Serre Ridge in November 1916.

Attar Khan, IOM
Subedar Attar Khan of 33RD Punjabis was awarded the 3RD Class IOM for displaying gallantry on the first day of the Battle of Loos on 25TH September 1915, by controlling No. 1 Company under enemy machine-gun fire during the regiment's retirement.

Indian Order of Merit

1ˢᵀ World War

Western Front

Monbara Khan, IOM
Lance Daffadar Monbara Khan of 9TH Hodson's Horse was awarded the 3RD Class IOM for gallantry and devotion to duty while serving with the Indian Army Corps, British Expeditionary Force on the Western Front.

Sarfaraz Khan, IOM
Daffadar Sarfaraz Khan of 10TH Lancers was awarded the 3RD Class IOM for gallantry and devotion to duty while serving with the Indian Army Corps, British Expeditionary Force on the Western Front.

Amir Mohammad, IOM
Daffadar Amir Mohammad of 11TH Lancers was awarded the 3RD Class IOM for gallantry and devotion to duty while serving with the Indian Army Corps, British Expeditionary Force on the Western Front.

Mohammad Hyattt and Alla Ditta, IOM
Lance Daffadar Mohammad Hyattt and Sowar Alla Ditta of 19TH Lancer were awarded the 3RD Class IOM for gallantry and devotion to duty while serving with the Indian Army Corps, British Expeditionary Force on the Western Front.

Sadik Mohammad Khan, IOM
Risaldar Sadik Mohammad Khan of 36TH Jacob's Horse was awarded the 2ND Class IOM. In the fighting near Croisilles on 19TH March 1917, Risaldar Sadik Mohammad Khan Skilfully withdrew C Squadron which had come under very heavy fire, whilst making a dismounted advance towards the village. He displayed greatest coolness in doing so and also succeeding in getting the wounded away under heavy fire.

Alam Sher Khan, IOM
Jemadar Alam Sher Khan of 37TH Lancers was awarded the 2ND Class IOM. Jemadar Alam Sher Khan from 37TH Lancers was attached to the 36TH Horse. In an action near Croisilles on 19TH March 1917, Jemadar Alam Sher Khan assisted Risaldar Sadik Mohammad Khan in withdrawing the dismounted C Squadron from action and getting the wounded back safely.

Indian Order of Merit

1ST World War

Western Front

Nur Ahmed Khan, IOM
Ressaidar Nur Ahmed Khan of 9TH Hodson's Horse was awarded the 3RD Class IOM for gallantry and devotion to duty while serving with the Indian Army Corps, British Expeditionary Force on the Western Front. The IOM was awarded for a raid on the St. Helene trenches.

Mohammad Azam, IOM
Lance Daffadar Mohammad Azam of 9TH Hodson's Horse was awarded the IOM 2ND Class for France in raid on St. Helene trenches and the 1ST Class for an action at Cambrai on 30TH November 1917. He subsequently received an MC in Palestine.

Sardar Khan, IOM
Jemadar Sardar Khan of 9TH Hodson's Horse was awarded the 2ND Class IOM. He was severely wounded at Gauche Wood near Gouzeaucourt on the 30TH November 1917 and that the IOM was for this action.

Mohammad Khan, IOM
Daffadar Mohammad Khan of 18TH Lancers was awarded the 2ND Class IOM for gallantry and devotion to duty while serving with the Indian Army Corps, British Expeditionary Force on the Western Front.

Liakat Hussain, IOM
Sowar Liakat Hussain of 2ND Lancers was awarded the 3RD Class IOM for gallantry and devotion to duty while serving with the Indian Army Corps, British Expeditionary Force on the Western Front.

Fateh Khan, IOM
Daffadar Fateh Khan of 11TH Lancers was awarded the 2ND Class IOM for gallantry and devotion to duty while serving with the Indian Army Corps, British Expeditionary Force on the Western Front.

Mohammad Khan and Jemadar Adalat Khan, IOM
Jemadar Mohammad Khan and Jemadar Adalat Khan of 18TH Lancers were awarded the 2ND Class IOM for services while serving with the Indian Army Corps, British Expeditionary Force on the Western Front.

Fiaz Mohammad Khan, IOM
Lance Daffadar Fiaz Mohammad Khan of 38TH Central India Horse was awarded the 2ND Class IOM for services while serving with the Indian Army Corps, British Expeditionary Force on the Western Front.

Indian Order of Merit

1ST World War

Western Front

Dilwar Khan, IOM
Risaldar Dilwar Khan of 38TH Central India Horse was awarded the 2ND Class IOM. Risaldar Dilwar Khan was wounded in June 1917: 'where the greatest danger, there was he'. He was awarded the IOM for gallantry near Villers Gauslain on 1ST December 1917 when he commanded C Squadron. He worked his Hotchkiss gun and refused to retire until he had to be taken by the scruff of the neck and shoved to the rear. (Dilwar Khan, Hon. Lt., Bahadur, OBI).

Lihaz Gul Khan, IOM
Ressaidar Lihaz Gul Khan of 38TH Central India Horse was promoted to the 2ND Class IOM. During the action at Villers Gauslain on 1ST December 1917, armed only with walking stick he moved about directing the operations of his half-squadron as if no bullets were flying, and conducted the retirement in good order and with few casualties.

Ata Mohammad Khan, IOM
Assistant Surgeon Ata Mohammad Khan was awarded the 2ND Class IOM for services while serving with the Indian Army Corps, British Expeditionary Force on the Western Front.

Shah Nawaz Khan, IOM
Naik Shah Nawaz Khan of 3RD Sappers & Miners was awarded the 2ND Class IOM. During the attack on Neuve Chapelle on the 28TH October 1914, Captain McCleverly 47TH Sikhs, was shot dead in house-to-house fighting. Several men of the 47TH and Sappers & Miners tried to stalk his slayer and one of the latter pushed his way to the middle of the bullet-swept road, kneeled down, and awaiting his opportunity, shot the man dead, a fine example of cool courage. Attempts to identify the Sapper & Miner involved in this action failed at the time because their officers had all become casualties. But long afterwards on February 1921, an officer recognised Naik Shah Nawaz Khan, and obtained for him the Indian Order of Merit which he had earned on the 28TH October 1914. The story is confirmed in the unit history.

Indian Order of Merit

1ST World War

Gallipoli

The Gallipoli Campaign of 1915-16, also known as the Battle of Gallipoli or the Dardanelles Campaign, was an unsuccessful attempt by the Allied Powers to control the sea route from Europe to Russia during World War I. The Indian Brigade was sent late in August 1915 to the Sulva front, to reinforce the army attempting to gain foothold there. Concerns about the loyalty of Muslim soldiers led to the withdrawal of the two Punjabi battalions. Although 400,000 Muslim soldiers had fought on all the fronts of the Great War, earning multitude of gallantry awards! In the fighting the British made some local gains, but nothing of advantage was achieved, and it was decided to evacuate the Gallipoli peninsula. The British government authorized the evacuation to begin from Sulva Bay on December 7; the last troops left Helles on January 9TH, 1916. In all, some 480,000 Allied forces took part in the Gallipoli Campaign, at a cost of more than 250,000 casualties, including some 46,000 dead.

Jan Mohammad, IOM
Gunner Naik Jan Mohammad of 21ST Mountain Battery was awarded the 3RD Class IOM for distinguished service on the 21ST June near Gheba Tepe. He was the gun layer in a cramped underground emplacement, sides of which were blown in by a high-explosive shell. In spite of clouds of dust and extreme difficulties of the position, 7 rounds of the 21ST fire went straight into the enemy's gun posts and the two guns therein were knocked out.

Fazal Ilahi, IOM
Gunner Fazal Ilahi of 26TH Mountain Battery was awarded the 2ND Class IOM for exceptional bravery on the 13TH June 1915, near Gaba Tepe, in assisting to extinguish a fire in an emplacement containing ammunition. He was not only under heavy fire but extreme danger owing to the explosion of the ammunition.

Hashmet Ali, IOM
Jemadar Hashmet Ali of 1ST Mule Corps was awarded the 3RD Class IOM for gallantry and distinguished service while serving with the Indian Expeditionary Force at the Dardanelles.

Bahadur Shah, IOM
Lance Naik Bahadur Shah of 9TH Mule Corps was awarded the 3RD Class IOM for gallantry and distinguished service while serving with the Indian Expeditionary Force at the Dardanelles.

Indian Order of Merit

1ST World War

Gallipoli

Ghaus Mohammad, IOM
Assistant Surgeon Ghaus Mohammad was awarded the 1ST Class IOM for gallantry and distinguished service while serving with the Indian Expeditionary Force at the Dardanelles with effect from 1ST January 1916.

Mohammad Baksh, IOM
Havildar Mohammad Baksh 21ST Mountain Battery was awarded the 3RD Class IOM for gallantry and distinguished service in the field while serving with the Indian Expeditionary Force at the Dardanelles.

Mohammad Baksh, IOM
Jemadar Mohammad Baksh of 26TH Mountain Battery was awarded the 3RD Class IOM for gallantry on the 25TH June 1915, the day the battery had landed, and Jemadar Mohammad Baksh was one of the first to land and one of the last to leave.

Mesopotamia

Turkey's entry into the war on 29TH October 1914 immediately prompted Britain to open a new military front in the remote Ottoman province of Mesopotamia (present-day Iraq). British and Indian troops, sent to the Persian Gulf early November to protect British oil interests at Abadan, took military action against the Turks.

Feroz Ali, IOM
Jemadar Feroz Ali of 3RD Sappers & Miners was awarded the 2ND Class IOM for the conspicuous manners in which he handled his company during the action at Sahil on the 17TH November 1914, after the Company Commander and the Subedar were wounded, and with about 100 men did splendid work in spite of heavy casualties. (Subedar Major Feroz Ali, Honorary Captain, Bahadur, OBI).

Hashan and Sher Baz, IOM
Driver Hashan and Driver Sher Baz of 13TH Mule Corps were awarded the 3RD Class IOM for his conspicuous bravery while under fire during the action at Sahil on 17TH November 1914, in assisting though wounded, the Regimental Sergeant Major, Dorsetshire Regiment, in removing ammunition from a wounded mule and loading it onto another animal and in filling the ammunition carriers at a time when the supply of ammunition was of the first importance.

Indian Order of Merit

1ST World War

Mesopotamia

The following men of 3RD Sappers & Miners were awarded 3RD Class IOM at Kurna on the 8TH December 1914. Volunteers being called for to swim the River Tigres about 150 yards wide, and carry a line to the opposite bank, the above named volunteered and swam across with the line, thus enabling a flying bridge to be prepared for the passage of troops. The stream was flowing very rapidly and the work was attendant with great danger more especially as the tide was ebbing and the water was very cold. The opposite bank of the river was held by the enemy in considerable strength, Havildar Ghulam Nabi, Lance Naik Nur Dad, and Sapper Ghulam Haidar.

Maula Dad, IOM
Rifleman Maula Dad and other three riflemen of 104TH Rifles were awarded the 2ND Class IOM at Kurna on the 4TH December 1914. In December the machine-gun section was very heavily engaged with the enemy across the Tigris at range varying from 250 to 400 yards. Orders were given for the machineguns to retire with the first party. At the time, four men and the Officer Commanding the machine-gun section were left to take back two guns, ammunition boxes etc. The guns were carried some 250 yards back to the mules but some ammunition still remained behind. The Officer Commanding the machine-gun section called for volunteers to return for the ammunition. The four men including Rifleman Maula Dad at once volunteered and went back and gallantly recovered the whole of the ammunition on the face of heavy shell and rifle fire after the greater part of their own firing line had retired.

Haider Beg Ali, IOM
Lance Naik Haider Beg Ali of 110TH Mahratta Light Infantry was awarded the 2ND Class IOM for the conspicuous gallantry at Mazera on the 7TH December 1914. Lance Naik Haider Beg received instructions to signal the artillery a very important message from the Officer Commanding of the 110TH Mahratta Light Infantry. To do this, Lance Naik Haider Beg gallantly stood up about 500 yards from the enemy and, in the face of considerable rifle fire, successfully accomplished his task.

Indian Order of Merit

1ST World War

Mesopotamia

Habib Khan Ali, IOM
Havildar Habib Khan Ali of 22ND Mountain Battery was awarded the 3RD Class IOM, for conspicuously gallantry and devotion to duty near Ahwaz on the 3RD March 1915, in continuing to work his gun with great coolness and ability after one of his fingers had been badly shattered and subsequently amputated.

Latif Ali, IOM
Havildar Latif Ali of 23RD Mountain Battery was awarded the 3RD Class IOM for gallantry and ability at Barjisiyah on the 14TH April 1915, in commanding his section for some hours after his section commander and senior Havildar had been wounded. He displayed great coolness and initiative. He was mentioned on a previous occasion for his gallant conduct.

Mohammad Din Ali, IOM
Jemadar Mohammad Din Ali of 3RD Sappers & Miners was awarded the 3RD Class IOM for gallantry at Shaiba on the 12TH April 1915, under heavy shell and rifle fire, in directing the fire of his men in most trying circumstances at a particularly exposed part of the defence.

The following muleteers of 21ST Mule Corps were awarded 3RD Class IOM for conspicuous gallantry and devotion to duty at Barjisiyah on the 14TH April 1915. The 2ND Battalion, Dorsetshire Regiment, being in want of ammunition, the General Officer Commanding the 16TH Infantry Brigade sent up 16 mules with ammunition boxes. The gallant behaviour of drivers of these mules has been brought to notice by the Officer Commanding the 2ND Battalion, Dorsetshire Regiment and the Officer Commanding the 24TH Punjabis and the latter describing them as heroes. Nine mules were killed and three drivers wounded. The greater part of the ammunition reached the firing line, the drivers showing great courage. One driver was seen holding on to his mules, some of which were wounded, although wounded he and under heavy fire. The driver's names were, Lance Naik Allahdad, Lance Naik Sher Baz, and Driver Khwaja.

Indian Order of Merit

1ST World War

Mesopotamia

Ajab Khan Ali, IOM
Subedar Major Ajab Khan Ali of 76TH Punjabis was awarded the 2ND Class IOM for conspicuous gallantry at Khafajiyah on the 15TH May 1915, in courageously leading a party who swam the Karkheh River, a rapid stream 150 yards wide, supported by covering fire but in face of a heavy fire from the enemy on the opposite bank. He was also one of the first who under heavy fire rushed the doorway into a fort which was stubbornly held by some 50 armed Arabs. On both occasions he set a fine example. (Ajab Khan was a remarkable officer who is repeatedly mentioned in the regimental history. He displayed conspicuous gallantry in the attack on Turkish trenches at Nasiriyeh in July 1915. Ajab Khan retired in 1916 later became first Indian officer to sit on the Viceroy's Legislative Council. He was one of the notables who visited his former regiment when it was on active service in Palestine in 1943). (Ajab Khan, Honorary Captain, Sardar Bahadur, OBE, OBI).

Mehdi Khan Ali, IOM
Jemadar Mehdi Khan Ali of 76TH Punjabis was awarded the 2ND Class IOM for conspicuous gallantry at Khafajiyah on the 15TH May 1915, in being one of the first who, under heavy fire, rushed the doorway into a fort which was being stubbornly held by some 50 armed Arabs. Jemadar Mehdi Khan was wounded twice wounded while doing so.

Karam Dad Ali, IOM
Lance Naik Karam Dad Ali of 76TH Punjabis was awarded the 2ND Class IOM for conspicuous gallantry at Khafajiyah on the 15TH May 1915, in courageously swimming the Kharkeh River, a rapid stream 150 yards wide, supported by covering fire but in the face of heavy fire from the enemy on the opposite bank.

Burhan Ali Shaheed, IOM
Sepoy Burhan Ali of 76TH Punjabis was awarded 3RD Class IOM for conspicuous gallantry at Khafajiyah on the 15TH May 1915, in being one of a small party who, under heavy fire, rushed the doorway into a fort which was being stubbornly held by some 50 armed Arabs. Sepoy Burhan Ali was shot dead in doing so and posthumously awarded the IOM.
(Burhan Ali was Subedar Major Ajab Khan's orderly and his charred rifle with the butt completely burned off and the blackened bayonet still fixed was preserved in the Officer's Mess of the Battalion).

Indian Order of Merit

1ST World War

Mesopotamia

Sheikh Mohammad Dadsahib, IOM
Assistant Surgeon Sheikh Mohammad Dadsahib admitted to 3RD Class IOM for conspicuous gallantry and devotion to duty at Barjisiyah on the 14TH April 1915. He showed exceptional zeal in attending the wounded throughout the action under heavy shell and rifle fire.

Gheba Khan Shaheed and Feroz Khan Shaheed, IOM
Sepoy Gheba Khan and Sepoy Feroz Khan of 24TH Punjabis were killed an action near Nasiriyeh on the 14TH July 1915. They were posthumously awarded the 2ND Class IOM for very conspicuous gallantry in the action.

Nasim Khan, IOM
Subedar Major Nasim Khan of 20TH Punjabis was promoted to the 2ND Class IOM for conspicuous gallantry and ability at Kut-al-Amara on the 28TH September 1915 in leading his company and directing its fire without regard to his own safety and continuing to lead his men with great dash after his company had lost one third of its strength in casualties and he was wounded.

Fazal Husain, IOM
Havildar Fazal Husain of 22ND Punjabis was promoted to the 2ND Class IOM for conspicuous gallantry and devotion to duty at Kut-al-Amara on the 28TH September 1915 in fighting his machine-guns most gallantly under heavy fire both in the morning and in the evening attacks. He had no British officer over him and showed great determination and courage.

Sarfaraz Khan, IOM
Subedar Sarfaraz Khan of 119TH Infantry was posthumously awarded the 2ND Class IOM for conspicuous gallantry and devotion to duty at Kut-al-Amara on the 28TH September 1915, in leading his company forward under heavy fire to the attack on a redoubt and assisting to capture the first line of trenches. He then coolly reformed under fire and advanced on the second line, which was successfully stormed. On the edge of the second line he was treacherously shot down by the Turks after they had showed the white flag.

Gul Mohammad, IOM
Havildar Gul Mohammad of 119TH Infantry was admitted to 3RD Class IOM for conspicuous gallantry at Kut-al-Amara on the 28TH September 1915.

Indian Order of Merit

1ST World War

Mesopotamia

Afridi and Allah Ditta, IOM
Driver Afridi and Driver Allah Ditta of 30TH Mule Corps were admitted to 3RD Class IOM for conspicuous gallantry and devotion to duty at Kut-al-Amara on the 28TH September 1915, when each had a charge of 4 ammunition mules. When two mules were shot, both drivers under heavy fire, collected the ammunition, loaded it on the other mules and pressed on with it to the firing line.

Mazhar Khan, IOM
Sowar Mazhar Khan of 33RD Cavalry was admitted to 3RD Class IOM for conspicuous steadiness and courage when firing his gun under difficult circumstances, especially on the 18TH January 1916, when he continued firing with greatest steadiness and courage though himself under a heavy rifle fire which he was at last mortally wounded.

Khan Zaman, IOM
Sepoy Khan Zaman of 53RD Sikhs was awarded the 2ND Class IOM for great gallantry on the 7TH January 1916 at Shaikh Saad in bringing up ammunition from the rear to the most forward trench of all. Throughout his progress from the rear, there was no cover available. On arrival at the forward trench, which as less than 100 yards from the enemy, he personally saw that his Company was replenished with ammunition and later himself brought up water and fresh supplies to the regiment. Sepoy Khan Zaman had also to be restrained from making a premature dash before the final assault.

Fateh Mohammad, IOM
Havildar Fateh Mohammad of 53RD Sikhs was admitted to 3RD Class IOM. At the action of Shaikh Saad on the 6TH and 7TH January 1916, Havildar Fateh Mohammad was very specially conspicuous for the gallantry with which he led his section in the advance and assault, for the coolness and resource with which he handled his men.

Khwaja Mohammad, IOM
Jemadar Khwaja Mohammad of 56TH Rifles was admitted to 3RD Class IOM. At the action at Fort Chibibat on the 13TH January, Jemadar Khwaja Mohammad led his men in the most gallant manner and during the night when all ranks were worn out with fatigue and when only personal encouragement could make the men realise the urgency of the work, he completed some arduous entrenchments under fire.

Indian Order of Merit

1ST World War

Mesopotamia

Allah Ditta, IOM
Naik Allah Ditta of 56TH Rifles was admitted to 3RD Class IOM. During all the actions in which the 28TH (Frontier Force) Brigade had been engaged, Naik Allah Ditta has commanded the regimental scouts. He has shown throughout the finest personal courage and resource in independent reconnaissance and has performed his duties with greatest ability.

Abdul Latif Khan, IOM
Jemadar Abdul Latif Khan of 128TH Pioneers was admitted to 3RD Class IOM for very conspicuous gallantry when working under heavy gun fire while making a crossing for the 72ND Battery, Royal Garrison Artillery, in the action of Shaikh Saad on the 7TH January 1916. The work took about ten minutes and the enemy's artillery fire during the whole period was directed onto his party.

Ghulam Ali, IOM
Lance Naik Ghulam Ali of 90TH Punjabis was admitted to 3RD Class IOM for great gallantry and devotion to duty on the 7TH February 1916 at Butaniyeh, when he was always the last to leave the firing line and particularly for returning with Lieutenant Brewer to assist Jemadar Mewa Singh of the same regiment who was wounded. It was during this last act that Lance Naik Ghulam Ali was shot through the head.

Adam Khan, IOM
Naik Adam Khan of 28TH Punjabis was awarded the 2ND Class IOM for gallantry during the operations on the 6TH April 1916, when he went out with a party under heavy fire to try bringing their Commanding Officer who had been wounded and lying in an exposed position. The party were unable to bring away the wounded officer at first owing to the heavy fire being opened on them when they lifted the stretcher. Later they went out a third time under heavy fire and brought in a wounded Indian officer who was lying in front of the firing line.

Gulmir, IOM
Subedar Major Gulmir of 28TH Punjabis was awarded the 2ND Class IOM for great gallantry during the action at Shaikh Saad on the 7TH January 1916. By his personal bravery and example he materially assisted the advance of a reinforcing battalion.

Indian Order of Merit

1ST World War

Mesopotamia

Mahmud Ali Khan, IOM
Sepoy Mahmud Ali Khan of 5TH Light Infantry was awarded the 2ND Class IOM for conspicuous gallantry on the 12TH April 1916, when the water in the marsh was blown into forward trenches, filling them rapidly and forcing the garrison to evacuate them. The enemy took advantage of this opportunity to pour in a heavy shell and machine-gun fire. He erected a barricade in the trench with the assistance of Sepoy Mugli Khan, to enable two badly wounded men to be got away. There is no doubt that for this act the wounded men would have drowned.

Mugli Khan, IOM
Sepoy Mugli Khan of 9TH Bhopal Infantry was awarded the 2ND Class IOM for conspicuous gallantry on the 12TH April 1916, when the water in the marsh was blown into forward trenches, filling them rapidly and forcing the garrison to evacuate them. The enemy took advantage of this opportunity to pour in a heavy shell and machine-gun fire. On his own initiative, in full view of the enemy, regardless of personal risk, he erected a barricade in the trench with the assistance of Sepoy Mahmud Ali Khan, to enable two badly wounded men to be got away. There is no doubt that for this act the wounded men would have drowned.

Jan Baz, IOM
Lance Naik Jan Baz of 28TH Punjabis was awarded the 2ND Class IOM for conspicuous gallantry on the 6TH April 1916, when he went out with a party under heavy fire to try bringing their Commanding Officer who had been wounded and lying in an exposed position. The party were unable to bring away the wounded officer at first owing to the heavy fire being opened on them when they lifted the stretcher. Later they went out a third time under heavy fire and brought in a wounded Indian officer who was lying in front of the firing line.

Makhmand Din, IOM
Jemadar Makhmand Din of 51ST Sikhs was awarded the 2ND Class IOM for conspicuous gallantry on the 6TH April 1916, when left in command of a platoon, he led it forward under heavy machine-gun and rifle fire, and although he had only one man left, continued to do so until level with the troops on his left and right. He maintained his position within 60 yards of the enemy throughout the day and only withdrew at nightfall when ordered to do so.

Indian Order of Merit

1ST World War

Mesopotamia

Gul Khan, IOM
Jemadar Gul Khan of 53RD Sikhs was awarded the 3RD Class IOM for conspicuous gallantry on the 8TH March 1916. When Subedar in command of his company was wounded this newly promoted Jemadar took command and continued to handle it with skill and gallantry. He was especially helpful to his Double Company Commander during the difficult retirement when the company lost its way in the dark.

Gul Khan, IOM
Subedar Gul Khan of 59 Rifles was awarded the 3RD Class IOM for conspicuous gallantry and most valuable and loyal assistance on the 8TH March 1916, during the attack on the enemy's trench during their retirement. After his captain had been hit the third time, Subedar Gul Khan collected the remainder of the men and took up a position from which he covered the retirement of the left of the Brigade. Subedar Gul Khan had always set a fine example to his men, notably at Givenchy and Neuve Chapelle.

Kalandar Khan, IOM
Havildar Kalandar Khan of 59 Rifles was awarded the 3RD Class IOM for conspicuous gallantry on the 17TH -18TH April 1916 during the Turkish counter attack. Throughout the night he was engaged in carrying ammunition upto the front line and continually crossed and re-crossed the fire-swept zone. He was particularly successful in getting his tired men to work with energy and speed, himself displaying exceptional energy and daring.

Riyhazuddin, IOM
Assistant Surgeon Riyhazuddin was awarded the 2ND Class IOM for conspicuous gallantry during the operations on the 16TH -17TH April 1916. When some of the advanced troops in their first retirement passed through the aid post positions, forcing him to withdraw, he withstood the surrounding influences and despite the increasing closeness of the enemy's fire, established by far the most advanced post in that part of the field and worked throughout the night under the most trying conditions. At dawn he took the first opportunity of rejoining his regiment.

Indian Order of Merit

1ST World War

Mesopotamia

Zaman Shah, IOM

Subedar Zaman Shah of 89TH Punjabis was awarded the 3RD Class IOM for conspicuous gallantry on the 12TH-13TH April 1916, while commanding a platoon; he maintained his position at the most critical time as the enemy made several attempts to dislodge him and were unable to do so, owing to his excellent fire control. He inspired his men with confidence and refused to yield and of the ground gained in the advance.

Subedar Major Farman Ali, IOM

Subedar Major Farman Ali of 92ND Punjabis was awarded the 3RD Class IOM for conspicuous gallantry and meritorious service in action on the 6TH January 1916, when in command of his half company, he was twice wounded and carried on until completely disabled. Also for gallantry and initiative he showed on 7TH April 1916, under heavy shell, rifle and machine-gun fire. He was in charge of the 1ST Line Supports of No. 4 Company when No. 2 Double Company Commander was dangerously wounded in the firing line. He at once pushed up his supports and took over command of No. 2 Company. He continued to advance until ordered to halt and dig in. On the line he then formed at rest of the Brigade was aligned. His example and initiative were most valuable and conspicuous throughout the day. (Farman Ali must have been one of the most decorated soldiers of the Indian Army receiving in addition to the IOM, OBI, and IDSM for Egypt and the Military Cross for Mesopotamia).

Mohammad Baksh, IOM

Subedar Major Mohammad Baksh of 93RD Burma Infantry was awarded the 3RD Class IOM for conspicuous gallantry on the 17TH-18TH April 1916, during the Turkish counter-attack, in controlling and reforming parties of all units under heavy fire. He once wrestled with a Turk and killed him without using any firearms.

Mahtab Khan, IOM

Sapper Mahtab Khan of 3RD Sappers & Miners was awarded the 2ND Class IOM, in March 1916, when engaged in sapping operations against the enemy lines. He specially distinguished himself on the 22ND-23RD March 1916, in crawling out in the open under a heavy close range fire and in removing one of the enemy's land mines which menaced the safety of the working party and the progress of the sap.

Indian Order of Merit

1ST World War

Mesopotamia

Lal Khan, IOM
Lance Naik Lal Khan of 19TH Punjabis was awarded the 3RD Class IOM for conspicuous gallantry on the 8TH March 1916, when he fought with magnificent courage in the enemy's trenches. He was one of the parties who met the hostile bombers and held them back while the supply of grenades lasted, though attacked from both sides. They were the last of their company to leave the enemy's trenches. During the retirement the officer was wounded and the men refused to leave him and brought him in under heavy fire and a great risk of capture.

Khan Khel, IOM
Naik Khan Khel of 51ST Sikhs was awarded the 3RD Class IOM for conspicuous gallantry on the 8TH March 1916. When the regiments in the firing line were running short of ammunition, Naik Khan Khel with several others volunteered to take up an extra supply under heavy fire from rifles and machine-guns.

Ghulam Hassan, IOM
Naik Ghulam Hassan of 52ND Sikhs was awarded the 3RD Class IOM for conspicuous gallantry on the 8TH March 1916, when he fought with magnificent courage in the enemy's trenches. He was one of the parties who met the hostile bombers and held them back while the supply of grenades lasted, though attacked from both sides. They were the last of their company to leave the enemy's trenches. During the retirement the officer was wounded and the men refused to leave him and brought him in under heavy fire and a great risk of capture.

Ali Faqir, IOM
Lance Naik Ali Faqir 59TH Rifles was awarded the 2ND Class IOM for conspicuous gallantry on the 8TH March 1916, when he fought with magnificent courage in the enemy's trenches. He was one of the parties who met the hostile bombers and held them back while the supply of grenades lasted, though attacked from both sides. They were the last of their company to leave the enemy's trenches. During the retirement the officer was wounded and the men refused to leave him and brought him in under heavy fire and a great risk of capture.
(See also Naik Ghulam Hassan, 52ND Sikhs and Lance Naik Lal Khan 19TH Punjabis).

Indian Order of Merit

1ST World War

Mesopotamia

Mahtab Ali, IOM
Naik Mahtab Ali of 89th Punjabis was awarded the 2nd Class IOM for conspicuous gallantry on the 11th March 1916, when he went forward five times from the trench in which he was brought in wounded from a small fold in the ground 150 yards away from the enemy under intense rifle fire. He was severely wounded when bringing in the last man. He was previously recommended for an award for good work in France.

Abdul Akbar, IOM
Jemadar Abdul Akbar of 92nd Punjabis was awarded the 2nd Class IOM for conspicuous gallantry during the attack on the 22nd April 1916, when he led his company to the furthest point reached in the attack under very heavy rifle and machine-gun fire. When the British officer was killed and all the Indian officers of the company severally wounded, he took command of the company and directed them with ability until ordered to retire. He did good service in the action on the 6th January 1916, where he was wounded and again in the action of the 7th April 1916, where he was again wounded.

Sher Khan, IOM
Havildar Sher Khan of 125th Rifles was awarded the 2nd Class IOM for conspicuous gallantry during the attack on the 22nd April 1916, when he led his men forward under heavy shell and rifle fire. Notwithstanding being hit through both cheeks he continued to advance and twice wounded through the arm; he still continued to lead his men forward and was shot through the left lung. He again went forward and was only stopped when the bullet hit him in the leg. Even then he went to the Aid Post unassisted.

Ghulam Khan, IOM
Naik Ghulam Khan of 26th Punjabis was awarded the 2nd Class IOM for conspicuous gallantry in action. While a block was being constructed in a communication trench he maintained a position in front of the block with two other bombers and kept back the enemy who were trying to work down the trench. When badly wounded in the arm and unable to throw bombs himself, he continued to command the party and pass bombs to the two remaining men.

Indian Order of Merit

1ST World War

Mesopotamia

Mohammad Khan, IOM
Havildar Mohammad Khan of 62ND Punjabis was awarded the 2ND Class IOM for conspicuous gallantry while serving in Mesopotamia.

54TH Sikhs Havildar Buta Khan,	IOM 3RD Class (No citation given).
93RD Burma Infantry Havildar Shah,	IOM 2ND Class (No citation given).
93RD B Infantry Subedar Karam Dad,	IOM 3RD Class (No citation given).

Bhullen Khan, IOM
Naik Bhullen Khan of 1ST Sappers & Miners was awarded the 2ND Class IOM for conspicuous gallantry. On the night of the 4TH April 1916, when in charge of parties joining up a gap of 350 yards the front line, Naik Bhullen Khan with Naik Sawan Singh, freely exposed themselves under rifle and machine-gun fire as they cleared the casualties. It was mainly due to their action that the line was successfully consolidated. They had previously rendered good service by the energy with which they pushed forward saps against the enemy's positions.

Malik Khan, IOM
Naik Malik Khan of 104TH Rifles was awarded the 3RD Class IOM for conspicuous gallantry in the action on the 21ST April 1917. He commanded a Lewis Gun section and when within 500 yards of the enemy's line and his whole section except himself and two ammunition carriers had been killed or wounded, he brought up a Lewis gun under very heavy fire and brought it into action on the enemy who were collecting for a counter-attack. Naik Malik Khan was killed in this action.

2ND Sappers & Miners Sapper Saiyid Abdul Wahab,	2ND Class IOM (No citation given).
51ST Sikhs Sepoy Imam Din,	3RD Class IOM (No citation given).
56TH Rifles Sepoy Jafar Khan,	2ND Class IOM (No citation given).
128TH Pioneers Subedar Musa Khan, 51ST Sikhs	2ND Class IOM (No citation given).

Indian Order of Merit

1ST World War

Mesopotamia

Saiyid Hussain, IOM
Naik Saiyid Hussain of 3RD Sappers & Miners was awarded the 2ND Class IOM for conspicuous gallantry in the action on 25TH September, when although twice wounded he remained in the firing line.

Abdul Aziz, IOM
Sapper Abdul Aziz of 3RD Sappers & Miners was awarded the 3RD Class IOM for conspicuous gallantry on the 7TH December 1915, when he assisted in the demolition of an enemy bridge.

Fazal Hussain Shaheed, IOM
Havildar Fazal Hussain of 22ND Punjabis was awarded the 2ND Class IOM for conspicuous gallantry on the 22ND November 1915. He took command of the machie-gun section after the officer with the guns was killed. Although the teams were either killed or wounded, and he was severely wounded, Havildar Fazal Hussain kept his gun in action until he was killed.

Hussain Shah, IOM
Subedar Major Hussain Shah of 76TH Punjabis was awarded the 3RD Class IOM for conspicuous gallantry and devotion to duty on the 22ND November 1915 at Ctesiphon. Hussain Shah displayed the greatest coolness and bravery in leading his company. His personal example kept his company steady during the most trying period of the battle when the enemy's counter-attack developed on the flank of the battalion, which was held by Subedar Major Hussain Shah's company. The battalion was on the exposed flank of the force and any wavering at the critical moment might have led to disaster.

Hussain Shah Shaheed, IOM
Lance Daffadar Hussain Shah of 32ND Lancers was awarded the 3RD Class IOM for conspicuous gallantry in action on the 28TH June 1917. During the retirement of his squadron under heavy fire, Lance Daffadar Abdul Rahman was one of the rear parties. Seeing that his officer, whose horse had been shot under him, was left behind with the enemy closing in on him from every side, he at once turned back to aid him. In doing so, Lance Daffadar Abdul Rahman Khan had his horse shot under him. He was last seen fighting by the side of the officer against and overwhelming number of the enemy, both he and the officer were killed.

Indian Order of Merit

1ST World War

Mesopotamia

Khitab Gul, IOM
Subedar Major Khitab Gul of 120TH Rajputs was awarded the 2ND Class IOM for conspicuous gallantry and devotion to duty at Ctesiphon on the 22ND November 1915 while in a very exposed position.

Ata Mohammad, IOM
Sepoy Ata Mohammad of 91ST Punjabis was awarded the 3RD Class IOM for conspicuous gallantry in action on the 15TH April 1917, in swimming across a canal, under fire, taking ammunition to a patrol which was being attacked on the other side. He then brought back a boat moored between the enemy and the patrol and later returned and brought back the patrol itself. This gallant action was performed in the face of heavy fire.

Feroz Khan Mohammad, IOM
Lance Naik Feroz Khan Mohammad of 125TH Rifles was awarded the 3RD Class IOM for conspicuous gallantry in action on the 21ST April 1917. When his company commander was wounded and lying in the open, Feroz Khan Mohammad dug him a shelter trench and placed him in it. He then went forward to the company to find out the situation and returned to his company commander to report. Seeing his Adjutant lying fatally wounded in the open, he went and dressed his wound. He continued to liaison between his company and his commander throughout the day, freely exposing himself to the enemy's fire.

Ali Akbar, IOM
Naik Ali Akbar of Mule Corps was awarded the 3RD Class IOM for conspicuous gallantry when in charge of part of a bridging train in action on the 25TH March 1917. In the early morning the train came under heavy shell fire and Naik Ali Akbar was wounded but by his courage and perseverance he largely assisted in getting the bridging equipment to a place of safety. Later in the day when it became necessary to make a second bridge over a canal he was set up in charge of the material. The pontoons were again heavily shelled and damaged and three out of four mules badly wounded. However, he went back again and brought up fresh pontoons and mules and succeeding in delivering the material on site, thereby enabling the bridge to be made.

Indian Order of Merit

1ST World War

Mesopotamia

Mohammad Umar Faruk Khan, IOM
Jemadar Mohammad Umar Faruk Khan of 1ST Lancers was awarded the 2ND Class IOM for conspicuous gallantry in action on the 19TH December 1916. He showed great courage in extricating his rearguard under heavy fire. He engaged hand-to –hand with the enemy and his horse was badly cut under him. He displayed soldiery qualities on all occasions.

Sultan Mohammad Shaheed, IOM
Sowar Sultan Mohammad of 21St Cavalry was awarded the 3RD Class IOM for conspicuous gallantry in action on the 27TH March 1917.Though dangerously wounded by shell which killed his horse and nearly blew his right hand off besides causing other injuries about his body, he volunteered to ride, thus liberating the four men who were carrying him on a stretcher to join the firing line. He suffered immense pain but by sticking to his horse for two miles under heavy fire he enabled the squadron, which had been considerably delayed, to withdraw slowly to position from which it could check the enemy's advance. He was previously brought to notice for gallantry. He afterwards died of his wounds.

Alam Khan, IOM
Jemadar Alam Khan of 1ST Sappers & Miners was awarded the 2ND Class IOM for conspicuous gallantry, determination in action during bridging operations when forcing a passage of a river on the 23RD February 1917. Throughout the day he was in charge of work at the head of the bridge and set a fine example both early in the day under heavy shell fire and later on when shells were falling on each side of the bridge. He has done excellent work throughout the operations.

Abbaz Khan, IOM
Sepoy Abbaz Khan of 19TH Punjabis was awarded the 3RD Class IOM for conspicuous gallantry in action on the 22ND February 1917. He brought ammunition under heavy fire, being the only carrier left. He remained with the guns and on the enemy counter-attacking and materially assisted in holding them back by his great courage and determination.

Mohammad Zaman, IOM
Sepoy Mohammad Zaman of 84TH Punjabis was awarded the 3RD Class IOM for conspicuous gallantry in action on the 26TH February 1917. He volunteered to carry across the open under heavy fire a fresh supply of bombs to the firing line; he was wounded in delivering them.

Indian Order of Merit

1ST World War

Mesopotamia

Hayat Mohammad, IOM
Jemadar Hayat Mohammad of 46TH Punjabis was awarded the 3RD Class IOM for conspicuous gallantry in action on the 24TH February 1917. His platoon came under heavy flanking fire from some buildings and all except 12 became casualties. Seeing that the fire was hampering the whole of the advance, he rallied his men and took the buildings with six officers and 183 men taken prisoners. His gallantry all through the action has been most marked.

Tika Khan, IOM
Subedar Tika Khan of 51ST Sikhs was awarded the 3RD Class IOM for conspicuous gallantry in action on the 2ND February 1917, in taking his platoon, which was leading one, into the enemy's second line with a rush during the attack on the enemy's position and later in assisting his Company Commander to steady the men and make them hold on when the companies on the right had fallen back.

Jodh Khan, IOM
Subedar Jodh Khan of 56TH Rifles was awarded the 2ND Class IOM for conspicuous gallantry, determination in action on the 22ND February and the 9TH March 1917. He acted as Jemadar Adjutant in all the actions in which his regiment took part and always displayed great coolness and devotion to duty. On one occasion he displayed great courage in leading his men under heavy fire. He was of considerable assistance to his Company Commander in consolidating the position gained, till finally wounded.

Ali Mohammad, IOM
Sepoy Ali Mohammad of 87TH Punjabis was awarded the 2ND Class IOM for conspicuous gallantry, determination in action on the 7TH and 8TH February 1917.

Mohammad Ali, IOM
Subedar Mohammad Ali of 102ND Grenadiers was awarded the 2ND Class IOM for conspicuous gallantry in action on the 12TH February 1917 and notably on one occasion when though wounded, he went to the assistance of his Commanding Officer. Whilst dressing his wound, he was wounded again and his Commanding Officer killed.

Indian Order of Merit

1ST World War

Mesopotamia

Bahadur Khan Shaheed, IOM
Ressaidar Bahadur Khan 21ST Cavalry was awarded the 3RD Class IOM on the 27TH April 1918. He led his troop with great daring and skill throughout the day. Coming suddenly on a machine-gun round a corner in a river bed, he charged and captured it alone as he was well ahead of his troop. He was killed after leading his troop against the body of the enemy, who were enfilading the advancing troops.

Mohammad Akbar Khan, IOM
Risaldar Major Mohammad Akbar Khan of 7TH Lancers was awarded the 3RD Class IOM for conspicuous gallantry on the 22ND November 1915, in carrying messages under very heavy fire after the Woodie Major had been killed. He set an excellent example at all times by his coolness and on two former occasions his gallantry was brought to notice. He was wounded during the operations.

Darweza Khan, IOM
Subedar Darweza Khan of 124TH Infantry was awarded the 3RD Class IOM for conspicuous bravery on the 5TH November 1917, when he led and handled his platoon under heavy fire with marked skill, inspiring the young and inexperienced soldiers composing the company to which he had been specially attached. Always a reliable officer, he rendered most valuable assistance throughout the operations. He also distinguished himself on a previous occasion when although wounded he continued to command his platoon throughout the action.

Gulab Din, IOM
Jemadar Gulab Din of 28TH Punjabis was awarded the 2ND Class IOM for conspicuous gallantry and initiative on the 5TH November 1917 in leading his platoon throughout the day under fire. When remainder of the regiment had been held up he attempted to get his platoon forward to the enemy's strong point, only desisting when he was left with only one Sepoy.

Sahib-i-Haq, IOM
Subedar Sahib-i-Haq of 59TH Rifles was awarded the 2ND Class IOM for conspicuous gallantry and devotion to duty on the 5TH November 1917. Though severely wounded he continued to command his platoon with marked skill until again severely wounded. He has repeatedly been recommended for gallantry and good work.

Indian Order of Merit

1ST World War

Mesopotamia

Sarwar Khan, IOM
Sepoy Sarwar Khan of 124TH Infantry was awarded the 3RD Class IOM for conspicuous gallantry and devotion to duty on the 5TH November 1917. Orders were given to put out aeroplane signals at a time when a heavy fire was sweeping over the captured trench. Without hesitation or direct order, Sepoy Makhmand Khan Shah stepped out of the trench with the signals and within fifteen seconds he was hit by three bullets and staggered back into the trench. On his own initiative and without hesitation Sepoy Sarwar Khan deliberately completed the signal, during which he was wounded. He displayed conspicuous bravery and determination.

Mukhmad Khan, IOM
Sepoy Mukhmad Khan of 126TH Infantry was awarded the 3RD Class IOM for conspicuous gallantry and devotion to duty on the 5TH November 1917. Orders were given to put out aeroplane signals at a time when a heavy fire was sweeping over the captured trench. Without hesitation or direct order, Sepoy Makhmand Khan Shah stepped out of the trench with the signals and within fifteen seconds he was hit by three bullets and staggered back into the trench. On his own initiative and without hesitation Sepoy Sarwar Khan deliberately completed the signal, during which he was wounded. He displayed conspicuous bravery and determination.

Karam Illahio, IOM
Jemadar Karam Illahio of 24TH Punjabis was awarded the 3RD Class IOM for conspicuous gallantry and devotion to duty on the night of the 25TH - 26TH March 1918. He led his platoon under heavy fire against the enemy position which resulted in the capture of two lines of trenches. He was wounded in the chest, yet in spite of his wound walked back two miles and reported himself.

Abdullah Khan Shaheed, IOM
Ressaidar Abdullah Khan Guides Cavalry was awarded the 2ND Class IOM for conspicuous gallantry and devotion to duty on the 28TH and 29TH October 1918. In the defence of an exposed, untrenched position, repeatedly attacked by the enemy and under continues heavy fire, Ressaidar Abdullah Khan displayed energy and determination of the highest order. He was killed by a shell when fearlessly exposing him in order to obtain better command of his men. His grand example will ever be remembered by those under his command.

Indian Order of Merit

1ST World War

Mesopotamia

Shah Zada Shaheed, IOM
Daffadar Shah Zada of Guides Cavalry was awarded the 2ND Class IOM for conspicuous gallantry and devotion to duty on the 28TH and 29TH October 1918. As No. 1 of the Hotchkiss gun team, he brought his gun into action under heavy enfilade fire with marked ability. To obtain a good field of fire, the configuration of the ground necessitated taking up an exposed position. He handled his gun for fourteen hours with great determination until killed whilst clearing a stoppage in his gun.

Khan Bahadur, IOM
Kot-Daffadar Khan Bahadur of Guides Cavalry was awarded the 3RD Class IOM for conspicuous gallantry and devotion to duty on the 28TH and 29TH October 1918. In the defence of an exposed, untrenched position, repeatedly attacked by the enemy and under continues heavy fire, he rendered the utmost assistance in rapidly conveying messages along an extended fire-swept line, regardless of personal danger. He assisted the wounded with great bravery until he himself became a casualty. His conduct throughout was admirable.

Rahim Baksh, IOM
Assistant Surgeon Rahim Baksh was awarded the 2ND Class IOM for conspicuous gallantry and devotion to duty on the 27TH October 1918. He attended the wounded under heavy fire within 300 yards of the enemy's position with a total disregard of danger. On seeing some wounded lying near the enemy's line he at once volunteered to go out and bring them in but was forbidden to do so.

Rahim Khan, IOM
Naik Rahim Khan of 114TH Mahrattas was awarded the 3RD Class IOM for conspicuous gallantry and devotion to duty on the 29TH October 1918. He was commanding a Lewis gun section when the enemy made a strong counter-attack. In spite of heavy fire and the onrush of the enemy, he maintained his position most courageously and continued to fire his gun although almost overwhelmed. His bold and determined stand was in a great measure instrumental in restoring the line.

Din, IOM
Jemadar Din of 1ST Sappers & Miners was awarded the 3RD Class IOM for conspicuous gallantry from 1ST to the 4TH December 1915 in the defence of a bridge on the 9TH December 1915, against a powerful enemy attack.

Indian Order of Merit

1ˢᵀ World War

North West Frontier

In the early 19ᵀᴴ century, the Frontier was taken over by the East India Company when it annexed the Punjab in 1849. Between 1849 and 1947 the military history of the frontier was a succession of punitive expeditions against offending Pashtun tribes, punctuated by three wars against Afghanistan.

Sarwar Ali, IOM
Sowar Sarwar Ali of Kurram Militia was awarded the 2ᴺᴰ Class IOM for conspicuous bravery while under fire during and engagement between the Jagis and the Kurram Militia which took place at Lakkatigga Post on the 4ᵀᴴ October 1914, when he dragged Lt. Boyle, who was wounded, for a considerable distance until they were under cover. This act was performed under close fire.

Darim, IOM
Daffadar Darim of North Waziristan Militia was awarded the 2ᴺᴰ Class IOM for conspicuous courage during the action at Spina Khaisora on 7ᵀᴴ January 1915, when after escaping from and extremely dangerous situation, he stopped half way to place of safety and took up a position by himself to cover the retirement of his comrades, which act proved of the greatest assistance.

Makhmand Jan, IOM
Daffadar Makhmand Jan of North Waziristan Militia was awarded the 2ᴺᴰ Class IOM for conspicuous courage during the action at Spina Khaisora on 7ᵀᴴ January 1915, when he led his men in the attack under very heavy fire.

Pat Khan Jan, IOM
Jemadar Pat Khan Jan of North Waziristan Militia was awarded the 2ᴺᴰ Class IOM for conspicuous gallantry in action at Dredoni on the 27ᵀᴴ March 1917, when his personal leading was mainly responsible for the successful action of the party he commanded. During the pursuit of the enemy, it became necessary to seize a hill directly overlooking their line of retreat. This hill was held by the enemy and Jemadar Pat Khan on his own initiative, advanced with a section and rushed the hill, he himself reaching the top at least fifty yards ahead of his men. From the position thus gained, he was able to bring an effective fire to bear on the retreating enemy thereby inflicting considerable loss on them.

Indian Order of Merit

1st World War

North West Frontier

Faiz Mohammad Khan, IOM
Risaldar Faiz Mohammad Khan of 1st Lancers was awarded the 2nd Class IOM for conspicuous gallantry at Hafiz Khor on 18th April 1915. In face of an advancing enemy, Risaldar Faiz Mohammad Khan with 2nd Lt, Harrison, searched a nullah in which two wounded Sepoys had informed them, where a wounded man was lying. They were unable to find the wounded man, and came back to the spot where the two Sepoys were awaiting their return. The two Sepoys were exhausted and unable to move. Risaldar Faiz Mohammad Khan and a Sowar lifted them onto their horses and galloped away. After some 150 yards the Sowar's horse fell and Risaldar Faiz Mohammad Khan dismounted to help the Sowar. They mounted again and rode off with the exhausted Sepoys, under close and heavy rifle fire.

Mohammad Fazil, IOM
Kot-Daffadar Mohammad Fazil of 6th Mule Corps was awarded the 2nd Class IOM for conspicuous gallantry at Hafiz Khor on 18th April 1915. Kot-Daffadar Mohammad Fazil brought in badly wounded man from the firing line, under fire from distance of about 150 yards. He was cool and collected, showed great resource throughout and rendered valuable assistance in collecting ammunition mules which would otherwise had been lost.

Alam Khan, IOM
Subedar Major Alam Khan of Corps of Guides Infantry was awarded the 2nd Class IOM for exceptionally fine leadership in action, and for conspicuous bravery in action near Hafiz Khor on the 8th October 1915, when by his coolness, courage and good example he succeeded in getting away a large number of dead and wounded men of his company together with their rifles and equipment, whilst in an exposed position under fire.

Gul Rakhim, IOM
Jemadar Gul Rakhim of North Waziristan Militia was awarded the 2nd Class IOM for gallantry in an encounter with gang of raiders on the 24th August 1916. Jemadar Gul Rakhim was entirely responsible for the success of the operation which led to the rounding up of the gang. Jemadar Gul Rakhim was himself wounded at a range of 70 yards from the raider's sangars but continued to conduct the operations under a hot fire with coolness and skill until final success was achieved.

Indian Order of Merit

1st World War

North West Frontier

Turra Baz, IOM
Subedar Turra Baz of South Waziristan Militia was awarded the 2nd Class IOM for personal gallantry in an encounter with a gang of Mahsuds raiders on the 9th April 1917. By his promptitude in taking up a position at the commencement of the action and his bravery in maintaining his position under heavy fire at close range, although he had lost one third of his party killed and wounded, Subedar Turra Baz enabled a piquet which had been attacked to retire to a position of comparative safety.

Bir Khan, IOM
Subedar Major Bir Khan of Frontier Constabulary was awarded the 2nd Class IOM for conspicuous gallantry in action on the 26th May 1917. When in command of a patrol he engaged a party of the enemy and personally led the pursuit of them, inflicting heavy loss, and by his energy and tenacity set a fine example to the men under his command.

Qambar Ali, IOM
Havildar Qambar Ali of Frontier Constabulary was awarded the 2nd Class IOM for distinguished leadership and gallantry in action. His excellent example encouraged his men at a trying time; he was mortally wounded while advancing across an exposed area.

Qasim Ali, IOM
Jemadar Qasim Ali of 54th Sikhs was awarded the 2nd Class IOM for conspicuous gallantry in action on the 24th June 1917. During a withdrawal of troops, he assisted to bring in a wounded comrade under close and accurate fire from the enemy. This was during the action by the 43rd Brigade to seize the heights above the Shrawani Pass; the 54th Sikhs were conspicuous for their gallantry that day.

Subedar Hukum Dad, IOM	54th Sikhs
Havildar Ali Bahadur, IOM	54th Sikhs
Havildar Feroz Khan Shaheed, IOM	54th Sikhs

The above were awarded the 2nd Class IOM for conspicuous gallantry in defence of a piquet. Between two hundred and three hundred of the enemy made three determined efforts at night to rush the piquet and were only stopped within five yards of its position which was successfully held until dawn. The piquet lost one third of its strength.

Indian Order of Merit

1ST World War

Gulf and Persian Theatres

The Persian Campaign or Invasion of Persia also known as Invasion of Iran was a series of engagements in Iranian Azerbaijan and western Iran (Persia) involving the forces of the Ottoman Empire against those of the British Empire and Russian Empire, especially Transcaspsia, and also involving local population elements, beginning in December 1914 and ending with the withdrawal of the Indian forces in

Jafar Ali, IOM
Subedar Jafar Ali of 102ND Grenadiers was awarded the 2ND Class IOM for conspicuous gallantry during the operations at Muscat on 11TH January 1915, in conducting and leading a small party of men under heavy fire along a very difficult path on a precipitous hillside to dislodge a party of the enemy who were impeding the advance, during which for a short time, Subedar Jafar Ali with some Sepoys, Sultan Ahmed, Karamdad Khan all Sepoys of 102ND Grenadiers, were isolated with the enemy immediately above them. By his exceptional skill in handling his men, his personal courage and absolute disregard of his life, Subedar Jafar Ali set an example of the highest soldierly quality.

Sepoy Abdul Karim, IOM   124TH Baluchis
Sepoy Inayat Ali Khan, IOM   124TH Baluchis
They were awarded the 2ND Class IOM for conspicuous gallantry in the action at Saidabad on 28TH September 1916. In the absence of any non-commissioned officers, they advanced of their own accord from the supports to the firing line, over a distance of 150 yards under very hot and close fire from the enemy, thereby setting an example to the rest of the supports.

Ghulam Hussain, IOM
Sepoy Ghulam Hussain of 106TH Pioneers was awarded the 2ND Class IOM for conspicuous gallantry in charging the enemy single handed.

Kurban, IOM
Sepoy Kurban of 106TH Pioneers was awarded the 2ND Class IOM for conspicuous gallantry when surprised by three of the enemy in low jungle in Seistan operations. Although severally wounded, he killed two of them and put the third to flight.

Indian Order of Merit

1ST World War

Gulf and Persian Theatres

Ibrahim, IOM
Sowar Ibrahim of Gwalior State Lancers was awarded the 2ND Class IOM for conspicuous gallantry during the Seistan operations.

Sijawal Khan, IOM
Naik Sijawal Khan of 124TH Baluchis was awarded the 2ND Class IOM for conspicuous gallantry during an action on the 24TH October 1918; he was commander of the scouts of C Company who were sent forward under heavy fire to ascertain the enemy's dispositions. Naik Sijawal Khan led his scouts forward gallantly and after being severely wounded came back and made an accurate report to his Company Commander of the enemy's dispositions before having his wound dressed. The Company Commander was thereby able to give information to the artillery and get artillery support which materially helped in the subsequent advance.

Imam Din, IOM
Havildar Imam Din of 19TH Punjabis was awarded the 2ND Class IOM for conspicuous gallantry on the 14TH October 1918 when in charge of a machine-gun, brought into action under very heavy gun and rifle fire, he successfully silenced one of the enemy's guns, against the Bolsheviks at Dushak, Transcaspsia region. When finally severally wounded and unable to move, he refused all assistance and ordered his gun back into safety. He had previously done exceedingly well with his gun on 11TH August.

Mohammad Akbar, IOM
Lance Naik Mohammad Akbar of 19TH Punjabis was awarded the 2ND Class IOM for conspicuous bravery and initiative when in command of a Lewis gun on the 14TH October 1918, against the Bolsheviks at Dushak, Transcaspsia. He climbed onto the roof of a house with his gun, 40 yards in advance of all other troops and in spite of heavy fire and his exposed position, kept up concentrated fire on the enemy. Later, from the same position, he fired on one of the enemy's trains and forced it to retire.

Aziz Ullah, IOM
Subedar Aziz Ullah 19TH Punjabis was awarded the 2ND Class IOM for conspicuous bravery and ability in the leading of his platoon when out of touch with his company commander on the 16TH January 1919, for the fighting against the Bolsheviks in the action at Annevenkovo, Transcaspsia. He also behaved with conspicuous bravery on two former occasions.

Indian Order of Merit

1ST World War

Gulf and Persian Theatres

Manawar Khan, IOM
Lance Daffadar Manawar Khan of 28TH Light Cavalry was awarded the 2ND Class IOM for conspicuous gallantry and dash on the 2ND March 1919; when in command of a patrol of 13 men, he was surrounded by about 150 of the enemy's cavalry; he without hesitation led his patrol to the charge and broke through the enemy's ranks, spearing all opposed to them. Later, when pursued by the enemy, he himself halted, took up a position and opened rapid fire on the enemy, shooting three of them and checking the pursuit, thereby saving the lives of the remainder of the patrol with him.

Farid Khan Shaheed, IOM
Havildar Farid Khan of 19TH Punjabis was awarded the 2ND Class IOM for conspicuous gallantry and dash on the 16TH January 1919 in pressing forward at the head of his section under heavy fire fighting against the Bolsheviks in the action of Annenkovo, Transcaspsia. His total disregard of danger on this and former occasions was of the greatest assistance to his platoon commander and an example to his men. Havildar Farid Khan was killed in action.

Egyptian Expeditionary Force, 1919-1920

Mohammad Hussain Shaheed, IOM
Sepoy Mohammad Hussain of 28TH Punjabis was awarded the 3RD Class IOM for conspicuous gallantry at Giaour, Dagh Mountains, Cilicia, on the 11TH October 1919. When a column advancing in difficult mountainous and thickly wooded country, was heavily fired into from dominating heights, the gallant Mohammad Hussain took his Lewis gun to the only open space from which fire could be brought to bear. Sepoy Mohammad Khan from this position he took the Lewis gun on his back in order to allow proper aim to be taken by Sepoy Umar Din, his No. 1, at the enemy, remaining thus although twice wounded until he received the third wound which caused his death.

Nur Dad Shaheed and Art Nawab Khan, IOM
Sapper Nur Dad and Sapper Art Nawab Khan of 1ST Sappers & Miners were awarded the 2ND Class IOM for conspicuous gallantry on the 21ST April 1920. While serving with the Egyptian Expeditionary Force Sapper Nur Dad was killed and Sapper Art Nawab Khan captured, but he succeeded in escaping later.

Indian Order of Merit

Between the two World wars

Dil Sukh Shaheed, IOM

On 9TH June 1937, a platoon of 2ND Battalion, 8TH Punjab Regiment was ordered to establish a piquet on a hill commanding the Sham Plain on the North West Frontier of India. As the platoon was nearing the top, it was ambushed by about thirty tribesmen concealed in the rocks and bushes. One Sepoy was immediately killed. The tribesmen then charged down the hill but were driven back by heavy fire. Naik Dil Sukh, although mortally wounded, continued to encourage his men, and as the platoon advanced up the hill, the tribesmen fled, having suffered about ten casualties. For conspicuous gallantry Naik Dil Sukh was awarded a posthumous IOM.

Sardar Khan, IOM

After spending the next three months on road protection duties the 2ND Battalion, 8TH Punjab Regiment, moved to Suleiman Khel against Bhittanis, who had been raiding villages in the plains. The Battalion was engaged in some minor encounters. By now the tribesmen were getting tired of the incessant fighting, and by the end of the year the revolt had largely died down. For the operations in Waziristan, Subedar Major Sardar Khan was awarded the IOM.

Allah Dad, IOM

Major Girdhari Singh and Lance Naik Allah Dad of 3RD Battalion, 8TH Punjab Regiment, occupied a trench alongside a haystack and covered the German dugout with a Bren gun, in Italy. A burst from the dugout struck Allah Dad and cost him a finger. He refused to be evacuated until he had gotten even with the Germans. Major Girdhari gave him two grenades, and provided covering fire, as the gallant soldier crawled towards the enemy position. On arriving there, he threw one of the grenades inside the dugout, which was the signal for Major Girdhari and the other men of the platoon to cease firing. Allah Dad immediately rushed the dugout, throwing in the other grenade. Three Germans were killed and five surrendered, even though Allah Dad was by now unarmed. For this incredible act of bravery, Lance Naik Allah Dad was awarded the Indian Order of Merit.

Indian Order of Merit

Between the two World wars

The following officers and men were awarded the IOM while serving on the North West Frontier of India.

Risaldar Mohammad Amin,	Probyn's Horse	N. W. Frontier
Risaldar Hayat Khan	10TH Lancers	N. W. Frontier
Gunner Lal Khan	Mountain Artillery	N. W. Frontier
Subedar Ghulam Hussain	Mountain Artillery	N. W. Frontier
Subedar Alam Khan	Mountain Artillery	N. W. Frontier
Subedar Sada Din	Bengal S&M	N. W. Frontier
Sapper Nawab Khan	Bengal S&M	N. W. Frontier
Subedar Sultan	6TH Infantry	N. W. Frontier
Havildar Ghulam Mohd.	51ST Sikhs	N. W. Frontier
Sepoy Faqir Ali	57TH Rifles	N. W. Frontier
Jemadar Daud Shah	1ST Punjab Regt.	N. W. Frontier
Subedar Mohd. Baksh	2ND Punjab Regt.	N. W. Frontier
L/N Ghulam Rasool	2ND Punjab Regt.	N. W. Frontier
Subedar Imam Ud Din Khan	4TH Bombay Gren.	N. W. Frontier
Jemadar Hadi Khan	4TH Bombay Gren	N. W. Frontier
Subedar Abdul Aziz Khan	4TH Bombay Gren	N. W. Frontier
Subedar Allah Ditta	6 Raj Rif	N. W. Frontier
Subedar Sardar Khan	8TH Punjab Regt.	N. W. Frontier
Jemadar Mohd. Hussain	9 Jat Regiment	N. W. Frontier
Jemadar Mawaz Khan	10TH Baluch	N. W. Frontier
Subedar Umar Khan	10TH Baluch	N. W. Frontier
Naik Atta Mohammad	10TH Baluch	N. W. Frontier
Naik Illah Mohammad	10TH Baluch	N. W. Frontier
Subedar Mustafa Khan	10TH Baluch	N. W. Frontier
Havildar Shahzad Khan	10TH Baluch	N. W. Frontier
Jemadar Allah Ditta	11TH Sikhs	N. W. Frontier
Subedar Awalnur	12TH FF Regt.	N. W. Frontier
Jemadar Sohbat	12TH FF Regt.	N. W. Frontier
Havildar Yusuf	12TH FF Regt.	N. W. Frontier
Jemadar Shah Nawaz	13TH FF Rifles	N. W. Frontier
Sepoy Sultan Khan	15 Punjab Regt.	N. W. Frontier
Sepoy Sher Zarin	15 Punjab Regt.	N. W. Frontier
Sepoy Farman Ali	15 Punjab Regt.	N. W. Frontier
Naik Diwan Ali	15 Punjab Regt.	N. W. Frontier
Subedar Sardar Khan	15 Punjab Regt.	N. W. Frontier
Havildar Janjua	16 Punjab Regt.	N. W. Frontier

Indian Order of Merit

Second World War

Mohammad Abbas, IOM

' At Taungtha in Burma, on the night 26/27TH March 1945, a battalion of the 1ST Punjab Regiment was ordered to attack and capture a very rocky and dominating feature which was devoid of cover, and with very restricted lines of approach on the feature itself, believed to be strongly defended with bunker positions. Before the attack, and was to be led by 'C' Company. Subedar Mohammad Abbas, who was second in command of the Company, asked to be allowed to go with the forward Platoon as he was experienced at hill fighting. As the Company reached the foot hill, an enemy LGM opened fire from close range. Telling the platoon commander to go round it he silenced the position with grenades, killing the one remaining Japanes who tried to run. Another Japanese post was encountered on the right flank, and Subedar Mohammad Abbas organised an attack on it, killing four more Japanese. The advance continued until held up by intense fire from mortars, MMGs, LMGs and Grenade Dischargers. Subedar Mohammad Abbas then asked to do a reconnaissance, working his way along the knife-edged feature through intense fire. He did his reconnaissance and came back and guided the platoon. The platoon pushed forward under heavy fire sustaining heavy casualties, including the Platoon Commander. Subedar Mohammad Abbas again went forward to reconnoitre and to bring back the body of the Platoon Commander, but was unable to do so. Taking Command of the platoon, Subedar Mohammad Abbas repulsed an attack made by the enemy, and followed it with immediate counter attack. The enemy put in another attack which he held and also led counter attack on the enemy LMG post which was doing the most damage, killing everyone on the post. By now all the section commanders of Subedar Mohammad Abba's platoon had been killed and orders came to disengage. The enemy however put in another attack and he managed to stop it with his handful of men, which earned the approbation of the enemy. Subedar Mohammad Abba's platoon was now doing rear guard to the Company. He was the last to withdraw, killing two Japanese who rushed him while he was carrying a wounded man. He killed one with his rifle and bayoneted the other. Throughout this action Subedar Mohammad Abbas set an example of unparallel heroism and leadership. His encouragement to his men was personally responsible for the Company holding ground that was almost untenable and so gaining valuable information that was vital for the success of the future operation.' For his incredible act of gallantry and leadership, he was awarded the Indian Order of Merit on 20/9/1945.

Indian Order of Merit

Second World War

Walayat Khan, MC, IOM
'On the 27TH March 1944, Subedar Walayat Khan was senior Indian Officer in the company position on a hill dominating the exit from the Litan Box in Burma. For the successful evacuation of the box it was vital that this position should not fall into enemy hands. The enemy commenced to attack the position at dusk but the defenders successfully broke up the attacks. At midnight the Company Commander was killed and Subedar Walayat Khan took command. From then on the enemy launched attack after attack from every direction with the utmost disregard for casualties. All these attacks were repulsed. Through all this fierce fighting Subedar Walayat Khan's voice could be heard above the noise of battle, encouraging his men, urging them to kill and leading them to their war cry. Inspired by his leadership, his men fought magnificently and repulsed every attack with heavy loss to the enemy. At 0300 hours this most gallant man covered with wounds, had to hand over command of the post to another VCO. This was one of the fiercest fights yet seen in the campaign and the indomitable courage of Subedar Walayat Khan merits the highest praise.' Subedar Walayat Khan of the 1ST Punjab Regiment was awarded the IOM on 22ND June 1944.

Jemadar Qurban Ali of 1ST Punjab Regiment was awarded the IOM on 22ND June 1944, for gallantry in action in Burma. (No Citation)

Mohammad Zarin Shaheed, IOM
'Jemadar Mohammad Zarin of 1ST Punjab Regiment was in command of a platoon detailed to attack an enemy post which was known to be strongly garrisoned by a determined enemy. Before the attack Jemadar Mohammad Zarin was full of confidence and inspired his men with his enthusiasm. When the attack started Jemadar Mohammad Zarin rushed forward at the head of his men and succeeded in reaching the post, and had the Japanese suing for peace with up-stretched arms but with grenades in their hands. His shouts of encouragement to his men,   exhorting to kill the enemy, were heard over the battle field. Jemadar Mohammad Zarin was killed as he stood at the entrance to the enemy post. His example was superb. His fearlessness and utter disregard of danger was inspiration to all the men in his command and the battalion. The courage he displayed was magnificent and the highest order.' Jemadar Mohammad Zarin was posthumously awarded the IOM. His widow is admitted to the pension of the Second Class of the order with effect from the date of his death.

Indian Order of Merit

Second World War

Mir Afzal Shaheed, IOM
'On the 4TH February 1943, at 0245 hours Jemadar Mir Afzal's platoon of 1ST Punjab Regiment, was attacked in a Jungle country by a party o 15-20 Japanese, in Burma. Jemadar Mir Afzal seized a Bren gun and immediately opened fire on the attackers. His prompt action drove back the attack and resulted in six enemy bodies being recovered later in addition to two wounded Japanese. On 18TH February 1943, Jemadar Mir Afzal was in command of a Platoon detailed to attack an enemy post, which was known to be very strong and heavily armed with Machine Guns. Jemadar Mir Afzal led his platoon with the utmost vigour and in a most fearless manner. He succeeded in capturing the post and then pushed on through it to the further position. On the way he encountered very heavy fire and most of his platoon wiped out. As no assistance was immediately available he was forced to retire with the remnants of his platoon which then consisted of the Platoon Havildar and four men. On the way back he found two wounded British Officers and still under very heavy fire brought them back to cover. The Platoon Havildar carried back the Second officer. Jemadar Mir Afzal went forward on several occasions after this to bring back wounded men and to try and collect what remained of the company. He was later killed by a burst of Machine Gun fire. Jemadar Mir Afzal displayed courage and leadership of a very high order throughout the operations in which this unit had been engaged.' Jemadar Mir Afzal was posthumously awarded the IOM. His widow is admitted to the pension of the Second Class of the Order of Merit.

Mohammad Ayub Khan Shaheed, IOM
'During an attack on November 30TH, 1941, Sepoy Mohammad Ayub Khan was a Company runner of 1ST Punjab Regiment in the Middle East. He was wounded in the back but refused to go to the Regimental Aid Post. As the advance continued he followed slowly owing to his wound. The enemy fire increased in intensity and the advance was held up, whereupon Sepoy Mohammad Ayub Khan at once crawled forward on his stomach and reached the enemy Machine Gun, killing and wounding all the crew. Sepoy Mohammad Ayub Khan was afterwards killed fighting most gallantly against another enemy Machine Gun Post. He showed courage, devotion to duty and fortitude of the highest order and set a magnificent example to his Company.' Sepoy Mohammad Ayub Khan was posthumously awarded the IOM. His widow is admitted to the pension of the Second Class of the order with effect from the date of his death.

Indian Order of Merit

Second World War

Mohammad Akbar, IOM
Subedar Mohammad Akbar of 1ST Punjab Regiment was awarded the IOM on 30TH December 1941, for gallantry in action in the Middle East. (No Citation)

Khani Zaman, IOM
Havildar Khani Zaman of 1ST Punjab Regiment was awarded the IOM on 30TH December 1941, for gallantry in action in the Middle East. (No Citation)

Sabit Ullah, IOM
Sepoy Sabit Ullah of 1ST Punjab Regiment was awarded the IOM on 30TH December 1941, for gallantry in action in the Middle East. (No Citation)

Nur Khan, IOM
Havildar Nur Khan of 2ND Punjab Regiment was awarded the IOM on 22ND July 1943, for gallantry in the field. (No Citation)

Khan Mohammad, IOM
Jemadar Khan Mohammad of 2ND Punjab Regiment was awarded the IOM on 16TH November, 1944 for gallantry in Burma. (No Citation)

Ibrahim Khan Shaheed, IOM
'On 1ST November 1944, during the operations against Vital Corner, Sepoy Ibrahim Khan of 2ND Punjab Regiment was ordered to capture an objective on an important enemy position on the Tiddim-Fort White Road in Burma. Although one platoon had already penetrated the enemy perimeter, the position was still precarious. Realising that the utmost endeavour and speed in reaching his own platoon objective was vital if the leading platoon were to establish its gains, Sepoy Ibrahim Khan who was the LMG number one in leading section, moving well in advance of his section up the precipitous hill-side led the platoon attack. Single-handed firing his Bren gun from his hip, he charged into the enemy position inflicting casualties and preventing the enemy from occupying their trenches. Although severely wounded by a burst of fire in the chest he continued to engage the enemy until his ammunition ran out. In spite of his severe injuries he maintained his position close to the enemy and was calling for more ammunition when he collapsed and died. The action of the gallant Sepoy Ibrahim Khan not only inspired his section and platoon by his determination, leadership and stamina, but proved decisive in the capture and consolidation of the Company position.' Sepoy Ibrahim Khan was posthumously awarded the IOM.

Indian Order of Merit

Second World War

Ghulam Mustafa, IOM
'On 7TH December 1945, during a mobile column South East of Surabaya, in the Far East, a platoon of 2ND Punjab Regiment advanced astride a railway was held up by the enemy, in considerable strength, in a very strong natural position consisting of a series of double banks in thick bamboo. The two forward sections of the battalion were pinned down to the ground by heavy automatic fire; any attempt to move resulted in casualties. Efforts to outflank the position from the right with the third section failed, this section also came under very heavy automatic fire. Subedar Ghulam Mustafa was now ordered to attack the left flank of the enemy position with his platoon. The attack was made in the face of the heavy enemy fire but by his personal leadership and skilful manoeuvring of his sections, carried out at great risk to himself, Subedar Ghulam Mustafa succeeded in getting his men forward to within 30 yards of the enemy. The intensity of fire from one particular LMG had become so great that it was virtually impossible to advance any further. All three section commanders and a number of men of the platoon had become casualties. Realizing the seriousness of the situation and determine to capture the enemy position without further harm to his men, Subedar Ghulam Mustafa, quite regardless of his own life, charged forward alone firing his Sten Gun. Still firing his Sten, he kept up onto the top of the double banks which formed the enemy position and hurled grenades at the occupants. He completely wiped out the post, killing seven and mortally wounded the rest of the enemy. As a result of this and inspired by the incredible gallantry of their commander, the platoon was able to advance and eventually secured the whole enemy position. Twenty-five enemy dead were counted and many more were killed and wounded as they fled. Subedar Ghulam Mustafa's utter disregard for his own safety and his superb leadership throughout the action were magnificent example of courage and devotion to duty, worthy of the very highest traditions of the Indian Army.' Subedar Ghulam Mustafa was awarded the IOM on 1ST August 1946.
Subedar Fateh Mohammad of 11TH Sikh Regiment was awarded the IOM on 30TH December 1941 for gallantry in the Middle East. (No Citation).

Indian Order of Merit

Second World War

Fazal Illahi, IOM
'Since the battalion came on service in the Middle East, Jemadar Fazal Illahi of 2ND Punjab Regiment had taken part in at least eight night or dawn attacks and was in the leading elements of each occasion. During the operation he was a tower of strength, displaying coolness, determination and imperrtubality. He always kept his platoon well in hand and by sheer good leadership played a most essential part without which the Company would not performed the tasks allotted. His coolness, steadiness and devotion to duty have been an example and encouragement to all. In an attack on a fort he kept his platoon staunch and steady, when they came under artillery fire led and captured the first position of the fort area, and organized an excellent rallying point for the future. After capture of the fort, he took a small patrol which captured a 20 mm Gun and the gun crew.' Jemadar Fazal Illahi was awarded the IOM on 9TH September 1942.

Mohammad Akbar Shaheed, IOM
The 5TH Battalion, 8TH Punjab Regiment sailed for Java on 15TH October 1945, and its companies were dispersed all over the island, to disarm the Japanese and to contain frequent attacks by the Indonesians. On 17TH December, a Company was ambushed by insurgents concealed in a rubber plantation outside Buitenzorg. A platoon under Company Havildar Major Mohammad Akbar carried out an attack on the position. But as the platoon neared the position, it was surrounded by armed insurgents eight times their number. A desperate hand-to-hand struggle ensued in which Akbar killed at least ten insurgents. Despite being wounded four times, he continued to fight with great valour. Seeing Lance Naik Jalal Shah surrounded by eight men, Akbar rushed to his aid and saved him from certain death. However in the process he was killed by a sword thrust. For his act of gallantry, Company Havildar Mohammad Akbar was awarded a posthumous Indian Order of Merit. His widow is admitted to the pension of the Second Class of the order with effect from the date of his death.
Jemadar Gul Mohammad of 13TH Frontier Force Rifles was awarded the IOM on 21ST June, 1945, for gallantry in Italy. (No Citation).

Indian Order of Merit

Second World War

Sowar Khan, IOM
'On the 1ST November 1943, a Company under the command of Subedar Sowar Khan of 13TH Frontier Force Rifles was ordered to cross the River Trigno in Italy, and secure a part of bridgehead to cover the crossing of the remainder of the Brigade. Enemy opposition proved to be much greater than had been anticipated; in fact the objective would never have been reached had not Subedar Sowar Khan led his Company with greater skill and personal leadership. Throughout the next 48 hours the Company position was held against three successive counter-attacks. On the 4TH November, Subedar Sowar Khan was wounded badly, for the third time, by crossing a very exposed ground under close range enemy fire, to restore the situation on a point of his post, knowing full well that in doing so he was risking his life. Throughout the operation, Subedar Sowar Khan's personal example of courageous leadership was an inspiration to his men, enabling them to carry out their allotted task.' For his gallant leadership, Subedar Sowar Khan was awarded the IOM on 20TH April 1944.

Bostan Khan Shaheed, IOM
'On the night of 3/4TH November 1943, Naik Bostan Khan of 13TH Frontier Force Rifles, was in charge of a Section of a Company holding a position covering the forming up place of the remainder of the battalion for an attack, in Italy. His post was involved in three successive counter attacks, for the dispersal of which he and his Section were largely responsible. Later in the night he took over the command of a platoon which was one of the few to reach the enemy main position, having filtered through enemy machine gun posts and strong points over very difficult country. Having reached the objective he covered the arrival of further platoons of the battalion onto the enemy position, who likewise filtered through the enemy lines. Finally, when the enemy over ran a small force collected on the enemy position, he was last seen leading his men in a charge straight at the oncoming enemy. He was killed during the ensuing fight. Throughout the last stages of this grim fight his voice could be heard urging his men on to follow him and to 'Maro' (kill) the enemy. The personal courage and leadership of Subedar Sowar Khan were of the highest order.' Naik Bostan Khan was posthumously awarded the IOM. His widow is admitted to the pension of the Second Class of the order with effect from the date of his death.

Indian Order of Merit

Second World War

Abdul Hamid, IOM
'On the 13TH May 1944, a Company of the 13TH Frontier Force Rifles was given the task of widening the River Gari Bridgehead from the South of and the platoon commanded by Jemadar Abdul Hamid was given the task to advance along the road to a certain point. When his platoon was 150 yards from its objective, however, it came under very heavy MMG fire from two pill-boxes on either side of the road and suffered casualties. Jemadar Abdul Hamid at once collected 12 hand grenades from the casualties, and single -handed attacked first the left pill-box and then the right, succeeded in destroying them and killing 7 of the enemy and capturing 25 more. In this action Jemadar Abdul Hamid showed the highest example of leadership and bravery to his men by destroying a well defended enemy post single-handed, which was holding up the Company's advance.' For his gallantry and leadership Jemadar Abdul Hamid was awarded the IOM on 26TH October 1944.

Isa Khan Shaheed, IOM
'On the night 17/18TH March 1941, in the Middle East, the enemy after, shelling our position heavily for 45 minutes, attacked and penetrated the centre of the Company sector. Sepoy Isa Khan of the 13TH Frontier Force Rifles, although already wounded, joined up with a small part of his Company which delivered a counter-attack and evicted the enemy at the point of the bayonet. During their counter-attack he was always in the lead and was seen to kill the enemy himself. He was mortally wounded in the counter-attack. His gallant and stout hearted action contributed in no small measure to the complete success of our attack.' Sepoy Isa Khan was posthumously awarded the IOM. His widow is admitted to the pension of the Second Class of the order with effect from the date of his death.

Hakim Khan, IOM
'During the attack on 8TH May 1941, Lance Naik Rakhim Gul and Sepoy Hakim Khan of 13TH Frontier Force Rifles were with the Company which captured the hill. The enemy began to counter attack. In order to enable the Company to consolidate its position, it was essential to occupy the spur. Under heavy and close fire, the Lance Naik Rakhim Gul and Sepoy Hakim Khan got their Bren gun forward into action and engaged the enemy for two hours until both were killed. Their gallant conduct enabled the Company to consolidate a difficult position under constant pressure from the enemy.' Their widows were admitted to the pension of the Second Class of the Order of Merit.

Indian Order of Merit

Second World War

Rakhim Gul Shaheed, IOM
'During the attack on 8TH May 1941, Lance Naik Rakhim Gul and Sepoy Hakim Khan of 13TH Frontier Force Rifles were with the Company which captured the hill. The enemy began to counter attack. In order to enable the Company to consolidate its position, it was essential to occupy the spur. Under heavy and close fire, the Lance Naik Rakhim Gul and Sepoy Hakim Khan got their Bren gun forward into action and engaged the enemy for two hours until both were killed. Their gallant conduct enabled the Company to consolidate a difficult position under constant pressure from the enemy.' Lance Naik Rakhim Gul and Sepoy Hakim Khan were awarded the Posthumous IOM. Their widows were admitted to the pension of the Second Class of the Order of Merit.

Gul Din Khan Shaheed, IOM
'On 12TH February 1942, the enemy got between 13TH F.F. Rifles and Garhwal Rifles. The Pathan Company was sent forward. Subedar Gul Din Khan advanced with the forward section of the right platoon, and while they were advancing along the forward slope of the hill, came under heavy fire from the enemy who were entrenched and numerically superior. Subedar Gul Din Khan ordered the remaining section to move round the enemy's flank, while he kept them occupied from his position. During the manoeuvre, although four of his section had become casualties, he continued working forward until he arrived at close quarters. He then ordered his men to charge the LMG post, and during the charge the four remaining men became casualties, yet Subedar Gul Din Khan carried on alone until he was killed a few yards from the position. By his action the flanking operation was successful and the enemy was forced to withdraw. Contact with the Garhwal Rifles was re-established. Throughout the Malayan Campaign Subedar Gul Din Khan's bearing in action and his disregard for personal safety were at all times an inspiration to his men. In one action he personally accounted for seven of the enemy. On many occasions his steadiness under heavy enemy pressure were of the greatest value in the situation which might have proves difficult.' Subedar Gul Din Khan awarded the Posthumous IOM. His widow was admitted to the pension of the Second Class of the Order of Merit, from the date of his death.

Sepoy Sadat Khan of 14TH Punjab Regiment was awarded the IOM on 29TH September 1942 for his gallantry in action in Southwest Pacific/ Malaya.

Indian Order of Merit

Second World War

Feroze Khan, IOM
'On the 5TH May 1944, Jemadar Feroze Khan's platoon of 14TH Punjab Regiment was posted to Khoijuman village in Burma, to watch and oppose any Japanese infiltration north. On the night of 5/6TH May, he left behind a section and took out the remainder to raconteur Japanese positions in Potsangram. On return at daylight his section which had remained behind reported movement in the Western edge of the village. Jemadar Feroze Khan immediately made reconnaissance and spotted two anti-tank guns with a strong escort being brought into position. Without hesitation Jemadar Feroze Khan collected his platoon and attacked. Going in with great dash the platoon killed the gunners and prevented the enemy removing the two guns. The speed and ferocity of the attack, so disorganised the enemy, that they were unable to organise their superior numbers to re-capture the guns. On the arrival reinforcements Jemadar Feroze Khan again ordered his platoon to advance and in conjunction with the other platoon completely drove the enemy out of the gun area. He then held on to his sector round the guns till part of the remainder of the Battalion arrived. His initiative and splendid dash enabled his platoon to pin down superior enemy force and resulted, on the arrival of the reinforcements, in the eventual capture of the enemy 4.7 anti-tank gun intact, a two pounder anti-tank gun and a 75 mm Battalion gun, two ammunition dumps, valuable documents, two live unwounded prisoners and the destruction by the enemy of a 75 mm Mountain Gun. The initiative of this young Jemadar and his gallant bearing throughout has been an inspiration to his Battalion.'

Wazir Badshah, IOM
'During an attack on the 3RD February, 1943, Naik Wazir Badshah of 15TH Punjab Regiment led his section in the first wave on to the Japanese position in Burma, when it was held up by heavy MG fire and shower of grenades. Naik Wazir Badshah then went forward and single-handed, attacked a Japanese LMG position with grenades killing or wounding the entire crew. He then proceeded to fire his Tommy gun into nearby Japanese positions until shot through the shoulder and later wounded by a grenade. Naik Wazir Badshah by his own initiative, determination and utter disregard for his own personal safety, set an example of the highest order to his men.' Naik Wazir Badshah for his gallantry was awarded the IOM on 22ND April 1943.

Indian Order of Merit

Second World War

Sarfraz Khan, IOM
'On the night of 17/18TH October 1944, Subedar Sarfraz Khan of 15TH Punjab Regiment, was commanding a Company during an attack on Groce Daniele, in Italy. His Company having already lost two VCO platoon commanders went in with three platoons commanded by Havildars. On crossing the start line the Company came under heavy mortar and MG fire and two of the platoon commanders were wounded. Subedar Sarfraz Khan led his Company on with unshaken determination. Shortly afterwards the third platoon commander was wounded by a burst of automatic fire. At this stage the Company was seriously disorganised owing to the severe casualties who were particularly heavy in NCOs, but Subedar Sarfraz Khan rallied the Company in the darkness, reorganised it into two platoons and disposed it so as to hold the ground already gained against any enemy counter- attack. Subedar Sarfraz Khan then led the Company forward and captured his objective just as the dawn was breaking. During this advance the leading sections came against an enemy post and the advance was halted by its fire; Subedar Sarfraz Khan threw two grenades into the trench whereby killing two Germans and enabling the advance to continue. While consolidating the Company came under heavy fire from a spur and suffered nine casualties in a short time. Subedar Sarfraz Khan seized a Bren gun and kept possession and got adequate cover. Throughout this action under most difficult conditions and during a very dark night, Subedar Sarfraz Khan showed the greatest personal bravery and disregard of danger and quite exceptional coolness, determination and leadership.'

Mahboob Ali Khan, IOM
Daffadar Mahboob Ali Khan of Indian Armoured Corps was awarded the IOM on 13TH August 1942 in the Middle East. His widow was admitted to the pension of the Second Class of the Order of Merit, from the date of his death.

Yunus Khan, IOM
Risaldar Yunus Khan of Indian Armoured Corps was awarded the IOM on 30TH December 1941 in the Middle East. His widow was admitted to the pension of the Second Class of the Order of Merit, from the date of his death.

Indian Order of Merit

Second World War

Malik Mohammad Allahdad Khan, IOM
'In his capacity of Squadron VCO Risaldar Malik Mohammad Allahdad Khan served throughout the recent operations in the Western Desert. On the 25TH November 1941 when his Squadron was attacked by a column of enemy tanks his coolness and disregard of fire in the execution of his duty was specially commented on by his Squadron Commander. In this action 3 enemy tanks were knocked out. On the same day he also controlled a successful feint by a troop which, approaching within 1,200 yards of the enemy tanks under heavy shell and MG fire succeeded in drawing them away from his Squadron. During the attack on 3RD December, 1941, he saw one of our planes shot down, and quickly collecting a motor section he led them to the crashed plane and rescued the pilot, his section killing several enemy infantry who came to interfere in the rescue work. During an advance he took prominent part in the actions of his Squadron which resulted in the capture of 200 enemy prisoners on the 9TH and 10TH December 1941, also several Lorries and Breda guns. On the 15TH December, 1941, he organised the survivors of his Squadron HQ with all the British Officers captured, and had patrols working as usual the following morning. His steadiness under fire and exceptional tactical ability was of inestimable value to his Squadron Commander in operations.' Risaldar Malik Mohammad Allahdad Khan was awarded the IOM on 9TH September 1942.

Ismail Khan, IOM
'During his period of captivity Risaldar Major Ismail Khan continuously withstood pressure both physical and mental, put upon him by Japanese and members of the Indian National Army to forswear his allegiance and to join and persuade others to join the Indian National Army. His splendid example as senior VCO of his Regiment was an inspiration to those entire junior to him and held them loyal despite the barbaric treatment meted out to him and then by their own compatriots backed by the Japanese. His detailed history discloses a succession of brutal beatings and physical injuries until the point of collapse, starvation and indignities. In spite of all he resolutely resisted all efforts to suborn his men and time and again maintained his resistance until his captors ceased their efforts and desisted from their illegal demands. His history is one of magnificent example of fortitude and determination which is deserving of the highest praise and permanent recognition.' Risaldar Major Ismail Khan was awarded the IOM on his release from captivity on 18TH April 1946.

Indian Order of Merit

Second World War

Abdul Sadiq, IOM
'On the night of 22ND March 1944, Jemadar Abdul Sadiq of Indian Engineers, showed a supreme example of courage, self-sacrifice and determination in the face of the enemy, while laying mines near Cassino in Italy. The minefield was raked by enemy machine gun and mortar fire, which became so intense, that Jemadar Abdul Sadiq, in order to avoid casualties, ordered his infantry covering party and most of his sappers to retire, keeping only two sappers to assist him in laying remainder of the mines. When most of the mines were laid, a mortar bomb exploded amongst the party, killing one sapper, seriously wounded Jemadar Abdul Sadiq in both legs, the remaining sapper although wounded was able to walk. Jemadar Abdul Sadiq gallantly determined to save the man's life at the risk of losing his own, so he ordered the sapper to go back to the A.D.S., and he remained out, unprotected and alone. Later a German doctor and stretcher party arrived and asked the Jemadar if he would like to be taken to the German A.D.S. in Cassino. Jemadar Abdul Sadiq although wounded and in great pain, realised that this would involve being taken prisoner, so he sternly refused the offer. Jemadar Abdul Sadiq was not located by our troops until first light, and by that time he had lost lot of blood, on seeing the stretcher party approaching him showed sufficient concern for their lives to direct them with the greatest care through the minefield. Although suffering intense pain, Jemadar Abdul Sadiq even after his task was finished refused to give in, and showed magnificent of cold courage.' Jemadar Abdul Sadiq was awarded the IOM on 21ST September 1944.

Hakim Khan, IDSM Shaheed, IOM
'Subedar Hakim Khan of Indian Artillery was singled out for his outstanding courage, discipline and devotion to duty at all times, throughout the campaign in Burma. The example he set was an inspiration to all ranks of the battery and the inititiative and reliability he displayed was always of the utmost value to his Battery Commander. His coolness and gallant bearing under fire on all occasions had an effect on all ranks which no isolated example of extreme bravery could ever have done. He was killed in action against the Japanese.' Subedar Hakim Khan was posthumously awarded the IOM on 9TH March 1943. His widow was admitted to the pension of Second Class Indian Order of Merit, with effect from the date of his death.

Indian Order of Merit

Second World War

Nur Khan, IOM

'Subedar Nur Khan, of Indian Artillery, showed conspicuous ability and courage throughout the campaign in Burma. Although wounded on the 8TH March, 1942, he did not disclose the fact lest undue anxiety or lack of confidence should result among his men. Later on April 19TH 1942, he was in-charge of Troop HQ. He manned the Bren gun, hitting one enemy plane. He personally led his personnel of Troop HQ on foot having previously destroyed all vehicles and the Wireless Set. Throughout the withdrawal he was always calm and ready to rally the troops.' For his gallant leadership, Subedar Nur Khan was awarded the IOM on 9TH March 1943.

Subedar Rehmat Khan IOM, of Indian Engineers was awarded the IOM, for gallantry against the Japanese in Burma on 30TH December 1941.

Mohammad Amin Shaheed, IOM

'Sepoy Mohammad Amin of 16 Punjab Regiment, was carrying a Bren gun with the leading platoon in Burma, which came under heavy fire. Sepoy Mohammad Amin sprang to the front and encouraged the men onwards. When his Section Commander was wounded he took over the command. Almost immediately he was wounded in the leg. Undaunted he struggled forward. He was wounded again. Despite his wounds he brought his gun into action at a range of 15 yards from the Japanese trenches. There he continued to fire and cheer his comrades on until a third bullet killed him.' Sepoy Mohammad Amin was posthumously awarded the IOM. His widow was admitted to the pension of Second Class Indian Order of Merit, with effect from the date of his death.

Allah Ditta, IOM

'On the morning of 8TH December 1941 as the 3RD Battalion, 16TH Punjab Regiment was engaged in Krool Operations in Malaya. The first task was to seize the Thai Customs Post and cut the telephone wire to Betong. The first man to put foot across the frontier was shot dead as a concealed road block, was cleverly covered with fire. By the time enemy position was reached the Thais had inflicted several casualties. Small arms fire increased and several Thais burst out of the bushes in fanatical to kill British Officers. Major Robinson's life was saved by Naik Allah Ditta, who clubbed the assailant to death, being badly wounded in doing so.' Naik Allah Ditta was awarded the Indian Order of Merit for his gallant action.

Indian Order of Merit

Second World War

Bahadur Khan, IOM
'On the 9TH October, 1941, in Malaya, a Company of the 16TH Punjab Regiment clashed with the Japanese. After some preliminary skirmishing the Company reached the road beyond the bend. There they saw some enemy tanks, of about 4 in number in the first batch; they were followed by infantry in considerable strength. Subedar Sher Khan let the tanks go and then ordered the Company to attack. The most noticeable feature of this action was the bravery of Havildar Bahadur Khan, who kept an LMG in action despite of being wounded several times, till he was killed. One Naik and eight Sepoys got back to the Company with whom they continued to server most admirably until they were nearly all killed. Company casualties were extremely heavy, but Jemadar Teja Khan and some men survived only to be captured later.' Havildar Bahadur Khan was posthumously awarded the IOM. His widow was admitted to the pension of Second Class Indian Order of Merit, with effect from the date of his death.

Amir Khan, IOM
Naik Amir Khan 7TH Battalion, 10TH Baloch Regiment, won a posthumous Indian Order of Merit in Burma in 1942. His widow was admitted to the pension of Second Class Indian Order of Merit, with effect from the date of his death.

Gul Din Khan, IOM
Subedar Gul Din Khan of 1ST Battalion, 13TH Frontier Force Rifles died in action on 11TH February 1942 against the Japanese in Hong Kong and was awarded a posthumous Indian Order of Merit. His widow was admitted to the pension of Second Class Indian Order of Merit, with effect from the date of his death.

Ghulam Nabi, IOM
Jemadar Ghulam Nabi of 7TH Rajput Regiment died the prisoner of Japanese on 28TH October 1943 in Hong Kong. He was awarded a posthumous Indian Order of Merit. His widow was admitted to the pension of Second Class Indian Order of Merit, with effect from the date of his death.

Indian Order of Merit

Second World War

Makhmad Anwar, IOM
'The Punjabis fought rear-guard actions mostly by themselves, as the Dutch units tended to pull out before contact with the enemy was made, Dutch West Borneo The Indian soldiers surrendered to a Japanese Naval Brigade on 3RD April 1942. In captivity it was the Indian officers and soldiers who suffered the most from Japanese atrocities in the camps. Most men, led by their Indian officers, refused to join the Japanese-sponsored Indian National Army led by the collaborator Subhas Chandra Bose. This infuriated the Japanese, and in the Kuala Belait camp in Brunei Subedar Makhmad Anwar IDSM was flogged and hung by his heels until he was dead. Four Jemadars in Kuala Belait camp (Akram Khan, Mohamed Anwar, Nazir Hussain and Lachman Singh) were made to dig their own graves before they were beheaded. It appears that fifty Sepoys who had refused to collaborate were tied up and bayoneted or otherwise murdered.' Subedar Makhmad Anwar was awarded a posthumous Indian Order of Merit. His widow was admitted to the pension of Second Class Indian Order of Merit, with effect from the date of his death.

Kamal Khan, IOM
Naik Kamal Khan of 12TH Frontier Force awarded posthumously the Indian Order of Merit in July 1945. His widow was admitted to the pension of Second Class Indian Order of Merit, with effect from the date of his death.

Indian Order of Merit

List of recipients of IOM (No Citations)

Subedar Mohammad Atta	Corps of Indian Engineers	Italy
Subedar Mohammad Gul	13 Frontier Force Rifles	Italy
Havildar Khan Sher,	15 Punjab Regiment	Italy
Naik Khan Bahadur,	12 Frontier Force Regiment	Italy
Sepoy Rangin Khan	15 Punjab Regiment	Italy
Subedar Mohammad Yusuf	6 Rajputana Rifles	Middle East
Subedar Bahadur Khan	6 Rajputana Rifles	Middle East
Risaldar Malik Khan,	Indian Armoured Corps	Middle East
Havildar Mohabbat Ali	10 Baluch Regiment	Middle East
Havildar Mohammad Akbar	6 Rajputana Rifles	Middle East
Havildar Mohammad Sadiq	10 Baluch Regiment	Middle East
Havildar Mohammad Khan	10 Baluch Regiment	Middle East
Havildar Han Fatteh.	6 Rajputana Rifles	Middle East
Jemadar Ghulam Sarwar	9 Jat Regiment	Middle East
Jemadar Jan Ghulam	Indian Army Service Corps	Middle East
Naik Khushal Khan	12 Frontier Force Regiment	Middle East
Subedar Ahmed Khan	12 Frontier Force Regiment	Burma
Subedar Hakim Khan	Indian Army	Burma
Subedar Kalandar Khan	12 Frontier Force Regiment	Burma
Subedar Naz Mohammad	7 Rajput Regiment	Burma
Havildar Ali Abid	9 Jat Regiment	Burma
Jemadar Mohammad Hayat	7 Rajput Regiment	Burma
Jemadar Mohammad Khan	3 Punjab Regiment	Burma
Sepoy Taj Mohammad	7 Rajput Regiment	Burma
Havildar Nawaz Khan	7 Rajput Regiment	Hong Kong
Jemadar Ali Mohammad	Singapore Artillery	Hong Kong

The India Distinguished Service Medal

Instituted in 1907, the Indian Distinguished Service Medal was awarded for distinguished services in the field for Indian commissioned and non commissioned officers and men of the Indian regular forces. The order was removed when India became independent in 1947.

The India Distinguished Service Medal 1907-1922

1ˢᵀ Lancers Skinner's Horse

The following soldiers of the regiment were awarded the India Distinguished Service Medal for their gallantry on the North West Frontier and France.

Rank	Name	Campaign
Sowar	Nishan Ali	N.W.Frontier (1915)
Jemadar	Ruknuddin	N.W.Frontier (1916)
Trumpeter	Abdul Majid Khan	N.W.Frontier (1916)
Sowar	Ghulam Mohd, Khan	Mesopotamia (1916)
L. Daffadar	Ali Hussain	France 1918
Jemadar	Mohammad Tagi Khan	Mesopotamia (1920)

2ᴺᴰ Lancers Gardner's Horse

The following soldiers of the regiment were awarded the India Distinguished Service Medal for their gallantry in France.

Rank	Name	Campaign
Risaldar	Abdul Latif Khan	France (1917)
Daffadar	Atta Mohammad Khan	France (1918)

4ᵀᴴ Cavalry

During the regiment's service in Mesopotamia Lance Daffadar Abdul Majid Beg was awarded the India Distinguished Service Medal for his gallantry in battle.

Rank	Name	Campaign
Lance Daffadar	Abdul Majid Beg	Mesopotamia (1916)

5ᵀᴴ Cavalry

The following soldiers were awarded the India Distinguished Service Medal for their gallantry in battle.

Rank	Name	Campaign
Daffadar	Mazhr Ali Shah	France (1917)
Sowar	Yakub Khan	France (1917)
Risaldar	Khurshid Mohammad Khan	France (1918)
Ressaidar	Amir Mohammad Khan	Mesopotamia (1917)
L.Daffadar	Abdul Aziz	Mesopotamia (1919)
Daffadar	Hoshiar Ali	Mesopotamia (1920)
Sowar	Maqbal Ahmed Khan	Mesopotamia (1921)

The India Distinguished Service Medal 1907-1922

6TH Cavalry

During the Great War the following men Distinguished Service Medal for their gallantry in battle.

Orderly	Abdul Wahab Khan	France (1917)
Sowar	Ghafur Ali Khan	Egypt (1919)

7TH Hariana Lancers

During the regiments service in Mesopotamia the following Sowars were awarded the India Distinguished Service Medal for his gallantry in battle.

Sowar	Abdul Shakur Khan	Mesopotamia (1917)
Sowar	Ghulam Khan	Mesopotamia (1917)
Sowar	Ghulam Mohammad	Mesopotamia (1917)

8TH Cavalry

The following Sowars were awarded the India Distinguished Service Medal for his gallantry in France and Mesopotamia.

Jemadar	Kale Khan	France (1918)
Jemadar	Nur Mohammad Khan	France (1919)
Jemadar	Fazl Ali Khan	Mesopotamia (1920)

9TH Hodson's Horse

The following officers and sowars were awarded the Indian Distinguished Service Medal for their gallantry in France and Mesopotamia.

Daffadar	Nawab Ali Khan	France (1917)
Sowar	Hashim Khan	France (1917)
Ferrier	Wali Mohammad	France (1917)
Sowar	Shamsudin Khan	France (1917)
Jemadar	Habib Gul	France (1918)
Jemadar	Sardar Khan	France (1918)
Daffadar	Abdul Satar Khan	France (1918)
Sowar	Firoz Khan	France (1918)
Sowar	Ramzan Khan	France (1918)
Risaldar	Mohammad Alam Khan	Egypt (1919)
Daffadar	Sher Shah	Egypt (1919)
Daffadar	Sikander Khan	Egypt (1918)
Sowar	Mir Badshah	Egypt (1919)

The India Distinguished Service Medal 1907-1922

10TH Lancers (Hodson's Horse)

The following officers and Sowars were awarded the Indian Distinguished Service Medal for their gallantry in Mesopotamia.

Rank	Name	Campaign
Daffadar	Sonbat Khan	Mesopotamia (1919)
Daffadar	Ghulam Bartr Khan	Mesopotamia (1919)
Daffadar	Ghulistan Khan	Mesopotamia (1920)
Sowar	Mir Akbar Khan	Mesopotamia (1920)
Sowar	Mazammal Khan	Mesopotamia (1920)
Daffadar	Gullistan Khan	Mesopotamia (1921)
Daffadar	Ghulam Baqir Khan	Mesopotamia (1921)
Trumpeter	Kaim Din	Mesopotamia (1921)
Cook	Waziru	Mesopotamia (1921)
Sowar	Yashin Khan	Mesopotamia (1923)
Sowar	Sher Dil	Mesopotamia (1923)

11TH Lancers (Probyn's Horse)

The following officers were awarded the Indian Distinguished Service Medal for his gallantry in Tibet and France.

Rank	Name	Campaign
Jemadar	Shahzad Mir	Tibet (1907)
Daffadar	Fateh Khan	France (1918)

12TH Cavalry

The following officers were awarded the Indian Distinguished Service Medal for his gallantry in Mesopotamia and France.

Rank	Name	Campaign
Risaldar	Ashak Ali Khan	Mesopotamia (1917)
Daffadar	Fateh Khan	France (1918)
Daffadar	Sangar Khan	France (1918)

13TH Lancers (Watson's Horse)

The following soldiers were awarded the Distinguished Service Medal for their gallantry in East Africa and Mesopotamia.

Rank	Name	Campaign
Daffadar	Kaim Din	East Africa (1917)
Daffadar	Kaim Din	Mesopotamia (1917)
Jemadar	Barhan Ali	Mesopotamia (1917)
L.Daffadar	Dost Mohammad	Mesopotamia (1917)
L.Daffadar	Ghul Mohammad	Mesopotamia (1919)
Sowar	Atta Mohammad	Mesopotamia (1919)

The India Distinguished Service Medal 1907-1922

15TH Lancers (Cureton's Multanis)

The following officers and men were awarded were awarded the Distinguished Service Medal for their gallantry in France, and Mesopotamia.

L.Daffadar	Allah Dad Khan	France (1916)
L.Daffadar	Ranmatullah Khan	Mesopotamia (1916)
Sowar	Dost Mohd. Khan	Mesopotamia (1916)

17TH Cavalry

The following officers were awarded were awarded the Distinguished Service Medal for their gallantry in N.W. Frontier, France and East Africa.

L.Daffadar	Khan Sahib	East Africa (1916)
Jemadar	Malik Alam Sher Khan	France (1918)
Risaldar	Rakhmat Sher Khan	N.W. Frontier (1920)

18TH Lancers

During the Great, the following officers and men were awarded the Distinguished Service Medal for their gallantry in France and Egypt.

Sowar	Hidayat Khan	France (1917)
K. Daffadar	Khuda Baksh Khan	France (1917)
L. Daffadar	Baz Khan	France (1917)
Daffadar	Allah Ditta Khan	France (1918)
Daffadar	Zahid Khan	France (1918)
Jemadar	Adalat Khan	France (1918)
L.Daffadar	Ghulam Mohammad	France (1918)
L.Daffadar	Hyat Khan	France (1918)
Sowar	Sultan Khan	France (1918)
Sowar	Makan Khan	France (1918)
Sowar	Talib Hussein	France (1918)
Sowar	Mohammad Sharif Khan	France (1918)
Driver	Fateh Khan	France (1918)
Jemadar	Khuda Baksh Khan	France (1919)
Risaldar	Malik Sultan Khan	France (1919)
Sowar	Ghiba Khan	Egypt (1919)
Daffadar	Ahmed Yar Khan	Egypt

The India Distinguished Service Medal 1907-1922

19TH Lancers (Fane's Horse

The following officers and a Sowar were awarded the Distinguished Service Medal for their gallantry in Peshawar, France and Egypt.

Rank	Name	Location (Year)
Risaldar	Abdul Aziz Khan	Peshawar (1909)
Daffadar	Mohammad Juma Khan	Peshawar (1909)
Sowar	Amir Khan	Peshawar (1909)
Risaldar	Ghulam Hussain	France (1917)
Daffadar	Gulbar Khan	France (1917)
L. Daffadar	Hussain Ali	France (1917)
Daffadar	Ghazni Khan	France (1918)
L.Daffadar	Musali Khan	France (1918)
Sowar	Nadir Khan	France (1918)
Jemadar	Sarbuland Khan	Egypt (1918)
Daffadar	Ali Mohammad	Egypt (1918)
Jemadar	Abdul Jabar Khan	Egypt (1919)
Jemadar	Abdul Majid	Egypt (1919)
Daffadar	Jehan Dad Khan	Egypt (1919)

20TH Deccan Horse

The following Sowars and officers were awarded the Indian Distinguished Service Medal for their gallantry in France and Egypt.

Rank	Name	Location (Year)
Risaldar	Ali Sher	France (1917)
Daffadar	Kasim Khan	France (1917)
Daffadar	Mohd Mohammad	France (1917)
Jemadar	Yusuf Ali Khan	France (1918)
Risaldar	Khurshid Mohammad Khan	France (1918)
Risaldar	Shaikh Faiz-ud-Din	France (1918)
Daffadar	Shaikh Ahmed Hussein	France (1918)
L.Daffadar	Mir Ranuk Ali	France (1918)
Salutri	Sayyid Ghulam Mahbub	France (1918)
Sowar	Sayed Abdul Majid	France (1918)
Sowar	Subhan Khan	Egypt (1919)
Daffadar	Abdul Karim Khan	Egypt (1919)

The India Distinguished Service Medal 1907-1922

21ST Cavalry (Frontier Force)

The following Sowar and officers were awarded the Indian Distinguished Service Medal for their outstanding feat of arms in Mesopotamia, Egypt and France.

Kot Daffadar	Bahadur Shah	Mesopotamia (1917)
Daffadar	Rasul Khan	Mesopotamia (1918)
Risaldar	Farzand Ali	Mesopotamia (1918)
Orderly	Mahmud Ali Khan	France (1918)
Daffadar	Ghulam Haider	Egypt (1919)

22ND Cavalry (Frontier Force)

During the Great War the following officers and sowars were awarded the Indian Distinguished Service Medal for their gallantry in Egypt, France and Mesopotamia.

Risaldar	Azam Ali	France (1917)
Daffadar	Wajid Ali	Mesopotamia (1917)
Daffadar	Abdullah Khan	Mesopotamia (1918)
Sowar	Akbar Khan	Mesopotamia (1918)
Sowar	Suraj Din	Mesopotamia (1918)
Risaldar	Kasim Raza	Mesopotamia (1919)
Jemadar	Fateh Mohammad	Mesopotamia (1919)
Jemadar	Baiham Khan	Mesopotamia (1919)
Daffadar	Gushtabaf Khan	Egypt (1919)

23RD Cavalry (Frontier Force)

The following officers were awarded the Indian Distinguished Service Medal for their gallantry in Waziristan, and Mesopotamia.

Ressaidar	Hasanmuddin Khan	NWF (1908)
Jemadar	Sahib Dad	Mesopotamia (1916)
Daffadar	Ismail Jan	Waziristan (1917)
Sowar	Mohammad Sayyid	Mesopotamia (1919)
Daffadar	Daud Khan	Mesopotamia (1919)
Daffadar	Mohammad Akbar	Mesopotamia (1920)
Daffadar	Tafazal Hussain	Mesopotamia (1920)
Risaldar	Yusuf Khan	Mesopotamia (1920)
Sowar	Ghulam Hussain	Mesopotamia (1920)

The India Distinguished Service Medal 1907-1922

25TH Cavalry

The following soldiers were awarded the Indian Distinguished Service Medal for their gallantry in East Africa, Mesopotamia and on the North West Frontier of India.

Daffadar	Mansur Khan	NWF (1907)
Risaldar	Kale Khan	Bannu (1913)
Daffadar	Ali Shan Khan	Bannu (1913)
Daffadar	Diwan Khan	Bannu (1913)
Ressaidar	Sher Ali Khan	NWF (1916)
Daffadar	Ibrahim Khan	East Africa (1918)
Daffadar	Pahlwan Khan	East Africa (1918)
Daffadar	Alam Sher	Mesopotamia (1919)
Sowar	Ghulam Mohammad	Mesopotamia (1919)
Daffadar	Mohammad Ayub	Egypt (1919)
Sowar	Mohammad Yar Khan	Mesopotamia (1921)

26TH Light Cavalry

The following officers were awarded the Indian Distinguished Service Medal for their gallantry in Aden and a volunteer in France.

Daffadar	Sher Mohammad	Aden (1917)
Daffadar	Fateh Khan	Aden (1917)
Daffadar	Khader Nawaz	France (1917)
Daffadar	Nawab Khan	Aden (1919)
Daffadar	Faiz Mohammad	Aden (1919)
Daffadar	Habib Ullah Khan	Aden (1919)
Daffadar	Khan Mohammad	Aden (1919)

27TH Light Cavalry

The following soldiers were awarded the Indian Distinguished Service Medal for their gallantry in Waziristan and a volunteer in Egypt.

Jemadar	Aulia Khan	Waziristan (1919)
Sowar	Karam Khan	Waziristan (1919)
Risaldar	Ghulam Mohammad Khan	Egypt (1919)
Daffadar	Khadir Khan	Waziristan (1920)

The India Distinguished Service Medal 1907-1922

28TH Light Cavalry

The following soldiers were awarded the Indian Distinguished Service Medal for their gallantry while serving in Salonika and Transcaspsia (against the Bolshevik Russians).

Daffadar	Fazal Khan	Salonika (1919)
Trumpeter	Murad Ali	Salonika (1919)
Daffadar	Lal Khan	Transcaspsia (1920)
Sowar	Yar Khan	Transcaspsia (1921)

29TH Lancers (Deccan Horse)

The following officers were awarded the Indian Distinguished Service Medal for their gallantry and leadership in France with a Daffadar in Egypt.

Daffadar	Imdad Ali	France (1917)
Daffadar	Mohammad Hafiz	France (1917)
Daffadar	Qasim Ali	France (1918)
Daffadar	Abdul Rahim Khan	France (1918)
Daffadar	Mir Hyder Ali	Egypt (1919)

31ST Lancers

The following soldiers were awarded the Indian Distinguished Service Medal for their conspicuous gallantry in Waziristan and a volunteer in France.

Jemadar	Arjun Khan	France (1917)
Daffadar	Abdul Wadood	Waziristan (1919)
Daffadar	Aziz Khan	Waziristan (1920)
Risaldar	Ghufar Rahman	Waziristan (1920)
Sowar	Dost Mohd. Khan	Waziristan (1920)

32ND Lancers

The following soldiers were awarded the Indian Distinguished Service Medal for their gallantry in Mesopotamia.

Sowar	Asghar Ali Khan	Mesopotamia (1917)
Daffadar	Fateh Mohammad Khan	Mesopotamia (1917)
Daffadar	Fazar Ali Khan	Mesopotamia (1918)
Daffadar	Abdul Gafar Khan	Mesopotamia (1919)
Daffadar	Munimud-din Khan	Mesopotamia (1919)

The India Distinguished Service Medal 1907-1922

32ND Lancers (Cont)

Risaldar	Mohammad Hayat Khan	Mesopotamia (1919)
Jemadar	Adam Khan	Mesopotamia (1919)
Sowar	Wali Mohammad Khan	Mesopotamia (1919)
Naik	Munir Khan	Mesopotamia (1921)

33RD Light Cavalry

The following officers and Sowars were awarded the Indian Distinguished Service Medal for their gallantry in Mesopotamia.

Risaldar	Hidayat Ali Khan	Mesopotamia (1915)
Risaldar	Abdul Satar Khan	Mesopotamia (1915)
Sowar	Sadulla Khan	Mesopotamia (1915)
Daffadar	Alam Ali Khan	Mesopotamia (1916)
Ressaidar	Allau Din Khan	Mesopotamia (1916)
Sowar	Ismail Khan	Mesopotamia (1916)
Daffadar	Mazhar Ali Khan	Mesopotamia (1918)
Daffadar	Yusuf Khan	Mesopotamia (1918)

34TH Poona Horse

The following officers and Sowars were awarded the Indian Distinguished Service Medal for their gallantry in France.

Sowar	Abdullah Khan	France (1915)
Sowar	Fateh Khan	France (1915)
Sowar	Firman Khan	France (1915)
Risaldar	Sattar Khan	France (1917)
Salutri	Abdullah Khan	France (1917)
Sowar	Qasim Ali Khan	France (1917)
Daffadar	Safdar Khan	France (1917)
Daffadar	Ghulam M. Khan	France (1917)
Daffadar	Allah –ud-Din Khan	France (1917)
Daffadar	Budha Khan	France (1917)
Daffadar	Sher Baz Khan	France (1917)
Daffadar	Fateh Mohammad Shah	France (1917)
Daffadar	Sher Bahadur Khan	France (1918)
Daffadar	Nadir Ali Khan	France (1918)
Jemadar	Taj Mohammad Khan	France (1918)
Ressaidar	Amir Khan	France (1918)
Ressaidar	Shamshir Ali Khan	France (1919)
Jemadar	Annu Khan	France (1922)

The India Distinguished Service Medal 1907-1922

36TH *Jacob's Horse*

The following officers and Sowars were awarded the Indian Distinguished Service Medal for their gallantry in France and Egypt.

Jemadar	Maqbul Shah	France (1917)
Sowar	Fakir Khan	France (1917)
K.Daffadar	Abdul Khalik	France (1917)
Sowar	Hazrat Shah	France (1917)
L.Daffadar	Saleh Mohammad	France (1917)
Daffadar	Jehan Khan	France (1918)
L. Daffadar	Akram Khan	France (1918)
Daffadar	Inzar Gul	France (1918)
Sowar	Lalla Jan	France (1918)
L.Daffadar	Rahim Khnn	Egypt (1919)
L. Daffadar	Fateh Khan	Egypt (1919)
K. Daffadar	Jan Mohammad	Egypt (1919)
Daffadar	Khanan Khan	Egypt (1919)
Sowar	Zaighin Shah	Egypt (1919)
Sowar	Aibala Khan	Egypt (1919)

37TH *Lancers (Baluch Horse)*

This regiment was an all-Muslim unit made up of Pathans and Baluchis. The following officers and Sowars were awarded the Indian Distinguished Service Medal for their gallantry in Persia and Mesopotamia.

Daffadar	Mohamand Khan	Persia (1917)
Daffadar	Mohamand Khan	Persia (1919)
Risaldar	Khan Alam Khan	Mesopotamia (1921)
Daffadar	Hussain Khan	Mesopotamia (1921)
Daffadar	Ali Murad Khan	Mesopotamia (1921)
Sowar	Ghulam Hussain	Mesopotamia (1921)
Sowar	Kambar Ali	Mesopotamia (1921)
Sowar	Mardan Ali	Mesopotamia (1921)
Ressaidar	Yakub Khan	Mesopotamia (1921)
Jemadar	Lawang Shah	Mesopotamia (1921)
Daffadar	Abdul Ghafur	Mesopotamia (1921)

The India Distinguished Service Medal 1907-1922

38^(TH) Central India Horse

The following officers and sowars were awarded the Indian Distinguished Service Medal for their gallantry and leadership in France and Egypt.

Rank	Name	Theatre
K. Daffadar	Chilzai Khan	France (1917)
Daffadar	Lal Khan	France (1917)
Daffadar	Sherjam Khan	France (1917)
L. Daffadar	Nur Mohammad Khan	France (1917)
L. Daffadar	Hastam Khan	France (1917)
Daffadar	Fateh Khan	France (1917)
Jemadar	Juma Khan	France (1917)
Sowar	Dost Mohammad Khan	France (1917)
L. Daffadar	Shah Nawaz Khan	France (1918)
Ressaidar	Bostam Khan	France (1918)
Sowar	Aslam Khan	France (1918)
Daffadar	Mohammad Aslam Khan	Egypt (1918)
L. Daffadar	Fateh Mohammad Khan	Egypt (1919)
Trumpeter	Abdul Sattan Khan	Egypt (1919)
L. Daffadar	Feroz Khnan	Egypt (1921)

39^(TH) Central India Horse

Following cavalrymen were awarded the Indian Distinguished Service Medal for their gallantry.

Rank	Name	Theatre
Jemadar	Abdul Rehman Khan	Persia (1911)
Sowar	Ali Mohammad Khan	Egypt (1918)
L.Daffadar	Feroz Khan	Aden (1919)

Corps of Guides, Cavalry (FF)

The following soldiers were awarded the Indian Distinguished Service Medal for their gallantry in N.W. Frontier, Mesopotamia and Persia.

Rank	Name	Theatre
Sowar	Sher Mohammad	Persia (1913)
Risaldar	Khwaja Mohammad Khan	NWF (1908)
L.Daffadar	Sharif Khan	Mesopotamia (1919)
K. Daffadar	Khan Bahadur	Mesopotamia (1920)
Risaldar	Zaidar Khan	Mesopotamia (1920)
Ressaidar	Abdullalh Khan	Mesopotamia (1920)
Sowar Shah	Shah Zada	Mesopotamia (1920)
L. Daffadar	Karbact	Persia (1921)

The India Distinguished Service Medal 1907-1922

Aden Troop

The following cavalrymen were awarded the Indian Distinguished Service Medal for his gallantry in this sorry affair.

Jemadar	Diwan Ali Khan	Aden (1917)
L.Daffadar	Najaf Khan	Aden (1917)
Risalder	Malik Dad Khan	Aden (1919)
L.Daffadar	Abdul Ghani	Aden (1920)

Royal Horse Artillery

The following soldiers were awarded the Indian Distinguished Service Medal for their gallantry while serving the guns in France and Mesopotamia.

Jemadar	Sultan Ali	Mesopotamia (1917)
Naik	Sultan Khan	Mesopotamia (1917)
Havildar	Manowar Khan	Mesopotamia (1917)
Naik	Mohammad Alam	Mesopotamia (1917)
Havildar	Munga Khan	Mesopotamia (1919)
Havildar	Tunda Khan	Mesopotamia (1919)
Naik	Jalal Khan	Mesopotamia (1919)
Driver	Fazal Din	Mesopotamia (1919)
Bhisti	Abdul Aziz	N.W.Frontier (1919)
Havildar	Tarja Khan	France (1917)
Driver	Alla Dad	France (1918)

Royal Field Artillery

The following officers and drivers were awarded the Indian Distinguished Service Medal for their gallantry while serving the guns France and Mesopotamia.

Havildar	Ilam Din	France (1919)
Havildar M.	Saif Ali	France (1919)
Havildar	Bahadur Khan	France (1919)
Driver	Gunga Din	France (1919)
Havildar	Najib Khan	France (1919)
Naik	Bag Hussain	France (1919)
Havildar M.	Palanwar Khan	France (1919)
Havildar	Bostan Khan	France (1919)
L.Naik	Islam Ali	France (1919)
Driver	Fateh Khan	France (1919)

The India Distinguished Service Medal 1907-1922

Royal Field Artillery (Cont)

Driver	Abdul Qayaum	France (1918)
Driver	Bashir Ahmed	France (1918)
Driver	Jumma	France (1919)
Havildar	Mohammad Alum	France (1919)
Havildar M.	Nawaz Ali	Mesopotamia (1919)
Jemadar	Hasham Ali	Mesopotamia (1919)
Naik	Hagat Ali	Mesopotamia (1919)
Havildar	Mohammad Hussain	Mesopotamia (1921)

Royal Garrison Artillery

Naik Nabi Baksh served with the Royal Garrison Artillery during the Salonika campaign was awarded the Indian Distinguished Service Medal for their gallantry against the Serbs.

Naik	Nabi Baksh	Salonika (1919)

Indian Coast Artillery

Havildar Langar Khan served with the Indian Coast Artillery in the defence of Aden during the Great War and was awarded the Indian Distinguished Service Medal for their gallantry against the Turks.

Havildar	Langar Khan	Aden (1915)

21ST Kohat Mountain Battery (Frontier Force)

Jemadar Sultan Ali and Driver Sarwar Khan awarded the Indian Distinguished Service Medal for their gallantry against the Turks in Mesopotamia and Egypt.

Jemadar	Sultan Ali	Mesopotamia (1916)
Driver	Sarwar Khan	Egypt (1917)

22ND Derajat Mountain Battery (Frontier Force)

The following gunners were awarded the Indian Distinguished Service Medal for their gallantry against the Germans in East Africa.

Havildar	Ghazan Khan	East Africa (1918)
Gunner	Aurangzeb	East Africa (1918)
Lance Naik	Puaind Khan	East Africa (1937)

The India Distinguished Service Medal 1907-1922

23RD Peshawar Mountain Battery (Frontier Force)

The following gunners were awarded the Indian Distinguished Service Medal for their conspicuous gallantry in South Persia and Mesopotamia.

Driver Naik	Sher Khan	Mesopotamia (1915)
Jemadar	Ali Akbar	Mesopotamia (1916)
Subedar M.	Fateh Din	South Persia (1918)

24TH Hazara Mountain Battery (Frontier Force)

The following gunners were awarded the Indian Distinguished Service Medal for their conspicuous gallantry in East Africa.

Gunner	Mughal Khan	East Africa (1917)
Driver	Mohammad Afsar	East Africa (1918)

25TH Mountain Battery

Jemadar Haidar Khan was awarded the Indian Distinguished Service Medal for his conspicuous gallantry against the Turks.

Jemadar	Haidar Khan	Mesopotamia (1917)

26TH Jacob's Mountain Battery

The following gunners were awarded the Indian Distinguished Service Medal for their conspicuous gallantry against the Turks in Egypt and Mesopotamia.

Havildar M.	Ghulam Mohammad	Egypt (1917)
Q. Master	Liakat Ali	Egypt (1917)
Havildar	Ghulam Jilani	Mesopotamia (1919)
Jemadar	Ghulam Hassan	Mesopotamia (1917)
Naik	Ahmed Khan	Mesopotamia (1919)
Gunner	Fazal Elahi	Mesopotamia (1919)

27TH Mountain Battery (Cont)

The following gunners were awarded the Indian Distinguished Service Medal for their conspicuous gallantry in Waziristan and East Africa.

Havildar	Kutab Din	Waziristan (1921)
Gunner	Mohammad Khan	Waziristan (1921)
Havildar	Jahan Dad	East Africa (1917)
Havildar	Shah Nawaz	East Africa (1917)
Lance Naik	Iman Din	East Africa (1917)

The India Distinguished Service Medal 1907-1922

28ᵀᴴ Mountain Battery

The following gunners were awarded the Indian Distinguished Service Medal for their conspicuous gallantry in East Africa against the Germans.

Gunner	Mehr Khan	East Africa (1915)
Lance Naik	Fateh Ali	East Africa (1917)
Gunner	Rajwali	East Africa (1917)

30ᵀᴴ Mountain Battery

The following gunners were awarded the Indian Distinguished Service Medal for their gallantry in Mesopotamia and Waziristan.

Havildar	Lal Beg	Mesopotamia (1916)
Gunner	Sardar Khan	Mesopotamia (1916)
Gunner	Hakim Khan	Mesopotamia (1916)
Havildar	Imam Ali Khan	Waziristan (1917)

32ᴺᴰ Mountain Battery

Jemadar Kifayat Allah was awarded the Indian Distinguished Service Medal for his conspicuous gallantry in Egypt.

Jemadar	Kifayat Allah	Egypt (1919)

34ᵀᴴ Mountain Battery

The following gunners were awarded the Indian Distinguished Service Medal for their gallantry in Mesopotamia and Persia.

Jemadar	Haidar Khan	Seistan (1917)
Havildar	Fazal Dad	Mesopotamia (1919)
Naik	Nader Ali	Mesopotamia (1920)

35ᵀᴴ Mountain Battery

Subedar Abbas Khan was awarded the Indian Distinguished Service Medal for his conspicuous gallantry in Persia.

Subedar	Abbas Khan	Persia (1919)

36ᵀᴴ Mountain Battery

Havildar Habib Khan was awarded the Indian Distinguished Service Medal for his conspicuous gallantry in South Persia.

Havildar	Habib Khan South	Persia (1919)

The India Distinguished Service Medal 1907-1922

38TH Mountain Battery

Lance Naik Mohammad Khan and Lance Naik Ali Sher were awarded the Indian Distinguished Service Medal for his conspicuous gallantry in Baluchistan.

Lance Naik	Mohammad Khan	Baluchistan (1919)
Lance Naik	Ali Sher	Baluchistan (1919)

Hong Kong-Singapore Mountain Battery

Assistant Surgeon Chandri Maula Baksh was awarded the Indian Distinguished Service Medal for his care of the injured gunners in Egypt.

A. Surgeon	Chandri Maula Baksh	Egypt, (1919)

Royal Engineers

Inspector Nadu Khan was awarded the Indian Distinguished Service Medal for his gallant works in East Africa.

Inspector	Nadu Khan	East Africa (1917)

1ST Sappers and Miner

The following sappers were awarded the Indian Distinguished Service Medal for their conspicuous gallantry in France, Mesopotamia, South Persia, Bushire and Aden.

1ST Sappers and Miners

Subedar	Fazl Shah	France (1916)
Jemadar	Abdul Aziz Khan	France (1915)
Jemadar	Mehr Baksh	France (1915)
Jemadar	Niamatullah	France (1915)
Naik	Bhullan Khan	France (1916)
Naik	Nawab Khan	France (1916)
Naik	Khairullah	France (1916)
Sapper	Bostan	France (1916)
Sapper	Nur Hussain	France (1916)
Naik	Sharaf Din	Mesopotamia (1916)
Jemadar	Alam Khan	Mesopotamia (1916)
Subedar	Fazal Shah	Mesopotamia (1917)
Havildar	Feroze Khan	Mesopotamia (1917)
Jemadar	Yakhuddin	Mesopotamia (1917)
Jemadar	Allah Rakha	Mesopotamia (1917)

The India Distinguished Service Medal 1907-1922

1ST Sappers and Miners (Cont)

Jemadar	Allah Rakha	Mesopotamia (1917)
Naik	Amir Ali	Mesopotamia (1917)
Naik	Khair Din	Mesopotamia (1917)
Sapper	Haidar Zaman	Mesopotamia (1917)
Naik	Sarfaraz	Mesopotamia (1917)
Havildar	Nur Akhmed	Mesopotamia (1918)
Naik	Ghulam Akbar	Mesopotamia (1918)
Havildar	Nowsher Khan	Mesopotamia (1918)
Subedar	Mehr Din	South Persia (1918)
Subedar	Saidam Shah	Bushire (1919)
Naik	Alla Dad	Aden (1919)
Naik	Karam Ilah	Mesopotamia (1920)

2ND Sappers and Miners

Sappers Said Ghafar and Shaikh Imam were awarded the Indian Distinguished Service Medal for their conspicuous gallantry in carrying out their work in Mesopotamia.

Sapper	Said Ghafar	Mesopotamia (1917)
Sapper	Shaikh Imam	Mesopotamia (1917)

3RD Sappers and Miners

The following sappers were awarded the Indian Distinguished Service Medal for their conspicuous gallantry in France, Mesopotamia, Egypt, Salonika and South Persia.

Jemadar	Nur Alam	France (1915)
Jemadar	Mohammad Baksh	France (1915)
Havildar	Saiyid Hussain	Mesopotamia (1915)
Subedar	Ismail Khan	France (1915)
Subedar	Ali Bahadur	France (1915)
Jemadar	Fateh Khan	Mesopotamia (1915)
Havildar	Ghulam Khadir	France (1916)
Naik	Shaikh Ramzam	France (1916)
Naik	Salah Mohammad	France (1916)
Havildar	Mohammad Din Khan	Mesopotamia (1916)
Havildar	Mohammad Juma	Mesopotamia (1917)
Havildar	Samundar Khan	Mesopotamia (1917)
Naik	Taj Din	Mesopotamia (1917)

The India Distinguished Service Medal 1907-1922

3RD Sappers and Miners (Cont)

Jemadar	Habib ullah Khan	Mesopotamia (1918)
Naik	Rahmat Khan	Mesopotamia (1918)
Havildar	Bahadur Khan	Salonika (1919)
Jemadar	Nur Alam	Egypt (1919)
Havildar	Samandur Khan	Mesopotamia (1920)
Havildar	Mahmud Khan	Mesopotamia (1920)

Railway Battalion-Sappers and Miners

The Sappers served in East Africa for four years, and were highly praised for their work. The following sappers were awarded the Indian Distinguished Service Medal for their conspicuous gallantry in East Africa.

Subedar	Fateh Khan	East Africa (1917)
Subedar	Alif Khan	East Africa (1917)
Lance Naik	Mohammad Sadiq	East Africa (1917)
Havildar	Ahmed Ali	East Africa (1918)
Subedar	Amir Zaman Khan	East Africa (1918)
Subedar	Sher Baz	East Africa (1918)
Subedar	Fazal Din	East Africa (1918)
Subedar	Nathe Khan	East Africa (1919)
Jemadar	Mir Baz Khan	East Africa (1919)

Signal Company

The following signallers were awarded the Indian Distinguished Service Medal for their conspicuous gallantry during the Great War.

Subedar	Bagh Ali	NWF (1920)
Havildar	Ismail Khan	Mesopotamia (1917)
Havildar	Pahlawan Khan	Mesopotamia (1917)
Naik	Mohammad Khan	Mesopotamia (1915)
Naik	Allah Dad Khan	Mesopotamia (1916)
Naik	Mohammad Fazal	Mesopotamia (1918)
Naik	Nur Mahi	Mesopotamia (1919)
Lance Naik	Saif Ali	Mesopotamia (1916)
Sapper	Abdul Jabbar	Mesopotamia (1916)
Sapper	Khan Bahadur	Mesopotamia (1915)
Sapper	Syed Abdul Raim	Mesopotamia (1915)
Sapper	Sowar Khan	Mesopotamia (1916)
Sapper	Baram Muddin	Mesopotamia (1917)

The India Distinguished Service Medal 1907-1922

Signal Company (Cont)

Sapper	Feroz Khan	Mesopotamia (1919)
Sepoy	Mohammad Sarwar	Mesopotamia (1919)
Havildar	Mawaz Din	France (1916)
Havildar	Mushtak Hussain	France (1915)
Naik	Khan Zaman	France (1915)
Sapper	Ghulam Aiyuddin	France (1915)
Sapper	Wali Dad	France (1916)
Sepoy	Ismail Khan	France (1917)

Guides (Lumsden's) Infantry

The following officers and men were awarded the Indian Distinguished Service Medal for their conspicuous gallantry during the Great War.

Subedar	Anil Gul	Tibet (1903)
Havildar	Ghafur Shah	Persia (1913)
Havildar	Taj Mohammad	N.W.Frontier (1915)
Havildar	Arsala Khan	Mesopotamia (1916)
Naik	Ahmed Khan	Mesopotamia (1917)
Lance Naik	Alam Khan	France (1917)
Lance Naik	Gul Haidar	France (1917)
Subedar	Ahmed Khan	Egypt (1919)
Subedar	Alam Khan	Egypt (1919)
Havildar	Hussain Khan	Egypt (1919)
Havildar	Faujun	Egypt (1919)
Lance Naik	Zamir Khan	Egypt (1919)
Sepoy	Ahmed Khan	Egypt (1919)
Sepoy	Amir Ali	Egypt (1919)

5TH Light Infantry

The following soldiers were awarded the Indian Distinguished Service Medal for their conspicuous gallantry during their service in West and East Africa.

Havildar	Ajmeri	West Africa (1916)
Jemadar	Raumat Khan	West Africa (1916)
Lance Naik	Mazhar Khan	West Africa (1916)
Sepoy	Munsab Khan	West Africa (1916)
Sepoy	Faiz Mohammad Khan	West Africa (1916)

The India Distinguished Service Medal 1907-1922

5TH Light Infantry (Cont)

Sepoy	Rahim Dad Khan	East Africa (1917)
Subedar	Aziz-ud-Din Khan	East Africa (1917)
Havilar	Ghulam Naib Khan	East Africa (1918)
Havildar	Maula Baksh	East Africa (1918)
Jemadar	Sikandar	East Africa (1918)
Naik	Maru Khan	East Africa (1918)
Lance Naik	Rustam Khan	East Africa (1918)
Lance Naik	Karam Ilahi Khan	East Africa (1918)

9TH Bhopal Infantry

The following soldiers were awarded the Indian Distinguished Service Medal for their conspicuous gallantry during their service in France and Mesopotamia.

Naik	Sheikh Abdul Latif	France (1915)
Havildar	Sheikh Ramzan	Mesopotamia (1916)
Subedar	Sher Mohammad Khan	Mesopotamia (1917)

12TH Pioneers

The following soldiers were awarded the Indian Distinguished Service Medal for their conspicuous gallantry during their service in Seistan.

Subedar	Mohammad Hassan	Seistan (1917)
Havildar	Kalbi Hussain	Seistan (1917)
Lance Naik	Abdul Hakim	Seistan (1917)

17TH Infantry

The following soldiers were awarded the Indian Distinguished Service Medal for their conspicuous gallantry during their service in East Africa and Egypt.

Sepoy	Murad Ali Khan	East Africa (1917)
Sepoy	Almanat Khan	East Africa (1917)
Jemadar	Yakub Ali Khan	East Africa (1917)
Havildar	Niaz Mohammad Khan	East Africa (1917)
Subedar	Ali Bahadur Khan	East Africa (1917)
Subedar	Hayat Khan	East Africa (1918)
Havildar	Abdul Rahman Khan	East Africa (1918)
Naik	Ghulam Maula Khan	East Africa (1918)
Naik	Ibramim Khan	East Africa (1918)

The India Distinguished Service Medal 1907-1922

17TH Infantry

Rank	Name	Location
Naik	Mohammad Ali Khan	East Africa (1918)
Sepoy	Babu Khan	East Africa (1918)
Sepoy	Mohammad Ali Khan	East Africa (1918)
Sepoy	Niamat Khan	East Africa (1918)
Sepoy	Munshi Khan	East Africa (1918)
Sepoy	Allah Nur Khan	East Africa (1918)
Sepoy	Qadir Baksh	East Africa (1918)
Sepoy	Allah Nur Khan	East Africa (1918)
Sepoy	Allah Ditta Khan	East Africa (1918)
Sepoy	Karim Baksh	East Africa (1918)
Sepoy	Qasim Ali Khan	East Africa (1918)
Subedar	Fiaz Mohammad Khan	East Africa (1919)
Naik	Ghulam Hussain Khan	East Africa (1919)
Havildar	Khong Baksh	East Africa (1919)
Sepoy	Niaz Mohammad	East Africa (1919)
Sepoy	Diwan Ali Khan	East Africa (1919)
Sepoy	Hashim Ali Khan	Egypt (1918)

19TH Punjabis

The following soldiers were awarded the Indian Distinguished Service Medal for their conspicuous gallantry during their service in Transcaspsia, Persia and Salonika.

Rank	Name	Location
Subedar	Ghulam Mohammad	Persia (1917)
Havildar	Sher Ahmed	Persia (1917)
Subedar	Aziz Ullah	Transcaspsia (1919)
Havildar	Must Amir	Transcaspsia (1919)
Havildar	Tora Khan	Transcaspsia (1919)
Lance Naik	Gulab Khan	Transcaspsia (1919)
Lance Naik	Shah Sowar	Transcaspsia (1919)
Sepoy	Chrigh Din	Transcaspsia (1919)
Sepoy	Karim Shah	Transcaspsia (1919)
Sepoy	Fazal Khan	Salonika (1919)
Sepoy	Gulab Khan	Salonika (1919)

The India Distinguished Service Medal 1907-1922

20TH Infantry (Brownlow's Punjabis)

Havildar Sher Ali and Naik Ghulam Haider were awarded the Indian Distinguished Service Medal for their conspicuous gallantry during their service in Mesopotamia.

Havildar	Sher Ali	Mesopotamia (1915)
Naik	Ghulam Haider	Mesopotamia (1915)

21ST Punjabis

The following soldiers were awarded the Indian Distinguished Service Medal for their conspicuous gallantry during their service in Waziristan, France and Mesopotamia.

Havildar	Fateh Ali	France (1917)
Sepoy	Mohammad Shah	France (1917)
Subedar	Habib Khan	Waziristan (1917)
Lance Naik	Said Amir	Waziristan (1917)
Jemadar	Ghulam Hussein	Mesopotamia (1919)
Naik	Nur Badshah	Waziristan (1920)
Sepoy	Hayat Mohammad	Waziristan (1921)
Jemadar	Mehdi Khan	Waziristan (1921)
Sepoy	Amir Khan	Waziristan (1921)
Havildar	Mian Ahmed	Waziristan (1921)

22ND Punjabis

The following soldiers were awarded the Indian Distinguished Service Medal for their conspicuous gallantry in Baluchistan and Mesopotamia.

Subedar	Allah Nur	Mohmad (1908)
Havildar	Sarfaraz Khan	Mohmad (1908)
Havildar	Badr Din	Mohmad (1908)
Havildar	Jenhandad	Mohmad (1908)
Havildar	Said Ahmed	Mesopotamia (1915)
Havildar	Fateh Jang	Mesopotamia (1915)
Jemadar	Hakim Khan	Mesopotamia (1915)
Lance Naik	Bostan Khan	Mesopotamia (1917)
Havildar	Yaqub Khan	Mesopotamia (1920)
Havildar	Gul Sher	Mesopotamia (1920)
Sepoy	Sardar Khan	Mesopotamia (1920)
Subedar	Ali Beg	Baluchistan (1920)

The India Distinguished Service Medal 1907-1922

24TH Punjabis

The following soldiers were awarded the Indian Distinguished Service Medal for their conspicuous gallantry during their service in Mesopotamia.

Naik	Sardar Khan	Mesopotamia (1915)
Naik	Ulas Mir	Mesopotamia (1915)
Naik	Haider Khan	Mesopotamia (1915)
Sepoy	Yar Akhmad	Mesopotamia (1915)
Sepoy	Nawab Ali	Mesopotamia (1915)
Havildar	Aksar Khan	Mesopotamia (1915)
Sepoy	Zawari	Mesopotamia (1919)

25TH Punjabis

The following soldiers were awarded the Indian Distinguished Service Medal for their conspicuous gallantry during their service in Mesopotamia.

Subedar	Hakim Khan	Mesopotamia (1916)
Havildar	Mir Afzal	Mesopotamia (1916)
Havildar	Kajir Khan	Mesopotamia (1916)
Jemadar	Sher Bahadur	Mesopotamia (1918)
Sepoy	Malik Din	Mesopotamia (1919)
Naik	Abdul Qadir	Mesopotamia (1921)

26TH Punjabis

The following soldiers were awarded the Indian Distinguished Service Medal for their conspicuous gallantry during their service in East Africa and Mesopotamia.

Lance Naik	Ghulam Haider	Mesopotamia (1917)
Havildar	Mir Dast	East Africa (1917)
Subedar	Mawaz Khan	Mesopotamia (1919)
Subedar	Sardar Khan	Mesopotamia (1919)

27TH Punjabis

The following soldiers were awarded the Indian Distinguished Service Medal for their conspicuous gallantry during their service in Egypt and Mesopotamia.

Subedar	Mir Akbar	Mesopotamia (1916)
Havildar	Fateh Khan	Mesopotamia (1916)

The India Distinguished Service Medal 1907-1922

27ᵀᴴ Punjabis (Cont)

Lance Naik	Makhumad Din	Mesopotamia (1916)
Sepoy	Mohammad Khan	Mesopotamia (1916)
Havildar	Zain Din	Mesopotamia (1917)
Sepoy	Dullah Khan	Mesopotamia (1917)
Subedar	Aman Gul	Egypt (1919)
Sepoy	Sajwal Khan	Egypt (1919)

28ᵀᴴ Punjabis

The following soldiers were awarded the Indian Distinguished Service Medal for their conspicuous gallantry during their service in Egypt and Mesopotamia.

Havildar	Multan	Mesopotamia (1916)
Havildar	Nikab Gul	Mesopotamia (1917)
Jemadar	Raja Khan	Mesopotamia (1917)
Jemadar	Imam Ali	Mesopotamia (1919)
Lance Naik	Gul Baz	Mesopotamia (1916)
Sepoy	Isa Khan	Mesopotamia (1916)
Sepoy	Amir Khan	Mesopotamia (1916)
Sepoy	Mohammad Amin	Mesopotamia (1916)
Havildar	Abbas Ali	Egypt (1919)
Jemadar	Ghafur Khan	Egypt (1919)
Lance Naik	Gul Khan	Egypt (1919)
Sepoy	Umar Din	Egypt (1921)
Sepoy	Sardar Khan	Waziristan (1921)
Sepoy	Ahmed Khan	Waziristan (1921)
Sepoy	Jiwan Khan	Waziristan (1921)
Seoy	Sheikh Mohammad	Waziristan (1921)
Havildar	Adalat Khan	Waziristan (1922)

29ᵀᴴ Punjabis

Jemadar Baz Khan was awarded the Indian Distinguished Service Medal for conspicuous gallantry during his service in East Africa.

Subedar	Mohammad Khan	N.W.Frontier (1916)
Jemadar	Baz Khan	East Africa (1918)

The India Distinguished Service Medal 1907-1922

30ᵀᴴ Punjabis

The following soldiers were awarded the Indian Distinguished Service Medal for their conspicuous gallantry during their service on the N.W.Frontier and East Africa.

Havildar	Sher Khan	N.W.Frontier (1916)
Lance Naik	Ismail Khan	East Africa (1917)
Havildar	Ali Ahmed	East Africa (1918)
Lance Naik	Said Mohammad	East Africa (1918)
Sepoy	Fateh Ali	East Africa (1918)
Subedar	Abbas Ali	Waziristan (1921)
Sepoy	Sher Khan	Waziristan (1921)
Subedar	Bhag Ali	Waziristan (1922)

31ˢᵀ Punjabis

Sepoy Ibrahim was awarded the Indian Distinguished Service Medal for his conspicuous gallantry during the action in Waziristan

Sepoy	Ibrahim	Waziristan (1920)

33ᴿᴰ Punjabis

The following soldiers were awarded Indian Distinguished Service Medal for their conspicuous gallantry in France and East Africa.

Subedar	Muzarab Shah	France (1916)
Naik	Farman Ali	France (1916)
Sepoy	Mowaz	France (1916)
Sepoy	Chowdre Khan	France (1917)
Havildar	Sakhi Zaman	East Africa (1918)
Naik	Abbas	East Africa (1918)
Naik	Ali Akbar	East Africa (1918)
Sepoy	Lal Khan	East Africa (1918)
Sepoy	Roshan Khan	East Africa (1918)

40ᵀᴴ Pathans

The following soldiers were awarded Indian Distinguished Service Medal for their conspicuous gallantry in France and East Africa.

Jemadar	Shiraj	France (1915)
Sepoy	Haider Ali	France (1916)
Naik	Sahib Shah	East Africa (1917)
Sepoy	Gafar Khan	East Africa (1917)

The India Distinguished Service Medal 1907-1922

46^(TH) Punjabis

The following soldiers were awarded the Indian Distinguished Service Medal for their gallantry.

Subedar	Abdul Ghafar Khan	N.W.Frontier (1916)
Subedar	Habib Ullah Khan	N.W.Frontier (1916)
Subedar	Badi-ul-Zaman	N.W.Frontier (1916)
Subedar	Firoz Khan	N.W.Frontier (1918)
Havildar	Mian Mohammad	Egypt (1919)
Lance Naik	Nur Alam	Egypt (1922)
Sepoy	Saugar Khan	Egypt (1922)

51^(ST) Sikhs (Frontier Force)

The following soldiers were awarded Indian Distinguished Service Medal for their conspicuous gallantry in Mesopotamia.

Subedar	Sher Gul	Mesopotamia (1916)
Subedar	Akbar Khan	Mesopotamia (1916)
Havildar	Khan Khel	Mesopotamia (1916)
Havildar	Barkat Shah	Mesopotamia (1916)
Jemadar	Amir Khan	Mesopotamia (1916)
Naik	Khial Zada	Mesopotamia (1916)
Naik	Jalal Khan	Mesopotamia (1916)
Naik	Gul Badshah	Mesopotamia (1916)
Naik	Sher Mohammad	Mesopotamia (1916)
Sepoy	Sahib Din	Mesopotamia (1916)
Sepoy	Habib Shah	Mesopotamia (1916)
Havildar	Gul Badshah	Mesopotamia (1918)
Subedar	Akbar Khan	Egypt (1918)
Naik	Sher Mohammad	Mesopotamia (1919)
Sepoy	Sahib Din	Mesopotamia (1919)

52^(ND) Sikhs (Frontier Force)

The following soldiers were awarded Indian Distinguished Service Medal for their conspicuous gallantry in N.W.Frontier, France and Mesopotamia.

Subedar	Karam Khan	N.W.Frontier (1915)
Lance Naik	Chur Khan	France (1915)
Subedar	Sahib Gul	Mesopotamia (1919)
Lance Naik	Haider Khan	Mesopotamia (1919)
Havildar	Hakim Shah	Mesopotamia (1920)

The India Distinguished Service Medal 1907-1922

53RD Sikhs (Frontier Force)

The following soldiers were awarded Indian Distinguished Service Medal for their conspicuous gallantry in Egypt and Mesopotamia.

Rank	Name	Campaign
Sepoy	Nurudin	Gumati Fort (1902)
Subedar	Sayyid Ali	Bazar Valley (1908)
Havildar	Gul Akhmed	NW Frontier (1908)
Havildar	Umar Din	NW Frontier (1908)
Havildar	Jamal Din	Mesopotamia (1916)
Sepoy	Allah Dad	Mesopotamia (1916)
Sepoy	Bazm Ali	Mesopotamia (1916)
Sepoy	Farman Ali	Mesopotamia (1916)
Sepoy	Painda Khan	Mesopotamia (1916)
Bugler	Fateh Mohmand	Mesopotamia (1916)
Sepoy	Gama Khan	Egypt (1919)

54TH Sikhs (Frontier Force)

The following soldiers were awarded Indian Distinguished Service Medal for their conspicuous gallantry during the Great War.

Rank	Name	Campaign
Havildar	Golodu	Mohmad (1908)
Havildar	Hashmat Ali	Mohmad (1908)
Sepoy	Mian Khan	Mohmad (1908)
Jemadar	Mohammad Sher	Mesopotamia (1917)
Naik	Sultan Baksh	Waziristan (1918)
Lance Naik	Pinnu Khan	Waziristan (1918)
Lance Naik	Mir Zaman	Waziristan (1918)
Lance Naik	Mohammad Khan	Waziristan (1918)
Lance Naik	Mohd. Baksh	Waziristan (1918)
Sepoy	Walayat Khan	Waziristan (1918)
Havildar	Mowaz Khan	Waziristan (1918)
Havildar	Firoz Khan	Somaliland (1920)
Subedar	Janas Khan	Egypt (1919)
Havildar	Sher Ullah	Egypt (1919)
Havildar	Faiz Alam	Egypt (1919)
Havildar	Bakhtawar Khan	Egypt (1919)
Sepoy	Lakhmir Khan	Egypt (1919)

The India Distinguished Service Medal 1907-1922

55TH Rifles (Frontier Force)

The following soldiers were awarded the Indian Distinguished Service Medal for their conspicuous gallantry in the actions fought during the Great War and before.

Jemadar	Shah Gul	Waziristan (1901)
Sepoy	Nazir Din	Tibet (1903)
Subedar	Zargun Shah	Waziristan (1901)
Subedar	Mansur Khan	NW Frontier (1908)
Jemadar	Daud Shah	NW Frontier (1908)
Sepoy	Summer Gul	NW Frontier (1908)
Sepoy	Mir Bad Shah	France (1915)
Sepoy	Mehr Khan	France (1915)
Subedar	Ibrahim Khan	East Africa (1918)
Naik	Umbrass Khan	East Africa (1917)
Lance Naik	Ghulam Nabi	East Africa (1918)
Sepoy	Mawiz Khan	East Africa (1918)
Subedar	Isa Khan	Bushire (1919)
Havildar	Jehan Khan	Bushire (1919)
Havildar	Gulab Khan	Waziristan (1920)
Havildar	Fazal Illahi	Waziristan (1920)
Havildar	Gheba Khan	Waziristan (1920)
Havildar	Gulab Akbar	Waziristan (1920)
Naik	Zarin Khan	Waziristan (1920)

56TH Punjabi Rifles (Frontier Force)

The following soldiers were awarded the Indian Distinguished Service Medal for their conspicuous gallantry in the actions fought in France, Somaliland and Mesopotamia.

Jemadar	Firoz Khan	Somaliland (1915)
Sepoy	Dheru Khan	Mesopotamia (1916)
Havildar	Sajwal Khan	Mesopotamia (1916)
Lance Naik	Nur Hamed	Mesopotamia (1916)
Sepoy	Allah Ditta Khan	Mesopotamia (1916)
Sepoy	Gulab Khan	Mesopotamia (1916)
Sepoy	Mirzada	Mesopotamia (1917)
Naik	Samundar Khan	Mesopotamia (1917)
Naik	Hakim Ali Khan	Mesopotamia (1918)

The India Distinguished Service Medal 1907-1922

57TH Rifles (Frontier Force)

The following officers and men of the 57TH Rifles were awarded the Indian Distinguished Service Medal for their gallantry in France and East Africa.

Rank	Name	Campaign
Jemadar	Munir	NW Frontier (1908)
Sepoy	Bahadur	NW Frontier (1908)
Sepoy	Bazid Khan	NW Frontier (1908)
Sepoy	Lal Mir	NW Frontier (1908)
Havildar	Gulzada	NW Frontier (1908)
Subedar	Fateh Jang	France (1915)
Havildar	Karim Khan	France (1915)
Havildar	Sahib Sher	France (1915)
Havildar	Sar Mast	France (1915)
Sepoy	Alvaz Khan	France (1915)
Sepoy	Mir Badshah	France (1915)
Sepoy	Mir Baz	France (1915)
Sepoy	Bahadur Khan	France (1915)
Sepoy	Sher Mohammad	East Africa (1918)
Naik	Kala Khan	East Africa (1920)
Havildar	Amir Shah	Waziristan (1920)

58TH Rifles (Frontier Force)

The following officers and men of the regiment were awarded the Indian Distinguished Service Medal for their gallantry in France, Egypt and East Africa.

Rank	Name	Campaign
Subedar	Hamid Khan	France (1915)
Subedar	Raj Talab	France (1915)
Havildar	Bai Dullan	France (1915)
Havildar	Sarfaraz	France (1915)
Jemadar	Mir Mast	France (1915)
Naik	Sergun Shah	France (1915)
Naik	Zar Baz	France (1915)
Lance Naik	Said Asghar	France (1915)
Sepoy	Azam Khan	France (1915)
Havildar	Fazal Dad	Egypt (1918)
Lance Naik	Mohammad Amin	Egypt (1918)
Lance Naik	Rahim Ali	Egypt (1918)
Havildar M.	Var Khan	East Africa (1918)

The India Distinguished Service Medal 1907-1922

59TH Rifles (Frontier Force)

The following officers and men of the regiment were awarded the Indian Distinguished Service Medal for their gallantry in France, Mesopotamia, Egypt and Somaliland.

Rank	Name	Campaign
Subedar	Jan Mohammad	NW Frontier (1908)
Jemadar	Jahan Dad Khan	NW Frontier (1908)
Jemadar	Mir Nabbi Hussain	NW Frontier (1908)
Havildar	Mobil Khan	NW Frontier (1908)
Sepoy	Madat Ali	NW Frontier (1908)
Sepoy	Haidar Ali	NW Frontier (1908)
Subedar	Mohammad Khan	France (1915)
Havildar	Niaz Gul	France (1915)
Havildar	Amir Ali	France (1915)
Havildar	Nur Ali	France (1916)
Jemadar	Ghamai Khan	France (1915)
Jemadar	Zaman Ali	France (1915)
Sepoy	Lal Khan	France (1915)
Sepoy	Abkar Khan	France (1915)
Subedar	Ali Akbar	Mesopotamia (1919)
Havildar	Abuzar Khan	Mesopotamia (1919)
Havildar	Hazrat Khan	Mesopotamia (1917)
Havildar	Niaz Gul	Mesopotamia (1918)
Jemadar	Malang Khan	Mesopotamia (1919)
Lance Naik	Saida Khan	Mesopotamia (1916)
Naik	Alwal Khan	Mesopotamia (1919)
Sepoy	Hasham Khan	Mesopotamia (1919)
Havildar	Hukum Dad	Mesopotamia (1919)
Naik	Rasul Khan	Egypt (1919)
Jemadar	Burhan Ali Khan	Somaliland (1920)

61ST Pioneers

The following officers of the regiment were awarded the Indian Distinguished Service Medal for their gallantry in East Africa.

Rank	Name	Campaign
Subedar	Mohammad Abdul Aziz	East Africa (1917)
Subedar	Lal Khan	East Africa (1917)
Havildar	Abdul Rahim	East Africa (1917)
Havildar	Saiyed Ahmed	East Africa (1917)

The India Distinguished Service Medal 1907-1922

62ND Punjabis

The following officers and men of the regiment were awarded the Indian Distinguished Service Medal for their gallantry in France and Mesopotamia.

Naik	Bari Sher	France (1915)
Naik	Imam Shah	France (1915)
Subedar	Sher Zaman Khan	Mesopotamia (1917)
Jemadar	Sher Gul Khan	Mesopotamia (1917)

64TH Pioneers

The following soldiers were awarded the Indian Distinguished Service Medal for their gallantry in action in the Kachin Hills.

Havildar	Rahman Sharif	Kachin Hills (1915)
Lance Naik	Qadir Beg	Kachin Hills (1916)

66TH Punjabis

During the fighting many deeds of gallantry were performed including the Indian Distinguished Service Medal awards to the following officers.

Subedar	Mohammad Khan	Mesopotamia (1917)
Havildar	Muzaffar Khan	Mesopotamia (1917)
Subedar	Akbar Khan	Mesopotamia (1920)

67TH Punjabis

The following soldiers were awarded the Indian Distinguished Service Medal for their conspicuous gallantry in Mesopotamia.

Subedar	Ahmed Khan	Mesopotamia (1917)
Havildar	Sharif Khan	Mesopotamia (1915)
Havildar	Ali Ahmed	Mesopotamia (1917)
Naik	Gauhar Ali	Mesopotamia (1915)
Naik	Khoja Khan	Mesopotamia (1917)
Sepoy	Allah Ditta	Mesopotamia (1915)
Sepoy	Nur Khan	Mesopotamia (1917)
Sepoy	Mehr Din	Mesopotamia (1917)

The India Distinguished Service Medal 1907-1922

69^(TH) Punjabis

The following soldiers were awarded the Indian Distinguished Service Medal for their conspicuous gallantry N.W.Frontier, France, Aden and Mesopotamia.

Havildar	Ghulam Ali	France (1916)
Jemadar	Gheba Khan	France (1916)
Sepoy	Mohammad Fazal	Mesopotamia (1916)
Lance Naik	Muhammad Din	Aden (1917)
Lance Naik	Zaman Ali	Mesopotamia (1918)
Havildar	Mohammad Baksh	Aden (1918)
Havildar	Allah Ditta	Aden (1919)
Naik	Asgar Ali	Aden (1919)
Sepoy	Ali Dad	Aden (1919)
Lance Naik	Bahadur Khan	N.W.Frontier (1920)

72^(ND) Punjabis

The following soldiers were awarded the Indian Distinguished Service Medal for their conspicuous gallantry Egypt and Mesopotamia.

Naik	Feroz Khan	Mesopotamia (1917)
Sepoy	Baz Khan	Mesopotamia (1916)
Subedar	Latif Khan	Egypt (1919)
Subedar	Jilal Din	Egypt (1919)
Naik	Karam Ali	Egypt (1919)
Naik	Feroz Khan	Egypt (1919)

74^(TH) Punjabis

Naiks Ghzi Khan and Jehan Dad were awarded the Indian Distinguished Service Medal for their conspicuous gallantry in Egypt.

Naik	Ghazi Khan	Egypt (1919)
Naik	Jehan Dad	Egypt (1919)

75^(TH) Infantry

The following NCOs were awarded the Indian Distinguished Service Medal for their conspicuous gallantry in Mesopotamia.

Lance Naik	Shaikh Farid	Mesopotamia (1915)
Naik	Abdul Basith	Mesopotamia (1920)

The India Distinguished Service Medal 1907-1922

76^(TH) Punjabis

The following soldiers were awarded the Indian Distinguished Service Medal for their conspicuous gallantry in during the siege in Mesopotamia and their gallantry in Waziristan.

Rank	Name	Campaign
Subedar	Bahadur Shah	Mesopotamia (1915)
Subedar	Hussein Shah	Mesopotamia (1915)
Havildar	Hukam Dad	Mesopotamia (1915)
Havildar	Said Zaman	Mesopotamia (1915)
Havildar	Hamid Ullah	Mesopotamia (1915)
Lance Naik	Lal Khan	Mesopotamia (1915)
Lance Naik	Nawais Ali	Mesopotamia (1915)
Lance Naik	Bari Sher	Mesopotamia (1915)
Naik	Firoze Khan	Mesopotamia (1915)
Naik	Shah Khan	Somaliland (1915)
Sepoy	Karim Khan	Mesopotamia (1915)
Sepoy	Sujawal Khan	Mesopotamia (1915)
Sepoy	Sher Dil	Mesopotamia (1915)
Sepoy	Firoz Khan	Mesopotamia (1915)
Sepoy	Madar Ali	Mesopotamia (1915)
Sepoy	Afsar Ali	Mesopotamia (1915)
Sepoy	Bostan Khan	Mesopotamia (1915)
Sepoy	Sultan Mohammad	Mesopotamia (1915)
Sepoy	Baker Khan	Mesopotamia (1915)
Bugler	Gul Sher	Mesopotamia (1915)
Lance Naik	Zaman Khan	Mesopotamia (1916)
Subedar	Ghulam Khan	Mesopotamia (1917)
Havildar	Kalandar Khan	Mesopotamia (1920)
Havildar	Karam Khan	Waziristan (1920)
Jemadar	Mahmud Khan	Waziristan (1920)
Havildar	Firoze Khan	Mesopotamia (1920)

79^(TH) Carnatic Infantry

Rank	Name	Campaign
Lance Naik	Syed Madar	Persia (1911)
Sepoy	Shaikh Imam	Persia (1911)
Sepoy	Abdul Basid	Persia (1911)
Sepoy	Abdul Khadar	Persia (1911)

The India Distinguished Service Medal 1907-1922

80TH Carnatic Infantry

The following soldiers were awarded the Indian Distinguished Service Medal for their conspicuous gallantry during the fighting in Mesopotamia.

Subedar	Daud Beg	Mesopotamia (1919)
Lance Naik	Mohammad Abdul Sabhan	Mesopotamia (1919)
Subedar	Mohammad Ismail	Mesopotamia (1921)
Havildar	Shaikh Ahmad	Mesopotamia (1923)

82ND Punjabis

The following soldiers were awarded the Indian Distinguished Service Medal for their conspicuous gallantry in Waziristan and Mesopotamia.

Subedar	Ghulam Muhiddin	Mesopotamia (1917)
Havildar	Abdul Khan	Mesopotamia (1917)
Havildar	Khawas Khan	Mesopotamia (1917)
Lance Naik	Mehmed Khan	Waziristan (1919)
Jemadar	Aziz Khan	Waziristan (1920)

84TH Punjabis

Naik Burham Ali was awarded the Indian Distinguished Service Medal for his conspicuous gallantry against the Germans in France.

Naik	Burham Ali	France (1916)

87TH Punjabis

The following soldiers were awarded the Indian Distinguished Service Medal for their conspicuous gallantry in Mesopotamia.

Subedar	Karam Din	Mesopotamia (1917)
Havildar	Allah Dad	Mesopotamia (1917)
Sepoy	Nadir Ali	Mesopotamia (1917)
Sepoy	Allah Dad	Mesopotamia (1919)
Havildar	Munshi Khan	Mesopotamia (1921)
Naik	Sultan Ali	Mesopotamia (1921)
Lance Naik	Imam Din	Mesopotamia (1921)
Jemadar	Mohammad Sadiq Khan	Mesopotamia (1921)
Lance Naik	Nur Mohammad	Mesopotamia (1921)

The India Distinguished Service Medal 1907-1922

89TH Punjabis

The following soldiers of the regiment were awarded the Indian Distinguished Service Medal for their conspicuous gallantry in France and Mesopotamia.

Havildar	Mohammad Sadiq	France (1915)
Naik	Karam Dad	France (1916)
Sepoy	Mohammad Khan	France (1916)
Havildar	Ghulam Mohammad	Mesopotamia (1916)
Sepoy	Sher Mohammad	Mesopotamia (1916)
Naik	Amir Dad	Mesopotamia (1916)
Sepoy	Sher Mohammad	Mesopotamia (1916)
Subedar	Allah Ditta	Mesopotamia (1919)
Lance Naik	Khuda Baksh	Mesopotamia (1919)

90TH Punjabis

The following soldiers were awarded the Indian Distinguished Service Medal for their conspicuous gallantry in Mesopotamia.

Lance Naik	Garkhar Khan	Mesopotamia (1918)
Sepoy	Mehtab Ali	Mesopotamia (1920)

91ST Punjabis

The following soldiers were awarded the Indian Distinguished Service Medal for their conspicuous gallantry in Egypt and Mesopotamia.

Subedar	Amir Ali	Egypt (1915)
Sepoy	Mustafa Khan	Mesopotamia (1918)
Lance Naik	Karam Dad	Egypt (1919)
Subedar	Amir Ali	Egypt (1919)
Sepoy	Mohammad Khan	Egypt (1919)
Subedar	Sher Khan	Waziristan (1922)

92ND Punjabis

The following soldiers were awarded the Indian Distinguished Service Medal for their conspicuous gallantry in Egypt and Mesopotamia.

Subedar	Farman Ali	Egypt (1915)
Sepoy	Fateh Mohammad	Mesopotamia (1916)
Sepoy	Manga Khan	Mesopotamia (1916)

The India Distinguished Service Medal 1907-1922

101ST Grenadiers

The following soldiers were awarded the Indian Distinguished Service Medal for their conspicuous gallantry in Aden, East Africa and Egypt.

Rank	Name	Campaign
Sepoy	Sabdal Khan	East Africa (1915)
Lance Naik	Abdul Sattar Khan	Egypt (1918)
Sepoy	Umar Khan	Egypt (1918)
Sepoy	Dilbar Shah	Egypt (1918)
Jemadar	Wahid Ali	Aden (1919)
Havildar	Abdul Karim Khan	Aden (1919)
Naik	Sattar Ali	Egypt (1919)
Naik	Wali Dad	Egypt (1919)
Subedar	Raj Wali Khan	Egypt (1919)
Subedar	Ahmed Din	Egypt (1920)
Havildar	Mohammad Yusuf	Egypt (1920)
Lance Naik	Mohd, Yusuf Khan	Egypt (1920)
Lance Naik	Gowhar Ali Khan	Egypt (1920)

102ND Grenadiers

The following soldiers were awarded the Indian Distinguished Service Medal for their conspicuous gallantry in Muscat and Mesopotamia.

Rank	Name	Campaign
Private	Sultan Ahmed	Muscat (1916)
Private	Karam Dad Khan	Muscat (1916)
Havildar	Mansare Ali	Mesopotamia (1916)
Jemadar	Khan Mohammad	Mesopotamia (1916)
Private	Feroz Khan	Mesopotamia (1917)
Havildar	Niamat Khan	Mesopotamia (1918)
Subedar	Mansar Ali	Mesopotamia (1920)

103RD Light Infantry

The following soldiers were awarded the Indian Distinguished Service Medal for their conspicuous gallantry in Mesopotamia.

Rank	Name	Campaign
Havildar	Shaikh Maqtum	Mesopotamia (1916)
Havildar	Hamid Khan	Mesopotamia (1916)
Havildar	Haider Khan	Mesopotamia (1920)
Subedar	Ilyasdar Khan	Mesopotamia (1923)

The India Distinguished Service Medal 1907-1922

104TH Rifles

The following soldiers were awarded the Indian Distinguished Service Medal for their conspicuous gallantry in Waziristan and Mesopotamia.

Rank	Name	Campaign
Bugler	Kala Khan	Mesopotamia (1915)
Subedar	Rahim Baksh	Mesopotamia (1916)
Havildar	Rahim Dad	Mesopotamia (1916)
Naik	Maula Baksh	Mesopotamia (1916)
Havildar	Sharaf Khan	Mesopotamia (1917)
Havildar	Rahim Dad Khan	Mesopotamia (1917)
Havildar	Barkhader	Waziristan (1920)
Rifleman	Nawab Ali	Waziristan (1921)
Naik	Sher Mohammad	Waziristan (1921)

106TH Hazara Pioneers

The following pioneers were awarded the Indian Distinguished Service Medal for their conspicuous gallantry in South Persia, Seistan and Mesopotamia.

Rank	Name	Campaign
Subedar	Dost Mohammad	Bahadur (1907)
Subedar	Ali Dost	Kelat Column (1910)
Sepoy	Raz Ali	Mesopotamia (1916)
Havildar	Haider Ali	Mesopotamia (1917)
Subedar	Wali Mohammad	Seistan (1917)
Subedar	Ali Dost	Seistan (1917)
Jemadar	Ali Juma	Seistan (1917)
Naik	Abdul Karim	Seistan (1917)
Naik	Ali Nazar	Seistan (1917)
Sepoy	Haji Mohammad	Seistan (1917)
Subedar	Ali Shafa	Mesopotamia (1918)
Havildar	Haidar Khan	Mesopotamia (1918)
Havildar	Haidar	Mesopotamia (1918)
Lance Naik	Sayed Mohammad	Mesopotamia (1918)
Sepoy	Kurban	Mesopotamia (1919)
Sepoy	Abdul Hussein	Mesopotamia (1920)
Naik	Raz Ali	Mesopotamia (1920)
Sepoy	Abdul Hasan	Mesopotamia (1921)
Naik	Musharaf Khan	Mesopotamia (1921)
Sepoy	Said Rehmat	Mesopotamia (1921)
Naik	Hassan	Mesopotamia (1921)
Jemadar	Ibrahim	Mesopotamia (1921)

The India Distinguished Service Medal 1907-1922

107TH Pioneers

The following Pioneers were awarded the Indian Distinguished Service Medal for their conspicuous gallantry in France, Egypt and Mesopotamia.

Rank	Name	Location (Year)
Subedar	Hashmat Dad Khan	France (1915)
Subedar	Fateh Mohammad Khan	France (1916)
Havildar	Nasir Ullah Kham	Mesopotamia (1916)
Jemadar	Abdul Rahman	Mesopotamia (1916)
Jemadar	Habib Khan	Mesopotamia (1916)
Havildar	Nizam Khan	Mesopotamia (1916)
Naik	Sohbat Khan	Mesopotamia (1916)
Havildar	Zota Khan	Egypt (1919)
Havildar	Imam Din	Egypt (1919)

108TH Infantry

Rank	Name	Location (Year)
Sepoy	Allah Ditta	Mesopotamia (1917)
Sepoy	Munshi Khan	Egypt (1919)
Sepoy	Fazal Dad	Mesopotamia (1919)
Sepoy	Muzaffar Khan	Mesopotamia (1919)
Naik	Sardar Khan	Mesopotamia (1921)
Jemadar	Mir T Hussain	Mesopotamia (1921)
Sepoy	Murad Ali	Mesopotamia (1921)
Sepoy	Arshad Khan	Mesopotamia (1921)
Jemadar	Ghulam Qadir	Mesopotamia (1922)

109TH Infantry

Rank	Name	Location (Year)
Sepoy	Dost Mohammad	Aden (1916)
Sepoy	Fateh Mohammad	Egypt (1919)
Subedar	Amar Ali Khan	Waziristan (1921)
Subedar	Karram Khan	Waziristan (1921)
Naik	Mehtab Khan	Waziristan (1921)
Naik	Bakhtawar Khan	Waziristan (1921)
Sepoy	Sher Khan	Waziristan (1921)

110TH Light Infantry

Rank	Name	Location (Year)
Sepoy	Shaikh Umar	Mesopotamia (1915)
Subedar	Sayed Razak	Mesopotamia (1916)
Subedar	Shaikh Yasin	Mesopotamia (1917)

The India Distinguished Service Medal 1907-1922

112TH Infantry

Sepoy	Mehr Khan	Mesopotamia (1918)
Subedar	Karam Din	Mesopotamia (1919)
Subedar	Fazal Karim	Waziristan (1920)

113TH Infantry

Sepoy	Mohammad Zaman	Waziristan (1920)
Havildar	Sadar Din	Mesopotamia (1921)
Havildar	Rehmat Khan	Mesopotamia (1921)

114TH Mahrattas

Jemadar	Shaikh Khalil	Mesopotamia (1919)
Sepoy	Sayyid Bale	Mesopotamia (1919)
Sepoy	Shaikh Ladie	Mesopotamia (1919)

116TH Mahrattas

Jemadar	Sayad Shams-ud-Din	Mesopotamia (1919)
Sepoy	Mohammad Hussain	Mesopotamia (1919)
Sepoy	Din Mohammad	Mesopotamia (1921)

117TH Mahrattas

Sepoy	Abdul Ghaffar	Mesopotamia (1915)

119TH Infantry (The Mooltan Regiment)

The following soldiers were awarded the Indian Distinguished Service Medal for their conspicuous gallantry in Mesopotamia.

Sepoy	Nabi Baksh	Mesopotamia (1915)
Havildar	Mohammad Safi Khan	Mesopotamia (1915)
Naik	Imtiaz Khan	Mesopotamia (1919)
Havildar	Usman Gani Khan	Mesopotamia (1920)
Sepoy	Abdul Ghafur Khan	Mesopotamia (1920)

120TH Rajputana Infantry

Sepoy	Juma Baksh	Mesopotamia (1916)
Havildar	Asghar Ali	Mesopotamia (1916)
Sepoy	Ghafur Khan	Mesopotamia (1916)
Sepoy	Yusuf Ali	Mesopotamia (1916)
Sepoy	Zaid Gul	Mesopotamia (1916)

The India Distinguished Service Medal 1907-1922

121ST Pioneers

The following soldiers were awarded the Indian Distinguished Service Medal for their conspicuous gallantry in Egypt and Mesopotamia.

Havildar	Dal Khan	France (1916)
Sepoy	Chota Khan	Mesopotamia (1917)
Havildar	Phul Khan	Mesopotamia (1917)
Havildar	Shadi Khan	Egypt (1919)
Subedar	Abdul Ghani Khan	Mesopotamia (1921)

123RD Rifles

The following soldiers were awarded the Indian Distinguished Service Medal for their conspicuous gallantry in the Great War.

Jemadar	Ghulam Mohammad	Persian Gulf (1910)
Jemadar	Mubarik Ali	France (1916)
Rirleman	Ladu Khan	Egypt (1918)
Sudedar	Feroz Khan	N.W.Frontier (1920)
Naik	Ahmed Khan	Mesopotamia (1920)
Naik	Alif Khan	Mesopotamia (1921)
Naik	Kabai Khan	Mesopotamia (1921)

124TH Baluchistan Infantry

The following soldiers were awarded the Indian Distinguished Service Medal for their conspicuous gallantry in Mesopotamia, Baluchistan and South Persia.

Sepoy	Ghulam Hussein	France (1915)
Sepoy	Abdula Khan	East Africa (1917)
Naik	Juma Khan	East Africa (1918)
Subedar	Mehdi Khan	South Persia (1918)
Havildar	Fateh Khan	South Persia (1918)
Sepoy	Kasim Khan	South Persia (1919)
Havildar	Nur Khan	Mesopotamia (1919)
Lance Naik	Rahim Khan	South Persia (1919)
Havildar	Bahadur Ali Shah	South Persia (1919)
Subedar	Sallah Mohammad	South Persia (1919)
Havildar	Boota Khan	South Persia (1919)
Havildar	Mohammad Karim	South Persia (1919)
Havildar	Nur Khan	Mesopotamia (1919)
Sepoy	Jiwan Khan	NW Frontier (1920)

The India Distinguished Service Medal 1907-1922

124TH Baluchistan Infantry (Cont)

Havildar	Alam Khan	South Persia (1920)
Naik	Hussien Mohammad	South Persia (1920)
Subedar	Ghulam Unis	Baluchistan (1920)
Subedar	Mirza Khan	Baluchistan (1920)
Havildar	Ghafur Khan	Baluchistan (1920)
Naik	Jaffar Khan	Baluchistan (1920)
Sepoy	Allan Ditta	Baluchistan (1920)
Sepoy	Sajawal Khan	Baluchistan (1920)

125TH Rifles

The following soldiers were awarded the Indian Distinguished Service Medal for their conspicuous gallantry in Egypt and Mesopotamia.

Rifleman	Gul Sher	France (1916)
Havildar	Hakim Khan	Mesopotamia (1916)
Jemadar	Nizam-ud-Din	Mesopotamia (1919)
Subedar	Allah Dad Khan	Egypt (1919)
Havildar	Madat Khan	Egypt (1919)
Rifleman	Nawab Khan	Egypt (1919)

126TH Baluchistan Infantry

The following soldiers were awarded the Indian Distinguished Service Medal for their conspicuous gallantry in Aden and Mesopotamia.

Jemadar	Guldar Shah	Aden (1916)
Naik	Ahmed Khan	Aden (1916)
Naik	Wazir Khan	Aden (1916)
Lance Naik	Kampoo Khan	Mesopotamia (1918)
Subedar	Umar Khan	Mesopotamia (1919)
Jemadar	Ajab Gul	Mesopotamia (1919)
Jemadar	Arz Mohammad	Mesopotamia (1920)
Naik	Ahmed Din	Mesopotamia (1920)
Naik	Fazal Khan	Mesopotamia (1920)
Naik	Malik Shah	Mesopotamia (1920)
Sepoy	Shahza Khan	Mesopotamia (1920)
Sepoy	Ahmed Khan	Mesopotamia (1920)
Sepoy	Nikab Gul	Mesopotamia (1920)

The India Distinguished Service Medal 1907-1922

127TH Baluchistan Infantry

The following soldiers were awarded the Indian Distinguished Service Medal for their conspicuous gallantry in France, East Africa, Mesopotamia, Bushire and Waziristan.

Rank	Name	Campaign
Jemadar	Raj Wali	Baluchistan (1907)
Havildar	Dad Khan	France (1917)
Lance Naik	Mustkin	France (1917)
Subedar	Karam Shah	East Africa (1918)
Havildar	Mir Shah	East Africa (1918)
Lance Naik	Mohammad Sadiq	East Africa (1918)
Naik	Hayat Mohamand	East Africa (1918)
Naik	Torsum	East Africa (1918)
Lance Naik	Mohammad Sadiq	East Africa (1918)
Sepoy	Jamadar	East Africa (1918)
Sepoy	Alam Mir	East Africa (1918)
Havildar	Mohammad Sher	Mesopotamia (1919)
Sepoy	Fateh Mohammad	Mesopotamia (1919)
Havildar	Khan Zada	Bushire (1919)
Sepoy	Allah Dad	Waziristan (1920)
Sepoy	Nizam Din	Waziristan (1920)

128TH Pioneers

The following soldiers were awarded the Indian Distinguished Service Medal for their conspicuous gallantry in Mesopotamia.

Rank	Name	Campaign
Subedar	Sher Afzal	Mesopotamia (1917)
Jemadar	Malle Khan	Mesopotamia (1916)
Jemadar	Hakim Khan	Mesopotamia (1919)
Lance Naik	Rakkmat Shah	Mesopotamia (1916)
Lance Naik	Mohammad Issa	Mesopotamia (1917)
Naik	Dhunde Khan	Mesopotamia (1917)
Private	Ghosi Khan	Mesopotamia (1916)
Private	Sardar Khan	Mesopotamia (1916)
Private	Sheikh Hubdar Ali	Mesopotamia (1917)
Sepoy	Kamal Khan	Mesopotamia (1919)
Sepoy	Said Amir	Mesopotamia (1917)

The India Distinguished Service Medal 1907-1922

129ᵀᴴ Baluchis

The following soldiers were awarded the Indian Distinguished Service Medal for their conspicuous gallantry in France and East Africa.

Rank	Name	Location (Year)
Jemadar	Ghulam Jilani	France (1916)
Sepoy	Kassib	France (1915)
Sepoy	Lal Sher	France (1915)
Sepoy	Afsar Khan	France (1915)
Sepoy	Said Ahmed	France (1915)
Sepoy	Auliya Khan	France (1915)
Sepoy	Mehrab Gul	France (1915)
Subedar		France (1915)
Subedar	Durani Khan	East Africa (1917)
Naik	Fateh Khan	East Africa (1917)
Naik	Sahib Jan	East Africa (1917)
Sepoy	Boota Khan	East Africa (1917)
Naik	Najib Khan	Somaliland (1919)
Lance Naik	Roshan Ali	Baluchistan (1920)
Sepoy	Waryam Khan	Baluchistan (1920)
Havildar	Fateh Khan	Waziristan (1920)

130ᵀᴴ Baluchis

The following soldiers were awarded the Indian Distinguished Service Medal for their conspicuous gallantry in East Africa.

Rank	Name	Location (Year)
Havildar	Mohammad Ali	East Africa (1916)
Subedar	Sultan Khan	East Africa (1917)
Lance Naik	Fateh Mohammad	East Africa (1917)
Naik	Mohammad Hussein	East Africa (1917)
Naik	Mustaffa Khan	East Africa (1917)
Sepoy	Lal Khan	East Africa (1917)
Sepoy	Mirza Khan	East Africa (1917)
Sepoy	Sultan Baksh	East Africa (1917)
Private	Chaman Khan	East Africa (1917)
Private	Shah Baz Khan	East Africa (1917)
Subedar	Now Shere	East Africa (1918)
Lance Naik	Waris Khan	East Africa (1918)
Naik	Rajwali	East Africa (1918)
Sepoy	Kadir Din	East Africa (1919)
Havildar	Bagga Khan	East Africa (1919)

151 Sikh Infantry

Sepoy	Mohammad Khan	Egypt (1919)
Naik	Mohammad Fazal	Waziristan (1920)

152ND Punjabis

The following soldiers were awarded the Indian Distinguished Service Medal for their conspicuous gallantry in Egypt.

Jemadar	Jahan Khan	Egypt (1919)
Naik	Raj Wali	Egypt (1919)
Sepoy	Ahmed Ji	Egypt (1919)
Sepoy	Ghulam Ali	Egypt (1919)

153RD Punjabis

The following soldiers were awarded the Indian Distinguished Service Medal for their conspicuous gallantry in Baluchistan and Egypt.

Subedar	Ali Mohammad Shah	Egypt (1919)
Havildar	Amir Ali	Egypt (1919)
Jemadar	Mir Afzal Khan	Egypt (1919)
Lance Naik	Jumma Khan	Egypt (1919)
Sepoy	Mohammad Zaman	Egypt (1919)
Sepoy	Shah Mohammad	Egypt (1919)
Subedar	Lahir Khan	Baluchistan (1920)
Naik	Ghasita Khan	Baluchistan (1920)
Sepoy	Fateh Mohammad	Baluchistan (1920)

155TH Indian Pioneers

The following soldiers were awarded the Indian Distinguished Service Medal for their conspicuous gallantry during the Great War.

Subedar	Fateh Khan	Egypt (1919)
Havildar	Adam Khan	Egypt (1919)

Indian Medical Department

A. Surgeon	Mohamand Umar	France (1915)
A. Surgeon	Zaffar Hussein	France (1915)
A. Surgeon	Saif ud Din	France (1915)
A. Surgeon	Fazal Ahmed	Mesopotamia (1915)
A. Surgeon	Sayid Abdul Basit	Mesopotamia (1917)
A. Surgeon	Mubarak Shah Khan	Mesopotamia (1917)
A. Surgeon	Mehdi Hussein Khan	Mesopotamia (1917)

The India Distinguished Service Medal 1907-1922

Indian Medical Department (Cont)

A. Surgeon	Barktullah	Mesopotamia (1916)
A. Surgeon	Wahidyar Khan	Mesopotamia (1917)
A. Surgeon	Abdul Ghafur	East Africa (1917)
A. Surgeon	Sayid Mohammad Ezar	East Africa (1917)
A. Surgeon	Mohammad Ishak	Mesopotamia (1918)
A. Surgeon	Ghulam Haidar	East Africa (1918)
A. Surgeon	Abdul Majid	East Africa (1918)
A. Surgeon	Shaikh Farid	Mesopotamia (1919)
A. Surgeon	Mohammad Hussain	South Persia (1919)
A. Surgeon	Mohammad Reza Khan	Bushire (1919)
A. Surgeon	Mohammad Hussain	Mesopotamia (1919)

Army Bearer Corps

The following bearers were awarded the Indian Distinguished Service Medal for their conspicuous gallantry during the Great War.

Naik	Sher Ahmed Khan	Mesopotamia (1916)
Naik	Fateh Mohammad	Gallipoli (1916)
Bearer	Mohammad Khan	Mesopotamia (1916)
Bearer	Sattar Mohammad Khan	France (1916)
Bearer	Mohammand Ismail	France (1917)
Bearer	Mohammad Kasim	France (1917)
Naik	Karim Baksh	France (1918)
Naik	Gunga Din	France (1918)
Naik	Mohammad Nur	France (1918)
Bearer	Firoze	France (1918)
Bearer	Hussein Baksh	France (1918)
Bearer	Data Din	Mesopotamia (1918)
Bearer	Rehmat Khan	Mesopotamia (1919)
Bearer	Ali Bahadur	Aden (1919)
Bearer	Ali Sher	N.W. Frontier (1920)

Burma Military Police

The following soldiers were awarded the Indian Distinguished Service Medal for their conspicuous gallantry in Burma, Aden and East Africa.

Havildar	Umar Din	Burma (1920)
Subedar	Mir Fazal	Burma (1920)
Jemadar	Fateh Mohammad	Burma (1920)
Jemadar	Ahmed Khan	East Africa (1917)
Lance Naik	Jalal Din	Aden (1919)

The India Distinguished Service Medal 1907-1922

Mule Corps

Rank	Name	Theatre (Year)
Naik	Painda Khan	France (1915)
Lance Naik	Rafi-ud-Din	France (1915)
Driver	Choo Beg	France (1915)
Driver	Faqir Mohammad	France (1915)
Driver	Abdulla	Egypt (1915)
Naik	Hiram Baksh	France (1915)
Naik	Sahib Din	Gallipoli (1915)
Driver	Wilayat Khan	Mesopotamia (1916)
Driver	Abdulla	France (1916)
Jemadar	Fateh Khan	France (1916)
Jemadar	Bahawal Din	France (1916)
Daffadar	Khan Gul	France (1916)
Driver	Mohammad Hussain	Mesopotamia (1916)
Ressaidar	Mohammad shah	Mesopotamia (1916)
Daffadar	Pir Khan	Gallipoli (1916)
Lance Naik	Ghulam Haider	Mesopotamia (1916)
Naik	Mir Zaman	Mesopotamia (1916)
Daffadar	Firman Ali	Egypt (1917)
Naik	Sahib Din	Mesopotamia (1917)
Daffadar	Ali Akbar	Mesopotamia (1917)
Daffadar	Ibrahim Khan	Mesopotamia (1917)
Driver	Khair Din	Mesopotamia (1917)
Driver	Kiam Din	Mesopotamia (1917)
Naik	Mir Said	Mesopotamia (1917)
Jemadar	Samundar Khan	Mesopotamia (1917)
Driver	Bagh Hussain	Mesopotamia (1918)
Naik	Ibrahim	Mesopotamia (1918)
Jemadar	Jehan Khan	Mesopotamia (1918)
Naik	Gul Zaman	Aden (1918)
Lance Naik	Akbar Ali	Mesopotamia (1919)
Driver	Saidullah	Mesopotamia (1919)
Jemadar	Sardar Khan	Egypt (1919)
Jemadar	Ali Mohammad	Mesopotamia (1919)
Jemadar	Jehan Dad	Mesopotamia (1919)
Jemadar	Baz Khan	Mesopotamia (1919)
Daffadar	Abdullah Khan	Mesopotamia (1919)
Driver	Wali Mohammad	Waziristan (1919)
Naik	Hussaina	NW Frontier (1919)

The India Distinguished Service Medal 1907-1922

Mule Corps (Cont)

Jemadar	Painda Khan	Mesopotamia (1919)
Jemadar	Karam Ali	Mesopotamia (1920)
Naik	Allah Dad	Waziristan (1920)
Daffadar	Azim Khan	Mesopotamia (1920)
Daffadar	Shalu Khan	Waziristan (1923)

Transport Corps

Risaldar	Nazir Mohammad	NW Frontier (1908)
Jemadar	Mohammad Ismail	Salonika (1917)
Daffadar	Fazal Elahi	Salonika (1917)
Risaldar	Nur Din	NW Frontier (1920)
Daffadar	Sarwar Khan	Waziristan (1921)
Ressaidar	Ghulam Qadir	Waziristan (1921)
Ressaidar	Fazal Dad	Waziristan (1921)
Daffadar	Mir Mohammad	Waziristan (1922)
Risaldar	Ashraf Ali Khan	Waziristan (1922)
Risaldar	Dadan Khan	Waziristan (1924)

Burma Military Police

Jemadar	Ahmed Khan	East Africa (1917)
Lance Naik	Mohammad Khan	East Africa (1918)
Lance Naik	Jalal Din	Aden (1919)
Subedar	Mir Fazal	Assam/Burma (1920)
Jemadar	Fateh Mohammad	Assam/Burma (1920)
Havildar	Umar Din	Assam/Burma (1920)

Burma Mounted Rifles

The following officers of the Burma Mounted Rifles were awarded the Indian Distinguished Service Medal for their conspicuous gallantry South Persia.

Daffadar	Saif Ali	South Persia (1918)
Daffadar	Abdullah Khan	South Persia (1919)
Risaldar	Farman Ali	South Persia (1918)
Risaldar	Farman Ali Khan	South Persia (1918)

The India Distinguished Service Medal 1907-1922

Frontier Constabulary

The following policemen were awarded the Indian Distinguished Service Medal for their conspicuous gallantry in Waziristan and on the N.W.Frontier.

Subedar	Zaffar Khan	Waziristan (1920)
Jemadar	Mad Asgar	Waziristan (1920)
Jemadar	Mohammad Azam	Waziristan (1920)
Havildar	Nazir Khan	N.W.Frontier (1917)
Jemadar	Turab Shah	N.W.Frontier (1920)
Lance Naik	Sher Ali	N.W.Frontier (1920)
Lance Naik	Ghulam Ali	N.W.Frontier (1920)
Sepoy	Pir Mohammad	N.W.Frontier (1920)
Sowar	Mubarak Shah	N.W.Frontier (1920)
Sowar	Ayub Khan	N.W.Frontier (1920)
Sowar	Zarif Khan	N.W.Frontier (1920)
Havildar	Niaz Khan	N.W.Frontier (1920)
Said	Nakki	N.W.Frontier (1920)

Khyber Rifles

The following soldiers were awarded the Indian Distinguished Service Medal for their conspicuous gallantry on the N.W.Frontier.

Subedar	Khan Sahib	N.W.Frontier (1908)
Jemadar	Tans Khan	N.W.Frontier (1917)
Havildar	Shamal	N.W.Frontier (1917)
Jemadar	Gul Zir	N.W.Frontier (1923)

Kohat Border Military Police

Havildar	Abdullah Khan	N.W.Frontier (1909)
Lance Naik	Ali Khan	N.W.Frontier (1909)
Sepoy	Said Kasim	N.W.Frontier (1909)
Sepoy	Sohbat Khan	N.W.Frontier (1909)

Chitral Scouts

The following Scouts were awarded the Indian Distinguished Service Medal for their conspicuous gallantry on the N.W.Frontier.

Subedar	Rehmat Zaman	N.W.Frontier (1920)
Havildar	Mania	N.W.Frontier (1920)
Havildar	Mir Khan	N.W.Frontier (1920)

The India Distinguished Service Medal 1907-1922

Northern Waziristan Militia

The following Militiamen were awarded the Indian Distinguished Service Medal for their conspicuous gallantry in Waziristan and on the N.W.Frontier.

Rank	Name	Campaign
Lance Naik	Khushal Khan	N.W.Frontier (1905)
Subedar	Malham Khan	N.W.Frontier (1909)
Jemadar	Zar Khan	N.W.Frontier (1909)
Subedar	Sardar Khan	Spinwarm (1913)
Naik	Nawab Khan	Spinwarm (1913)
Havildar	Khial Din	N.W.Frontier (1915)
Sepoy	Zaman Ullah	N.W.Frontier (1915)
Sepoy	Tawalhe Din	N.W.Frontier (1915)
Sepoy	Ain ud Din	N.W.Frontier (1915)
Sepoy	Mir Shah Jan	N.W.Frontier (1915)
Sepoy	Mohi Khan	N.W.Frontier (1915)
Jemadar	Zarif Khan	N.W.Frontier (1916)
Naik	Zar Khan	N.W.Frontier (1916)
Naik	Syad Akhmud	N.W.Frontier (1916)
Sepoy	Tor Khan	N.W.Frontier (1916)
Sepoy	Amir Khan	N.W.Frontier (1916)
Havildar	Malang Khan	N.W.Frontier (1917)
Subedar	Tor Khan	Waziristan (1920)
Naik	Saddar Khan	Waziristan (1920)
Bugler	Sher Ali	Waziristan (1920)
Compounder	Haq Nawaz Khan	Waziristan (1920)
Sepoy	Nur Shamal	Waziristan (1909)

Southern Waziristan Militia

The following Militiamen were awarded the Indian Distinguished Service Medal for their conspicuous gallantry in Waziristan and on the N.W.Frontier.

Rank	Name	Campaign
Jemadar	Mohibulla	Waziristan (1901)
Subedar	Kwan Khan	N.W.Frontier (1908)
Havildar	Gul Anar	N.W.Frontier (1908)
Jemadar	Ayub Khan	N.W.Frontier (1909)
Havildar	Gulakal	N.W.Frontier (1914)
Nai	Ghulam Khan	N.W.Frontier (1914)
Subedar	Maquam Khan	N.W.Frontier (1917)
Jemadar	Zari Gul	N.W.Frontier (1917)
Jemadar	Taza Gul	Waziristan (1920)

The India Distinguished Service Medal 1907-1922

Southern Waziristan Militia (Cont)

Naik	Sarwar	Waziristan (1920)
Jemadar	Sarwar	Waziristan (1920)
Risaldar	Ilaudin	Waziristan (1922)
Subedar	Mir Akhmad	Waziristan (1920)
Havildar	Khabib	Waziristan (1920)

Mohmand Militia

Sepoy Umar Gul was awarded the Indian Distinguished Service Medal for his conspicuous gallantry on the N.W.Frontier.

Sepoy	Umar Gul	N.W.Frontier (1920)

Kurram Militia

The following men of the Kurram Militia were awarded the Indian Distinguished Service Medal for their conspicuous gallantry on the N.W.Frontier.

Havildar	Sherbat Ali	N.W.Frontier (1905)
Subedar	Mohammad Hassan	N.W.Frontier (1908)
Subedar	Akbar Ali	N.W.Frontier (1911)
Subedar	Said Asghar	N.W.Frontier (1914)
Sudedar	Gul Khan	N.W.Frontier (1920)
Jemadar	Faqir Hussain	N.W.Frontier (1915)
Risaldar	Ali Mohsin	N.W.Frontier (1920)
Sepoy	Mir Abdullah Jan	N.W.Frontier (1920)

Zhob Militia

The following Militiamen were awarded the Indian Distinguished Service Medal for their conspicuous gallantry on the N.W.Frontier.

Naik	Awal Khan	Baluchistan (1920)
Lance Naik	Mir Bad Shah	Baluchistan (1920)
Lance Naik	Said Akbar	Baluchistan (1920)

1ST Hyderabad Lancers

The following Lancers were awarded the Indian Distinguished Service Medal for their conspicuous gallantry in Egypt.

Jemadar	Mohammad Faqir ud Din	Egypt (1918)
Jemadar	Safdar Khan	Egypt (1918)
Jemadar	Iqbal Ali Beg	Egypt (1918)
Daffadar	Abdul Basira Khan	Egypt (1918)

The India Distinguished Service Medal 1907-1922

Mekran Levy Force

The following men were awarded the Indian Distinguished Service Medal for their conspicuous gallantry while serving with the Mekran Force.

Jemadar	Sayyid Mohammad	Mekran Force (1916)
Jemadar	Gwaram Khan	Mekran Force (1916)
Daffadar	Nabi Baksh	Mekran Force (1916)
Lance Naik	Dad Khuda	Mekran Force (1916)

Levy Corps

The following men were awarded the Indian Distinguished Service Medal for their conspicuous gallantry while serving in Seistan and Baluchistan.

Risaldar	Edoo Khan	Seistan (1917)
Jemadar	Barat Ali	Seistan (1917)
Jemadar	Juma Jalal	Seistan (1917)
Havildar	Ramzan	Baluchistan (1920)
Naik	Lala Khan	Baluchistan (1920)
Jemadar	Shahbaz Khan	Baluchistan (1920)
Jemadar	Akbar Khan	Baluchistan (1920)
Subedar	Gul Badshah	Baluchistan (1920)

Alwar Imperial Troops

Alwar Imperial Troops The following men were awarded the Indian Distinguished Service Medal for their conspicuous gallantry while serving in Mesopotamia and Egypt.

Risaldar	Mohammad Ali Khan	Mesopotamia (1917)
Subedar	Zulfikar Ali	Egypt (1918)

Bharatpur Imperial Troops

The following men were awarded the Indian Distinguished Service Medal for their conspicuous gallantry while serving in East Africa.

Naik	Hasan Hussain	East Africa (1917)
Lance Naik	Zamal	East Africa (1918)

Bikaner Imperial Troops

The following men were awarded the Indian Distinguished Service Medal for their conspicuous gallantry while serving in East Africa.

Sepoy	Faiz Ali Khan	Egypt (1914)
Jemadar	Khwaja Bux	Egypt (1917)

The India Distinguished Service Medal 1907-1922

Jaipur Imperial Troops

The following men were awarded the Indian Distinguished Service Medal for their conspicuous gallantry while serving in Mesopotamia.

Jemadar	Faqir Mohammad	Mesopotamia (1918)
Driver	Nawab Khan	Mesopotamia (1918)

Malay States Guides Artillery

The following gunners were awarded the Indian Distinguished Service Medal for their conspicuous gallantry while serving in Aden.

Gunner	Abdul Rahim	Aden (1920)
Gunner	Roshan Din	Aden (1920)

Indian Postal Corps

The following officers were awarded the Indian Distinguished Service Medal for their conspicuous gallantry while serving in East Africa and Mesopotamia.

Subedar	Faqir Hussain	East Africa (1918)
Subedar	Muzaffar Ahmed	East Africa (1918)
Havildar	Abdul Karim	East Africa (1918)
Havildar	Bindraban	East Africa (1918)
Havildar	Shah Ghafur Khan	East Africa (1918)
Subedar	Jehangir	East Africa (1918)
Subedar	Abdul Aziz	East Africa (1918)
Inspector	Fazal Din	Mesopotamia (1919)
Inspector	Sher Khan	Mesopotamia (1919)

Survey of India

The 'Survey of India' set up in 1767 to help consolidate the territories of the British East India Company; it is one of the oldest Engineering Departments. During the Great War the following officers surveyed the conquered territories.

Jemadar	Abdul Azim	Salonika (1919)
Jemadar	Ghulam Rasul	Salonika (1919)
Jemadar	Laltan Khan	Mesopotamia (1919)
Jemadar	Mohammad Nasir Khan	Mesopotamia (1919)

The India Distinguished Service Medal 1923-1947

Indian Armoured Corps

The following men were awarded the Indian Distinguished Service Medal for their conspicuous gallantry while serving with the Indian Armoured Corps.

Rank	Name	Campaign
Daffadar	Faiz Mohammad Khan	N.W.Frontier (1930)
Sowar	Alam Ali Khan	N.W.Frontier (1930)
Ferriar	Mustaffa Khan	N.W.Frontier (1936)
Daffadar	Mohammad Sharif Khan	Middle East (1941)
Daffadar	Bajid Khan	Middle East (1941)
Daffadar	Mohd Munir Khan	Middle East (1942)
Risaldar	Hasham Ali Khan	Middle East (1941)
Sowar	Abdi Khan	Middle East (1941)
Sowar	Bhure Khan	Middle East (1941)
Daffadar	Mohd Bashir	Western Desert (1942)
Daffadar	Ghulam Rabbani	Western Desert (1942)
Daffadar	Khuda Baksh	Western Desert (1942)
Daffadar	Bahadur Khan	Western Desert (1942)
Risaldar	Rafiq Khan	Western Desert (1942)
Risaldar	Ali Musa Khan	Western Desert (1942)
Risaldar	Sardar Khan	Western Desert (1943)
Sowar	Mohammad Afzal	Western Desert (1942)
Sowar	Alim Khan	Western Desert (1942)
Risaldar	Abdulla Khan	Field (Escape) (1943)
Jemadar	Sher Ahmed	Italy (1944)

Royal Indian Artillery

The following Gunners were awarded the Indian Distinguished Service Medal for their conspicuous gallantry during the Second World War.

Rank	Name	Campaign
Lance Naik	Ghulam Hussein	Mesopotamia (1936)
Havildar	Fazal Elahi	Burma (1936)
Jemadar	Ghulan Mohi-ud-Din	Waziristan (1937)
Havildar	Hakim Khan	Waziristan (1937)
Subedar	Nawab Khan	N.W.Frontier (1939)
Signaller	Inyatt Ullah	East Africa (1941)
Naik	Mohd Khan	Syria (1941)
Havildar	Bahadur Khan	Western Desert (1942)
Havildar	Ghulam Ali	Western Desert (1942)
Havildar	Hakim Khan	Burma (1943)
Mechanic	Rehmat Ullah	Burma (1943)

The India Distinguished Service Medal 1923-1947

Royal Indian Artillery (Cont)

Havildar	Ali Bahadur	Burma (1943)
Havildar	Waris Khan	Burma (1943)
Naikk	Lal Hussain	Field (Escape) (1943)

Corps of Royal Indian Engineers

The following Engineers were awarded the Indian Distinguished Service Medal for their conspicuous gallantry during the Second World War.

Subedar	Fazk Haq	Waziristan (1924)
Subedar	Noor Mohammad	Waziristan (1924)
Havilar	Said Akbar	East Africa (1941)
Subedar	Hussain Shah	Western Desert (1942)
Havildar	Mohammad Ismail	Western Desert (1943)
Havildar	Nur-ul-Haq	Western Desert (1942)
Jemadar	Imdad Khan	Western Desert (1942)
Naik	Taj Mohammad	Western Desert (1943)
Havildar	Fazal Shah	Middle East (1943)
Subedar	Aslam Khan	Burma (1943)
Havildar	Fazal Elahi	Burma (1944)
Havildar	Masal Khan	Burma (1945)
Havildar	Mohammad Wilayat	Burma (1946)
Havildar	Salmat Ali	Burma (1944)
Naik	Ghulam Qadir	Burma (1942)
Naik	Qadam Ali	Burma (1943)
Lance Naik	Abdul Majid	Burma (1943)
Sapper	Mohammad	Burma (1945)
Driver	Abdul Hakim	Malaya (1942)
Lance Naik	Ghulam Hassan	South East Asia (1946)

Indian Signal Corps

The following Signallers were awarded the Indian Distinguished Service Medal for their conspicuous gallantry during the Second World War.

Jemadar	Mahbub Khan	Mohmand (1934)
Jemadar	S.Z. Hussain Shah	Middle East (1941)
Naik	Bostan Khan	Middle East (1942)
Havildar	Mohammad Habib	Italy (1944)
Signalman	Mohammad Aslam	Italy (1944)
Naik	Mohammad Akbar	Burma (1945)

The India Distinguished Service Medal 1923-1947

1ST Punjab Regiment

The following soldiers of the regiment were awarded the Indian Distinguished Service Medal for their conspicuous gallantry during the Second World War.

Rank	Name	Campaign
Subedar	Abdul Jabbar	N.W. Frontier (1936)
Sepoy	Ghafar Shah	N.W. Frontier (1936)
Subedar	Atta Mohammad	Middle East (1940)
Jemadar	Mohammad Sher	East Africa (1941)
Havildar	Abdul Aziz	Syria (1941)
Havildar	Kala Khan	Syria (1941)
Havildar	Mohammad Alam Khan	Syria (1941)
Havildar	Rasul Khan	Syria (1941)
Havildar	Abbas Khan	Syria (1941)
Naik	Abdul Rehman	Syria (1941)
Naik	Dost Mohammad	Syria (1941)
Sepoy	Fazal Rahman	Syria (1941)
Sepoy	Mohammad Shah	Syria (1941)
Sepoy	Mir Ahmed	Syria (1941)
Naik	Rahim Dad	Western Desert (1942)
Jemadar	Mohammad Abbas	Western Desert (1942)
Havildar	Gul Rehman	Burma (1943)
Jemadar	Musaffar Khan	Burma (1943)
Jemadar	Abdul Latif	Burma (1943)
Jemadar	Mohammad Azad	Burma (1943)
Naik	Mohammad Yakub	Burma (1944)
Naik	Ghulam Qayum	Burma (1944)
Sepoy	Mohammad Akbar	Burma (1944)
Sepoy	Sajawal Shah	Burma (1944)
Naik	Qalander Khan	Burma (1945)
Havildar	Gul Zaman	Burma (1945)
Sepoy	Zaid Baksh	Italy (1945)
Sepoy	Barkhat Khan	Italy (1945)
Naik	Mohd Riaz	Italy (1945)
Naik	Sardar Khan	Italy (1945)
Naik	Mishal Khan	Italy (1945)
Havildar	Fazal Rehman	Burma (1946)
Jemadar	Karim Khan	Burma (1947)

The India Distinguished Service Medal 1923-1947

2ⁿᵈ Punjab Regiment

The following soldiers of the regiment were awarded the Indian Distinguished Service Medal for their conspicuous gallantry during the Second World War.

Rank	Name	Campaign
Subedar	Itbar Khan	Tauda Chin (1932)
Naik	Sheraf Din	N.W. Frontier (1934)
Havildar	Mohmad Khan	Agra (1936)
Lance Naik	Farman Ali	Agra (1936)
Subedar	Maula Baksh	N.W. Frontier (1936)
Sepoy	Tor Baz	N.W. Frontier (1937)
Subedar	Badar-ud-din	East Africa (1941)
Naik	Munsab Khan	Somaliland (1941)
Naik	Ajaib Khan	Middle East (1941)
Sepoy	Khan Zada	Middle East (1941)
Sepoy	Itbar Khan	Western Desert (1942)
Havildar	Abdul Malik	Western Desert (1943)
Jemadar	Allah Din	Burma (1943)
Havildar	Nur Illahi	Burma (1944)
Naik	Ghulam Qadir	Burma (1944)
Naik	Mohd Mirza	Burma (1944)
Naik	Mohd Yakub	Burma (1944)
Sepoy	Akbar Khan	Burma (1944)
Sepoy	Dasswandi Khan	Burma (1944)
Sepoy	Sher Mohammad	Burma (1944)
Naik	Nur Khan	Burma (1945)
Lance Naik	Kala Khan	Burma (1945)
Havildar	Ahmed Khan	Italy (1945)
Havildar	Gulam Khan	Italy (1945)
Lance Naik	Walyat Khan	Italy (1945)
Lance Naik	Lal Khan	Italy (1945)
Naik	Habib Khan	Italy (1945)
CQMH	Khan Bahkadur	Italy (1945)
Haviladar	Guran Ditta	South East Asia (1946)
Naik	Karan Khan	South East Asia (1946)

The India Distinguished Service Medal 1923-1947

4th Bombay Grenadiers

The following Grenadiers of the regiment were awarded the Indian Distinguished Service Medal for their conspicuous gallantry in N.W. Frontier and Burma.

Rank	Name	Campaign
Naik	Dilwar Khan	N.W. Frontier (1937)
Havildar	Mumtaz Khan	Burma (1945)
Havildar	Ismail Khan	Burma (1945)
Naik	Fateh Mohammad	Burma (1945)

6TH Rajputana Rifles

The following soldiers of the regiment were awarded the Indian Distinguished Service Medal for their conspicuous gallantry during the Second World War.

Rank	Name	Campaign
Subedar	Feroz Khan	Middle East (1941)
Jemadar	Gulab Khan	Middle East (1941)
Naik	Suba Khan	Middle East (1941)
Jemadar	Lall Khan	Western Desert (1941)
Havildar	Inayat Khan	Western Desert (1942)
Rifleman	Fida Hussain	Western Desert (1944)
Rifleman	Inayat Ali Khan	Western Desert (1942)
Havildar	Mohammad Niwaz	North Africa (1943)
Sepoy	Khushi Mohammad	North Africa (1943)
Havildar	Sultan Mumraiz	North Africa (1943)
Havildar	Atta Mohammand	North Africa (1943)
Lance Naik	Aziz Khan	North Africa (1943)
Naik	Ali Akbar	Burma (1945)
Lance Naik	Walli Dad	Burma (1944)
Rifleman	Mohammad Yusuf	Burma (1943)
Naik	Mumtaz Ali	Italy (1944)

7TH Rajput Regiment

The following soldiers of the regiment were awarded the Indian Distinguished Service Medal for their conspicuous gallantry during the Second World War.

Rank	Name	Campaign
Subedar	Abdul Majid Khan	N.W. Frontier (1932)
Jemadar	Rehmat Khan	N.W. Frontier (1934)
Lance Naik	Jahan Dad	N.W. Frontier (1936)
Lance Naik	Abdul Haq	N.W. Frontier (1936)

The India Distinguished Service Medal 1923-1947

7TH *Rajput Regiment (Cont)*

Sepoy	Sahib Din	N.W. Frontier (1936)
Subedar	Jemadar Khan	N.W. Frontier (1937)
Subedar	Raza Mohammad	Waziristan (1937)
Subedar	Dilwar Ali Khan	N.W. Frontier (1938)
Sepoy	Ghulam Rabani	Middle East (1941)
Sepoy	Allah Ditta	Burma (1941)
Havildar	Amanant Alii	Hong Kong (1941)
Havildar	Shah Mohammad	Western Desert (1942)
Havildar	Nur Abdullah	North Africa (1942)
Subedar	Mohammad Yusuf	Burma (1943)
Subedar	Mohammad Aziz	Burma (1943)
Havildar	Mohammad Shariff	Burma (1943)
Jemadar	Ayub Khan	Burma (1943)
Lance Naik	Mohammad Khan	Burma (1943)
Lance Naik	Jalal Din	Burma (1943)
Naik	Sher Ali	Burma (1943)
Naik	Raja Khan	Burma (1943)
CHM	Fazal Hussein	Burma (1943)
Sepoy	Faqir Mohammad	Field (1943)
Sepoy	Mohammad Said	Burma (1944)
Sepoy	Niaz Mohammad	Burma (1945)
Naik	Fazal Hussein	Field (1944)

8TH *Punjab Regiment*

The following soldiers of the regiment were awarded the Indian Distinguished Service Medal for their conspicuous gallantry during the Second World War.

Sepoy	Rang Baz	Waziristan (1923)
Lance Naik	Nawab Ali	Waziristan (1937)
Lance Naik	Sukruh Khan	Waziristan (1937)
Naik	Mohammad Khan	Waziristan (1937)
Sepoy	Amir Ali	Waziristan (1937)
Subedar	Atta Mohammad	N.W. Frontier (1937)
Havildar	Sajwal Khan	N.W. Frontier (1938)
Sepoy	Fazal Dad	N.W. Frontier (1941)
Lance Naik	Mohammad Khan	Burma (1943)
Lance Naik	Sultan Ahmed	Burma (1943)
Sepoy	Said Akbar	Burma (1943)

The India Distinguished Service Medal 1923-1947

8TH Punjab Regiment (Cont)

Rank	Name	Campaign
Naik	Gulzar Khan	Field (1943)
Havildar	Allah Dad	Italy (1943)
Naik	Fazal Hussein	Italy (1944)
Lance Naik	Akbar Khan	Italy (1944)
Lance Naik	Raja Khan	Italy (1944)
Sepoy	Sadiq Hussein Shah	Italy (1944)
Naik	Mohammad Azam	Italy (1946)
Lance Naik	Mohammad Akram	Italy (1946)
Naik	Fazal Khan	Italy (1946)

9TH Jat Regiment

The following soldiers of the regiment were awarded the Indian Distinguished Service Medal for their conspicuous gallantry during the Second World War.

Rank	Name	Campaign
Sepoy	Alum Beg	Waziristan (1933)
Sepoy	Amir Ali	N.W. Frontier (1933)
Subedar	Hassan Ali	Burma (1944)
Jemadar	Nawab Khan	Burma (1944)
Naik	Maksud Ali	Burma (1944)
Naik	Atta Ullah	Burma (1944)
Naik	Abdul Razak	Burma (1944)
Subedar	Mohammad Sherif	Western Desert (1946)

10Th Baluch Regiment

The following soldiers of the regiment were awarded the Indian Distinguished Service Medal for their conspicuous gallantry during the Second World War.

Rank	Name	Campaign
Subedar	Ghulam Mohammad	N.W. Frontier (1934)
Havildar	Sher Hassan	N.W. Frontier (1936)
Subedar	Abdar Rehman	N.W. Frontier (1936)
Subedar	Nur Mohammad	N.W. Frontier (1937)
Subedar	Nek Mohammad	N.W. Frontier (1937)
Havildar	Mohammad Yusuf	N.W. Frontier (1938)
Naik	Khan Zaman	N.W. Frontier (1938)
Sepoy	Sher Zaman	N.W. Frontier (1938)
Sepoy	Abdulla Khan	N.W. Frontier (1938)
Sepoy	Abul Malik	N.W. Frontier (1938)

The India Distinguished Service Medal 1923-1947

10Th Baluch Regiment (Cont)

Rank	Name	Campaign
Subedar	Asmatullah Khan	N.W. Frontier (1939)
Naik	Khan Zaman	N.W. Frontier (1939)
Subedar	Allah Dad	N.W. Frontier (1939)
Naik	Zari Marjan	Middle East (1941)
Sepoy	Sher Khan	Middle East (1941)
Subedar	Nawab Khan	East Africa (1941)
Jemadar	Mir Ali	East Africa (1941)
Havildar	Fazal Hussein	East Africa (1941)
Subedar	Sher Khan	Western Desert (1942)
Naik	Mian Gul	Western Desert (1942)
Subedar	Ahmed Khan	Burma (1943)
Jemadar	Sardar Khan	Burma (1943)
Havildar	Wais Mohammad	Burma (1944)
Havildar	Ghulam Hussain	Burma (1943)
Havildar	Anar Khan	Burma (1943)
Havildar	Balawal Khan	Burma (1943)
Havildar	Ali Bahadur	Burma (1944)
Lance Naik	Haji Mohammad	Burma (1944)
Naik	Abdul Khaliq	Burma (1944)
Naik	Mani Khan	Burma (1944)
Naik	Sikander Khan	Burma (1944)
Naik	Qurban Hussain	Burma (1944)
Sepoy	Abdul Nabi	Burma (1944)
Havildar	Zar Ullah	Italy (1944)
Lance Naik	Bal Bahadur	Italy (1944)
Sepoy	Khan Malik	Italy (1944)
CHM	Allah Dad	Field (1943)
Subedar	Khan Bahadur	Field (1946)

11TH Sikh Regiment

The following soldiers of the regiment were awarded the Indian Distinguished Service Medal for their conspicuous gallantry during the Second World War.

Rank	Name	Campaign
Naik	Surkhru Khan	N.W. Frontier (1930)
Subedar	Mohammad Khan	Western Desert (1942)
Sepoy	Ghazi Khan	Middle East (1942)
Havildar	Mohammad Ashraf	Italy (1945)
Naik	Manawar Din	Italy (1945)
Sepoy	Ghulam Hassan	Italy (1945)

The India Distinguished Service Medal 1923-1947

12TH Frontier Force Regiment

The following soldiers of the regiment were awarded the Indian Distinguished Service Medal for their conspicuous gallantry during the Second World War and the N.W. Frontier.

Rank	Name	Campaign
Havildar	Palwan Khan	N.W. Frontier (1930)
Subedar	Barkat Shah	N.W. Frontier (1932)
Jemadar	Shah Zaman	N.W. Frontier (1933)
Jemadar	Abdul Ghani	N.W. Frontier (1935)
Subedar	Bahadur Jung	N.W. Frontier (1935)
Havildar	Lal Mast	N.W. Frontier (1935)
Havildar	Fateh Khan	N.W. Frontier (1935)
Sepoy	Ghuncha Gul	N.W. Frontier (1935)
Subedar	Dost Mohammad	Waziristan (1937)
Jemadar	Khan Mir	Middle East (1944)
Jemadar	Shandi Gul	Middle East (1941)
Naik	Mir Hassan	Middle East (1941)
Naik	An Mir	Middle East (1941)
Naik	Din Sher	Middle East (1942)
Jemadar	Allah Yar Khan	Burma (1942)
Sepoy	Karamat Hussain	Burma (1942)
Jemadar	Azim Ullah	Burma (1943)
Havildar	Qaim Shah	Burma (1944)
Jemadar	Maqurrab Khan	Italy (1944)
Naik	Habib Ullah	Italy (1944)
Naik	Jalal Khan	Italy (1944)
Lance Naik	Sajawal Khan	Italy (1944)
Sepoy	Makhamad Rasul	Italy (1944)
Havildar	Janab Gul	Burma (1945)
Havildar	Abdul Qayum	Burma (1945)

13TH Frontier Force Regiment

The following soldiers of the regiment were awarded the Indian Distinguished Service Medal for their conspicuous gallantry during the Second World War.

Rank	Name	Campaign
Havildar	Dheru Khan	Waziristan (1923)
Subedar	Nur Akhmed	Waziristan (1923)
Sepoy	Ayub Khan	Waziristan (1923)
Subedar	Allah Ditta	Waziristan (1924)
Havilar	Abdulla Nur	Waziristan (1930)
Sepoy	Manawar Khan	Waziristan (1930)

The India Distinguished Service Medal 1923-1947

13TH Frontier Force Regiment (Cont)

Sepoy	Sultan Khan	Waziristan (1930)
Havildar	Daftar Khan	Waziristan (1934)
Havildar	Gulab Hussain	Waziristan (1935)
Sepoy	Mohammad Khan	Waziristan (1937)
Lance Naik	Spin Gul	N.W. Frontier (1937)
Havildar	Mohammad Khan	Middle East (1941)
Subedar	Amir Khan	Italy (1944)
Havildar	Mohammad Naqqi	Italy (1944)
Havildar	Gulma Din	Italy (1944)
Havildar	Sial Baz	Italy (1944)
Havildar	Mir Zaman	Italy (1944)
Havildar	Abdul Rehman	Italy (1944)
Havildar	Allah Dad	Italy (1944)
Havildar	Fateh Khan	Italy (1944)
Havildar	Alam Gul	Italy (1944)
Naik	Mohammad Azam	Italy (1944)
Lance Naik	Gul Hassan	Italy (1944)
Sepoy	Chaudhri Khan	Italy (1944)
Sepoy	Ali Zaman	Italy (1944)
Sepoy	Abid Ali	Italy (1944)
Sweeper	Mehr Din	Italy (1944)
Havildar	Ali Akbar	Burma (1945)
Havildar	Zarin Shah	Burma (1944)
Naik	Khaista Gul	Burma (1944)
Naik	Gulistan Khan	Burma (1945)
Lance Naik	Makhmad Nabi	Burma (1944)
Sepoy	Inzat Gul	Burma (1944)
Naik	Mohammad Khan	Burma (1944)
Sepoy	Gul Amir	Burma (1944)
Sepoy	Rakhim Gul	Sudan (1940)

14TH Punjab Regiment

The following soldiers of the regiment were awarded the Indian Distinguished Service Medal for their conspicuous gallantry during the Second World War.

Subedar	Hukmal Khan	N.W. Frontier (1935)
Subedar	Karam Khan	N.W. Frontier (1936)
Sepoy	Mohammad	N.W. Frontier (1936)
Sepoy	Nawab Khan	N.W. Frontier (1936)

The India Distinguished Service Medal 1923-1947

14TH Punjab Regiment (Cont)

Rank	Name	Campaign
Sepoy	Mir Badshah	N.W. Frontier (1939)
Havildar	Sobhat Khan	Burma (1943)
Lance Naik	Sultan Mahmud	Burma (1943)
Naik	Imam Khan	Burma (1943)
Havildar	Ranghin Khan	Burma (1944)
Naik	Sher Mohammad	Burma (1944)
Naik	Gul Mohammad	Burma (1944)
Naik	Dost Mohammad	Burma (1944)
Havildar	Khan Bahaduar	Burma (1945)
Naik	Baz Khan	Burma (1945)
Lance Naik	Maqbul Hussain	Burma (1945)
Havildar	Mobil Khan	Malaya (1947)

15TH Punjab Regiment

The following soldiers of the regiment were awarded the Indian Distinguished Service Medal for their conspicuous gallantry during the Second World War.

Rank	Name	Campaign
Jemadar	Bostan Khan	N.W. Frontier (1935)
Havildar	Subha Khan	N.W. Frontier (1935)
Lance Naik	Alla Yar	N.W. Frontier (1935)
Subedar	Bagh Ali	N.W. Frontier (1935)
Jemadar	Mohammad Anwar	N.W. Frontier (1936)
Jemadar	Sahib Gul	N.W. Frontier (1937)
Subedar	Gul Wahid	Burma (1943)
Havildar	Fateh Khan	Burma (1943)
Havildar	Mohammad Salim	Burma (1943)
Jemadar	Makhmad Ali	Burma (1943)
Havildar	Sher Khan	Italy (1944)
Lance Naik	Mustaqin	Italy (1944)
Sepoy	Mehr Mohammad	Italy (1944)
Havildar	Mohammad Afzal	Burma (1945)
Havildar	Ghanam Gul	Burma (1945)
Jemadar	Anwar Shah	Burma (1944)
Jemadar	Banaras Khan	Burma (1944)
Naik	Sifarsh Khan	Burma (1945)
Sepoy	Said Mohammad	Burma (1945)
Havildar	Mahbub Khan	Italy (1945)
Sepoy	Sarwar Khan	Italy (1945)

The India Distinguished Service Medal 1923-1947

16TH Punjab Regiment

Rank	Name	Location (Year)
Sepoy	Saddar Din	Iraq (1923)
Subedar	Badshah	N.W.Frontier (1937)
Naik	Sultan Khan	N.W.Frontier (1937)
Subedar	Atta Mohammad	N.W.Frontier (1938)
Havildar	Abdur Rehman	N.W.Frontier (1938)
Jemadar	Raja Khan	N.W.Frontier (1938)
Naik	Mugarrab Khan	N.W.Frontier (1938)
Jemadar	Akbar Ali	N.W.Frontier (1939)
Sepoy	Hassain	Western Desert (1941)
Havildar	Gul Shaid	Western Desert (1941)
Havildar	Chasm-i-Nazir	Western Desert (1941)
Sepoy	Hukum Dad	North Africa (1942)
Subedar	Ghulam Mohammad	Burma (1942)
Havildar	Aslam Khan	Western Desert (1942)
Subedar	Mian Mohammad	Western Desert (1943)
Havildar	Mohammad Aslam	Western Desert (1943)
Havildar	Sakhi Mohammad	Western Desert (1943)
Sepoy	Mohammad Niwaz	Western Desert (1943)
Sepoy	Ghulam Rasul	North Africa (1943)
Lance Naik	Mohammad Khan	Italy (1944)
Naik	Allah Yar	Burma (1944)
Havildar	Shah Wali	Burma (1944)
Naik	Mohammad Yaqub	Burma (1944)
Naik	Mohammad Hassan	Burma (1944)
Lance Naik	Fateh Khan	Burma (1944)
Naik	Mohammad Hussein	Burma (1945)

Royal Indian Army Service Corps

The following officers and drivers were awarded the Indian Distinguished Service Medal for their conspicuous gallantry in battle.

Rank	Name	Location (Year)
Risaldar	Samundar Shah	N.W.Frontier (1926)
Clerk	Abdul Rashid	Burma (1932)
Risaldar	Saif Ali	N.W.Frontier (1934)
Daffadar	Halim Bux	N.W.Frontier (1934)
Risaldar	Ali Haider	N.W.Frontier (1936)
Jemadar	Mohammad Ashraf	N.W.Frontier (1936)
Risaldar	Dewan Shah	Waziristan (1937)
Lance Naik	Sharaf Ali	Waziristan (1937)

The India Distinguished Service Medal 1923-1947

Royal Indian Army Service Corps (Cont)

Naik	Mohammad Akbar	Waziristan (1937)
Naik	Suleman	Waziristan (1937)
Jemadar	Fazal Khan	N.W.Frontier (1937)
Jemadar	Nizam Din	N.W.Frontier (1939)
Jemadar	Maula Dad Khan	B.E.F. (1940)
Jemadar	Gulzar Khan	B.E.F. (1940)
Naik	Abdulla	B.E.F. (1940)
Sepoy	Abdul Rahim	Middle East (1941)
Clerk	Mohammad Bux	East Africa (1941)
Subedar	Allah Jan	Middle East (1942)
Naik	Rehmat Khan	Middle East (1942)
Daffadar	Painda Khan	Field (1943)
Naik	Mir Alam Khan	Field (1943)
Naik	Mohammad Abbas	Field (1943)
Havildar	Mohammad Iqbal	North Africa (1943)
Lance Naik	Lal Khan	North Africa (1943)
Sepoy	Pehelwan Shah	North Africa (1943)
Jemadar	Sher Mohammad	Burma (1943)
Risaldar	Fazal Elahi	Burma (1943)
Risaldar	Qurban Ali	Burma (1943)
Lance Naik	Nazar Hussain	Burma (1943)
Naik	Anwar Khan	Burma (1943)
Driver	Imam Baksh	Burma (1943)

Indian Army Medical Corps

The following soldiers of the Indian Medical Service were awarded the Indian Distinguished Service Medal for their conspicuous gallantry in attending to the wounded while still under enemy fire.

Jemadar	Abdul Latif	N.W. Frontier (1936)
Lance Naik	Amar Din	North Africa (1941)
Amb Sepoy	Mohammad Yaqub	North Africa (1943)
Amb Sepoy	Mohamand Yusuf	North Africa (1943)
Naik	Bostan Khan	Burma (1943)
Amb Sepoy	Kala Khan	Burma (1943)
Lance Naik	Ali Afsar	Burma (1944)
Amb Sepoy	Mohammad Ibrahim	Italy (1944)
Amb Sepoy	Sheikh Rahim	Italy (1944)
Dhobi	Baz Mir	Italy (1944)

The India Distinguished Service Medal 1923-1947

Burma Military Police

Jemadar Anar Khan and Sepoy Sher Khan were awarded the Indian Distinguished Service Medal for their conspicuous gallantry on Burma China Border.

Jemadar	Anar Khan	Burma China Border (1935)
Sepoy	Sher Khan	Burma China Border (1935)

Frontier Constabulary

The following policemen were awarded the Indian Distinguished Service Medal for their conspicuous gallantry on the North West Frontier.

Lance Naik	Hamzulla	Waziristan (1923)
Havildar	Shahmir	Waziristan (1923)
Sepoy	Nawaz Ali	N.W.Frontier (1925)
Sepoy	Mohammad Nur	N.W.Frontier (1925)
Sepoy	Rehmat AlI	N.W.Frontier (1925)
Sepoy	Sher Ali	N.W.Frontier (1925)
Sepoy	Khair Ali	N.W.Frontier (1925)
Lance Naik	Said Nur	N.W.Frontier (1926)
Sepoy	Jhangi Khan	N.W.Frontier (1926)
Havildar	Ali Mardan	N.W.Frontier (1933)
Subedar	Taza Gul	N.W.Frontier (1936)
Subedar	IIam Din	N.W.Frontier (1936)
Subedar	Lal Zada	N.W.Frontier (1937)
Jemadar	Sher Ali	N.W.Frontier (1937)
Sepoy	Mohammad Azam	N.W.Frontier (1937)
Jemadar	Arman Shah	N.W.Frontier (1938)
Naik	Mohammad Ali	N.W.Frontier (1938)
Sepoy	Zakim	N.W.Frontier (1939)
Sepoy	Said Askar	N.W.Frontier (1939)
Sepoy	Salim Khan	N.W.Frontier (1939)
Subedar	Hasham Gul Khan	N.W.Frontier (1939)
Jemadar	Said Jalal	N.W.Frontier (1939)
Jemadar	Mada Mir Khan	N.W.Frontier (1939)
Lance Naik	Sardi Khan	N.W.Frontier (1939)
Lance Naik	Jaffar Ali	N.W.Frontier (1940)
Sepoy	Ali Majan	N.W.Frontier (1940)
Havildar	Hassan Nawaz	N.W.Frontier (1942)
Naik	Sher Ali Khan	N.W.Frontier (1942)

The India Distinguished Service Medal 1923-1947

Kurram Militia

The following Militiamen were awarded the Indian Distinguished Service Medal for their conspicuous gallantry in the Kurram Valley.

Havildar	Mohammad Akbar	Kurram Valley (1930)
Jemadar	Miram Shah	Kurram Valley (1930)
Jemadar	Mohammad Hassan	Kurram Valley (1930)
Jemadar	Abbas Khan	Kurram Valley (1930)
Jemadar	Mir	Kurram Valley (1930)
Jemadar	Nasser Khan	Kurram Valley (1930)
Lance	Naik Shah Zada	Kurram Valley (1930)
Sepoy	Hanif Jan	Kurram Valley (1930)

Mekran Levy Corps

The following officers were awarded the Indian Distinguished Service Medal for their conspicuous gallantry in the Kurram Valley.

Havildar	Ali Mohammad	Baluchistan (1924)
Jemadar	Hassan Khan	Baluchistan (1930)
Havildar	Aziz Mohammad	Baluchistan (1935)
Jemadar	Jalal Khan	Baluchistan (1935)

South Waziristan Scouts

Following Scouts were awarded the Indian Distinguished Service Medal for their conspicuous gallantry.

Subedar	Shaadat	Waziristan (1923)
Subedar	Shah Khan	Waziristan (1924)
Sepoy	Maskin	N.W.Frontier (1924)
Havildar	Said Abbas	N.W.Frontier (1925)
Jemadar	Niyaz Gul	N.W.Frontier (1930)
Naik	Samar Din	N.W.Frontier (1930)
Jemadar	Suleiman Khan	N.W.Frontier (1934)
Havildar	Said Anwar	N.W.Frontier (1934)
Subedar	Gul Majid	Waziristan (1937)
Daffadar	Jullundur Shah	Waziristan (1937)
Sepoy	Haider Shah	Waziristan (1937)
Subedar	Mohabbat Khan	N.W.Frontier (1937)
Subedar	Akhmed Shah	N.W.Frontier (1937)
Jemadar	Shah Zaman	N.W.Frontier (1937)
Sepoy	Haider Shah	N.W.Frontier (1937)

The India Distinguished Service Medal 1923-1947

South Waziristan Scouts (Cont)

Sepoy	Ghilaf Gul	N.W.Frontier (1937)
Jemadar	Sahib Nur	N.W.Frontier (1938)
Jemadar	Biland Shah	N.W.Frontier (1938)
Lance Naik	Gul Khayat	N.W.Frontier (1938)
Naik	Surat Min	N.W.Frontier (1938)
Sepoy	Faqir Khan	N.W.Frontier (1938)
Sepoy	Khaista Jan	N.W.Frontier (1938)
Lance Naik	Ali Nazar	N.W.Frontier (1940)
Sepoy	Khawas Khan	N.W.Frontier (1940)
Jemadar	Musalli Khan	N.W.Frontier (1942)
Jemadar	Jalal Khan	N.W.Frontier (1942)
Sowar	Badshah Khan	N.W.Frontier (1942)

Tochi Scouts

Following Tochi Scouts were awarded the Indian Distinguished Service Medal for their conspicuous gallantry in Waziristan and the N.W.Frontier.

Havildar	Sinak	Waziristan (1923)
Subedar	Qudrat Shah	Waziristan (1923)
Subedar	Mohammad Yaqub	Waziristan (1923)
Sepoy	Ayam ud din	Waziristan (1930)
Sepoy	Gul Zedah	Waziristan (1930)
Havildar	Manawar Din	Waziristan (1930)
Havildar	Sher Dil	Waziristan (1933)
Naik	Mir Shah	Waziristan (1933)
Lance Naik	Wazir Khan	Waziristan (1935)
Daffadar	Ahmed Khan	Waziristan (1936)
Subedar	Jan Bahadur	Waziristan (1937)
Jemadar	Shad Amir	Waziristan (1937)
Jemadar	Makhed Gul	Waziristan (1937)
Risaldar	Guli Lal	Waziristan (1937)
Havildar	Udin Shah	Waziristan (1937)
Havildar	Mad Azam	N.W.Frontier (1937)
Jemadar	Shad Amir	N.W.Frontier (1937)
Subedar	Baz Mohammad	N.W.Frontier (1938)
Subedar	Bagh Khan	N.W.Frontier (1938)
Subedar	Mir Afzal	N.W.Frontier (1939)
Jemadar	Kabul Khan	Waziristan (1939)
Subedar	Wulayat Shah	N.W.Frontier (1940)

The India Distinguished Service Medal 1923-1947

Zhob Militia

Following Tochi Scouts were awarded the Indian Distinguished Service Medal for their conspicuous gallantry in the N.W.Frontier.

Havildar	Said Badshah	N.W.Frontier (1930)
Sepoy	Zarif Khan	N.W.Frontier (1930)
Sepoy	Khair Mohammad	N.W.Frontier (1931)
Sepoy	Balghar	N.W.Frontier (1931)
Subedar	Iqbal Khan	N.W.Frontier (1931)
Subedar	Said Baz	N.W.Frontier (1933)

1ST Hyderabad Infantry

Following officers were awarded the Indian Distinguished Service Medal for their conspicuous gallantry in Malaya.

Subedar	Shaikh Mohammad	Malaya (1942)
Jemadar	Shaik Ahmed	Malaya (1942)

Jammu and Kashmir Infantry

The following soldiers were awarded the Indian Distinguished Service Medal for their conspicuous gallantry in the Middle East.

Lance Naik	Qabala Khan	Middle East (1941)
Havildar	Rehmat Ali	Burma (1945)

Malerkotla Sappers & Miners

Havildar Sayed Khan awarded the Indian Distinguished Service Medal for their conspicuous gallantry in Burma.

Havildar	Sayed Khan	Burma (1942)

Royal Indian Navy

The following sailors were awarded the Indian Distinguished Service Medal for their conspicuous gallantry while serving in the Indian Ocean.

Able Seaman	smail Baba	Indian Ocean (1942)
Able Seaman	Ismail Mohammad	Indian Ocean (1943)
Able Seaman	Mohammad Khan	Indian Ocean (1943)
Able Seaman	Punna Khan	Burma Waters (1943)
Able Seaman	Shadi Khan	Burma Waters (1943)

Victoria Cross

The Victoria Cross (VC) is the highest recognition for valour "in the face of the enemy" that can be awarded to members of the British and some Commonwealth armed forces (British Empire personnel prior to the Commonwealth). In 1911 King George V extended this to include officers and men of the Indian Army. Previously the equivalent award for which these soldiers were eligible was the Indian Order of Merit.

Subedar Khudadad Khan, VC.
Khudadad Khan was born on 20 October 1888 into a Minhas Rajput family in the village of Dab in Chakwal District of the Punjab Province (now Pakistan) Khudadad Khan enlisted in the 129th Duke of Connaught's Own Baluchis, Indian Army, on 3RD August 1914.at a time when the regiment was recruiting on the North-West Frontier. Initially, Sepoy Khan was sent to the Suez Canal Zone but he was then diverted to France because of the urgent need for more Allied troops. On 18TH October 1914 he moved with the Firozepur Brigade from Orleans, France, to be attached to the British Cavalry Corps that was attempting to hold the line between Zandvoorde and Ploegsteert wood, Belgium. On 22ND October, his regiment joined the 3RD Cavalry Brigade. By late October 1914, the Germans launched a major offensive in northern Belgium, in order to capture the vital ports of Boulogne in France and Nieuport in Belgium. In what came to be known as the First Battle of Ypres, the newly arrived 129th Baluchis were rushed to the frontline to support the hard-pressed British troops. On 31 October, two companies of the Baluchis bore the brunt of the main German attack near the village of Gheluvelt in Hollenbeck Sector. The out-numbered Baluchis fought gallantly but were overwhelmed after suffering heavy casualties. Sepoy Khudadad Khan's machine-gun team, along with one other, kept their guns in action throughout the day; preventing the Germans from making the final breakthrough. The other gun was disabled by a shell and eventually Khudadad Khan's own team was overrun.

Victoria Cross

Subedar Khudadad Khan, VC (Cont)

One by one, Havildar Ghulam Mohammad, Sepoy Lal Sher, Sepoy Said Ahmed, Sepoy Kassib and Sepoy Afsar Khan were killed by bullets or bayonets, except Khudadad Khan who, despite being badly wounded, had continued working his gun. He was left for dead by the enemy but despite his wounds he managed to crawl back to his regiment during the night. Thanks to his bravery, and that of his fellow Baluchis, the Germans were held up just long enough for Indian and British reinforcements to arrive. They strengthened the line, and prevented the German Army from reaching the vital ports. For his matchless feat of courage and gallantry, Sepoy Khudadad Khan was awarded the Victoria Cross. He is regarded as the first Indian recipient of the Victoria Cross

Khudadad Khan retired as a Subedar. He died in 1971 and is buried in Chak No. 25, Mandi Bahauddin. His Victoria Cross is on display at his ancestral house in Village Dab (Chakwal), Pakistan. A statue of Khudadad Khan Minhas is at the entrance of the Pakistan Army Museum in Rawalpindi.

Jemadar Mir Dast, VC.

Jemadar Mir Dast was born in 1874 in the Maidan valley in a province of British India that is now part of Pakistan. He was a member of the Afridi tribe of Pashtun. Like many Afridis, Mir Dast joined the Indian Army in 1894, enlisting in the 55TH Coke's Rifles. By the time of the First World War, Mir Dast was already an experienced and decorated soldier. The North West frontier was an area of frequent tension, and he fought in several campaigns. In 1908 he was awarded the Indian Order of Merit, at that time considered the Indian equivalent to the Victoria Cross. He was also promoted to Jemadar, the most junior officer rank of the Indian Army. Mir Dast was not among the first wave of Indian Army soldiers who travelled to the Western Front in 1914, as his regiment remained stationed in India. But as Indian casualties mounted, he was among a number of men that transferred from Coke's to be attached to the 5TH Wilde's Rifles, a brigade that was fighting in Europe. Mir Dast joined his new unit in France in January 1915. Mir Dast's great moment of gallantry came through his actions during the Second Battle of Ypres in April 1915. On 26TH April, he led a platoon on a counter-attack against German lines, across difficult undulating terrain. The attack was thwarted by heavy artillery fire and poison gas, at a time when the latter was still unfamiliar to most soldiers — the first major gas attack on the Western Front had taken place just four days previously. In spite of the confusion, Mir Dast held his position until nightfall.

Victoria Cross

Jemadar Mir Dast, VC (Cont)

When ordered to retire he led numerous men back to the British lines, and at great personal risk he carried eight British and Indian officers back to safety. Mir Dast was severely injured by the gas attack, and like many other wounded Indian soldiers he was hospitalised in Brighton. He was admitted to the Royal Pavilion Hospital and it was here that he learned that he was to be awarded the Victoria Cross for his actions in Ypres, and was also promoted to the rank of Subedar.

The Victoria Cross made Mir Dast not only a hero but a celebrity too. He was presented to numerous eminent men of the day, including the Secretary of State for India, Austen Chamberlain, and Lord Kitchener, the Secretary of State for War, who was also a former Commander in Chief of the Indian Army.

While this was an obvious source of pride, Mir Dast's pleasure was tempered by his physical suffering. 'I have got the Victoria Cross. The Victoria Cross is a very fine thing, but this gas gives me no rest. It has done for me.'

On 25TH August Mir Dast received his award from the King-Emperor George V at a ceremony in the Royal Pavilion Garden. Although he still required the use of a wheelchair, Mir Dast insisted on standing to receive the Victoria Cross from the king. In conversation, he asked the king to release wounded Indian soldiers from further active duty once they had recovered — a request that was not carried out. In a letter written two days after the ceremony, Mir Dast displayed a very different tone to his previous letter: By the great, great, great, kindness of God, the King with his royal hand has given me the decoration of the Victoria Cross. God has been very gracious, very gracious, very gracious, very gracious. The desire of my heart is accomplished.' Curiously, Mir Dast's fame and honour stand in stark contrast to the infamy and disgrace attained by his brother, Mir Mast. Another experienced and decorated soldier, Mir Mast had been promoted to Jemadar shortly after the outbreak of the First World War. Arriving in France in October 1914, he had fought for several months under British command before deciding to desert. On 3RD March 1915, Mir Mast led a small band of fellow Afridis to defect to the Germans. It is unclear whether this defection was motivated by personal or political grievances: the entry of Turkey into the war in November 1914 placed a strain on the loyalty of some Muslim troops. A rumour was circulated that Mir Mast had been awarded the Iron Cross by the Kaiser as a reward for his desertion, but this was probably a myth or a deliberate piece of propaganda by the Germans.

Victoria Cross

Iron Cross

Jemadar Mir Mast, IC

A forgotten hero in Pakistan is Jemadar Mir Mast Afridi from the 58th Frontier Force (Vaughan's Rifles). Mir Mast was an Afridi Pathan from tribal areas of modern Pakistan. In 1914 his unit was shipped to France as part of the Indian Infantry Corps, which played a major role in stopping the German advance in France in 1914 in Ypres Sector. Mir Mast Afridi seems to have been a far more politically aware and resolute man as compared to many Muslims educated at MAO College Lahore, Aligarh or at many prestigious British universities and Legal Inns! Mir Mast decided that he must not fight the Britisher's war and crossed over to the German lines on a rainy night in March 1915 along with 14 other Afridi Tribal Pathan. Mir Mast was awarded one of the highest German gallantry award Iron Cross by the German Kaiser Willhelm II. The British in order to equalize the insult awarded Mir Mast's real brother Mir Dast Afridi (from 55TH Coke's Rifles) a Victoria Cross in April 1915. Mir Mast was sent to Turkey by the Germans, to meet with the Mufti, and by late in the war was back in Afghanistan apparently trying to discourage his Muslim countrymen from joining up to fight for the Raj.

The Turko-German mission failed in 1915 to gain the support of the Afghan government. However, the Mission members succeeded in establishing a centre for the anti-British activities in Bagh (Tirah), in the tribal belt. In June 1916, two Turkish emissaries arrived at Tirah and they were welcomed by Mast. By the middle of 1916 a large number of the Pashtun soldiers, mainly deserters from the British Indian army had swelled the ranks of the Turkish emissaries. They started recruitment of the locals as well. By July 1916, the total number of the Afridi recruits was reported to have reached about four hundreds. They were posted in three different places and drilled every day by Mir Mast Khan. The tribes who were supporting the Turkish emissaries inflicted losses on those who were accused of supporting the British. In retaliation, other tribes also organised themselves under the leadership of Khan Bahadur Zaman Khan Kuki Khel and attacked and burnt the village in which the two Turkish emissaries and their Afghan followers were living in Tirah. In June 1917 the Turks finally left the tribal territory and crossed over to Afghanistan.

Mir Mast is believed to have died in the flu epidemic of 1919, having been stripped of his previous medals.

Victoria Cross

Naik Shahamad Khan, VC

Shahamad Khan, sometimes spelt Shahmed, a Punjabi Muslim, was born on the 1st July 1879, in Takht, in the Rawalpindi district of then India. Little is known of his formative years. He joined the army in 1904. He served with the 89TH Punjabis, British Indian Army (now 1ST Battalion the Baloch Regiment, Pakistan Army) and on the outbreak of the war his unit were stationed at Dinapore. The battalion was made up of two companies of Punjabi Musalmans, one of Sikhs and one of Rajputana Hindus.

The regiment had provided drafts to other regiments and those that had escaped being sent to other units were ordered to leave for overseas duty in October 1914. They were to leave from Karachi, and assigned to the 29TH Brigade and made their way to Egypt, though they were in action at Sheikh Saad where they captured Fort Turba and relieved the island of Prim. Following these actions they continued to Egypt, landing at Suez and then moving by train to Port Said where they took over guard duties at a salt works and the northern section of the Suez Canal. The 29TH Brigade were then despatched to Kantara and the 89th Punjabis held an outpost line which came under attack from the Turks in February 1915. Two months later the regiment were sent to Gallipoli, but only stayed on the peninsula for 15 days due to concerns by the authorities about Muslims in the Indian Army fighting against fellow Muslims on the Turkish side. They were sent back to Alexandria, where they eventually received orders to embark for France. The regiment were in and out of the trenches for the next five months, including a period in the Battle of Loos, and in December 1915 they left France for Mesopotamia.

On the 12TH of April, the 89TH Punjabis advanced against the Turkish positions at Beit Ayeesa, in which action three officers became casualties, one being killed and Acting Captain James assumed command. The ground to the west of the Indian soldiers was flooded and this held up a planned advance and the dispersal of picquets by the 9th and 37th Brigades for a few hours. At 7.30pm the Turks launched an attack on the Punjabi left flank which was dealt with by rapid fire from the picquets and the 27TH Punjabi's moved forward to support the left flank, along with the 1st Connaught Rangers. At 9pm "A" Company reported back that the 36th Sikhs had retired and the Turks were probing along the right flank. A small force of the enemy were being held up by machine gun fire from the Punjabi machine guns, in particular that of Naik Shahamad Khan for which he was awarded the Victoria Cross.

Victoria Cross

Naik Shahamad Khan, VC (Cont)

His citation for the award of Victoria Cross read – "He was in charge of a machine-gun section in an exposed position and covering a gap in our new line within 150 yards from the enemy's entrenched position. He beat off three counter attacks, and worked his gun single-handed after all his men, apart from two belt-fillers, had become casualties. For three hours he held the gap under very heavy fire while it was being made secure. When his gun was knocked out by enemy fire he and his two belt fillers held their ground with their rifles till ordered to withdraw. With three men sent to assist him he bought back his gun, ammunition and one severely wounded man unable to walk. Finally he himself returned and removed all existing arms and equipment except two shovels. But for his great gallantry and determination our line must have been penetrated by the enemy." – London Gazette 26TH September 1916

In August 1916, the regiment returned to India, and once again were used as a holding regiment with numerous men being moved to other regiments, especially the officers, though they did occasionally provide troops for duty on the Mohamand Blockade, which was a blockade formed by a series of blockhouses and barbed wire defences, along the Mohamand border on the North West Frontier by the Indian Army during the war, and began after a number of Mohamand raids into Peshawar. In the summer of 1917, the regiment were posted to Chital, the largest district in the Khyber-Pakhtunkhwa province, and where they provided escorts to the reliefs. They were then sent back to Mesopotamia, landing in December 1917. The regiment were active in the spring fighting and finished the war in Salonika, though they did not take part in any fighting there. They were then moved to Batum in the Caucasus area, where they guarded a 200 mile section of railway lines, bridges and stations between Batum and Tiflis. The area they guarded was later extended and when the British finally withdrew from the area the 89TH Punjabis and two other units were left behind to continue garrison duties in Batum. They were then moved to Turkey in July 1920, and then back to India in the October. During this period Khan had been to England and presented with his VC on the 13th November 1919 at Buckingham Palace and was promoted to the rank of Jemadar in January 1920.

Khan died in his home village of Takhti and was buried in the local cemetery. His medal group is now part of the Lord Ashcroft Collection held at the Imperial War Museum.

Victoria Cross

Jemadar Abdul Hafiz Khan, VC

He was 18 years old, and serving as Jemadar in the 9TH Jat Regiment, British Indian Army during World War II, when he performed the deeds for which he was awarded the VC.

On 6TH April 1944, during the Battle of Imphal, Burma, Jemadar Abdul Hafiz Khan was ordered to attack with his platoon a prominent position held by the enemy, the only approach to which was across a bare slope and then up a very steep hill. The Jemadar led the assault, himself killing several of the enemy, pressing on regardless of machine-gun fire. He received two wounds, the second of which was fatal; but he had succeeded in routing an enemy vastly superior in numbers, and had captured a most important position.

The citation reads as follows:

The KING has been graciously pleased to approve the posthumous award of the VICTORIA CROSS to:–

Jemadar Abdul Hafiz Khan, 9TH Jat Regiment, Indian Army.

In Burma, in the early hours of the 6th April, 1944, in the hills 10 miles North of Imphal, the enemy had attacked a standing patrol of 4 men and occupied a prominent feature overlooking a Company position. At first light a patrol was sent out and contacted the enemy, reporting that they thought approximately 40 enemies were in position. It was not known if they had dug in during the hours of darkness.

The Company Commander ordered Jemadar Abdul Hafiz Khan to attack the enemy, with two sections from his platoon, at 0930 hours. An artillery concentration was put down on the feature and Jemadar Abdul Hafiz Khan led the attack. The attack was up a completely bare slope with no cover, and was very steep near the crest. Prior to the attack, Jemadar Abdul Hafiz Khan assembled his sections and told them that they were invincible, and the entire enemy on the hill would be killed or put to flight. He so inspired his men that from the start the attack proceeded with great dash. When a few yards below the crest the enemy opened fire with machine-guns and threw grenades. Jemadar Abdul Hafiz Khan sustained several casualties, but immediately ordered an assault, which he personally led, at the same time shouting the Mohammedan battle-cry. The assault went in without hesitation and with great dash up the last few yards of the hill, which was very steep. On reaching the crest Jemadar Abdul Hafiz Khan was wounded in the leg, but seeing a machine-gun firing from a flank, which had already caused several casualties, he immediately went towards it and seizing the barrel pushed it upwards, whilst another man killed the gunner.

Victoria Cross

Jemadar Abdul Hafiz Khan, VC

Jemadar Abdul Hafiz Khan then took a Bren gun from a wounded man and advanced against the enemy, firing as he advanced, and killing several of the enemy. So fierce was the attack, and all his men so inspired by the determination of Jemadar Abdul Hafiz Khan to kill all enemy in sight at whatever cost, that the enemy, who were still in considerable numbers on the position, ran away down the opposite slope of the hill. Regardless of machine-gun fire which was now being fired at him from another feature a few hundred yards away, he pursued the enemy, firing at them as they retired. Jemadar Abdul Hafiz Khan was badly wounded in the chest from this machine-gun fire and collapsed holding the Bren gun and attempting to fire at the retreating enemy, and shouting at the same time "Re-organise on the position and I will give covering fire." He died shortly afterwards.

The inspiring leadership and great bravery displayed by Jemadar Abdul Hafiz Khan in spite of having been twice wounded, once mortally, so encouraged his men that the position was captured, casualties inflicted on the enemy to an extent several times the size of his own party, and enemy arms recovered on the position which included 3 Lewis Machine-guns, 2 grenade dischargers and 2 officers' swords. The complete disregard for his own safety and his determination to capture and hold the position at all costs was an example to all ranks, which it would be difficult to equal'.

Jemadar Abdul Hafiz was buried in the Imphal Indian Army War Cemetery, Manipur State. His VC is on display in the Lord Ashcroft Gallery at the Imperial War Museum, London.

Naik Sher Shah, VC

He was 27 years old, and a Lance Naik in the 7TH Battalion of the 16TH Punjab Regiment, (the battalion was raised in Sialkot in May 1941) when the following deed took place for which he was awarded the VC.

'On 19/20 January 1945 at Kyeyebyin, Kaladan, Burma (now Myanmar), Lance Naik Sher Shah was commanding a left forward section of his platoon when it was attacked by overwhelming numbers of Japanese. He broke up two attacks by crawling right in among the enemy and shooting at point-blank range. On the second occasion he was hit and his leg shattered, but he maintained that his injury was only slight and when the third attack came, he again crawled forward engaging the enemy until he was shot through the head and killed'.

Sher Shah's Battalion 7/16 Punjab Regiment, affectionately known as "Saat Solah Punjab" is now a part of the Pakistan Army, proudly known as the "Sher Shah Battalion".

Victoria Cross

Naik Fazal Din, VC

Fazal Din was 23 years old, and an Acting Naik in the 7TH Battalion 10TH Baluch Regiment, British Indian Army (now 15th Battalion The Baloch Regiment of Pakistan Army) during World War II when the following deed took place for which he was awarded the VC.

'During the Second World War, Fazal Din's battalion, 7TH Battalion 10TH Baluch Regiment, fought against the Japanese Army in the Burmese Campaign. On 2ND March 1945, near Meiktila, Burma, Naik Fazal Din was commanding a section during a company attack on a Japanese bunkered position. His section was held up by machine-gun fire and grenades from several bunkers. Unhesitatingly, he attacked the nearest position with grenades and silenced it; but as he led his men against the other bunkers, six Japanese soldiers rushed from a nearby house, led by two officers wielding swords. The section Bren gunner shot one officer and an enemy soldier, but ran out of ammunition and was killed by the second officer. Naik Fazal Din rushed to the assistance of his stricken comrade but the Japanese ran his sword through his chest. As he withdrew the sword, Fazal Din, despite his terrible wound, seized the sword from the Japanese officer and killed him with it. He then killed two more Japanese soldiers with the sword. Continuing to encourage his men, he staggered to his Platoon Headquarters to make his report. He collapsed there, and died soon after reaching the Regimental Aid Post. His action was seen by the whole platoon, who, inspired by his gallantry, continued the attack and annihilated the Japanese garrison of fifty-five men. Such supreme devotion to duty even when fatally wounded, presence of mind and outstanding courage have seldom been equalled and reflect the unquenchable spirit of a singularly brave and gallant NCO. For his incredible feat of valour, Naik Fazal Din was awarded a posthumous Victoria Cross'.

Naik Fazal Din has no known grave; however his name is inscribed on the Rangoon Memorial, Burma.

His VC is on display in the Lord Ashcroft Gallery at the Imperial War Museum, London.

Victoria Cross

Sepoy Haidar Ali, VC

Haidar Ali was born in 1913 in present-day Pakistan. He served as a Sepoy (Private) in the 13TH Frontier Force Rifles. In 1944, his platoon was tasked with crossing the River Senio under heavy enemy fire. The crossing was part of the Allied spring offensive and much depended upon the assault. However, the banks of Senio had been built up three metres high, and whilst Haidar's assault section travelled in vulnerable boats, the Germans were securely dug-in and heavily armed. The Rifles were cut to pieces by intense machine fire, and only Haidar and two fellow soldiers survived the crossing – the rest of his men laid injured or dead in the water. Undaunted, Haidar Ali seized the initiative, and covered by his two colleagues, charged the nearest machinegun post. He threw a grenade but was met by another, thrown by the enemy. He sustained a severe wound to his back, but in spite of this, continued his attack, silencing the machine gun and taking four Germans prisoner. Not content, he charged onto the next machinegun nest, sustaining further injuries in the right leg and right arm. Weakened by the loss of blood, but utterly determined to continue the battle, Haidar crawled closer and lobbed in another grenade, destroying the enemy position. Having subdued immediate opposition, the river was crossed and a vital bridgehead established. Haidar's bravery and devotion to duty saved the rest of his company. Found lying on the ground next to the river; Haidar Ali was carried back to his regiment with serious wounds. He recovered sufficiently to receive his Victoria Cross from King George VI at Buckingham Palace in October 1945.

His Victoria Cross citation read: "The conspicuous gallantry, initiative and determination, combined with a complete disregard for his own life, shown by this very brave Sepoy in the face of heavy odds, were an example to the whole company. His heroism saved an ugly situation which would, but for his personal bravery, have caused the battalion serious casualties at a critical time and delayed the crossing of the river."

He returned to Pakistan after the war, where he and his wife worked at a small farmstead. He died in 1999, at the age of 86, a short while after his wife's death, leaving behind no children.

On 9TH April 2017 the Mayor of Lugo di Romagna Davide Ranalli unveiled a Memorial dedicated to VC Haidar Ali upon the Senio River western bank in the vicinity of Sabbioni area. The ceremony was attended by Brigadier Yogi Sheoran, Defence Wing Attaché of the Indian Embassy in Rome.

George Cross

The *George Cross* (GC) is the second highest award of the United Kingdom honours system. It is awarded 'for acts of the greatest heroism or for most conspicuous courage in circumstance of extreme danger'. It is for acts not in the presence of the enemy to members of the British armed forces and to British civilians. The George Cross superseded the Medal of the Order of the British Empire for Gallantry (commonly known as the Empire Gallantry Medal).

Abdus-Samad Abdul-Wahid Golandaz Shaheed, GC
Abdus-Samad Abdul-Wahid Golandaz was an Indian landowner who received the Empire Gallantry Medal (later converted to the George Cross), the highest non-combat gallantry decoration of the British Empire, in the 1934 Birthday Honours. Citation read:
Mr. Golandaz owns a fleet of boats and trained boatmen which he places at the disposal of the authorities whenever Surat, Rander or the surrounding districts are threatened by the floods, and on frequent occasions he has risked his own life in leading his men to works of rescue. He has shown conspicuous personal bravery on several occasions. In particular on the 16TH of September 1933, when the Tapti River had swollen to such proportions that one of the sluices in the city wall had been damaged and water was pouring in through it, threatening to flood the city, he volunteered to dive into the flooded river and ascertain the nature and extent of the damage. He accomplished this brave feat successfully and blocked the sluice with sandbags at considerable risk to his own life. In 1930 he had also performed an act of conspicuous bravery in rescuing the boys of the Government High School and the family of the Excise Inspector, whose bungalows had been cut off by the floods.

George Cross

Lance Naik Islam-ud-Din Shaheed, GC

Lance-Naik Islam-ud-Din was a soldier of the British Indian Army during World War II, who was posthumously awarded the George Cross for sacrificing his own life to save others. He was serving in the 6TH Battalion, 9TH Jat Regiment, when on 12TH April 1945 at Pyawbwe, central Burma; a live grenade went astray and threatened to cause a large number of casualties in his unit. Islam-ud-Din threw himself on the grenade at once, showing no hesitation. Saving the lives of his comrades, he was killed instantly, aged only 19 or 20 and leaving behind a widow in India. He was described as steadfastly courageous and a good leader by his superior officers after his death. He was gazetted on 5TH October 1945.

Captain Mateen Ahmed Ansari Shaheed, GC

Captain Mateen Ahmed Ansari was serving in the 5TH Battalion, 7TH Rajput Regiment, in the Indian Army, during World War II. He was awarded the George Cross posthumously. He was taken prisoner when Japan occupied Hong Kong in December 1941 after the Battle of Hong Kong. After the Japanese discovered that he was related to the ruler of one of the Princely States they demanded that he renounce his allegiance to the British and foment discontent in the ranks of Indian prisoners in the prison camps. He refused and was thrown into the notorious Stanley Jail in May 1942 where he was starved and brutalised. When he remained firm in his allegiance to the British on his return to the prison camps he was again incarcerated in Stanley Jail where he was starved and tortured for five months. He was then returned to the original camp, where he continued in his allegiance to the British, and even helped to organise escape attempts by other prisoners. He was sentenced to death, with over thirty other British, Chinese and Indian prisoners and beheaded on 20TH October 1943. He is buried in Stanley Military Cemetery in Hong Kong.

Captain Muhammad Azad Khan, GC

Captain Muhammad Azad Khan, 1ST Punjab Regiment was awarded the George Cross in 1943 for fighting bravely against the Japanese Army. He took the railway station captured by the enemy during World War II in Java, Sumatra. He also received the 1939/45 Star, War Medal, Burma Star, Indian Service Medal (ISM), G.S. Medal, IDSM, OBI Class II, N.W. Frontier of India 1930 & Waziristan 1936-1937. He also fought in Kashmir during Indo-Pak war in 1948.

George Cross

Lieutenant Colonel Mahmood Khan Durrani, GC

Lieutenant Colonel Mahmood Khan Durrani after completing his schooling, he joined the Army of Bahawalpur State. When the Second World War broke out, he was posted to North Malaya in March 1941. During the British retreat, Captain Mahmood Khan Durrani and a small party of soldiers managed to evade capture for three months before their location was betrayed to the Japanese sponsored Indian National Army (INA). On his release he was awarded the George Cross. Citations read: "For outstanding courage, loyalty and fortitude whilst a prisoner-of-war. With a small party he was cut off during the withdrawal in Malaya. They succeeded in remaining free in hiding for three months until betrayal, when they were arrested and confined. Refusing to join the I.N.A this officer devoted himself to rendering valuable service. He then conceived and put into execution, a plan for thwarting the Japanese plans for infiltrating agents into India. After many delays and setbacks due to falling under suspicion he ultimately achieved much of his objective. Presumably as a result of the suspicion that he had been responsible for the failure of their plans, he was arrested by the Japanese. For ten days he was subjected to third degree methods including starvation, deprivation of sleep and physical torture such as the application of burning cigarettes to his legs. Subsequently he was given a mock trial and condemned to death but the execution was postponed in order that information should be extracted. He was then tortured by various particularly brutal methods continuously for several days. The exact time is uncertain as there were periods of unconsciousness, but it was certainly lasted for some days. No information whatever was obtained from him. Thereafter he was kept in solitary confinement for several months, with occasional interrogations and was given little medical treatment and just enough food to sustain life. When finally liberated he was found to be permanently affected in health and still bears the marks of physical torture. He will never be the same again. Throughout he was fully aware of the possible consequences of his actions and, when discovered, he preferred to undergo protracted and cruel torture rather than confess his plans and save himself, because he still hoped that he might achieve his purpose. To confess would have endangered others' lives and might have influenced the enemy to change their plans. His outstanding example of deliberate cold-blooded bravery is most fully deserving of the highest award." Captain Durrani was presented with his George Cross by Field Marshal Lord Wavell in 1946 at a special investiture ceremony held at the Red Fort, Delhi

George Cross

Noor-un-Nisa Inayat Shaheed, GC

Noor-un-Nisa Inayat Khan) was a British heroine of World War II renowned for her service in the Special Operations Executive. She also went by the name Nora Baker and was a published author of Indian and American descent who was posthumously awarded the George Cross for her service in the SOE, the highest civilian decoration in the UK. As an SOE agent she became the first female wireless operator to be sent from Britain into occupied France to aid the French Resistance during World War II, and was Britain's first Muslim war heroine. Inayat Khan was taken prisoner and transferred to Dachau concentration camp and at dawn on the, 13TH September, she was executed.

The full citation of the award of the George Cross reads:

The KING has been graciously pleased to approve the posthumous award of the George Cross to: Assistant Section Officer Nora Inayat Khan, Women's Auxiliary Air Force. Assistant Section Officer Nora Inayat Khan was the first woman operator to be infiltrated into enemy occupied France, and was landed by Lysander aircraft on 16TH June, 1943. During the weeks immediately following her arrival, the Gestapo made mass arrests in the Paris Resistance groups to which she had been detailed. She refused however to abandon what had become the principal and most dangerous post in France, although given the opportunity to return to England, because she did not wish to leave her French comrades without communications and she hoped also to rebuild her group. She remained at her post therefore and did the excellent work which earned her a posthumous Mention in Despatches.

The Gestapo had a full description of her, but knew only her code name "Madeleine". They deployed considerable forces in their effort to catch her and so break the last remaining link with London. After 3 months, she was betrayed to the Gestapo and taken to their H.Q. in the Avenue Foch. The Gestapo had found her codes and messages and were now in a position to work back to London. They asked her to co-operate, but she refused and gave them no information of any kind. She was imprisoned in one of the cells on the 5TH floor of the Gestapo H.Q. and remained there for several weeks during which time she made two unsuccessful attempts at escape. She was asked to sign a declaration that she would make no further attempts, but she refused and the Chief of the Gestapo obtained permission from Berlin to send her to Germany for "safe custody". She was the first agent to be sent to Germany.

George Cross

Noor-un-Nisa Inayat Khan, GC (Cont)
Assistant Section Officer Nora Inayat Khan, was sent to Karlsruhe in November 1943, and then to Pforzheim where her cell was apart from the main prison. She was considered to be a particularly dangerous and uncooperative prisoner. The Director of the prison has also been interrogated and has confirmed that Assistant Section Officer Nora Inayat Khan, but when interrogated by the Karlsruhe Gestapo, refused to give any information whatsoever, either as to her work or her colleagues.

She was taken with three others to Dachau Camp on the 12TH September 1944. On arrival, she was taken to the crematorium and shot. Assistant Section Officer Nora Inayat Khan displayed the most conspicuous courage, both moral and physical over a period of more than 12 months.

Nora Inayat Khan was posthumously awarded the George Cross in 1949, and a French Croix de Guerre with Silver Star (avec étoile de vermeil). As she was still considered "missing" in 1946, she could not be recommended for a Member of the Order of the British Empire, but was mentioned in Despatches instead in October 1946. At the beginning of 2011, a campaign was launched for a bronze bust of her in central London close to her former home. It was claimed that this would be the first memorial in Britain to either a Muslim or an Asian woman, but Inayat Khan had already been commemorated on the FANY memorial in St Paul's Church, Wilton Place, Knightsbridge, and London, which lists the 52 members of the Corps who gave their lives on active service. The unveiling of the bronze bust by HRH the Princess Royal took place on 8TH November 2012 in Gordon Square Gardens, London. Inayat Khan is commemorated on a stamp issued by the Royal Mail on 25 March 2014 in a set of stamps about "Remarkable Lives".

Havildar Abdul Rehman Shaheed, GC
Havildar Abdul Rahman GC was a soldier of the British Indian Army who was posthumously awarded the George Cross, the highest British (and Commonwealth) award for bravery not in combat. He was awarded the decoration for the gallantry he showed while saving three other men from a burning vehicle on 22ND February 1946 in Kletek in Java. He was serving with the 3rd Battalion of the 9th Jat Regiment, which had fought in the Battle of Cauldron against Rommel's forces and saw action at Imphal in 1943. His award was announced in the London Gazette of 10 September 1946.

George Cross

Lance Naik Islam-ud-Din Shaheed, GC

Lance-Naik Islam-ud-Din GC) was a soldier of the British Indian Army during World War II, who was posthumously awarded the George Cross for sacrificing his own life to save others. He was serving in the 6th Battalion, 9TH Jat Regiment, when on 12TH April 1945 at Pyawbwe, central Burma, a live grenade went astray and threatened to cause a large number of casualties in his unit. Islam-ud-Din threw himself on the grenade at once, showing no hesitation. Saving the lives of his comrades, he was killed instantly, aged only 19 or 20 and leaving behind a widow in India. He was described as steadfastly courageous and a good leader by his superior officers after his death He was gazetted on 5TH October 1945.

The Distinguished Conduct Medal

The Distinguished Conduct Medal was instituted by Royal Warrant on 4 December 1854, during the Crimean War, as an award to Warrant Officers, Non-Commissioned Officers and men for "distinguished, gallant and good conduct in the field". It was the second highest award for gallantry in action after the Victoria Cross. Prior to the institution of this decoration, there had been no medal awarded by the British government in recognition of individual acts of gallantry in the Army.

The Hong Kong and Singapore Royal Garrison Artillery (HKSRA) operated in Palestine during the Great War and saw actions in the Battle of Magdabah, Battle of Rafa and Gaza, and the Capture of Jerusalem. The following Punjabi Musalmans officers were awarded the DCM for their gallant leadership. They were an exclusive band as no other Indian soldiers have been so honoured with the award of DCM.

Havildar Nawab Khan, DCM	(Battle of Magdabah)
Havildar Sultan Mohammad, DCM	(Battle of Magdabah)
Havildar Piran Ditta 712, DCM	(Battle of Magdabah)
Havildar Piran Ditta 1081, DCM	(Battle of Gaza)

George Medal

The George Medal (GM), instituted on 24 September 1940 by King George VI, is a decoration of the United Kingdom and Commonwealth, awarded for gallantry "not in the face of the enemy".

Jemadar Jahan Dad, GM
On the 16TH September, 1944, near the Tiddim Road, Burma, a Sapper who was attempting to swim the Manipur River to join an Indian Infantry Regiment in their advance, was caught in a whirlpool, carried under, and drifted haplessly into a series of further whirlpool and rapids. Fully aware of the danger in this treacherous stretch of water, which claimed fiver victims the previous day; Jemadar Jahan Dad of the Indian Engineers, plunged into the river and after a terrific with the current succeeded in bringing the drowning man to safety.

Subedar Mohammad Azad, GM
On the 19TH November,1945, after 'C' Company of 1ST Punjab Regement had captured Tramway Workshops and Power Station area, No. 8 Platoon commanded by Subedar Mohammad Azad, was put in position East of Workshops to consolidate. While the Platoon was still digging its positions, a large ammunition dump containing heavy anti-aircraft and mortar ammunition blew up at a distance of less than 75 yards from the Platoon position. The explosion was tremendous and the whole area occupied by the forward section was covered with bricks, debris, fragments of bursting shells and even solid shot. Trenches were shattered, and casulties were caused; Subedar Mohammad Azad himself being wounded in the head. Heedless of wounds and shock, he six times traversed 50 yards of open ground in the midst of continous voilent explosions, flying debris and bursting shells, and over a period of one hour with complete disregard for his own personal safety in circumstances of very great danger, and indifferent to exhaustion, and pain and shock of his wounds, Subedar Mohammad Azad displayed resolute gallantry and devotion to duty of the highest order which will live in the history of his Regiment. As a result of his untiring efforts the lives of five men of his Platoon were saved. He also fought in Kashmir during Indo-Pak war in 1948 with Capt. Sarwar Shaheed. He died in 1989.

Distinguished Service Order (DSO)

The Distinguished Service Order (DSO) is a military decoration of the United Kingdom, and formerly of other parts of the Commonwealth of Nations, awarded for meritorious or distinguished service by officers of the armed forces during wartime, typically in actual combat.

Major General Akbar Khan, DSO
Akbar Khan was born 1ST December 1912 in a fairly affluent Pashtun family. He was the son of Muhammad Akram Khan. He belonged to a village named Utmanzai (Parichkhail Family) in the district of Charsadda. He received his education at Islamia College, Peshawar and the Royal Military College, Sandhurst. He was commissioned a Second Lieutenant onto the Indian Army on 1ST February 1934. He returned to India and he was attached to a battalion of the Hampshire Regiment from 1934-35, after which he was admitted to the Indian Army on 18TH March 1935 and was posted to the 6TH battalion, 13TH Frontier Force Rifles. He took part in operations in Waziristan war during 1937–1938. During the Second World War he served with the 14TH battalion, 13TH Frontier Force Rifles, part of 100TH Indian Infantry Brigade of the 20TH Indian Division during active combat operations against the Imperial Japanese Army in Burma. As a Captain and temporary Major he was awarded the Distinguished Service Order for conspicuous gallantry and leadership displayed during the Battle of Kwanlan Ywathit.

As a Brigadier-in-Charge, he participated in the Indo-Pakistani War of 1947. He also served as a commander of the Pakistan Army's division to stop the first Baloch insurgency of 1948. Khan had also served as appointed *Chief of National Security* under Prime Minister Zulfikar Ali Bhutto. Under his guidance, the Army had quelled the Baloch Insurgency during the early and mid-1970s. In spite of his engaging military career, Khan is mostly known in Pakistan as the main conspirator of the first but failed coup attempt of 1951, which came to be known as the *Rawalpindi Conspiracy*. Muhammad Akbar Khan died in 1993 at the age of 81 in Karachi. He was buried in Defence Military graveyard Karachi.

Distinguished Service Order (DSO)

Lieutenant Colonel Mohammad Aslam Khan, DSO
In the early stages of the operations in then Jhelum Valley, it was Major Mohammad Aslam Khan's outstanding leadership audacity and determination which inspired our forces to continue fighting against heavy odds. During the advance of the Indian force towards Muzzafarabad, this officer with a very small band was the sole nucleus of resistance. Burt for his superb leadership and bravery the Indian forces would have reached Muzzafarabad. Subsequently in the Northern Areas he with numerically inferior force organised and conducted under most difficult conditions, a brilliant operation thought be impossible in winter conditions which annihilated the garrisons of Gurez, Dras and Kargil, thus isolating Skardu and Leh, it was thanks to this officer that particularly the entire Northern Area of the line Gurez-Zojila- Padan, approximately 12,000 square miles was cleared of the opposing forces and Baltistan and Gilgit Agency kept out of enemy's reach. Throughout this officer displayed initiative, leadership and bravery of a very high order throughout. Very strongly recommend for Pakistan equalent of a DSO, General Gracy.

Vice-Admiral Syed Mohammad Ahsan, HQA, SPk, DSO
Syed Mohammad Ahsan was born in Hyderabad Deccan, Indian Empire, to an Urdu-speaking family in December 1920. After being schooled in Hyderabad, he attended the Nizam College of the Osmani University and gained B.A. degree and decided to join the Royal Indian Navy (RIN) in 1938 as a Sub-Lieutenant. In 1938, he joined the Britannia Royal Naval College in United Kingdom and was given commission as Lieutenant in Executive Branch of the Royal Indian Navy. He specialized in Signals and was an instructor at the Combined Cadet Force in Liverpool, England. His military career saw his participation in the World War II as a RIN naval officer and saw actions in the Atlantic battle against German Krieg marine. Upon posting back to British India, he participated in Arakan Campaign in 1942–43 and later served well in the Mediterranean theatre in 1944–45. His actions of valour earned him to be decorated with the Distinguished Service Order by the United Kingdom after the end of World War II in 1945. In 1946, he was appointed as aide-de-camp to Viceroy of India, Lord Mountbatten and assisted him in cabinet meetings to resolve political crises in the British Indian Empire. When the United Kingdom announced its intentions to partition of India in 1947, Ahsan decided to opt for Pakistan and was introduced by Lord Mountbatten to Muhammad Ali Jinnah as his aide-de-camp.

Distinguished Service Order (DSO)

Vice-Admiral Syed Mohammad Ahsan (Cont)

In a meeting with Jinnah, Lord Mountbatten reportedly quoted: [President] Jinnah, I give you Pakistan, I give you my Aide'd camp, Lieutenant Ahsan." At the time of his joining the Pakistan Navy, the Indian Navy sent the military seniority list to Pakistan's Ministry of Defence (MoD) where Lt. Ahsan was the 4TH ranking officer in the Executive Branch in terms of seniority. He was assigned as military adviser and ADC to founding father and the first Governor-General M.A. Jinnah. In 1947, Lt. Ahsan was the first person at the Jinnah Terminal to receive Lord Mountbatten's when they first arrived to Karachi to meet Jinnah. On 30 September 1949, he witnessed the commissioning of the PNS *Tippu Sultan* from the Royal Navy and was subsequently promoted as Lieutenant-Commander. He was made First Executive officer of *Tippu Sultan* and later commanding the PNS *Tariq* as Commander in 1950. He participated in Task Force 92 alongside with Commander A.R. Khan who commanded the *Tippu Sultan* and made a first goodwill visit to Malta, Middle East and Eastern Europe.

In 1951, he commanded the HMS *Tughril* which became a part of the 25TH Destroyer. In 1955–56, he was posted in the MoD's diplomatic assignment as the naval attaché at the Pakistan Embassy in the Washington D.C. In 1957, he was promoted as Captain and assigned to command the cruiser warship, the PNS *Baber*, that sailed in Karachi the following year. His first assignment included his role as Deputy Director of Naval Intelligence at the Navy NHQ while establishing his intelligence department. At December 1952, he was asked to send a priority report that compiled detail discussions with Pakistani military personnel on the basic principles of the ISI. In addition, he was also asked for military's reaction towards the Basic Principles Committee where he ultimately warned of the theocracy and concluded that the economic disparities between East and West Pakistan must be addressed to prevent the breaking-up of the nation's unity. In 1959–60, he served as chief of staff of the Navy NHQ under the Navy Commander in Chief. In 1960, he was promoted to the one-star rank, Commodore, and directed the Naval Intelligence during this time. In 1961–62, he again served on the diplomatic assignment when he was appointed as deputy chief military planning officer of Southeast Asia Treaty Organization (SEATO) in Bangkok and later became its chief military officer. In 1962, he was promoted as Rear Admiral and established the Logistics Command to resolve the logistics problems in both East and West Pakistan

Distinguished Service Order (DSO)

Vice-Admiral Syed Mohammad Ahsan (Cont)

In 1964, he was sent to Dacca and took over the chairmanship of the East-Pakistan Inland Water Transport Authority where he had begun training of East-Pakistani military on riverine tactics with the absence of the strong naval presence. During this time, he became the principle military secretary to President Ayub Khan. In a short time, Rear-Admiral Ahsan gained influence on President Ayub Khan and advised him on important military issues concerning on the defence of the nation at the cabinet meeting chaired by the President Ayub. While in East, he played a crucial role in deployment of Eastern Command and prevented the East-Pakistani military to involve in East-Pakistani politics while opposing any military action against East Pakistani activists after the riots in 1964 despite the calls. In 1965, he was stationed back to Pakistan and assumed the command of Naval Intelligence as Director-General, and participated in second war with India in 1965. Rear-Admiral Ahsan and his staff at the Navy NHQ helped planned out the naval offense in Dwarka and partially leading the fleet as its Commander. The operation met with mixed results but it stopped the Indian Air Force raiding Karachi and Pakistan's coastal areas as Admiral Ahsan collated the intelligence reports on the Indian Navy's strategic western naval positions, and orchestrated naval operations against the Indian Navy. After the war, he was most senior admiral serving in the navy and was nominated for navy's chief of staff by outgoing naval chief Admiral A.R. Khan in 1966. His nomination papers were approved by President Ayub Khan in 1966, and appointed him as commander in chief of Navy. In 1967, he was promoted to the three-star rank, Vice-Admiral, and was honoured with Sitara-e-Pakistan by President Ayub. As a naval chief, he oversaw the induction of the Daphné submarines procured from France in 1966 in navy's submarine branch. In 1966, he held successful negotiation with Turkish Navy to refit and upgraded the submarine PNS *Ghazi*. Since 1966–68, Admiral Ahsan knew of Indian Navy massive procurement and acquisitions of weapon systems being acquired from the Soviet Union and United Kingdom. On multiple meetings with President Ayub, he raised the issue of modernizing the navy against India, and kept warning the Army GHQ of potential and possible Indian Navy's attack on West and East region of the country; his reservations were bypassed on every meeting and warnings were not heed due to the financial reasons. His Navy NHQ staffs were in brief conflict with the Air AHQ staff over the establishment of naval aviation by induction of fighter jets in 1968.

Distinguished Service Order (DSO)

Vice-Admiral Syed Mohammad Ahsan (Cont)

The Air AHQ staff bypassed his recommendation over the loss of jets and their pilots in seas in an event of conflict with India. He succeeded in convincing President Ayub in acquiring the missile boats only, and permissions were granted to procure the Soviet-built *Osa-class* missile boat in 1968. He led series of unsuccessful talks with the Soviet Navy and Russian Marshal Andrei Grechko in 1969 due to their warming of relations with India. From 1966–69, his Navy NHQ staff tussle with the Finance ministry over the issues of budget and financial support for modernization of navy without any success. He established the Special Services Group Navy (SSG) and commissioned the Pakistan Marines in 1966 after commissioning the naval facilities for training purposes in the special operations. In 1966, he further accepted the recommendation from United States Navy to train its Special Forces unit, an equivalent organization to that of U.S. Navy SEALs.

In Karachi, he went on to commission the Naval Academy to provide teaching of the naval staff and cadets instead of sending cadets to United Kingdom for training and education. From 1966–68, he served on the served on the Board of Governors of Cadet College Petaro. Vice-Admiral Ahsan is also credited with founding Port Qasim – Pakistan's second port – after exploring the coast around Phitti Creek, when he was Chief of Naval Staff. He immediately met with then–Foreign Minister Zulfikar Ali Bhutto where he convinced Bhutto in 1972 to locate the port there. He supervised the construction and establishment of the port where he set up the main industries and machineries at the Port.[28] The main channel of this port bears his name. From 1966–69, he established the East-Pakistan Navy and commissioned the warships, *PNS Sylhet* and *PNS Tughril*, in its arm. However, he struggled with expanding the East-Pakistan Navy's capabilities as many sailors and officers had defected to India to join the Awami League's military wing– the *Mukti Bahini*. After President Ayub Khan tendered resignation, and invited army chief General Yahya Khan to take over the presidency. In 1969, he relieved the naval command to Admiral Muzaffar Hassan to be appointed as deputy CMLA under Yahya administration. In August 1969, he joined the Yahya administration as cabinet minister of finance, statistics, commerce, industry, and planning commission. However, this was short-lived and Admiral Ahsan was appointed as Governor of East-Pakistan on 1ST September 1969. The assignment was considered very difficult by the Pakistani military when many senior officials in West were reluctant to accept appointments in East Pakistan.

Distinguished Service Order (DSO)

Vice-Admiral Syed Mohammad Ahsan (Cont)

The law and order situation was quickly deteriorating under the martial law enforced by Major-General Muzaffaruddin in East. In the Cabinet meeting, President Yahya was told that the situation in East is at a critical, and his government needed an administrator with a good reputation in the province. In an attempt to control the law and order in the country, Admiral Ahsan's service was extended and appointed governor in East. He took over the command of Eastern Command and appointed Lieutenant-General Yaqub Ali Khan as his principle staff officer (PSO) in 1969.

In 1969, he paid a state visit to the United States to meet with Elliot Richardson to gain foreign support for East Pakistan and sustainability in the region. In addition, he also arranged the visit of U.S. Navy officials to visit him at the Governor's House, Dhaka to strengthened military relations with the United States. In 1970, his government coordinated efforts to rehabilitate the infrastructure after the deadly cyclone and used the military coordinate to relief operations after meeting with President Yahya who had instruct him to "take charge". In February 1971, Admiral Ahsan, together with Lieutenant-General Yaqub Ali Khan, attended the cabinet meeting President Yahya Khan, which Admiral Ahsan described as "tense", where the atmosphere was highly "anti-Bengali", with no representation from East Pakistan in the policy and decision-making. He provided his intelligence analysis on military option over political one which he preferred the political solution.

His stand of view was not well supported which made him highly unpopular at the meeting and returned to Dhaka immediately with his principle staff officer Lieutenant-General Ali Khan. On 22 February 1971, Admiral Ahsan attended the last meeting over the issue of the East Pakistan. When it became apparent that the military actions and Indian interventions were inevitable, Admiral Ahsan renewed his offer to President Yahya, Rahman, and Bhutto to work out an arrangement where the Pakistani military deployments to support the Eastern Command could get out intact, without being humiliated. Known as Admiral's Formula, the East Pakistan would eventually gained independence through a co-federation where Yahya would serve its President with East Pakistanis moving to East and Western Pakistanis moving to Pakistan. National assets would equally be divided between Pakistan and East Pakistan as Pakistani military deployments would continue to support the East-Pakistani military. It was reported that Bhutto supported the idea but later vetoed it due to Yahya's maintaining the presidency.

Distinguished Service Order (DSO)

Vice-Admiral Syed Mohammad Ahsan (Cont)

On February 1971, he supervised the military deployments in East that were already preparing to conduct a military operation to curb the movement. He became aware of Yahya administration's decision of taking military actions despite his staff officer Lieutenant-General Yaqub Khan's recommendations. Disheartened and isolated by his colleagues, Admiral Ahsan returned to East Pakistan to pick up his personal belongings and tried getting in telephoned with President Yahya without success. On March 7TH, 1971, Admiral Ahsan resigned in protest and immediately requested to be posted back Navy NHQ in Karachi, Pakistan. At the Dhaka International Airport, he was asked by Bengali journalists about how it felt to be back in a land where he had once wielded authority.

His response was as profound as it was coruscating as he intoned: *Kaise kaise rang badalte hain asmaan ke* (lit. How the skies change colour! Nothing else needed to be said.") He participated in the war with India in 1971 but without an assignment of any command at the Navy NHQ and sought honourable discharge from the navy after the war ended in the winter of 1971. In an article titled *A nation's shame* published in the *Newsline magazine* of September 2000, the Admiral Ahsan concluded:

But who was responsible for creating this hostile atmosphere and hatred among the people? The situation deteriorated further after General Yahya Khan postponed the first session of the newly elected constituent assembly. It became very clear immediately after the election results that the generals were not prepared to transfer power to the Awami League. First the delay in summoning the National Assembly session and later its postponement confirmed the Bengalis' worst fears, that the election results were not acceptable both to the generals and to the majority of West Pakistani politicians. Zulfikar Ali Bhutto publicly called for a boycott of the assembly session. Such a transgression was bound to further fuel public resentment. He welcomed the formation of the War Enquiry Commission that was to be chaired by Chief Justice Hamoodur Rahman in 1972, and attended its proceedings. He confessed in the War Enquiry Commission and aptly described the hostile mood of the military leadership when they decided to postpone the assembly session and launch a military operation in the eastern province. Admiral Ahsan publicly stated: 'On arrival in Rawalpindi, I was alarmed to notice the high tide of militarism flowing turbulently. There was open talk of a military solution according to plan. I was caught quite unaware in this atmosphere for I know of no military solution which could possibly solve whatever crisis was supposed to be impending in the minds of the authorities.

Distinguished Service Order (DSO)

Vice-Admiral Syed Mohammad Ahsan (Cont)

It was evident from the statement that the decision to launch a military operation was taken without consulting the Governor of East Pakistan who was the only sane voice in the government. The President presided over the meeting of the governors and martial law administrators attended as usual by the military and the civilian officers of the intelligence community. It is relevant to record that among the tribe of governors and MLAs, I was the only non-army governor and the only active naval officer in the midst of active service men. I was the only person, though a non-Bengali, who had to represent the sentiments of seventy million Bengalis to a Pakistani government. During the past 17 months, in meetings and conferences, my brief ran counter to the cut-and-dried solutions of Pakistan representatives and civil servants. The president invariably gave decisions which accommodated East Pakistan's viewpoint, at least partially. This made me unpopular with my colleagues who probably thought I was "difficult at best" and "sold" to the Bengalis at worst. After retiring from Navy in 1971, Admiral Ahsan remained one of the notable naval chief of Pakistan Navy and key figure who witnessed notable events in the military history of South Asia. He was appointed chairman of Port Qasim Authority in 1972 and later chairman of National Shipping Corporation from 1975–76. After leaving the public service in 1976, he spent his remaining years in quietness and put himself out of public eye during his last years. During his last years, Admiral Ahsan learned French and played bridge. Ahsan died peacefully in 1989 in his villa located in Islamabad and was given an honorary guard of honour by the Government of Pakistan and buried in military graveyard in Karachi per accordance to his will. His death was mourned by Prime Minister Benazir Bhutto, President Ghulam Ishaq, Chairman joint chiefs Admiral Iftikhar Ahmed Sirohey, and Chiefs of Staff of Army, Navy, and Air Force. In 1990, the Pakistan Navy announced of establishing a naval base in Baluchistan and commissioned in 1991 as PNS Ahsan to honour his services. The base was given commissioned by Chief of the Naval Staff Admiral Yastur-ul-Haq Malik. The main channel of the Port Qasim bears his name, as it known as Ahsan Channel, which was inaugurated by Prime Minister Benazir Bhutto who acknowledged Admiral Ahsan's as the founder of Port Qasim at a speech on the occasion of the opening of a new terminal at Port Qasim on 4TH August 1989. Ahsan died peacefully in 1989 in his villa located in Islamabad and was given an honorary guard of honour by the Government of Pakistan and buried in military graveyard in Karachi per accordance to his will.

Military Cross

The Military Cross (MC) is the third-level military decoration awarded to officers and (since 1993) other ranks of the British Armed Forces, and used to be awarded to officers of other Commonwealth countries. The MC is granted in recognition of "an act or acts of exemplary gallantry during active operations against the enemy on land to all members, of any rank in Our Armed Forces"

Risaldar Nur Ahmed Khan, MC, IOM
9TH Hodson's Horse
Citation:
'Risaldar Nur Ahmed Khan of 9TH Hodson's Horse, Indian Army. Egypt. On 19TH September 1918, he as in charge of the advance troop and acted with great dash and gallantry. He made several personal reconnaissances and sent back clear information. When checked by fire from the orchard just north of Wadi Falik he collected his troop and cleared the place, securing two guns, 1 machine gun, some transport, 3 officers and about 40 other ranks. He did splendid work.' Risaldar Nur Ahmed Khan was awarded the Military Cross on 8TH March 1919.
Risaldar Nur Ahmed Khan was born on 20TH December 1881. During the Great War, he served in France and Palestine from 1914 to 1920 and saw action in 1917 during the various raids on trenches in St. Helene. He earned the 1ST Class of the Indian Order of Merit for the actions at Cambrai, 30TH November 1917. Woodie Major, 1ST April 1914. He was Orderly officer to General Allenby and Appointed ADC to Commander-in- Chief in India, 1ST April 1921. He was Quartermaster 4TH Hodson's Horse, 1924-27 and Assistant Recruiting Officer, Rawalpindi, 16TH November 1927.

Military Cross 1914-1921

Jemadar Hasan Shah, MC
9TH Hodson's Horse
Mention in Despatches from General Wingate from 1916 to 1919 to Secretary of State:
'In my second despatch, I also referred to the outstanding services rendered by the small detachment of Indian Moslem Gunners under the able command of Jemadar Hasan Shah, who was promoted Risaldar and granted the award of the Military Cross for gallantry and devotion to duty. I cannot speak too highly of the behaviour of this detachment, 'which', in the words of Major Davenport, 'never complained in spite of great hardships, and did all the arduous service they were called upon to perform with a willing smile. This detachment specially distinguished itself at the defence of Zumrud Fort and displayed a military zeal and resource in action was most praiseworthy'. In the words of T.E. Lawrence: 'This refers to a detached unit of Indian Army machine-gunners who were engaged, under his command, in a relatively unconventional form of warfare. They had volunteered to serve in the desert force supporting the Arab Revolt against the Ottoman Empire in 1917 and 1918. These men came from regular Indian Army cavalry regiments fighting on the Western Front. They were formed into a camel-mounted machine gun section with two Vickers guns. On 6TH July 1917 Davenport raided Zumrud on the Hajaz railway, destroying three miles of track, rail by rail, in one of the most successful raids of the whole campaign; it was carried out with the support of the Indian gunners. Although Lawrence did not recount the services of the Indian gunners in any detail, he made numerous references to them and to Hasan Shah personally, speaking of him in generous terms for his camaraderie and well as his professional competence. In December 1917, a little over fourteen years after joining the Indian Army, Hasan Shah was commissioned Jemadar in the 9TH Hodson's Horse. He remained with Hodson's Horse throughout his career, received the Military Cross for gallantry, and was twice mentioned in despatches. He was appointed Honorary Lieutenant upon retirement in February 1927. Most significant to the determination of his services during the Great War, he was decorated with the 4TH Class Order of El Nahda by HM the King of Hejaz. He was the only Indian officer to be thus decorated. Most probably Hasan and his gunners were once again on horseback, when this regiment marched into Damascus'.
The other cavalry volunteer who joined Hasan Shah's command was from his very own regiment: Lance Daffadar Sher Shah. This officer was awarded the Indian Distinguished Service Medal for gallantry in Egypt.

Military Cross 1914-1921

Ressaidar Laurasib Khan, MC
10TH DCO Lancers (Hodson's Horse)
Citation:
'Ressaidar Laurasib Khan, 10TH Lances (Hodson's Horse), Indian Army, Mesopotamia. For conspicuous gallantry and devotion to duty on the 1ST March 1920, at Safrah, when in command of a squadron after his squadron leader had been killed. His squadron was suddenly attacked, and, almost surrounded and outnumbered, by skilful leadership and sound judgement he extricated the squadron with little loss from extremely critical situation. His gallant conduct and coolness throughout the action were beyond all praise'. Ressaidar Laurasib Khan was awarded the Military Cross on 12TH July 1920. He went on the pension establishment on 16^{THE} January 1929 as Honorary Lieutenant.

Ressaidar Munsabdar Khan, MC
13TH DCO Lancers (Watson's Horse)
Citation:
'Ressaidar Munsabdar Khan, 13TH Lancers, Mesopotamia. For conspicuous gallantry and devotion to duty on 27TH November 1917, he was with patrol, which penetrated the enemy lines at night, gaining much valuable information and bringing back four prisoners, including two officers. He was of great assistance to his British officer and extracting the patrol from a position of considerable danger'. The Military Cross was presented by HM King George V in the gardens at Buckingham Palace on 2ND August 1919. He went on pension establishment in October 1921.

Risaldar Kamaluddin Khan, MC, OBI
38TH KGO Central India Horse
Citation:
For distinguish service in connection with military operations in Egypt and Palestine'. In recognition of his distinguished service in the field was promoted to the rank of 2ND Lieutenant at the end of the Great War. He had graduated the hard way, for he had enlisted in the regiment 6TH February 1904 and proved he had proved himself on service, and was a valuable officer in the years that followed. He was a great favourite with all ranks and especially with his brother officers, and occupied a special privileged position in the regiment, until he went of pension establishment on 1ST November 1933 with the rank of a Captain.
Risaldar Kamaluddin Khan was awarded the Military Cross on 12TH December 1919 for distinguish service in connection with military operations in Egypt and Palestine.

Military Cross 1914-1921

Subedar Amir Khan Bahadur, MC, OBI
2ND Battalion, 21ST Punjabis
Citation:
'Subedar Amir Khan Bahadur, 2ND Battalion, 21ST Punjabis, Indian Army. During operations at Jandola, on 29TH June 1921, his company commander was killed, whereupon he took charge of the company, and handled it with great skill and coolness. At the time, he took over command; the company was just starting to cross the Sagar Algard, being on the extreme right of the Battalion. The enemy had held up this advance at this point by heavy fire and by carrying out outflanking movement in force. The situation at this time was critical; if this company had not defeated the enemy flanking movement, the remainder of the Regiment would have taken the rear. Although short of ammunition he defeated the flanking movement, after which, still under heavy fire, he got in all the wounded, rifles and equipment. When the retirement was started the enemy charged; in face of this he completely broke the enemy's rush and carried out most skilful retirement. His company did not lose a single rifle or piece of equipment, and brought in the equipment of a Lewis Gun, the soldiers of which had been killed. It was mainly due to the courage, skill, and coolness of this Indian Officer that the Regiment was able to effect a successful retirement without the heavy loss in men and rifles, which at one time seemed inevitable. He displayed great personal bravery and set an excellent example to his men'. Subedar Amir Khan Bahadur was awarded the Military Cross on 29TH March 1922. He went on pension establishment on 17TH September 1922 as Subedar-Major.

Subedar Ghulam Ali, MC
40TH Pathans
Citation:
'For conspicuous gallantry and devotion to duty, he conducted the withdrawal of a rear-guard with exceptional gallantry and skill. He sent a magnificent example to his men'. Subedar Ghulam Ali was awarded the Military Cross on 25TH August 1917
On 18TH April 1917, the burden of the retreat fell on the Punjabi Mussulman Company acting as rear-guard under Subedar Ghulam Ali, who for his skill in handling the rear-guard, as well his own disregard of danger, was awarded the Military Cross. (Regimental History).
Subedar Ghulam Ali went on pension establishment in 1922.

Military Cross 1914-1921

Subedar Gul Akbar Bahadur, MC, OBI
53RD Sikhs (Frontier Force)
Citation:
'Conspicuous gallantry when at Sannaiyat on 7TH April at about 11.00 AM, under heavy shell, Machine Gun and Rifle fire he applied first aid to a wounded British Officer in an exposed position, assisted in removing him to a less exposed position and in digging him in, further advance having been stopped by orders, attended to him until it was possible to remove him after dark'. Subedar Gul Akbar Bahadur was awarded the Military Cross on 22ND December 1916. He went on pension establishment in 1922 as an Honorary Captain.

Subedar Arsla Khan Bahadur, MC, IOM, OBI
57TH Wilde's Rifles (Frontier Force)
Citation:
'For service in the Field'
Military Cross and the OBI medals were presented to him by HM Queen Mary at Buckingham Palace on 12TH November 1915. An incredible soldier to have earned the MC and IOM and was awarded the OBI! Subedar Arsla Khan Bahadur went on pension establishment in 1921 as Subedar-Major.

Subedar-Major Farman Ali, MC, IOM, IDSM, OBI
92ND Punjabis
Citation:
'For marked gallantry and distinguished service and ability in the attack on Sannaiyat on 2ND April 1916, when under very heavy Rifle and Machine Gun fire, he commanded the remnants of the regiment after the British Officers had been killed or dangerously wounded. He kept men of all companies together and hung on to the furthest point reached, though no support came, with a handful of men to the last minute. When it was clear that the final counter attack would overwhelm his party, he maintained rapid fire until the enemy reached bombing distance, arranged for covering his retirement, hurled bombs checking the enemy, and withdrew his men under cover of the confusion that ensued. Though the regiment suffered 84 percent casualties of those engaged, he was the last to retire. His example in action is always an inspiration to the men of all castes, and his military coolness are always conspicuous'. Subedar-Major Farman was awarded the Military Cross on 22ND December 1916. He went on pension establishment in 1921 as Honorary Captain, Sardar Bahadur.

Military Cross 1914-1921

Subedar Shaikh Abdulla, MC, IDSM
93RD Burma Infantry
Citation:
'Service in the Field'
His medal for the Military Cross was presented to him by HM King George-V in the gardens at Buckingham Palace on 2ND August 1919. Subedar Shaikh Abdulla went on pension establishment in 1922.

Subedar Jiwan Khan, MC and Bar
2ND Battalion, 101ST Grenadiers
Citation:
'Subedar Jiwan Khan, 2ND Battalion, 101ST Grenadiers, Indian Army. For conspicuous gallantry and the magnificent example he set to all ranks during the attack on the 20TH September 1918. Subedar Jiwan Khan was continually under very heavy and accurate fire from Rifle and Machine Gun for nine hours and never stopped a moment to rest. He was not content with the capture of the objective allotted to his company, but by pressing on materially aided in the capture of another place. His coolness and clear-headedness were as remarkable as his courage. In the face of the heaviest Machine Gun fire, he retained a splendid grasp of the situation and was indefatigable in re-organising the line and that the Lewis Guns were kept supplied with ammunition, often carrying the ammunition himself'. Subedar Jiwan Khan was awarded the Military Cross on 8TH March 1919.
Citation to Bar to MC:
'Subedar Jiwan Khan, 2ND Battalion, 101ST Grenadiers, Indian Army. For conspicuous gallantry and skilful leading on the 14TH December 1918. Under heavy Machine Gun and Rifle fire, Subedar Jiwan Khan led his platoon with great enterprise and courage, even after being wounded, and affected the capture of five Nordenfelt Guns'. He was awarded the Bar to his Military Cross on 10TH February 1925.
Military Cross was presented to him by HM King George V in the gardens of Buckingham Palace on 2ND August 1919. On 21ST January 1921, the 2ND Battalion was disbanded. Two Indian officers, one of whom was Subedar Jiwan Khan had earned during the World War the distinction to a bar to his Military Cross, and eighty three men were transferred to the 1ST Battalion. Subedar Jiwan Khan went on pension establishment on 1928 as Subedar Bahadur.

Military Cross 1914-1921

Jemadar Pola Khan, MC
1ST Battalion, 101ST Grenadiers
Citation:
'Jemadar Pola Khan 1ST Battalion, 101ST Grenadiers, Indian Army. On the night of 18TH and 19TH June, he was in command of a patrol of twelve other ranks. When nearing village the patrol came across the enemy. They called on the enemy to surrender, but they showed no sign of doing so, instead made ready to throw bombs and open fire. Seeing this Jemadar Pola Khan, at once dashed forward, seizing the bomber with one hand and the rifle of another man with the other, and calling on his men to follow. All three men captured, a party of the enemy about thirty-five strong, who were apparently out as an ambush a short distance off, immediately charged, but were repulsed with a loss. There is no doubt that but for Jemadar Pola Khan's cool courage and prompt action both in capturing the prisoners and conducting his fighting retirement with prisoners to guard, the patrol would have suffered badly, both casualties and morale. He showed splendid example of leadership, many of the men being under fire for the first time'. Jemadar Pola Khan was awarded the Military Cross on 7TH November 1918. Jemadar Pola Khan and went on pension establishment as Honorary Lieutenant.

Jemadar Lal Shah Gul, MC, OBI
126TH Baluchistan Infantry
Citation:
'Jemadar Lal Shah Gul, 126TH Baluchistan Infantry, Mesopotamia. For conspicuous gallantry and devotion to duty at Sheranis on 17TH September 1919, when with two sections he attacked and captured a point within close range of the enemy Sangars at Khantur. Although heavily fired on he maintained his position unsupported for two hours until ordered to withdraw. Whilst holding the position he showed great gallantry in moving wounded men, and controlled his command most skilfully throughout'. Jemadar Lal Shah Gul was awarded the Military Cross on 15TH January 1920. Jemadar Lal Shah Gul went on pension establishment on 1922 as Subedar Bahadur Lal Shah Gul.

Captain Haji Suleiman Ghulam- Hussein Haji, MC
Indian Medical Service
He was awarded the Military Cross for his services in East Africa in 1918

Major Haji Mohammad Salamat Ullah, MC
He was awarded the Military Cross for his services on the NW Frontier in 1919.

Military Cross 1914-1921

Subedar Sher Afzal, MC, IDSM
128TH Pioneers
Citation:
'Service in the Field'   x
The medal for Military Cross was presented by HM King George V in the garden at Buckingham Palace on 2ND August 1919. He went on pension establishment in 1922 as Khan Sahib, Honorary Lieutenant.

Khan Sahib Sher Afzal Khan, MC, IDSM, Extra Assistant Commissioner, Banu, was the son of Khan Bahadur Abdul Qadir Khan, Jagirdar, Jhanda, district Mardan in the NWFP. Born in July 1896 he was permanent resident of Jhanda, Tehsil Swabi in the district of Mardan. Well versed in Pashto, Persian, Arabic, and English, he was directly commissioned Jemadar and served in the army from 1912 to 1922. After retiring from the army, he joined the Civil Services in 1925. He was conferred with the title of Khan Sahib for excellent services in Kalam against odds and intrigue where he initiated government control at great personal risk. He worked on the Anglo-Afghan Commission of 1936 and 1938. His great-grandfather, Sher Khan, was in the service of Akbar the Mogul King of India and received Jagir at Attock. Sher Afzal's father, Khan Bahadur Abdul Qadir Khan, did political work at the border for sixty years with great success and credit. He also helped the government during the Sepoy mutiny in 1857.

Subedar Zaman Khan, MC, OBI
129TH DCO Baluchis
Citation:
'Awarded the Military Cross for Service in the Field'.
On the 23RD-24TH November occurred the action of Festubert, in which both the Lahore and Meerut Divisions took part. The 34TH Pioneers were first to take the train. The 129TH then saved the critical situation and Subedar Zaman Khan found an opportunity to add the OBI to his Military Cross he had already won. Subedar Zaman Khan was wounded in action on 30TH November 1914. He received the Military Cross for the same action in which Sepoy Khudadad Khan received the Victoria Cross. At the end of this action then Baluchis had suffered 114 killed and wounded and 64 missing. Subedar Zaman Khan enrolled in the Army on 24TH March 1890 and went on pension establishment in 1922 as Honorary Captain.

Military Cross 1914-1921

Subedar Mohammad Khan, MC
3RD Battalion, 152ND Punjabi
Citation:

'Subedar Mohammad Khan, 3RD Battalion 152ND Punjabis, Egypt. For conspicuous gallantry on the 19TH September 1918, when at Khan Abu Malul he took command of a company, his company commander having become a casualty. He showed great coolness moving up and down the line under heavy fire encouraging the men after they had been checked in the first assault. He organised a second attack but was incapacitated at the outset by a grenade wound to the head'. Subedar Mohammad Khan was awarded the Military Cross on 8TH March 1919. He went on the pension establishment, when the battalion was disbanded in late 1919.

Military Cross 1922-1947

Jemadar Mohammad Shabir Khan, MC
Skinner's Horse (1ST Duke of York's Own Cavalry)
Citation:

'During the period 1ST January to 2ND May 1945, Jemadar Mohammad Shabir Khan has shown consistently excellent qualities of leadership and initiative in commanding his Troop in action. He has commanded the Infantry Troop of his squadron for the whole period under review, and has shown qualities of leadership and courage beyond praise. A particular instance was on the night 4TH-5TH February, when his troop was in position on the River Senio within one hundred yards of the enemy. The enemy attacked from both front and rear of his position and Jemadar Mohammad Shabir Khan, realizing that his Troop were inexperienced in this type of action, deliberately showed much complete fearlessness turning his fire and his own personal courage throughout the action. The above is but one example when the success of his Troop can be attributed directly to his personal example, which he inspired the utmost confidence in his men'. Jemadar Mohammad Shabir Khan was awarded the Military Cross on 13TH December 1945. He was promoted to the rank of Jemadar on 26TH April 1944. At the independence of the sub continent in 1947 into Indian and Pakistan, Jemadar Mohammad Shabir Khan opted for the new Independent State of Pakistan.

Military Cross 1922-1947

Lieutenant Hazur Ahmed Khan, MC
Skinner's Horse (1ST Duke of York's Own Cavalry)
Citation:
'During the period from 1ST September to 31ST December 1944, Lieutenant Hazur Ahmed Khan has shown has shown consistently excellent qualities of leadership and initiative in commanding his Troop in action. He has commanded the Infantry Troop of his squadron for the whole period under review, and had personally led many difficult and dangerous patrols. A particular instance was on 2ND September 1944.when operating forward from Bibblona he led a patrol deep into the enemy's line and besides inflicting several casualties brought back very valuable information of the enemy's position. Again on 30TH September 1944, he personally led another patrol to Monte Gignolo, when similar result was obtained. The success of his Troop, which has been considerable, is directly attributed to his personal example, which has inspired the utmost confidence in his men'. Lieutenant Hazur Ahmed Khan was awarded the Military Cross on 28TH June 1945.
After the war and the independence of the sub continent in 1947 into Indian and Pakistan, Lieutenant Hazur Ahmed Khan opted for the new Independent State of Pakistan.

Risaldar Mohammad Sharif, MC, IDSM
Skinner's Horse (1ST Duke of York's Own Cavalry
Citation:
'In the early afternoon of 22ND April 19454, Risaldar Mohammad Sharif, was ordered to take his armoured car troops along a road just west of Route -64 up to River Reno. He was told that if he could make good going he might succeed in cutting off the rear-guard of enemy who were trying to withdraw across this road. He led his own armoured car and ignored the risk of mines and 'panzer fasts', though he knew that both were likely to be met. Three badly concealed mines were soon seen by him in time. These he cleared personally by hand. His dash was rewarded, and he caught up with the enemy rear-guard. As he met each party, he drove straight into them. His troop followed his example, and by the time, he had reached the river he had over-run three complete Spandau positions and captured 39 Germans with their arms'. Risaldar Mohammad Sharif was awarded the Military Cross on 19TH July 1945. After the war he opted for the Pakistan Army in 1947.

Military Cross 1922-1947

Captain Riaz Ul Karim Khan, MC
Probyn's Horse
Citation: 'At Meiktila on 3RD March 1945, Captain Riaz Ul Karim Khan was in command of a troop of tanks of a squadron detailed to clear up an enemy squadron came under heavy fire from the enemy 75 mm and 37 mm guns, and two tanks received direct hits. Captain Riaz Ul Karim Khan's was then sent forward, unescorted by infantry, to locate the extent of the enemy's position and destroy the guns. Captain Riaz Ul Karim Khan led his troop round the enemy's right flank into the gun position, where he was engaged at 70 yards range by 75 mm guns. His leading tank received four direct hits and was set on fire and his own tank received two direct hits. With extreme coolness, this officer then engaged the enemy causing the crew of the burning tank to evacuate the tank whilst he gave supporting fire. He then withdrew his troop and gave such a clear report of the extent of the position and the location of the guns, that the position was subsequently captured without further casualties together with three 75 mm guns and one 37 mm gun. The courage and coolness, and initiative of this troop leader were beyond praise and example to all ranks'. Captain Riaz Ui Karim Khan was awarded an immediate Military Cross.
Captain Riaz Ul Karim Khan opted for Pakistan Army in 1947 and as Brigadier commanded the 4TH Armoured Brigade during the India-Pakistan War 1965.

Jemadar Fazal Dad, MC
6TH DCO Lancers (Watson's Horse)
Citation:
'On 26TH April 1945, during the advance on Rovigo, Jemadar Fazal Dad was commanding the leading troop of his squadron. On approaching the site of the wooden bridge over the Canale Bianco south of Villa Marzana, he came under heavy enemy fire and found that the end span of the bridge on the enemy side of the Canale was burning. Jemadar Fazal Dad took immediate action, crossed the burning bridge on foot in full view of the enemy, organised the damping of the fire and drove the enemy away. The bridge was saved and was used as the primary axis for the whole of 17TH Brigade during the following days advance. Jemadar Fazal Dad's prompt action his section in saving the bridge was of prime importance in the subsequent advance'. Jemadar Fazal Dad was awarded an immediate Military Cross.

Military Cross 1922-1947

Risaldar Ali Khan, MC
7TH Light Cavalry
Citation:
'Risaldar Ali Khan was commander of a Troop when it was attacked at Litan Saddle on 15TH June 1944. He attacked and demolished two Japanese bunker positions with the help of Infantry. Later the Infantry was held up by a third bunker, which stopped the whole advance along the front. Risaldar Ali Khan went forward with his tank, engaged this obstacle, and completely destroyed it, thereby enabling the whole front to advance. In doing so, his tank became stuck. He made every effort to extricate but if failed, and finally received a direct hit from enemy anti-tank weapons, which jammed his turret and disabled his gun. He kept cool and calm, dismounted his Browning guns from the tank and prepared to defend his tank from the ground. All this time he was under heavy fire from the enemy. He refused to leave the vicinity of his tank until definitely ordered to do so. When he did come away, he destroyed everything, and brought back his guns. Risaldar Ali Khan had already been recommended for his bravery'. Risaldar Ali Khan was awarded the Military Cross for his gallantry September 1944.

Risaldar Nazar Mohammad Khan, MC
PAVO Cavalry (11TH Frontier Force)
Citation:
'At Myinmu, Burma, on 22ND January 1945, Risaldar Nazar Mohammad Khan was in command of an Armoured Car Troop being used in a tank role in support of 10TH Ghurkha Rifles. On numerous occasions, he took his Car within 10 yards of Bunkers under heavy small arms and grenade fire and destroyed them. He was ordered to capture two Japanese who were dug in a position. He took his Car up to seven yards of the position, and shouted at them to come out; when they replied with grenades, he leaned out of his turret and shot them both with his Tommy Gun, as the car was too close to bring its armament to bear. Again at Miyoung on 25TH January Risaldar Nazar Mohammad Khan set a very high example of dash and leadership. His personal courage, by exposing himself to enemy fire to engage targets when his periscope was damaged, was an inspiration to all ranks and deserving of the highest praise'. Risaldar Nazar Mohammad Khan was awarded an immediate Military Cross for his gallantry and leadership.

Military Cross 1922-1947

Jemadar Mohammad Zaman, MC
Central India Horse (21ST KGVO Horse)
Citation:

'On the night of 5TH/ 6TH October 1944, Jemadar Mohammad Zaman led his troop on a fighting raid to cut the main Savignano- Strigara road just North of Mount Galli, at a point strongly held by the enemy, in Italy. Guiding his troop through the darkness over the difficult country Jemadar Mohammad Zaman crossed the road at the appointed place and disposed his men on either side of it. Within ten minutes the ambush thus laid as successful, three enemies being killed and three wounded before his quarry disappeared again into the darkness. The noise of the firing had revealed his presence, however, and hail of accurate Spandau fire commenced from the four houses on either side of the troop and at a distance of under 200 yards. Having anticipated this new danger before any damage had been done, by frequent changes and by switching the fire of his section now to one house and now another, he managed to convey an impression of strength greater than he had in reality. After half an hour, the fire fight ceased. All four houses had been cleared at the cost of one man wounded. The Troop then searched the building and the surrounding countryside before returning. Throughout this action, Jemadar Mohammad Zaman showed and coolness that well merits the recognition, himself moving about fearlessly over the fire-swept ground, keeping the situation under his control and passing his orders to his second leaders. By his example of courage under withering enemy fire and his complete disregard for his personal safety, he mastered a very difficult situation. The close control he established over his section at the risk of his own safety undoubtedly saved many lives.'

The Regiment had served in India, North Africa, Italy and Greece. At independence in 1947 Mohammad Zaman transferred to 19TH KGO Lancers a regiment destined for Pakistan. He served in the Regiment during the India-Pakistan war of 1965 and was awarded the gallantry awards of Sitara-e-Shujat and Imitiazi-i-Khidmat by the Pakistan Army.

Military Cross 1922-1947

Risaldar Abdul Razak Khan, MC, OBI
16TH Light Cavalry
Citation:
'On 3RD and 4TH March 1945, two armoured car patrols were sent out on the Meiktilla-Wudwin road. The strength and position of the enemy were unknown but it was known that the enemy had guns of a calibre that could completely destroy an armoured car with any sort of hit and that these guns were trained on the road. Despite this information Risaldar Abdul Razak Khan who was in the point car throughout acted with consummate boldness and skill. Even under heavy fire, which he saw completely destroy another car of his patrol, Risaldar Abdul Razak Khan carried on coolly with his task, which was to determine the strength and limits of the enemy positions. In fact, the main method by which he could gain this information was by drawing fire on him. His conduct on both these days was an inspiration to other members of his patrol and a tremendous example to troops of his squadron of which he was the senior VCO. This example had had a big effect on all ranks of the unit'. He was awarded an immediate Military Cross.

Acting Major Mohammad Adalat, MC
Royal Indian Artillery
Citation:
'During the periods under review 16TH May to 15TH August and throughout the whole period of operations November 1944- August 1945, Major Mohammad Adalat has done outstanding work as Foo, and an Infantry have more than once praised the exceptional skill, courage, and energy, which he has invariably shown. On operation Sunshine when the Division was advancing over the very difficult country of Mawachi Road, in most trying climate conditions, it was reported as largely due to the timely and accurate artillery fire brought down by Major Mohammad Adalat that casualties to our forces, which, if numerous would have seriously jeopardised the success of the operation, were so slight. On one occasion, an attack upon a strongly held enemy position, the Company Commander was killed within a few of Major Mohammad Adalat, who then went forward with the leading troops, under heavy fire, and helped to encourage them in assault. By his untiring keenness, cheerful coolness in the face of enemy fire, he has shown on several occasions throughout the campaign that there are few officers, in whom confidence that is more complete can be placed.' He was deservedly awarded the MC.

Military Cross 1922-1947

Jemadar Hakim Ali, MC
Royal Indian Artillery
Citation:

'On 25TH May 1944, the Brigade executed a night march across country through enemy held territory to Moirang Khunou. The Battery ran into an enemy ambush and sustained heavy. The Subedar-Major was seriously wounded in the first volley, leaving Jemadar Hakim Ali in charge of the guns. He was wounded himself but despite the general confusion, he managed to get his guns into action and to put out local protection by first light. He then proceeded to inflict heavy casualties on the enemy from point blank range, his well-sited local protection parties driving off repeated enemy attempts to attack the guns, until the Battery was ordered to withdraw. This young VCO's magnificent handling of so vulnerable a column as a mountain battery on the move deserves the very highest praise. His coolness and fine example to his men undoubtedly saved the Battery from what might have easily led to almost complete annihilation'. He was awarded an immediate Military Cross.

Jemadar Imam Ali, MC
Royal Indian Artillery
Citation:

'At Wazonzeik, near Prome on 14TH May 1945, a report was received of 200 Japanese in a village a miles north. Jemadar Imam Ali, with two sections of infantry, was sent to locate this party and engage them with artillery. On nearing the village, he realised that his presence had been given away by the locals. Undeterred he proceeded to make a detour thereby avoiding an ambush to reach his selected viewpoint. Here he saw a party of Japanese and then engaged another party with gunfire, as a result which 10 Japanese were definitely seen to be killed. The Japanese then started to work round both flanks of the Jamadar's position, and his party came under fire. Though fully realising the threat from the greatly superior Japanese party, Jemadar Imam Ali coolly carried on with his task of shelling the village. He then turned his fire on the advancing enemy and when almost surrounded, with excellent judgement he skilfully withdrew his party, covering his withdrawal by the fire of his guns. In attending his objective in spite of knowing that his presence had been given away to the enemy, Jemadar Imam Ali showed initiative and determination and leadership of a high order. His coolness and courage under fire and in face of the Japanese as was conferred by the patrol the next day'. Jemadar Imam Ali was awarded an immediate the Military Cross.

Military Cross 1922-1947

Lieutenant Mohammad Aslam, MC, OBI, ADC to the King.
Royal Indian Artillery
Citation:
'At Ngangkha Lowai on 26TH May, 1944, and again at Ningthoukhong Kha Khundu on 29TH May, while acting as FOO he displayed determination, Skill and coolness under the heaviest fire and in continuous close contact with the enemy. On both occasions though slightly wounded, he contrived repeatedly to bring down the fire of the whole regiment on the enemy defences despite the fact that the three Signallers who were with him either killed or wounded. Owing to the high rate of officer and VCO casualties in his battery, Lieutenant Mohammad Aslam borne responsibilities much beyond his rank and service and have had to remain unrelieved in forward positions for very long periods. In his continued cheerfulness, enthusiasm, and well founded confidence.' Lieutenant Mohammad Aslam was awarded the Military Cross on 28^T July 1945. *He joined the Pakistan Army in 1947 and retired in 1978 as a Major General.*

Jemadar Maula Dad, MC
Royal Indian Artillery
Citation:
'Central Burma. On 29TH April 1945, 'B' Company, 6TH South Wales Borders was given the task of capturing Myitha Gap. The Company advanced and when 10 yards from the objective, came under heavy small arms fire. Jemadar Maula Dad who was the OP for the 32ND Mountain Battery and 25 Pounders attached to 'B' Company at once went to the forward section, and regardless of his own safety brought accurate fire on the enemy positions. During the action Jemadar Maula Dad was sniped and wounded, and although in pain, he continued to direct accurate fire onto the enemy at a crucial time. When he was advised to return to the RAP, he refused to leave his post and insisted that he remain the night, until it was possible for him to be relieved in the morning. His courage and resourcefulness throughout the entire action was responsible for inflicting heavy casualties upon the enemy and allowing the Company to take up positions. His disregard for personal safety, unselfish devotion to duty and persistence in inflicting casualties to the enemy while aiding the Company was example to all.' Jemadar Maula was awarded an immediate the Military Cross.

Military Cross 1922-1947

Subedar Wali Dad, MC
Royal Indian Artillery
Citation:
'September 1944, Subedar Wali Dad, was attached as FOO with 1ST Battalion, 17TH Dogras, who were holding a roadblock at Milestone 139 on the road Tonzang-Tiddim Road, Burma. Subedar Wali Dad left the safety of his trench and from an exposed position remained in observation of the enemy gun until he had silenced it with the power of his own guns. At about 0200 hours on the night of $19^{TH}/20^{TH}$ September 1944, the position was subjected to heavy automatic and grenade fire, and the Japanese were heard forming up for an assault. Again, Subedar Wali Dad was seen moving about in the open; and with complete disregard for his own safety, selecting positions from which he could best observe and direct the defensive fire of his guns onto the most threatened points. The attack was repulsed and the success achieved by the roadblock was due in large degree to Subedar Wali Dad's high sense of duty and his skilful handling of the artillery in the face of danger. His example of cool courage and complete disregard for personal safety were inspiration to all.' He was awarded an immediate the Military Cross.

Jemadar Fazal Dad Khan, MC
Royal Indian Artillery
Citation:
'The work of Havildar Major (now Jemadar) Fazal Dad Khan has been outstanding during the whole campaign. Owing to the shortage of officers in his battery during May and June 1944, Jemadar Fazal Dad Khan was called on to carry out the duties in a most zealous and highly distinguished manner. In both Bishenpur and the Ukhrul Road areas, he was frequently employed as OP Officer, in which capacity he displayed initiative and a ready acceptance of risk when close to the enemy. He carried out many successful shoots, particularly against enemy gun positions in the Bishenpur area, during which he boldly moved his OP to positions from which the best view of his targets could be obtained, though this often entailed moving over ground covered by enemy fire to positions in close proximity to the enemy. In carrying out these duties, he showed judgement, skill, leadership and sense of responsibility beyond that normally expected of his rank. During the whole period his cheerfulness, efficiency and gallant conduct have been an inspiration to all ranks'. Jemadar Fazal Dad Khan was awarded the Military Cross in 1946.

Military Cross 1922-1947

Subedar Liaquat Hussein, MC
Royal Indian Artillery
Citation:
'Subedar Liaquat Hussein without a break took part in the battle from Tiddim to Bishenpur, and then with 89TH Brigade, he fought at Ukhrul and later in the advance from Meiktila to Pegu. Whether as a Forward Observation Officer or in charge of the Gun position he has always shown not only great technical ability but coolness and a total disregard for his own personal safety. The following are examples of his work. As Forward Observation Officer when attacking a roadblock, he crawled forward with telephone on to the forward slope of a hill covered by accurate enemy machine-gun fire. From this position, he registered targets for a fire plan. Later the fire plan was so accurate that the roadblock was broken by our attack. Once when returning from Wet to Meiktila with his Battery it was ambushed, the enemy firing machine guns onto the Battery transport. Then an enemy section charged towards the vehicles throwing grenades. Subedar Liaquat Hussein taking a Bren gun killed three of them and wounded one; the remainder fled. He then got his gun into action and held the enemy until help from the Infantry arrived. On another occasion, he was Forward Observation Officer supporting an Infantry battalion attacking and enemy heavy defended locality. It was impossible to carry out registration as the only point of vantage was covered by enemy fire. Subedar Liaquat Hussein waited until it was nearly dark and crawling forward under heavy fire carried out his registration.' Subedar Liaquat Hussein was awarded the Military Cross on 6TH June 1946

Jemadar Raza Mohammad, MC
Royal Indian Artillery
Citation:
'Jemadar Raza Mohammad was with the Regiment throughout the operations in Tiddim and Bishenpur and during the 1945 advance through Burma. Most of his work has been done in the operations. On every occasion, he has used his guns to the greatest effect in helping forward infantry and his bravery has been an inspiration to the all ranks of the Regiment. This officer has shown him fearless in action throughout the operations and his accurate fire has proved invaluable to the infantry on many occasions. Jemadar Raza Mohammad was awarded the Military Cross on 6TH June 1946.

Military Cross 1922-1947

Jemadar Mohammad Hussain, MC
Royal Indian Artillery
Citation:

'At Chawai on 12TH June 1944, Jemadar Mohammad Hussain was Forward Observation Officer with an Infantry Company in position astride a Japanese line of communication. During the afternoon, the Company moved off to engage a Japanese supply convey seen resting in nearby village. The Company Commander asked for artillery fire on the convoy. In order to secure good observation, Jemadar Mohammad Hussain moved forward alone save for one Signaller and took up a position upon a feature overlooking the village from a distance of 100 yards. At the time, he was to engage the target; it was concealed from view by a heavy mist. Realising the success of the attack depended upon the assistance he could give from his guns; Jemadar Mohammad Hussain proceeded to engage the target despite the mist, ranging by the sound of the fall of the shot. As the Infantry moved into the village, they found the convoy had been split by the artillery fire and their task made much easier. The following morning another attack was launched on the village where the Japanese had reorganised. Once again Jemadar Hussain was with the leading platoon, which was held up by heavy light machine-gun, rifle and grenade fire. He brought down immediate and accurate fire upon the village from an exposed observation post approximately 30 yards from the Japanese who, when they saw him immediately started throwing grenades in his direction. Undaunted Jemadar Mohammad Hussain remained where he was. Against Sirurukhong on 14TH June 1944, Jemadar Mohammad Hussain was the Gun Position Officer with the guns which were firing over open sight from a position overlooking the village. Throughout the action, Jemadar Mohammad Hussain gave very able support to the attacking Company and was chiefly responsible for the success of the attack. On one occasion he saw the Company was held up and could not advance due to heavy machine-gun fire. Jemadar Mohammad Hussain from his gun position saw the position from which the medium machine-gun was firing and without awaiting further orders Jemadar Mohammad Hussain turned his guns and them and opened fire. The result was that the Medium Machine Gun stopped firing and the Company was able to continue the advance. Throughout the operation Jemadar Mohammad Hussain showed self-control, initiative, and courage of a very high order.'
Immediate MC was recommended by the Corps Commander and C-in-C Army Group approved the award of an Immediate Military Cross for Jemadar Mohammad Hussain.

Military Cross 1922-1947

Subedar Fatteh Khan, MC
Royal Indian Artillery
Citation:
'At Milestone-52 on the Tiddim-Fort White road on 14TH December 1943, Subedar Fatteh Khan was in command of a Forward Observation party in support of 1ST Battalion, Ghurkha Regimen. This Battalion as attacking a strongly fortified enemy position for the first time under cover of artillery barrage. Early in the attack the FOO commanding a second party was wounded. Subedar Fatteh Khan immediately assumed command this second observation party also. The infantry got close to their objective but the enemy MMG mortar fire continued to prove stumbling blocks. As the attack was held up enemy fire increased, and sniping as rife. Subedar Fatteh Khan then proceeded to set an example to all ranks both infantry and artillery, of coolness and leadership. He showed complete disregard of the enemy fire by openly exhorting of the enemy fire by openly encouraging his troops, and showing defiance of the enemy. The infantry regrouped and went into attack again. Owing to the proximity of our own troops, the artillery could not be employed but not to be outdone his share of the battle, Subedar Fatteh Khan took part assisting the infantry officers in whatever way he could in the second attack. His determination to get to close grips with the Japanese was an inspiration to all taking part in the attack. This has not been an exceptional case. Subedar Fatteh Khan has been throughout the period under review was consistently in the forefront of battles, outstanding in excellent work during recent operations on the Tiddim road.' Subedar Fatteh Khan was the Military Cross on 8TH February 1945.

Jemadar Sher Ali, MC
Corps of Royal Engineers
Citation:
'On 5TH November 1943, Jemadar Sher Ali was in charge of a party engaged on road construction in Monte Falcone, Italy. The work was heavily shelled and the party had to withdraw temporarily. Jemadar Sher Ali seeing and ambulance with wounded which had to get through the village, stayed on the work although already wounded, and helped the ambulance through. Again in November, when wounded on the road at Mozzagrogna, he insisted on remaining with his men until the task was completed.' Jemadar Sher Ali was awarded the Military Cross on 24TH August 1944.

Military Cross 1922-1947

Jemadar Chaudhari Khan, MC
Corps of Royal Engineer
Citation:
'On 11TH May 1944, Jemadar Chaudhari Khan was in charge of an engineer assault party accompanying the infantry, when they made an attack on hill feature south of Kohima. They were all pinned down by heavy fire from the Japanese. Jemadar Chaudhari Khan with complete disregard for the intense enemy fire organised his engineer party and temporarily neutralized the Japanese attack. He then rallied what remained of his party and with the cry *'Nagra-El-Hadri'* joined in the infantry assault which was successful. The success of the attack on this vital position was undoubtedly due to the exemplary bravery and disregard of his safety of Jemadar Chaudhari Khan.' Jemadar Chaudhari Khan was awarded the Military Cross on 31ST August 1946.

Jemadar Mohammad Shah, MC
Corps of Royal Engineer
Citation:
'On 29TH November 1944, Jemadar Mohammad Shah was detailed with two sections of his platoon to carry out the engineer work in connection with an 'Ark' crossing over the Viacuva canal north of Forli, Italy. From the outset, he came under small arms fire, as his party had followed up close behind the leading infantry. Lying flat on the ground, they worked their way forward and cleared the site mines. When the leading fascine-carrying tank came up, the enemy commenced to shell the area. In order to position the fascines correctly it was found necessary to manhandle them. Undeterred by shelling and by coolness of the water, Jemadar Mohammad Shah immediately led his men waist deep into the canal, where sheer strength and determination they were able to manoeuvre the very heavy fascines into the correct place. By his leadership and fine example, Jemadar Mohammad Shah inspired his men to carry out their difficult task with complete success. Jemadar Mohammad Shah has consistently over very long period displayed the very highest qualities of leadership and determination and has repeatedly carried out essential recces in the most exposed positions.' Jemadar Mohammad Shah was awarded the Military Cross in April 1946.

Military Cross 1922-1947

Subedar Jahan Dad, MC
Corps of Royal Engineers
Citation:
'During the period under review, Subedar Jahan Dad has been outstanding in all Engineer tasks carried out his Company and also commanding his Punjabi Muslim Platoon after the platoon commander's death in action. He has shown great coolness in operations when in command of sapper mine lifting detachment operating with the forward tanks and infantry and during two assault tank crossings south of Singu. He was in command of his platoon of sapper's n the Brigade Group, which captured Maymyo and was highly commended for his work in this operation.' Subedar Jahan Dad was awarded the Military Cross on 17TH January 1946.

Subedar Ramzan Khan, MC. MBE
Corps of Royal Engineer
Citation:
'Subedar Ramzan Khan, who had been Senior Subedar for the Field Company for the last 20 months, has particularly distinguished himself during the advance into Burma this year by his outstanding leadership and courage, selfless devotion to duty and his magnificent personal example and encouragement to all ranks at the most critical and serious moment. At the crossing of the Irrawaddy near Myinmu, where his OC was evacuated wounded, when the Sappers who were operating the rafts were continually driven off the beaches by accurate shell fire, he continuously over the period of four days and nights of heavy Sapper casualties led them back to the beaches, re-organised them, repaired the rafts, and re-started the flow of men and equipment across the river. His continuous presence on the beaches, his drive and energy were an inspiration to all ranks. Later in the advance to Rangoon, he was always forward urging his men to work faster under fire, to ensure the minimum delay to the advance.' Subedar Ramzan Khan was awarded MC on 6TH June 1946.

Jemadar Mohammad Riaz, MC
Corps of Royal Engineer
Citation:
'Jemadar Mohammad Riaz commands the Punjabi Mussulman platoon, which he took over after it had been badly shaken and suffered heavy casualties at Cassino. In spite of deficiencies in numbers, he kept his platoon at very high standard of efficiency throughout the advance north of Aresso, across the River Arno and finally through the Gothic Line at Urbine, Montescudo, and San Marino. Every task given to him to do with his platoon was completed successfully in the quickest possible time.

Military Cross 1922-1947

Jemadar Mohammad Riaz (Cont)
Corps of Royal Engineer
Citation:

Due to the large commitments in recognisance required from platoon officers most of Jemadar Mohammad Riaz's tasks were carried out without supervision. At Gemmano on 16TH September 1944, the platoon cleared mines and filled in craters on the roadway leading down to the Conca Valley. This work was under complete observation from the enemy and the party came under almost constant shellfire. Due to the leadership of Jemadar Riaz and excellent example set by him, the work was completed in a few hours without a single casualty being sustained. Later on 21ST September 1944, below San Marino, the platoon was detailed to make the crossing of the River Marechia between Montebbelo and Scorticarta. While clearing lines in order to construct a division near the main river Jemadar Mohammad Riaz saw party of the enemy on the far bank. He immediately organised a party to hunt them down and succeeded in taking three prisoners without loss to his own party. Work by day eventually to be abandoned due to Spandau fire from across the valley; nevertheless as soon as the dusk came he resumed his work and completed the task despite the proximity of the enemy. This resulted in tanks being able to pass onto Montenbello-Scorticarta ridge in the morning thus providing invaluable support for the infantry in the subsequent attack. On these occasions Jemadar Mohammad Riaz was in charge of works and due to his courage and fine leadership, he earned the highest respect of officers and men of the Divisional Sappers and Miners.' Jemadar Mohammad Riaz was awarded the Military Cross on 28TH June 1945.

Jemadar Atta Mohammad, MC
Corps of Royal Engineer
Citation:

'On the night of 20/21 February 1944, immediately after a collision at sea between his ship and the Staffordshire, Subedar Atta Mohammad, on board the Dunzra displayed high courage and an officer's best qualities. By taking complete control of the situation regardless of his own safety and exercising initiative, determination and high powers of leadership, he established order from panic. The evacuation of his troops to boat stations was remarkable for each man being in procession of his rifle. OC Troops commented in the highest terms upon his courage and the excellence of his example to officers as well as men.' Jemadar Atta Mohammad was awarded the Military Cross on 21ST December 1944.

Military Cross 1922-1947

Subedar Mohammad Afsar, MC
1ST Punjab Regiment
Citation:
'As leader of the Guerrilla Platoon Subedar Mohammad Afsar has done most valuable work during the period under review. Personally leading fifteen long distance patrols under the worst possible conditions and over most difficult country he has, besides inflicting loss on the enemy and causing confusion, brought back information, which had been of vital importance in the operations. It was due to his skill and leadership that blocks were established on all the three tracks leading from Kennedy Peak eastwards to the Japanese base on Hungvung Maui. By constantly harassing and twice destroying the enemy post near the latter position, he caused the enemy to withdraw thus giving another battalion freedom of action. Subedar Mohammad Afsar has throughout shown outstanding zeal, skill and bravery and has materially assisted to oust the enemy from his strong positions.' Subedar Mohammad Afsar was awarded the Military Cross on 13TH September 1945.

Jemadar Mohammad Fazil, MC
1ST Punjab Regiment
Citation:
'On 11TH October 1944, Jemadar Mohammad Fazil's was ordered to capture a Japanese position and cut their Line of Communication. The first attack was held up by heavy LMG fire. In spite of the fact that there was only one approach, Jemadar Mohammad Fazil made a fresh plan and again attacked. He personally led the charge and was the first into the position causing the enemy to abandon it in disorder. Jemadar Mohammad Fazil by his sound planning, disregard for personal safety and determination to carry out his difficult task enabled the Battalion to securely close the enemy's Line of Communication.' Jemadar Mohammad Fazil was awarded an immediate Military Cross.

Lieutenant Adam Khan, MC
1ST Punjab Regiment
In March 1937, the 2ND Battalion, 1ST Punjab Regiment moved to Waziristan for taking part in the operations against the Faqir of Ippi. It was during these operations that Lieutenant Adam Khan was awarded the Military Cross for gallant and distinguished service in action at Engamal near Razmak on 23RD July 1937.
(In 1947, Adam Khan opted to join the Pakistan Army and attained the rank of Major-General).

Military Cross 1922-1947

Captain Mohammad Aslam, MC
1ST Punjab Regiment
Citation:

'Captain Mohammad Aslam has been in continuous command of a Rifle Company throughout operations from 1ST July 1944 to date. He has earned the respect of all ranks for his qualities of leadership and coolness of command in the face of the enemy. During the Battalion attack on the ridge area overlooking Promano on the evening of 10TH July 1944, his Company, while in occupation of Colle Di Pozzo, a feature vital to the success of the operation, was subjected to an enemy counter attack from two directions. Appreciating that one was a faint to ensure the success of the other, Captain Mohammad Aslam quickly reorganised his Company, left a platoon to deal with the faint attack, and personally led another to successfully repel the enemy's main effort. His bold action made secure the left flank of the Battalion at a time when any enemy success would have prejudiced the safety of three remaining companies who had not consolidated their objectives. On the night of 3RD August 1944, while the Battalion was in operation of the high ground south of T. Sovora, he was given the task of establishing his Company on Point 600, a feature devoid of any cover, to protect the digging of artillery OP. During the operation, the feature was heavily shelled, and just before dawn, he was ordered to withdraw his Company. It was due to his cool and skilful direction in the execution of this order that the Company as able to carry out this difficult operation under fire, without suffering a casualty. By the above acts and his conduct in subsequent actions, Captain Mohammad Aslam has proved himself a courageous and fearless leader of men, outstanding in quick and cool appreciation when in close contact with the enemy. He set an example to all officers in the Battalion.' Captain Mohammad Aslam was awarded the Military Cross on 19TH April 1945.

Subedar Abdul Ghani, MC, MBE
1ST Punjab Regiment
Citation:

'Subedar Abdul Ghani has commanded his platoon consistently well throughout the Arakan and Assam campaigns. At Akhaungbaukywa (Arakan) in the initial attack, he displayed skill and daring. On 17TH January 1944, he went on a patrol in enemy occupied territory and brought back valuable information, gaining of which entailed lying up for a complete day within 200 yards of the enemy post. On 25TH January 1944, during the battle for a feature called Squiggle he led his platoon with success in the face of heavy opposition.

Military Cross 1922-1947

Subedar Abdul Ghani (Cont)
1ST Punjab Regiment
Citation:
On 13TH March 1944, his platoon ejected the enemy from the West Oyster. At Tuphema on 30TH March, during the battle of the Jeeps, Subedar Abdul Ghani personally took command of a section during the confused fighting and inflicted very heavy casualties on the enemy. After two hours of heavy fighting, Subedar Abdul Ghani whose platoon had become scattered and cut off in the confusion, gathered his section together, and fought his way back to the remainder of the Company. In all engagements Subedar Abdul Ghani has led his platoon with consistent courage and skill.' Subedar Abdul Ghani was awarded an immediate Military Cross.

Subedar Karim Khan, IDSM, MC
1ST Punjab Regiment
Citation:
'On 11TH January 1946, Subedar Karim Khan moved forward from Brihgnang to Domas. When 300 yards south of Domas Subedar Karim Khan and his platoon were ambushed and the Battalion Commander and five soldiers were killed and several were wounded. Although wounded, Subedar Karim Khan reformed the remainder of the platoon under heavy MG fire showing total disregard for personal safety. Throughout this engagement Subedar Karim Khan had no communication ad was unable to call for mortar or artillery support. Subedar Karim Khan's personal gallantry and high standard of leadership were a great inspiration to his men. His actions without doubt saved the lives of his platoon and enabled the wounded to be evacuated. It was entirely due to the coolness and courage under fire of Subedar Karim Khan that the lives of all the men were saved. The gallantry of Subedar Karim Khan and his devotion to duty merits a high reward'. Subedar Karim Khan was awarded the Military Cross on 4TH April 1946.

Military Cross 1922-1947

Major Mohammad Jamshed, MC and Bar
1ST Punjab Regiment
Citations:

'Throughout the Assam-Burma operations, Major Jamshed has shown outstanding courage, skill, and determination. As leader of the Guerrilla Platoon in September and October 1944, Major Mohammad Jamshed was almost permanently out on long distance patrols. In spite of the worst possible weather conditions, he invariably completed his mission with success, causing confusion to the enemy and bringing back valuable information, which greatly assisted the operations. At the end of October 1944, although suffering from a very severe attack of fever, Major Jamshed with great skill placed blocks on all three approaches to Kennedy Peak from the East. From these blocks, he harassed the strong enemy positions at either end of the track, giving them no rest and inflicting many casualties. He was also able to secure the neutralising of two 75 MM guns, which he discovered near his position. He led his men in the destruction of enemy supply camp near Kennedy Peak capturing large quantities of supplies and arms and killing or putting to flight to all in the camp. His energetic leadership, enthusiasm and daring have been a great example to the men of his command and he was a great factor in forcing the enemy to leave his immensely strong position on Kennedy Peak and Hungvung Maul thus opening the way for the advance of another Brigade. Major Mohammad Jamshed was awarded the MC on 13TH September 1945.

Citation (Bar to MC):
'Major Mohammad Jamshed was Company Commander two armoured cars and was ordered to attack a party of 100 Japanese dug in at Letpanzaul. The enemy opened fire with LMGs on the Company forming up for the attack. Major Mohammad Jamshed immediately engaged the enemy with such speed and dash that the enemy left his bunkers in disorder, only to run into the fire of the other 2 platoons and the armoured cars. The bodies of 2 officers and 59 men of the Japanese were found. Major Mohammad Jamshed led his company again on 8TH April 1945 in a successful attack against the Japanese bunkered position at Nuagyan. On 17TH April 1945, his Company was engaged with a strong force of enemy, and he managed to subdue the enemy fire and ensured that all casualties were brought in. Throughout the operations Major Mohammad Jamshed has commanded his Company with singular skill and success. His enthusiasm and personal gallantry have been such that his men will follow him anywhere.'

Military Cross 1922-1947

Jemadar Khurshid Khan, MC
1ST Punjab Regiment
Citation:
'Jemadar Khurshid Khan took over command of the position the hill dominating the exit from the Lintan Box on 27TH March 1944, after his Company Commander had been killed and the senior VCO severely wounded. In the action that followed, very heavy casualties were inflicted on the Japanese, estimated 100 killed and only about 10 men of his Company were wounded. Jemadar Khurshid Khan had only been promoted a few days ago and completely inexperienced, but his conduct at the defence of the slopes was in the highest traditions of the Indian Army and a great example and inspiration to his men'. Jemadar Khurshid Khan was awarded the Military Cross in October 1946.

Jemadar Nawab Khan, MC
1ST Punjab Regiment
Citation:
'During the period 16TH November 1944 to February 1945, in India and Ramree Island, Burma, Jemadar Nawab Khan was a platoon commander in a rifle company. On 26TH January 1945, his platoon took part in a heavily opposed assaulted crossing of the Yanbauk Chaung. The craft were under heavy machine-gun and mortar fire all the way across the tidal Chaung. Regardless of enemy fire, Jemadar Nawab Khan stood up in the boat and cheered his men to greater endeavours, and reaching the enemy shore the Jemadar immediately led his men in a bayonet charge on the enemy position, which drove them out of it. He then reorganised his platoon into defensive positions. Despite heavy enemy counter attacks throughout the night of January 1945 the position was held. Wherever the fight was the fiercest Jemadar Nawab Khan was there and it was his superb example and disregard to personal safety, which was the inspiration to his platoon to hold their position. When orders came to withdraw on 27TH January 1945, Jemadar Nawab Khan collected his platoon and showed such skill and determination was of very high order and fine example to all. Throughout the whole period he has proved himself a fine leader and has shown a high devotion to duty against the enemy'. Jemadar Nawab Khan was awarded the Military Cross on 15TH November 1945.

Military Cross 1922-1947

Subedar Walayat Khan, MC, IOM
1ST Punjab Regiment
Citation:
'Subedar Walayat Khan is the senior Subedar in 'C' Company. On 22ND February 1944, this Company was leading the advance of the Battalion on to Sugar Loaf and Ione Three. At 1400 hours when the leading troops were approaching the feature, two parties of enemy each numbering 12 to 15 opened fire with Light Automatics and grenades from the north and south. Immediately Subedar Walayat Khan shouting his war cry charged the enemy in the trenches to the south and drove them out. Hardly had he done this when another party of 10 were spotted by him moving near their supply dump in the nala. At once Subedar Walayat Khan rushed in with two sections but the terrified enemy disappeared into very thick jungle leaving behind them two dead including one WO and vast quantities of ammunition, equipment, arm, and rice. These two gallant charges led by Subedar Walayat Khan saved the Battalion numerous casualties and inflicted a heavy loss on an already starving enemy by depriving them of vast stocks of rice to say nothing of numerous casualties. He then set fire to this huge dump and having cleared the area made the pass impassable to the enemy by means of exploding rounds and bombs. This most inspiring leader of men then returned with his party cheerfully and the Battalion's advance to its final objective was continued.' Subedar Walayat Khan was awarded the Military Cross on 22ND June 1944.

Subedar Din Mohammad, MC
1ST Punjab Regiment
Citations:
'Subedar Din Mohammad, commands No.-11 Platoon of 'B' Company. On 23RD February 1944, B Company was ordered to attack and capture a difficult hill and spur feature commanding a large stretch of the Ngakyadauk Pass. An earlier attempt was beaten off by the Japanese with heavy casualties to the British. Subedar Din Mohammad led the advance and gradually edged near the enemy and judging the moment very carefully shouted his war cry and led a gallant, irresistible charge onto the enemy position. The Japanese were taken completed by surprise and fled although they were in strength and suffered many casualties and left much equipment behind. The success of the operation was due to the very gallant Subedar Din Mohammad, whose behaviour had been exemplary throughout the whole campaign.' Subedar Din Mohammad was awarded an immediate Military Cross.

Military Cross 1922-1947

Subedar Jan Mohammad, MC
1ST Punjab Regiment
Citation:

'During the period 16TH November 1944-15TH February 1945, in India and on Ramree Island, Burma, Subedar Jan Mohammad had been Platoon Commander of a Rifle Company throughout the operations against Japanese. On 6TH January 1945, two platoons of Subedar Jan Mohammad's Company carried out a heavily opposed assault crossing of the Yanbauk Chaung. Despite the fast flowing tidal current and the heavy machine-gun fire, he led his platoon in assault boats and standing up in leading craft in full view of all, advanced on his objective. Throughout the night of 26/27 January 1945, Subedar Jan Mohammad taking command of both platoons, organised and held the captured position until ordered to withdraw on the morning of 27TH morning. During the night the area was under continuous enemy mortar and machine-gun fire, and was repeatedly counter attacked when hand-to –hand bayonet fighting took place. All attacks were repulsed, and casualties inflicted on the enemy. On 27TH January 1945, he successfully disengaged his command and withdrew it across the Chaung under heavy enemy fire without loss. On 7TH February 1945, Subedar Jan Mohammad's platoon moved out to destroy an enemy sniper position, which was holding up the movements of another Company on its flank. The position was located in extremely thick and difficult jungle and the leading patrols Commander were severely wounded. From a different direction, Subedar Jan Mohammad personally led a second party, which killed the sniper and cleared the opposition. On 9TH February Subedar Jan Mohammad's platoon was engaged in clearing an enemy LMG position located in a very thick jungle on a feature overlooking the road into Ramree. He engaged the enemy by day, and when at night he was withdrawn, he personally led a patrol to pinpoint the position and ascertain its strength. This he achieved, and at dawn the next day, attacking the enemy stronghold through the most difficult country, he succeeded in driving them from their position. Throughout this period, and in every action with the enemy in which he has been engaged, Subedar Jan Mohammad has shown outstanding courage and bravery and complete disregard for his own safety. His aggressive spirit, determination, initiative, and fine leadership have been an inspiration to all, and have played an important part in the enemy's decisive defeat. His devotion to duty was in keeping with the best traditions of Indian Army.' Subedar Jan Mohammad was awarded the Military Cross on 15TH November 1945.

Military Cross 1922-1947

Major Ghulam Qadir, MC
1ST Punjab Regiment
Citation:

'Major Ghulam Qadir was in command of a 'D' Company during four attacks in which the Company was involved on the 5TH, 25TH, 26TH, and 28TH January 1944, near Maugdaw, Burma. On each of these occasions, Major Ghulam Qadir has been the inspiration to his men. He has powers of leadership and command of an exceptional high standard and the complete calm, which he displayed particularly on those occasions when the situation became critical, that inspired the men of his Company to perform feats of real gallantry on many occasions during these four attacks. Although the Company suffered over forty casualties, their morale could not possibly higher.' Major Ghulam Qadir was awarded the Military Cross on 20TH April 1944.

Jemadar Mohammad Rafiq, MC
1ST Punjab Regiment
Citation:

'At Kohima (Assam) on 9TH April 1944, Jemadar Mohammad Rafiq commanded a platoon, which was ordered to counter-attack a party of the enemy who had infiltrated within the perimeter and seized some bunkers. His three section commanders were killed in early stages of the attack. Jemadar Mohammad Rafiq with cool disregard for his personal safety, moved from section to section over fire swept ground, encouraging the men and preparing them for the final assault. He personally led the final assault and the enemy position was taken after a fierce struggle. Jemadar Mohammad Rafiq showed a fine spirit of determination, courage, and devotion to duty.' Jemadar Mohammad Rafiq was awarded the Military Cross on 31ST August 1944.

Subedar Mohammad Yusaf, MC
1ST Punjab Regiment
Citation:

'On 3RD November 1944, Subedar Mohammad Yusaf attacked an enemy camp near Kennedy Peak (Burma). He took the enemy by surprise, killing four and causing the remainder to flee leaving their arms, equipment, and large quantities of stores. Throughout the period under review, Subedar Mohammad Yusaf has shown outstanding bravery, cheerfulness, determination, and initiative and has great influence on the Company.' Subedar Mohammad Yusaf was awarded the MC on 13TH September 1945.

Military Cross 1922-1947

Jemadar Mohammad Arshad, MC
2ND Punjab Regiment
Citation:
'On the night of 5/6 September 1944, Jemadar Mohammad Arshad was in the command of the leading platoon of his Company when the Company HQ came under heavy small arms and mortar fire. Having received orders from his Company Commander to work his platoon forward into an assault position without disclosing his intentions, he made such skilful use of ground that he advanced some 600 yards and brought his platoon within striking distance of the main enemy position without being discovered. He then led his platoon with the utmost dash and gallantry in a bayonet charge up a very steep slope, cleared the crest, killing six enemy on the spot, and maintaining the impetus of his surprise onslaught drove the enemy out of their reverse slope positions, The inspiration of his leadership in acknowledged by all ranks of his platoon, who state that his coolness, gallantry and control was magnificent. Having beaten the first and immediate counter attack he handed over to his Company Commander, but continued to show utmost disregard for his personal safety throughout the remainder of the operation.' Jemadar Mohammad Arshad was awarded an immediate Military Cross.

Jemadar Maula Baksh, MC
2ND Punjab Regiment
Citation:
'On 23RD November 1945, Jemadar Maula Baksh was commanding one of the leading platoons of a company advancing in the Negemplak area of Surabaya. The platoons advance was repeatedly checked by LMG and sniper fire from concealed position in the houses. On each occasion Jemadar Maula Baksh dashed forward to the section being held up and by skilful manoeuvring if his reserve section, which he led personally, either destroyed the enemy or forced them to retire, thus enabling the advance to continue. On one of these occasions he led a magnificent charge on to a strongly entrenched MMG. The section commander was killed and two men wounded n this charge, but Jemadar Maula Baksh carried on and killed the three enemies in the post with a burst from his Sten gun at a range of 10 yards. Jemadar Maula Baksh's leadership throughout the day was of the highest order and his courage, utter disregard for his own safety and determination to get on and destroy the enemy was an inspiration to all.' Jemadar Maula Baksh was awarded an immediate Military Cross.

Military Cross 1922-1947

Jemadar Fazal Dad, MC
2ND Punjab Regiment
Citation:
'During the operation in Arakan (Burma) Jemadar Fazal Dad has consistently shown himself to be a fine leader always at the head of his men. He has distinguished himself on many occasions. On 21ST January 1944, he was in command of the forward platoon on 'Three Pimples' although off for 36 hours without water, ammunition or supplies, he hung on to his positions inflicting casualties on the enemy and encouraging the men under his command. It was due to his determination and leadership that the whole position was retaken. On 14TH March 1944, on Boomerang he led his platoon into attack against heavy opposition and accounted for four of the enemy. The next day his platoon was counter attacked many times but each enemy attack was repulsed with heavy losses. He was always a fine example of courage and leadership.' Jemadar Fazal Dad was awarded the Military Cross on 8TH February 1945.

Jemadar Qadar Dad, MC
2ND Punjab Regiment
Citation:
'On the night of 11/12 March 1944, the Battalion HQ on Boomerang was attacked and its Security threatened by the enemy. 'A' Platoon commanded by Jemadar Qadar Dad was ordered to counter-attack. In this attack, Jemadar Qadar Dad inspired the men under his command by his personal example of leadership, courage, and disregard of his own life and led the foremost Section in a charge in to the enemy position, killing five Japanese and destroying the enemy strong point. After that charge though badly injured in right knee he continued to encourage his men to go forward, and throughout he was fine example to his platoon.' Jemadar Qadar Dad was awarded an immediate Military Cross.

Lieutenant Sardar Mohammad Afzal Khan, MC
2ND Punjab Regiment
Citation:
'On 22ND July 1942, during the Battalion's successful attack on Point 63, at the west end of the El Ruweisat Ridge, Lieutenant Sardar Mohammad Afzal Khan displayed courage and leadership of the highest order and complete disregard of personal danger.' Lieutenant Sardar Mohammad Afzal Khan was awarded an immediate Military Cross on 23RD September 1942.

Military Cross 1922-1947

Jemadar Ghulam Din, MC
2ND Punjab Regiment
Citation:
'On 30TH March 1945, Burma during operations east of Irrawaddy at Kabyu Jemadar Ghulam Din's Platoon was given the task of making a recce of a track along which the remainder of the Company was to proceed. The Platoon debussed at Kybyu and one section moved off the road, and started advancing west of the village when it suddenly came under heavy enemy LMG and rifle fire from under the trees and behind a cactus hedge. Jemadar Ghulam Din was at this time on the road with remaining two sections; on seeing and hearing the enemy fire he immediately ordered his two sections into open formation, ordered them to fix bayonets and charge the enemy. He himself led the two sections shouting in Punjabi Mussulman war cry, *'Nara Haidar Ya ALI'*, This completely demoralised the Japanese who broke and fled towards a Chaung about 500 yards south of the village resulting in the Japanese losing several men killed. On reaching the Chaung, Jemadar Ghulam Din's Platoon came under heavy mortar, MMG and LMG fire but he dispersed his sections so that they dominated the enemy and commenced to knock out enemy posts by fire. The battle lasted from 0830 to 1630 hours. During the whole of this time Jemadar Ghulam Din never wasted a moment but immediately after the initial action he commenced to hunt out the enemy, locate their positions and guns, and annihilate them. This was no set piece battle but a sudden encounter when this Platoon was part of a column looking for Japanese blood. It was afterwards ascertained that the Japanese strength was 130 moving up to position from which to attack Kingcol firm base that night. By his immediate action in seizing the initiative by a bayonet charge, he knocked the enemy off his stride and enabled the rest of Kingcol to have an overwhelming victorious battle. During the course of 8 hours battle Jemadar Ghulam Din's Platoon killed over 40 Japanese without loss to them. His personal conduct, dash, bravery and leadership combined with the skilful tactics in out manoeuvring enemy gun positions was an inspiration to all around him and to his whole Battalion. Jemadar Ghulam Din himself magnificently followed by his Platoon dominated the battle.'
Jemadar Ghulam Din, commanding the leading platoon in the action, was given the Military Cross, as an immediate award, and four others mentioned in dispatches.

Military Cross 1922-1947

Subedar Zulaf Din, MC
2ND Punjab Regiment
Citations:

'Subedar Zulaf Din in his capacity as Company's 2ND in command during the total period of his Company defence of our northern position, from 28TH January to 5TH February 1945, has shown outstanding courage and devotion to duty. On the night of 28/29 January 'A' Company then under command of 16/10 Baluch was attacked five times, each attack being supported strongly by 78 mm shellfire. During these attacks Subedar Zulaf Din constantly visited the forward troops of his Company regardless of the sustained bombardment and small arms fire, displaying complete disregard for his own safety and by quite coolness and courage and encouragement of the hard pressed troops imbued them with fresh determination to repel the fanatical attempts made by the enemy to gain entry into the Company position. On the morning of 29TH January it became necessary to bury the dead, Subedar Zulaf Din ignoring further enemy shelling personally buried the dead in accordance with Muslim customs. Again on the night of 1-2 February when the enemy repeatedly attacked, Subedar Zulaf Din again and again went forward to the troops on the outer defences to encourage and cheer them to greater effort.' Subedar Zulaf Din was awarded the Military Cross on 21ST June 1945.

Jemadar Mahbub Illahi, MC
2ND Punjab Regiment
Citation:

'On 29TH October 1944, a reconnoitring patrol was sent out to investigate the possibility of placing one company on each side of the corner and thus isolating the enemy posted there. Seen through glasses, the approaches to the objective seemed impossible even to the smallest patrol, let alone a company encumbered with ammunition, radio equipment, and other stores. The patrol was however, entirely successful. On 1ST November 1944, Jemadar Mahbub Illahi guided his Company to the same area and leading forward his Platoon killed the enemy sentry and rushed part of the enemy position completely surprising the remainder who were caught in this rest area. He then reorganised his Platoon, himself handling a Bren gun, and beat off the enemy counter attacks until the remainder of his Company could come up and seize the rest of the peon. Jemadar Mahbub Illahi by his quick grasp of the situation aggressiveness and gallant determination contributed largely to the success of the whole operation.' Jemadar Mahbub Illahi was awarded the Military Cross on 22ND March 1945.

Military Cross 1922-1947

Subedar Major Ahmed Khan, MC
2ND Punjab Regiment
Citation:
'Subedar Major Ahmed Khan commanded a Company with outstanding success during the operations in Malaya from 8TH December 1941 until 25TH January 1942. His courage and morale during the difficult period of the campaign was an outstanding example to the personnel of his Company, whilst his leadership was of a very high standard. On the Grik Road on 20TH December 1941, on hearing that one of his platoons guarding the rear flanks of the Argyll and Sutherland Highlanders were being attacked, he proceeded at once to the position and by his leadership and courage inspired the platoon to hold on sufficiently long enough to permit the Argyll and Sutherland Highlanders readjusting their position to meet this threat. The platoon suffered twenty casualties in holding this attack.' The award of MC was gazetted in 1946 for actions fought in 1942 ties in the fact that Subedar Major Ahmed Khan was taken POW by the Japanese and this citation was initiated upon his release from captivity.

Jemadar Fateh Mohammad Khan, MC
2ND Punjab Regiment
Citations:
'The Pioneer Platoon under command of Jemadar Fateh Mohammad Khan was attached to 'A' Rifle Company on 26TH and 27TH December 1941. At dawn, 27TH December 1941, the enemy attacked with two Battalions the position held by 'A' Company. In the hand-to –hand fighting which ensued, Jemadar Fateh Mohammad Khan fought with great gallantry setting up a wonderful example to his platoon and others. He accounted for many Japanese including three officers, whose swords he brought with him on the withdrawal of 'A' Company being ordered.' Jemadar Fateh Mohammad Khan was awarded the MC on 19TH December 1946.

Subedar Saghar Khan, MC
2ND Punjab Regiment
Citation:
'On the night of 3/4 October 1944 at S. Donato Subedar Saghar Khan while in command of his Company showed most skilful and resourceful leadership during a night operation, entailing searching for and destroying enemy posts which had not yet been reconnoitred nor in some case located.' For his endures Subedar Saghar Khan was awarded an immediate Military Cross on 8TH March 1945.

Military Cross 1922-1947

Jemadar Fazal Rehman, MC
2ND Punjab Regiment
Citation:

'Jemadar Fazal Rehman was in command of No. 8 Platoon of 'B' Company. Throughout the action at Sheldon's Corner at Sangshak, on 18TH-26TH March 1944, Jemadar Fazal Rehman, displayed exceptional power of command and leadership. His great personality has at all times inspired the men under his command. During the period of reorganisation at Imphal, Jemadar Fazal Rehman by his complete loyalty and hard work, had been the inspiration to the men of his platoon, and trained them upto a high standard. On 10TH June 1944, B Company was ordered to join 100 Brigade in the Saddle area. The Company arrived late at night and bivouacked for the night acting as protection for the guns. Early on the morning of 11TH June, the Company was ordered up the Brigade HQ area in order to attack and recapture the Bastion position, which had been occupied by the enemy previous day and a counter attack on the position had failed which had necessarily made the situation Brigade HQ very precarious. The position had been dug at the end of a spur running due south of the Keep position and 250 yards away. The attack was to be supported by three Stewart tanks of 7TH Cavalry and all available covering fire from the perimeter posts of the Keep position. The leading No. 8 platoon was to follow behind the first tank then swing out to the right, followed by the second tank. The third tank followed by No. 7 platoon was commanded by Jemadar Fazal Rehman, who was to assault the position frontally. Jemadar Fazal Rehman led his platoon with great dash and complete disregard of his own safety. Yelling their war cry, he allied the LMG, Rifle, and grenade fire, and throughout the short action and directing his section personally against the enemy posts. By his own bravery and complete disregard of the enemy fire, he inspired his platoon that they took all the positions and inflicted heavy casualties on the Japanese. The complete co-ordination of the plan and the zeal of the men enabled the position to be captured and the enemy evicted within fifteen minutes of the commencement of the attack. Very few casualties were inflicted on the Company but the enemy suffered heavily. The Company Commander and the senior VCO of the Company had been wounded during the action; Jemadar Fazal Rehman immediately assumed command of the Company and consolidated the position. Jemadar Fazal Rehman, throughout the operations has proved himself to be a leader of the highest order.' Jemadar Fazal Rehman was awarded an immediate Military Cross.

Military Cross 1922-1947

Jemadar Attar Khan, MC
4TH Bombay Grenadiers
Citation:
'At Chaunggyin in Assam on the Burma front on 26TH November 1944, Jemadar Attar Khan was in command of No. 18 Platoon 'D' Company 4TH Bombay Grenadiers, which was escorting the leading troop of tanks. The enemy withheld his fire until the leading tank was on top of his position, and then opened fire with small arms, grenades, and mortars. Jemadar Attar Khan leading his platoon immediately assaulted the enemy position engaging in a hand-to- hand fight. Due to the spirited attack of his platoon, the enemy evacuated his forward position. The platoon followed up killing ten of the enemy. The success of this action was very largely due to the fact that Jemadar Attar Khan as always n the forefront, leading his men. Throughout recent operations, Jemadar Attar Khan has consistently displayed a high standard of leadership, and his personal courage and example has been an inspiration to all ranks in his platoon.' Jemadar Attar Khan was awarded an immediate Military Cross on 22ND March 1945.

Subedar Mamur Khan, MC
4TH Bombay Grenadiers
Citation:
'On 23RD April 1945, 'D' Company 4TH Bombay Grenadiers met stiff and determined opposition when mopping up of Pyagale village as part of an advance guard. Despite heavy fire from medium and light machine-guns in the bunkers, which caused casualties, Subedar Mamur Khan was continuously to the forefront of his platoon, which killed twenty-three Japanese. Later he took two sections and protected a tank severely damaged by a mine. The position was under heavy fire from a large number of Japanese located in houses to his front. These he dealt with by directing personally in the open fire by tank, which set the houses, alight, burning the occupants alive, and forcing others into open where they were shot to pieces. Throughout the whole operation, Subedar Mamur Khan exposed himself with complete disregard for his own safety. On at least four occasions, Subedar Mamur Khan has shown marked personal gallantry and strong aggressive spirit, which has been an inspiration to all.' Subedar Mamur Khan was awarded an immediate Military Cross on 20TH September 1945.

Military Cross 1922-1947

Subedar Sabdal Khan, MC
4TH Bombay Grenadiers
Citation:
'In central Burma in February and May 1945, Subedar Sabdal Khan greatly distinguished himself by outstanding personality, leadership, and courage. Mutual respect, trust, and affection between his company and Gordon Highlanders are complete; both units' personnel are one. Personal esteem between the BORs and IORs is most remarkable and has been rarely equalled. For the above, Subedar Sabdal Khan's tact and strong cheery personality are mainly responsible. His outstanding leadership and bravery were shown at Yanaung on 9TH April. B-echelon vehicles of 255 Indian Tank Brigade could not reach harbour and had to spend the night on the road. Unprotected by wire or defences they were attacked frequently during the night by MMG, small arms, grenade and bayonet. Subedar Sabdal Khan organised and led the defence of his Battalion's vehicles under the most trying confused and dangerous conditions. His men consisted of administration personnel, never previously engaged. He walked up and down waving a Kukri and personally inspired and encouraged every man with a strong offensive spirit. He exercised close fire control; whenever the Japanese seemed to be gathering for a rush, he shouted bogus orders to imaginary MGs and troops. He was undoubtedly responsible for the fact that his unit vehicles were never rushed and that no casualties were sustained among his men who remained perfectly steady due to his example. His complete coolness under fire has been frequently shown during the whole period.' Subedar Sabdal Khan was recommended with the award of MBE but awarded the Military Cross.

Jemadar Mohammad Sawar, MC
4TH Bombay Grenadiers
Citation:
'Jemadar Mohammad Sawar, 'C 'Company of Bombay Grenadiers , in support of 'C' Squadron of 3 Carabineers, has been almost continuously in action for several months, from the Chindwin to present area. During this time, he has displayed fine qualities of leadership, initiative, and personal bravery, on several occasions himself accounting for number of enemy, gaining valuable information. During an assault on the village of Saye, Jemadar Mohammad Sawar was badly wounded but remained until the final capture of the village, and was then ordered by the Squadron Commander to be taken to the Regimental Aid Post.' Jemadar Mohammad Sawar was awarded the Military Cross on 17TH January 1946.

Military Cross 1922-1947

Lieutenant Bashir Ahmed, MC
6TH Rajputana Rifles
Citation:
'Lieutenant Bashir Ahmed on reaching his forward platoon that the VCO and the most senior NCOs had been killed or wounded. The enemy were in occupation of a strongly entrenched and loop holed position about 70 or 80 yards away. He immediately seized a rifle and fired at a hostile who had crawled up the bodies of the casualties which were lying in the open some 60 yards from that of the enemy. He continued to fire and covers the bodies although twice wounded. His action set a fine example to his men and enabled the bodies of the casualties and their arms, including one VB Gun, to be retrieved later when the counter-attack had dislodged the enemy.' For conspicuous gallantry in this snappy action Lieutenant Bashir Ahmed was awarded the Military Cross.

Jemadar Anwar Beg, MC
6TH Rajputana Rifles
Citation:
'At Kyugono on 4TH March 1945, Jemadar Anwar Beg was in command of his platoon in an attack. Intense enemy fire has held up the forward company and pinned it to the ground. Accordingly, his company was ordered to attempt to out-manoeuvre the enemy by envelopment. Immediately the troops were met by very heavy fire, Jemadar Anwar Beg dashed forward ahead of his men and with great élan led his platoon in a vicious bayonet charge killing 24 Japanese and capturing two. He then continued to lead his men with bravery enabling the rest of his company to take up the assault routing the enemy and killing over 60 Japanese in that portion of the field. This action was fought by his battalion without supporting arms, and it is without doubt due to Jemadar Anwar Beg's great personal courage and dash that an assault could be pressed home so rapidly, saving many casualties and liquidating the Japanes force in the area.' Jemadar Anwar Beg was awarded the Military Cross in October 1946.

Military Cross 1922-1947

Subedar Usman Ghani, MC
6TH Rajputana Rifles
Citation:

'During the campaign in the Cassino-Monastery Hill area n March 1944, the 9TH Ghurkha Rifles, had reached Point 435 on the slopes of Monastery Hill, where they were cut off and isolated from rest of the Brigade without supplies or ammunition. Subedar Usman Ghani was commanding a platoon in a Company 4TH Raj Rif, which had orders to fight a supply column through the 9TH Ghurkha Rifles. After reaching its objective, this Company was retained to assist 9TH Ghurkha Rifles, in the defence of their position. The Jamadar's platoon was cited in one of the forward positions where they stayed for seven days, being supplied from the air. They were very short of food, water, and sleep. Despite these conditions, Subedar Usman Ghani continued to hold the position, although under constant fire until order came to withdraw. In front of his position approximately 100 yards was an enemy MG post that fired across the only route along which supplies could arrive. This post covered the line of communication to the enemy's forward troops. On the night 22/23 March 1944, the Jemadar went out alone to silence this post. Advancing with great courage and determination, he attacked the post with grenades and Tommy gun and killed or wounded all its occupants. As a result of this fearless and surprise attack the post was silenced thereby greatly effecting the security of the whole of this isolated detachment. Throughout the operation, Subedar Usman Ghani showed outstanding powers of leadership, endurance and devotion to duty.' Subedar Usman Ghani was awarded the MC on 26TH October 1944.

Captain Mian Khan, MC
6TH Rajputana Rifles
Citation:

'On 15TH July 1942, Captain Mian Khan and his Company attacked the enemy on Ruweisat Ridge. In the confusion of attack the forward Companies withdrew. Captain Mian Khan collected two men and he manned an abandoned MMG and carried on firing at the enemy guns for over an hour. During this period, he was alone with his two men. This cool and collected action was mainly responsible for silencing the enemy guns and allowing the Battalion to reorganise in rear and launch another attack.' Captain Mian Khan was awarded the Military Cross on 24TH September 1942.

Military Cross 1922-1947

Jemadar Mohammad Sarwar, MC
6TH Rajputana Rifles
Citation:
'On 17TH January 1942, south of Muar River when the Battalion had lost all but two British Officers killed or wounded and nearly two thirds of the other ranks killed, wounded, or missing, Jemadar Mohammad Sarwar, by his personal example and leadership, and by his energetic and aggressive leading of patrols contributed incalculably to the restoration of morale. Again on 19TH January 1942 at Bakri, when a Company of the Battalion had been driven in by a Japanese attack, Jemadar Mohammad Sarwar, at first coolly withholding the fire of his platoon, then directed it accurately onto the flank of the enemy, contributed greatly to the success of the subsequent counter attack. The example of Jemadar Mohammad Sarwar has been an inspiration to all'. Jemadar Mohammad Sarwar was awarded the Military Cross on 19TH December 1946.

Captain Syed Abdul Wadud, MC
Indian Medical Service (attached to 6TH Rajputana Rifles)
Citation:
'During the period under review 16TH May to 15TH August 1945, Captain Syed Abdul Wadud, has shown outstanding skill and devotion to duty as a Regiment Medical Officer. On many occasions he has saved many lives by his unusual skill. Captain Syed Abdul Wadud has carried out successful operations and blood transfusions not only under enemy fire, but also under most unfavourable hygienic conditions. His RAP has always been forward and many times under enemy fire. The coolness and outstanding example set by this officer has inspired confidence in all ranks and has at all times been of the highest order.' Captain Syed Abdul Wadud was awarded the Military Cross on 6TH June 1946.

Jemadar Nasir Ahmed, MC
7TH Rajput Regiment
Citation:
'From the beginning of the campaign in Arakan in December 1943, until the capture of Kalemyo in November 1944, Jemadar Nasir Ahmed commanded No. 6 Platoon of 'C' Company, and later during the advance from Meiktila to Rangoon, he was performing the duties of JQM. Throughout these two campaigns, he showed personal courage, powers of leadership, and a standard of battle discipline of the highest order.

Military Cross 1922-1947

Jemadar Nasir Ahmed, MC (Cont)
Citation:
'On 31ST December 1943, when ordered to attack a strong point covering Point 124 in Arakan, Jemadar Nasir Ahmed's platoon came under withering MMG and LMG fire and sustained heavy casualties. He however, immediately rallies the balance of his men and led them to their objective, and himself being the first to reach the enemy's trenches. Again on the 11TH June 1944 when B Company had attacked and taken a hill feature covering the Jesami Track at about Milestone 21 his platoon was detached and on the flank of the remainder of the Company. Shortly after the objective was taken, enemy put on a strong counter attack, and Jemadar Nasir Ahmed, realizing the immediate danger to his Company, on his own initiative, took one section from his platoon and personally led them against the flank of the enemy, taking them completely by surprise and dispersing their counter attack. On these numerous occasions and throughout his tour of duty, Jemadar Nasir Ahmed's devotion to duty, constant cheerfulness under adverse conditions and example of personal bravery have been an example and inspiration to all who had served with him.' Jemadar Nasir Ahmed was awarded the Military Cross on 6TH June 1946.

Subedar Abdul Jabar, MC
7TH Rajput Regiment
Citation:
'From the 9TH to 11TH December 1941, Subedar Abdul Jabar commanded one of the platoons ordered to stop the threatened Japanese break through between the Royal Scots and 14TH Punjab Regiment. Throughout this continuous and heavy engagement, he inflicted heavy casualties on the enemy by superior tactical handling of his Platoon and an uncommon degree of fearlessness and determination. On the night 18/19 December 1941, through the hand-to-hand fighting, he again skilfully and fearlessly commanded his Platoon, which stood its ground gallantly until overwhelmed. Though wounded in the head, arm and leg, he remained with his Platoon throughout until evacuated to hospital. He was back again in action on 22ND December 1941, commanding a composite platoon in the fierce and confused fighting in Wanchai, and remained in command until capitulation. In the bitter fighting, regardless of personal safety he was always in the forefront and was a constant source of inspiration and encouragement to the tired troops under his command.' On his repatriation, Subedar Abdul Jabar was awarded the Military Cross on 22ND March 1945.

Military Cross 1922-1947

Jemadar Abdul Karim, MC
7TH Rajput Regiment
Citation:
'Jemadar Abdul Karim was a Platoon Commander at a night attack in the Des Sherin depression on the night 21/22 July 1942. He led his Platoon with utmost gallantry and dash. At one time, his Platoon was pinned down by heavy machine-gun fire from three sides; he rose to his feet and urged the platoon forward and being immediately hit by two bursts of machine-gun fire. The platoon, however, carried the position, and for the remainder of the night though disabled he encouraged the platoon to hold out against frequent enemy counter-attacks. His gallantry and fortitude were an example to all.' Jemadar Abdul Karim was taken prisoner by the Japanese and at his repatriation was awarded the Military Cross.

Captain Amir Abdullalh Khan, MC
7TH Rajput Regiment
Citation:
'On 11TH June 1944, in the Kikrima area on the Jessami Road on the Assam-Burma front, Captain Amir Abdullalh Khan was ordered to take his company on a wide outflanking movement with a view to ascertaining the enemy strength on a hill feature covering the road at about the Milestone 21, which as holding up the units advance along the Jessami track. Having got round the feature without being observed, he reported to the Battalion HQ that in his opinion he could achieve surprise if he attacked and that though several bunkers had been located, he was not of the opinion that they were strongly held. He was told to carry on the attack. The company strength at that time was only thirty-five and he was told that if resistance proved stronger than anticipated he was not to press home the attack and get involved. He organised the attack with such skill that his leading platoon succeeded in achieving complete surprise over the enemy holding the first three bunkers, destroying the occupants inside with grenades. The other bunkers then opened up from the crest of the feature and casualties began to occur in his leading platoon. Captain Amir Abdullalh Khan then personally led the second platoon in a small outflanking movement and took on three bunkers, destroying the occupant's one and killing two of the occupants of the second as they ran out. The element of surprise by this time had been lost and two parties each of about 60 enemies were seen to be forming up, one on each side of the crest of the feature. Two further bunkers had also disclosed themselves and casualties were occurring'.

Military Cross 1922-1947

Captain Amir Abdullalh, MC (Cont)
Citation:
Captain Amir Abdullalh Khan with great coolness left the senior platoon commander of his two committed platoons to engage the left hand group of enemy while he detailed his reserve platoon to take on the new bunkers. He himself took a rifle-bunker, a spare EY rifle, and crawled forward under heavy fire until he reached a position from which and the rifle-bomber could fire their grenades. They fired in all five rounds, most of it fell in the centre of the right hand group of the enemy, who were forming up in line for a counter-attack, causing at least 30 casualties and completely dispersing the attack. He then returned to see how his other platoons were fairing and discovered though they had held the enemy, they were almost completely out of ammunition owing to the weak strength of the initial sections and the consequent small number of magazines and grenades that could be carried. He discovered that this was also the case with the third platoon, which had been successful in silencing the two bunkers they had attacked and near the loophole of which two wounded were lying. He therefore first put in a small diversionary attack by which he succeeded in extracting the wounded, and under cover of which he withdrew two of his platoons. He then with great skill and coolness withdrew his last platoon section by section, he himself remaining with the rearmost section in each case. It was entirely due to Captain Amir Abdullalh Khan's personal leadership, bravery, and complete disregard for his own personal safety that the Japanese lost a minimum of 60 casualties when at a time they could ill afford them and it was undoubtedly due to a very large extent to this very spirited action that they withdrew from that feature the following night and enabled the speed of the advance to be continued'. Captain Amir Abdullalh Khan was awarded an immediate Military Cross.

Captain Amir Abdullalh Khan opted to join the newly created Pakistan Army in 1947. He rose to the rank of lieutenant-general in the Pakistan Army and the last Governor of East Pakistan known for commanding the Eastern Command of Pakistani military in East Pakistan during the third war with India. He was decorated with the gallantry awards of Hilal-i-Jurat with Bar and Sitara-i-Jurat. He passed away in February 2004 aged 90 years in Lahore, Punjab, Pakistan. He was buried at the Military Graveyard in Lahore.

Military Cross 1922-1947

Subedar Mehr Khan, MC
7TH Rajput Regiment
Citation:
'Subedar Mehr Khan was commanding a forward platoon when the enemy attacked the Mau Tong position on the evening of 12TH December 1941, and by his well controlled fire he broke up this attack. Later when his Company to Hai Wan, the fact that the enemy failed it up was in the main to his dogged and determined handling of his platoon as covering troops, and his ability in disengaging them without being pinned down to the ground. Later in the operations in Hong Kong after his Company Commander had been killed on 20TH December and his Company cut off from his Battalion he took over command not only of his own Company but also of remnants of 'D' Company he could find and placed himself under the orders of OC 1ST Middlesex Regiment, until the arrival of his own Commanding Officer on the morning of 21ST December some 36 hours later. From then until the surrender though very tired he proved himself able leader completely dependable, assets which were invaluable in the fighting round Leighton Hill.' Subedar Mehr Khan was taken prisoner by the Japanese and at his repatriation was awarded the Military Cross.

Subedar Mohammad Afsar Khan, MC
7TH Rajput Regiment
Citation:
'From the beginning of the Campaign in February 1945 to the conclusion on 15TH May 1945, Subedar Mohammad Afsar Khan had been the 2ND in command of his Company ad later when the Company Commander was killed, he commanded. The Company has taken part in many stiff actions in village and close country fighting. Throughout he has shown himself to be a great leader with plenty of initiative and dash. Especially during the later stages as a Company Commander, he proved himself to be Commander of a very high order. I have always had complete confidence in him and known that the task given him will be carried out thoroughly. His leadership has been excellent and his calmness and tactical handling of the Company has been first class. At Yindaw where his Company suffered some 40 casualties his conduct throughout was magnificent both in the attack and later in the evacuation of the wounded under difficult circumstances after under extremely heavy fire.' Subedar Mohammad Afsar Khan was awarded the Military Cross on 17TH January 1946.

Military Cross 1922-1947

Subedar Mohammad Qasim Khan, MC
7TH Rajput Regiment
Citation:
'On the night 22/23 March 1945, during the operations to secure the bridgehead over Tanlwe Chaung, Subedar Mohammad Qasim Khan's platoon secured and occupied a feature on the South Bank. At about midnight, the enemy put on a determined attack. Though beaten off, he again and succeeded in breaking in after causing casualties on one face of the perimeter. Subedar Mohammad Qasim Khan immediately dashed forward at the enemy approaching the gap using his Sten gun to good effect. One enemy however, got into the position, and Subedar Mohammad Qasim Khan being unable to use his Sten gun within his own perimeter, hurled himself on the Japanese and after struggle subdued him. Subedar Mohammad Qasim Khan immediately followed him out of his own position in spite of being between our own and the enemy's fire and succeeded again in capturing the prisoner and bringing him back to the platoon position. Further attacks were made at intervals during the night, and all were beaten off until dawn when the enemy withdrew. By Subedar Mohammad Qasim Khan's devotion to duty, leadership and courage, a position vital to the security of the bridgehead was saved.' Subedar Mohammad Qasim Khan was awarded an immediate Military Cross.

Subedar Mushrif Khan, MC
7TH Rajput Regiment
Citation:
'In Burma on 8TH April 1945, the Company of which Subedar Mushrif Khan was 2ND in command was ordered to occupy a feature overlooking Taungup Chaung. The leading platoon almost immediately came under heavy fire and the Company Commander was killed. Subedar Mushrif Khan immediately came forward and assumed command of the Company. In spite of continuous fire he reorganised the forward elements himself, by his complete disregard of personal danger. Subedar Mushrif Khan so skilfully disposed his platoon and extricated the forward platoon, with two wounded from an extremely difficult position, and so restricted further enemy attacks by bold and skilful manoeuvre, that his Company was withdrawn in good order and reorganised in very short time. Acting in a capacity higher than his own, the courage, skill and coolness shown by Subedar Mushrif Khan were of a high order and his prompt and successful action saved the Company from grave and perilous position.' Subedar Mushrif Khan was awarded an immediate Military Cross.

Military Cross 1922-1947

Captain Nur Khan, MC, MBE
7TH Rajput Regiment
Citation:
'During the action of 31ST December 1942, Captain Nur Khan was invaluable as the Adjutant and 2ND in command of the Battalion. The situation was such that all the Battalion HQ personnel were involved in fighting and I had to rely on him to convoy instructions personally to the Company Commanders. On several occasions the crossing of open ground as exposed to heavy enemy fire as unavoidable but Captain Nur Khan was more concerned for my own safety than his. He displayed complete disregard of danger throughout the battle. His conduct and efficiency over a long period and particularly during the present operations have materially contributed to the high morale of the unit and the credible performance it put up its first action in this campaign. I consider this most deserving case of an immediate award of the DSO.' Although immediate DSO was recommended, Captain Nur Khan was instead awarded the Military Cross on 8TH April 1943.'

Subedar Major Khan Mohammad, MC
7TH Rajput Regiment
Citation:
'Subedar-Major Khan Mohammad was 2ND in command of a Company during a night attack in the Dier El Shein depression on the night of 21/22 July 1942. The Company Commander was wounded early in the action and the Command delved on Subedar-Major Khan Mohammad, who led the Company, to the assault against heavy opposition. When the position had been taken, it was repeatedly and heavily counter-attacked throughout the night. Communication with the Battalion HQ, and the neighbouring Companies was severed. The leadership and example of Subedar-Major Khan Mohammad, were now an example to all, and under him the Company held its ground until with 35 men left, many of them wounded and its ammunition exhausted, it was overrun at dawn by an overwhelming force of tanks and Infantry.'
Subedar Major Khan Mohammad most likely taken prisoner by the Japanese and the recommendation for the award of the Military Cross was made after his release from enemy captivity in 8TH February 1946. Subedar-Major Khan Mohammad was awarded the Military Cross on 23RD January 1947.

Military Cross 1922-1947

Jemadar Shah Mohammad, MBE, MC
7TH Rajput Regiment
Citation:
'Jemadar Shah Mohammad as Battalion Intelligence Officer was tireless and by his daring obtained much valuable information. He showed great courage and coolness during confused fighting in extricating elements of Battalion HQ from Taikoo on nigh 18/19 December, was undoubtedly responsible for saving many lives. Later, throughout the operation round Leighton Hill and Wanchai from 21ST to 25TH December, he showed fine example of courage and skilful leadership when commanding a platoon at both Cemetery Ridge and Parish Hill and proved himself resourceful and reliable in the most trying conditions. Throughout the operations, he displayed courage and leadership of a very high order.' Jemadar Shah Mohammad was awarded the Military Cross in October 1946.

Subedar Abdul Sattar, MC
7TH Rajput Regiment
Citation:
On 29TH February 1944, Subedar Abdul Sattar commanded a platoon attacking a knife-edge feature known as Hamborne, south of Tatmin Che. He led his platoon with great gallantry to a position immediately below the crest and was unable to move further forward owing to the steepness of the ascent. He held on this position, until the Japanese were forced to withdraw by a thrust of another platoon. Throughout this period, his platoon was subjected to continuous grenading from the Japanese from above. On the night of 3/4 March, Subedar Abdul Sattar's platoon was attacked by a large force of Japanese estimate to be around 150, it broke up these attacks, inflicting 16 dead Japanese on the ground. On 3RD April 1944, on a feature known as Rabbit, Subedar Abdul Sattar's platoon attacked a position about 100 yards south of the forward troops. Subedar Abdul Sattar was severally wounded having his leg shattered. Although in great pain and unable to stand, he refused to be brought back, and remained on the feature, encouraging his platoon forward. He only allowed himself to be brought back when ordered by his Company Commander. The courage and devotion to duty and qualities of leadership displayed throughout these operations have been an inspiration and example to all.' Subedar Abdul Sattar was awarded an immediate Military Cross.

Military Cross 1922-1947

Jemadar Mohammad Sharif, MC
7TH Rajput Regiment
Citation:
'Since January 1945, Jemadar Mohammad Sharif has been commanding a platoon which had been conspicuous successful throughout the operations terminating in the capture of Rangoon. On 17TH April 1945, at Shewmyo Jemadar Mohammad Sharif's and a troop of tanks were acting as a fighting patrol, when the platoon was engaged by and enemy gun. The tanks were completely exposed and enable to engage the enemy. Jemadar Mohammad Sharif immediately mounted an infantry attack on the gun. This attack was executed with such skill and speed that the gun was captured intact and the entire crew killed. On 29TH May 1945, at Myitkyina, his platoon was again engaged as a fighting patrol in clearing villages west of Sittang River. In Pyunmagan, he received information that a large number of Japanese were resting in Basha. He immediately attacked this Basha and by his prompt and forceful decision, complete surprise was achieved resulting in two officers and 15 Japanese other ranks killed, the remainder fleeing in disorder. The success of these two and other operations was entirely due to the outstanding initiative, drive and devotion to duty, and invariable example of coolness and personal bravery under fire displayed by Jemadar Mohammad Sharif, on every one of the numerous occasions he has been in contact with the enemy.' Jemadar Mohammad Sharif was awarded the Military Cross on 6TH June 1946.

Jemadar Mohammad Khan Bahadur, IDSM, OBI, MC
8TH Punjab Regiment
Citation:
'Jemadar Mohammad Khan was Intelligence Officer of the Regiment. On the evening of February 12TH 1942, under very heavy mortar and artillery fire, he carried out a particularly daring and dangerous reconnaissance in an enemy infested area through most difficult terrain in Malaya. By virtue of this reconnaissance, he enabled to guide the Battalion successfully to its new position on Buenovista road.' Jemadar Mohammad Khan was taken prisoner and on his release was awarded the Military Cross on 25TH September 1947.

Military Cross 1922-1947

Jemadar Ghazan Khan, MC
8TH Punjab Regiment
Citation:

On the night of 20TH May 1944, in the Japanese attack on the Mule camp at Bishenpur Jemadar Ghazan Khan's party got caught between the fire of our own troops and a group of Japanese who had infiltrated into the Camp. Only half of his detachment was armed with rifles. The Jemadar however, single handed by skilful handling of a LMG (No. 2 of the gun had been killed early in the action) kept the enemy at bay. He was wounded in the foot and his Daffadar did his best to persuade the Jemadar to be taken away to safety, but Jemadar Khan insisted on staying on. By this time the position had become untenable and Jemadar Ghazan Khan ordered his two Daffadars to collect as many of the unarmed men as possible and lead them to safety, while he engaged the enemy to cover their withdrawal. He continued firing with his LMG but eventually his position was rushed by 30 Japanese. With 10 men who had remained with him, he stood to fight with the bayonet, handicapped by the wound in his foot and sustaining another bullet wound and also bayonet wounds, he fell into a trench. All his party except himself and two others were killed; he was rescued next morning from under the dead and wounded bodies which were piled on top of him. This Jemadar showed a truly wonderful fighting spirit; with complete disregard to his own life he faced the enemy almost single handed and finally with a rifle and bayonet was prepared to die fighting. As VCO of a Mule Company, his display of cool courage and self-sacrifice is the more remarkable and is inspiring example to all ranks.'

Major Nazar Hussein, MC
8TH Punjab Regiment
Citation:

'During the North Burma campaign 2ND Battalion, 8TH Punjab Regiment holding the left sector of the bridgehead which 26TH Brigade had recently captured at Myitson on the South bank of the Shweli River. The position on the previous four days had been subjected to enemy shelling and also considerable fire from machine guns and mortars, and a series of small counter attacks. On account of these, they were not able to enlarge their position sufficiently and the main Battalion position was somewhat cramped. 'A' Company commanded by Major Nazar Hussein, was one of the companies holding the outside perimeter. At 0730 hours, the Japanese counter-attacked the whole perimeter, but especially against 'A' Company.

Military Cross 1922-1947

Major Nazar Hussein, MC (Cont)
Citation:
The enemy shelled and mortared the position and then laid down a thick smoke screen, under which he brought up flamethrowers, and with them completely wiped out the two most forward sections. On seeing this, in spite of heavy fire from the enemy, Major Nazar Hussein constantly crossed the open ground, encouraging his men in each post and holding them steady. He filled the gaps as they occurred and continued to hold off the enemy until they withdrew after four hours bitter fighting. The attack was made by at least a battalion of the enemy and 139 Japanese bodies were picked up on the perimeter the next day, mostly in front of A Company and many more recovered later. Had the enemy broken through the Company, the whole Battalion position would have been seriously jeopardised. By his personal bravery and excellent handling of his Company, Major Nazar Hussein greatly encouraged his men in this hard fight, and his own example was undoubtedly one of the main factors in this defeat of the enemy.' Major Nazar Hussein was awarded an immediate Military Cross.

Subedar Raj Wali Khan, MC
8TH Punjab Regiment
Citation:
'On 9TH February 1945, 'D' Company, 8TH Punjab Regiment arrived on South Bank of the Shweli River. During the night, the Company was subjected to repeated enemy attacks. Throughout the night, Subedar Raj Wali Khan shouted encouragement to his men and kept up their spirits, setting a magnificent example to all present. From 12TH to 17TH February the Company was detached from the Battalion. On the 14TH February during a determined enemy attack, Subedar Raj Wali Khan, saw wounded Japanese about 25 yards outside the perimeter. Realising the importance of a prisoner, he left his dugout and personally drove off the Japanese covering the body with hand grenades from an exposed position under heavy fire. He then went outside the perimeter and dragged in the body, all the time under very heavy fire. Later it was learned that valuable information was obtained from this prisoner. Subedar Raj Wali Khan has all times proved himself a most courageous and inspiring leader, and set a magnificent example to his company.' Subedar Raj Wali Khan was awarded an immediate Military Cross.

Military Cross 1922-1947

Subedar Ali Dad, MC
8TH Punjab Regiment
Citation:

'During the North Burma campaign on 7TH February 2ND Battalion, 8TH Punjab Regiment holding the left sector of the recently won bridgehead at Myitson on the south bank of Shweli River. For six days previously, the whole bridgehead had been subjected to small but very determined counter-attacks supported by gun and mortar fire. Although the Battalion had yielded no ground, it not has been able to make any progress. At 0730 hours, the Japanese counter-attacked the entire Battalion perimeter, with what was subsequently proved to be at least a battalion. The attack was commenced by smoke screen under the cover of which the enemy brought up flamethrowers, and aided by these and heavy automatic fire from close range; they succeeded in almost wiping out one platoon of 'A' Company. Subedar Ali Dad, who was in the HQ Company behind 'A' Company, saw the enemy had penetrated into the platoon position and were using our trenches for their own protection. He spotted a Japanese officer waving his men on to the attack, and immediately shot him, and emptied the rest of his magazine into the advancing enemy. He then rushed forward to the platoon trenches over 50 yards through the hail of bullets and fired off his magazine into the enemy who were then concentrating a rush through the gaps they had made. When he ran out of ammunition he ran back to his Company HQ, collected as many grenades as he could carry and hurled them into the advancing Japanese. This finally broke up that attack and the enemy dispersed in some confusion. Subedar Ali Dad then manned a 2 inch mortar and let drive with that short range into the retreating enemy. By his brave actions so encouraged the other men in the vicinity that at once seized the old platoon position, led by Subedar Ali Dad. He continued firing his Tommy gun and hurled hand grenades, and they held this important post until midday when the enemy finally withdrew. The bitterness of the fighting on the perimeter can be judged by fact that 129 Japanese bodies were picked up on the next day and many more later. A large number of these were in front of 'A' Company and Subedar Ali Dad must have killed at least a dozen Japanese. There can be no doubt that Subedar Ali Dad personally saved the situation in the A Company sector had the enemy broken through the entire Battalion would have been jeopardised. Subedar Ali Dad's magnificent action so inspired the other men in the vicinity that they faced the enemy with renewed vigour and assisted in inflicting the defeat on them.' Subedar Ali Dad was awarded an immediate Military Cross.

Military Cross 1922-1947

Subedar Musahib Khan, MC
8TH Punjab Regiment
Citation:
'On the night 29/30 May 1945, Subedar Musahib Khan was ordered to take his platoon as a fighting patrol to Kwethe, to find out the strength of the Japanese n the village. Forming a base near the area, he took forward two men and penetrated deep into the enemy's position. Having ascertained that there was a large concentration of the Japanese in the village, and from personal observation accurately pinpointed their positions, he came back, contacted the artillery forward observation officer, returned to his position and directed what afterwards proved to be a most successful concentration. Having sent accurate details of the enemy strength and dispositions, he decided to stay in the area and harass the enemy. For a further 36 hours, he remained in the area, continuously taking out patrols during which he inflicted heavy casualties on the enemy. Many attempts were made by the Japanese to cut off his patrols, but on every occasion, he skilfully out witted the enemy and extricated his men only total of three casualties throughout the operation. After continuous harassing for 36 hours, the enemy still alive evacuated the area, which he immediately occupied. The final estimate found by counting the dead Japanese bodies was fifty-two. Throughout these four days, Subedar Musahib Khan, who, during April and the first half of May had three times led his platoon in successful attacks at Gwegon and Pobhaingsanu, displayed personal bravery , skill and tenacity above the standard of a Platoon Commander. Due to his leadership, more than fifty Japanese were killed and the area cleared of the enemy. His conduct throughout was worthy of the highest praise.' Subedar Musahib Khan was awarded an immediate Military Cross.

Major Wisal Mohammad Khan, MC
8TH Punjab Regiment
Citation:
'During the Burma campaign Major Wisal Mohammad Khan took over the command of 'C' Company on 13TH February 1945, during the battle of the Myitson Bridgehead. From the moment his Company started digging astride the road south of Myitson village, it came under shell fire and continuous sniping for four days. On 17TH February 1945, his Company position was heavily shelled and an artillery smoke screen was put down to his south and south-west. Major Wisal Mohammad Khan realising the significant of the smoke, ordered his Company to stand to, which took the element of surprise from the fierce Japanese attack.

Military Cross 1922-1947

Major Wisal Mohammad Khan, MC (Cont)
Citation:

The attack was heavily supported by MMG and LMG fire that most of the platoon, which bore brunt of it, was casualties. Major Wisal Mohammad Khan quickly reorganised his perimeter and thus saved his position from being overrun in the second attack. The action lasted until 0700 hours by which time his Company had suffered thirteen killed and twenty wounded. Three others including Major Wisal Mohammad Khan was slightly wounded remained at their posts and refused to be evacuated. His Company can claim a large share of the three hundred and fifty Japanese killed in this action. He fought another successful action on 10TH March1945. Then he became second-in-command of the Battalion and on two occasions on 9TH and 24TH May 1945, on the Zalon Bridgehead he commanded two Company operations with considerable tactical skill.' Major Wisal Mohammad Khan was awarded the Military Cross on 6TH June 1946.

Jemadar Gul Mohammad, MC
8TH Punjab Regiment
Citation:

'During the Italian campaign Jemadar Gul Mohammad commanded a platoon of 'A' Company 3RD Battalion, 8TH Punjab Regiment. On 11TH May 19454, he led a raid into an enemy occupied house, and succeeded in demoralising and inflicting casualties on the enemy. On 10TH April 1945, when his Company was attacking the Scolo di Tratturo, and before the platoon had time to consolidate the enemy counter-attacked strongly from close quarters. They were repulsed with losses and several prisoners taken. In clearing the banks of the River Santerno near San Bernardino on 12TH and 13TH April 1945, Jemadar Gul Mohammad again took out several fighting patrols and mopped up enemy posts still holding out there. Again in the village of San Micolo Ferrarse on 21ST April 1945, Jemadar Gul Mohammad saw a small party of enemy infiltrate into the Battalion area near his platoon. Realising that the enemy if not dealt with immediately might slip into a house in the village and cause casualties, and his nearest section was some yards away, Jemadar Gul Mohammad took two men with him and stalked the enemy, killing two while the remainder fled. These are but a few instances of Jemadar Gul Mohammad's unfailing resource and courage. He has always been outstanding in a class renowned for bravery and initiative and he can invariably be relied upon to inspire all ranks under him to magnificent efforts.' Jemadar Gul Mohammad was awarded the Military Cross in October 1946.

Military Cross 1922-1947

Jemadar Ali Akbar, MC
9TH Jat Regiment
Citation:
'On 17TH August 1944, spearheads of 5TH Indian Division advancing south down the Tiddim Road in Burma, made contact with a roadblock, which had been established by 1ST Royal. Subsequently 1ST Royal Jats was ordered to seize the village of Khuaivum and to re-establish a road block further south on the Tiddim road to assist the advance of 5TH Indian Division. The only practicable approach to Khuaivum lay along a narrow ridge and the task of leading the advance fell to a platoon of D Company commanded by Jemadar Ali Akbar. The platoon advanced with considerable speed although the visibility was frequently no more than ten yards. Series of Japanese ambushes were encountered during the advance and these had, owing to the nature of the ground, to attack frontally. Jemadar Ali Akbar now led his platoon forward with such courage and determination, and inspired so his men by his example and his splendid leadership that in each case the Japanese were driven off the ridge at the fist onset, and the momentum of the advance was maintained in a remarkable manner. Jemadar Ali Akbar's courage and tenacity of purpose played a large part in ensuring the occupation of Khuaivum and the successful establishment of the road block in the short time given for the operation, thereby materially assisting 5TH Indian Division in its advance south. Both before and after this operation Jemadar Ali Akbar has in successful patrols displayed a determination to come to grips with the enemy, and power of leadership and grasp of the tactical handling of his platoon, which has stamped him as an officer of the highest quality and which has been an example to his Company and to the Battalion.' Jemadar Ali Akbar was awarded the Military Cross on 6TH June 1946.

Jemadar Fazal Ali, MC
9TH Jat Regiment
Citation:
'In the Rangoon Delta area on 4TH May 1945, Jemadar Fazal Ali led his platoon to attack a party of the enemy. This party were positioned on the Bank of the river. In spite of heavy fire and over ground devoid of cover, Jemadar Fazal Ali pressed on and despite the loss of six killed and three wounded, captured the position intact. Jemadar Fazal Ali was severely wounded and he would not agree to be evacuated until his was satisfied that the position he had won was suitably consolidated.' Jemadar Fazal Ali was awarded the Military Cross on 20TH September 1945.

Military Cross 1922-1947

Jemadar Ghulam Akbar, MC
10TH Baluch Regiment
Citation:
'On 25TH April 1944, Jemadar Ghulam Akbar, was out with a fighting patrol in the vicinity of a strong Japanese position in Burma. Unable to find a clear way into the position himself with a small recce patrol climbed a precipice with the aid of rifles and slings and got into the position. He took the enemy completely by surprise and he killed six of them. He extricated the patrol under heavy fire and brought back valuable information concerning the enemy's layout. He was out again with his patrol on 1ST May 1944, in the area, when he contacted body of enemy which were dug in. Although his patrol came under heavy LMG fire and grenades from short range, by piece of cool leadership he annihilated them. He was under heavy fire from the enemy main position at that time. His cool leadership resulted in the killing of at least 8 Japanese and the wounding of many more. He brought back a British Bren Gun complete with magazine and ammunition. The gun had been troubling his Company for some days previously. The three Japanese working this gun were all killed. He killed the Japanese platoon commander and brought back in his satchel valuable papers and identification. Finally with great coolness he extricated his platoon and casualties. It was a fine example of platoon command and personal gallantry under heavy fire.' Jemadar Ghulam Akbar was awarded an immediate Military Cross.

Subedar Moghal Baz, MC
10TH Baluch Regiment
Citation:
(From History of the Baloch Regiment)
'Another box position called 'Richmond' had been established about 2000 yards east of Tonforce and was just taken over by a company of 7/10 Balochis, when it was attacked on the morning of 16TH March 1944 by a strong Japanese column and was overrun, resulting in forty three casualties including Major Pat Dunn who was wounded and two VCOs killed. The remnants, included the wounded, were brought back to the battalion by a splendid rear-guard action by Subedar Moghal Baz.'
Throughout the fighting in the Imphal Plain, the personal example, devotion to duty, indifference to danger and resourceful leadership set by Subedar Moghal Baz have been quite inspiring, setting a standard of gallant and distinguished conduct abnormally encountered. Subedar Moghal Baz was awarded the Military Cross on 28TH June 1945.

Military Cross 1922-1947

Major Sardar Ali, MC
10TH Baluch Regiment
Citation:
'On 29TH August 1944, the Battalion of the Baluch Regiment reached River Foglia in Italy, in front of Monte Croce, Monte Calvo Bastian to the Gothic Line. Orders were issued for an immediate attempt to be made to rush the position before the Germans came aware of our strength in front of them. Major Sardar Ali, after organising a night's very active patrolling, led his Company forward by day, up the steep slopes of Monte Calvo, co-ordinating the move that of another Company, and generally directing the advance of two forward companies. Although it was hoped that the position was not yet fully manned, patrols reported that it was partially defended. Air photographs had revealed the extent to which it was wired, mined, and elaborately dug in, so the advance, though fully justifiable in the circumstances, was hazardous, and Major Sardar Ali knew this. By skilful use of ground, the advance continued unopposed half way up the spur towards Monte Croce, and then the crossfire of Spandau came down the Company from the ground above and positions on both flanks. These machines were sighted in cunningly concealed permanent positions in orchards, vineyards and houses. Almost at once extremely heavy enemy artillery and mortar defensive fire started. At this stage, an enemy forward defended locality, round a house opened fire onto Major Sardar Ali's Company. It had been impossible to get the supporting tanks across the ground so they were in action in the last available positions, four thousand yards back. Everything dependence upon Major Sardar Ali's resolution, skill and courage, and decided to force the pace. He called down the artillery concentrations, and swept over the enemy defenders, and took six prisoners. He immediately exploited the success. He passed around minefields and belts of wire and seized Monte Croce feature, six hundred feet above he had crossed the River, and thus earning a great honour of having the first to break into the Gothic Line. The enemy reacted violently and immediately counter-attacked the feature under cover of elaborate pre-arranged fire plans, which included all nature of weapons. All that day Major Sardar Ali hung on to the vital ground and inspired his men to perform many acts of courage. By his example, Monte Croce position was held and later, when the companies could not get forward, a firm secure base was already in our hands for the final assault and capture of Monte Calvo. In this action and the next day Major Sardar Ali led his Company with distinction.' Major Sardar Ali was awarded an immediate Military Cross.

Military Cross 1922-1947

Subedar Lall Badshah, MC
10TH Baluch Regiment
Citation:
'At Ngwedaung in Burma on 17TH February 1945, Subedar Lall Badshah was commanding a leading platoon, when it came under heavy small arms fire from tree snipers and from automatics covering open ground, also mortar and grenade discharge fire. An attack was supported by light tanks was developed. While crossing the open ground two light tanks were hit and set on fire by anti-tanks guns. Subedar Lall Badshah's platoon was ordered to cover the evacuation of the casualties and the crews of the light tanks. The enemy maintained intense small arms, mortar, and artillery fire, all with direct observation at close range. With great skill and daring, Subedar Lall Badshah led his platoon forward to a position from which they were able to extricate the tanks crews successfully. Throughout this period Subedar Lall Badshah moved from section to section encouraging his men and with complete disregard for his personal safety. Finally when the evacuation of the wounded was nearly completed, Subedar Lall Badshah went forward and carried one of the wounded back to cover. The coolness, courage, and the leadership of Subedar Lall Badshah was instrumental in the successful extrication of the wounded from the very exposed position was in the highest tradition of the Service.' Subedar Lall Badshah was awarded an immediate Military Cross.

Jemadar Abdul Hakim, MC
10TH Baluch Regiment
Citation:
'Jemadar Abdul Hakim has been in command of a platoon throughout all the fighting in Italy and has always shown dauntless courage and excellent leadership. During the period from Ortona to Arezzo, he was a patrol platoon commander and carried out first class patrols in a very difficult country. During the more recent fighting on the River Senio and in the Monte De; Verro, he set a very high standard of courage and leadership both under shellfire and on patrol. One of the patrols, which he commanded, brought back two prisoners including one German Officer'.
Jemadar Abdul Hakim was awarded the Military Cross on 20TH September 1945.

Military Cross 1922-1947

Major Gul Mawaz Khan, MC
10TH Baluch Regiment
Citation:

'In operations against the enemy in Kangwa, Arakan, Major Gul Mawaz Khan by his complete disregard of personal safety, sound planning, and utter contempt for the enemy, proved himself to be a courageous and outstanding leader. On 14TH February 1945, one Company of Baluch Regiment and one Company of 2ND Punjab Regiment had moved out from a feature Melrose to discover whether the enemy were in occupation of certain features East and South of Melrose. The Company of 2ND Punjab Regiment entered a re-entrant, whilst the Company of Baluch Regiment was searching a feature on the right flank of the re-entrant. Enemy, estimated strength of two platoons was found on the features, and owing to the line of approach being overlooked, this Company which had suffered casualties was ordered to withdraw. 'A' Company commanded by Major Gul Mawaz Khan was immediately ordered to assault and capture Northern tip of the feature but were pinned down by withering fire from a knoll, which overlooked their position. Major Gul Mawaz Khan rushed upto his leading Platoon and under heavy enemy fire, and having surveyed the situation, ordered it to remain in position and hold the enemy with fire. He then returned to his second Platoon, and ordering them to follow him, and charged the enemy from the right flank, inflicting heavy casualties on them. Two immediate enemy counter-attacks were beaten off, the enemy suffering heavily. Heavy enemy fire was now directed on to his Platoon from the next feature, which overlooked it, and the Platoon was unable to advance without accepting heavy casualties. Major Gul Mawaz Khan then noticed the enemy moving into new position, which covered the re-entrant, on which the 2ND Punjab Company was due to return. He then rushed back to his third Platoon and under heavy and accurate fire; this Platoon led him, charged the enemy from the left flank, and drove them off. Only when he saw that the Company of 2ND Punjab Regiment had regained its base unmolested, did Major Gul Mawaz Khan extricate his Company from positions overlooked by the enemy and under heavy fire, bringing back his dead and wounded. At least 15 enemies were killed and 20 wounded during this engagement. Major Gul Mawaz Khan's magnificent example of cool courage, bravery, determination, and skilful leadership was of the highest order.' Major Gul Mawaz Khan was awarded an immediate Military Cross.

Military Cross 1922-1947

Jemadar Hamid Ullah Khan, MC
10TH Baluch Regiment
Citation:
'Throughout the period under review, Jemadar Hamid Ullah Khan has conducted himself with the highest courage and has shown a very high standard of leadership, inspiring all who work with him. At Pear Hill on the morning of 26TH January 1945, a party of the enemy had managed to infiltrate on to one end of the Hill during the night and found in a strong position in Pagoda about 40 yards from the perimeter. Two attempts were made to clear up this centre of resistance but both failed. Jemadar Hamid Ullah Khan was then ordered to eject the Japanese. His handling of the attack was admirable, and skilful by placing one of his sections where it was able to launch his attack with the bayonet which he personally led with great dash, ejecting the Japanese who were compelled to leave their dead behind. His action enabled his Company to reorganise and repair the damage caused to its position by heavy enemy bombardment during the previous night's engagement. Jemadar Hamid Ullah Khan by his determination and leadership was material help in enabling the situation on Pear Hill to be restored.' Jemadar Hamid Ullah Khan was awarded the Military Cross o 15TH November 1945.

Subedar Misri Khan, MC
10TH Baluch Regiment
Citation:
'In Kangwa, Arakan, on 28TH January 1945, in the attack on a strongly held Japanese bunkered position; Subedar Misri Khan was the Platoon Commander of the leading Platoons of his Company. In the initial attack, when under fire, Subedar Misri Khan led the Platoon with great courage and determination screaming and shouting encouragements to his men, he dashed into the attack with his Platoon, and was responsible for directing fire and knocking out three Japanese bunkers ad at least 20 Japanese. Taking his leading Section, he carried out on to the top, indifferent to the fire and grenades flung at him from all directions. Undeterred he and his Section carried on, the enemy was taken completely by surprise. The Section accounted for at least 10 Japanese, 4 of whom were bayoneted by Subedar Misri Khan himself. It was only after this Section had been reduced to himself and one man could be prevailed upon to join that the rest of Company. Throughout the action his fearlessness, dash, daring and offensive spirit were outstanding. His every action inspired confidence and his personality dominated his Platoon.' Subedar Misri Khan was awarded an immediate Military Cross.

Military Cross 1922-1947

Major Mohammad Abdul Latif Khan, MC
10TH Baluch Regiment
Citation:
'In the heavy fighting in the Irrawaddy Bridgehead in Burma, at Pear Hill during 22ND to 27TH January 1945. Major Mohammad Abdul Latif Khan was in command of the Dogra Company. This Company bore the brunt of both Japanese attacks on Pear Hill on the nights 23/24 January and 25/26 January, and sustained heavy casualties including all three platoon commanders. The Japanese pressed home their attacks with fanaticism, and at one occasion obtained a lodgement in the Company perimeter, but were ejected by our counter-attacks. Throughout this period Major Mohammad Abdul Latif Khan, under very difficult conditions, by his coolness, example, and understanding of his men, was able to encourage men and enabled them to hold on to their positions under heavy fire, and in spite of their losses to the Japanese. His example was an encouragement and inspiration to the whole garrison and was responsible for our protection of this vital position.' Major Mohammad Abdul Latif Khan was awarded an immediate Military Cross.
Major Mohammad Abdul Latif Khan opted out for Pakistan Army in 1947, and attained the rank of Brigadier.

Subedar Nauroze Khan, MC
10TH Baluch Regiment
Citation:
'On 8TH January 1945, Subedar Nauroze Khan was second-in-command of 'B' Company, which had been ordered to attack a heavily bunkered feature called Merose. The attack was met by strong Japanese heavy MMG, LMG, mortars, and rifle fire. Subedar Nauroze Khan rushed forward to the leading platoon and organised the destruction of six enemy bunkers. Whilst attacking at close range by a Japanese officer whom he shot and killed with his rifle. He then turned on two other Japanese and shot them down. When the Company had consolidated its position, Subedar Nauroze Khan did admirable work organising the evacuation of the wounded, whilst the position was still under heavy automatic fire. Throughout the engagement in spite of heavy fire of all arms from strongly held position, Subedar Nauroze Khan gave example of leadership and personal bravery of the highest order. The conduct of this platoon under his direction led in no small measure to the success of the attack and the ultimate success f a vital operation.' Subedar Nauroze Khan was awarded an immediate Military Cross.

Military Cross 1922-1947

Jemadar Satara Khan, MC
10TH Baluch Regiment
Citation:

'Jemadar Satara Khan commanded the support group in a staged attack on the enemy FDLs. Having silenced the enemy MMGs, he came forward and joined the assault. Showing complete disregard for personal danger he killed six Germans and captured two. He was blown up by an exploding mine, which killed one of his men but despite this he, continued fighting and by his coolness and leadership inspired his men to greater effort. His personal gallantry and leadership went to ensure the success of an enterprising and most successful engagement.' Jemadar Satara Khan was awarded an immediate Military Cross.

Lieutenant Sayed Safdar Ali Khan, MC
Indian Medical Service attached to 10TH Baluch Regiment
Citation:

'Lieutenant Sayed Safdar Ali Khan has been the Battalion Medical Officer throughout the present campaign, including the battle of Gallabat, Barentu, Cheren, and Massawa. In all these battles, his work has been above praise, At Gallabat when neighbouring hospital was compelled to fall back by enemy fire, he carried on unperturbed and attended to the overflow of the wounded. At Barentu, he attended the wounded of another unit in addition to his own when their Medical Officer was hard pressed. During a period of heavy casualties at Cameron Ridge, on the night of 16/17 March 1941, he was called to treat a man in another unit who had lost a leg. Before he had finished there, he was urgently called to deal with some 60 casualties in his own Battalion in very difficult ground under fire, and in the dark. These casualties, he successfully cleared before the Battalion advanced that night to attack Brig's Peak. In this attack his RAP was of necessity exposed and evacuation on very steep slopes exposed to fire extremely difficult. All were successfully treated, and evacuated. Again in the battle 25 to 27 at Cheren he ran his Aid Post with conspicuous efficiency. Lieutenant Sayed Safdar Ali Khan's conscientious work in battle inspires a great confidence with the men, most of whom he knows by name, and who know that if wounded they will receive the prompted possible attention. His personal gallantry and disregard of danger are worthy of the highest praise.' Lieutenant Sayed Safdar Ali Khan was awarded the Military Cross on 30TH December 1941.

Military Cross 1922-1947

Subedar Atta Mohammad, MC
10TH Baluch Regiment
Citation:
'On 3RD July 1944, during the advance of 10TH Indian Infantry Division on the Citta Di Castello, Subedar Atta Mohammad was in command of a small force consisting of 2 NCOs and 17 IORs, positioned on the slopes of Mount Acuto. The force had been in action for 12 hours. All communications with the Company and the Battalion HQ had failed. The force was attacked by a numerically superior enemy force and Subedar Atta Mohammad immediately severely wounded in the left arm. He remained however, to direct the fight under his leadership and this small force inflicted many casualties and held off the enemy for one and half hours. During this time Subedar Atta Mohammad was again wounded in the right leg and the force suffered a further 8 casualties. Ammunition ran very low and Subedar Atta Mohammad decided to disengage from the fight. During the next half hour by sending men back one by one and organising an accurate covering fire he broke the contact with the enemy taking all the casualties with him. To reach HQ entailed an arduous march over difficult mountain country and there were no stretchers for the wounded. Subedar Atta Mohammad displayed great courage throughout this march and by his efforts, every man got back. He refused all medical treatment until he had given full report of the action and the whereabouts of the remainder of his company to his Battalion Commander. Through Subedar Atta Mohammad's super display of leadership, courage and real fighting spirit this small force had fought a numerically superior enemy for more than two hours inflicting heavy casualties. The morale of his troop throughout the action remained high due to the Subedars magnificent spirit and example.' Subedar Atta Mohammad was awarded an immediate Military Cross.'

Subedar Fateh Mohammad, MC
10TH Baluch Regiment
Citation:
'During the period under review 15TH February to 15TH May 1945, Subedar Fateh Mohammad had shown exceptionally high standard of leadership, and throughout the operations, he has been a tower of strength in his Company. Subedar Fateh Mohammad has shown and unusually high degree of courage and spared himself no effort to encourage his men throughout the operations.' Subedar Fateh Mohammad was awarded the Military Cross on 17TH January 1946.

Military Cross 1922-1947

Jemadar Sakhi Mohammad, MC
10TH Baluch Regiment

Jemadar Sakhi Mohammad was awarded the Military Cross while serving in Greece in 1944 to contain the eruption of civil war. Military Cross was awarded on 10TH May 1945 for 'Gallant and Distinguished Service'.

Subedar Sultan Mohammad, MC
10TH Baluch Regiment
Citation:

'At Maingleze on the Mandalay Canal on 13TH March 1945, Subedar Sultan Mohammad was commanding a platoon of the Company, which was ordered to hold a roadblock on the track junction at this point. During the advance to the position, the enemy estimated at about 50 were seen on the opposite bank of the canal. The enemy was engaged by a Bren group, while the Company pushed on to secure their objective. On their arrival at the objective, it was found to be held by some twenty of the enemy. Subedar Sultan Mohammad commanding the leading platoon rushed the position on the west bank, killing two and wounding three. Fire was opened on him from the east bank, where there were some ten of the enemy with Lorries. He led his platoon in an attack on this position under heavy fire, but routed the enemy, capturing two of the trucks intact the other being by the enemy before their retreat. Subedar Sultan Mohammad then he led his platoon against the party first seen and being fired on by the Bren group. On nearing the position, he immediately led his platoon in a third bayonet assault and once again, the enemy broke in utter confusion and retired to the comparative of the jungle round the village of Nasu. On reaching his objective, he ordered his platoon to collect the booty captured, while he with another NCO and two Sepoys covered their evacuation. The enemy counter attacked on three separate occasions endeavouring to recover their transport. Subedar Sultan Mohammad with his companions gallantly beat off every attack and enabled the booty to be evacuated to the defended locality held by the remainder of the Company. Subedar Sultan Mohammad by his initiative, complete disregard of his own safety, powers of leadership and outstanding character was instrumental in maintaining surprise and destroying the enemy and capturing a very valuable convoy of medical supplies. His actions on all occasions were superb and in the highest traditions of the service'. Subedar Sultan Mohammad was awarded an immediate Military Cross.

Military Cross 1922-1947

Subedar Taj Mohammad, MC
10TH Baluch Regiment
Citation:
'On the night 7/8 February 1945, Subedar Taj Mohammad was second-in-command 'B' (Pathan) Company 10TH Baluch Regiment, displayed personal courage and gallantry in the highest degree. In an immediate counter-attack led by his Company Commander, he moved forward at his commander's side. In the ensuing fierce hand-to-hand engagement, Subedar Taj Mohammad was seen in the very centre of things grappling with Japanese and shouting encouragement to his men. His own personal determination to get in grips with the enemy was in accord with the highest qualities of his race.' Subedar Taj Mohammad was awarded an immediate Military Cross.

Jemadar Mohammad Nawaz, MC
10TH Baluch Regiment
Citation:
'At Sangshak during the night of 24/25 March 1944, Jemadar Mohammad Nawaz was commanding a mortar platoon which was in position on the left flank of a very exposed company position. Throughout the night, his platoon was subjected to continuous and accurate mortar and small arms fire. Shortly before daylight on 25TH March, he was wounded in the arm but continued to command his platoon until active enemy resistance died down and only then did he go down to the ADS to have his wound dressed. He then returned to his position and immediately re-assumed command of his platoon. His platoon's position was subjected to heavy shelling by artillery and several men being wounded. During the night 25/26 March his position was heavily attacked, the attack was driven off, but at dawn the enemy overran the forward positions of his company. Gradually he was compelled to withdraw to a position further in rear. The movement was carried out under enemy fire and was successful. Later in the morning when the company position had been retaken, he took his platoon forward again and remained in position until relieved. This he did on his own initiative as his Company Commander had previously been killed. The personal bravery of Jemadar Mohammad Nawaz and his devotion to duty was an outstanding example of leadership and inspiration to all ranks of his platoon. Although wounded his courage, skill and leadership never failed.' Jemadar Mohammad Nawaz was awarded the Military Cross on 16TH November 1944.

Military Cross 1922-1947

Jemadar Ghulam Sarwar, MC
10TH Baluch Regiment
Citations:

'On the night 17/18 December 1944, Jemadar Ghulam Sarwar was ordered to attack and capture a house known as Casa Madonna, and enemy defensive positron on the bank of River Senio. A skilful approach followed by a determined attack led to the capture of the platoon's objective without a loss, and three enemies, including a section commander, were taken prisoner. By day break the enemy had brought up SP guns and heavy shelling of the platoon position continued incessantly. This however, did not prevent Jemadar Ghulam Sarwar from passing back bearings and other information, which resulted in a successful artillery shoots. At approximately 1230 hours 18TH December 1944 the enemy counter-attacked the platoon position. This attack was repulsed and three more prisoners were taken. At 1400 hours the enemy brought up a MK IV tank and two SP guns within 250 yards of the house and after five minutes firing, scored a direct hit on the platoon Piat Killing No. 1 and wounding No. 2; the house was then set on fire and Jemadar Ghulam Sarwar decided to evacuate as many of his men as possible remaining behind himself with a covering party. Courageous Jemadar Ghulam Sarwar was still at his post covering the withdrawal of the remainder of his platoon, when enemy rushed the position he was either killed or captured.' Jemadar Ghulam Sarwar was taken prisoner and at the end of the hostilities was awarded the Military Cross.

Subedar Mohammad Razak, MC
10TH Baluch Regiment
Citation:

'At Shwebo on 8TH January 1945, Subedar Mohammad Razak was in command of the leading platoon of the Company detailed to occupy a position on a bridge. The platoon surprised the enemy, and inflicted heavy casualties on them, and prevented them occupying their prepared positions. He then occupied a block on the road, covering the occupation of the objective by another platoon and preventing the enemy from counter attacking the position won. He continued to cover the consolidation of the position under heavy fire from three sides until ordered to withdraw into the box for the night. Subedar Mohammad Razak personally directed the withdrawal of his platoon under heavy fire and it was largely to his leadership and personality that the operations were carried out and casualties inflicted on the enemy.' Subedar Mohammad Razak was awarded an immediate Military Cross.

Military Cross 1922-1947

Subedar Ghulam Yasin, MC
10TH Baluch Regiment
Citation:
'Subedar Ghulam Yasin was in command of two sections of a piquet on Point 2926. On the night of 21/22 May he was attacked by a force of two Companies of the enemy. The attacks beginning about 2200 hours and continuing fiercely throughout the night, they were all repulsed with heavy losses to the enemy. Subedar Ghulam Yasin with complete disregard for personal safety moved round his position under heavy fire, a magnificent example of devotion to duty. `Through his personal control, the fire control of his men was excellent, a determining factor in the battle, as it is certain that without this control the force would have run out of ammunition. His telephone reports throughout gave a cool and most accurate estimate of the enemy strength and movement which were of the highest value; to obtain this information Subedar Ghulam Yasin had frequently exposed himself to the enemy fire. Reinforced the next morning, he remained in command of the position for six more days and by his gallant and skilful leadership repulsed several determined attacks, inflicted losses on the enemy and continued to send most valuable and reliable information. The courage, the devotion to duty, example, and complete disregard of danger shown by Subedar Ghulam Yasin was not only inspiration to all his men but averted what might have become a most serious situation.' Subedar Ghulam Yasin was awarded an immediate Military Cross.

Jemadar Ahmed Khan, MC
11TH Sikh Regiment
Citation:
'During the night 14/15 December 1945, in an attack of Casseti, Jemadar Ahmed Khan was given an objective, a line of hay stacks around the enemy held positions. As he advanced he was met with a hail of grenades from the enemy. He immediately established himself in rear of the enemy. There he organised the firing of the Bren gun and finally smashed into the house, himself in the forefront and occupied the upstairs rooms which had been strongly held by the enemy. Throughout the operations in the Gothic Line and in recent operations Jemadar Ahmed Khan has repeated shown outstanding qualities of steadiness, leadership and courage. The last operation in particular, carried out under difficult circumstances, proved his courage and reliability to be worthy of the highest praise.' Jemadar Ahmed Khan was awarded the Military Cross in October 1946.

Military Cross 1922-1947

Jemadar Nawab Khan, MC
11TH Sikh Regiment
Citation:

'During the period under review 16TH February to 15TH May 1945, Jemadar Nawab Khan has shown in action courage and organising ability of high order which has been an inspiration to his machine gunners. During an infantry attack on a key Pagoda position in the Singu area, Jemadar Nawab Khan without hesitation placed his guns in an exposed position in order to give the infantry the maximum supporting fire possible. His control whilst under enemy shellfire, machine gun supporting fire with coolness and skill until the leading infantry were within one degree of the machine guns supporting fire, our own infantry suffering one causality only. On entering the objective 20 Japanese bodies were discovered, mainly killed by the effective and accurate machine gun supporting fire. In March 1945, during the mopping up operations out of Mandalay, Jemadar Nawab Khan was commanding 6 machine guns during an attack on a village. His machine guns came under heavy enemy shellfire and automatic fire whilst supporting the infantry. Jemadar Nawab Khan again showed courage under fire. He kept his guns successfully in action during whole of the infantry advance, which finally aided in the capture of the village. During April 1945, Jemadar Nawab Khan's platoon of machine guns was successful on two night ambushes resulting in the killing of six of the enemy. Jemadar Nawab Khan's courage and his ability in action during the period of operation under review have been of the highest order giving his men the utmost confidence at all times.' Jemadar Nawab Khan was awarded the Military Cross on 17TH January 1946.

Jemadar Samundar Khan, MC
11TH Sikh Regiment
Citation:

'Jemadar Samundar Khan was in command of a strong raiding party near Castle Bolognese in Italy. Jemadar Samundar Khan was in command of a strong raiding party sent out to raid some occupied enemy houses. He led his party undected close to the enemy. Then with a Sepoy he charged a dugout by the side of the house from which fire was coming. He silenced the enemy post and then led his men to other positions. In one action he killed an enemy and took two prisoners. Though wounded in the back and neck, he completed his task, brought out his party with few casualties. Jemadar Samundar Khan proved himself over a long period to be a first class officer.' Jemadar Samundar Khan was awarded the Military Cross in 7TH April 1945.

Military Cross 1922-1947

Captain Taj Mohammad Khanzada, MC
11TH Sikh Regiment
Citation:
'For conspicuous gallantry and devotion to duty during the recent operations in Waziristan, a piquet was heavily attacked. Captain Taj Mohammad Khanzada was ordered to take two platoons and secure the piquet feature, evacuate the casualties, and cover the withdrawal of the piquet. In carrying out this operation, he displayed great coolness and carried out his task with great determination in spite of heavy opposition. On 6TH August 1940, when Razcol was attacking Tappi village, Captain Taj Mohammad Khanzada's Company was opposed by a party of some 30 hostiles who stood their ground. He immediately organised, led an attack under heavy fire over 200 yards of open country, routed the party with bayonet and grenade. His leadership and gallantry caused heavy casualties to be inflicted on the enemy who withdrew leaving seven dead. This prompt action lowered the enemy's morale and resistance and had a decisive effect on the situation.' Captain Taj Mohammad Khanzada was awarded the Military Cross 29TH November 1940.

Captain Mohammad Siddiq, MC
11TH Sikh Regiment
Citation:
'Lieutenant Mohammad Siddiq, was commanding a Company which ordered to capture Left Bump, the first objective in the Battalion's attack on the Samana Ridge. In spite of heavy machine gun, mortar, and rifle fire, he led his company into the attack and captured the objective under a shower of hand grenades. Under continued heavy fire, he organised the consolidation of the position and fire support the companies attacking the Middle and Right Bumps. It was largely owing to the speed and resolution with which his attack was made that his company suffered comparatively light casualties. Later, owing to a company commander being wounded, he was given command of another company after its attack on the Middle Bump was repulsed, and successfully reorganised it. He commanded this company during the night attack on Middle Bump, in the course of which he was twice wounded when closed to an enemy Sanger. Throughout the action Lieutenant Mohammad Siddiq displayed the highest courage and powers of organisation and leadership. His example and coolness under fire undoubtedly had great effect on the men under his command.' Lieutenant Mohammad Siddiq was immediately awarded the Military Cross. Bar to his Military Cross follows on the next page.

Military Cross 1922-1947

Captain Mohammad Siddiq, Bar to MC
11TH Sikh Regiment
Citation:

'Throughout the periods of operations, Lieutenant Mohammad Siddiq had played an outstanding part in command of a Company and his bravery and his determination to close with the enemy and his inspired leadership and his handling of his Company with complete disregard for his personal safety have been of the highest praise. During the attack on Haqfet El Qineiqina on 24TH November 1941, when his Company was held up by very heavy fire, both artillery, MG and rifle addition to an hitherto unsuspected minefield, he did not hesitate for a moment but led his Company to the assault, and there is no doubt that his leadership and personal example were mainly responsible for the capture of the objective in very short time and with comparatively few casualties. Again during the attack on and the capture of the Derna Landing Ground on 15TH December 1941, Captain Mohammad Siddiq's Company was one of those which carried out the attack. Although confronted with not only the enemy occupying in position covering the LG but also with an enemy convoy of two tanks, 20 Lorries full of troops and three guns he did not hesitate for a moment but disposed his Company to take on both tasks and again inspiring skill and determination he displayed were largely responsible for their successful achievement and led to the subsequent capture of the Landing Ground.'

Major Mian Hayaud Din, MC
12Th Frontier Force Regiment
Citation:

(From 'The Frontier Force Regiment)
On 6TH March 1932, the first young officers from Sandhurst to be posted to the Battalion nationalization scheme arrived. They were 2ND Lts. M Hayauddinand K Sheikh and Sardar Har Narain Singh. All three achieved distinguish and rose to high rank in their careers. Hayauddinand Sheikh commanded the 9TH and 8TH Battalions of the Regiment respectively in the Second World War, the former being decorated with Hilal-e-Jurat, MBE, the French Legion of Honour and MC, and was mentioned three times in despatches. Both officers became General officers in Pakistan Army, and Sardar Har Narain Singh a Major-General in the Indian Army. Major Mian Hayauddin was awarded Military Cross in 24TH May 1945 for his services in the Burma campaign. The citations of the other awards to Mian Hayaud are recorded in the relevant sections of in this book.

Military Cross 1922-1947

Major Mohammad Attiqar Rahman, MC
12Th Frontier Force Regiment
Citation:
'On 10TH June 1944, during the operations in the hills southwest of Imphal Major Mohammad Attiqar Rahman's Company (Pathans) was ordered to capture and hold a feature now known as Piffer Hill against which numerous previous attacks had failed with heavy casualties. After a long tiring approach march and a night of great discomfort in rain in the open, the attack opened with an airstrike and artillery bombardment. Major Mohammad Attiqar Rehman, had deployed his Company and led them forward closely following up the barrage. The ground over which the Company had to advance was bare steep hillside exposed on both flanks to enemy MMG and LMG fire. When the barrage lifted, Major Rehman shouted the Pathan war cry and the Company doubled forward with fix bayonets in the face of heavy enemy fire from the flanks and front. Such was the dash and gallantry with which Major Rehman led his Company that they arrived at their objective with very few casualties, and the hand-to-hand fight which then ensued, though fierce, was brief and resulted in the complete extermination of the Japanese garrison. The Company then consolidated under heavy enemy gun, mortar, and MMG fire and so well and quickly was the task carried out that the position was held during the night against the determined and persistent attacks. During the whole action Major Rehman showed a high degree of dash and gallantry which combined with cool leadership so inspired his men that the action was a complete success resulting in the capture of one enemy MMG and several LMGs while thirty dead Japanese were picked up on the position at a very low cost to our own troops.'

Jemadar Gul Mohammad, MC
12Th Frontier Force Regiment
Citation:
'On 4TH June 1944, Jemadar Gul Mohammad was ordered to attack and capture an enemy bunkered position on a hill just west of Bungte in Burma. Jemadar Gul Mohammad led his platoon with Pathan war cry, when he was badly wounded. He continued to encourage his men, and the enemy trenches overrun. It was only due to the capture of this feature that the company was enabled to go through and in turn capture the second objective that was made secure. Throughout the present operations the conduct and devotion to duty of Jemadar Gul Mohammad has been beyond praise.' Jemadar Gul Mohammad was awarded the Military Cross on 28TH June 1945.

Military Cross 1922-1947

Captain Atta Ullah, MC
12Th Frontier Force Regiment
Citation:
'On 11TH April 1945, during the assault across the River Santerno, Captain Atta Ullah commanded 'B' Company of the Regiment. During the advance to the River heavy casualties were suffered from mines, shelling and machine gun fire, and one platoon commander was killed and another wounded. However, positions were established on the rear bank. Captain Atta Ullah then sent out one platoon across the River to seize the far bank. This platoon immediately came under intense machine gun fire from both flanks and suffered heavy casualties. Captain Atta Ullah then led two remaining platoons through the wire, mines, and waist deep water, leaving only a few men in the rear bank to give the necessary covering fire, and secured a firm hold on the far bank. By now the Company was reduced to less than half to its original strength and was still under heavy fire from the flanks and the houses in front. Realizing that an advance over the far bank was not possible without further heavy casualties Captain Atta Ullah, accompanied by only a signaller with an 18-set. Together with the Signaller, he rushed the post and two prisoners were taken, but he was hit in the leg. His Signaller and two prisoners then helped him back to area of his Company, during which he was again hit in the leg. Although unable to move, he continued to encourage his men until he was finally evacuated several hours later. This gallant officer by his courage, determination, leadership, and devotion to duty played a great part in the success of this hard fought operation.' Captain Atta Ullah was awarded an immediate Military Cross.

Jemadar Shandi Gul, MC
12Th Frontier Force Regiment
Citation:
Jemadar Shandi Gul was in command of a section at Sangshak on the night 25/26 March 1944. He engaged the enemy throughout the night inflicting many casualties on the advancing Japanese. The position was surrounded but Jemadar Shandi Gul, kept on firing on all-round traverse until the guns were rendered useless, either by shrapnel or bullets and the crews wounded or killed. He then fought his way out, with the remaining members of his section, with grappling with the Japanese, wrenching his rifle and bayonet and killing him. By this action of courage and initiative, his section was able to retire to another position. Jemadar Shandi Gul eventually retiring and bringing remainder of the platoon with him. Jemadar Shandi Gul was awarded the Military Cross on 27TH July 1944.

Military Cross 1922-1947

Lieutenant Ameer Mohammad Khan, MC
12Th Frontier Force Regiment
Citation:
'Lieutenant Ameer Mohammad Khan was the Company officer with the leading convoy attacking an enemy village in Assam. The Company was caught in the open by an un-located enemy Medium Machine Gun and the Company Commander was seriously wounded. The Company went to ground but Lieutenant Ameer Mohammad Khan at once assumed command and went forward to the leading platoon. This platoon he got going by encouragement and personal example, and completely regardless of heavy enemy fire he led it by hand to hand fighting through the enemy's front line of defences into the village and attained the Company's first objective. Although the remainder of the Company was not able to cross, the open bullet swept area, and only a small portion of the Company on his left had succeeded in crossing, though by this time he was wounded in three places, but continued to engage with the highest offensive spirit, the enemy in the village. Only his personal example of gallantry kept his small force in action, and though continuously forced to withdraw after heavy casualties, he brought out the remainder in good order. He refused to go to the Regimental Aid Post to have his wounds dressed until he had reorganised the Company and later returned to the scene of action after only hasty attention by the Battalion Medical Officer. Due to Lieutenant Ameer Mohammad Khan's conspicuous gallantry in clearing the enemy away from the forward edge of the enemy defended locality and the personal example set in front of the remainder of his troops engaged , a two Company attack was launched immediately afterwards was successful and the Battalion objective gained.' Lieutenant Ameer Mohammad Khan was awarded an immediate Military Cross.

Subedar Mansabdar Khan, MC
12Th Frontier Force Regiment
Citation:
'Subedar Mansabdar Khan was second in command of 'B' Company. The Company took part in the piercing of the Gothic Line North of Florence in Italy, the advance to Marradi and North of Modigliani. Throughout this period in the face of most difficult country, appalling weather and bitter enemy Subedar Mansabdar Khan displayed unfailing determination to close in with the enemy. In two highly successful patrols he obtained valuable information of enemy dispositions.' Subedar Mansabdar Khan was awarded the Military Cross on 28TH June 1945.

Military Cross 1922-1947

Subedar Sultan Ali, MC
12Th Frontier Force Regiment
Citation:

'On 25TH March 1945, Subedar Sultan Ali was the commander of No. 7 Platoon, 'C' Company ordered to attack and clear village of Kyigon. The Company went with No. 7 Platoon as spearhead, as the degree of enemy resistance was not known, and had to be ascertained. A troop of tanks was in support, but took no part in the first phase of the attack, and remained behind outside the village. On entering the village Subedar Sultan Ali's platoon soon came under fire from the Japanese in trenches and foxholes in the vicinity of the Pagoda to their front. By skilful manoeuvring of his section Subedar Sultan Ali soon overcame this opposition, about one section strong, and destroyed the enemy. He then continued his advance into the village and came under automatic fire from a strong bunker to his front, and heavy sniping from both flanks. The platoon was pinned down and almost at once the enemy began to shell the position from close range, with great accuracy, and casualties to the platoon began to mount. A lesser man might have withdrawn from such predicament, and gone in again with tank support, but Subedar Sultan Ali at once decided that the solution in swift and determined attack to destroy the enemy and occupy his position. Subedar Sultan Ali was badly wounded by a shell splinter in the stomach before reaching the enemy position, but continued to direct the men under cover. Not till then he allowed himself to be dragged away and evacuated. The platoon suffered 2 killed and 9 wounded in this action, but secured a firm base in the centre of the enemy resistance, and it was from here that the further operations of the Company as launched, with tank support, and the village completely cleared in spite of constant shelling. Kyigon was not again occupied after our men were withdrawn in the evening. This Subedar has shown determination and skilled leadership of the highest order, and his courage has inspired his men to give their utmost throughout the recent operations.' Subedar Sultan Ali was awarded an immediate Military Cross.

Military Cross 1922-1947

Subedar Sultan Ali, MBE, MC
12Th Frontier Force Regiment
Citation:

'Subedar Mian Gul was VCO of 52 Company 'D' Force throughout all the operations on the Arakan Coast during the period from November 1944 until the capture of Rangoon in May 1945. Throughout this period Subedar Mian Gul has shown himself to be a man possessed of the highest military qualities. He is fearless in battle, leader of resource and great initiative, and excellent disciplinarian who gained both the respect and admiration of the Pathans as an outstanding example. The Company was heavily engaged with the enemy on many occasions and on every occasion Subedar Mian Gul very much distinguished himself. In November 1944, at the time when 25TH Indian Division was carrying out a reconnaissance in force, Subedar Mian Gul led a section into the enemy held strong position known as Massif where he laid deceptive effects and remained behind till daybreak in order to set off the effects personally, thus exposing himself to very great danger. On the Ramree Island during the hazardous operation on the Yan Bauk Chaung when 52 Company was part of the force covering the outflanking movement of 71 Brigade on Ramree town, Subedar Mian Gul section was specially selected from 52 Company, and was the first man to cross the Yan Bauk Chaung successfully. The left bank of the Chaung to which he crossed was strongly held by the enemy with infantry, supported by mortars, MMGs and 75 mm guns. Subedar Mian Gul with his section isolated enemy post, and finally brought back a great deal of most useful information concerning enemy positions. In February 1945, while 52 Company was covering the landings 25 Indian Division at Ru-Ywa, Subedar Mian Gul carried out several daring raids from an LCA, penetrating up the Chaungs in enemy held territory and sinking enemy supply Sampans, carrying both supplies and troops. In March 1945, when operating ahead of 4 Indian Brigade in the small islands and mangrove swamps in the approaches to Taungup, Subedar Mian Gul was again responsible for sinking several more enemy supply Sampans and also attacked and wiped out an enemy post on the island of Padin Kyun. In this encounter Subedar Mian Gul killed three Japanese and bringing back a prisoner. Subedar Mian Gul's great capacity for hard work, his powers of physical endurance and his courage under fire have indeed been inspiration to his men at all times under the most trying conditions.' Subedar Mian Gul was awarded the Military Cross in October 1946.

Military Cross 1922-1947

Subedar Mada Mir, MC
12Th Frontier Force Regiment
Citation:
'On 10TH June 1944, when 'D' Company (Pathans), attacked and captured Piffer Hill, Subedar Mada Mir of the left forward platoon of the Company. He led his platoon in a magnificent bayonet charge under heavy grenade and LMG fire and the position which had defied three previous attacks, was taken by storm, many dead Japanese left in the field. Thereafter he was prominent in directing consolidation operations under constant shell, mortar, and MMG fire. At 0315 hours on 11TH June 1944, the position was fiercely counter attacked by a large boy of enemy who persisted vigorously until dawn. Throughout this attack the situation on several occasions became critical, but Subedar Mada Mir so inspired his men that they remained firm, even when the enemy had penetrated the wire. He went from trench to trench personally replenishing the ammunition, and for his devotion to duty and disregard for personal safety, the position might have deteriorated. Every NCO in Subedar Mada Mir's platoon was wounded on this occasion, and it was his example that kept his men so staunchly at their posts. Throughout the present operations the conduct of Subedar Mada Mir has been beyond praise'. Subedar Mada Mir was awarded the Military Cross on 28TH June 1945.

Jemadar Feroz Khan, MC
12Th Frontier Force Regiment
Citation:
'Jemadar Feroz Khan was in command of the detachment from 'B' Company supplying boatmen for the crossing of the River Gariu in Italy, during the night 11/12 May 1944. Just after opening of the barrage, many of his men were wounded by airbursts. At the same time, the riverbank came under severe machine gun and small mortar fire. Jemadar Feroz Khan entirely regardless of his own safety, in the midst of shells and bullets went from boat to boat superintending the launching. On three occasions it was due to Jemadar Feroz Khan's personal example and direction under heavy fire that a reserve boat was able to replace the one lost. In one instance, it entailed jumping into the river to retrieve a rope. Exposed to a continuous fire for a long period and in spite of casualties around him Jemadar Feroz Khan never failed to direct and control the men ferrying the boats with the result that two battalions were able to cross under most difficult circumstances without much loss. Jemadar Feroz Khan's coolness under fire and personal example were outstanding.' Jemadar Feroz Khan was awarded an immediate Military Cross.

Military Cross 1922-1947

Subedar Pehlwan Khan, MC
12Th Frontier Force Regiment
Citation:
During September and early October 1944, Subedar Pehlwan Khan was second in command of a company, which was continuously engaged in driving back the Germans through the mountains after the main Gothic Line defences had been broken. Throughout the period, Subedar Pehlwan Khan's courage and ability were shining example to all. In four days, the battle of Castelnuovu, his company played main part in the attack on a hill feature, which was the key to the whole defensive system of the enemy in that sector, and his mortaring and shelling of our forward areas was continuous and intense. Again and again, the enemy tried to infiltrate back into our newly won position and during the battle, he mounted four major counter attacks against us. During these long and confused operations Subedar Pehlwan Khan was in sole charge of the administration of first his own company and later two additional companies, which were placed under command of his company commander. Continuously for four days, of under heavy fire he was an ubiquitous figure, organising the supply of urgently needed ammunition to the forward companies, collecting and organising the evacuation to the RAP of a stream of casualties, directing forward line parties, managing large number of mules with food water and supplies. As at Castelnuovu, so, throughout the long arduous advance, on foot, with mule transport, in hilly country where the enemy had Ops covering the line of approach, our roads and tracks only fit for jeeps and mules, in rain and in cold and in mud, he performed his duties with such untiring energy, initiative and energy and ability in spite of all difficulties, that everything possible to be done for the comfort of the men and the vigorous prosecution of the operations against the enemy. His company commander, relieved of all the administrative problems, left entirely free to deal with operational matters. On two occasions during the period of his company commanders went sick and Subedar Pehlwan Khan taking over command, again distinguished himself, once by leading the whole battalion to its objective on a night approach march of four miles and again by leading his company in to the attack in the successful assault on the Montebello ridge. Cool and brave, energetic and resourceful, alert and decisive, thoughtful for his men, absolutely reliable, Subedar Pehlwan Khan throughout the period, showed himself the possessor of every military virtue to a degree that did honour to himself his battalion, and his race.' Subedar Pehlwan Khan was awarded the Military Cross on 28TH June 1945.

Military Cross 1922-1947

Jemadar Nauroze Khan, MC
12Th Frontier Force Regiment
Citation:

'On the Arezzo sector in Italy during the Battalion's attack on Campriano on 24/25 July 1944, 'B' Company held up all night by intense mortar and shellfire. At 0500 hours, the Company was ordered to attack the final objective, which was a strong enemy position on high ground, with well-sited defences in houses and trenches. The position was held by approximately 30 men with three Spandaus. Jemadar Nauroze Khan's platoon was ordered to pass through another platoon and capture the objective, which was 100 yards distant. 25 yards from the objective the leading section was wiped out to a man. Then Jemadar Nauroze Khan with great courage and determination spurred the survivors of his platoon maintaining the momentum of the attack. He led the assault on to the objective. In face of this fierce encounter, the enemy fled, leaving behind 17 prisoners and a number of dead. There is no doubt that the momentum of the attack at the critical stage and the subsequent capture of the objective was highly due to the personal courage, determination and leadership of Jemadar Nauroze Khan.' Jemadar Nauroze Khan was awarded an immediate Military Cross.

Jemadar Nur Khan, MC
12Th Frontier Force Regiment
Citation:

On 20TH June 1944, Jemadar Nur Khan was ordered to attack a ridge East of Belvedere. During his recce, he was subjected to heavy and accurate mortar fire and further advance seemed impossible. With complete disregard for personal safety, he rallied his platoon and led them forward. As he advanced fire was opened on him from three Spandau's and shelling continued. Nevertheless, he continued his advance and so great was his courage and skill in handling his platoon that the ridge was eventually taken under point blank Spandau fire. Had he once wavered the ridge would have remained in enemy hands and no advance on Belvedere would have been made. The following morning he was ordered forward to mop up the enemy machine gun positions on Belvedere ridge. The position was located in tall crops with no covered approaches and his platoon was held up by concentrated Spandau fire. Without hesitation Jemadar Nur Khan led his men forward and although immediately wounded, burst into the position and forced the enemy to surrender and a firm position was established on Belvedere ridge. Jemadar Nur Khan was awarded an immediate Military Cross.

Military Cross 1922-1947

Jemadar Sultan Ahmed Khan, MC
12Th Frontier Force Regiment
Citation:
'On 28TH February 19454, 'D' Company of this Battalion was ordered to capture the village of Yezin in Burma. The village was captured with Jemadar Sultan Ahmed Khan commanding one of the leading platoons, who cleared the enemy snipers out of the village with bayonets. Soon after this, the platoon was fired upon from a bunker position, which was on the flank overlooking the nullah through which the remainder of the Battalion was moving to Yezin. Realising the threat, and the necessity to deal with it promptly, Jemadar Sultan Ahmed Khan immediately leading his men, charged straight in to the enemy position in spite of the enemy fire. When the enemy realised, that he was being overrun, ran out of the bunker into the open where they were all killed. A total of 23 Japanese were killed in this action, Jemadar Sultan Ahmed Khan accounting for three of them. The success of this operation was entirely to the prompt action, gallantry, and leadership of Jemadar Sultan Ahmed Khan who liquidated this enemy position before it could inflict any casualties. The company having cleared the village was later ordered to help 'C' Company of this Battalion in the capture of Inya village which was the next objective. Jemadar Sultan Ahmed Khan's platoon was again detailed as one of the leading platoons. Whilst leading his platoon through the open fields they were suddenly fired upon by enemy light machine gun at point blank range from concealed position hidden in the grass. Jemadar Sultan Ahmed Khan standing in the open, with bullets flying all round ordered his platoon to charge the enemy position shouting encouragement. The enemy inflicted some casualties on the platoon but failed to stop them from charging. The Japanese light machine gun was overrun and knocked out, and the crew killed. Jemadar Sultan Ahmed Khan distinguished himself again by killing with bayonet a Japanese officer. The elimination of this enemy position made safe the advance of the remainder of the company. Throughout this action, Jemadar Sultan Ahmed Khan showed an outstanding example of leadership, courage, and devotion to duty in complete disregard to his own life in face of great danger. He displayed a very high standard of initiative. His prompt and immediate action in annihilating the enemy on occasions saved the rest of the company from suffering casualties and made the operation a success.' Jemadar Sultan Ahmed Khan was awarded the Military Cross on 21ST June 1945.

Military Cross 1922-1947

Jemadar Amir Shah, MC
12Th Frontier Force Regiment
Citation:

'On 24TH March 1945, Jemadar Amir Shah's platoon was holding a position on the east flood bank of the River Senio near Bagna Cavallo, in Italy, with a section posts on the bank on the west flood bank, and also had further positions on the same flood bank which enabled him to cover the platoon from both flanks. The platoon was harassed continually by mortars, grenades and snipers. At 0900 hours, medium guns and rockets on the neighbouring localities, and by Spandau from the flanks, the enemy launched a sudden raid. Rushing to the top of the bank, preceded by a shower of HE and smoke grenades and firing Bazookas, the enemy demolished two posts, killing two men and wounding a third. Jemadar Amir Shah disregarding the hail of bullets and grenades ran forward to the threatened section, with Thomson sub-machine gun and grenades killed two enemies, and forced the remainder to withdraw. He then ran form post to post encouraging his men and hurling grenades until the attack had been completely smashed. Seven enemies were killed on the bank and other casualties were certainly inflicted, but covering fire from the far bank prevented a detailed count. The magnificent leadership and contempt for danger of Jemadar Amir Shah were the major factors in the decisive defeat of this bold and well-organised raid.' Jemadar Amir Shah was awarded an immediate Military Cross.

Jemadar Nurab Shah, MC
12Th Frontier Force Regiment
Citation:

'Jemadar Nurab Shah was second in command of 'C' Company it its advance from River Gari on 12TH May 1944. The company came under extremely heavy fire from its flank and rear. Commanders of the leading in addition to many NCOs became casualties. Some men started to withdraw. Jemadar Nurab Shah, in view of the enemy, rushed from section to section rallying the men. The enemy mortared and shelled the company, preparatory to counter attack. Jemadar Nurab Shah continued to move amongst the men in the midst of this fire, completely reorganised the company, which succeeded in beating off the counter attack. The intrepid manner, completely regardless of personal safety, displayed by Jemadar Nurab Shah was an inspiration to all ranks under his command and was largely responsible for the successful issuer of this action.' Jemadar Nurab Shah was awarded an immediate Military Cross.

Military Cross 1922-1947

Jemadar Qaim Shah, MC
12Th Frontier Force Regiment
Citation:
'On 4TH March 1945, Jemadar Qaim Shah was in command of the leading platoon, embused, of a force ordered to make a wide sweep of the area of the landing ground, east of Meiktila as far as Kondaung in Burma. On approaching the village of Nyaungkaya, the leading truck in which Jemadar Qaim Shah was leading the column, was heavily fired upon by the enemy automatics and mortars, and it was apparent that the village was held by at least company of the enemy. Jemadar Qaim Shah immediately debussed his platoon and directed them to positions on the ground, which out in front of the village was open and bare cultivation. Six of his men were shot down at once, but no thought of anything but attacking entered Jemadar Qaim Shah's mind, and he at once prepared to attack. At this juncture, the No. I of his 2" mortar was knocked out, but without hesitation Jemadar Qaim Shah manned it, while his platoon deployed, and actually silenced the enemy mortars that had previously pinned down the men. He then led his platoon in to the attack, but it was not till many hours later, after an artillery concentration and arrival of a troop of tanks from Meiktila area, that the enemy was finally silenced. Throughout these hours of hard fighting in the open, against enemy entrenched and under cover, and surrounded by snipers, Jemadar Qaim Shah never gave an inch of ground, and his stubborn determination to beat the Japanese was the deciding factor which enabled the deployment of the rest of the column to proceed, and valuable time to be gained until the arrival of troop of tanks, and the final assault. Forty-five enemy dead were counted as a result of this action, and the major credit of this success must go to Jemadar Qaim Shah, whose fine leadership and dauntless courage so inspired his men that the enemy were at first held and finally liquidated. His actions on this day are worthy of the highest tradition of the service.' Jemadar Qaim Shah was awarded an immediate Military Cross.

Major Mohammad Sher Khan, MC
13TH Frontier Force Rifles
In 1941, during the battle of Cheren in (Eritrea) the Horn of Africa against the Italians, Major Mohammad Sher Khan was the Adjutant of his Battalion and was frequently under heavy shellfire. He invariably organised and supervised the work of Battalion Headquarters with coolness and diligence for which he was awarded the Military Cross on 18TH July 1941.

Military Cross 1922-1947

Major Rakhman Ghul, MC
13TH Frontier Force Rifles
Citation:

'On 31ST February 1945, having just marched seven miles, the company under Major Rakhman Ghul's command attacked a hill feature near Yanthitgyi on Ramree Island. This contained about eighty enemies in prepared positions. In spite of being twice held up, the attack was completely successful, the position was consolidated, and an enemy counter attack was repulsed. Very heavy casualties were inflicted on the enemy, twenty seven bodies being eventually recovered. On 19TH March 1945, the company under Major Rakhman Ghul again attacked approximately forty enemies in prepared positions on a high feature overlooking the Sabyin bridgehead. The enemy were well dug in and in addition to normal small guns had two MGs in position. The leading platoon was held up twice by extremely heavy and accurate fire. Under this Major Rakhman Ghul went forward extremely unconcerned to reconnoitre means of approach and reorganise his company after casualties sustained. The third attempt, in which heavy casualties were inflicted on the enemy, was successful. The position was captured and consolidated and enemy infiltration by night beaten off. Over the period of three months the tactical skill shown by Major Rakhman Ghul had been most outstanding. He possesses great personal courage and has the power of imparting this and his confidence to his men. His possession, of the more important attributes of the soldier, including that of personal bravery, is reflected in the spirit of the men whom he commands and their continuous success in battle.' Major Rakhman Ghul was awarded the Military Cross on 17TH January 1946.

At the independence in 1947, most of the Frontier Force units were allotted to Pakistan; Rakhman Ghul being domicile of the NWFP was automatically transferred to the Pakistan Army and continued service with his Battalion. He participated in the Indo-Pak war of 1948, and was mentioned in despatches and awarded the Imtiaz Sanad. He eventually attained the rank of Lieutenant General. In 1972 after retiring from the army Rakhman Ghul served as the Ambassador to Afghanistan and after this assignment he was appointed Ambassador to Libya. For his long distinguished and meritorious service in the army and to his country Rakhman Ghul received the Sitara-i-Pakistan, Sitara-i-Quaid-i-Azam, and Sitara-i-Khidmat, some of the highest awards of the Republic of Pakistan. Rakhman Ghul finally retired in 1980 and settled in Peshawar where he passed away on 15TH June 1998.

Military Cross 1922-1947

Major Jehangir T Sataravala, MC
13TH Frontier Force Rifles
Citation:
'Major Jehangir T Sataravala has proved an outstanding in every way during the difficult operation, which the Battalion has undertaken during last three months and during which time he was Adjutant. His tireless energy, cheerful nature, and eagerness to get to grips with the crossing of the River Trigno on 3/4 November 1943, when the Battalion was fighting the enemy at close quarters in the dark, his duties entailed crossing the enemy MG fixed lines of fire frequently and over ground covered by accurate mortar fire. Later he rescued the Battalion No. 18 Set when the Signaller had been wounded, and altogether that night he did countless actions under heavy fire for the good of his Battalion. He has since in stiff actions and has invariably displayed the greatest efficiency, regardless of personal risk, and contributed in no small measure to the success of his Battalion'. For his gallant leadership Major Jehangir T Sataravala was awarded the Military Cross.

Captain Tor Gul, MC
13TH Frontier Force Rifles
Citation:
'Captain Tor Gul has repeated displayed exceptional gallantry in action whilst commanding 'B' Company especially when 'B' Company attacked and captured Mount Alto on 16TH September 1944 and again when the Company carried out a successful raid on the enemy position on German Mountain Division for the first time in Italy. The attack on Mount Alto was strongly resisted by the enemy and 'B' Company suffered many casualties but managed to on to the West end of the feature during the night, and just before light with a spirited bayonet charge cleared the summit of the Eastern slopes. Captain Tor Gul was with his two forward platoons all the time, and by coolness under fire and disregard for his personal safety, set a magnificent example to his men. B Company operated under command of the 1ST Battalion Scots Guards from 2ND December to 9TH December 1944 and their CO stated later that he and his officers were much impressed by Captain Tor Gul's powers of leadership and cool behaviour in action. Enemy shelling and mortaring of the locality held by B Company was intense during this period. Captain Tor Gul is an officer who inspires his men by his cool courage and confident handling of his Company in action.' Captain Tor Gul was awarded the Military Cross on 13TH December 1945.

Military Cross 1922-1947

Lieutenant Fazl Wahid Khan, MC
13TH Frontier Force Rifles
Citation:

'At Khampat, Kabaw Valley in Burma on 7TH March 1944, Lieutenant Fazl Wahid Khan was in command of a fighting patrol of one platoon. Two days previously a section in that area had fought an action from which four men were still missing and Lieutenant Fazl Wahid Khan had received orders to go in and maintain contact with the enemy, and if possible search the scene of the previous action for the missing men. At about 1045 hours, the platoon observation point reported seven Japanese going South on the track for Khampat towards Nangadeik. The fighting patrol at once followed this party, and after about a mile, came under fire from the Japanese party astride the track. Lieutenant Fazl Wahid Khan got his platoon into position. In the engagement that followed, by skilful tactics and quick appreciation he succeeded in inflicting some 20 to 25 casualties on the enemy who were estimated to be one platoon. At the commencement, casualties were inflicted on the party astride the track, and heavy automatic fire was brought down on several bodies of the enemy who attempted to remove these casualties. An ambush party was discovered and driven out of adjacent Chaung, with loss, and an enemy attempt at encirclement was countered by a wider encircling move by two sections. Finally when his scouts reported the rapid advance of Japanese reinforcements, Lieutenant Fazl Wahid Khan still under heavy grenade fire, withdrew this platoon, with his two wounded men, and returned to his role of watching for any enemy to follow up. On 9TH March, Lieutenant Fazl Wahid Khan, now reinforced by a second platoon, decided to resume his search of scene of the previous action, and moved southwards to do so. He reached the area, and his covering platoon was about to move forward, when heavy fire was opened from the front and from both flanks, and shortly afterwards an armoured car moved towards them, and enemy tree snipers became very active. The advance of the armoured cars was stopped by the fire from two Bren guns from the flanks and from then on the vehicles stayed silent and out of action. Four tree snipers were shot and fell to the ground. Fire from the mortars continued to crater the track, but enemy automatic and grenade fire had lessened, and Lieutenant Fazl Wahid Khan decided to carry out an encircling attack with two sections. He was forced however to discontinue this movement, by a report from a rear platoon that they were being steadily outflanked by the enemy estimated at one platoon, which threatened his rear whilst at that moment two men in his forward section were wounded.

Military Cross 1922-1947

Lieutenant Fazl Wahid Khan (Cont)
13TH Frontier Force Rifles

Lieutenant Fazl Wahid Khan decided to break contact, which he did, the sections covering each other's movement and effectively preventing any attempt by the enemy to follow up. From individual reports it is estimated that the enemy casualties were not less than 30. On the following morning Lieutenant Fazl Wahid Khan was occupying an all-round defensive position west of the track with his two platoons with observers watching the track to Nangadeik, and on Chaung on his south flank. At about 1000 hours, some rather obvious groans from the direction of the Chaung and track junction aroused suspicion and a party was sent to withdraw observation posts. Shortly after this party left, enemy platoon approached from the direction of the track and halted, still in a 'two up' formation, some fifty yards from the position, which they clearly had not seen. A Japanese officer then proceeded to give out verbal orders to six or seven subordinates, in full view of Lieutenant Fazl Wahid Khan who waited for a few moments before turning on the fire of three Bren and six machine carbines, which practically wiped out the other group and two forward sections. Fire then switched to the rear section, which had taken cover, and made only a weak return. Shortly afterwards, two sections of the enemy were seen moving round the north flank, and simultaneously heavy automatic opened and further movement was observed from Chaung on the south. Lieutenant Fazl Wahid Khan now realised that he was certainly opposed by a Japanese company making double encirclement, and as his ammunition was running low, after three engagements in four days, decided to withdraw which he successfully carried out having again inflicted some 30 to 40 casualties on the enemy. He remained in position at BP 30, covering the track to the patrol base at Holkhom until relieved. During these four days of almost constant contact with the enemy, the conduct of Lieutenant Fazl Wahid Khan, himself under fire for the first time, is worthy of the highest praise. His cool and accurate appreciations and his skilful handling of his troop enabled him to inflict severe losses on a superior enemy and to impose a considerable delay on their advance; He set an example of gallant and determined leadership, which has inspired all ranks. Lieutenant Fazl Wahid Khan was awarded an immediate Military Cross.

Military Cross 1922-1947

Lieutenant Mohammad Yusuf Khan, MC
13TH Frontier Force Rifles

'For conspicuous gallantry against the tribesmen in Waziristan, Lieutenant Mohammad Yusuf Khan was awarded the Military Cross on 10TH December 1937. Following his tour in South Waziristan, Mohammad Yusuf Khan transferred to the Political Department remaining in South Waziristan as Assistant Political Agent'. At independence in 1947, he opted for Pakistan.

Lieutenant Sadiqullah Khan, MC
13TH Frontier Force Rifles
Citation:

'On 8TH and 9TH May 194, during the battle of Amba Alagi, in Middle East, Lieutenant Sadiqullah Khan commanded a Company, which captured Centre Hill. The Company on his left was driven off Castle Hill by a very heavy counter attack early in the morning of 8TH May. This left his Company in a difficult position enfiladed in close range from higher ground on the left. Throughout 8TH and 9TH May he ceaselessly visited his Section posts, often under heavy fire, on every difficult ground and in bad weather, encouraging his men at great personal risk. Thanks largely to his Company in spite of twenty percent casualties were able to hold an important position under pressure from enemy counter attacks and patrols until relieved on night of 10TH May.' Lieutenant Sadiqullah Khan was awarded an immediate Military Cross.

Lieutenant Fazle Rahim Khilji, MC
13TH Frontier Force Rifles
Citation:

'Lieutenant Fazle Rahim Khilji commanded many fighting patrols on the Arakan front in Burma during the monsoon period. These patrols have been carried out under most difficult conditions, and due to Lieutenant Fazle Rahim Khilji's determination and devotion to duty, have proved most successful. This officer was in command of a fighting patrol on the West Mayu Front which successfully ambushed and enemy patrol, killing 13 of the enemy. The success of this action was largely due to the sill of Lieutenant Fazle Rahim Khilji, who showed a high order of leadership and coolness.' Lieutenant Fazle Rahim Khilji was awarded the Military Cross on 19TH October 1944.

In 1947 Fazle Rahim Khilji opted to join the Pakistan Army and eventually attained the rank of Brigadier.

Military Cross 1922-1947

Captain Bahadur Sher, MC
13TH Frontier Force Rifles
Citation:
'On 19TH December 1943, Captain Bahadur Sher's Company was one of the leading Companies in Battalion attack to clear a village commanding the cross tracks on Item track on the main approach cross roads east of Tollo in Italy. The position to be attacked was strongly held by four enemy heavy MMGs and two enemy anti-tank 75 mm guns. On this occasion, this officer's leadership and gallantry carried his Company, in spite of heavy casualties, through on to his objective. Four heavy MMGs and enemy half track vehicle was captured and destroyed. Some of the enemy teams, unable to make their gateway, were taken prisoners. During the following four days, his Company was subjected to very heavy shelling and enemy counter attacks. In spite of depleted numbers, he held his Company on their position, which was vital to the success of the plan. To a Company somewhat shaken by days and nights of severe fighting and heavy enemy shelling and many casualties this officer's outstanding examples of fearlessness and leadership were an inspiration.' Captain Bahadur Sher was awarded an immediate Military Cross.
In 1947 at the time of independence, Bahadur Sher opted to join the Pakistan Army, attained the rank of Lieutenant General, and became one of the outstanding general officers of the Pakistan Army. He retired in 1972 and passed away in 1983.

Subedar Ghulam Abbas, MC
13TH Frontier Force Rifles
Citation:
'On 12TH December 1944, the Battalion position on Mount Carere in Italy was attacked by German paratroopers. After an intense bombardment, the greater part of a whole Parachute Battalion threw themselves on to Subedar Ghulam Abbas's Company, of which he was second in command. His Company position was almost overrun, one platoon having only five men left in it. Subedar Ghulam Abbas rallied the remains of his Company and by means of an immediate counter attack, carried out with great dash, restored the situation, and threw the enemy from his Company position before they had time to consolidate. His Company on this occasion accounted for a certain 23 German paratroopers killed, 14 prisoners taken. Many wounded which for the next three nights were being collected by the Germans. His Company suffered seven killed and 40 wounded.' Subedar Ghulam Abbas was awarded an immediate Military Cross.

Military Cross 1922-1947

Subedar Habib Khan, MC
13TH Frontier Force Rifles
Citation:

'Subedar Habib Khan as a platoon commander in the Pathan Company has continually throughout the advance from the Irrawaddy in Burma, led his platoon with conspicuous gallantry and marked leadership. In the advance south of his tactical handling of platoon and coolness under fire have been very high order and an inspiration to all ranks. On two occasions his leadership has been without doubt instrumental in inflicting heavy losses on the Japanese and the quick stabilising of the situation. At Pyo he was despatched suddenly on a local report as a scratch force and his platoons, only 28 strong, with five Lee Tanks, engaged 400 of the enemy killing 81 and only sustaining one slightly wounded. He returned, having captured mortars and Light Machine Guns, and his action in these particular operations was superb, himself showing complete disregard to his own personal safety throughout this operation. Later on, he assumed the appointment of second in command of his Company and at times, he commanded the Company most efficiently. At all times he has been a tower of strength and fine example of dash and cool calculated leadership to all men in his Company.' Subedar Habib Khan was awarded the Military Cross on 6TH June 1946.

Subedar Mohammad Khan, MC
13TH Frontier Force Rifles
Citation:

'On 20TH February 1945, a Company attack was put it on a prepared position containing about 80 enemies at Yanthitgyi. Subedar Mohammad Khan was in command when one platoon was held up and had several men wounded, who fell in the deep nullah between platoon and the enemy. The latter covered the nullah with intense LMG and grenade fire from the range of fifteen yards. Subedar Mohammad Khan with five men twice charged the enemy positions, enabling the wounded to be successfully recovered. When the enemy counter attacked he and few men again rushed forward to engage them, inflicting heavy casualties, some of which seemed to be caused by Subedar Mohammad Khan. Throughout the action the determination, control, and complete disregard of personal danger shown by Subedar Mohammad Khan in more than fulfilling his duty as Company senior VCO was an inspiration to all ranks, and contributed largely to the success of the attack and subsequent consolidation of the attack.' Subedar Mohammad Khan was awarded an immediate Military Cross.

Military Cross 1922-1947

Subedar Yar Mohammad, MC
13TH Frontier Force Rifles
Citation:
'During the period under review Subedar Yar Mohammad has commanded a MG platoon. The platoon took a very effective part in the attack on and consolidation of Kanhla and Pakokku in Burma. On 22ND February 1945, Subedar Yar Mohammad's platoon was detached from its Company and placed under the command 28TH East African Brigade. To mention three of this platoon's many actions, on 25TH February the platoon was heavily engaged with the enemy; commandant of 4TH Battalion. 4TH Punjab Regiment in his report states, 'Subedar Yar Mohammad remained at the OP throughout the action which lasted five hours, coolly moving his MG's into a succession of alternative positions whenever the enemy got the MG position taped. He refused to be rattled.' On the night 26/27 February 1945, one of the MG sections decimated a Japanese fighting patrol, which they allowed to approach to within 15 yards before opening fire. On 20TH March 19454, the other MG section was largely instrumental in repelling the heavy Japanese attack on the Letse box, inflicting on the enemy casualties, which may well have been over 100. On 7TH April 1945, the platoon was joined by the rest of its Company. Subedar Yar Mohammad had then been exercising his detachment command for over six weeks and had been continuously in the front line with his platoon for over two months. Throughout this period, Subedar Yar Mohammad proved himself as a MG platoon commander of the first order, as possessing great personal courage, and being born a leader of men.' Subedar Yar Mohammad was awarded the Military Cross on 17TH January 1946.

Subedar Mohammad Sardar, MC
13TH Frontier Force Rifles
Citation:
'Subedar Mohammad Sardar commanded a force against the enemy in the hills southwest of Pale in Burma, from 5TH May 1944. During this time his detachment fought five most successful actions, four of which were planned and personally directed by Subedar Mohammad Sardar. On each occasion his troops were greatly outnumbered, by brilliant use of ground, bold offensive action and absolute control of his various small detachments Subedar Mohammad Sardar caused the complete disintegration of a force estimated to be no less than 300.' Subedar Mohammad Sardar was awarded an immediate Military Cross.

Military Cross 1922-1947

Jemadar Abdul Gafoor, MC
13TH Frontier Force Rifles
Citation:

'On 25TH February 1944, at a hill feature East Finger, Arakan in Burma, Jemadar Abdul Gafoor's platoon was moving forward to occupy a knoll, which had previously reported clear of the enemy. However, on drawing near they were fired on by LMGs. Placing two sections to hold the enemy, he led out a flanking movement. The route lay across open country, but though fired on both from the original enemy position and now also from a second one on the opposite side of his line of advance, by sheer force of personality and leadership, he got his party to its destination which though wounded in the leg, he kept his men in action until more than half were casualties and ammunition had almost run out. After successfully withdrawing all his party, including his casualties, he offered to lead another counter-attack. On 15TH March 1944, Jemadar Abdul Gafoor led a charge on the enemy bunker position on Ticker Hill with great gallantry and continued to hold the position he reached, which was only ten yards from the enemy, for an hour in spite of receiving permission to withdraw. In this action he more than lived up to the standard of determination and leadership he had set in the action of 25TH February 1944.' Jemadar Abdul Gafoor was awarded an immediate Military Cross.

Jemadar Sardar Khan, MC
13TH Frontier Force Rifles
Citation:

'On 18TH March 1944, near Htidaw, Arakan in Burma, Jemadar Sardar Khan commanded the leading platoon in the assault on Ticker Hill. Mindful of an unsuccessful attack three days previously, Jemadar Sardar Khan personally led the attack on the first bunker, which was completely destroyed, throwing grenades into it and silenced the defenders. Though LMG fire opened suddenly from the flank, he continued to lead the charge up the remainder of the slope, shouting to his men to follow him at all costs before the enemy has the time to re-organise. He himself took leading part in the hand to hand fighting that took place before the top could be reached, and there is no doubt that his personal efforts, combined with unflinching determination and complete disregard of danger, were the outstanding feature that led to the success of the operation when the issue hung in balance thus enabling the rest of the Company to follow up and consolidate the ground won.' Jemadar Sardar Khan was awarded the Military Cross in April 1946.

Military Cross 1922-1947

Jemadar Mohammad Shafi, MC
13TH Frontier Force Rifles
Citation:
'During the nine months that the Battalion had been in action in Italy. Jemadar Mohammad Shafi has during the actions in which he has taken part, always shown a high standard of devotion to duty, courage, and powers of leadership. The following is an example of the excellent work done by Jemadar Mohammad Shafi. On the night of 12TH April 1945, Jemadar Mohammad Shafi was in command of a fighting patrol of platoon strength. His orders were to patrol the village of San Martino and if possible occupy it. From previous reports, it was known that the enemy held this village, and also that it was heavily mined and booby-trapped. Approaching the village the patrol encountered a minefield and one Section Commander lost a foot and had to be evacuated. Jemadar Mohammad Shafi personally recced the route round this field, and eventually the patrol proceeded. On reaching the outskirts of the village, the patrol was engaged by the enemy with Spandau and machine gun fire. Jemadar Mohammad Shafi displayed such powers, leadership and initiative, and by example of his own personal courage that resistance was overcome and the village was soon in our hands. Jemadar Mohammad Shafi rapidly consolidated and asked his Company Commander for reinforcements in order to hold the village. The Company Commander was only able to send out one more section. However, Jemadar Mohammad Shafi so disposed of his troops and so dominated the village that he held on for two days under very trying conditions, the village being constantly subjected to heavy shelling, mortaring and small arms fire. The presence of our troop in the village was a continued embarrassment to the enemy, and great importance to the Brigade plan for the general offensive that commenced the next night. Two hours before he was to be relived Jemadar Mohammad Shafi was wounded by a mortar bomb. This is the second time this gallant officer had been wounded in four months. The above is the typical of the extremely fine work done by Jemadar Mohammad Shafi in action. At all times he has shown himself to possess great courage, initiative and leadership, always extremely cheerful, however the trying the situation he has always been a great influence in his Company.' Jemadar Mohammad Shafi was awarded the Military Cross on 13TH December 1945.

Military Cross 1922-1947

Jemadar Gul Zarin, MC
13TH Frontier Force Rifles
Citation:
'On the night of 14/15 February 1944, the platoon which Jemadar Gul Zarin commands was holding an important position on the flank of the Brigade in front of Orsogna in Italy. The position which was only half prepared, was situated around the cave, tip of which was only available cover. Movement by day was impossible owing to heavy MG fire from enemy posts situated less than 150 yards distant. Jemadar Gul Zarin's orders were to consolidate this position by day light. This task he was unable to do. Throughout the night, he was mortared and machine-gunned, extremely and accurately and heavily by the enemy. By 15TH February the enemy had brought up a tank and from close range, the cave was continually pounded. Jemadar Gul Zarin was ordered to withdraw to another position. This he did after dark and asked permission to retake his old position and himself, after the moon has gone down, sneaked and rushed the post with one section driving out a party of enemy and consolidated the position for three days and nights until relieved. During this time he drove off determined attack by the enemy.' Jemadar Gul Zarin was awarded the Military Cross on 29TH June 1944.

Jemadar Ran Gul, MC
13TH Frontier Force Rifles
Citation:
At Aishan, Imphal area in Burma on 2ND June 1944, Jemadar Ran Gul was in command of a section of a fighting patrol with orders to harass the enemy and if possible to collect identification. On arriving in the Aishan areas, Jemadar Ran Gul that the enemy had advanced one mile ahead of their original position and were busily digging bunkers under cover of the night. Jemadar Ran Gul moved his section forward to within 30 yards of the enemy and gave the section orders to cover him. He then crawled forward to within 3 yards of the enemy, where he remained for some minutes, searching for cast of clothing etc. This proved unsuccessful so he withdrew to his section and sent back information to his Company Headquarters. Two sections were sent out immediately from Headquarters with orders to contact Jemadar Ran Gul and make a surprise combined assault on the enemy. The party now full platoon strength, moved to the enemy position.

Military Cross 1922-1947

Jemadar Ran Gul (Cont)
13TH Frontier Force Rifles

Jemadar Ran Gul with one section moved to the right of the enemy position, leaving two sections o the left to fire direct in to the enemy. Closing to 30 yards range, he observed 40 to 50 Japanese moving in the middle of the bunker position, Jemadar Ran Gul then prepared 12 grenades, which he threw into midst of the enemy. He then personally led the section in a bayonet assault on the bunker. As he came out in the open, he was met by heavy LMG fire from the bunker position and was forced to withdraw. With great skill Jemadar Ran Gul withdrew his section under heavy fire and determined to carry out his orders to the full, he closed his men on the main body of the platoon where he reorganised and again with courage led his men in a double section assault. The enemy by this time had concentrated most of their fire power on the attackers, killing one of Jemadar Ran Gul's men, wounding two and finally Jemadar Ran Gul was shot through the leg, completely disabling him. Jemadar Ran Gul then displayed all the qualities of a born Commander. Under intense enemy fire, and himself badly wounded, he rallied his men, organised the evacuation of the wounded, and then ordered his men back into defensive position with the remaining section. Inspired by the fine example set by Jemadar Ran Gul the platoon then repulsed three determined attacks made by two platoons of enemy ad finally after inflicting very heavy casualties on the Japanese withdrew. Throughout the action, Jemadar Ran Gul displayed skill, judgement, and courage of the highest order with complete disregard for his own personal safety. His valour and devotion to duty has won the respect and admiration of all ranks.' Jemadar Ran Gul was awarded an immediate Military Cross.

Jemadar Ran Gul (Bar to his MC)

Jemadar Ran Gul was in command of a small fighting patrol of six men with orders to harass the Japanese, in a most the most important sector of the conflict. Throughout this daring and very successful patrol, Jemadar Ran Gul, displayed courage determination and skilled leadership of a very high order. He led his men with complete disregard for personal safety, and his conduct and devotion to duty under very difficult conditions have been an inspiration to all ranks. Jemadar Ran Gul was awarded the Bar to his existing gallantry award of Military Cross.

Military Cross 1922-1947

Major Mohammad Sadiq Khan, MC
14TH Punjab Regiment
Citation:
'On 30TH May 1945, at Sagaung a Company under Major Mohammad Sadiq Khan working in the thick and previously unrecorded jungle surprised a Japanese party and destroyed a gun and tankettes. A heavy counter attack was put in by the Japanese and one platoon became separated. Major Mohammad Sadiq Khan first assured himself of the safety of his platoon, personally directed the repulse of the counter attack and then safely withdrew his Company through heavy all round opposition. During the next week, he conducted close personal recces of Japanes positions and was able to report accurately on their dispositions. Again on 29/30 June while in command of a detached force of six platoons, this officer in 48 hours led his party some 20 miles through flooded paddy and jungle finally surrounding and destroying a Japanese party of 40 men. Throughout operations during May and June 1945 this officer's initiative, leadership and personal example have been of the highest order.' Major Mohammad Sadiq Khan was awarded the Military Cross in October 1946.
At independence in 1947, Mohammad Sadiq Khan opted to join the Pakistan Army and attained the rank of Acting Brigadier.

Captain Sarfaraz Khan, MC
14TH Punjab Regiment
Citation:
'On the night o f17/18 August 1943, in Arakan, Burma, Captain Sarfaraz Khan was in command of a platoon of his Battalion attached to a company of 12TH Frontier Force Regiment holding Ngakyadauk Pass. Between 1830 and 0430 hours, the enemy made four separate attacks on the company position. On one occasion, the enemy fired one red very light. Captain Sarfaraz Khan realising that this might be taken for our withdrawal signal, mortar, and LMG fire to prevent the possible accidental withdrawal of one of his section and throughout the night moving from post to post encouraging his men. His leadership, courage and devotion to duty set a fine example to his men.' Captain Sarfaraz Khan was awarded an immediate Military Cross.
At independence in 1947, Sarfaraz Khan opted to join the Pakistan Army and attained the rank of Lieutenant Colonel. He at one time commanded the 2ND Battalion 14TH Punjab Regiment.

Military Cross 1922-1947

Lieutenant (Dr.) Bashir Ahmad, MC
14TH Punjab Regiment
(Indian Army Medical Corps attached to 14TH Punjab Regiment).
Citation:
'This officer is the Regimental Medical Officer of 4TH Battalion, 14TH Punjab Regiment. During the action on Windwin in Burma on 7TH February 1944, he went forward and established his advance Regimental Aid Post with the leading company, and throughout the day, he dealt with casualties from this unit and Sappers and Miners with great coolness under fire. Again on 22ND February 1944, he displayed great coolness in dealing with casualties of two companies in an attack on enemy positions o Long Ridge. On both these occasions he has shown complete disregard for personal safety in order to deal with the wounded efficiently in the forward area. His quick and capable methods of dealing with large numbers wounded, and his personal calm and steadiness have had a calming influence on wounded of all classes and his conduct has had a very great influence in keeping up morale throughout the Battalion.'
Lieutenant (Dr.) Bashir Ahmad awarded an immediate Military Cross.

Lieutenant Said Shah, MC
14TH Punjab Regiment
Citation:
'On 2ND April 1943, Lieutenant Said Shah was commanding two platoons in a defensive position on Shamdak Pass in Burma. A section of one of these platoons had been sent forward on patrol when a strong force of enemy about 600 strong made a surprise attack on the position. During the engagement which followed, a complete withdrew upon the orders of a Havildar, thus leaving Lieutenant Said Shah with only two sections to defend the pass. The officer held on the position throughout the night by driving off the enemy patrols, and only withdrew the following morning when practically all his ammunition had been expended, and when his men were almost surrounded.' Lieutenant Said Shah was awarded the Military Cross on 30TH September 1943

Military Cross 1922-1947

Lieutenant Mohammad Yusuf, MC
14TH Punjab Regiment
Citation:
'On the 10TH February 1944, during the attack on the Japanese position at Milestone 26 Datweyauk track in Burma, Lieutenant Mohammad Yusuf's company led the Battalion attack. In the face of heavy and accurate fire, he led his men with such dash and determination that he finally attained his objective despite many casualties. His fearless courage and selfless determination maintained in his Company in what proved to be a position exposed to heavy fire for an hour, when he received orders to withdraw. He set about this difficult operation with calm, deliberate organising the collection of wounded, and arms until all men were clear, when he withdrew last of all. His courageous example inspired his Company to keep on hammering at the enemy even after 60 percent casualties had been suffered, and this intrepid gallantry and resolution has inspired the whole Battalion.' Lieutenant Mohammad Yusuf was awarded an immediate Military Cross.

Subedar Mohammad Anwar, MC
14TH Punjab Regiment
Citation:
'On 18TH January 1945, Subedar Mohammad Anwar, was detailed to attack the Japanese position at Setyon in Burma, with his platoon. Leading his platoon with skill under artillery concentration and dashed in. So spirited was his attack that the Japanese fled from well dug and wired position. On 20TH January 1945, Subedar Mohammad Anwar's platoon was again in the lead in the attack on the Japanese main defence line at Monywa. Leading his platoon with dash, he got through the smoke across the open space in front of the enemy position and right up to the enemy wire. Here the platoon ran into very heavy grenade and automatic fire and suffered eleven casualties. Subedar Mohammad Anwar however, attempted to press on and not until the attack had been halted by further casualties and the order to withdraw, did he coolly get his wounded and weapons and withdraw his platoon to the start line. In getting the wounded from the open ground in front of the enemy position, he displayed courage of very high order. On his return, he was able to draw a valuable sketch map of the enemy position where the attack had been halted. Subedar Mohammad Anwar displayed courage and dash on both occasions which has been worthy of the highest praise.' Subedar Mohammad Anwar was awarded an immediate Military Cross.

Military Cross 1922-1947

Subedar-Major Haider Rehman Khan, MC
14TH Punjab Regiment
Citation:
'On 18TH December 1941, Rear Bn. HQ, was bombed and shelled in Hong Kong. Subedar-Major Haider Rehman Khan organised and conducted the rescue of men trapped in the miniature ranges and the evacuation of the injured and dying men. He assisted in rallying the Chinese firemen and salvage corps and in suppressing fires. Throughout the operation from 8TH to 25TH December, whilst under almost continuous bombardment, the work of Subedar-Major Haider Rehman Khan was beyond praise. The example he set under shellfire and serial bombing and his work in maintenance of the Battalion in the Field upheld morale of those around him in a manner that aroused the utmost admiration and respect.' Subedar-Major Haider Rehman Khan was awarded the Military Cross on 4TH April 1946.

Subedar Major Mussaik Khan, MC
14TH Punjab Regiment
Citation:
'On the night 15/16 February, the Kyigon bridgehead and boat unloading point in Burma, were heavily attacked. While the action was in progress, a series of boats approaching the beach were heavily fire on and heavy casualties ensued. Subedar-Major Mussaik Khan immediately organised the stretcher bearers and under heavy fire supervise the removal of the wounded to safety. His prompt and gallant action undoubtedly saved the lives of several men, who would otherwise died from loss of blood. On the night 17/18 February, the Kyigon bridgehead was again heavily attacked throughout the night. The Beach-Master and his assistant were killed. Subedar-Major Mussaik Khan immediately took over as assistant. Under very heavy shellfire he supervised the unloading of stores and the distribution of vital ammunition to companies. To do this he frequently crossed the camp area, which was also swept by bullets as well as exploding shells. Throughout the night he worked untiringly, unloading the boats, encouraging the stretcher-bearers and organising the supply of ammunition. Following his inspired leadership, the men under him worked devotedly and vital requirements for the battle reached where they were required. For nearly ten hours, he displayed cool bravery which set a splendid example. Throughout the operations he was a tower of strength and the greatest single factor in the maintenance of morale.' Subedar-Major Mussaik Khan was awarded an immediate Military Cross.

Military Cross 1922-1947

Subedar Tor Khan, MC
14TH Punjab Regiment
Citation:

'I am speaking on behalf of my late CO, Lt. Col. Stokes, to whom I was Adjutant, when I say that I cannot praise too highly the conduct of Subedar Tor Khan during the Malayan Campaign of 8TH December 1941 to 15TH February 1942. He not only by leadership and personal example kept a young and inexperienced Pathan Company together, but also distinguished himself in two actions, on 15 km position on the Kroh-Pattnani Road and in an ambush position south of Kampar, in the latter of which actions Lt. Col. Stokes recommended him for decoration, which recommendation was lost in the subsequent sack of Singapore. This action took place on 3RD January 1942, and resulted in the destruction of Japanese tanks and motor vehicles carrying Japanese infantry. Subedar Tor Khan was second-in-command of Pathan Company under Lt. Ringer, and was wounded in the hand when proceeding to inspect destroyed Japanese vehicles. He refused to leave his Company when advised to the Unit MO. When taken prisoner by the Japanese Subedar Tor Khan resisted all efforts to force him to join the INA, and compiled a list of notes on the actions of certain members of the INA in dealing with their comrades, which list he succeeded in keeping safe, to the end, which has proved most useful in helping to separate white from black ones. He also ran across news service, records of which had to be destroyed due the danger of Japanese Military Police searches. He deserves the highest praise for his loyalty and integrity during this difficult period, when he had every chance to take the easy way and join the INA. Lt. Col. Lewis second in command 5TH Battalion, 14TH Punjab Regiment, to Col. Stokes will vouch for the truth of his statement. Captain Iyapp, No. 1 Signal Section, Malaya\ Command and Captain Hari Budhwar 3RD Cavalry, will testify to Subedar Tor Khan's loyalty during his POW years, and more difficult for him as the Indian officers of 1 Battalion, 14TH Punjab Regiment went over to the INA to a man.' At the end of the hostilities and the release of Subedar Tor Khan, he was awarded the Military Cross on 19TH December 1946.

(The Indian National Army was an armed force formed by Indian nationalists in 1942 in Southeast Asia during World War II. Its aim was to secure Indian independence from British rule. It formed an alliance with Imperial Japan in the latter's campaign in the Southeast Asian theatre of WWII. Many Indian soldiers who were prisoners of the Japanese were coerced to join the INA).

Military Cross 1922-1947

Subedar Abdul Majid, MC
14TH Punjab Regiment
Citation:
'From 30TH August to 15TH September 1944, Subedar Abdul Majid was operating against the enemy on the Tiddim Rod, in Burma. The patrol was out in very bad monsoon conditions and without cover from the weather. During this operation the patrol covered over 100 miles of the most difficult jungle country and was subject to heavy mortar and LMG fire almost every night directed by Japanese CPs. Due to good leadership in series of ambush, this officer's patrol succeeded in inflicting serious casualties on the enemy amounting to 192 killed or wounded and 18 Lorries damaged or destroyed. Subedar Abdul Majid showed outstanding determination in pressing home his attacks in face of most difficult conditions ad enemy counter fire and thereby made a valuable contribution to the disorganisation of a vital enemy line of communication.' Subedar Abdul Majid was awarded the Military Cross in October 1946.

Subedar Sarfaraz, MC
14TH Punjab Regiment
Citation:
'From 15TH to 26TH August 1944, Subedar Sarfaraz was operating against the enemy on the Tiddim Rod, in Burma. The patrol was out in very bad monsoon conditions and without cover from the weather. During this operation the patrol covered over 100 miles of the most difficult jungle country and was subject to heavy mortar and LMG fire almost every night directed by Japanese Ops. Due to good leadership in series of ambush, this officer's patrol succeeded in inflicting serious casualties on the enemy amounting to 177 killed or wounded and 12 Lorries damaged or destroyed. Subedar Abdul Majid showed outstanding determination in pressing home his attacks in face of most difficult conditions ad enemy counter fire and thereby made a valuable contribution to the disorganisation of a vital enemy line of communication.' Subedar Sarfaraz was awarded the Military Cross on 13TH September 1945.

Jemadar Pir Gul, MC
14TH Punjab Regiment
Jemadar Pir Gul was awarded the Military Cross on 22ND June 1944 for conspicuous gallantry in an action against the Japanese column on 4TH February 1944 at Kwazon Ridge in Burma.

Military Cross 1922-1947

Subedar Falak Sher, MC
14TH Punjab Regiment
Citation:

'On the night of 25/26 February 1944, Subedar Falak Sher was ordered to lay and ambush with his platoon in order to prevent parties of enemy withdrawing back to their own lines. At about 2300 hours, a party of about a hundred enemy approached his position covered by an advanced of two sections. Subedar Falak Sher held the fire of his platoon until the main body of the enemy were within a hundred yards of his position. He then opened up on the advanced guard killing four of the enemy, at the same time opening up with mortar, grenade dischargers, and LMGs on the main body. The fire was very accurate and caused great confusion and heavy casualties to the enemy. Not satisfied with this Subedar Falak Sher moved two of his sections round the enemy's flank and inflicted more casualties on them. By his own display of courage and excellent planning, he was able to inflict heavy casualties on the enemy while only having two of his men slightly wounded.' Subedar Falak Sher was awarded an immediate Military Cross.

Subedar Mohammad Zaman, MC
14TH Punjab Regiment
Citation:

'On the 5TH May 1944, Subedar Mohammad Zaman's platoon was posted at Kwa Sepabi in Burma. Early next morning, hearing firing at Khoijuman, he left behind a small OP and proceeded at all speed to the spot. Finding Jemadar Feroze Khan with a Punjabi platoon fighting for the possession of two guns and hard pressed, he immediately ordered a charge. He led his platoon with fire and dash, and drove the enemy back 200 yards and captured a third gun. His advance enabled Jemadar Feroze Khan to advance and complete the box round the guns. He then held on to his sector and kept the enemy off until part of the remainder of the Battalion arrived and cleared up the area. His quick appreciation of the situation when Jemadar Feroze Khan was hard pressed and his magnificent leadership during the charge were outstanding and resulted in the capture, in conjunction with Jemadar Feroze Khan's platoon, of three enemy guns, two arm dumps, valuable documents, two unwounded prisoners and the destruction by the enemy of a fourth gun. The courage and dash of this young Jemadar was quite outstanding and undoubtedly saved the guns being recaptured by the enemy.' Subedar Mohammad Zaman was awarded an immediate Military Cross.

Military Cross 1922-1947

Subedar Shahi Beg, MC
14TH Punjab Regiment
Citation:
'On the morning of 11TH April 1944, east of Imphal in Burma, Subedar Shahi Beg was in command of his company's leading platoon. The platoon marching through extremely difficult and mountainous country, in darkness for three hours suddenly contacted the enemy in a strong defensive position. He led his platoon with great determination into an attack. In the ensuing action the position was captured, at least twenty five casualties inflicted on the enemy, one three inch mortar and much booty taken without a single causality to his platoon. This extremely successful result was entirely due to Subedar Shahi Beg's ready initiative, skilful manoeuvre, and fine leadership. Under enemy fire, he reorganised his platoon on the position with great coolness and complete disregard for his own safety. During the next 24 hours, when the company was heavily engaged with the enemy, although wounded, he continued to act aggressively against the enemy and set an example of superb courage and devotion to the whole country.' Subedar Shahi Beg was awarded an immediate Military Cross.

Jemadar Ali Akbar, MC
14TH Punjab Regiment
Citation:
'Jemadar Ali Akbar has throughout the period 15TH February to 15TH May 1945, proved to be a man of iron nerves, a first class leader and extremely courageous. During the period in which the Battalion was at Letse in Burma, he commanded a number of ambushes on the Japanese Line of Communication and all were successful. On one occasion he followed a Japanese bullock cart convoy for three miles, controlling the eagerness of his men to dash into attack, until the convoy reached a steep slope at which he knew that it would automatically close up and thus became liable to heavier punishment. As result of this ambush, 20 casualties were caused and much equipment either destroyed or captured. Since this occasion he successfully commanded many ambushes and sweeps on the Japanese Line of Communication at Letse using natural cunning, a fine sense of timing and excellent control over his men to inflict the maximum number of casualties on the enemy. It is his platoon that inflicted over 60 casualties on the Japanese. This VCO has throughout the period in question for nearly 2 years of operations maintained an extremely high standard of bravery, leadership and organising powers.' Jemadar Ali Akbar was awarded an immediate Military Cross.

Military Cross 1922-1947

Jemadar Mohammad Amin, MC
14\ths Punjab Regiment
Citation:

'Jemadar Mohammad Amin has commanded his platoon in every action fought by the Battalion since crossing the Irrawaddy in Burma. His inspiration, leadership and complete disregard for danger have been a fine example to all. On 15th May 1945 at Thingadon his platoon was leading the Company, came under heavy and accurate fire from all arms including a 75 mm gun. Although blown off his feet by a shell burst, badly shaken and deafened he continued to lead his platoon and took the village. He refused all personal attention and when ordered to withdraw he personally conducted the withdrawal with great skill and gallantry. The next day at Letwaywa his platoon was holding a corner of the village under heavy and accurate enemy fire. Appreciating the most threatening part of the enemy position, he personally led his platoon with bayonet charge and cleared a strongly held enemy post. Again at Minzu on 1st April 1945, his personal example and leadership was largely responsible for extricating his Company from very dangerous position. This officer had been twice severely wounded but always volunteered for any dangerous mission. His leadership is the admiration of all ranks.' Jemadar Mohammad Amin was awarded the Military Cross on 6th June 1946.

Jemadar Gul Baz Khan, MC
14th Punjab Regiment
Citation:

On 11th May 1944, in the Imphal area this Platoon Commander skilfully determinedly led his platoon on to an enemy position in the face of fierce opposition. The cool handling and encouragement of this Platoon while under heavy LMG and Mortar fire, during the ensuing counter attack by the enemy enabled the platoon to hold on to the position. He resolutely fought the Platoon until nearly every VCO was either killed or wounded; even under this handicap maintained his position until ordered by his Company Commander to withdraw. His withdrawal from the position was skilfully carried out. The conduct of this NCO during the whole period of this campaign showed his excellent powers of leadership, determination to destroy the Japanese whenever possible

Military Cross 1922-1947

Jemadar Khan Sherin, MC
14TH Punjab Regiment
Citation:
'When in command of No. 15 Platoon 'C' Company, Jemadar Khan Sherin was given the task of left flank protection to the main body of forward troops, who were covering the demolition from the frontier to the 'Guiddrinkers' Line in Hong Kong. His line of retirement was through an intricate piece of country consisting of scrub-covered hills and valleys. His task he carried out with complete success and displayed complete coolness and great courage. In spite of being virtually surrounded on one occasion, bombed from the air, and attacked by greatly superior force the whole time of his command without any serious loss while inflicting heavy casualties on the enemy. It was largely to this officer's powers of leadership, courage and tenacity the task of the forward troop was so successfully carried out against heavy odds.' Jemadar Khan Sherin was awarded the Military Cross on 29TH August 1946.

Jemadar Mohammad, MC
14TH Punjab Regiment
Citation:
'On 3RD February 1944 at Milestone 26 Datweyauk Road when patrol with artillery OP his leading section ran into a Japanese bunker position and one man was killed and two wounded and the remainder of his patrol pinned down by snipers. Jemadar Mohammad steadied his men who had not been under fire before and personally took over the Bren gun at a critical stage. He maintained his position for four hours under continuous fire while the target was being registered. He later organised the withdrawal, got a dead body and wounded safely away. On the 9TH February when his Company attacked the Japanese position at Milestone 26, Jemadar Mohammad's platoon led the attack. Coming under heavy fire from LMG's and grenades from hitherto unsuspected bunker, he rallied his men, led his platoon throughout with great dash , and got into the Japanese trenches with only five unwounded men left. He maintained his position there for an hour under heavy grenade and LMG fire and only came out on orders to do so, the last man away from the position, last of all and alone. His dash and courage inspired the attackers to reach the enemy bunker and his splendid determination as a prime factor in their maintaining their position between two enemy bunkers during a most vital phase of the attack.' Jemadar Mohammad was awarded the Military Cross on 8TH February 1945.

Military Cross 1922-1947

Jemadar Khan Badshah, MC
14TH Punjab Regiment
Citation:
'On 11TH January 1945, Jemadar Khan Badshah was ordered to take out a special patrol to report whether the town of Alon in Burma, was clear of Japanese. Jemadar Khan Badshah took his patrol and worked it unseen into the middle of the town, and reported it clear and brought out his patrol on the evening of 12TH January 1945. On the evening of 15TH January 1945, he again volunteered to take a patrol behind the Japanese defended line of Monywa. He moved out by night and got his patrol right inside the Japanese outpost screen. From there he sent back most valuable information. During his patrol, he located two enemy held roadblocks; three other occupied positions, personally searched all villages in the area, and kept continuous watch on the road. He kept his patrol working throughout in spite of continual movement of Japanese parties in the vicinity, made daring reconnaissance and sent back most detailed and accurate report of Japanese dispositions and movements in the area. He brought back his patrol back intact on the fourth day. Jemadar Khan Badshah's skill and personal initiative in getting his patrol right upto and behind Japanese positions and maintaining continuous watch for period up to four days at a stretch has made a vital contribution to the reconnaissance of the Japanese dispositions round Monywa and has been an example of continued and calculated courage and determination.'

Remarks of the Brigade Commander:
Jemadar Khan Badshah was sent out on an extremely dangerous patrol mission. The information he gained, all of which has proved accurate, and all of which was of immense value in planning the Brigade assault on Monywa, could have been obtained by leadership, initiative and personal courage of the very high order. In remaining out, after knowing the added risk he was running from our artillery registration, which had started, he displayed a selfless devotion to duty and a determination, which merits the highest praise, and in view, he deserves richly the IOM which I have upgraded his CO's recommendation.
Jemadar Khan Badshah was recommended to receive the gallantry award of Indian Order of Merit but instead was awarded an immediate award of the Military Cross.

Military Cross 1922-1947

Subedar Kalandar Khan, MC
14TH Punjab Regiment
Citation:
'On 21ST May 1944, No. 4 Company commanded by Subedar Kalandar Khan was detailed to locate and drive out the Japanese party, which had over run the Mule Company in Bishenpur wood during the night before. While making his reconnaissance the Company Commander was killed. Subedar Kalandar Khan immediately took over, proceeded forward and having made his reconnaissance put an attack by the south flank. The attack was held up. Subedar Kalandar Khan therefore regrouped his Company and put in an attack by west of the road. This again was held up but Subedar Kalandar Khan, undaunted, continued attempts to get patrols forward for four hours until relieved by a British Officer. During that night, the enemy attempted, on several occasions to rush the position taken by his Company. Subedar Kalandar Khan throughout the night encouraged and steadied his men, who only a few days previously, suffered heavy casualties in action on two successive days, and beat back the enemy. Until his Company was relieved on 23^{RD,} he displayed magnificent courage and fortitude. His bold and determined attitude on the first day of the action in maintaining continues attacks and holding on all night allowed the enemy no freedom of movement and materially assisted in their being surrounded in their virtual annihilation on 24TH May. After the action, 125 Japanese bodies were counted on the field. On 24TH May No. 4 Company was ordered to clear the area to the village of Irengham. Subedar Kalandar Khan was in Command of the Company, which moved through the foothills supported by tanks from the road. As the Infantry approached Wainen, the leading elements reported enemy in ravines in the foothills. He immediately led the Company in a bayonet charge. This proved too much for the enemy who fled. Four dead were left in the nullah and eight more were killed by fire from the tanks. On 6TH July, No. 4 Company was detailed to attack and capture the Japanese held roadblock on the Silchar Track. After long and difficult approach march, the platoon reached a spot close to the objective. Under heavy sniping he led his platoon up on to a bluff overlooking the road, drove off the enemy, and consolidated with speed and skill. His dash virtually completed the task of opening the track to Youyangtak. Throughout these operations his Company has behaved with exemplary steadiness and fortitude. This has in the main been due to the spirit infused into them by the vitality of and the example set by Subedar Kalandar Khan.' Subedar Kalandar Khan was awarded the Military Cross on 28TH June 1945.

Military Cross 1922-1947

Major Khurshid Alam Khan, MC
15TH Punjab Regiment
Citation:

'Major Khurshid Alam Khan, Commander of the Sikh Company, assaulted and captured Point 121 a high feature near Singohnbyin, Arakan in January 1944. Throughout the operations, Major Khurshid Alam Khan displayed outstanding leadership and ability to command. His plans, which resulted in the capture of Point 121, a key point on the river, were an excellent example of his capabilities. His patrols having reported a portion of the hill unoccupied in the morning, he occupied this portion in the evening with a platoon and put in main attacks o the occupied feature. The attack here was very difficult owing to the precipitous slope and when the result appeared doubtful Major Khurshid Alam Khan ordered his flank platoon to the Sikh battle cry thereby distracting the defenders attention and enabling the main part of the Company to gain its objective. Besides this action Major Khurshid Alam Khan's initiative, control, and very sound tactical ability have been most outstanding.' Major Khurshid Alam Khan was awarded the Military Cross on 8TH February 1945.

Captain Mohammad Ahmad, MC
15TH Punjab Regiment
Citation:

'Captain Mohammad Ahmad handled his Company with admirable skill and coolness and displayed leadership of a very high order during the attack on North Top, a very high feature near Maunggyihtaung on 14TH December 1943. The enemy dispositions caused him to readjust his plan during the action, this he did and displayed initiative in re-appreciating the situation. His control throughout was noteworthy and the subsequent high morale of his Company was largely due to the excellent example set by the young Captain Mohammad Ahmad to his men during his first action under fire. Subsequently his Company position was attacked four nights in succession, again Captain Mohammad Ahmad displayed coolness in his handling of the situation and his behaviour throughout has been an inspiration to all ranks.' Captain Mohammad Ahmad was awarded an immediate Military Cross.

Military Cross 1922-1947

Lieutenant Syed Ghaffar Mehdi, MC
15TH Punjab Regiment
Citation:
'At Buthidaung, Burma on 2ND May 1943 Lieutenant Mehdi led a small recce patrol to find out if the enemy were in a certain nullah in Buthidaung area. He discovered abundant evidence of the enemy, and also to destroy an enemy signal cable. Not satisfied with this, he pushed further into the enemy position, until his scouts gave warning of the approach of the Japanese. Placing his men in an ambush Lieutenant Mehdi allowed the enemy scouts to pass through about 12 yards in front of him before opening fire at 10 yards range on the main body. He personally killed five of the enemy. In all seven were definitely killed. Lieutenant Mehdi was unable to bring back any identification, owing to the approach of a much larger body of Japanese. However, his blood soaked shoes amply testified to a daring act which was not only an inspiration to the men but also an example to his fellow officers.' Lieutenant Mehdi was awarded an immediate Military Cross. At independence in 1947, Lieutenant Mehdi opted to join the Pakistan Army and attained the rank of Lieutenant Colonel.

Subedar Safdar Ali, MC
15TH Punjab Regiment
Citation:
'On 27TH May 1945, 'D' Company 4/15 Punjab Regiment were ordered to cut the Japanese Line of Communication in the Zelon Bridgehead in Central Burma. During the operation Subedar Safdar Ali was given the task of bringing up ammunition and stores to the forward platoons. Whilst on his convoy was heavily attacked. A battle ensued for about 15 minutes, after which the Japanese fled leaving four dead. During the night, the Japanese started putting strong attacks on the company position, and the ammunition began to run short. Subedar Safdar Ali volunteered to go back for more ammunition. This time he was attacked more heavily and he once more counter attacked the enemy, and although three men were wounded, he carried on the fight until the Japanese ran away. The ammunition was brought up to the company and the personal bravery and sense of duty of Subedar Safdar Ali enabled the company to have enough ammunition to hold off all the fanatical attacks of the enemy. Apart from fighting his way through, he visited all the trenches throughout the night under very heavy fire to encourage the men. Throughout the action he set a magnificent example.' Subedar Safdar Ali was awarded an immediate Military Cross.

Military Cross 1922-1947

Subedar Ghulam Ullah Khan, MC
15TH Punjab Regiment
Citation:

'During the period under review 16TH November 1944 to 15TH February 1945, Subedar Ghulam Ullah Khan has consistently shown powers of leadership as second-in-command of 'C' Company. On 17TH January 1945, the enemy counter attacked in about one company strength. 'C' Company was holding Gin feature and the nullah on the right of the Brandy feature. The Company front was strongly attacked and the enemy supported by MMGs and mortars pushed to within 50 yards of the Company position, where he suffered considerable casualties and the enemy attempted to withdraw his force, but a party of them were cut off by our flanking fire. To wipe out this pocket, mortar and grenade fire was brought down, but without success. It was then that Subedar Ghulam Ullah Khan volunteered to lead a bayonet attack on the enemy. This attack of two sections by the Subedar shouting the Pathan battle cry completely routed the enemy who fled leaving his dead behind. The Subedar followed the attack up and many more enemies were wounded while escaping. Throughout Subedar Ghulam Ullah Khan showed leadership of a very high order and his fighting spirit and utter disregard for personal safety was example to the whole Company.' Subedar Ghulam Ullah Khan was awarded the Military Cross on 15TH November 1945.

Jemadar Lal Khan, MC
15TH Punjab Regiment
Citation:

'Jemadar Lal Khan was commanding a platoon which supported by tanks attacked a most strongly defended Japanese position in the north of Meiktila on 5TH March 1945. During the assault, Jemadar Lal Khan was wounded in the left arm and his platoon sustained one killed, eight wounded, including two section commanders. The assault was held up, so he got his wounded back and reorganised his sections. At the head of his platoon he led a second assault and after much bitter fighting secured firstly the outer line of bunkers and finally the objective itself. Throughout the action which lasted four hours, Jemadar Lal Khan showed outstanding leadership and total disregard of danger. Although bleeding profusely during this period he refused medical attention. His gallant conduct as an inspiration to his platoon, and was mainly responsible for the capture o a very strong enemy position at a time when the success of the operation appeared most doubtful.' Jemadar Lal Khan was awarded an immediate Military Cross.

Military Cross 1922-1947

Subedar Khan Zaman, MC
15TH Punjab Regiment
Citation:
'North of Mandalay on the night of 4/5 March 1945, Subedar Khan Zaman was commanding a platoon of C Company, was ordered to capture a key height in a mountain massif. It was a night operation over difficult country and opposition was encountered early in the advance, and the troops were subjected to heavy fire. Subedar Khan Zaman, however, with his coolness and courage dealt with the situation decisively and containing the enemy to his front, personally led an outflanking movement over very difficult jungle-covered mountain and led an assault on the Japanese from a surprise direction, routing them and inflicting many casualties. He then surprised another party of the Japanese who withdrew in haste leaving stores and equipment, and we captured the hill. Though he was badly wounded during the final charge, Subedar Khan Zaman refused to be evacuated and continued to direct the operations until he was assured of final success. His conspicuous leadership, quick thinking, and personal gallantry were responsible for the seizure of a key position necessary to the success of the operations and were and inspiration to his men. His courage and leadership have always been marked in previous actions.'
Subedar Khan Zaman was awarded an immediate Military Cross.

Subedar Mohammad Zaman, MC
15TH Punjab Regiment
Citation:
'During the period under review 16TH May to the cessation of hostilities n Burma, Subedar Mohammad Zaman of D Company 1/15 Punjab Regiment has consistently displayed great courage, sound decision and a tireless energy and determination despite his age and length of service. At times when younger men were tempted to flag, he was always an encouragement under arduous and dangerous circumstances. In action, he has always been to the fore and shown coolness and complete indifference to personal danger. In this, in his fighting spirits and his unfailing cheer fullness and ability to install cheerfulness into his men, no matter what the occasion of danger and fatigue, Subedar Mohammad Zaman has been a great factor in maintain the offensive spirit and morale of his Battalion. He has frequently commanded his Company when his Company Commander has been knocked out and has set a superb example throughout this campaign.'
Subedar Mohammad Zaman was awarded an immediate Military Cross.

Military Cross 1922-1947

Jemadar Anar Gul, MC
15TH Punjab Regiment
Citation:

On 17TH March 1945, at Myingyan in Central Burma the 4/15 Punjab Regiment and a squadron of tanks was ordered to break out of the area South of Myingyan across a nullah bounding to the area to the North and East and form a bridgehead across the nullah which was a natural tank obstacle, so that the armoured column could close with the enemy in Myingyan and elsewhere. Throughout the day, various efforts were made to find and force a crossing, all of which failed. As it was vital to find this bridgehead for armoured operations the following day, it was decided to try and force a direct crossing across the nullah, which was some 100 yards wide due North in Myingyan itself. The north bank of the nullah was known to be very strongly held by the enemy. B Company of the regiment was ordered to make the crossing. Owing to mines, the only possible tank crossing, it was only possible for the tanks to give support from the southern bank. After ten minutes of tank fire on the enemy position, the leading section of Jemadar Anar Gul's platoon raced across the nullah only to be brought to halt by hail of enemy fire. Jemadar Anar Gul without a moment's hesitation, with complete disregard for his own safety, doubled forward to the leading section accompanied by his orderly, led the section up the steep bank of the nullah under continues heavy fire, on to the objective, scattering the superior enemy force, and capturing a MMG. With the arrival of his two remaining sections, Jemadar Anar Gul energetically pushed the enemy back in spite of the loss of his three section commanders. His leadership so inspired what was left of platoon, that the bridgehead was quickly enlarged to take the rest of the Company. By this time, it was dark, but with tremendous drive and vigour under fire, Jemadar Anar Gul fully wire and consolidated his part of the perimeter. Throughout the night Jemadar Anar Gul was continually moving about his position under heavy small arms and grenade discharger fire encouraging and directing the fire of his men. Two heavy counter-attacks were repulsed. It is safe to say that the courage, the inspiring leadership and determination of Jemadar Anar Gul was directly responsible for the seizing of a tank able crossing, which allowed the armoured forces to close with the enemy, the following day to clear Myingyan and the surrounding country of the Japanese. Jemadar Anar Gul was awarded the Military Cross on 2ND August 1945.

Military Cross 1922-1947

Jemadar Banaris Khan, MC
15TH Punjab Regiment
Citation:
'On 11TH May 1944, 4/5 Punjab Regiment were ordered to attack a feature Lis in the Kohima Area in Burma, Two companies put in the attack but were only partially successful owing to heavy opposition from a bunker on the far crest. Jemadar Banaris Khan went forward round a flank with a party from the reserve company and located the bunker. He crawled forward to a position within 10 yards of the bunker with only a Bren gunner and directed the fire of the Bren gunner on to the bunker and on to snipers who were covering the bunker. Several Japanese were killed and during this period Jemadar Banaris Khan was under constant heavy fire from the bunker and the snipers. Several men of his party were wounded behind him and not until they had all been pulled away would leave his position. The same afternoon Jemadar Banaris Khan went forward to the same position with an MMG Section and again directed fire on the enemy. This time heavy casualties were inflicted on the party and again he insisted in remaining behind until all possible casualties had been evacuated. The same evening he went as protection party of Sappers and was sent to clear mines of the road in front of the tanks, which were vital for assisting in the Brigade operations. The protection party under Jemadar Banaris Khan inflicted more casualties on the Japanese and ensured complete protection for the mine clearing party, who cleared the minefields and enabled the tanks to move forward. The tanks having freed from the minefield ensured complete success for the Brigade operations. Throughout these actions Jemadar Banaris Khan showed initiative, devotion to duty and complete disregard for his own safety and set an admirable example to all ranks.' Jemadar Banaris Khan was awarded the Military Cross on 31ST August 1944.

Jemadar Gul Rang Khan, MC
15TH Punjab Regiment
Citation:
'On 9TH April 1945, Jemadar Gul Rang Khan was commanding a platoon and was ordered to secure the bridgehead on the river Senio in Italy. While advancing they came under attack from both banks and suffered casualties. Only five men reached the objective. He assisted the five men in dealing with several enemy posts on the banks of the river, and chased some Germans away with grenades. Throughout this critical stage of the operation displayed highest standard of personal courage.' Jemadar Gul Rang Khan was awarded an immediate Military Cross.

Military Cross 1922-1947

Jemadar Anar Gul, (Bar to MC)
Citation:
'On 28TH March 1945, 4/15 Punjab Regiment and a squadron of
was employed on the task of clearing Natogi-Taunthar road, an(
Company had the protection of Battalion Headquarters, and a long N
Transport Column. As the column reached a consolidated area north (
village Legaing, the advance section of the forward platoon rep
enemy movement west of the road. Jemadar Anar Gul who
commanding the forward platoon made a quick recce and disco
platoon strength of enemy occupying trenches covering the
Realising the danger to the long Motor Transport Column close to
position and that quick action was imperative, Jemadar Anar Gul de(
to make full use of the element of surprise and before the enemy coul
fully prepared put in a very bold platoon attack in the enemy positio
leading the attack. Seeing the Jemadar leading the charge, the w
platoon fell on the enemy with full weight, killing 16 Japanese and for
the rest to flee in great disorder across the road. They were mopped u
other platoon in position there. While Jemadar Anar Gul was clearin
the enemy, trenches one by one an enemy 105 mm gun opened
shelling the road where the long Motor Transport Column was halted.
gun was firing from a very close range and over open sights. Jem;
Anar Gul with only two men, as the rest of the platoon was still dea
with the fleeing Japanese, dashed forward, and located the gun in a s
nullah 100 yards away from the enemy position. Realising the g
danger to the Motor Transport Column from this gun, Jemadar Anar
with complete disregard of his personal safety charged the gun and kil
the gun crew of two while they were still engaged in firing the g
Throughout this action Jemadar Anar Gul showed outstanding cour;
and power of command. His quick fearless action and inspired leaders
resulted in the destruction of an enemy gun and 16 Japanese and th
removed a real danger to a long vulnerable Motor Transport Colum
Jemadar Anar Gul was awarded Bar to the Military Cross on 3RD Ap
1945.

Military Cross 1922-1947

Jemadar Rakhmat Ullah, MC
15TH Punjab Regiment
Citation:
'During the period under review 16TH November 1944 to 15TH February 1945, Jemadar Rakhmat Ullah has consistently shown powers of leadership as second-in – command of 'C' Company. On 17TH January 1945, the enemy counter attacked in about one company strength. 'C' Company was holding Gin feature and the nullah on the right of Brandy feature, supported by MMGs and mortars pushed to within 50 yards of the Company positions, where he suffered considerable casualties and attempted to withdraw his force, but a party of them was cut off by our flanking fire. To wipe out this pocket, mortar and grenade fire was brought down, but without success. It was then that Jemadar Rakhmat Ullah who had all along been walking around the Company positions, volunteered to lead a bayonet attack on the enemy position. This attack of two sections led by the Subedar shouting his Pathan battle cry completely routed the enemy who fled leaving his dead behind. The Subedar followed the attack up and many more enemies were wounded in escaping. Throughout Jemadar Rakhmat Ullah showed leadership of very high order and his fighting spirit and utter disregard for personal safety were example to the whole Company.' Jemadar Rakhmat Ullah was awarded the Military Cross 15TH November 1945.

Subedar Lal Khan, MC
15TH Punjab Regiment
Citation:
On 27TH May 1945, 'D' Company 4/15 Punjab Regimen was ordered to advance and cut the main track used by the Japanese withdrawal from the Zalon Bridgehead in Central Burma. Subedar Lal Khan's platoon was given the task of capturing a hill feature overlooking the track and denying it to the enemy until remainder of the Company arrived. Whilst approaching the hill his platoon came under heavy LMG and rifle fire. Without stopping the advance, he put one section in position with 2" mortar, and leading the other two shouted 'Charge', and dashed up the hill; the enemy position was assaulted and all the Japanese in the enemy position killed. Subedar Lal Khan himself accounted for four. After capturing his objective, he was placing his platoon in position when about 40 Japanese put in a determined counter attack. Taking up a position on the perimeter, the attack was repulsed, and many casualties inflicted on the enemy. The remainder of the Company then arrived and whilst there was digging in, the Japanese started attacking in large numbers.

Military Cross 1922-1947

Subedar Lal Khan (Cont)
Citation:
'They attacked the Company position seven times. Four of these attacks were directed against Subedar Lal Khan's platoon. At one time the Japanese got into his trenches. At this time Subedar Lal Khan took his platoon forward shouting 'Charge', and went into attack. After hand-to-hand fighting, during which Subedar Lal Khan encouraged the remainder of his men with shouts, and the entire enemy were killed or driven off. Throughout these attacks, Subedar Lal Khan showed absolutely no regard for his personal safety; it was mainly due to his gallantry and leadership that his platoon was able to hold their ground and beat off all the attacks.'
Subedar Lal Khan was awarded an immediate Military Cross.

Captain Ishaq Mohammad, MC
16TH Punjab Regiment
Citation:
'Captain Ishaq Mohammad commanded his Company detachment at Mizawa in Burma. Fighting started at 0800 hours on 7TH March 1944. During the period 7TH to 11TH March 1944, he beat off three determined Japanese attacks inflicting total of 40 casualties seen killed. Short of ammunition and rations, he withdrew with all arms and equipment on 11TH March 1944, having sustained a total of five casualties. Of his personal bravery his VCOs says, 'Ishaq Sahib was everywhere- we told him not to expose himself unnecessary as we could hang on all right but he was always around not worrying about his personal safety.'
Captain Ishaq Mohammad had been specially selected to Command this Company two months previously as the general state was unsatisfactory. He has shown outstanding leadership, highest sense of devotion to duty, which he instilled in his Company in a short time. His personal bravery and self-sacrifice, remarked by his VCOs are of the highest order.'
Captain Ishaq Mohammad was recommended for the award of DSO but was awarded an immediate Military Cross.
At the time of independence in 1947 Ishaq Mohammand opted to join the Pakistan Army and attained the rank of Lieutenant Colonel. However he was involved in the military coup attempt against the government and consequently he arrested by the authorities. He was sentenced to four years rigorous imprisonment and cashiered from the Army.

Military Cross 1922-1947

Lieutenant Ifthikar Ahmad Chaudri, MC
16TH Punjab Regiment
Citation:
'During the early hours on 26TH January 1944, three platoons were pushed out from the forward companies of the Battalion position south of Arielle in Italy to ascertain the depth and location of the enemy positions and if possible to gain identifications. At the first light Lieutenant Chaudri as Battalion Intelligence Officer went to the left forward company and on arriving there discovered that the officer and VCO who had taken the platoon out from this sector were missing and believed to be Prisoner of War. Unhesitatingly Lieutenant Chaudri decided to go forward to the platoon locality, especially as the most recent information showed that the platoon's position had become critical in the face of unexpectedly strong enemy position. Moving through the morning rain, across the FDLs in the face of well-concentrated enemy mortar fire, he arrived at the platoon to find the situation desperate with ammunition running low. He at once reorganised the position and carefully detailed the future expenditure of the remaining ammunition. At this stage an enemy counter attack developed and a Bren gunner was badly wounded. Lieutenant Chaudri immediately took over the gun and cheerfully encouraging the men around him, ordered fire to be held until the advancing enemy were within forty yards, when fire was opened. Lieutenant Chaudri himself killed or mortally wounded at least three Germans and the remainder were forced to go to the ground. The attack was held and Lieutenant Chaudri buoyed up the morale of his men by cheering encouragement despite the fact that the position was under accurate machine gun and mortar fire. The withdrawal of the platoon was ordered from Brigade HQ, under a smokescreen, and this Lieutenant Chaudri successfully carried out without further loss also safely evacuated seven wounded men. By his initiative and daring Lieutenant Chaudri was able to avoid a situation that was becoming critical, and also brings back very useful and detailed information regarding the enemy positions. By his doggedness and cool calculation, he was able to maintain the platoons position for over four hours and provide protection and prevented localities on his right from being encircled. His conduct throughout was highly exemplary and fully in keeping with the tradition of Indian fighting men.' Lieutenant Chaudri was immediately awarded the military Cross. Lieutenant Chaudri opted to join the Pakistan Army and had an illustrious career attain the rank Lieutenant Colonel and served the Pakistan government in many different diplomatic posts. Lieutenant Colonel Chaudri passed away in 2ND June 2015.

Military Cross 1922-1947

Lieutenant Ajaib Khan, MC
16TH Punjab Regiment
Citation:

'On 28TH April 1944, Lieutenant Ajaib Khan was directed to raid Shongphel village Burma, which was suspected as Japanese HQ. Leading his Company with great dash and courage he drove the Japanese force out of the village capturing a 3" mortar, a discharger cup and 2.2" mortars. While directing the further advance of his Company with cool disregard of the enemies cup grenade. The steel dash and courage displayed by this officer animated his whole Company and were responsible for the success of this raid.' Lieutenant Ajaib Khan was awarded the Military Cross on 16TH November 1944.

Lieutenant Mohammad Zarif Khan, MC
16TH Punjab Regiment
Citation:

'This young officer led with great gallantry his Company in a bayonet charge, which dislodged the Japanese from a hill feature overlooking the ledge position on the Pattani Road in Thailand on 10TH December 1941. For this action, this enabled the Battalion to check the Japanese advance for further two days, Lt. Col. Moorhead recommends an immediate award of Military Cross. Lieutenant Mohammad Zarif Khan continued to command his Company of Musalmans with determination and skill until he was badly wounded in the face during the Singapore fighting on 11TH February 1942. He has believed to have been killed but actually stayed in the jungle for over a fortnight, assisting a wounded Sepoy who was unable to move more than few yards per day.' Lieutenant Mohammad Zarif Khan was awarded the Military Cross on 19TH December 1946. Mohammad Zarif Khan opted to join the Pakistan Army in 1947 and eventually attained the rank of Lieutenant Colonel.

Military Cross 1922-1947

Subedar Sultan Ahmed Bahadur, MC
16TH Punjab Regiment
Citation:
'Subedar Sultan Ahmed Bahadur 4/16 Punjab Regiment, who is 50 years of age, has total service of 34 years in the Army. He served in France and Palestine in the last war. In September 1940, he proceeded overseas with his unit and served in Sudan, Eritrea, and the Western Desert Campaigns. He was captured near Benghazi on 20TH January 1942, with many others o his Battalion, including the CO. He was sent to Tarhuna and in March 1942 to Bari in Italy. Afterwards he was sent to various camps in Italy, finishing up at Avezzano in August 1943. Subedar Sultan Ahmed had always had the thought of escape in mind, and when the Germans took over this camp in 19TH September 1943, he gave serious consideration to the possibility of escape, particularly as it became known that all the prisoners in this camp were to be transferred to Germany. On 18TH September 1943, the first party of POW for transfer to Germany was taken down the railway station. This party consisted of approximately 163 VCOs and 1,000 IORs, including Subedar Sultan Ahmed. They entrained and this escaper found himself sitting in a goods wagon. When the train was being shunted, he and another POW jumped out and ran towards a house close by where they hid until dark. They left the house and walked throughout the night until they reached Collelongo. They lay here for about a fortnight, hiding in the mountains by day coming down the village at night, where they obtained food from the villages. About, 10TH October 1943, after a fortnight in hiding and under the most uncomfortable conditions, they lay up here for about a fortnight, hiding where they accompanied to Gusano Mutri, where they reported to the American forces. Subedar Sultan Ahmed was in enemy hands for one year and eight months. A man of his age might be excused, after this long period of impoundment if the will to escape ceased to exist. But evidence of escape was ever present, and it is very highly to his credit that he took the first available opportunity of putting it to test. Bearing mind his age, his many years of service coupled with the determination and courage shown by him in effecting his escape, it is therefore recommended that he be awarded the Military Cross'. Subedar Sultan Ahmed awarded the Military Cross on 14TH September 1944.

Military Cross 1922-1947

Subedar Bahadur Khan, MC
16TH Punjab Regiment
Citation:

'Throughout the operation s in Burma-Arakan from December 1943 to April 1945 Subedar Bahadur Khan has always been in the thick of the fighting as Company 2 i/c and Platoon Commander. On two occasions he has been recommended for an immediate Military Cross but has received no recognition. On the first occasion on 16TH January 1945, he commanded a patrol to Kyeyebyin village for contacting an enemy platoon. By his good leadership and skilful manoeuvring he drove them back causing heavy casualties. His platoon suffered no casualties. On the night 19/20 January 1945, his platoon was in position in Kyeyebyin, This officer was repeated attacked by an enemy company and was continuously under MMG, mortar and 75 mm fire. With total disregard for his own safety and twice narrowly missing death, he encouraged his platoon and by his courage inspired them to outstanding deeds of gallantry. The enemy company suffered heavy casualties and withdrew. On the second occasion in the Tamandu Area on 9TH March 1945, Subedar Bahadur Khan was ordered to take a fighting patrol to a hill feature occupied by the enemy. In spite of heavy shelling and fire, he coolly manoeuvred his platoon to 37 mm gun which was subsequently liquidated. His offensive spirit, example and devotion to duty were astounding. He was always in the forefront of any action. Throughout his courage and leadership, his devotion to duty and personal example had been an inspiration to all under his command. I strongly recommend him for the award of the Military Cross for his invaluable services to his Battalion.' Consequently Subedar Bahadur Khan was awarded the Military Cross.

Jemadar Akbar Ali, MC
16TH Punjab Regiment
Citation:

'On 19TH April 1944 in the Ukhrul area in Burma, Jemadar Akbar Ali was in command of a platoon ordered to carry out a raid on a Japanese position. Jemadar Akbar Ali led his platoon into the middle of the position, taking the enemy by surprise his platoon killed twelve and inflicted many more casualties. The enemy attempted to counter attack but were driven off, and Jemadar Akbar Ali successfully withdrew his platoon. The enemy suffered such casualties that they were unable to continue. During this action Jemadar Akbar Ali at the head of his platoon and by his personal courage was responsible for the success of the raid.' Jemadar Akbar Ali was awarded an immediate Military Cross.

Military Cross 1922-1947

Subedar Major Noor Khan, MC
16TH Punjab Regiment
Citation:
During the whole period between 11TH February and 25TH March 1944, Subedar Major Noor Khan was responsible for getting forward the supply of ammunition, rations, water, and stores from B-Echelon to the Battalion, which was operating in the hills North of North West of Cassino in Italy. On the night 12/13 February, the Battalion moved forward from its forward concentration area into the hills with 160 mules loaded with ammunition and equipment. At this critical time, the enemy brought heavy artillery fire on to the area. In the darkness, many of the mules scattered and others became casualties, only 40 remained under control and unhurt. The Subedar Major immediately took control and organise parties to reassemble the mules. Although the shelling continued the mules were collected and the Battalion was able to complete taking over its positions. Therefore it was his responsibility the supply by mule and jeep of the Battalion. The routes to the forward companies was steep and difficult and after rain and snow slippery with ice. Enemy harassing fire throughout the area was heavy and the physical exhaustion of the men and animals considerable, nevertheless inspired by Noor Khan's determination, courage and endurance, supplies reached forward troops every night. It was also necessary for him to cross the Rapido frequently both by day and night. The enemy had full observation of this crossing and frequently shelled it but this never deterred him from his duties. His jeep received a direct hit from a shell on one occasion and he was wounded in the shoulder. In spite of this he refused to be evacuated and continued to work without giving any indication of the pain he was suffering. Subedar Major Noor Khan insisted on making frequent visits to the forward positions and his constant cheerfulness and complete disregard of enemy shelling had most encouraging and steadying effect on the men. He toured positions where casualties were being suffered and his example and experienced advice were of the greatest assistance to the officers and VCOs of the Battalion. He showed exceptional powers of organisation and leadership as well personal courage of a high order and earned the admiration of all who came into contact with him.' Subedar Major Noor Khan was immediately awarded the Military Cross.

Military Cross 1922-1947

Subedar Sher Mohammad, MC
16TH Punjab Regiment
Citation:

The Battalion took over the right forward sector of the Brigade south of Arielle in Italy, on the night of 11/12 April 1944. Subedar Sher Mohammad commanded a platoon in the left forward company of the area situated I a salient flanking the Carloni feature to the south. Shortly after the takeover was complete, the enemy commenced to concentrate the fire of a heavy gun on Jock's House, a foremost locality, occupied only by night, in which Subedar Sher Mohammad was in position with his HQ and one section. Desultory fire continued during which the house received several direct hits. Towards the end of this period, the enemy increased the rate of its fire. The roof of the house was completely destroyed and three men who were on top storey were killed and buried in the debris. Subedar Sher Mohammad was pinned to the ground by a falling beam. Having extracted himself with difficulty Subedar Sher Mohammad ordered five of his remaining men to occupy the trenches outside while he would hold the house with three others; their only weapon was a Tommy gun and few grenades. At this juncture, the enemy attack developed and those who had been ordered to vacate the house were virtually surrounded. The enemy attacked in determined fashion, shouting as they came. The Subedar and his three men at the crucial moment fired a short burst from the Tommy gun and hurled grenades. The enemy was forced to withdraw to a stone-wall some hundred yards away. Subedar Sher Mohammad in the pitch darkness then commenced a search for the post telephone, which he succeeded in unearthing from the rubble. It was still in working order and the VCO was able to direct mortar fire on to the enemy who were again preparing to take the house. During this time Subedar Sher Mohammad was wounded in the leg and though now severally wounded and by concussion, he was able to hold on till just before dawn when he was ordered to withdraw and successfully evacuating the wounded with him. By Subedar Sher Mohammad outstanding conduct, the Battalion was able to retain its hold on a key position n the Brigade sector, as without the possession of Jock's house the salient would become untenable. This alone was due to Subedar Sher Mohammad's tenacity and leadership.' Subedar Sher Mohammad was awarded an immediate Military Cross.

Military Cross 1922-1947

Subedar Ghulam Rasul, MC
16TH Punjab Regiment
Citation:
'Subedar Ghulam Rasul commanded a Company during the operation leading to the capture of Libyan Omar from 22ND November to 1ST December 1941. The position was very strongly entrenched and the four attacks launched against it, he led his Company under extremely heavy MG and mortar fire, and inflicted severe punishment on the enemy. On the night of 24/25 November by his coolness and resourcefulness his Company stopped an enemy counter attack round his left flank which had it had been successful would have seriously undermined the position of the Battalion.' Subedar Ghulam Rasul was awarded an immediate Military Cross. At the Pakistan independence in 1947, Ghulam Rasul opted to join the Pakistan Army and attained the rank of Major and participated in the India-Pakistan war of 1947-48.

Jemadar Mohammad Hussain, MC
16TH Punjab Regiment
Citation;
'On 6TH June 1944, the Japanese heavily shelled the position held by Jemadar Mohammad Hussain's Company in Imphal area of Burma. The left flank platoon of the Company suffered 50 percent casualties and the position was destroyed. The Company Commander being wounded and the HQ knocked out. Jemadar Mohammad Hussain took over the command of the Company and reorganised the position. As a result when the Japanese attack came in it was replied with heavy loss. The great courage and leadership displayed by Jemadar Mohammad Hussain was responsible for the holding of the position at very critical time.' Jemadar Mohammad Hussain was awarded the Military Cross on 5TH October 1944.

Jemadar Atta Mohammad, MC
16TH Punjab Regiment
Citation:
Jemadar Atta Mohammad was the Intelligence officer and the Company Second- in- Commander. He was the only VCO of the Battalion to come through the whole campaign in Malaya. At Rengat when his platoon was cut off by the enemy, he hung on until the section was wiped out. He then organised the withdrawal back of the remnants complete with their arms. Eventually he was taken prisoner by the Japanese and on his release from captivity he was awarded the Military Cross on 19TH December 1946.

Military Cross 1922-1947

Jemadar Mohammad Shafayat Khan, MC
The Bihar Regiment
Citation:
'On 5TH March and again on 23RD March Jemadar Mohammad Shafayat Khan, was commanding his platoon in raids on Japanese prepared positions, west of Haka in Burma. Both these raids involved long approaches through a Booby-trapped area. Both raids were successful in causing heavy casualties to the enemy, largely due to the coolness and personal example of Jemadar Mohammad Shafayat Khan.' Jemadar Mohammad Shafayat Khan was awarded the Military Cross for his conspicuous gallantry in Burma.

Lieutenant Saiyed Anwar Hasan Rizvi, MC
The Bihar Regiment
Citation:
'On 16TH October 1944, Lieutenant Rizvi when leading a patrol of four sections came across signs of recent evacuation of Pioneer camp in Burma. He saw about 150 Japanese and INA, including three officers in the area about 150 yards away. Disregarding the numerical superiority of the enemy and at considerable risk to himself and his men he advanced within 50 yards, opened fire on the enemy, and took them completely by surprise causing nine casualties. By his cool and determined action in the face of great danger, he was great inspiration to his men.' Lieutenant Saiyed Anwar Hasan Rizvi was awarded an immediate Military Cross. At the time of the independence in 1947 Lieutenant Saiyed Anwar Hasan Rizvi opted to stay with the Indian Army, and eventually attained the rank of Brigadier.

Subedar Illahi Baksh, MC
Indian Pioneer Corps
Subedar Illahi Baksh was awarded the Military Cross in Italy for continuous devotion to duty, acting as Detachment Commander and for inspiring leadership and cheerfulness with his men, getting the maximum amount of work from them under shelling and dive bombing.

Subedar Mauz Ali Shah, MC
Indian Pioneer Corps
Subedar Mauz Ali Shah was awarded the Military Cross in Italy for continuous devotion to duty, acting as Detachment Commander and for inspiring leadership and cheerfulness with his men, getting the maximum amount of work from them under shelling and dive bombing.

Military Cross 1922-1947

Jemadar Saddiq Ahmed, MC
Indian Army Service Corps
Citation:
'Jemadar Saddiq Ahmed having proceeded on active service to France, during December 1939, was later attached to Animal Transport Company, RIASC; this unit was forced to surrender o 24TH June 1940. He remained in captivity until March 1943. On 23RD February he was with other of his countrymen, being sent to Bayonne from prison camp in Germany. Before leaving Germany, Jemadar Saddiq Ahmed determined to take the next available opportunity to escape. The President of the Camp's Escape Committee provided him with French money and advice. Risaldar Abdullah Khan and Jemadar Rattan Singh agreed to attempt to escape with him. In March 1943, the train transporting the POW stopped at a small station called Ste Marie; the guards were then asleep. As the train pulled out, they jumped off, and ran away unseen. Principally owing to the ability Jemadar Saddiq Ahmed to speak French, they were able to obtain food from farms and local inhabitants, and pass themselves as Algerians. Despite the ad verse and trying conditions, they managed to successfully to travel on foot, train, and bus to a town called Esterase near the Spanish Frontier, where they had been advised to contact a certain guide to take them into Spain. Unfortunately the guide was away and the house under German suspicion. They therefore decided to attempt the journey unaided except or a Shell Co. Tourist Map, and go in the direction of Andorra State. This was on 12TH March. Owing to the German garrisons in the Frontier towns, it necessitated to cover most of the journey using hill paths. The weather was extremely cold they found it difficult to obtain food, living for three days on two potatoes each. To add to their misfortune, Risaldar Abdullah Khan's feet became ulcerated and frostbitten. After a trek lasting some ten days they eventually reached Escalades in Andorra, where the proprietress of the local hotel gave them food and accommodation. She also paid services of a doctor to attend to Risaldar Khan's feet and arranged with HBM Council General in Barcelona for their transfer to that city. Risaldar Khan was sent to the hospital to Barcelona. He later followed Jemadar Saddiq Ahmed and Jemadar Rattan Singh who had returned to India via Madrid, Gibraltar and Cairo. Jemadar Saddiq Ahmed's initiative and conduct under most trying conditions and his ability as the leader of the party through territories foreign to his nature are worthy of high praise and recognition and I therefore recommend that he should be awarded the Military Cross'.
Jemadar Saddiq Ahmed was awarded an immediate Military Cross.

Military Cross 1922-1947

Risaldar Ghulam Hussain, MC
Indian Army Service Corps
Citation:
'During the whole of the Arakan Campaign in Burma, 1943/44 this unit has been continuously on active service. Furthermore from the 4TH February 1944 this unit with 114 Indian Infantry Brigade was isolated by enemy action of the Kalapanzin in Kawazan area. During this period, Risaldar Ghulam Hussain's personal example to all ranks did much to keep moral at the highest when the situation was tense. He spared himself not at all despite being ill and in great pain due to severe colic caused stones in the kidney. His bearing throughout this very trying period was exemplary in every way. Again in March 1944, when this unit was manning the Brigade defence perimeter on Kawazan ridge, an attack was put in during the night of 7/8. The unit area was heavily machine-gunned and mortared the Second in Command being killed and several IOR's killed or wounded. Risaldar Ghulam Hussain showed conspicuous gallantry regardless of personal danger. He checked all defences under fire, rallied, and heartened his men; he was seen on several occasions moving about under heavy fire regardless of his personal safety until ordered by me to take cover. By his fine example the situation was kept well in hand. During the whole period, covering operations in Arakan the example of this officer has consistently been of the highest order.'
Risaldar Ghulam Hussain was awarded an immediate Military Cross.

Lieutenant Ata Mohammad, MC
The Sikh Light Infantry
Citation:
'On 7TH April 1945 Lieutenant Ata Mohammad was commanding the Battalion's Defence platoon in the attack on Thabyebin in the Yindaw area of Central Burma. This was his first command in action. He was the very spirit of aggressiveness throughout, leading his men through heavy fire, always in the lead, directing his sections, leading charges, and assisting the wounded. So well and with such determination did this young officer lead his men that his platoon gained its final objective killing 53 Japanese, in doing so and capturing three LMG's and two grenade dischargers through suffering twelve casualties themselves. Three days later, Lieutenant Ata Mohammad now commanding a Company after an advance march of 11 miles was ordered to capture Point 790 overlooking Hminlodaung, the Battalion's final objective, this he did with little trouble but immediately came under heavy fire from two 75 mm guns.

Military Cross 1922-1947

Lieutenant Ata Mohammad (Cont)
Citation:
'Quite undismayed Lieutenant Ata Mohammad carried on with his consolidation walking round his platoon in full view of the enemy and urging his men to hold on, as his position was the key to the attack. It was impossible to get food and water up but Lieutenant Ata Mohammad carried on. His men stayed there with him all night and all next day until the objective was captured. They had been without food for 36 hours without water for 18 hours when finally relieved, had walked 11 miles to their position, and were under consistent and accurate fire from the enemy the whole time. Throughout this very trying time the young officer was soul of the defence, cheering his tired and thirsty men and succouring his many wounded, making light of difficulties, fatigue alike, and proving himself a real leader. There is little doubt that this young officer's tenacity, bravery, and cheerful demeanour were the driving force that held the position and made the attack on Hminlodaung possible. He acted throughout with the greatest determination and courage in the finest tradition of an officer of the Indian Army.' Lieutenant Ata Mohammad was awarded an immediate Military Cross.

Indian States Forces

Jemadar Mohammad Jan, MC
Bhopal Infantry
The regiment could trace its origins to 1818, when it was raised at Sehore, as a mixed force of infantry and cavalry by the State of Bhopal for service with the British. It was known as the Bhopal Contingent and was employed to keep peace in the lawless regions of Central India. In 1878, the battalion participated in the Second Afghan War. During the First World War, the 9th Bhopal Infantry was dispatched to France in 1914. The regiment suffered heavy losses at the Battles of Neuve Chapelle, Festubert, Givenchy and the Second Ypres. In 1915, they arrived in Mesopotamia, where they were engaged in fierce fighting on the Tigris Front. During the Second World War Jemadar Mohammad Jan was awarded the Military Cross on 18TH October 1945 while maintaining the Lines of Communication duties in the South East Asia Command. In 1947, it was allocated to Pakistan Army. In 1948, the battalion fought in the war with India in Kashmir, while during the 1965 and 1971 Indo-Pakistan Wars, it again fought with great gallantry at Lahore, where Major Raja Aziz Bhatti was awarded the Nishan-i-Haider, Pakistan's highest gallantry award in 1965.

Military Cross 1922-1947

Indian States Forces

Major Hussain Khan, MC
Kashmir Infantry
Citation:
'Throughout the period under review the superb gallantry, devotion to duty, outstanding leadership, and inflexible determination of Major Hussain Khan has been an inspiration to all ranks. On 6TH November 1944, when the attacking company temporarily lost touch with the Battalion HQ, Major Hussain Khan, then the adjutant volunteered to cross the Japanese bullet swept area to regain touch. This he did with complete disregard for his personal safety. By this action, he was materially responsible for the capture of a vital hill feature, which was in enemy hands. During the night 22/23 March 1945, in Meiktila area, it was entirely to his indomitable spirit, untiring effort and personal example that a series of determined Japanese counter attacks were beaten off by his Company with very heavy loss to the enemy. He showed similar bravery again during night 24/25 March 1945, when his Company was attacked by an enemy tank. During the night 16/17 April 1945, at Magyiban area on Mandalay-Rangoon road, he managed to dislodge Japanese who he penetrated the position and applied first aid to his 2 i/c who was wounded while both were crawling from post to post to encourage their men. Throughout the period, Major Hussain Khan with complete disregard of his own safety gave an example of coolness and leadership of the highest order'. Major Hussain Khan was awarded the Military Cross on 6TH June 1946.

Major Hussain Khan opted to join the Pakistan Army in 1947. Many serving cadres were part of the Lashkars that Pakistan raised for war with India in 1947.48, Major Hussain Khan was one such man. He commanded the Northern Area Sector from 31ST October 1947 to 30TH November 1947. He was awarded the Pakistan Army's award of Fakhr-i-Kashmir is equivalent to Hilal-i-Jurat of the Pakistan regular army. He was arrested for being conspirator in the Rawalpindi Conspiracy case on 15TH May 1951.Major Hussain Khan was sentenced to four years rigours imprisonment in addition he was ordered to be cashiered from the Pakistan Army.

Military Cross 1922-1947

Indian States Forces

Major Mohammad Aslam Khan, MC
Kashmir Infantry
Citation:
'On 4TH to 6TH November 1944, in the Fort White area Major Mohammad Aslam Khan was commanding his Company in an attack on a thickly wooded feature, which was strongly held by the Japanese bunker positions. On the afternoon of 4TH November, with little time for recce he led his Company into the attack and captured a number of bunkers on the north slopes of the hill. He consolidated there as light was failing. Three times during the night his Company was counter attacked but owing to Major Mohammad Aslam Khan's example and determination all were beaten off. On 5TH November Major Mohammad Aslam Khan led his Company forward to 200 yards from the top of the hill and was preparing to charge when he received orders to retire to allow an air strike to go in. He was again heavily counter attacked during the night and again beat off all enemies. On 6TH November Major Mohammad Aslam Khan again led his Company to attack the hill, this time after hand to hand fighting near the crest the attack was successful. Major Mohammad Aslam Khan's example to his men and his powers of command and leadership was responsible for his Company's success on this heavily defended feature the capture of which cleared the way to Fort White'. Major Mohammad Aslam Khan was awarded an immediate Military Cross.

Jemadar Mohammad Nawaz Khan, MC
Kashmir Infantry
Citation:
On 4 to 6 November 1944, in the Fort White Area Jemadar Mohammad Nawaz Khan was commanding the leading Platoon of the Company attacking a thickly wooded hill, which was defended by Japanese bunker positions. On 4TH November he led his platoon up-close to the enemy LMG positions. He was allowed to withdraw to allow artillery concentration and an air strike to be put down on the enemy positions, not one of his sections was pinned down by the Japanese LMG firing from a concealed position. Jemadar Mohammad Nawaz Khan crawled forward through the jungle until he located the LMG and then threw grenades into the bunker until the post was wiped out. After this he successfully withdrew his section. During the night of 4/5 November he was the only VCO remaining in the Company and acted as 2 i/c of the Company, which was heavily counter attacked three times.

Military Cross 1922-1947

Indian States Forces

Jemadar Mohammad Nawaz Khan, MC (Cont)
Citation:
'Regardless of the enemy fire, he moved from platoon to platoon throughout the night encouraging his men. On 5 and 6 November, he again commanded the leading platoon in the attack on this hill feature, which eventually proved successful. By his outstanding courage and initiative, Jemadar Mohammad Nawaz Khan saved the lives of the men in one of his sections and later actions were a deciding factor in the capture of this vital hill'. Jemadar Mohammad Nawaz Khan was awarded the Military Cross on 22ND March 1945.

Jemadar Mohammad Nawaz Khan along with other Muslim elements of the Kashmir Infantry went over to the Pakistan Army in 1947. He was granted commission in the Pakistan Army, and attained the rank of Major. He commanded 18TH Azad Kashmir Battalion during the India-Pakistan war of 1948 and was awarded Mujahid-i-Hydri, which is equalent to Sitara-i-Jurat the third highest gallantry award of the Pakistan Army.

British Army 1914-1921

Jemadar Imam Din Khan, MC
Royal Garrison Artillery
Citation:
'Jemadar Imam Din Khan was awarded the Military Cross on 23RD December 1916, for conspicuous gallantry and devotion to duty. On two occasions he displayed great coolness and courage under heavy fire in Mahabat, Egypt. He has at all times set a fine example to his men'.

Subedar Alim Sher, MC
Royal Garrison Artillery
Citation:
No details about the gallant deed, He was awarded the Military Cross on 3RD June 1918 for gallantry in Egypt.

Military Cross 1922-1947

Burma Army

Jemadar Mohammad Hussain, MC
The Burma Regiment
Citation:
'During the initial attack by the Battalion on the 'Catacomb' position at Nyaungu on 15TH February 1945, Jemadar Mohammad Hussain was commanding his Platoon when it came under heavy fire and the Jemadar was wounded in the right leg. The platoon faltered and the attack was only partially successful. In spite of his wounds, he rallied his men and led them again into the assault. The platoon came under heavy MMG fire, which halted the attack. Jemadar Mohammad Hussain displaying outstanding endurance and devotion to duty again reorganised the remnants of his platoon; and led a third and successful assault. In spite of his wounds, he organised the consolidation of the objective, refusing to be evacuated until the position was secure. Jemadar Mohammad Hussain displayed outstanding powers of leadership, courage, tenacity, and devotion to duty, which was directly responsible for the success of this phase of the battle, and set a magnificent example to all ranks'. Jemadar Mohammad Hussain was awarded an immediate Military Cross on 24TH May 1945.

Lieutenant Fazal Karim Mian, MC
The Burma Regiment
Citation:
Prior to the advance, to capture Taungtha, Lieutenant Fazal Karim Mian was selected to carry out at reconnaissance of the town area. On the night of ¾ March 1945, he proceeded with two men and passed through Japanese positions, entered the town and returned with very valuable information. The accuracy of which was proved, when the Battalion was enabled to capture Taungtha with the minimum of casualties while inflicting heavy casualties on the enemy. Later it was decided to seize and occupy the feature Point 1788 known to be held by the enemy and on which was suspected Japanese Artillery Observation Post. Lieutenant Fazal Karim Mian volunteered to carry out a recce of the summit and find a route through the enemy's positions. With a small escort he proceeded, under cover of darkness, through the enemy lines and found a possible route. He sent the greater part of his escort back to report the fact while he lay up during the following day, watching the enemy movement and pinpointing their positions.

Military Cross 1922-1947

Burma Army

Lieutenant Fazal Karim Mian, MC (Cont)
Citation:
'Next night he continued up to the summit, completed that portion of his recce, and returned to the Battalion at dawn having been out for 36 hours. His detailed information was most valuable and 12 hours later, he guided a Company through to the summit, which was seized and occupied as a complete surprise to the enemy. An operation which would not been possible but for the information he had obtained. In the subsequent mopping up, he was wounded in the head and arm, but remained on the position until 18 hours later when he conducted the evacuation of the other wounded again through the enemy positions. His determination and resourcefulness has been displayed on other occasions and has set a very fine example of reconnaissance, patrolling and endurance to all ranks'. Lieutenant Fazal Karim Mian was awarded an immediate Military Cross on 2ND August 1945.

Subedar Ali Zaman, MC
The Burma Regiment
Citation:
'During March 1944, Subedar Ali Zaman was 2ND I/C of 'B' Company of the Regiment. He was ordered to dig up and occupy defensive positions and carry out intensive patrolling in the area of Phek. Later the Company was withdrawn to Kohima. On 6TH April his Officiating Commander Captain AN Lunn, was killed by enemy mortar bombing and the Subedar was wounded through the back. In spite of his wounds he rallied as many men of his Company as he could and occupied and defended the new position. Later, he was removed to the Advance Dressing Station, which came under heavy enemy mortar fire, and he was again wounded and lost two fingers. After remaining in the Advance Dressing Station for two days, he rejoined his Company and remained on the defensive perimeter and inspiring and encouraging his men until evacuated with the wounded seven days later. Subedar Ali Zaman, displayed courage of a very high order and displayed great initiative and devotion to duty throughout the operation although he was of advance age and must have been considerably weakened through loss of blood and severe illness he had suffered just prior to the opening of the campaign'. Subedar Ali Zaman was awarded the Military Cross on 8TH February 1945.

Military Medal

The Military Medal (MM) was (until 1993) a military decoration awarded to personnel of the British Army and other services, and formerly also to personnel of other Commonwealth countries, below commissioned rank for bravery in battle on land. The medal was established on 25 March 1916. It was the other ranks' equivalent to the Military Cross (MC), (which was awarded to commissioned officers and, rarely, to Warrant Officers, although WOs could also be awarded the MM). The MM ranked below the MC and the Distinguished Conduct Medal (DCM), which was also awarded to non-commissioned members of the Army. Recipients of the Military Medal are entitled to use the post-nominal letters "MM". In 1993 the Military Medal was discontinued. Since then the Military Cross has been awarded to personnel of all ranks.

Indian Armoured Corps
Daffadar Khan, A.
Daffadar Mohammad, K.
Lance Daffadar Hayat, M.
Lance Daffadar Khan, M.
Lance Daffadar Khan, N.
Lance Daffadar Shah, S.
Naik Ditta, A.
Sowar Ali, R.
Sowar Khan, M.S.
Sowar Mohammad, A.

Indian Army Engineers
Havildar Din, G.
Havildar Elahi, F.
Havildar Khan, J.
Havildar Khader, S.
Havildar Qadir, A.

Indian Artillery
Havildar Major Sadiq, M.
Havildar Abbas, G.
Havildar Ahmed, H.
Havildar Mohammad, G.
Havildar Hussain, A.
Havildar Khan, A.
Havildar Khan, L.
Havildar Ali, W.
Naik Ali, A.
Naik Ali, R.
Naik Khan, G.
Naik Khan, J.
Naik Khan, N.
Naik Mohammad, W.
Lance Naik Ajaib, M.
Lance Naik Akbar, M.

Military Medal

Indian Army Engineers
Naik Aziz, A.
Naik Badshah, K.
Naik Ali, A.
Naik Din, M.
Naik Ditta, A.
Naik Hussain, S.
Naik Rehman, F. *MM (Bar)*.
Naik Sharif, M.
Lance Naik Haq, A.
Lance Naik Khan, M.
Lance Havildar Madina, S.
Lance Naik Rehman, F.
Sapper Ali, T.
Sapper Balouch
Sapper Gul, K.M.
Sapper Hussain, M.
Sapper Ismail, M.
Sapper Khan, G.
Sapper Khan, S.
Sapper Latif, A.
Sapper Rafiq, M.

1ST Punjab Regiment
Havildar Akbar, M.
Havildar Akbar, M. MM (Bar)
Havildar Amir, M.
Havildar Dil, S.
Havildar Gul, A
Havildar Khan, G.
Havildar Mohammad, B.
Havildar Sarwar, M.
Lance Havildar Shafi, M.
Lance Havildar Shafi, M. MM(Bar)
Lance Havildar Haider, G.
Lance Havildar Shah, R.
Naik Ahmed, S.
Naik Ajab, M.
Naik Andaz, G.

Indian Artillery(Cont)
Lance Naik Amin, M.
Lance Naik Khan, A
Lance Naik Khan, M. (101154)
Lance Naik Khan, M. (21172)
Lance Havildar Khan, M
Lance Naik Mohammad, S.
Gunner Ali, Q.
Gunner Bux, K.
Gunner Khan, M.
Gunner Khan, Y.

Indian Signals
Naik Ali, B.
Havildar Khan, A.
Naik Khan, F.
Signalman Khan, M.S.
Naik Khan, S.
Signalman Mohammad, K.
Lance Naik Mohammad, G.
Havildar Rafiq, M.
Havildar Rehman, G.
Havildar Rehman, S.
Havildar Ullah, A.

2ND Punjab Regiment
Havildar Mohammad, M.
Havildar Mohammad, S.
Havildar Ali, N
Havildar Khan, A.
Havildar Khan, S.
Havildar Khan, S.
Naik Aurangzeb
Naik Baksh, K.
Naik Din, F.
Naik Khan, A.
Naik Khan, N.
Naik Khan, S.
Naik Khan, S. MM (Bar)
Naik Sadiq, M.

Military Medal

1ST Punjab Regiment(Cont)
Naik Dad, K.
Naik Khan, M.
Naik Khan, A.
Naik Shah, G.
Lance Naik Ahmed, S.
Lance Naik Khan, I.
Lance Naik Khan, S.
Lance Naik Rahim,
Sepoy Ishmael, M.
Sepoy Khan, A.G.
Sepoy Khan, B.
Sepoy Khan, F.
Sepoy Khan, K.
Sepoy Khan, Q.
Sepoy Sajwal
Sepoy Sarwar, M

4TH Bombay Grenadiers
Lance Naik Hussain, K.
Havildar Khan, C.
Naik Khan, I.
Naik Khan, M.A.
Sepoy Khan, S.

6TH Rajputana Rifles
Rifleman Ali, Z.
Rifleman Dad, A.
Rifleman Dad, K.
Lance Naik Elahi, K.
Naik Hussain, F.
Naik Khan, A.
Naik Khan, M.
Naik Khan, M. *MM (Bar)*
Naik Khan, M.
Naik Khan, Q.
Lance Naik, Z.
Lance Naik Rehman, A.
Rifleman Sharif, M.

2ND Punjab Regiment(Cont)
Lance Naik Sadiq, M.
Lance Naik Sarwar, G.
Lance Naik Yaqub, M
Lance Naik Ahmed, H.
Lance Naik Baksh, M.
Lance Naik Khan, M.
Lance Naik Sabar, M.
Lance Naik Khan, S.
Sepoy Dad, K.
Sepoy Karim, F.
Sepoy Khan, I.
Sepoy Khan, P.
Sepoy Khan, S.
Sepoy Niwaz, M.

7TH Rajputana Rifles
Lance Naik Afsar, M.
Naik Dad, F.
Havildar Dad, F.
Lance Naik Din, K.
Lance Naik Din, W.
Havildar Khan, J.
Naik Khan, M.
Lance Nail Mohammad, K.

10TH Baluch Regiment
Sepoy Ali, B.
Lance Naik Amin, M.
Sepoy Ashraf
Sepoy Badshah, Z.
Havildar Bahadur, K.
Sepoy Dad, F.
Lance Naik Din, M. (23359)
Lance Naik Din, M. (17962)
Lance Naik Din, S.
Naik Din, T.
Lance Havildar Ghani, A.
Sepoy Gul, K.

Military Medal

8TH Punjab Regiment
Havildar Afar, M.
Naik Akbar, M.
Lance Naik Ali, I.
Sepoy Ali, M.
Havildar Alam, M.
Havildar Baksh, Q.
Sepoy Bashir, M.
Sepoy Din, M.
Sepoy Din, S.
Sepoy Hussain, K.
Sepoy Hussain, M.
Sepoy Khan, C.
Sepoy Khan, F.
Sepoy Khan, P.
Lance Naik Khan, S.
Naik Khan, Y.
Sepoy Khan, Y.
Naik Mohammad, H.
Naik Ramzan
Naik Rehman, A.
Naik Sadiq, M.
Havildar Sarwar, M.
Sepoy Sher, A.

12TH Frontier Force Rifles
Havildar Afzal, S.
Havildar Khan, M.
Naik Baz, T.
Naik Din, G.
Naik Gul, I.
Naik Khan, A. (10208)
Naik Khan, A, *MM (Bar)*
Naik Khan, A. (16206)
Naik Khan, A. (14846)
Naik Khan, M.
Naik Khan, S.
Naik Khan, Y.

10TH Baluch Regiment (Cont)
Lance Naik Haider, A.
Lance Naik Hasna
Naik Hassan, S.
Sepoy Hayat
Lance Naik Hussain, F.
Sepoy Hussain, F.
Havildar Hussain, K.
Sepoy Ibrahim.
Naik Jahan, S.
Sepoy Khan, A. (17271)
Sepoy Khan, A. (29482)
Naik Khan, A.
Havildar Khan, A.
Havildar Khan, A. Y.
Sepoy Khan, B.
Lance Naik Khan, D.
Havildar Khan, M.
Sepoy Khan, M.
Havildar Major Khan, M.
Lance Naik Khan, M.
Lance Naik Khan, N.
Naik Khan, N.
Havildar Khan, N.
Havildar Khan, R.
Naik Khan, S. (16880)
Naik Khan, S. (11713)
Havildar Mohammad, S.
Naik Mohammad, H.
Naik Rasul, G.
Naik Khan, Z.
Sepoy Khitab,
Sepoy Mohammad, T.
Sepoy Shah, P.Z.
Sepoy Zaman, S.

Military Medal

12TH Frontier Force Rifles (Cont)
Naik Mehdi, G.
Naik Mohammad, A
Lance Nail Akbar, M.
Lance Naik Dad, M.
Lance Naik Gul, A.
Lance Naik Gul, J.
Lance Naik Gul, Z.
Lance Naik Mohammad, N.
Sepoy Abdul, M.
Sepoy Ali, B.
Sepoy Ashraf, M. (33034)
Sepoy Ashraf, M.(20468)
Sepoy Badshah, M.
Sepoy Ditta, M.
Sepoy Fazal, M.
Sepoy Hussain, M.
Sepoy Janan, G.
Sepoy Khan, C.
Sepoy Khan, D.
Sepoy Khan, H.
Sepoy Khan, J.
Sepoy Khan, Z.
Sepoy Maqbula
Sepoy Mohammad
Sepoy Mohammad, F.
Sepoy Mohammad, M

14TH Punjab Regiment
Havildar Khan, M.N.
Havildar Gul, P.
Havildar Khan, A.
Havildar Khan, B.
Havildar Khan, M.
Havildar Khan, P.
Havildar Shah, M.H.
Havildar Shah, P.
Naik Hussain, N.
Naik Khan, N.

11TH Sikh Regiment
Havildar Baksh, F.
Havildar Mulk, S.
Naik Bahadur, K.
Sepoy Ali, M.
Sepoy Khan, D.
BQMH Khan, N.
Sepoy Mahmud, S.

13TH Frontier Force Rifles
Havildar Major Khan, S.
Havildar Bahar, B.
Havildar Bahar, B. MM (Bar)
Sepoy Gul, H.
Sepoy Gul, S.
Sepoy Khabib, S.
Sepoy Khan, A.
Havildar Khan, I.
Sepoy Khan, K.
Sepoy Khan, M.
Naik Khan, R.
Havildar Major Khan, S.
Havildar Khan, Y.
Sepoy Khan, Z.
Naik Khel, K.
Naik Mansabdar
Sepoy Mohammad, F.
Lance Naik, Rehman, A.
Sergeant Rehman, A.
Lance Naik Shah, A.Military Medal

15TH Punjab Regiment
Havildar Ashraf, M.
Havildar Yusuf, M.
Naik Alam, M.
Naik Dad, J.
Naik Gul, B. (12621)
Naik Gul, B. (12310)
Naik Khan. T.

Military Medal

14TH Punjab Regiment(Cont)
Naik Khan, P.
Naik Sadiq, M.
Naik Yaqub, M.
Naik Mohammad, M.
Naik Ahmed, G.
Naik Khan, B. *MM (Bar)*
Naik Khan, B.
Lance Naik Ajaib, M.
Lance Naik Dad, R.
Lance Naik Din, K.
Lance Naik Din, T
Lance Naik Elahi, K.
Lance Naik Khan, M. (18804)
Lance Naik Khan, M. (19684)
Lance Naik Mir, J.
Lance Naik Khan, W.
Sepoy Ali, S.
Sepoy Aurangzeb
Sepoy Hussain, G.
Sepoy Karim, S.
Sepoy Khan, A.
Sepoy Khan, L.
Sepoy Khan, M.
Sepoy Khan, R.
Sepoy Khan, S.
Sepoy Malik, A.
Sepoy Nur, R.
Sepoy Zaman, S.

15TH Punjab Regiment (Cont)
Naik Khan, P.
Naik Sadiq, M.
Naik Yaqub, M.
Naik Mohammad, M.
Naik Ahmed, G.
Naik Khan, B. *MM (Bar)*
Naik Khan, B.
Lance Naik Ajaib, M.
Lance Naik Dad, R.
Lance Naik Din, K.
Lance Naik Din, T
Lance Naik Elahi, K.
Lance Naik Khan, M. (18804)
Lance Naik Khan, M. (19684)
Lance Naik Mir, J.
Lance Naik Khan, W.
Sepoy Ali, S.
Sepoy Aurangzeb
Sepoy Hussain, G.
Sepoy Karim, S.
Sepoy Khan, A.
Sepoy Khan, L.
Sepoy Khan, M.
Sepoy Khan, R.
Sepoy Khan, S.
Sepoy Malik, A.
Sepoy Nur, R.
Sepoy Zaman, S.

16TH Punjab Regiment
Lance Naik Ahmed, S., Lance Naik Ayaz, M., Sepoy Haider, G., Lance Naik Hussain, F, Sepoy Khan, A., Naik Khan, B., Lance Naik Khan, J., Naik Khan, J. *MM (Bar)*. Havildar Khan, K., Lance Naik Khan, S., Lance Naik Khan, T.B., Lance Havildar Khan, U., Havildar Khan, W., Sepoy Mohammad, B., Sepoy Mohammad, F., Lance Naik Mohammad, W., Lance Naik Sarwar, G., Sepoy Yaqub, M., Naik Yar, M.

Burma Gallantry Medal

The Burma Gallantry Medal (BGM) was a military decoration awarded to non-commissioned Officers and other ranks of the British Burma military, Frontier Force and military police for acts of personal bravery in war or peace. The Medal was established by royal warrant in 1940.

The Burma Regiment was formed in India on 1ST October 1942, mainly from non-Burmese survivors of the retreat from Burma. Composition was personnel of the 7TH and 8TH Battalions Burma Rifles (the men for these battalions originally largely having been found from the Burma Frontier Force and the Burma Military Police), units of the Burma Frontier Force and the Burma Military Police. The men were all Indian. The Burma Frontier Force was abolished. The 1st Battalion, the Burma Regiment consisted of Sikhs and Punjabi Musalmans in equal numbers. 1st Battalion, fought at Kohima as Corps Troops to XXXIII Corps and in the re-conquest of Burma with first 33 Indian Infantry Brigade (7 Indian Infantry Division) and then 9 Indian Infantry Brigade (5 Indian Infantry Division). At the end of the war the battalion went first to Singapore and then went on to serve at Palembang, Sumatra, landing on 25 October 1945 and leaving a year later. After the end of the war, 1st Battalion Burma Regiment was disbanded in 1947.

Two Muslim soldiers were awarded the Burma Gallantry Medal for their actions against the Japanese in Burma. Information about the citations as to how they won the Burma Gallantry Medal has been supplied by Mr. Nick Metcalfe from his forthcoming book: *For Gallantry, Volume 1, Burma Gallantry Medal*.

This new book will begin a series of volumes that examine some of the United Kingdom's lesser know gallantry awards. It will cover the status of Burma, its geography, people and armed forces prior to the Second World War and will examine the awards of the Burma Gallantry Medal in the context of the campaign in Burma from 1942 to 1945.

Burma Gallantry Medal

Sepoy Ghulam Mohammed, BGM

1st Burma Regiment went up against the bunker positions at Nyaungu on the Irrawaddy River on 15TH February 1945. This is Ghulam's citation:

At Nyaungu on 15TH February, 1945, 'C' Company was ordered to attack three enemy held features. It was vital to the operation that the approaches to the beaches were cleared quickly. The leading section was driven off their objective by enemy light machine gun. Subjected to enemy sniping and grenading and in great danger from tank and medium machine guns giving supporting fire to his company, Sepoy Ghulam Mohd held his position, climbed alone onto the top of the bunkered and tunnelled enemy feature and destroyed the light machine gun post with grenades. His presence on the enemy position was an inspiration and an example quickly followed by his platoon who rapidly secured their objective. He displayed courage, initiative and complete disregard for personal safety throughout the operation. Sepoy Ghulam Mohammad was awarded the Burma Gallantry Medal on 12TH July 1945.

Havildar Major Fateh Khan, BGM

Havildar Major Fateh Khan was wounded during the mopping up operation after the seizure of pt.1788. Despite his wound he personally killed three more Japanese who were survivors and still defending a strongly built building. During the day the Company on the position were subjected to constant enemy sniping and fire from Grenade Dischargers. Fateh Khan was indefatigable in encouraging those who were digging the defences and in keeping up morale generally. During the night 14/15 March 1945 the position was heavily counter-attacked in considerable strength. It was imperative to ascertain the situation and despite his wound Fateh Khan volunteered to leave his trench and through a hail of enemy Grenade Discharger and Small Arms fire he visited every post on the position. Later it was feared that the enemy had penetrated a part of the Perimeter. Fateh Khan went forward to confirm, he found that this was unfortunately so and personally killed two of the Japanese who had already infiltrated. He exhorted his men to hang on and returned to report the situation to his Coy Commander. Throughout the 36 hours during which the action lasted and although his wound warranted it, Fateh Khan steadfastly refused that any particular attention be paid to it and displayed a very high degree of initiative, endurance, tenacity and courage of a very high order. Havildar Major Fateh Khan was awarded The Burma Gallantry Medal on 2ND August 1945.

Order of the British Empire (OBE)

The Most Excellent Order of the British Empire was established on 4 June 1917 by King George V. Recommendations for appointments to the Order of the British Empire were at first made on the nomination of the United Kingdom, the self-governing Dominions of the Empire and later the Commonwealth. Most Commonwealth countries, such as India, and Pakistan, ceased recommendations for appointments to the Order of the British Empire when they created their own honours.

Vice-Admiral Haji Mohammad Siddiq Choudri, HPk, OBE, HI (M).
Haji Mohammad Choudhri was born in Batala, Punjab, and British India in 1912 in an Arain family. He was educated at the Rashtriya Indian Military College and later joined the Britannia Royal Naval College in the United Kingdom. He was trained as torpedo and anti-submarine specialist and held various officer's appointments both at sea and with land-based naval formations before and after the World War II. He participated in World War II's Pacific theatre as part of Royal Indian Navy. He witnessed the Japanese surrender in 1945 and commanded a naval division that consisted of the two-ship formation that represented the Royal Indian Navy. At the time of the partition of British India in 1947, Captain Choudhri was one of the senior-most Indian officer and decided to opted for Pakistan in 1947. He was among the first twenty naval officers who joined the Royal Pakistan Navy (RPN) as a Captain. He was the first most senior and the only Captain in the navy in terms of seniority list provided by the Royal Indian Navy to the Ministry of Defence (MoD) in 1947.
He did not actively participated in first war with India in 1947, instead he commanded a destroyer from Karachi to Mumbai to oversee the evacuation of Indian emigrants to Pakistan. In 1950, he was promoted to one-star rank, Commodore, and appointed to serve as deputy commander in chief under Rear-Admiral J.W. Jefford. The Pakistan government called for appointing a native chiefs of staff of army, air force, navy, and marines. He was the most senior officer to be appointed as an admiral in the navy.

Order of the British Empire

Vice-Admiral Haji Mohammad Siddiq Choudri (Cont)

Prime Minister Liaquat Ali Khan approved his nomination papers as navy's commander in chief on the condition that he would spend a year in commanding a squadron in sea, and then attend the Imperial Defence College. Upon returning to Pakistan in 1952, he was appointed as Deputy Commander-in-Chief at the NHQ where he established staff corps and administration. Although, the Pakistani government announced the appointment of navy's first native commander in chief in 1951 and Commodore Choudhri's nomination papers being approved by Prime Minister Ali Khan also in 1951, his appointment as navy's first native commander in chief came only in effect in 1953. He was promoted as Vice-Admiral and assumed the command of the navy.

In 1951, Admiral Choudri decided to built the submarines and warships at the Karachi Shipyard & Engineering Works, relaying his plans to the Ministry of Defence and Ministry of Finance, but was told by the civilian planners that the "second-hand ships from the United Kingdom would be better off for Pakistan", that eventually led the Navy to relay on the obsolete vessels that had to be acquire from the United Kingdom. From 1953–56, he bitterly negotiated with the U.S. Navy and Royal Navy over the acquisition of warship and made several unsuccessful attempts for the procurement of submarines imported from the United States.

In 1954, he convinced the U.S. government to provide monetary support for modernization of aging O–class destroyers and minesweepers, while commissioning the Ch–class destroyers from British Navy. In 1955, Admiral Choudhri cancelled and disbanded the British military tradition in the navy when the U.S. Navy's advisers were dispatched to the Pakistani military. British military tradition were only kept in the air force due to being under its British commander and major staff consisting of Royal Air Force officers. Despite initiatives, the Admiralty's influence slowly vanished from the navy until the native officers were educated and promoted to flag ranks to replace the Royal Navy's officers. In 1956, Admiral Choudhri sent recommendations for the construction of the seaport in Ormara and a naval base, but it was bypassed Ministry of Shipping that cited financial constraints. In 1957, he finalizes the sale of cruiser warship from the United Kingdom, and used the government's own fund to induct the warship that caused a great ire against Admiral Choudhri by the Finance ministry in the country. In 1958, his Navy NHQ staff began fighting with the Army GHQ staff and the Ministry of Defence (MoD) over the plans regarding the modernization of the navy.

Order of the British Empire

Vice-Admiral Haji Mohammad Siddiq Choudri (Cont)

He was in bitter conflict with General Ayub who saw the purchase of *PNS Baber* and his submarine procurement approaches had jeopardized the foreign military relations with the United States. The MoD did sanctioned to pay off the costly *PNS Baber* but halted the crucial funds for the operations of the navy which had been assembled since 1956. In another Joint Chiefs of Staff meeting chaired by General Ayub in 1958, he became involved with heated debate over the financial costs for the naval operations in deep sea. General Ayub reportedly reached out to the President Iskander Mirza and lodged a complained against Admiral Choudhri by noting the Admiral of "neither having the brain, imagination or depth of thought to understand such (defence) problems nor the vision or the ability to make any contribution." Admiral Choudhri then was called to meet with President Mirza to resolve the interservice rivalry between the army and navy but it was ended with "stormy interview" with the President. Upon returning to NHQ, Admiral Choudhry decided to tender his resignation to broke the interservice rivalry in protest as result of having differences with Navy's plans of expansion and modernization. He resigned from the command of navy on 26 January 1959 and cited to President: "major decision [which] have been taken with disagreement with the technical advice I have consistently tendered.... concerning the concept of our defence, the appointment of our available budget, and the size and shape of our Navy." In 1958, Vice-Admiral Afzal Rahman Khan, who was known to be confident of General Ayub Khan, was appointed as naval chief by President Mirza.

After retiring from Navy, he went on to establish Merchant Navy and promoted civilian shipping trade throughout his life. After retiring from Navy in 1959, he founded and became director of Pakistan Institute of Maritime Affairs (PIMA) which he remained associated with until his death in 2004.

He avoided politics and provided no commentaries on conflicts and wars with neighbouring India in successive years of 1965, 1971, and 1999. He died of old age on 27 February 2004 and was buried in a military graveyard in Karachi. In his honour, the government established the "HMS Choudhri Memorial Hall" at the National Defence University in Islamabad in 2005.

Member of the Most Excellent Order of the British Empire (MBE)

The Sovereign could appoint a person as a Commander, Officer or Member of the Order of the British Empire for gallantry.

Hony Captain Sher Dil Khan, *Sardar Bahadur*, MBE, OBI

Subedar-Major Sher Dil Khan commenced his military career in July 1908 when he joined the 29th Punjabis. He was promoted Jemadar in June 1921, Subedar in March 1928 and Subedar-Major in July 1938. During his service he has held the appointments of Head Clerk on active service with the 29th Punjabis, Q.M. Jemadar 2/15th Punjab Regiment and Q.M. 2/15th Punjab Regiment on active service in Borneo in 1941. He was admitted to the O.B.I. 1st Class in January 1941, and was promoted Honorary Lieutenant in August 1940, and Honorary Captain on 1 January 1942. Subedar-Major Sher Dil Khan served with "B.E." Force during the last war, Wazir Force June 1922 to May 1923 and served in the Burma Rebellion, Loe Agra and Mohmand Operations 1935. He went overseas with the 2/15th Punjab Regiment in October 1940 and served in Singapore, Sarawak, and Dutch West and South Borneo, being made a prisoner of war following the capitulation of the unit on 3 April 1942. At the age of 55 he fought a rearguard action with the Battalion through the swamps and mountains of Borneo for about 900 miles and by his courage and devotion to duty set a fine example to all ranks. As a prisoner of war, Subedar-Major Sher Dil Khan, together with some 500 men of the Battalion. He left Java for Singapore in July 1942 where he went into Saletar Camp. Being one of the most senior Punjab Musalman officers, every effort was made by the leaders of the I.N.A. to get him to join the movement. Captain Sher Dil Khan resisted all persuasions and in August 1942 was taken to the I.N.A. Detention Camp, Bida-Dari, where he was subjected to every form of menial indignity, mental and bodily torture and starvation. In January 1943, Sher Dil, since it was obvious that he did not intend to join the movement, was sent with 149 men of the Battalion to Rabaul, New Britain, remaining there as a prisoner of war until the end of the war. Captain Sher Dil Khan has just been awarded the M.B.E. in recognition of his loyalty

Member of the Most Excellent Order of the British Empire (MBE)

Ghazan Khan, MBE

The KING has been graciously pleased to give orders for the Captain Ghazan Khan of 16TH Punjab Regiment appointments to the Most Excellent Order of the British Empire for gallant and distinguished services whilst Prisoners of War in the Far East: - *To be Additional Members of the Military Division of the said Most Excellent Order.*

Gulistan Khan, MBE

The KING has been graciously pleased to give orders for the Subedar Gulistan Khan of 16TH Punjab Regiment appointments to the Most Excellent Order of the British Empire for gallant and distinguished services whilst Prisoners of War in the Far East.

The following officers were awarded the MBE by the British Sovereign:

Colonel Afridi Monawar Khan	Indian Medical Service
Lt. Col. Syed Mohammad Ishaq	Hyderabad Infantry
Lt. Col. Ahmed Jan	Indian Armoured Corps
Lt. Col. Ahmed Jan	Indian Armoured Corps
Lt. Col. Syed Mohammad Ishaq	Hyderabad Infantry
Major Ahmed Khan	Indian Armoured Corps
Major Mian Hayaud Din	12TH Frontier Force Regiment
Major Lall Khan	Indian Army
Major Mohammad Abdul Latif Khan	Indian Army
Major Ali Mohammad Pardiath	Indian Medical Service
Major Nawab Khan	Royal Indian Artillery
Major Said Ahmad	Camp Commandant
Major Sesha Salam	Indian Signal Corps
Major Altaf Qadir	Royal Air Force
Major WB Butt	8 Punjab Regiment
Major Ata Ulllah	Indian Field Ambulance
Major Fakhruddin Mir	Indian Pioneer Corps
Major Burki Wajid Ali	Indian Medical Service
Major Hamshad Khan	4 Bombay Grenadiers
Captain Gulzar Ahmed	10 Baluch Regiment
Captain Sardar Ahmed	Indian Medical Service
Captain Sardar Ahmed	Indian Medical Service
Captain Hafiz-ur-Rahman	Indian Medical Service
Captain Syed Baqir Hosain	Indian Medical Service
Captain Atta Mohd. Shah	14 Punjab Regiment
Captain Mohammad Zia-ud-Din	1 Punjab Regiment
Captain Feroz Khan	10 Baluch Regiment

MBE

The following officers were awarded the MBE by the British Sovereign:

Lieutenant Hussain Ali	Indian Medical Corps
Lieutenant Talibuddin	Royal Indian Service Corps
Lieutenant Liaqat Saeed Khan Lodi	Indian Army
Lieutenant Mohammad Sadiq	13 Frontier Force Rifles
Lieutenant Mohammad Shamin Ansari	Indian Signal Corps
Lieutenant, Sheikh Nazir Ahmed	Indian Pioneer Corps
Lieutenant Ahmed Khan	Indian Pioneer Corps
Lieutenant Mohammad Hussain Khan	Jat Regiment
Lieutenant Abrar Hussain	10 Baluch Regiment
Lieutenant Abrar Hussain	10 Baluch Regiment
Lieutenant Sajjad Ali Naqvi	Indian Army Service Corps
Subedar Major Ahmed Khan	Indian Army
Subedar Major Aziz-ur-Rahman	Indian Army
Subedar Major Abbas Ali	Jat Regiment
Subedar Major Mirza Sakhi Mohammad,	Indian Corps Signals
Subedar Major Karam Ilahi,	Indian Corps Signals
Subedar Major Khushi Mohammad,	Indian Engineers
Subedar Major Mohammad Feroze	1 Punjab Regiment
Subedar Major Mohammad Khan	Indian Artillery
Subedar Major Walayat Hussain	Indian Artillery
Subedar Major Atta Mohammad	8 Punjab Regiment
Subedar Major Haider Rahman	14 Punjab Regiment
Subedar Major Abdul Siddique	Royal Army Service Corps
Subedar Allah Ditta	Royal Army Service Corps
Subedar Fateh Mohammad	Royal Army Service Corps
Subedar Mohammad Din	Royal Indian Service Corps
Subedar Mohammad Hayat	Royal Indian Service Corps
Subedar Muzaffar Khan	Corps of Indian Engineers
Subedar Ramzan Khan,	Corps of Indian Engineers
Subedar Imam Ali	Corps of Indian Engineers
Subedar Walayat Khan	Corps of Indian Engineers
Subedar Fazal Ellami	Indian Field Company
Subedar Fazal Din	Indian Army
Subedar Gul Wahid Khan	15 Punjab Regiment
Subedar Kanwal Khan	Indian Field Company
Subedar Saif Ali	13 Frontier Force Rifles
Subedar Saif Ali	Indian Army
Subedar Abdul Gafoor	Bengal Sappers and Miners
Subedar Fazal Elahi	Indian Field Ambulance

MBE

The following officers were awarded the MBE by the British Sovereign:

Subedar Ahamat Ullah	1 Punjab Regiment
Subedar Gulistan Khan	16 Punjab Regiment
Subedar Mohammad Hayat	Jat Regiment
Subedar Yakub Khan,	Indian Pioneer Corps
Subedar Ahmed Khan	Indian Army
Subedar Imam Ali	Corps of Indian Engineers
Subedar Abdul Salam Siddiqiue	Indian Army Service Corps
Subedar Major T. Mohammad	8 Punjab Regiment
Subedar Gulistan Khan	16 Punjab Regiment
Subedar Khan Abdullah	ndian Army
Subedar Mohammad Khan	Indian Army Service Corps
Subedar Major Pehlwan Khan	12 Frontier Force Regiment
Risaldar Feroze Khan	Indian Armoured Corps
Risaldar Asul Shah	Indian Army Service Corps
Risaldar Abdulla Khan	Indian Army Service Corps
Risaldar Major Ali Musa Khan	Indian Armoured Corps
Risaldar Mehr Din	Indian Army
Risaldar Abdulla Khan	Royal Army Service Corps
Risaldar Mukhtiar Khan	Royal Army Service Corps
Risaldar Sikandar Khan	Royal Army Service Corps
Risaldar Sowar Khan	Royal Army Service Corps
Risaldar Zardan Khan	Royal Army Service Corps
Risaldar Mohammad Hanif	Army Remount Department
Risaldar Feroze Khan	Hong Kong Mule Corps
Jemadar Taj Ali	Royal Army Service Corps
Jemadar Warris Khan	Royal Army Service Corps
Jemadar Mohammad Sharif	Royal Army Service Corps
Jemadar Munshi Mohammad	Royal Army Service Corps
Jemadar Abdul Khan	Royal Army Service Corps
Jemadar Akbar Shah	Field Remount Section
Jemadar Ghulam Mohi-ud-Din	Indian Engineers
Jemadar Iniatullah	Indian Pioneer Corps
Jemadar Sher Zuman	Indian Pioneer Corps
Jemadar Mohammad Sayeed	Bihar Regiment
Jemadar Sardar Mohammad	Indian Field Company
Jemadar Ghulam Nabi	14 Punjab Regiment
Jemadar Karam Dad Khan	Indian Signal Corps
Jemadar Mohammad Jaffar Khan	Rajput Regiment
Jemadar Shah Mohammad	Rajput Regiment

The Empire Gallantry Medal

The Empire Gallantry Medal (officially called the Medal of the Order of the British Empire for Gallantry) was introduced on 29 December 1922. It was intended to recognise specific acts of gallantry, and was replaced by the George Cross. When the George Cross was introduced in September 1940, living recipients of the EGM could return their EGM and receive the George Cross.

Mohi-ud-Din Ghulam, EGM
Sub-Inspector Mohi-ud-Din Ghulam was awarded the Empire Gallantry Medal on 3RD June 1931.

Ahmed Muhammad Mirghany, EGM
Ahmed Muhammad Mirghany was awarded the Empire Gallantry Medal on 2ND January 1933.

Ahmed Yar, EGM
Havildar Ahmed Yar, British Army, was awarded the Empire Gallantry Medal on 19TH November 1935.

Hukam Dad, EGM
Lance Naik Hukam Dad of 8TH Punjab Regiment was awarded the Albert Medal on 19TH November 1935.

Firoze Khan, EGM
Lance Naik Firoze Khan of 8TH Punjab Regiment was awarded the Albert Medal on 19TH November 1935.

Mata Din
Lance Naik Mata Din, Indian Army, was awarded the Empire Gallantry Medal on 19TH November 1935.

Ashraf-un-Nisa Begum, EGM
Ashraf-un-Nisa Begum was awarded Empire Gallantry Medal on 1ST February 1937.

British Empire Medal

The British Empire Medal, which may be awarded posthumously, is granted in recognition of meritorious civil or military service.

The following officers were awarded the BEM by the British Sovereign:

Havildar Major Mir Badshah	Rajputana Rifles
Havildar Amin Chand	15 Punjab Regiment
Havildar Atta Mohammad	Indian Engineers
Havildar Khan Zaman	Indian Mountain Artillery
Havildar Mohammad Zaman	Royal Indian Artillery
Havildar Sher Khan	Indian Army
Havildar Abdul Khalaque	Corps of Indian Engineers
Havildar Mohammad Ayub Ali	Corps of Indian Engineers
Havildar Major Shraz Khan	Frontier Force Regiment
Havildar Allah Ditta	Indian Signal Corps
Havildar Mohammad Yusuf	Indian Army Service Corps
Havildar Imdad Nabi	Indian Army
Havildar Mohammad Ashraf	Indian Hospital Corps
Havildar Khan Zaman	Indian Artillery
Havildar Mohammad Din	Corps of Indian Engineer
Havildar Sher Khan	Indian Army
Havildar Ahmed Khan	2 Punjab Regiment
Havildar Inayat Ullah	14 Punjab Regiment
Havildar Ahmed Khan	16 Punjab Regiment
Havildar Baz Gul	16 Punjab Regiment
Havildar Mohammad Shaffi	Frontier Force Regiment
Havildar Major Hiraz Khan	Frontier Force Regiment
Daffadar Abdul Saboh	Indian Armoured Corps
Daffadar Gulab Khan	Indian Armoured Corps
Naik Abdul Razak,	Indian Army Service Corps
Naik Ghulam Haider	Indian Army Service Corps

British Empire Medal

The following officers were awarded the BEM by the British Sovereign:

Naik Fazal Khan	Indian Army
Naik Mohammad Sharif	Indian Engineers
Naik Abdul Razak	Royal Indian Army Service Corps
Naik Munir Khan	Indian Army Ordnance Corps
Naik Munshi Khan	Corps of Indian Engineers
Lance Naik Mohammad Sadiq	Indian Field Ambulance
Lance Naik Ullah Mohib	Indian Army Medical Corps
Lance Naik Ali Hyder	Indian Pioneer Corps
Lance Naik Mohammad Ahmed	Corps of Indian Engineers
Lance Naik Nur Hussain	Corps of Indian Engineers
Lance Daffadar Gulab Khan	Indian Armoured Corps
Sapper Mohammad Sharif	Corps of Indian Engineers
Sapper Said Ullah	Corps of Indian Engineers
Sepoy Dost Mohammad	16 Punjab Regiment
Pioneer Zain Abdi	Indian Pioneer Corps
Pioneer Akram Shah	Indian Army
Fitter Abdul Aziz	Indian Engineers
Ward Orderly Shahbaz Khan	Indian Medical Corps
Serang Abdul Khalaque	Corps of Indian Engineers
Saddler Mohammad Khan	Indian Army Service Corps
Foreman Mohammad Ibrahim	Corps Indian Engineers

Order of the Nile

The Order of the Nile is Egypt's highest state honour. The following officers were awarded the Nishan al-Nil by the Sultan of Egypt.

Major Mohammad Azmatullah Khan, Nishan al-Nil	Egypt
Captain Abdul Sattar, Nishan al-Nil	Egypt
Subedar Zulfikar Ali, Nishan al-Nil	Egypt
Subedar Mohammad Abdul, Nishan al-Nil	Egypt
Ressaidar Hassan Shah, MC, Nishan al-Nil	Egypt

MacGregor Medal

In 1888 the medal was instituted in the memory of its founder Sir Charles Metcalfe MacGregor. The MacGregor Medal was awarded to Indian Armed Forces personnel for valuable military reconnaissance.

Subedar Havildar Ramzan Khan, 12TH Frontier Force Regiment	(1891)
Daffadar Fazaldad Khan, Bengal Cavalry	(1893)
Sepoy Ghulam Nabi, Corps of Guides, Frontier Force	(1896)
Risaldar Shahzad Mir, of the Probyn's Horse	(1897)
Daffadar Shahzad Mir, Scinde Horse	(1897)
Havildar Adam Khan, Corps of Guides, Frontier Force	(1898)
Naik Mihr Din, The Corps of Bengal Sappers and Miners	(1899)
Lance Daffadar Ghulam Hussain, Corps of Guides, Frontier Force	(1903)
Daffadar Moghal Baz Khan Afridi, Corps of Guides Cavalry,	(1904)
Lance-Naik Ghafur Shah, Corps of Guides, Frontier Force	(1906)
Havildar Sheikh Usman 103RD Light Infantry	(1907)
Havildar Muhammad Raza, 106TH Hazara Pioneers	(1909)
Subedar Khan Bahadur Sher Jang, 55TH Coke's Rifles (FF),	(1910)
Lance-Daffadar Mohibullah, Corps of Guides, Frontier Force	(1912)
Sowar Sirdar Khan, Central India Horse	(1912)
Sepoy Sirdar Khan 39TH Horse	(1913)
Naik Haidar Ali Shah, 106TH Hazara Pioneers	(1914)
Havildar Ali Juma, 106TH Hazara Pioneers	(1915)
Naik Abdur Rahman, 1ST Battalion, 21ST Punjabis	(1916)
Havildar Zarghun Shah, 58TH Vaughan's Rifles (Frontier Force)	(1916)
Sepoy Mian Afraz Gul, The Khyber Rifles	(1917)
Jemadar Alla Sar, North East Frontier Corps	(1919)
Havildar Awal Nur, Corps of Guides Infantry, Frontier Force	(1920)
Sepoy Sher Ali, 106th Hazara Pioneers	(1921)
Lance Naik Nur Muhammad, Corps of Guides	(1922)
Captain Abdus Samad Shah, OBE, DCO Lancers	(1922)
Lance Naik Mian Badshah, Frontier Force Rifles	(1938)
Subedar MIA Qureshi, Corps of Indian Engineers	(1945)

The Knights

An Indian knight was a male indigenous British subject of a country under the British Raj before 1947. The following Muslims were knighted by the British Sovereign.

Sir Mir Turab Ali Khan, Salar Jung I

Sir Mir Turab Ali Khan, Salar Jung I, Indian statesman of Hyderabad. He was considered the greatest Prime Minister of Hyderabad. He was given the title Salar Jung and first of the three with that title. The British knighted him as Sir Salar Jung, and was addressed by that name. He was styled by native officials of Hyderabad the Mukhtar 'l-Mulk, and was referred to by the general public as the Nawab Sahib. He died at Hyderabad on 8TH February 1883.

Sir Hajji Nawab Kalb Ali Khan Bahadur

Sir Hajji Nawab Kalb Ali Khan Bahadur was a Nawab of the princely state of Rampur from 1865 to 1887. Succeeding his father, Sir Nawab Yusaf Ali Khan Bahadur, he continued his father's good works, expanding the Rampur library, constructing the Jama Masjid costing Rs.3 lakhs and encouraging the spread of education, architecture, literature and art in general. A gifted ruler, Sir Kalb Ali Khan was highly literate in Arabic and Persian and patronised scholars from across India and the Islamic world. He was a member of John Lawrence's council from 1878 to his death, attended the Delhi Durbar of Queen Victoria and was granted a personal salute of 17-guns. He was succeeded at his death in 1887, aged 55, by his son, Muhammad Mushtaq Ali Khan Bahadur.

The Knights

Sir Abdul Karim Ghaznavi

Sir Abdul Karim Ghaznavi (25TH August 1872 – 24TH July 1939) was a British Indian politician, traveller, minister, member of Bengal Governor's Executive Council, Bengal Provincial Council and Central Legislative Assembly, reformer of Muslim education and one of the pioneer of Muslim renaissance in Bengal. He was involved in Central National Mohammedan Association founded by Syed Ameer Ali. He was awarded Knighthood in 1928. Later in 1933 he received Nawab Bahadur title. Sir Abdul Karim Ghaznavi died on 24TH July 1939 at his home in Baliganj, Calcutta. He was buried in his family graveyard of his village.

Sir Sheikh Sir Abdul Qadir

Sheikh Sir Abdul Qadir (15TH March 1874 – 9TH February 1950) was a newspaper and magazine editor and a Muslim community leader in British India. He led the famous Muslim organization, Anjuman-i-Himayat-i-Islam and used his position as the leader of this organization to form other, pro-partition, organizations. He was an early activist of the Pakistan Movement. Qadir was born in Ludhiana on 15TH March 1872. He was the editor of The Observer, the first Muslim newspaper published in English in 1895. In 1901, he launched the magazine Makhzan, an Urdu language publication. This magazine published the early works of Allama Muhammad Iqbal. In 1904, Qadir went to study law in London, and was called to the bar in 1907 after which he returned to India, where he served as a member of the Punjab Legislative Council and the minister of education in Punjab, British India in 1925. Qadir was knighted by the British in the 1927 Birthday Honours and in 1935 became a member of the governing council of India He died on 9TH February 1950 at the age of 77 and was buried in Miani Sahib Graveyard, Lahore. His son Manzur Qadir was a prominent Pakistani jurist who served as the Foreign Minister of Pakistan during the military rule of Ayub Khan.

Sir Nawab Sir Muhammad Ali Beg

Sir Nawab Sir Muhammad Ali Beg, KCIE, MVO, (1852 - 1930). He was the son of the late Mirza Vilayet Ali Beg, Ressaidar 3RD Lancers, and Hyderabad Contingent. From 1897 he commanded H. H. the Nizam's Regular forces, and from 1884 he was aide-de-camp to H. H. the Nizam of Hyderabad, in the Ressaidar Hyderabad Contingent. He was Commander of the Golconda Brigade since 1885, in the Hyderabad Imperial Service Troops since 1893, and Commander of Regular Troops since 1897, Jagirdar, Hyderabad State. He passed away in 1930.

The Knights

Sir Sultan Muhammed Shah, Aga Khan III

Sir Sultan Muhammed Shah, Aga Khan III (2ND November 1877 – 11TH July 1957) was the 48TH Imam of the Nizari Ismailia community. He was one of the founders and the first president of the All-India Muslim League (AIML). He shared Sir Syed Ahmad Khan's belief that Muslims should first build up their social capital through advanced education before engaging in politics. Aga Khan called on the British Raj to consider Muslims to be a separate nation within India, the so-called 'Two Nation Theory'. Even after he resigned as president of the AIML in 1912, he still exerted major influence on its policies and agendas. He was nominated to represent India to the League of Nations in 1932 and served as President of the League of Nations from 1937–38. He was awarded multiple honours by the British Sovereign for example:- 1ST January 1934 appointed a member of His Majesty's Most Honourable Privy Council by 26TH June 1902 Knight Grand Commander of the Order of the Indian Empire, GCI. 1ST January 1955 Knight Grand Cross of the Order of St Michael and St George, GCMG. He passed away on 11TH July 1957.

Mir Sir Ahmad Yar Khan Ahmedzai

Mir Sir Ahmad Yar Khan Ahmedzai GCIE (1902-1979) was the last Khan of Kalat, a semi-autonomous state within Britain's Indian Empire, serving from 10TH September 1933 to 14TH October 1955. Despite his nationalist aspirations, Muhammad Ali Jinnah was Yar Khan's legal adviser in the early 1940s. Jinnah pressured Yar Khan to accept Pakistani rule but the Khan stalled for time. Out of impatience, on 27TH March 1948, Pakistan formally annexed Kalat. Yar Khan's eldest son, Mir Suleman Dawood Jan, assumed the title of Khan of Kalat upon his father's death in 1979. On Dawood Jan's death his son Suleman Daud Jan became new Khan of Kalat. He has lived in exile in London since the Pakistani Army killed tribal leader Akbar Bugti in battle in 2006. Officially, the Pakistani government does not recognize his authority but unofficially his voice still carries tremendous weight with much of the populace and leading politicians like Chief Minister Abdul Malik Baloch and Sanaullah Zehri have asked him to return to Pakistan to pacify the restless Baloch. Yar Khan's younger sons, Prince Muhiyddin Baloch and grandson Umar Daud Khan, are both politicians in Pakistan.

The Knights

Sir Syed Sultan Ahmed

Sir Syed Sultan Ahmed, KCSI (1880–1963, Patna, Bihar) was an Indian barrister and politician who had a very successful practice as a barrister, having victories over Motilal Nehru, Tej Bahadur Sapru and Sarat Chandra Bose. Sultan Ahmed was related to Sir Ali Imam and Syed Hasan Imam and like them was a Bihari Shia. While he was the first Indian Vice-Chancellor of Patna University (1923–30) he was included as a delegate from British India, to the Round Table Conference (1930–31) in London .He was Member of the Bihar Legislative Council in 1937 but resigned on the grounds of not getting enough time for politics. He joined the Viceroy's Executive Council (1941–43) and was made the Member for Information and Broadcasting. Later he was also Advisor to the Chamber of Princes (1945–47) in India. In the 1945 New Year Honours, he was appointed a Knight Commander of the Order of the Star of India (KCSI). Although Jinnah offered him a cabinet position in Pakistan, he stated that he could not leave India as it contained the graves of his forefathers. After Indian Independence, Sir Sultan turned to his law practice. In 1950 he became the President of the All India Shia Conference. Sir Sultan passed away in 1963.

Sir Ziauddin Ahmad

Sir Ziauddin Ahmad CIE, MP (13TH February 1878 – 23RD December 1947) was a mathematician, parliamentarian, logician, natural philosopher, politician, political theorist, educationist and a scholar. He was a member of the Aligarh Movement and was a professor, Principal of MAO College, first Pro Vice-Chancellor, Vice Chancellor and Rector of Aligarh Muslim University, India. He served as Vice Chancellor of Aligarh Muslim University for three terms. In 1917, he was appointed a member of the Calcutta University Commission also known as the Sadler Commission. He was also a member of Skeen Committee also known as Indian Sandhurst Committee and Shea Commission for the Indianisation of the British Indian Army. He was appointed a Companion of the Order of the Indian Empire (CIE) in the 1915 King's Birthday Honours list. During World War II he served as a lieutenant colonel. He died in London on 22ND December 1947. His body, as he had requested, was sent back to Aligarh.

The Knights

Sir Nawab Khwaja Ahsanullah

Sir Nawab Khwaja Ahsanullah (1846–1901), Khan Bahadur KCIE, was the Nawab of Dhaka. Ahsanullah was an ardent advocate for Muslims. He created a number of mosques and Madrasas including the Madaripur and Begambari mosques and Madrasas. He also restored and rebuilt over 15 Dargahas and mosques. He was a member of the Central Northern Muhammadan Association and this played a large role in his works. He also was an ardent supporter of the Partition of Bengal (1905) which his son Khwaja Salimullah facilitated. Both he and his father were noted allies of the British Raj. Khwaja Ahsanullah died on 16TH December 1901 of heart failure. The Nawab was buried in the family plot in Begumbazar.

Sir Ahmad Yar Khan Ahmedzai

Sir Ahmad Yar Khan Ahmedzai was the last Khan of Kalat, a semi-autonomous state within Britain's Indian Empire, serving from 10TH September 1933 to 14TH October 1955. Mir Ahmad Yar assumed his throne in 1933, and was decorated by the British in the 1936 New Year Honours as a Knight Grand Commander of the Most Eminent Order of the Indian Empire (GCIE). He declared Kalat's independence from the British Empire on 15TH August 1947, hoping British would honour his pledge to respect the self-determination of the Princely States. Kalat was recognized by the UK and India but not Pakistan. Despite his nationalist aspirations, Muhammad Ali Jinnah was Yar Khan's legal adviser in the early 1940s. Jinnah pressured Yar Khan to accept Pakistani rule but the Khan stalled for time. Out of impatience, on 27TH March 1948, Pakistan formally annexed Kalat. Yar Khan signed a treaty of accession, submitting to the federal government. Jinnah and his successors allowed Yar Khan to retain his title until the province's dissolution in 1955.

Sir Khan Bahadur Sayyid Sir Fazl Ali

Sir Khan Bahadur Sayyid Sir Fazl Ali (19TH September 1886 – 22ND August 1959) was an Indian judge. Fazl belonged to an aristocratic Zamindar (landlord) family of Bihar state. He studied law and began practicing. Eventually he was raised to the judiciary. Sir Fazl Ali was successively given the title of Khan Sahib first and of Khan Bahadur later. In 1918, he was made an Officer of the Order of the British Empire (OBE). He was knighted in the New Year's Honours list of 1941 and invested with his knighthood on 1ST May 1942 by the Viceroy, Lord Linlithgow. He died in 1985 while yet a sitting judge of the Supreme Court.

The Knights

Sir Syed Sultan Ahmed

Sir Syed Sultan Ahmed was an Indian barrister and politician who had a very successful practice as a barrister, having victories over Motilal Nehru, Tej Bahadur Sapru and Sarat Chandra Bose. Sultan Ahmed was related to Sir Ali Imam and Syed Hasan Imam and like them was a Bihari Shia. While he was the first Indian Vice-Chancellor of Patna University (1923–30) he was included as a delegate from British India, to the Round Table Conference (1930–31) in London. He was Member of the Bihar Legislative Council in 1937 but resigned on the grounds of not getting enough time for politics. He joined the Viceroy's Executive Council (1941–43) and was made the Member for Information and Broadcasting. Later he was also Advisor to the Chamber of Princes (1945–47) in India. In the 1945 New Year Honours, he was appointed a Knight Commander of the Order of the Star of India (KCSI). Although Jinnah offered him a cabinet position in Pakistan, he stated that he could not leave India as it contained the graves of his forefathers. After Indian Independence, Sir Sultan turned to his law practice.

Sir Ziauddin Ahmad

Sir Ziauddin Ahmad was a mathematician, parliamentarian, logician, natural philosopher, politician, political theorist, educationist and a scholar. He was a member of the Aligarh Movement and was a professor, Principal of MAO College, first Pro Vice-Chancellor, Vice Chancellor and Rector of Aligarh Muslim University, India. He served as Vice Chancellor of Aligarh Muslim University for three terms. In 1917, he was appointed a member of the Calcutta University Commission also known as the Sadler Commission. He was also a member of Skeen Committee also known as Indian Sandhurst Committee and Shea Commission for the Indianisation of the British Indian Army. Sir Ahmad was an originally member of the Independent Party, which included Hindus, Muslims and Sikhs. When this party dissolved he joined the Muslim League and served as its Parliamentary Secretary. Sir In 1917, he was appointed a member of the Calcutta University Commission also known as the Sadler Commission. He was also a member of Skeen Committee also known as Indian Sandhurst Committee and Shea Commission for the Indianisation of the British Indian Army. He was knighted in the 1938 New Year Honours list. In 1946, he was the chief whip of the Muslim League in the Central Assembly. He died in London on 22ND December 1947. His body, as he had requested, was sent back to Aligarh.

The Knights

Sir Shah Nawaz Bhutto

Sir Shah Nawaz Bhutto, was a politician and a member of Bhutto family hailing from Larkana in Sindh province of British India, which is now part of Pakistan. Shah Nawaz Bhutto, the son of Ghulam Murtaza Bhutto, was born in a Bhutto family of Sindh as the youngest brother of Nawab Nabi Bux Khan Bhutto. The British appointed him a Companion to the Order of the Indian Empire (CIE) and an Officer of the Order of the British Empire (OBE). The Bhutto family owned 250,000 acres of land spread over Larkana, Sukkur and Jacobabad. Shah Nawaz his land-ownership made him the wealthiest and most influential people in Sindh. Bhutto was a good friend of Governor General (later President) Iskander Mirza, who was a regular guest for the annual hunt in Larkana, staying at the Bhutto family home called Al-Murtaza. In the winter of 1955-1956, Mirza brought General Ayub Khan with him to Larkana for the hunt. Shah Nawaz's third son Zulfikar Ali Bhutto (1928-1979) founded the Pakistan People's Party (PPP) in 1967 and served as President and Prime Minister. His daughter, Benazir (1953-2007), also served as Prime Minister, while Benazir's husband, Asif Ali Zardari, later served as president from 2008 to 2013 CE. The Bhutto's continue to dominate the leadership of the PPP. Benazir's son Bilawal Bhutto Zardari became co-chairperson in 2007. The family has experienced many premature deaths, drawing comparisons to the Kennedy curse: Zulfikar was convicted and executed in 1979; Shahnawaz died in France in 1983; Murtaza was killed in a police encounter during his sister's government in 1996; and Benazir died in an assassination in 2007.

Nawab Sir Shahbaz Khan Bugti

Nawab Sir Shahbaz Khan Bugti (1897-1989) was a prominent tribal chief of the Bugtis in Baluchistan. He was knighted as a Knight Commander of the Order of the Indian Empire (KCIE) in November 1901 for fighting for the British Colonial Government of India and for his service to the British colonials. In addition, Sir Shahbaz received large gifts of land in Baluchistan. He passed away in 1989. He was the father of Nawab Mehrab Khan Bugti and Nawabzada Sardar Sohrab Khan Bugti. He was the grandfather of Nawabzada Abdul Rahman Bugti, Nawab Akbar Khan Bugti, Nawabzada Ahmad Nawaz Bugti, Nawabzada Hayat Bugti, Nawabzadi Sardar Bibi Bugti, Nawabzada Munawar Bugti, and Nawabzada Noor Jahan Bugti & Sardar Ghulam Mustafa Khan Bugti. He had 56 great grandchildren.

The Knights

Sir Muhammad Ahmad Said Khan Chhatari

Lieutenant Colonel Saeed ul-Mulk Nawab Sir Muhammad Ahmad Said Khan, Nawab of Chhatari GBE KCSI KCIE also generally referred to as Nawab of Chhatari (12TH December 1888 - 1982) was Governor of the United Provinces, Chief Minister of United Provinces, President of the Executive Council of the Nizam of Hyderabad (i.e. Prime Minister of Hyderabad) and Chief Scout of India. Nawab Chhatari attended the first Round Table Conference, held in St. James's Palace in London on 12TH November 1930. The Muslim Delegation was led by the Aga Khan and others, including Muhammad Ali Jinnah, Sir Mohammad Shafi, Maulana Muhammad Ali, Dr Shafat Ali, Sir Muhammad Zafarullah Khan, the Nawab of Chhatari, and Fazlul Huq. The Nawab of Chhatari was a member of India's National Defence Council from July to August 1941. He resigned from this to accept the post of President of the Hyderabad Executive Council, effectively Prime Minister of the important princely state of Hyderabad. The Nawab was also patron of Jamia Urdu, Aligarh. He also served as Chancellor of Aligarh Muslim University from December 1965 to 6TH January 1982 and as Chief Scout of the All India Boy Scouts Association from 1955 to 1982. Sir Muhammad Ahmad Said Khan passed away in 1982.

Sir (Fazalbhoy) Currimbhoy Ebrahim

Sir (Fazalbhoy) Currimbhoy Ebrahim, 1ST Baronet CBE (25TH October 1839 – 26TH September 1924) was a Gujarati Khoja businessman of the Nizari Ismailia faith based in Bombay credited with founding E. Pabaney & Co, whose ship owning family held trading interests as far as the Arabian peninsula and the African coast. Khojas based in Bombay, who had been active in Canton before the Opium War and long monopolized India's overseas merchandising, continued to maintain a considerable stake in the opium trade through branch offices springing up in Hong Kong and Shanghai during the latter half of the 19TH century. Sir Currimbhoy Ebrahim was knighted during the Prince and Princess of Wales's Indian tour of 1905 and created a baronet in 1910 and further granted lands to support that dignity by the Currimbhoy Ebrahim Baronetcy Act 1913 following the precedent set by the Cowasji Jehangir Baronetcy Act. Sir (Fazalbhoy) Currimbhoy Ebrahim passed away in 1924.

The Knights

Sir Fazal Ibrahim Rahimtoola

Sir Fazal Ibrahim Rahimtoola CIE (1895 - 1977) was an Indian politician. He was the Sheriff of Bombay in 1928. He was also a member of Bombay Legislative Council and Central Legislative Assembly. He was appointed a Companion of the Order of the Indian Empire (CIE) in the 1939 New Year Honours list, and was knighted in the 1946 Birthday Honours, thus becoming Sir Fazal Ibrahim Rahimtoola. On 20TH July 1946, he was invested with his knighthood at the Viceroy's House in New Delhi, by the Viceroy, Lord Wavell. Sir Fazal Ibrahim Rahimtoola passed away in 1977.

Sir Abdul Halim Ghaznavi

Sir Abdul Halim Ghaznavi (11TH November 1876 – 18TH June 1953) was a Bengali Muslim League politician and a former member of the Central Legislative Assembly of British Raj. In 1900 he became the chairman of Mymensingh Municipality and Honorary Magistrate. He joined the Indian National Congress in opposing the Partition of Bengal. He later left the congress and joined the All India Muslim League. He was elected to the Central Legislative Assembly from Dhaka as a Muslim League candidate. From 1939 to 1940 he was the president of the Muslim Chamber of Commerce and of the Indian Chamber of Commerce from 1925 to 1946. He was made Knight Bachelor by the British. He was involved in the publication of the newspapers The Musalman and The Star of India. Sir Abdul Halim Ghaznavi died on 18TH June 1953 in Delduar, Tangail, and East Pakistan.

Sir Muhammad Habibullah

Habibullah was born in Madras (now Chennai) to Aushukh Hussain Khan Saheb on 22ND September 1869. He was a member of the Arcot royal family and closely related to the Nawab of Arcot. He studied law at Zila High School in Saidapet and joined the bar at Vellore in July 1888. Habibullah was awarded the title of Khan Bahadur by the Indian government in 1905. He was made a Companion of the Indian Empire in 1920 and a Knight Bachelor in 1922. In 1924, he was made a Knight Commander of the Star of India and promoted from a Companion of the Indian Empire to a Knight Commander of the Indian Empire. Habibullah retired in 1936 and died in Travancore on 16TH May 1948.

The Knights

Sir Malik Ghulam Muhammad

Sir Malik Ghulam Muhammad (20TH April 1895– 29TH August 1956), was a Pakistani financier who served as the third Governor-General of Pakistan, appointed in this capacity in 1951 until being dismissed in 1955 due to health conditions. He hailed from a Punjabi Pathan family who traced their roots Kakazai tribe of Pashtuns and completing his schooling in Lahore, he went to Aligarh in Uttar Pradesh to attend the MOA College of the Aligarh Muslim University (AMU). At AMU he gained a BA degree in accountancy. Following the outbreak of the Second World War, Muhammad was successively appointed to increasingly important positions. His wartime services as a professional accountant were recognized by the British government that year when he was appointed a Companion of the Order of the Indian Empire (CIE) in the 1941 Birthday Honours list. After World War II, he was asked by Nawab of Bahawalpur, Lord Sadiq Mohammad Khan V to represent him at the Round Table Conferences, and during this time, he began formatting political relations with Liaquat Ali Khan. He left Hyderabad left to join the Ministry of Finance in 1946. In the 1946 Birthday Honours, the last honours list in which Indian civil servants were recognised, he received a knighthood. After witnessing the Partition of India in 1947, he decided to acquire the citizenship of Pakistan and permanently settled in his native city, Lahore, on 14TH August 1947. He was brought up in the Liaquat administration when Prime Minister Liaquat Ali Khan appointed him as country's first Finance Minister. In 1952 he was appointed as the Governor General of Pakistan. In 1953, he represented Pakistan as head of state at the Coronation of Elizabeth II in Westminster Abbey alongside with the Governors-General from Canada, Australia, New Zealand, South Africa and Ceylon. During this time, his health began to deteriorate as paralysis spread in his whole body, forcing him to take a leave of absence to seek treatment in the United Kingdom in 1955. In his capacity, he appointed Interior Minister Iskander Mirza as acting Governor-General, but Mirza dismissed him from his post in order to take his place, supported by the Constituent Assembly's legislators. On 29TH August 1956, Malik Sir Ghulam Muhammad died and was buried in Lahore.

The Knights

Sir Abdullah Haroon

Sir Abdullah Haroon was a British Indian politician who contributed a lot towards developing and defining the role of Muslims in economic, educational, social and political fields in the Indian subcontinent. Abdullah Haroon first joined the Indian National Congress party in 1917 and started to participate in the Independence movement of India. Soon he was disenchanted with the policies of the Congress party of India and joined the All-India Muslim League party and remained its strong supporter till his death. He was knighted by King George VI in the 1937 Coronation Honours list and came to be known as Sir Abdullah Haroon. The decline of the Sind United Party let him to organize the Muslim League in Sindh in 1938. Abdullah Haroon piloted the independence of Pakistan resolution in the Sindh Provincial Muslim League Conference in October 1938 under the presidency of the Quaid-i-Azam Muhammad Ali Jinnah. He also endorsed the 'Pakistan Resolution' on behalf of all Muslims of Sindh at the historic 27TH Session of the Muslim League at Lahore on 23RD March 1940. Abdullah Haroon died on 27TH April 1942 in Karachi.

Sir Ghulam Hussain Hidayutullah

Sir Ghulam Hussain Hidayutullah was a Pakistani politician from Sindh. He received the title of Khan Bahadur from the British government, which also knighted him in the 1926 New Year Honours and further appointed him a Knight Commander of the Most Exalted Order of the Star of India (KCSI) in the 1933 Birthday Honours. In 1938, the Sindh Assembly passed a resolution demanding a separate homeland for the Muslims of India. In 1943, the Sindh Government became the first Provincial Assembly of the sub-continent to pass an official resolution in favour of the creation of Pakistan. When the Muslim League in 1946 decided on a policy of renunciation of titles conferred by the British Government, Sir Ghulam renounced his British titles and honorific's. After independence Sir Ghulam Hussain Hidayutullah earned the unique distinction of being the only Pakistani Governor of a Province in Pakistan as all other Governors were British. This shows the faith and trust the Quaid-e-Azam laid in him. Within a month of the passing away of the Quaid-e-Azam, Sir Ghulam Hussain Hidayutullah the "Grand Old Man of Sindh" died in Karachi on the October 4TH, 1948.

The Knights

Sir Syed Shamsul Huda

Sir Syed Shamsul Huda was a Muslim political leader and scholar in British India. Syed Shamsul Huda obtained all kinds of institutional knowledge, and became one of the most eloquent, articulate and educated Muslims of his generation. He carried out a very important role of Muslim scholar, leader and politician in British India over the beginning of twentieth century. Syed Shamsul Huda was a member of 'Governor's Executive Council' between 1912 and 1919. He awarded Nawaab in 1913. He awarded KCIE in 1916. He designated Judge of Kolkata High Court in 1917 and became the second Muslim occupying the post after Justice Syed Ameer Ali. He died on 14TH October 1922 at the age of 61 and was buried in Tiljola Municipal graveyard.

Sir Mian Fazl-i-Husain

Sir Mian Fazl-i-Husain he entered Government College, Lahore and graduated with a BA in 1897. He travelled to Britain in 1898 to further his education. He was admitted to Christ's College, Cambridge in 1899 and graduated with a BA in 1901. He studied Oriental languages and law at Cambridge and was called to the Bar at Gray's Inn in 1901. Husain was elected President of the Cambridge Majlis in January 1901 and assisted in writing a telegram of condolence to Edward VII upon the death of Queen Victoria. Husain joined the Indian National Congress in 1905 and in 1916 he was elected election to the Punjab Legislative Council. He was made a Knight Commander of the Order of the Indian Empire in 1926. In 1930 he was promoted to the Viceroy's Executive Council in Delhi where he remained until 1935. He played an important part in organising the Round Table Conferences and influencing the views of the present Muslim delegates. The implementation of the Communal Award and Government of India Act, 1935, allowed the majority Muslims in Punjab and Bengal to retain their separate electorates yet also granted those more seats than any other community in their respective assemblies. Whilst this allowed Muslim politicians in the Punjab to increase their autonomy it brought them into conflict with Muslims in Hindu majority provinces, which would now look to Jinnah and the Muslim League for support. In 1932 he led the Indian delegation to the Indo-South African conference and was appointed a Knight Commander of the Order of the Star of India in 1932. January 1936, Jinnah offered him the annual presidency of the Muslim League, however before waiting for this he fell ill on 1ST July 1936, and died at Lahore nine days later. He was buried at the family graveyard in Batala.

The Knights

Sir Syed Wazir Hasan

Sir Syed Wazir Hasan was an Indian jurist and Secretary and later President of the All-India Muslim League. A practitioner in the Judicial Commissioner's Court, he was the first Indian Chief Justice of the Awadh Chief Court (1930–1934). He was knighted in the imperial 1932 New Year Honours list and invested with his knighthood by the Viceroy of India in New Delhi on 4TH March of that year. The Muslim League Presidential address was delivered by Sir Wazir Hasan at the Bombay Session held on 12TH April 1936. He died in Lucknow in August 1947.

Sir Muhammad Akbar Nazar Ali Hydari,

Sir Muhammad Akbar Nazar Ali Hydari was an Indian politician. He served as the Prime Minister of Hyderabad State from 18TH March 1937 to September 1941. In January 1936, he was appointed a member of the Privy Council of the United Kingdom. He was appointed, as a member of the Viceroy's Executive Council in 1941. Hydari was knighted by the British government in the 1928 Birthday Honours, and was formally invested with his knighthood at Hyderabad on 17TH December 1929 by the Viceroy, the Lord Irwin. Sir Muhammad Akbar Nazar Ali Hydari passed away in November 1941.

Sir Ibrahim Rahimtoola

Sir Ibrahim Rahimtoola GBE, KCSI, CIE (May 1862 - June 1942) was an eminent Indian politician, parliamentarian and mayor of Bombay (1899 - 1900) in British India. In November 1924, he was knighted by the British Raj. A Street in Bhendi Bazaar, Bombay is named after him. Overall Sir Ibrahim Rahimtoola remained a member of Bombay Legislative Council [1899-1912], Imperial Legislative Council [1913-1916], Government's Executive Council for Education and Local Self-Government [1918-1923], the President of Legislative Council Bombay [1923-1928], Member of Indian Legislative Assembly in 1931, President of the Indian Legislative Assembly [1931 to 1933], the Chairman of Indian Fiscal Committee [1921] - the first Indian Muslim to hold this post, the member of Royal Commission on Labour in 1929 and also delegated to Round Table Conference London in 1930. Ibrahim Rahimtoola died in June 1942 at Bombay, aged 80.

The Knights

Sir Mohammed Saleh Hydari

Sir Mohammed Saleh Hydari was the last British-appointed and the first Indian Governor of the Indian state of Assam. He entered the Indian Civil Service (ICS) in 1919 and began his career in Madras Presidency. He held many administrative positions in the states and at the centre. He was appointed a CIE in 1934, a CSI in 1941 and was knighted with the KCIE in 1944. From May 1947 he served as Governor of Assam until his death in 1948. He is remembered for entering accord with *Nagas*.

Sir Muhammad Iqbal,

Sir Muhammad Iqbal is called the "Spiritual Father of Pakistan." In 1923, he was knighted by King George V, granting him the title "Sir". While studying law and philosophy in England, Iqbal became a member of the London branch of the All-India Muslim League. Later, during the League's December 1930 session, he delivered his most famous presidential speech known as the Allahabad Address in which he pushed for the creation of a Muslim state in northwest India. In 1933, after returning from a trip to Spain and Afghanistan, Iqbal suffered from a mysterious throat illness. He spent his final years helping Chaudhry Niaz Ali Khan to establish the Dar ul Islam Trust Institute at Jamalpur estate near Pathankot, where there were plans to subsidise studies in classical Islam and contemporary social science. He also advocated for an independent Muslim state. Iqbal ceased practising law in 1934 and was granted a pension by the Nawab of Bhopal. In his final years, he frequently visited the Dargaha of famous Sufi Ali Hujwiri in Lahore for spiritual guidance. After suffering for months from his illness, Iqbal died in Lahore on 21ST April 1938. His tomb is located in Hazuri Bagh, the enclosed garden between the entrance of the Badshahi Mosque and the Lahore Fort, and official guards are provided by the Government of Pakistan.

Sir Mirza Muhammad Ismail

Sir Mirza Muhammad Ismail - Amin-ul-Mulq, KCIE, OBE (24TH October 1883 – 5TH January 1959) was the Diwan (Prime Minister) of the Kingdoms of Mysore, Jaipur and Hyderabad. He was appointed an OBE in 1922 by the British Government for his services to India, and was appointed a CIE in 1924. He was knighted in 1930 and was further appointed a KCIE in 1936. In 1938, he was appointed an Associate Commander of the Venerable Order of the Hospital of St. John of Jerusalem. Sir Mirza Muhammad Ismail passed away on 5TH January 1959 in Bangalore, Karnataka, India.

The Knights

The Jehangir Baronetcy

The Jehangir Baronetcy, of Bombay, is a title in the Baronetage of the United Kingdom. It was created on 16TH July 1908 for Cowasjee Jehanghir, an influential member of the Parsee community in Bombay. He was the nephew and adopted son and heir of the Parsee community leader, philanthropist and industrialist Cowasji Jehangir Readymoney. By Special Act of the Legislative Council of India in 1911, it was decided that all future holders were to assume the name of the first Baronet on succeeding. The first Baronet was succeeded by his son, the second Baronet, who became a prominent politician.

Sir Cowasji Jehangir, 1st Baronet (1853–1934)
Sir Cowasji Jehangir, 2nd Baronet (1879–1962)
Sir Hirji Jehangir, 3rd Baronet (1915–2000)
Sir Cowasji Jehangir (JHC), 4th Baronet (born 1953)

Sir Nizamat Jung Bahadur

Sir Nizamat Jung Bahadur (April 1871– 1955) was an Arab-Indian poet. Nizamuddin was the second son of the Late Nawab Rafath Yar Jung Bahadur (Moulvi Shaikh Ahmed Hussain), Subedar of Warangal, well known in his days as an ardent educational and social reformer and statesman of no mean order. Nawab Sir Nizamat Jung, was educated at the Madrasas-i-Aizza, a school founded by his father in 1878, and proceeding to England in 1887 joined Trinity College, Cambridge, and took the degrees of B. A., LL. B. Honours) in 1891 being the first Hyderabadi to achieve this. Later on he became a Barrister-at-Law, being called to the Bar from the Inner Temple in 1895 during his second visit to England. Nizamuddin built Hill Fort Palace on Naubat Pahar which was later purchased by the erstwhile Nizam HEH Mir Osman Ali Khan Siddiqi for his son Prince Moazzam Jah. Nizamuddin's first cousin Hakim-ud-Dowla was also a chief justice and he was the owner of the Bella Vista Palace located adjacent to Hill Fort Palace. Serving as an official of numerous prestigious posts, he was a political minister and served as the chief justice of the Hyderabad Deccan High Court during the reign of the Nizams. Sir Nizamat Jung Bahadur passed away in 1955.

The Knights

Jam Mir Sir Ghulam Qadir Khan Aliani

Jam Mir Sir Ghulam Qadir Khan Aliani, CIE, OBE Jam of Lasbela, was the last ruler of the State of Las Bela (Princely State) in Baluchistan of Pakistan. The State of Las Bela was founded in 1742 by Jam Ali Khan I. His descendants ruled Las Bela until 1955 when the state became part of Pakistan. Jam Mir Ghulam Qadir Khan was educated in the Aitchison Chiefs College, Lahore and succeeded his father Jam Mir Ghulam Muhammad Khan in October 1937. Jam Ghulam Qadir Khan succeeded his father in October 1937. He was the last ruler of the former state, had twice served as the Chief minister of Baluchistan and also Federal Minister for Health, Pakistan as well as being the Speaker of the Baluchistan Provincial Assembly. And also Minister for Auqaf and Jails for West Pakistan. Las Bela acceded to Pakistan in 1947. He was the last ruler of the Las Bela state until 1955, when the state was dissolved. In 1988, Jam Ghulam Qadir Khan was walking with his son Jam Akber and grandson Ali Ahmed Zai on a street in London, England. Around 10.20 pm, he felt pain in his left arm and fell on ground. He was taken by ambulance to nearby hospital where his condition deteriorated. At 2.30 am, he was pronounced death. He is buried in the Bara Bagh Cemetery, Lasbela

Sir Malik Mohammed Umar Hayat Khan

Major General Sir Malik Mohammed Umar Hayat Khan GBE KCIE MVO (1875–1944), was a Rajput soldier of the Indian Empire, one of the largest landholders in the Punjab, and an elected member of the Council of State of India. The son of Sir Malik Sahib Khan KB CSI, Khan was educated at Aitchison Chiefs College, Lahore. His family, from Khushab, were part of the Tiwana family of Shahpur. Khan served in the Somaliland War of 1902-1904, receiving the Jidballi medal and clasp, in the Tibet Expedition of 1903-1904 (for which he was Mentioned in Despatches, in the European theatre of the Great War, 1914-15 (during which he was Mentioned in Despatches a further six times), and then in the Third Anglo-Afghan War. He was attached to the 18th King George's Own Lancers and later the 19th King George's Own Lancers. Amongst the Honours awarded to him include thee : Member of the Royal Victorian Order, Fourth class (MVO), 1911· Knight Commander of the Order of the Indian Empire (KCIE), 1916CIE, Knight Grand Cross of the Order of the British Empire (GBE).He acted as an honorary aide-de-camp to George V, Edward VIII. Sir Malik Mohammed Umar Hayat Khan passed away in 1944.

The Knights

Sir Muhammad Faiyaz Ali Khan

Nawab Sir Muhammad Faiyaz Ali Khan Bahadur KCIE KCVO CSI CBE (1851–1922) was a Nawab of Pahasu, a member of the Governor General's Council and Member of the Legislative council of the United Provinces. Khan was appointed Foreign Minister of Jaipur State Council in 1901. In 1902, he was chosen to represent the United Provinces of Agra and Oudh at the coronation in London of King Edward VII and Queen Alexandra. His Honours included: January 1903: Companion of the Order of the Star of India (CSI)' June 1907: Knight Commander of the Order of the Indian Empire (KCIE)' December 1911: Knight Commander of the Royal Victorian Order (KCVO) and January 1919: Commander of the Order of the British Empire (CBE)' He founded an Anglo-vernacular school at Pahasu in 1899. He had donated large amount for public and charitable purposes. He also build the Mumtaz hostel of Aligarh Muslim University, and served as President of Board of Trustees of Aligarh Muslim University. Sir Muhammad Faiyaz Ali Khan passed away in 1922.

Sir Mohammad Yamin Khan

Sir Mohammad Yamin Khan CIE was a barrister-at-law, statesman and politician in the period before the partition of India. Khan served as a parliamentarian and one of the senior most members of the All India Muslim League. Muhammad Yamin Khan was a close confidant of Quaid-e-Azam. He was a member of the working committee of All India Muslim League. He also remained Deputy President of the Indian legislative Council. He also presided over the third "Kamboh Conference" held in Bareilly in 1936. Yamin Khan was prominent in raising the Indianisation debate in the Central Legislatures in which he demanded the admission of increasing numbers of Indians to the officer corps of the British Indian Army. The British Government recognized him for his outstanding social and legal services by appointing him a Companion of the Order of the Indian Empire (CIE) in the 1931 Birthday Honours list, and knighting him in the 1936 New Year Honours list. After the independence of Pakistan in 1947, Khan moved with his family to Karachi, Pakistan where he soon died. Muhammad Yamin Khan was the second Kamboj member to be knighted, and also was the second Kamboj member of the Indian Parliament (M.P.). He had also been a member of the Municipal Board of Meerut since 1918 and served it as Vice-Chairman and Chairman for a long time. The Chairmanship of the Meerut Municipal Board remained for the first half century of its existence with the Nawab family of the Meerut Kambohs.

The Knights

Sir Sadiq Muhammad Khan V Abbasi

General Nawab Sir Sadiq Muhammad Khan V Abbasi GCSI GCIE KCVO (29TH September 1904, in Derawar –24TH May 1966, in London) was the Nawab, and later Amir, of Bahawalpur State from 1907 to 1966. He became the Nawab on the death of his father, when he was only three years old. A Council of Regency, with Sir Rahim Bakhsh as its President, ruled on his behalf until 1924. The Nawab served as an officer with the British Indian Army, fighting in the Third Afghan War (1919) and commanding forces in the Middle East during the Second World War. Under his rule, Bahawalpur State comprised an area larger than Denmark or Belgium. By 1947, its institutions consisted of departments run by trained civil servants; there was a Ministerial Cabinet headed by a Prime Minister; the State Bank was the Bank of Bahawalpur, with branches outside the State, including Karachi; there was a high court and lower courts; a trained police force and an army commanded by officers trained at the Royal Indian Military Academy at Dehra Doon. The Nawab had a keen interest in education, which was free till a level and the State's Government provided scholarships of merit for higher education. In 1951, the Nawab donated 500 acres in Bahawalpur for the construction of Sadiq Public School. Nawab was known for his relationship with the Quaid-i-Azam (Muhammad Ali Jinnah), Founder of Pakistan. In August 1947, on the withdrawal of British forces from the subcontinent, the Nawab decided not to cede his State at once to the new Dominion of Pakistan. However, on 3RD October 1947, after some delay, he relented, and became the first ruler of a princely state to accede successfully. As tens of thousands of Muslim refugees flooded into the state from the new India, he set up the Ameer of Bahawalpur Refugee Relief and Rehabilitation Fund to provide for their relief. In 1953, the Ameer represented Pakistan at the coronation of Queen Elizabeth II. In 1955 he signed an agreement with the Governor-General of Pakistan, Malik Ghulam Muhammad, under which Bahawalpur became part of the province of West Pakistan, with effect from 14 October 1955, and the Ameer received a yearly privy purse of 32 lakhs of rupees, keeping his titles. The same year, he was promoted to the rank of General in the Pakistan Army. He died in 1966, aged 62.

The Knights

Sir Sikandar Hayat Khan

Sir Sikandar Hayat Khan was born on June 5TH, 1892 in Multan. He belonged to the Khattar Tribe of Attock. He was the son of Nawab Muhammad Hayat Khan, a police inspector in British Government. Later, he became Tehsildar and finally Assistant Commissioner. He went to Aligarh for education and admitted in Oriental College and High School. Sikandar Hayat went England for higher education but came back without degree. He joined the British Army in WW2 and reached to the position of Captain. After the war, he started his business and entered in local politics. Sir Sikandar Hayat Khan joined local politics as he return from England. He was elected as a member of Punjab Legislative Council from Attock District in 1920. He joined the secular unionist party of Sir Fazl-i-Hussain. It represented the interests of the landed gentry and landlords of Punjab including Muslims, Sikhs and Hindus. Sikander Hayat got victory in the elections of 1937 and became premier of Punjab. He carried out many reforms in favour of Punjabi Zamindar. Sir Sikandar Khan joined AIML in the wake of Jinnah-Sikander Pact in 1937. He believed in the policy of cooperation with the British for the independence of India and tried to maintain a balance in the Punjab political system. He guided other unionist members to counter congress totalitarianism. He was one of the chief supporters and architects of the Lahore Resolution. He resigned from National Defence Council on Jinnah recommendation in 1941. He also opposed Quit India Movement in 1942. Sir Sikandar supported the British struggle against Nazi Germany in WW2. He believed in cooperating with the British Government as it would help in independence. He was active in the recruitment of troops from the Punjab in WW2 as part of the 'War Effort'. The Muslim League leadership agreed with his perspective and cooperated with British Raj. Sikandar Hayat Khan was a great administrator. Sir Sikandar showed his strengths in the local administration in 1920. It resulted in his contacts with the unionist party. Unionist Party was a coalition of Hindu farmer in east Punjab and Muslim feudal and land owners of the west Punjab. Sikandar was also appointed as the revenue member in Punjab Government. He succeeded Sir Fazl-e-Hussain as the leader of Unionist Party and claimed victory in the first election of Punjab legislative Assembly in 1937. Sikandar remained the premier of the Punjab till his death. His main political contribution was the strong opposition of the Unionist Party toward the division of Punjab. His Administration was admired owing to various innovative form of taxation. This alarmed the money lenders.

The Knights

Sir Sikandar Hayat Khan (Cont)

He appealed for the collection of one rupee tax from all Muslims to renovate the Badshahi Mosque. Owing to this, he had been buried at the doorstep of Mosque. Sikandar Hayat Khan viewed India as collection of the states including Muslim majority and Hindu majority areas. Sikandar Hayat khan proposed a scheme of loose federation for Indio in 1939. India should be divided into regional and zonal legislatures to deal with local people problems while the state might continue to remain united. Punjab could not ignore the issue of partition as it was a Muslim majority area and Jinnah has strong foothold. Lahore Resolution promised adequate and effective safeguards for the minorities to protect their politics, culture, religious, and economics. Jinnah also made efforts to avoid clash between the Muslim Governor and Muslim led parties to ensure the security of Minorities. Sikandar Hayat, in this context, can be regarded as a strong voice for Punjab. He died in December, 1942. He is buried outside the Badshahi mosque. His numerous works were left half done especially British war efforts and his attempt to save Punjab from communal friction.

Sir Syed Ahmad bin Syed Muhammad Muttaqi

Sir Syed Ahmad bin Syed Muhammad Muttaqi KCSI (17TH October 1817 – 27TH March 1898), commonly known as Sir Syed, was an Indian Muslim pragmatist, Islamic reformist and philosopher of nineteenth century British India. He was awarded honorary LLD from the University of Edinburgh. In 1838, Syed Ahmad entered the service of East India Company and went on to become a judge at a Small Causes Court in 1867, and retired from service in 1876. During the Indian Rebellion of 1857, he remained loyal to the British Empire and was noted for his actions in saving European lives. Believing that the future of Muslims was threatened by the rigidity of their orthodox outlook, Sir Syed began promoting Western–style scientific education by founding modern schools and journals and organising Muslim entrepreneurs. In 1859, Syed established Gulshan School at Moradabad, Victoria School at Ghazipur in 1863, and a scientific society for Muslims in 1864. In 1875, founded the Muhammadan Anglo-Oriental College, the first Muslim university in South Asia. During his career, Syed repeatedly called upon Muslims to loyally serve the British Empire and promoted the adoption of Urdu as the lingua franca of all Indian Muslims. Syed heavily critiqued the Indian National Congress. Syed maintains a strong legacy in Pakistan and Indian Muslims. He strongly influenced other Muslim leaders including Allama Iqbal and Jinnah.

The Knights

Sir Syed Ahmad bin Syed Muhammad Muttaqi (Cont)

His advocacy of Islam's rationalist (Muʿtazila) tradition, and at broader, radical reinterpretation of the Quran to make it compatible with science and modernity, continues to influence the global Islamic reformation. Many universities and public buildings in Pakistan bear Sir Syed's name. Syed Ahmad is widely commemorated across South Asia as a great Muslim social reformer and visionary. At the same time, Syed Ahmad sought to politically ally Muslims with the British government. An avowed loyalist of the British Empire, he was nominated as a member of the Civil Service Commission in 1887 by Lord Dufferin. In 1888, he established the United Patriotic Association at Aligarh to promote political co-operation with the British and Muslim participation in the British government. Syed Ahmed was bestowed with the suffix of 'Khan Bahadur' and was subsequently knighted by the British government in 1888 and was awarded Knight Commander of the order of Star of India (KCSI) for his loyalty to the British crown, through his membership of the Imperial Legislative Council and in the following year he received an LL.D. honoris causa from the Edinburgh University. Sir Syed died on 27TH March 1898. He was buried besides Sir Syed Masjid inside the campus of the Aligarh University.

Nawab Sir Muhammad Faiz Ali Khan Bahadur

Nawab Sir Muhammad Faiz Ali Khan Bahadur, KCSI (26TH August 1821 – 5TH August 1894) was the Nawab of Pahasu, also a politician and administrator, who served as Prime Minister of Jaipur State. Nawab Sir Muhammad Faiz Ali Khan KCSI was scion of Muslim Rajput community of Lalkhani (Badgujar Rajput) lineage. He was born to Murad Ali Khan. He and his father both served in Jaipur Armed Forces and served British well in Indian Mutiny of 1857. He was rewarded for his loyalty with a large estate and title of Khan Bahadur and Knighted by the British. He served as Prime Minister of Jaipur State in 1863. He was an active member in public life and was member of Legislative council of United Provinces and member of Governors General's Legislative council. He was Jagirdar of Pahasu with title of Nawab of Pahasu. Also held jagir in Jaipur State located at Tazami. He also held one village in Sadabad Estate. He was succeeded by his able son Sir Muhammad Faiyaz Ali Khan, as Nawab of Pahasu.

The Knights

Sir Muhammad Mahabat Khanji III Rasul Khanji

Sir Muhammad Mahabat Khanji III Rasul Khanji, GCIE, KCSI (2ND August 1900 – 7TH November 1959) was the last ruling Nawab of Junagadh of the princely state of Junagadh in British India from 1911 to 1948. He was the father of Muhammad Dilawar Khanji – Former Governor of Sindh and his claimed successor. Famed for his extravagant lifestyle and his love of dogs, his decision to accede Junagadh to the Dominion of Pakistan following India's Independence led to the Indian Army taking military action. The Indian Army then took over Junagadh on 9TH November, installed a new state Governor, and called for a public referendum on the status of the state. The referendum, arranged by the Indian government, was held on 20TH February 1948. Of over 200,000 people who voted, 91 percent chose India while the rest chose Pakistan. The following year, on 20TH January 1949, Junagadh was merged into the new Indian state of Saurashtra. After his exile from Junagadh, Mahabat Khanji and his family settled at Karachi, where he died, aged 59 on 17TH November 1959.

Nawab Sir Muhammad Muzammilullah Khan

Nawab Sir Muhammad Muzammilullah Khan, Khan Bahadur KCIE OBE (1865–1935) was a noted Zamindar and politician from United Province of British India. He was former Vice Chancellor of Aligarh Muslim University. He was made one of the trustees of Muhammadan Anglo-Oriental College, Aligarh in 1886 and a fellow of Allahabad University. He was one of the signatories to the 1906 Muslim Memorial and was involved in 1909 agitation for separate electorates for Muslims and was among the member of all-India delegation of Muslims led by Sir Aga Khan III to meet with Viceroy Lord Minto in order to demand a separate Legislative Council for Muslims. He held his estate in Bhikampur in Aligarh district. He was nominated member of United Province Legislative Council for the years 1916-19. He was also a member of Viceroy's Council of State and twice home member of United Province government. He served as Secretary of the Zamindar's' Association, United Provinces and was also made Special magistrate by the government. He also served as president of UP Muslim Defence Association in 1917. He was made Khan Bahadur in 1904 and given personal title of the Nawab in 1910. He was appointed an Officer of the Order of the British Empire in the 1919 New Year Honours, and invested as a Knight Commander of the Order of the Indian Empire in the 1924 New Year Honours. He died in 1935.

The Knights

Sir Khawaja Nazimuddin

Sir Khawaja Nazimuddin (19TH July 1894 – 22ND October 1964), KCIE,CIE, was an East Pakistani politician and one of the leading founding fathers of Pakistan. He is noted as being the first Bengali leader of Pakistan who led the country as Prime Minister (1951–53), as well as the second Governor-General (1948–51). He was educated at the Aligarh Muslim University before pursuing his education at the Cambridge University. He started his political career on a Muslim League platform. From 1943–45, he served as the Prime Minister of Bengal and later becoming the Chief Minister in 1947 until 1948 when he ascended as Governor-General after Jinnah's passing. In 1951, he took over the control of the government as Prime Minister of Pakistan upon the assassination of Liaquat Ali Khan, and relinquished the post of Governor-General to Sir Malik Ghulam. As Prime Minister, he struggled to run the government effectively and struggled to maintain law and order in the country and instructed the military to impose martial law in Lahore due to religious riots and stagnation. Foreign relations with the United States, Soviet Union, Afghanistan, and India soured as republicanism and socialism gained popularity at home. Eventually, he was forced to step down in favour of diplomat Mohammad Ali Bogra by his own appointed Governor-General Sir Malik Ghulam and conceded defeat in elections held in 1954. Upon retiring from national politics, he suffered a brief illness and died in 1964. He was buried at a Mausoleum in Dhaka.

Sir Rafiuddin Ahmed

Moulvi Sir Rafiuddin Ahmed (1865–1954) was an Indian Muslim barrister, journalist and politician. He was generally known as the Moulvi. He was educated at Deccan College, Pune, and King's College London. In 1892, he became a barrister-at-law in the Middle Temple. He was a close friend of Abdul Karim (the Munshi), the Indian secretary of Queen Victoria. Victoria was instrumental in involving Ahmed in diplomatic approaches to Sultan Abdul Hamid II of the Ottoman Empire in the late 1890s, and unsuccessfully suggested that he be appointed to the British embassy in Constantinople. He was a prominent member of the Muslim Patriotic League, and under the Montagu–Chelmsford Reforms, which introduced greater self-government to British India; he was elected to the council of the Bombay Presidency. In 1928, he was appointed Minister of Agriculture and then as Minister of Education where he served till 1934. For his work in government, he was knighted in 1932. He died in his native Pune, where he had lived for the last 20 years of his life.

The Knights

Khan Bahadur Nawab Sir Liaqat Hayat Khan
Khan Bahadur Nawab Sir Liaqat Hayat Khan was an Indian official who served for most of his career as a minister and later Prime Minister of Patiala State, in British India. Liaqat Hayat found employment as a junior police officer in the Patiala princely state, and in due course, rose to be head of the police force. Later on, he was appointed state minister for Home Affairs and then, finally, as Chief or Prime Minister to the state. In his capacity of loyal representative of the interests of Patiala, he was nominated by the then Maharaja as a delegate to the Round Table Conferences in London, England, and put forward the case for independent princely states in the event of India's eventual freedom from British colonial rule. Liaqat Hayat, unlike his younger brother Sir Sikandar, was neither a supporter of the All India Muslim League nor of the idea of a separate or even autonomous Muslim state, along the lines of Pakistan. However, after Independence/Partition in August 1947, he did settle in the new Pakistani state and accepted the post of the new country's ambassador to France. Sir Liaqat Hayat died in 1948.

Sir Muhammad Zafarullah Khan
Sir Muhammad Zafarullah Khan was a Pakistani politician, diplomat, and international jurist, known particularly for his representation of Pakistan at the United Nations (UN). He practiced law in Sialkot and Lahore, became a member of the Punjab Legislative Council in 1926, and was a delegate in 1930, 1931, and 1932 to the Round Table Conferences on Indian reforms in London. In 1931-32 he was president of the All-India Muslim League He was knighted in 1935. He sat on the British viceroy's executive council as its Muslim member from 1935 to 1941. He led the Indian delegation to the League of Nations in 1939, and from 1941 to 1947 he served as a judge of the Federal Court of India. Prior to the partition of India in 1947, Zafarullah Khan presented the Muslim League's view of the future boundaries of Pakistan to Sir Cyril Radcliffe, the man designated to decide the boundaries between India and Pakistan. Upon the independence of Pakistan, Zafarullah Khan became the new country's minister of foreign affairs and served concurrently as leader of Pakistan's delegation to the UN (1947-54). From 1954 to 1961 he served as a member of the International Court of Justice at The Hague. He again represented Pakistan at the UN in 1961-64 and served as president of the UN General Assembly in 1962-63. Returning to the International Court of Justice in 1964, he served as the court's president from 1970 to 1973. He died in Lahore on 1ST September 1985 following a protracted illness.

The Distinguished Service Cross

The Distinguished Service Cross is the second highest military award that can be given to a member of the United States Army for extreme gallantry and risk of life in actual combat with an armed enemy force. Actions that merit the Distinguished Service Cross must be of such a high degree that they are above those required for all other U.S.

Sepoy Sher Ali, DSC

The Distinguished Service Cross is presented to Sher Ali, Sepoy, of the 1st Battalion, 2nd Punjab Regiment, Royal British Indian Army, for extraordinary heroism in action against the enemy near San Clemente, Italy on 22 February 1945. As a member of a six man patrol sent out to raid an enemy position on the forward slope of a hill, Sepoy Sher Ali charged an enemy trench, bayoneted its occupants and then assisted his patrol in killing two other enemy and capturing two prisoners. On the return journey, the patrol was suddenly attacked by 15 Germans, whereupon Sepoy Sher Ali without hesitating charged the Germans, killed two with his bayonet, and then turned to assist his comrades in killing three more. Upon seeing that there were only two members of his patrol left Sepoy Sher Ali ordered them to withdraw while he exposed himself to enemy fire in order to cover their return to allied lines. His gallantry and unswerving leadership reflect great credit upon himself and the Armed Forces of the Allied Nations.

Bronze Star

The Bronze Star Medal was instituted in February 1944 to be awarded to personnel, male or female, serving in any capacity with the Army, Navy, Marine Corps or Coast Guard of the USA, who 'on or after 7TH December 1941 shall have distinguished themselves by heroic or meritorious military achievements, or service in connection with military operations.

Sepoy Seemurgh Khan, BS
Citation:
'During the recent operations near Cesena and Faenza the courage and devotion to duty of Sepoy Seemurgh Khan of the 3RD Battalion, 1ST Punjab Regiment, a Battalion Linesmann, has been an outstanding example to all ranks. His determined efforts on numerous occasions had been responsi ble for the maintanance of vital communications under the most adverse conditions. On 17TH October, 1944, he in company with another Signaller was layibng a line form Battalion HQ, to a forward Company, some 1000 yards distance, on the Aquarola ridge, over ground which was under almost continous enemy Mortar, Artillery and Tank fire, when his companion was killed outright. With about 800 yards of cable still to lay, Sepoy Seemurgh Khan, single handed and despite the intense Morar fire, continud his task. He succeeded in reaching in within 100 yards of the Company HQ, when an enemy tank, observing his movements, opened up with accurate MG fire as to make further progress impossibl. From 7TH to 15TH December,1944, the Battalion positions on Duecento ridge were continously subjected to intense enemy Artillery concentaritlons, causing damage almost hourly to Signal Line communications, and making repair of the lines a most hazardous task. Despite this Sepoy Seemurgh Khan was often discovered to be out in the open in forward localitions repairing damaged cable, having time after time volunteeered to go out alone to do the task. On one occasion when it was necessary to relay the line from Tac HQ to the Exchange afer particularly heavy shelling, Sepoy Seemurgh Khan volunteered to go out and complete the task.

Bronze Star

Sepoy Seemurgh Khan, BS (Cont)

This continued moveing along an almost bare ridge for about 400 yards under enemy Artillery fire all the way. He successfully relaid this most vital communication. The personal courage, determination and high sense of duty displayed by this young Sepoy are beyond all praise. Sepoy Seemurgh Khan was awarded the Bronze Star by the grateful US Army.

Havildar Gheba Khan, BS
Citation

Havildar Gheba Khan, 3RD Battalion 8 Punjab Regiment for heroic achievement in connection with military operations near Ussinano Italy in November 1944. While recconnotering enemy positions on the night 17/18 November, 1944 a party consisting of one officer and 5 men were severly wounded by exploding mines close to the enemy forward positions. In the intense darkness another party sent out to find them failed to do so. Havildar Gheba Khan, platoon havildar of the platoon, volunteered to go out to find thbe recce party. After some searching he found all six of the party lying severely wounded in an enemy minefield. Heedless of his own safety he felt his way cautiosly along the trip wirers which were totally invisible in the dark and succeeded in carrying and dragging two of the wounded clear of the minefield. These two he and his companion carried back to the patrol base. He then returned with a rescue party to the same scene of the accident. Realising that if he allowed the party to enter the minefield there would by further casualties he ordered them to remain in a clear area while he himself, heedless of his own safety, entered the minefied again and again until he had succeeded in extricating all the casualties. He then organised the carrying back of casualties to the patrol base. Half way back the party suddenly came under close and accurate MG fire from the enemy patrol. Realising their helplessness the Havildar quickly and quietly got the party and casualties under cover and lay quiet while the enemy patrol searched around. No thought of abandoning the casualties arose. Later when the enemy had moved on Havildar Gheba Khan brought the party back to safety. Havildar Gheba Khan's complete disregard of his own safety, coolness and devotion to duty and the safety of his comrades is and inspirinag example of the high traditions of the Indian Army. Havildar Gheba Khan was awarded the Bronze Star by the grateful US Army.

Bronze Star

Subedar Mian Khan, BS
4TH Battalion, 10TH Baluch Regiment

Citation:

Subedar Mian Khan was second in command of a Company during the 12 days fighting from 8TH October 1944 to 19TH October 1944. This operation started with the capture of Strigara and finished with the capture of Monte Tuscola, a distance of 8 miles as the crow flies, but well over 15 miles over the route actually taken. The country was extremely difficult, being mountainous and intersected by deep ravines. Throughout the period the weather was appalling. A heavy mist flew over the hilltops and not infrequently torrential rain filled the trenches, soaked the men and made the progress doubly difficult. German resistance was strong and counter-attacks against positions were frequent and fierce, but inspite of this the Company gained all the objectives and never gave a foot of ground back to the enemy. Over 40 prisoners were taken by the Company alone. The success of the Company was largely due to Subedar Mian Khan's excellent example. In spite of heavy casualties he maintained the morale of the Company at the highest pitch. Always cheerful himself and he insisted on visiting all positions the Company was holding, in spite of heavy enemy artillery, mortar and small arms fire and by his courage and devotion to duty, maintained the offensive spirit of the men. On one occasion, seeing that the Company Commander with two platoons was held up by the enemy, he led the third platoon in an out-flanking movement and captured a key position. His initiative and bold action on this occasion enabled the Company to seize their final objective. Subedar Mian Khan's previous and subsequent service to the above action has been and is of the highest order. Throughout the period, his example of cool courage and under heavy fire and cheerfulness under all circumstances was a great inspiration to the men under his command. Subedar Mian Khan was awarded the Bronze Star by the grateful US Army.

The Legion of Merit

The Legion of Merit (LOM) is a military award of the United States Armed Forces that is given for exceptionally meritorious conduct in the performance of outstanding services and achievements.

Major General Mian Hayaud Din, LOM

Major General Mian Hayaud Din was awarded the American Medal of the Legion of Merit in Karachi on 12TH January 1961. At a ceremony at the American Embassy Residence, Major General Mian Hayaud Din, Director General Mineral Resources and former Military Attaché to the Embassy of Pakistan in the United States, received the Medal of the Legion of Merit, Degree Officer, from the American Ambassador William M Rountree. The text of the citation accompanying the medal was read by Lieutenant Colonel William D Ward, Assistant Army Attaché to the American Embassy said:

The President of the United States of America, authorised by Act of Congress, July 20TH, 1942, has awarded the Legion of Merit, Degree of Officer, to Major General Mian Hayaud Din, Pakistan Army, for exceptionally meritorious conduct in the performance of outstanding services. Major General Mian Hayauddinhas distinguished himself by exceptionally meritorious conduct in the performance of outstanding service as Military Attaché to the Embassy of Pakistan in the United States from July 1955 to September 1960. Through his tireless and selfless devotion to duty, he has contributed significantly to the attainment of the Free World's objectives of peace and security. His friendly and sincere cooperation with United State's military personnel has served to strengthen the spirit of friendship and mutual confidence, which characterizes the relationship between the Armed Forces of Pakistan and the United States of America. His outstanding leadership, sound judgement, and exceptional energy in the performance of his important duties reflect distinct credit upon himself and the military service of his country.

The Legion of Merit

Admiral Shahid Karimullah, LOM
Admiral Shahid Karimullah was bestowed Legion of Merit on July 21ST, 2004, for his steadfast support of American-Pakistan cooperation in regional maritime, security affairs, demonstrated superb resolve and unwavering dedication to the Global War on terrorism.

Admiral Afzal Tahir, LOM
Admiral Afzal Tahir was awarded Legion of Merit on January 23RD, 2006 in recognition of his efforts in conducting maritime security operations and strengthening of cooperation between the two navies in the 5TH Fleet area of responsibility.

Major General Mian Ghulam Jilani, LOM
In 1959, Major General Mian Ghulam Jilani was made an Officer of the Legion for exceptionally meritorious conduct in the performance of outstanding services to the Government of the United States, from October 1952 to June 1955.

Lieutenant General Tariq Khan, LOM
On December 9TH, 2007, Lieutenant General Tariq Khan received the award of Legion of Merit for meritorious services as a liaison officer at CENTCOM during Operations Enduring Freedom.

General Asfaq Parves Kayani, LOM
General Asfaq Parves Kayani is a retired four-star rank army general in the Pakistan Army who January 1ST, 2009, was awarded the Legion of Merit for strengthening the ties between the two countries.

Admiral Noman Bashir, LOM
Admiral Noman Bashir was awarded the Legion of Merit for distinguished service and strengthening American-Pakistani relations.

General Raheel Sharif, LOM
Chief of Army Staff General Raheel Sharif on November 19TH, 2014 was conferred with the US Legion of Merit Medal in recognition of his brave leadership and efforts to ensure peace in the region.

Admiral Mohammad Zakaullah, LOM
The Chief of Naval Staff the Admiral Muhammad Zakaulla was presented with the United States Legion of Merit for strengthen the relations between the two Navies of both countries.

The Legion of Honour

Created in 1802 by Napoleon Bonaparte, the Legion of Honour is the highest award given by the French Republic for outstanding service to France, regardless of the social status or the nationality of the recipients.

Major General Mian Hayaud Din, HJ, MBE, MC, Légion d'Honneur

At a ceremony at the French Embassy, Major General Mian Hayauddin was decorated with the Cross of Commander Legion of Honour by Major General Jean Marie Bezy. The speech of the French Ambassador to the USA:

Dear General Hayaud Din, it is indeed an honour and a great pleasure for me to bestow upon you the Cross of Commander de la Legion d'Honneur. The French Military ceremonies as a rule do not involve long speeches, therefore in a few short words; I will indicate the reasons, which merit this decoration. For a long time, France has desired to express to you her gratitude for your brilliant conduct in 1945-1946 during the campaign, which brought about the surrender of the Japanese forces and Communist elements by them in South Vietnam. At the head of your battalion you established bridgeheads, thus permitting the landing of Allied Forces in the Saigon area; you brought under control difficult regions at the price of heavy casualties; you succeeded everywhere. Your brilliant leadership became so well known that the Divisional Commander, General Gracy, chose you to receive the sabre of the Japanese Commander in Chief at the time of his surrender. By brave and vigorous action, which put a quick end to a murderous occupation, you spared the lives of numerous of our French Compatriots and of our Vietnamese friends, and in this way, you gave them liberty sooner. The Government of the French Republic is deeply grateful to you. The presence here today of His Excellency Aziz Ahmed, Ambassador of Pakistan to the United States, emphasis the concurrence of your own Government to this homage rendered to an outstanding officer who have served so magnificently the cause of Liberty, the Allied cause and the French cause. Dear general, with my personal congratulations, it is my pleasure to decorate you.

The Legion of Honour

Admiral Muhammad Asif Sandila, HI (M) , NI (M)) Légion d'Honneur
Muhammad Asif Sandila completed his primary education Sheikhupura, Punjab Province. Thereafter, he studied at the prestigious Cadet College Kohat where he gained a high school diploma. In 1971, shortly after the 1971 *winter war*, Sandila passed the university entrance exam and the officers' exam from Sheikhupura. Sandila was admitted to the Pakistan Naval Academy in 1972 and entered the Business Administration Department at the Naval Academy. Sandila also attended the Britannia Royal Naval College at Dartmouth, United Kingdom from where he is a certified surface warfare officer. In 1975, Sandila earned a B.B.A. degree in Business Administration and was commissioned as a Sub-Lieutenant in the Naval Operations Branch of the Navy. Sandila is also a graduate of Pakistan Naval War College from where he earned a M.Sc. in Naval strategy. While at the Naval College, Sandila went to Indonesia on a year's deputation where he attended the Indonesian Navy's Naval Command and Staff College and completed a Naval Staff course. Sandila also holds a M.Sc. in War studies from National Defence University (NDU). Asif Sandila joined the Pakistan Navy in 1972 as a non-commissioned officer and was commissioned into the Naval Operations Branch in June 1975. He specialized as a Principal Warfare Officer in United Kingdom. Throughout his naval career, Sandila has held challenging naval command and staff appointments. During the 1980s Sandila served as the ADC to former Chairman of the Joint Chiefs of Staff Committee and former Chief of Naval Staff Admiral Iftikhar Ahmed Sirohey. As Captain, Sandila commanded the *PNS Badr*, a guided-missile destroyer. As Commodore, Sandila commanded the 25th Destroyer Squadron during the Indo-Pakistani War of 1999. In 2002, Sandila was promoted to the 2-star rank of Rear-Admiral and served as the Chief of Staff of Pakistan Coast Guard which he commanded until 2005. From 2006 till 2007, Rear-Admiral Sandila served as the Commander of Naval Logistics (COMLOG) and commanded all logistic naval facilities of Pakistan Navy. In October 2008 Sandila commanded the Pakistan Naval Fleet. From 2008 till 2009, Sandila commanded the entire Pakistan's naval combatant fleet and entire naval combatant operations. In 2010, Sandila was promoted to the 3-star rank of Vice-Admiral and was made Chief of Staff of the Pakistan Navy.
Sandila has held several important staff positions during his career. He was awarded the Legion of Honour by the French President Jacques Chirac.

National Order of Merit (France)

The National Order of Merit (French: *Ordre national du Mérite*) is a French order of merit with membership awarded by the President of the French Republic, founded on 3 December 1963 by President Charles de Gaulle. The reason for the order's establishment was twofold: to replace the large number of ministerial orders previously awarded by the ministries; and to create an award that can be awarded at a lower level than the Legion of Honour.

Riaz Pirach, National Order of Merit
Riaz Pirach was foreign secretary of Pakistan from 1980 to 1982. He was awarded The National Order of Merit, by the French President François Mitterrand.

Major General Rahmat Khan, National Order of Merit
His Excellency Philippe Thiébaud, the Ambassador of France in Pakistan hosted a reception at his residence on the occasion of the award of the National Order of Merit to Major General Rahmat Khan, who has been the Managing Director of Lafarge Pakistan since January 2008 and non executive Chairman of Board of Directors of Lafarge Pakistan since January 2013.

Marvi Memon, National Order of Merit
A Pakistani politician in July 2017, she was conferred the French National Order of Merit by the French Ambassador to Pakistan in Islamabad.

Shabbir Ahmed, National Order of Merit
Shabbir Ahmed Chief Executive at D.l. Nash *(pvt)* Ltd. was conferred the French National Order of Merit by the French Ambassador to Pakistan in Islamabad.

Suhail Hameed, National Order of Merit
Commodore Suhail Hameed SI (M). Was conferred the French National Order of Merit by the French Ambassador to Pakistan in Islamabad.

Croix de Guerre (France)

The Croix de Guerre is bestowed on individuals who distinguish themselves by acts of heroism involving combat with enemy forces.

Subedar Hukam Dad, Croix de Guerre	France
Subedar Major Khitab Gil, Croix de Guerre	France
Subedar Bahadur Shah, Croix de Guerre	France
Subedar Ghulam Mohammad Khan, Croix de Guerre	France
Subedar Major Hassan Mohammad, Croix de Guerre	France
Subedar Major Hyasdar Khan, Croix de Guerre	France
Subedar Ali Dost, Croix de Guerre	France
Subedar Sadar Din, Croix de Guerre	Mesopotamia
Subedar Major Mohammad Din, Croix de Guerre	Mesopotamia
Subedar Major Alam Khan, Croix de Guerre	Mesopotamia
Subedar Major Mohibullah Khan, Croix de Guerre	Mesopotamia
Subedar Nishan Ali, Croix de Guerre	Mesopotamia
Subedar Major Boi Khan, Croix de Guerre	Mesopotamia
Subedar Ghulam Jilani, Croix de Guerre	East Africa
Subedar Mohammad Din, Croix de Guerre	East Africa
Subedar Saiyed Abdul Ghafur, Croix de Guerre	East Africa
Subedar Syed Mohammad Shah, Croix de Guerre	East Africa
Daffadar Zahur Ali, Croix de Guerre	France
Daffadar Sayed Hassan, Croix de Guerre	France
Daffadar Ahmed Khan, Croix de Guerre	France
Daffadar Rafik Hassan Khan, Croix de Guerre	Egypt
Daffadar Darin, Croix de Guerre	Mesopotamia
Kot Daffadar Mohammad Fazil, Croix de Guerre.	Mesopotamia
Lance Daffadar Asghar Ali, Croix de Guerre	France
Lance Daffadar Nur Ali, Croix de Guerre	France
Ressaidar Mohammad Amin, Croix de Guerre	France
Ressaidar Zaman Khan, Croix de Guerre	France
Jemadar Fez Talab, Croix de Guerre	France
Jemadar Zargir, Croix de Guerre	East Africa

Croix de Guerre (French) (Cont)

Jemadar Fateh Din, Croix de Guerre	Mesopotamia
Jemadar Pat Khan, Croix de Guerre	Mesopotamia
Sepoy Ghulam Hussain, Croix de Guerre	France
Sepoy Kurban, Croix de Guerre	France
Sepoy Inyat Ali Shah, Croix de Guerre	France
Sowar Sarwar Ali, Croix de Guerre	Mesopotamia
Sowar Ibrahim, Croix de Guerre	East Africa

Croix de Guerre (Belgium)

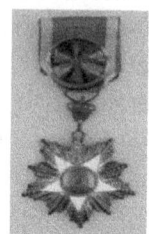

The Belgian Croix de Guerre (or War Cross) was instituted on 25 October 1915 as a means of formally recognising acts of heroism performed by individuals (of any of the Allied powers) during the First World War.

Daffadar Nawab Ali Khan, Croix de Guerre	France
Daffadar Adil Beg, Croix de Guerre	France
Sowar Sayyad Abdul Majid, Croix de Guerre	France
Daffadar Nadir Ali Khan, Croix de Guerre	France
Daffadar Nazir Mohammad Khan, Croix de Guerre	France
Kot Daffadar, Shahweli Khan, Croix de Guerre.	France

Cross of St. George (Russian)

The George Cross is the civilian counterpart of the Victoria Cross and the highest gallantry award for civilians as well as for military personnel in actions which are not in the face of the enemy or for which purely military honours would not normally be granted.

Naik Shahamad Khan, VC. 89TH Punjabis	Cross of St. George
Lance Naik Mohammad Din 27TH Punjabis	Cross of St. George
Subedar Mir Most VC, IOM 55TH Coke's Rifles (FF)	Cross of St. George
Daffadar Mohammad Yusuf 7TH Hariana Lancers	Cross of St. George
Jemadar Abdul Gafoor Khan 34TH Poona Horse	Cross of St. George
Havildar Ali Akbar 22ND Peshawar Mountain Battery	Cross of St. George
Subedar Ismail Khan 3RD Sappers and Miners	Cross of St. George
Naik Zar Baz 58TH Vaughan's Rifles (FF)	Cross of St. George
Sepoy Nek Amal, IOM 129TH DCO Baluchis	Cross of St. George
Daffadar Amanatullah Khan 4TH Cavalry	Cross of St. George

St George Medal for Bravery

The Medal for Bravery awarded to non-commissioned officers and enlisted men for bravery during peace or war. In 1913 the title of the medal was changed to 'St George Medal for Bravery'.

Havildar Major Rehmat Khan 21ST Kohat Mountain Battery	St George Medal for Bravery
Naik Ghulam Hassan 52ND Sikhs (FF)	St George Medal for Bravery
Subedar Major Nasir Khan 59TH Scinde Rifles (FF)	St George Medal for Bravery
Havildar Wasim Khan 129TH Baluchi	St George Medal for Bravery
Havildar Nowsher Khan 1ST Sappers and Miners	St George Medal for Bravery
Subedar Nazir Khan 9TH Bhopal Infantry	St George Medal for Bravery
Naik Ahmed Din 9TH Bhopal Infantry	St George Medal for Bravery
Havildar Abdul Wahab 59TH Scinde Rifles	St George Medal for Bravery
Naik Feroze Khan 66TH Punjabis	St George Medal for Bravery
Nail Bahadur Khan 93RD Burma Infantry	St George Medal for Bravery
Sowar Allah Dad Khan 12TH Cavalry	St George Medal for Bravery

St George Medal for Bravery (Russian)

Sepoy Nazir Din 22ND Punjabis	St George Medal for Bravery
Naik Safirullah 58TH Rifles	St George Medal for Bravery
Sepoy Mohammad Shafi 102ND Grenadiers	St George Medal for Bravery
Sepoy Sardar Khan 108TH Infantry	St George Medal for Bravery
Lance Naik Karim Dad Signal Company	St George Medal for Bravery
Sepoy Rahim Dad 57TH Light Infantry	St George Medal for Bravery
Sepoy Mukhrtiara 40TH Pathans	St George Medal for Bravery
Sepoy Dadum Khan 40TH Pathans	St George Medal for Bravery
Sepoy Sardar Din 59TH Scinde Rifles	St George Medal for Bravery
Jemadar Fateh Haidar 129TH Baluchis	St George Medal for Bravery
Sepoy Sultan Baksh 129TH Baluchis	St George Medal for Bravery
Driver Din Mohammad Mule Corps	St George Medal for Bravery
Sepoy Hafiz Ali 3RD Kashmir Rifles	St George Medal for Bravery
Sepoy Rahim Ali 3RD Kashmir Rifles	St George Medal for Bravery
Lieutenant Colonel Haidar Ali Khan 2ND Kashmir Rifles	St George Medal for Bravery
Private Sultan Baksh 130TH Baluchis	St George Medal for Bravery

Bibliography

Army Aviation Directorate (2008), *History of Pakistan Aviation*
The Army Press, Islamabad.

Sushil Talwar *(2017) Indian Recipients of the Military Cross*
KW Publishers Ltd. New Delhi.

P.P. Hypher (1925) *Deeds of Valour of the Indian Soldier*
Simla Times Press. (2 Vols)

Rana Chhina (2001) *The Indian Distinguished Service Medal*
Invica, India Publishers

Anthony Farrington (1986) *Second Afghan War 1878-1880*
London Stamp Exchange Ltd.

WO 373 Awards WO 373/6, *Honour and Awards*
National Archives, Kew, UK

The Register of the Victoria Cross (1988),
This England Books, Cheltenham, Gloucestershire, UK

Peter Duckers (1999), *Reward of Valour, The IOM 1914-1918*
Jade Publishing Ltd. Lancashire, UK.

INDEX

2ND Lieutenant Farooq Abdul Aziz 80
2ND Lieutenant Imran Ahmed Khan 122
2ND Lieutenant Mohammad Sabir Beg 80
A. Surgeon Abdul Ghafur 300
A. Surgeon Abdul Majid 300
A. Surgeon Barktullah 300
A. Surgeon Chandri Maula Baksh 271
A. Surgeon Fazal Ahmed 299
A. Surgeon Ghulam Haidar 300
A. Surgeon Mehdi Hussein Khan 299
A. Surgeon Mohamand Umar 299
A. Surgeon Mohammad Hussain 300
A. Surgeon Mohammad Hussain 300
A. Surgeon Mohammad Ishak 300
A. Surgeon Mohammad Reza Khan 300
A. Surgeon Mubarak Shah Khan   299
A. Surgeon Saif ud Din 299
A. Surgeon Sayid Abdul Basit 299
A. Surgeon Sayid Mohammad Ezar 300
A. Surgeon Shaikh Farid   300
A. Surgeon Wahidyar Khan 300
A. Surgeon Zaffar Hussein 299
Abdus-Samad Abdul-Wahid Golandaz 335
Able Seaman Ismail Mohammad 324
Able Seaman Mohammad Khan 324
Able Seaman Punna Khan 324
Able Seaman Shadi Khan 324
Able Seaman smail Baba 324
Acting Major Mohammad Adalat 363
Subedar Mohammad Suleiman Khan 185
Adjutant Kaleh Khan 169
Admiral Afzal Tahir 529
Admiral Karamat Rahman Niazi 101
Admiral Mohammad Shariff 64
Admiral Mohammad Zakaullah 529
Admiral Muhammad Asif Sandila 531
Admiral Noman Bashir 529
Admiral Shahid Karimullah 529
Admiral Shahid Karimullah 67
Ahmed Muhammad Mirghany 496

Index

Air Commodore Mohammad Zafar Masud 55
Air Commodore Mukhtar Ahmad Dogar 74
Air Marshal Abdur Rahim Khan 59
Air Marshal Inamul Haque Khan 61
Air Marshal Nur Khan 53
Amb Sepoy Kala Khan 320
Amb Sepoy Mohamand Yusuf 320
Amb Sepoy Mohammad Ibrahim 320
Amb Sepoy Mohammad Yaqub 320
Amb Sepoy Sheikh Rahim 320
Ashraf-un-Nisa Begum 496
Assistant Surgeon Abdul Rahim 190
Assistant Surgeon Ata Mohammad Khan 209
Assistant Surgeon Ghaus Mohammad 211
Assistant Surgeon Rahim 230
Assistant Surgeon Riyhazuddin 219
Assistant Surgeon Sheikh Mohammad Dadsahib 215
Bahawal Din 301
Baloch 7
Bangladesh 5
Bargheer Synd Shureef 166
Bearer Firoze 300
Bearer Ali Bahadur 300
Bearer Ali Sher 300
Bearer Hussein Baksh 300
Bearer Mohammad Kasim 300
Bearer Mohammad Khan 300
Bearer Mohammand Ismail 300
Bearer Rehmat Khan 300
Bearer Sattar Mohammad Khan 300
Bhisti Abdul Aziz 267
Bibi Sahiba 72
BQMH Khan 485
Brigadier Abdul Qayum Sher 47
Brigadier Ahsan Rashid Shami 43
Brigadier Amjad Ali Khan Chaudhry 41
Brigadier Jamal Mohammad 103
Brigadier M. Aslam Khan 73
Brigadier Masood Naveed 113
Brigadier Muhammad Aslam Khan 22

Index

Brigadier Muhammad Taj 102
Brigadier Nisar Ahmed Khan 75
Brigadier Sher Muhammad Khan 72
Brigadier Syed Hazoor Hasnain 102
Bugler Azum Gool 130
Bugler Chuddo Beg 178
Bugler Fateh Mohmand 282
Bugler Gul Sher   288
Bugler Kala Khan 292
Bugler Mahaboolah Khan 145
Bugler Shaik Soubrette 130
Bugler Sher Ali 304
Captain Abdul Jalil 81
Captain Abdul Sattar 498
Captain Abdus Samad Shah 499
Captain Adil Bahadur 115
Captain Ahsan Wasim Sadiq 115
Captain Amir Abdullalh Khan 393
Captain Atta Mohd. Shah 493
Captain Atta Ullah 422
Captain Bahadur Sher 437
Captain Farhat Haseeb Haider 115
Captain Farooq Nawaz Janjua 77
Captain Feroz Khan 493
Captain Gulzar Ahmed 493
Captain Gulzar Ahmed 493
Captain Hafiz-ur-Rahman 493
Captain Haji Suleiman Ghulam- Hussein Haji 356
Captain HUK Niazi 100
Captain Hussain Ahmed 115
Captain Iftikhar 123
Captain Ishaq Mohammad 464
Captain Karnal Sher Khan 15
Captain Kashif Khaleel 115
Captain Israr Haider 115
Captain Umair Iftikhar Ahmed 115
Lieutenant Faisal Zia Ghumman 115
Captain Kashif Khalil 115
Captain Mateen Ahmed Ansari 336
Captain Mian Khan 390

Index

Captain Mohammad Ahmad 456
Captain Mohammad Aslam 374
Captain Mohammad Siddiq 419
Captain Mohammad Siddiq 420
Captain Mohammad Zia-ud-Din   493
Captain Muazzam Ali Shah 100
Captain Muhammad Ammar Hussain 115
Captain Muhammad Azad Khan 336
Captain Muhammad Iqbal Khan 50
Captain Muhammad Sadiq 80
Captain Mujeeb Faqrullah Khan 104
Captain Nadeem Raza 123
Captain Nawazish Ali Khan 104
Captain Niamat Ali Khan 188
Captain Nisar Ahmed 79
Captain Nur Khan 397
Captain Raheel Hafeez Sehgal 113
Captain Raja Muhammad Sarwar 7
Captain Riaz Ul Karim Khan 360
Captain Rommel Akram 115
Captain Sardar Ahmed 493
Captain Sardar Ahmed 493
Captain Sardar Izhar Haider Baloch 115
Captain Sarfaraz Khan 444
Captain Sher Badshah Mahsud 72
Captain Syed Abdul Wadud 391
Captain Syed Baqir Hosain 493
Captain Taj Mohammad Khanzada 419
Captain Tor Gul 433
Captain Zafar 115
Captain Zaghir Hussain 80
Captain Zahoor Afridi 78
CHM Allah Dad   315
CHM Fazal Hussein 313
Clara Rosalind Kaur Dhesi 2
Clerk Abdul Rashid 319
Clerk Mohammad Bux 320
Colonel Afridi Monawar Khan 493
Colonel Mirza Hassan Khan 116
Colonel Sher Ur Rehman 103

Index

Commandant Ghulam Hussan Khan 167
Commander Azim Khan 140
Commander Zafar Muhammad Khan 101
Compounder Haq Nawaz Khan 304
Cook Waziru 258
Corporal Omar Ali 120
Corporal Sher Mohammad 120
Corporal Technician Ghulam Abbas 119
Corporal Technician Syed Shaukat Ali 119
CQMH Khan Bahkadur 311
Daffadar Abdool Rehman Khan 160
Daffadar Abdul Basira Khan 305
Daffadar Abdul Gafar Khan 263
Daffadar Abdul Ghafur 265
Daffadar Abdul Karim Khan 260
Daffadar Abdul Rahim Khan 263
Daffadar Abdul Saboh 497
Daffadar Abdul Satar Khan 257
Daffadar Abdul Wadood 263
Daffadar Abdullah Khan 261
Daffadar Abdullah Khan 301
Daffadar Abdullah Khan 301
Daffadar Abdullah Khan 301
Daffadar Abdullah Khan 302
Daffadar Adil Beg 534
Daffadar Ahmed Khan 323
Daffadar Ahmed Khan 533
Daffadar Ahmed Shah 162
Daffadar Ahmed Yar Khan 259
Daffadar Akbar Khan 148
Daffadar Akbar Nowaz Khan 177
Daffadar Alam Ali Khan 264
Daffadar Alam Sher 262
Daffadar Ali Akbar 301
Daffadar Ali Akbar 301
Daffadar Ali Akbar 301
Daffadar Ali Mohammad 260
Daffadar Ali Murad Khan 265
Daffadar Ali Shan Khan 262
Daffadar Allah Ditta Khan 259

Index

Daffadar Allah –ud-Din Khan 264
Daffadar Alum Ali Shah 175
Daffadar Amanatullah Khan 535
Daffadar Amir Mohammad 207
Daffadar Askur Ali 138
Daffadar Atta Mohammad Khan 256
Daffadar Aumzoolah Khan 164
Daffadar Azeem Beg Khan 169
Daffadar Azim Khan 160
Daffadar Azim Khan 302
Daffadar Aziz Khan 263
Daffadar Bahadur Khan 308
Daffadar Bajid Khan 308
Daffadar Bashir 308
Daffadar Bhurmadeen 163
Daffadar Budha Khan 264
Daffadar Burkut Ali 175
Daffadar Darim 231
Daffadar Darin 533
Daffadar Daud Khan 261
Daffadar Diwan Khan 262
Daffadar Faiz Mohammad 262
Daffadar Faiz Mohammad Khan 308
Daffadar Fateh Khan 208
Daffadar Fateh Khan 258
Daffadar Fateh Khan 258
Daffadar Fateh Khan 262
Daffadar Fateh Khan 266
Daffadar Fateh Mohammad Khan 263
Daffadar Fateh Mohammad Shah 264
Daffadar Fazal Elahi 302
Daffadar Fazal Khan 263
Daffadar Fazaldad Khan 499
Daffadar Fazar Ali Khan   263
Daffadar Firman Ali 301
Daffadar Firman Ali 301
Daffadar Firman Ali 301
Daffadar Fuzul Khan 150
Daffadar Ghazni Khan 260
Daffadar Gholam Muhammad Khan 125

Index

Daffadar Ghoolam Dustagheer 132
Daffadar Ghulam Baqir Khan 258
Daffadar Ghulam Bartr Khan 258
Daffadar Ghulam Haider 261
Daffadar Ghulam Jelani 174
Daffadar Ghulam M. Khan 264
Daffadar Ghulam Rabbani 308
Daffadar Ghulistan Khan 258
Daffadar Golam Huzrut Khan 160
Daffadar Gulab Khan 497
Daffadar Gulbar Khan 260
Daffadar Gullistan Khan 258
Daffadar Gushtabaf Khan 261
Daffadar Habib Ullah Khan 262
Daffadar Hajee Ahmed 206
Daffadar Halim Bux 319
Daffadar Hamudoollah Khan 177
Daffadar Himmat Khan 161
Daffadar Hoshiar Ali 256
Daffadar Hussain Khan 265
Daffadar Ibrahim Khan 262
Daffadar Ibrahim Khan 301
Daffadar Ibrahim Khan 301
Daffadar Ibrahim Khan 301
Daffadar Imdad Ali 263
Daffadar Inayat Ali Shah Khan 138
Daffadar Inayut Ali 160
Daffadar Inzar Gul 265
Daffadar Ismail Jan 261
Daffadar Jehan Dad Khan 260
Daffadar Jehan Khan 169
Daffadar Jehan Khan 265
Daffadar Jullundur Shah 322
Daffadar Kaim Din 258
Daffadar Kaim Din 258
Daffadar Kallie Khan 132
Daffadar Kasim Khan 260
Daffadar Khader Nawaz 262
Daffadar Khadir Khan 262
Daffadar Khan 481

Index

Daffadar Khan Gul 301
Daffadar Khan Gul 301
Daffadar Khan Gul 301
Daffadar Khan Mohammad 262
Daffadar Khanan Khan 265
Daffadar Khuda Baksh 308
Daffadar Kullunder Beg 166
Daffadar Kurrum Elahi 160
Daffadar Lal Khan 263
Daffadar Lal Khan 266
Daffadar Mahboob Ali Khan 249
Daffadar Makhmand Jan 231
Daffadar Mansur Khan 262
Daffadar Mazhar Ali Khan 264
Daffadar Mazhr Ali Shah 256
Daffadar Meer Ali Rasul 160
Daffadar Meer Kurramut Ali 168
Daffadar Meer Kurramut Ullee 125
Daffadar Meer Nasir Ali 160
Daffadar Mir Hyder Ali 263
Daffadar Mir Mohammad 302
Daffadar Mirza Abdul Beg 151
Daffadar Mirza Ahmed Ali Beg 168
Daffadar Moghal Baz Khan Afridi 499
Daffadar Mohamand Khan
Daffadar Mohamand Khan 265
Daffadar Mohammad 481
Daffadar Mohammad Akbar
Daffadar Mohammad Aslam Khan 266
Daffadar Mohammad Ayub 262
Daffadar Mohammad Buksh 165
Daffadar Mohammad Bux Khan 151
Daffadar Mohammad Hafiz 263
Daffadar Mohammad Hayat Khan 128
Daffadar Mohammad Hussain Khan 131
Daffadar Mohammad Ishak 175
Daffadar Mohammad Juma Khan 260
Daffadar Mohammad Khan 163
Daffadar Mohammad Khan 169
Daffadar Mohammad Khan 208

Index

Daffadar Mohammad Noor Khan 132
Daffadar Mohammad Sharif Khan 308
Daffadar Mohammad Yusuf 535
Daffadar Mohd Mohammad 260
Daffadar Mohd Munir Khan 308
Daffadar Morad Khan 157
Daffadar Munimud-din Khan 263
Daffadar Nabi Baksh 306
Daffadar Nadir Ali Khan 264
Daffadar Nadir Ali Khan 534
Daffadar Nahar Khan 162
Daffadar Nawab Ali Khan 257
Daffadar Nawab Ali Khan 534
Daffadar Nawab Khan 143
Daffadar Nawab Khan 262
Daffadar Nazir Mohammad Khan 534
Daffadar Nubbee Hussein 160
Daffadar Pahlwan Khan 262
Daffadar Painda Khan 320
Daffadar Pir Khan 301
Daffadar Pir Khan 301
Daffadar Pir Khan 301
Daffadar Qasim Ali 263
Daffadar Rafik Hassan Khan 533
Daffadar Rahim Khan 163
Daffadar Rasul Khan 261
Daffadar Safdar Khan 264
Daffadar Saif Ali 302
Daffadar Saleem Khan 156
Daffadar Sangar Khan 258
Daffadar Sarbulan Khan 206
Daffadar Sarfaraz Khan 177
Daffadar Sarfaraz Khan 207
Daffadar Sarwar Khan 302
Daffadar Sayed Hassan 533
Daffadar Shah Zada 230
Daffadar Shahzad Mir 499
Daffadar Shaick Hossain 158
Daffadar Shaikh Ahmed Hussein 260
Daffadar Shalu Khan 302

Index

Daffadar Sheik Golam Nubbee 132
Daffadar Sheik Hyder 132
Daffadar Sheikh Husirudin 160
Daffadar Sher Bahadur Khan 264
Daffadar Sher Baz Khan   264
Daffadar Sher Mohammad 262
Daffadar Sher Shah 257
Daffadar Sherjam Khan 266
Daffadar Sikander Khan   257
Daffadar Sonbat Khan 258
Daffadar Sultan Khan 168
Daffadar Syed Goolam Ghouse 132
Daffadar Tafazal Hussain 261
Daffadar Wajid Ali 261
Daffadar Wullee Mohammad 144
Daffadar Wullee Mohammad Khan 160
Daffadar Wuzeer Shah 162
Daffadar Yad Hussein 160
Daffadar Yakoob Khan 151
Daffadar Yusuf Khan 264
Daffadar Zahid Khan 259
Daffadar Zahur Ali 533
Daffadar Zubberdust Khan 160
Deputy Inspector Hyat Khan 145
Dhobi Baz Mir 320
Driver Abdul Hakim 309
Driver Abdul Qayaum 268
Driver Abdulla 301
Driver Abdulla 301
Driver Abdulla 301
Driver Abdulla 301
Driver Abdulla 301
Driver Abdulla 301
Driver Afridi 216
Driver Alla Dad   267
Driver Allah 216
Driver Bagh Hussain 301
Driver Bagh Hussain 301
Driver Bagh Hussain 301
Driver Bashir Ahmed 268

Index

Driver Choo Beg 301
Driver Choo Beg 301
Driver Choo Beg 301
Driver Din Mohammad 537
Driver Faqir Mohammad 301
Driver Faqir Mohammad 301
Driver Faqir Mohammad 301
Driver Fateh Jang 206
Driver Fateh Khan 259
Driver Fateh Khan 267
Driver Fazal Din 267
Driver Fuzl 172
Driver Gunga Din 267
Driver Hashan 211
Driver Imam Baksh 320
Driver Jumma 268
Driver Khair Din 301
Driver Khair Din 301
Driver Khwaja 213
Driver Kiam Din 301
Driver Kiam Din 301
Driver Kiam Din 301
Driver Mohammad Afsar 269
Driver Mohammad Hussain 301
Driver Mohammad Hussain 301
Driver Mohammad Hussain 301
Driver Naik Sher Khan 269
Driver Nawab Khan 307
Driver Saidullah 301
Driver Saidullah 301
Driver Saidullah 301
Driver Sarwar Khan 268
Driver Sayyid Abdulla 202
Driver Sher Baz 211
Driver Wali Mohammad 301
Driver Wali Mohammad 301
Driver Wali Mohammad 301
Driver Wilayat Khan 301
Driver Wilayat Khan 301
Driver Wilayat Khan 301

Index

Drummer Hussan Khan 139
East Pakistan 8
Ferriar Mudar Bux 152
Ferriar Mustaffa Khan 308
Ferriar Sirdar Khan 152
Ferrier Wali Mohammad 257
Field Marshal Mohd. Ayub Khan 25
Firoze Khan, Lance Naik 496
Fitter Abdul Aziz 498
Flight Lieutenant Abdul Karim Bhatti 121
Flight Lieutenant Abdul Samad Changezi 111
Flight Lieutenant Abdul Wajid Saleem 106
Flight Lieutenant Amanullah Khan 89
Flight Lieutenant Amjad Hussain Khan 88
Flight Lieutenant Arshad Sami Khan 91
Flight Lieutenant Cecil Chaudhry 89
Flight Lieutenant Chaudhry Rizwan Ahmed 94
Flight Lieutenant Dilawar Hussain 91
Flight Lieutenant Fazal Elahi 110
Flight Lieutenant Ghani Akbar 92
Flight Lieutenant Ghulam Murtaza Malik 118
Flight Lieutenant Iftikhar Ahmad Khan Ghauri 93
Flight Lieutenant Imtiaz Ahmad Bhatti 92
Flight Lieutenant Israr Ahmad 106
Flight lieutenant Javed Ahmed 107
Flight Lieutenant Javed Latif 121
Flight Lieutenant M. Tariq Habib Khan 92
Flight Lieutenant Maqsood Amir 121
Flight Lieutenant Mir Alam Khan 107
Flight Lieutenant Mohammad Akbar 91
Flight Lieutenant Nazir Ahmed Khan 95
Flight Lieutenant Saadat Mohammad Akhtar Khan 93
Flight Lieutenant Saeed Afzal Khan 110
Flight Lieutenant Saif-ul-Azam 95
Flight Lieutenant Saifullah Khan Lodhi 97
Flight Lieutenant Sikandar Mahmood Khan 90
Flight Lieutenant Syed Khalid Hasan Wasti 94
Flight Lieutenant Syed Manzoorul Hasan Hashmi 95
Flight Lieutenant Syed Saad Akhtar Hatmi 88
Flight Lieutenant Syed Safi Mustafa 111

Index

Flight Lieutenant Syed Shahid Raza 118
Flight Lieutenant Syed Shamsuddin 90
Flight Lieutenant Taloot Mirza 122
Flight Lieutenant Viqar Ahmed Abdi 96
Flight Lieutenant William D. Harney 93
Flight Lieutenant Yousaf Ali Khan 88
Flight Lieutenant Yousaf Hasan Alvi 90
Flight Lieutenant Yunus Hussain 98
Flight Lieutenant Zulfiqar Ahmed 111
Flying Officer Mohammad Shamsul Haq 107
Flying Officer Nasim Nisar Ali Baig 118
Flying Officer Riffat Jamil 108
Flying Officer Syed Shamshad Ahmed 108
Flying Officer Ziauddin Hasan 96
Foreman Mohammad Ibrahim 498
General Akhtar Abdur Rahman Khan 34
General Asfaq Parves Kayani 529
General Jilani Khan Ghulam Jilani Khan 77
General Mian Hayauddinhas 528
General Muhammad Musa Khan Hazara 28
General Raheel Sharif 529
General Shamim Alam Khan 75
General Tariq Mehmood 102
General Tariq Mehmood 76
Ghazan Khan 493
Group Captain Eric Hall 82
Gulistan Khan 493
Gun Lascar Ibrahim Beg 157
Gunner Abdul Rahim 307
Gunner Ali 482
Gunner Aurangzeb 268
Gunner Bux 482
Gunner Fazal Elahi 269
Gunner Fazal Ilahi 210
Gunner Hakim Khan 270
Gunner Khan 482
Gunner Khan 482
Gunner Lal Khan 238
Gunner Mehr Khan 270
Gunner Mohammad Khan 269

Index

Gunner Mughal Khan 269
Gunner Naik Jan Mohammad 210
Gunner Rajwali 270
Gunner Roshan Din 307
Gunner Sardar Khan 186
Gunner Sardar Khan 270
Haviladar Guran Ditta 311
Havilar Abdulla Nur 316
Havilar Said Akbar 309
Havildar Nur Abdullah 313
Havildar Abas Khan 204
Havildar Abbas 481
Havildar Abbas Ali 279
Havildar Abbas Khan 310
Havildar Abdool Kadir 169
Havildar Abdul Aziz 310
Havildar Abdul Karim 307
Havildar Abdul Karim Khan 291
Havildar Abdul Khalaque 497
Havildar Abdul Khan 186
Havildar Abdul Khan 289
Havildar Abdul Malik 311
Havildar Abdul Qayum 316
Havildar Abdul Rahim 285
Havildar Abdul Rahman Khan 275
Havildar Abdul Rehman 317
Havildar Abdul Rehman 339
Havildar Abdul Wahab 536
Havildar Abdullah Khan 303
Havildar Abdur Rehman 319
Havildar Abuzar Khan 285
Havildar Adalat Khan 279
Havildar Adam Khan 299
Havildar Adam Khan 499
Havildar Afar 484
Havildar Afzal 484
Havildar Ahmed 481
Havildar Ahmed Ali 273
Havildar Ahmed Khan 171
Havildar Ahmed Khan 311

Index

Havildar Ahmed Khan 497
Havildar Ahmed Khan 497
Havildar Ahmed Yar 496
Havildar Ajmeri 274
Havildar Akbar 482
Havildar Akbar 482
Havildar Aksar Khan 278
Havildar Alam 484
Havildar Alam Gul 317
Havildar Alam Khan 296
Havildar Ali 481
Havildar Ali 482
Havildar Ali Abid 255
Havildar Ali Ahmed 280
Havildar Ali Ahmed 286
Havildar Ali Akbar 317
Havildar Ali Akbar 535
Havildar Ali Bahadur 315
Havildar Ali Bahadur 233
Havildar Ali Bahadur 309
Havildar Ali Juma 499
Havildar Ali Mardan 321
Havildar Ali Mohammad 322
Havildar Allah Dad 289
Havildar Allah Dad 314
Havildar Allah Dad 317
Havildar Allah Ditta 287
Havildar Allah Ditta 497
Havildar Ally Hoosain 165
Havildar Amanant Ali 313
Havildar Amin Chand 497
Havildar Amir 482
Havildar Amir Ali 285
Havildar Amir Ali 299
Havildar Amir Shah 284
Havildar Anar Khan 315
Havildar Arsala Khan 274
Havildar Asghar Ali 294
Havildar Ashraf 485
Havildar Ashraf Khan 193

Index

Havildar Aslam Khan 319
Havildar Atta Mohammad 497
Havildar Atta Mohammand 312
Havildar Awal Nur 499
Havildar Azeem Beg 165
Havildar Azeez Khan 130
Havildar Aziz Mohammad 322
Havildar Badr Din 277
Havildar Bagga Khan 298
Havildar Bahadur 483
Havildar Bahadur Ali Shah 295
Havildar Bahadur Khan 253
Havildar Bahadur Khan 267
Havildar Bahadur Khan 273
Havildar Bahadur Khan 308
Havildar Bahar 485
Havildar Bahar, B. 485
Havildar Bai Dullan 284
Havildar Baichoo Khan 149
Havildar Bakhtawar Khan 282
Havildar Baksh 484
Havildar Baksh 485
Havildar Balawal Khan 315
Havildar Barkat Shah 281
Havildar Barkhader 292
Havildar Baz Gul 497
Havildar Bindraban 307
Havildar Bitind Khan 154
Havildar Boota Khan 295
Havildar Bostan Khan 267
Havildar Buccus Khan 155
Havildar Buta Khan 223
Havildar Buta Khan Ali 194
Havildar Chasm-i-Nazir 319
Havildar Dad 483
Havildar Dad Khan 297
Havildar Daftar Khan 317
Havildar Dal Khan 295
Havildar Dheru Khan 316
Havildar Dil 482

Index

Havildar Din 481
Havildar Elahi 481
Havildar Faiz Alam 282
Havildar Farid Khan 236
Havildar Fateh Ali 277
Havildar Fateh Haider 204
Havildar Fateh Jang 277
Havildar Fateh Khan 278
Havildar Fateh Khan 295
Havildar Fateh Khan 298
Havildar Fateh Khan 316
Havildar Fateh Khan 317
Havildar Fateh Khan 318
Havildar Fateh Mohammad 216
Havildar Faujun 274
Havildar Fazal 224
Havildar Fazal Dad 270
Havildar Fazal Dad 284
Havildar Fazal Elahi 308
Havildar Fazal Elahi 309
Havildar Fazal Husain 215
Havildar Fazal Hussein 315
Havildar Fazal Illahi 283
Havildar Fazal Rehman 310
Havildar Fazal Shah 309
Havildar Feroz Khan 233
Havildar Feroze Khan 271
Havildar Firoz Khan 282
Havildar Firoze Khan 288
Havildar Fukeeria 166
Havildar Futteh Deen 156
Havildar Ghafur Khan 296
Havildar Ghafur Shah 274
Havildar Ghanam Gul 318
Havildar Ghazan Khan 268
Havildar Gheba Khan 283
Havildar Gheba Khan 526
Havildar Gholam Mohammad Khan 152
Havildar Ghulam Ali 287
Havildar Ghulam Ali 308

Index

Havildar Ghulam Hussain 315
Havildar Ghulam Jilani 269
Havildar Ghulam Khadir 272
Havildar Ghulam Mohammad 290
Havildar Ghulam Mohammad 184
Havildar Ghulam Mohammad 200
Havildar Ghulam Mohammad 238
Havildar Ghulam Nabi 212
Havildar Ghulam Naib Khan 275
Havildar Gohur Shah 155
Havildar Golodu 282
Havildar Goolshah 127
Havildar Gul 482
Havildar Gul Akhmed 282
Havildar Gul Amir 199
Havildar Gul Anar 304
Havildar Gul Badshah 281
Havildar Gul Mohammad 215
Havildar Gul Rehman 310
Havildar Gul Shaid 319
Havildar Gul Sher 277
Havildar Gul Zaman 310
Havildar Gulab Hussain 317
Havildar Gulab Khan 283
Havildar Gulam Khan 311
Havildar Gulma Din 317
Havildar Gulzada 284
Havildar Habib Khan 270
Havildar Habib Khan 270
Havildar Habib Khan Ali 213
Havildar Haidar 292
Havildar Haidar Khan 292
Havildar Haider Ali 292
Havildar Haider Khan 291
Havildar Hakim Khan 296
Havildar Hakim Khan 308
Havildar Hakim Khan 308
Havildar Hakim Shah 281
Havildar Hamid Khan 291
Havildar Hamid Ullah 288

Index

Havildar Han Fatteh 255
Havildar Hashmat Ali 282
Havildar Hassan Nawaz 321
Havildar Hazrat Khan 285
Havildar Hubeeb Khan 154
Havildar Hukam Dad 288
Havildar Hukum Dad 285
Havildar Hussain 481
Havildar Hussain 484
Havildar Hussain Khan 274
Havildar Hyder Shah 152
Havildar Ilam Din 267
Havildar Imam Ali Khan 270
Havildar Imam Din 235
Havildar Imam Din 293
Havildar Imdad Nabi 497
Havildar Inayat Khan 312
Havildar Inayat Ullah 497
Havildar Ismail Khan 273
Havildar Ismail Khan 312
Havildar Jabar Khan 184
Havildar Jaffer Ally Khan 159
Havildar Jahan Dad 269
Havildar Jamal Din 282
Havildar Janab Gul 316
Havildar Janjua 238
Havildar Jehan Khan 283
Havildar Jemaun 167
Havildar Jenhandad 277
Havildar Kajir Khan 278
Havildar Kala Khan 310
Havildar Kalandar Khan 288
Havildar Kalandar Khan 219
Havildar Kalbi Hussain 275
Havildar Karam Ilahi 186
Havildar Karam Khan 288
Havildar Karim Khan 284
Havildar Khabib 305
Havildar Khader 481
Havildar Khan 481
Havildar Khan 481

Index

Havildar Khan 481
Havildar Khan 482
Havildar Khan 482
Havildar Khan 482
Havildar Khan 482
Havildar Khan 482
Havildar Khan 483
Havildar Khan 483
Havildar Khan 484
Havildar Khan 484
Havildar Khan 484
Havildar Khan 484
Havildar Khan 484
Havildar Khan 485
Havildar Khan 485
Havildar Khan 486
Havildar Khan 486
Havildar Khan Bahaduar 318
Havildar Khan Khel 281
Havildar Khan Sher 255
Havildar Khan Zada 297
Havildar Khan Zaman 497
Havildar Khan Zaman 497
Havildar Khani Zaman 242
Havildar Khawas Khan 289
Havildar Khial Din 304
Havildar Khoda Baksh 182
Havildar Khong Baksh 276
Havildar Kootub Deep 172
Havildar Kullunder Buksh 149
Havildar Kutab Din 269
Havildar Lal Beg 270
Havildar Lal Mast 316
Havildar Lalak Jan 16
Havildar Langar Khan 268
Havildar Latif Ali 213
Havildar M. Ghulam Mohammad 269
Havildar M. Nawaz Ali 268
Havildar M. Palanwar Khan 267
Havildar M. Saif Ali 267

Index

Havildar M. Var Khan 284
Havildar Mad Azam 323
Havildar Madat Khan 296
Havildar Mahbub Khan 318
Havildar Mahmud Khan   273
Havildar Maida Khan 190
Havildar Major Fateh Khan 488
Havildar Major Hiraz Khan 497
Havildar Major Khan 484
Havildar Major Khan 485
Havildar Major Khan 485
Havildar Major Mir Badshah 495
Havildar Major Mir Badshah 497
Havildar Major Rehmat Khan 536
Havildar Major Sadiq 481
Havildar Major Shaick Dyanut Allie 158
Havildar Major Shraz Khan 497
Havildar Malang Khan 304
Havildar Manawar Din 323
Havildar Mania   303
Havildar Manowar Khan 267
Havildar Mansare Ali 291
Havildar Masal Khan 309
Havildar Mata Deen 130
Havildar Maula Baksh 275
Havildar Mawaz Din 274
Havildar Meean Gool 152
Havildar Meer Hyder Allee 155
Havildar Mian Ahmed 277
Havildar Mian Mohammad 281
Havildar Mir Afzal 278
Havildar Mir Dast 278
Havildar Mir Khan 303
Havildar Mir Shah 297
Havildar Mir Zaman 317
Havildar Mirza Khan 184
Havildar Mobil Khan 285
Havildar Mobil Khan 318
Havildar Mohabbat Ali 255
Havildar Mohammad 481

Index

Havildar Mohammad 482
Havildar Mohammad 482
Havildar Mohammad 482
Havildar Mohammad 484
Havildar Mohammad Afzal 318
Havildar Mohammad Afzin 188
Havildar Mohammad Akbar 244
Havildar Mohammad Akbar 255
Havildar Mohammad Akbar 322
Havildar Mohammad Alam Khan 310
Havildar Mohammad Ali 298
Havildar Mohammad Alum 268
Havildar Mohammad Ashraf 315
Havildar Mohammad Ashraf 497
Havildar Mohammad Aslam 319
Havildar Mohammad Ayub Ali 497
Havildar Mohammad Baksh 211
Havildar Mohammad Baksh 287
Havildar Mohammad Din 497
Havildar Mohammad Din Khan 272
Havildar Mohammad Habib 309
Havildar Mohammad Hussain 268
Havildar Mohammad Iqbal 320
Havildar Mohammad Ismail 309
Havildar Mohammad Juma 272
Havildar Mohammad Karim 295
Havildar Mohammad Khan 144
Havildar Mohammad Khan 201
Havildar Mohammad Khan 223
Havildar Mohammad Khan 255
Havildar Mohammad Khan 317
Havildar Mohammad Naqqi 317
Havildar Mohammad Niwaz 312
Havildar Mohammad Ramzan Khan 197
Havildar Mohammad Sadiq 255
Havildar Mohammad Sadiq 290
Havildar Mohammad Safi Khan 294
Havildar Mohammad Salim 318
Havildar Mohammad Sawar 194
Havildar Mohammad Shaffi 497

Index

Havildar Mohammad Shariff 313
Havildar Mohammad Sher 297
Havildar Mohammad Wilayat 309
Havildar Mohammad Yacoob 169
Havildar Mohammad Yusuf 291
Havildar Mohammad Yusuf 314
Havildar Mohammad Yusuf 497
Havildar Mohammad Zaman 497
Havildar Mohmad Khan 311
Havildar Moodookistnah 147
Havildar Moosddee Khan 165
Havildar Mowaz Khan 282
Havildar Muhammad Raza 499
Havildar Mulk 485
Havildar Multan 279
Havildar Mumtaz Khan 312
Havildar Munga Khan 267
Havildar Mungal Khan 153
Havildar Munshi Khan 289
Havildar Mushtak Hussain 274
Havildar Must Amir 276
Havildar Muzaffar Khan   286
Havildar Najib Khan 267
Havildar Nasir Ullah Kham 293
Havildar Nawab Khan 340
Havildar Nawaz Khan 255
Havildar Nazir Khan 303
Havildar Niamat Khan 291
Havildar Niaz Gul 285
Havildar Niaz Gul 285
Havildar Niaz Khan 303
Havildar Niaz Mohammad Khan   275
Havildar Nikab Gul 279
Havildar Nitoolla Khan 156
Havildar Nizam Khan 293
Havildar Noor Khan 169
Havildar Nowsher Khan 536
Havildar Nowsher Khan 272
Havildar Nur Akhmed 272
Havildar Nur Ali 285

Index

Havildar Nur Illahi 311
Havildar Nur Khan 242
Havildar Nur Khan 295
Havildar Nur Khan 295
Havildar Nur-ul-Haq 309
Havildar Oomer 167
Havildar Pahlawan Khan 273
Havildar Palwan Khan 316
Havildar Peer Bux 152
Havildar Phul Khan 295
Havildar Piran Ditta (1081) 340
Havildar Piran Ditta (712) 340
Havildar Qadir 481
Havildar Qaim Shah 316
Havildar Qambar Ali 233
Havildar Rafiq 482
Havildar Rahim Ali 194
Havildar Rahim Dad 292
Havildar Rahim Dad Khan 292
Havildar Rahman Sharif 286
Havildar Ramzan 306
Havildar Ranghin Khan 318
Havildar Rasul Khan 310
Havildar Rehman 482
Havildar Rehman 482
Havildar Rehmat Ali 324
Havildar Rehmat Khan 294
Havildar Roshan Khan 201
Havildar Sadar Din 294
Havildar Saiad Gul 174
Havildar Said Abbas 322
Havildar Said Ahmed 277
Havildar Said Anwar 322
Havildar Said Badshah 324
Havildar Said Zaman 288
Havildar Saidak 201
Havildar Saif Ali 192
Havildar Saiyed Ahmed 285
Havildar Saiyid Hussain 272
Havildar Sajwal Khan 283

Index

Havildar Sajwal Khan 313
Havildar Sakhi Mohammad 319
Havildar Sakhi Zaman 280
Havildar Salim Khan 185
Havildar Salmat Ali 309
Havildar Samandur Khan 273
Havildar Samundar Khan 272
Havildar Sar Mast 284
Havildar Sarfaraz 184
Havildar Sarfaraz 284
Havildar Sarfaraz Khan 277
Havildar Sarwar 482
Havildar Sarwar 484
Havildar Savoo Deen 133
Havildar Sayed Khan 324
Havildar Shadi Khan 295
Havildar Shah 223
Havildar Shah 485
Havildar Shah Ghafur Khan 307
Havildar Shah Gool 144
Havildar Shah Mohammad 194
Havildar Shah Mohammad 313
Havildar Shah Nawaz 269
Havildar Shah Nawaz Khan 179
Havildar Shah Wali 319
Havildar Shah, P. 485
Havildar Shahgood Khan 172
Havildar Shahmir 321
Havildar Shahzad Khan   238
Havildar Shaick Hossein 167
Havildar Shaick Loll Mohammad 155
Havildar Shaick Qomaid 153
Havildar Shaik Abdool Cawdar 147
Havildar Shaik Abdool Cawdar 147
Havildar Shaik Emam Bux 136
Havildar Shaik Hyder 133
Havildar Shaikh Ahmad 289
Havildar Shaikh Maqtum 291
Havildar Shamal 303
Havildar Sharaf Khan 292

Index

Havildar Sharif Khan 286
Havildar Shazadah 144
Havildar Sheik Mokeem 146
Havildar Sheikh Khoda Buksh 149
Havildar Sheikh Ramzan 275
Havildar Sheikh Rujub Ullee 141
Havildar Sheikh Usman 499
Havildar Sher Ahmed 276
Havildar Sher Ali 277
Havildar Sher Dil 323
Havildar Sher Hassan 314
Havildar Sher Khan 222
Havildar Sher Khan 280
Havildar Sher Khan 318
Havildar Sher Khan 497
Havildar Sher Khan 497
Havildar Sher Ullah 282
Havildar Sherauz 167
Havildar Sherbat Ali 305
Havildar Sial Baz 317
Havildar Sinak 323
Havildar Sobhat Khan 318
Havildar Subha Khan 318
Havildar Sultan Bux 147
Havildar Sultan Mohammad 340
Havildar Sultan Mumraiz 312
Havildar Taj Mohammad 274
Havildar Tora Khan 276
Havildar Tunda Khan 267
Havildar Udin Shah 323
Havildar Ullah 182
Havildar Ullah 482
Havildar Umar Din 282
Havildar Umar Din 300
Havildar Umar Din 302
Havildar Usman Gani Khan 294
Havildar Wais Mohammad 315
Havildar Waris Khan 309
Havildar Wasim Khan 536
Havildar Wuzeer Khan 152

Index

Havildar Yakub Khan 200
Havildar Yaqub Khan 277
Havildar Yusuf   238
Havildar Yusuf 485
Havildar Zain Din 279
Havildar Zar Ullah 315
Havildar Zarghun Shah 499
Havildar Zarin Shah 317
Havildar Zota Khan 293
Hilal-e-Jurat 18
Honorary Captain Raja Sultan Sikandar 77
Hony Captain Sher Dil Khan 492
Hospital Assistant Haider Khan 174
Hospital Assistant Syed Noor Khan 170
Hussain Shah 224
Hyderabad 4
Inspector Fazal Din 307
Inspector Nadu Khan 271
Inspector Sher Khan 307
Jam Mir Sir Ghulam Qadir Khan Aliani 515
Jamadar Mohammad Khan 179
Jemadar 301
Jemadar Abbas Khan 322
Jemadar Abdul Akbar 222
Jemadar Abdul Azim 307
Jemadar Abdul Aziz Khan 271
Jemadar Abdul Gafoor 440
Jemadar Abdul Gafoor Khan 535
Jemadar Abdul Ghani 316
Jemadar Abdul Guffar Khan 198
Jemadar Abdul Hafiz Khan 331
Jemadar Abdul Hakim 408
Jemadar Abdul Hamid 246
Jemadar Abdul Jabar Khan 260
Jemadar Abdul Karim 393
Jemadar Abdul Khan 495
Jemadar Abdul Latif 217
Jemadar Abdul Latif 310
Jemadar Abdul Latif 320
Jemadar Abdul Majid 260

Index

Jemadar Abdul Rahman 293
Jemadar Abdul Rahman Khan 206
Jemadar Abdul Rehman Khan 266
Jemadar Abdul Sadiq 251
Jemadar Adalat Khan 208
Jemadar Adalat Khan 208
Jemadar Adalat Khan 259
Jemadar Adam Khan 264
Jemadar Ahmed Khan 300
Jemadar Ahmed Khan 302
Jemadar Ahmed Khan 417
Jemadar Ajab Gul 296
Jemadar Akbar Ali 319
Jemadar Akbar Ali 468
Jemadar Akbar Khan 306
Jemadar Akbar Shah 495
Jemadar Alam Khan 226
Jemadar Alam Khan 271
Jemadar Alam Sher Khan 207
Jemadar Ali Akbar 269
Jemadar Ali Akbar 405
Jemadar Ali Akbar 451
Jemadar Ali Juma 292
Jemadar Ali Mohammad 255
Jemadar Ali Mohammad 301
Jemadar Ali Mohammad 301
Jemadar Ali Mohammad 301
Jemadar Ali Shah Ali 198
Jemadar Alla Sar 499
Jemadar Allah Dad 151
Jemadar Allah Din 311
Jemadar Allah Ditta 183
Jemadar Allah Ditta 238
Jemadar Allah Rakha 271
Jemadar Allah Rakha 272
Jemadar Allah Rakka Khan 204
Jemadar Allah Yar Khan   316
Jemadar Allee Buccus 125
Jemadar Alluf Khan 162
Jemadar Alyar Khan 163

Index

Jemadar Amir Khan 281
Jemadar Amir Shah 430
Jemadar Anar Gul 460
Jemadar Anar Khan 321
Jemadar Annu Khan 264
Jemadar Anwar Beg 389
Jemadar Anwar Shah 318
Jemadar Arjun Khan 263
Jemadar Arman Shah 321
Jemadar Arz Mohammad 296
Jemadar Atta Mohammad 372
Jemadar Atta Mohammad 471
Jemadar Atta Ullah Khan 189
Jemadar Attar Khan 387
Jemadar Aulia Khan 262
Jemadar Ayub Khan 183
Jemadar Ayub Khan 203
Jemadar Ayub Khan 304
Jemadar Ayub Khan 313
Jemadar Azim Ullah 316
Jemadar Aziz Khan 289
Jemadar Baboo Khan 153
Jemadar Bahadoor Ally 126
Jemadar Bahadur Khan 178
Jemadar Bahawal Din 301
Jemadar Bahawal Din 301
Jemadar Baiham Khan 261
Jemadar Banaras Khan 318
Jemadar Banaris Khan 462
Jemadar Barat Ali 306
Jemadar Barhan Ali 258
Jemadar Baz Khan 279
Jemadar Baz Khan 301
Jemadar Baz Khan 301
Jemadar Baz Khan 301
Jemadar Beg Mohammad Khan 162
Jemadar Biland Shah 323
Jemadar Bostan Khan 318
Jemadar Burhan Ali Khan 285
Jemadar Cassim Sahib 159

Index

Jemadar Chaudhari Khan 370
Jemadar Dad Shere Khan 160
Jemadar Daud Shah 238
Jemadar Daud Shah 283
Jemadar Deedar Buksh Khan 166
Jemadar Din 230
Jemadar Diwan Ali Khan 267
Jemadar Dulel Khan 166
Jemadar Dur Khan Rahim 190
Jemadar Ellahee Bux 169
Jemadar Ellei Bux Khan 148
Jemadar Emam Bux 154
Jemadar Emam Bux Khan 146
Jemadar Faiz Talab 179
Jemadar Faqir Hussain 305
Jemadar Faqir Mohammad 307
Jemadar Fateh Din 534
Jemadar Fateh Haidar
Jemadar Fateh Khan 272
Jemadar Fateh Khan 301
Jemadar Fateh Khan 301
Jemadar Fateh Mohammad 261
Jemadar Fateh Mohammad 300
Jemadar Fateh Mohammad 302
Jemadar Fateh Mohammad Khan 385
Jemadar Fazal Ali 405
Jemadar Fazal Dad 360
Jemadar Fazal Dad 382
Jemadar Fazal Dad Khan 366
Jemadar Fazal Illahi 244
Jemadar Fazal Khan 320
Jemadar Fazal Rehman 386
Jemadar Fazl Ali Khan 257
Jemadar Feroz Ali 211
Jemadar Feroz Khan 426
Jemadar Feroze Khan 248
Jemadar Fez Talab 533
Jemadar Firoz Khan 283
Jemadar Futteh Mohammad 169
Jemadar Fuzl Achmud Ali 171

Index

Jemadar Ghafur Khan 279
Jemadar Ghamai Khan   285
Jemadar Ghazan Khan 400
Jemadar Gheba Khan 287
Jemadar Ghulam Akbar 406
Jemadar Ghulam Din 383
Jemadar Ghulam Hassan 269
Jemadar Ghulam Hussein 277
Jemadar Ghulam Jilani 298
Jemadar Ghulam Mohammad 295
Jemadar Ghulam Mohi-ud-Din 495
Jemadar Ghulam Nabi 253
Jemadar Ghulam Nabi 495
Jemadar Ghulam Qadir 293
Jemadar Ghulam Rasul 307
Jemadar Ghulam Sarwar 255
Jemadar Ghulam Sarwar 416
Jemadar Ghulam Shah 191
Jemadar Ghulan Mohi-ud-Din 308
Jemadar Goolam Hoosein Khan 161
Jemadar Gul Baz Khan 452
Jemadar Gul Khan 219
Jemadar Gul Mohammad 244
Jemadar Gul Mohammad 404
Jemadar Gul Mohammad 421
Jemadar Gul Rakhim 232
Jemadar Gul Rang Khan 462
Jemadar Gul Zarin 442
Jemadar Gul Zir 303
Jemadar Gulab Din 228
Jemadar Gulab Khan 312
Jemadar Guldar Shah 296
Jemadar Gulzar Khan 320
Jemadar Gungadeen 149
Jemadar Gwaram Khan 306
Jemadar Habib Gul 257
Jemadar Habib Khan 293
Jemadar Habib ullah Khan 273
Jemadar Hadi Khan 238
Jemadar Hafeezola 132

Index

Jemadar Haidar Khan 269
Jemadar Haidar Khan270
Jemadar Hakim Ali 364
Jemadar Hakim Khan 277
Jemadar Hakim Khan 297
Jemadar Hamid Ullah Khan 410
Jemadar Hasan Shah 351
Jemadar Hasham Ali 268
Jemadar Hashmet Ali 210
Jemadar Hassan Khan 322
Jemadar Hayat Ali Beg 200
Jemadar Hayat Mohammad 227
Jemadar Hazrat Shah 172
Jemadar Hidayutullah 165
Jemadar Hoosain Alli Khan 157
Jemadar Hossien Allee 146
Jemadar Ibrahim 292
Jemadar Imam Ali 279
Jemadar Imam Ali 364
Jemadar Imam Din Khan 478
Jemadar Imdad Khan 309
Jemadar Iniatullah 495
Jemadar Iqbal Ali Beg 305
Jemadar Ismail 169
Jemadar Jahan Dad 341
Jemadar Jahan Dad Khan 285
Jemadar Jahan Khan 299
Jemadar Jalal 306
Jemadar Jalal Khan 322
Jemadar Jalal Khan 323
Jemadar Jan Ghulam 255
Jemadar Jehan Dad 301
Jemadar Jehan Dad 301
Jemadar Jehan Dad 301
Jemadar Jehan Khan 301
Jemadar Jehan Khan 301
Jemadar Jewra Khan 155
Jemadar Juma Khan 266
Jemadar Kabul Khan 323
Jemadar Kale Khan 257

Index

Jemadar Kallee Khan 156
Jemadar Kalley Khan 154
Jemadar Karam Ali 302
Jemadar Karam Dad Khan 495
Jemadar Karam Illahio 229
Jemadar Karim Khan 310
Jemadar Khan 301
Jemadar Khan Badshah 454
Jemadar Khan Mir 316
Jemadar Khan Mohammad 291
Jemadar Khan Sherin 453
Jemadar Khooshud Allie 141
Jemadar Khuda Baksh Khan 259
Jemadar Khudiyar Khan 160
Jemadar Khurattee Khan 142
Jemadar Khurshid Khan 377
Jemadar Khwaja Bux 306
Jemadar Khwaja Mohammad 216
Jemadar Kifayat Allah 270
Jemadar Koorshaid Ali 160
Jemadar Kurreem Khan 154
Jemadar Lal Khan 458
Jemadar Lal Shah Gul 356
Jemadar Lall Khan 312
Jemadar Laltan Khan 307
Jemadar Lawang Shah 265
Jemadar Likayat Ali 204
Jemadar Mad Asgar 303
Jemadar Mada Mir Khan 321
Jemadar Mahboob Khan 148
Jemadar Mahboob Khan 168
Jemadar Mahbub Illahi 384
Jemadar Mahbub Khan 309
Jemadar Mahmud Khan 288
Jemadar Makhed Gul 323
Jemadar Makhmad Ali 318
Jemadar Makhmand Din 218
Jemadar Malang Khan 285
Jemadar Malik Alam Sher Khan
Jemadar Malik Mehr Khan 204

Index

Jemadar Malle Khan 297
Jemadar Maqbul Shah 265
Jemadar Maqurrab Khan 316
Jemadar Mattadeen 161
Jemadar Maula Baksh 381
Jemadar Maula Dad 365
Jemadar Maula Dad Khan 320
Jemadar Mawaz Khan 238
Jemadar Meer Akbur Ali 162
Jemadar Meer Hyat Mohammad 137
Jemadar Meer Kurrum Ali 161
Jemadar Meer Noor Ali 161
Jemadar Mehdi Khan 277
Jemadar Mehdi Khan Ali 214
Jemadar Mehr Baksh 271
Jemadar Mir 322
Jemadar Mir Afzal 241
Jemadar Mir Afzal Khan 299
Jemadar Mir Ali 315
Jemadar Mir Badshah 201
Jemadar Mir Baz Khan 273
Jemadar Mir Butt 170
Jemadar Mir Dast 326
Jemadar Mir Mast 284
Jemadar Mir Mast 328
Jemadar Mir Nabbi Hussain 285
Jemadar Mir T Hussain 293
Jemadar Mir Turab Ali 197
Jemadar Miram Shah 322
Jemadar Mirza Hatim Ali Beg 169
Jemadar Mirzaman Khan 192
Jemadar Mohammad 198
Jemadar Mohammad 211
Jemadar Mohammad 240
Jemadar Mohammad 453
Jemadar Mohammad Abbas 310
Jemadar Mohammad Akram 151
Jemadar Mohammad Amin 452
Jemadar Mohammad Anwar 318
Jemadar Mohammad Arabi 202

Index

Jemadar Mohammad Arshad 381
Jemadar Mohammad Ashraf 319
Jemadar Mohammad Azad 310
Jemadar Mohammad Azam 303
Jemadar Mohammad Baksh 204
Jemadar Mohammad Baksh 272
Jemadar Mohammad Deen Khan 161
Jemadar Mohammad Din 213
Jemadar Mohammad Faqir ud Din 305
Jemadar Mohammad Fazil 373
Jemadar Mohammad Hassan 322
Jemadar Mohammad Hayat 255
Jemadar Mohammad Hussain 368
Jemadar Mohammad Hussain 471
Jemadar Mohammad Hussain 479
Jemadar Mohammad Ismail 302
Jemadar Mohammad Jaffar Khan 495
Jemadar Mohammad Jan 475
Jemadar Mohammad Khan 174
Jemadar Mohammad Khan 208
Jemadar Mohammad Khan Bahadur 399
Jemadar Mohammad Nasir Khan 307
Jemadar Mohammad Nawaz 415
Jemadar Mohammad Nawaz Khan 477
Jemadar Mohammad Rafiq 380
Jemadar Mohammad Riaz 371
Jemadar Mohammad Sadiq Khan 289
Jemadar Mohammad Sarwar 391
Jemadar Mohammad Sawar 388
Jemadar Mohammad Sayeed 495
Jemadar Mohammad Shabir Khan 358
Jemadar Mohammad Shafayat Khan 472
Jemadar Mohammad Shafi 441
Jemadar Mohammad Shah 370
Jemadar Mohammad Sharif 399
Jemadar Mohammad Sharif 495
Jemadar Mohammad Sher 282
Jemadar Mohammad Sher 310
Jemadar Mohammad Tagi Khan 256
Jemadar Mohammad Umar Faruk Khan 226

Index

Jemadar Mohammad Wuzzeer Ally Khan 159
Jemadar Mohammad Zaman 362
Jemadar Mohd. Hussain 238
Jemadar Mohibulla 304
Jemadar Mubarik Ali 295
Jemadar Muddut Ali 147
Jemadar Mullick Surfraz Khan 151
Jemadar Munir 284
Jemadar Munshi Khan 186
Jemadar Munshi Mohammad 495
Jemadar Musaffar Khan 310
Jemadar Musalli Khan 323
Jemadar Nadir Shah 152
Jemadar Nasir Ahmed 391
Jemadar Nasser Khan 197
Jemadar Nasser Khan 322
Jemadar Nauroze Khan 428
Jemadar Nawab Ali Khan 195
Jemadar Nawab Khan 314
Jemadar Nawab Khan 377
Jemadar Nawab Khan 418
Jemadar Niamatullah 271
Jemadar Niyaz Gul 322
Jemadar Nizam Din 320
Jemadar Nizam-ud-Din 296
Jemadar Noor Khan 128
Jemadar Nubbee Buksh Khan 155
Jemadar Nur Alam 272
Jemadar Nur Alam 273
Jemadar Nur Khan 428
Jemadar Nur Mohammad Khan 257
Jemadar Nurab Shah 430
Jemadar Painda Khan 302
Jemadar Pat Khan 534
Jemadar Pat Khan Jan 231
Jemadar Peer Khan 156
Jemadar Pir Gul 449
Jemadar Pola Khan 356
Jemadar Qadar Dad 382
Jemadar Qaim Shah 431

Index

Jemadar Qasim Ali 233
Jemadar Qurban Ali 240
Jemadar Rahmut Ally Khan 155
Jemadar Raj Wali 297
Jemadar Raja Khan 279
Jemadar Raja Khan 319
Jemadar Rakhmat Ullah 463
Jemadar Ran Gul 442
Jemadar Raumat Khan 274
Jemadar Raza Mohammad 367
Jemadar Rehmat Khan 312
Jemadar Ruknuddin 256
Jemadar S.Z. Hussain Shah 309
Jemadar Saddiq Ahmed 473
Jemadar Safdar Khan 305
Jemadar Sahib Dad 261
Jemadar Sahib Gul 318
Jemadar Sahib Nur 323
Jemadar Said Jalal 321
Jemadar Sakhi Mohammad 414
Jemadar Samundar Khan 301
Jemadar Samundar Khan 301
Jemadar Samundar Khan 301
Jemadar Samundar Khan 418
Jemadar Sarbuland Khan 260
Jemadar Sardar Khan 205
Jemadar Sardar Khan 208
Jemadar Sardar Khan 257
Jemadar Sardar Khan 301
Jemadar Sardar Khan 301
Jemadar Sardar Khan 301
Jemadar Sardar Khan 315
Jemadar Sardar Khan 440
Jemadar Sardar Mohammad 495
Jemadar Sarwar 305
Jemadar Satara Khan 412
Jemadar Sayad Shams-ud-Din 294
Jemadar Sayyid Mohammad 306
Jemadar Shad Amir 323
Jemadar Shad Amir 323

Index

Jemadar Shah Gul 283
Jemadar Shah Mohammad 398
Jemadar Shah Mohammad 495
Jemadar Shah Nawaz 238
Jemadar Shah Zaman 316
Jemadar Shah Zaman 322
Jemadar Shahbaz Khan 306
Jemadar Shahzad Mir 258
Jemadar Shaick Jaffer 159
Jemadar Shaick Khoda Bux 153
Jemadar Shaik Ahmed 324
Jemadar Shaik Raheem Buksh 169
Jemadar Shaikh Khalil 294
Jemadar Shandi Gul 316
Jemadar Shandi Gul 422
Jemadar Sheik Abdoola Khan 166
Jemadar Sheikh Hidayut Ali 160
Jemadar Sheikh Nujjuf Ali 160
Jemadar Sheikh Rahimudin 163
Jemadar Sher Ahmed 308
Jemadar Sher Akhmed 184
Jemadar Sher Ali 321
Jemadar Sher Ali 369
Jemadar Sher Bahadur 278
Jemadar Sher Gul Khan 286
Jemadar Sher Mohammad 320
Jemadar Sher Zuman 495
Jemadar Shiekh Sobhan 154
Jemadar Shiraj 280
Jemadar Sikandar 275
Jemadar Sohbat 238
Jemadar Suffer Ally 152
Jemadar Suleiman Khan 322
Jemadar Suleman Khan 195
Jemadar Sultan Ahmed Khan 429
Jemadar Sultan Ali 267
Jemadar Sultan Ali 268
Jemadar Summund Khan 160
Jemadar Syud Mohammad 152
Jemadar Taj Ali 495

Index

Jemadar Taj Mohammad Khan 264
Jemadar Tans Khan 303
Jemadar Taza Gul 304
Jemadar Turab Shah 303
Jemadar Vilayut Ali Beg 161
Jemadar Wahid Ali 291
Jemadar Warris Khan 495
Jemadar Yakhuddin 271
Jemadar Yakub Ali Khan 275
Jemadar Yusuf Ali Khan 260
Jemadar Zaman Ali 285
Jemadar Zar Khan 304
Jemadar Zargir 533
Jemadar Zari Gul 304
Jemadar Zari Gul Khan 206
Jemadar Zarif Khan 304
Jemadar Zearut Khan 157
Junior Technician Muhammad Latif 119
K. Daffadar Chilzai Khan 266
K. Daffadar Jan Mohammad 265
K. Daffadar Khan Bahadur 266
K. Daffadar Khuda Baksh Khan 259
K.Daffadar Abdul Khalik   265
Kamal Khan 254
Kargil 6
Kashmir 4
Khan Bahadur Nawab Sir Liaqat Hayat Khan 523
Kot Daffadar Abdoola Khan 177
Kot Daffadar Bahadur Shah 261
Kot- Daffadar Ghunnee Khan 155
Kot Daffadar Goolam Allee Khan 166
Kot Daffadar Ibrahim Khan 156
Kot Daffadar Mazr Ali 178
Kot Daffadar Meer Ahmed Khan
Kot Daffadar Mohammad Fazil 533
Kot Daffadar Mookhtyar Ali 150
Kot Daffadar Shadil Khan 172
Kot Daffadar Soobhan Khan 149
Kot Daffadar, Shahweli Khan 534
Kot-Daffadar Khan Bahadur 230

Index

Kot-Daffadar Mohammad Fazil 232
L. Daffadar Akram Khan 265
L. Daffadar Ali Hussain 256
L. Daffadar Baz Khan 259
L. Daffadar Fateh Khan 265
L. Daffadar Fateh Mohammad Khan 266
L. Daffadar Feroz Khnan 266
L. Daffadar Hastam Khan 266
L. Daffadar Hussain Ali 260
L. Daffadar Karbact 266
L. Daffadar Nur Mohammad Khan 266
L. Daffadar Shah Nawaz Khan 266
L.Daffadar Abdul Aziz 256
L.Daffadar Abdul Ghani 267
L.Daffadar Allah Dad Khan 259
L.Daffadar Dost Mohammad 258
L.Daffadar Feroz Khan 266
L.Daffadar Ghul Mohammad 258
L.Daffadar Ghulam Mohammad 259
L.Daffadar Hyat Khan 259
L.Daffadar Khan Sahib 259
L.Daffadar Mir Ranuk Ali 260
L.Daffadar Musali Khan 260
L.Daffadar Najaf Khan 267
L.Daffadar Rahim Khnn 265
L.Daffadar Ranmatullah Khan 259
L.Daffadar Saleh Mohammad 265
L.Daffadar Sharif Khan 266
L.Naik Islam Ali 267
L/N Ghulam Rasool 238
Lance Daffadar Abdul Majid Beg 256
Lance Daffadar Abdul Karim 194
Lance Daffadar Asghar Ali 533
Lance Daffadar Fiaz Mohammad Khan 208
Lance Daffadar Ghulam Hussain 499
Lance Daffadar Gulab Khan 498
Lance Daffadar Hayat 481
Lance Daffadar Kala Khan 148
Lance Daffadar Khan 481
Lance Daffadar Khan 481

Index

Lance Daffadar Manawar Khan 236
Lance Daffadar Mohammad Azam 208
Lance Daffadar Mohammad Hyattt 207
Lance Daffadar Monbara Khan 207
Lance Daffadar Mowaz Khan 174
Lance Daffadar Nur Ali 533
Lance Daffadar Shah 481
Lance Havildar Ghani 483
Lance Havildar Haider 482
Lance Havildar Khan 482
Lance Havildar Khan 486
Lance Havildar Madina 482
Lance Havildar Shafi 482
Lance Havildar Shafi 482
Lance Havildar Shah 482
Lance Naik 486
Lance Naik Abdul Hakim 275
Lance Naik Abdul Haq 312
Lance Naik Abdul Majid 309
Lance Naik Abdul Sattar Khan 291
Lance Naik Afsar 483
Lance Naik Ahmed 483
Lance Naik Ahmed 483
Lance Naik Ahmed 486
Lance Naik Ajaib 481
Lance Naik Ajaib 486
Lance Naik Ajaib 486
Lance Naik Akbar 481
Lance Naik Akbar Ali
Lance Naik Akbar Ali 301
Lance Naik Akbar Ali 301
Lance Naik Akbar Khan 314
Lance Naik Alam Khan 274
Lance Naik Ali 484
Lance Naik Ali Afsar 320
Lance Naik Ali Faqir 221
Lance Naik Ali Hyder 498
Lance Naik Ali Khan 303
Lance Naik Ali Nazar 323
Lance Naik Ali Sher 271

Index

Lance Naik Alim Khan 182
Lance Naik Alla Yar 318
Lance Naik Allah Dad 237
Lance Naik Allahdad 213
Lance Naik Amar Din 320
Lance Naik Amin 482
Lance Naik Amin 483
Lance Naik Ayaz 486
Lance Naik Aziz Khan 312
Lance Naik Bahadur Khan 287
Lance Naik Bahadur Shah 210
Lance Naik Baksh 483
Lance Naik Bal Bahadur 315
Lance Naik Bari Sher 288
Lance Naik Biaz Gul and Zarif Khan 200
Lance Naik Bostan Khan 277
Lance Naik Chur Khan 281
Lance Naik Dad 485
Lance Naik Dad 486
Lance Naik Dad 486
Lance Naik Dad Khuda 306
Lance Naik Din 483
Lance Naik Din 483
Lance Naik Din 486
Lance Naik Din, K. 486
Lance Naik Din, T. 486
Lance Naik Elahi 483
Lance Naik Elahi 486
Lance Naik Elahi 486
Lance Naik Farman Ali 311
Lance Naik Fateh Ali 270
Lance Naik Fateh Khan 319
Lance Naik Fateh Mohammad 298
Lance Naik Fazal Ali 184
Lance Naik Feroz Khan Mohammad 225
Lance Naik Garkhar Khan 290
Lance Naik Ghulam Ali 217
Lance Naik Ghulam Ali 303
Lance Naik Ghulam Haider
Lance Naik Ghulam Haider 301

Index

Lance Naik Ghulam Haider 301
Lance Naik Ghulam Haider 301
Lance Naik Ghulam Hassan 309
Lance Naik Ghulam Hussein 308
Lance Naik Ghulam Khan 183
Lance Naik Ghulam Mohammad 192
Lance Naik Ghulam Nabi 283
Lance Naik Goolshair Khan 177
Lance Naik Gowhar Ali Khan 291
Lance Naik Gul Baz 179
Lance Naik Gul Baz 279
Lance Naik Gul Haidar 274
Lance Naik Gul Hassan 317
Lance Naik Gul Khan 279
Lance Naik Gul Khayat 323
Lance Naik Gul, J. 485
Lance Naik Gul, Z. 485
Lance Naik Gul 485
Lance Naik Gulab Khan 276
Lance Naik Habib Gul 201
Lance Naik Haider 484
Lance Naik Haider Beg Ali 212
Lance Naik Haider Khan   281
Lance Naik Haji Mohammad 315
Lance Naik Hamzulla 321
Lance Naik Haq 482
Lance Naik Hasna 484
Lance Naik Hukam Dad 496
Lance Naik Hussain 483
Lance Naik Hussain 484
Lance Naik Hussain 486
Lance Naik Hussain Buksh 155
Lance Naik Imam Din 289
Lance Naik Iman Din 269
Lance Naik Islam-ud-Din 336
Lance Naik Islam-ud-Din 340
Lance Naik Ismail Khan 280
Lance Naik Jaffar Ali 321
Lance Naik Jahan Dad 312
Lance Naik Jalal Din 300

Index

Lance Naik Jalal Din 302
Lance Naik Jalal Din 313
Lance Naik Jan Baz 218
Lance Naik Jumma Khan 299
Lance Naik Kala Khan 311
Lance Naik Kampoo Khan 296
Lance Naik Karam Dad 290
Lance Naik Karam Dad Ali 214
Lance Naik Karam Ilahi Khan 275
Lance Naik Karim Dad 537
Lance Naik Khan (21172) 482
Lance Naik Khan 482
Lance Naik Khan 482
Lance Naik Khan 482
Lance Naik Khan 483
Lance Naik Khan 483
Lance Naik Khan 483
Lance Naik Khan 484
Lance Naik Khan 484
Lance Naik Khan 484
Lance Naik Khan 486
Lance Naik Khan 486
Lance Naik Khan 486
Lance Naik Khan 486
Lance Naik Khan 486
Lance Naik Khan 486
Lance Naik Khan, M. 486
Lance Naik Khan, M. 486
Lance Naik Khuda Baksh 290
Lance Naik Khushal Khan 304
Lance Naik Khushi Muhammad 117
Lance Naik Lal 221
Lance Naik Lal Badshah 201
Lance Naik Lal Khan 288
Lance Naik Lal Khan 311
Lance Naik Lal Khan 320
Lance Naik Makhmad Nabi 317
Lance Naik Makhumad Din 279
Lance Naik Maqbul Hussain 318
Lance Naik Mazhar Khan 274

Index

Lance Naik Mehmed Khan 289
Lance Naik Mian Badshah 499
Lance Naik Mir 486
Lance Naik Mir 486
Lance Naik Mir Bad Shah 305
Lance Naik Mir Zaman 282
Lance Naik Mohammad 482
Lance Naik Mohammad 482
Lance Naik Mohammad 485
Lance Naik Mohammad 486
Lance Naik Mohammad Abdul Sabhan 289
Lance Naik Mohammad Ahmed 498
Lance Naik Mohammad Akbar 235
Lance Naik Mohammad Akram 314
Lance Naik Mohammad Amin 284
Lance Naik Mohammad Din 535
Lance Naik Mohammad Ghalib 147
Lance Naik Mohammad Issa 297
Lance Naik Mohammad Kassim 147
Lance Naik Mohammad Khan 271
Lance Naik Mohammad Khan 282
Lance Naik Mohammad Khan 302
Lance Naik Mohammad Khan 313
Lance Naik Mohammad Khan 313
Lance Naik Mohammad Khan 319
Lance Naik Mohammad Sadiq 273
Lance Naik Mohammad Sadiq 297
Lance Naik Mohammad Sadiq 297
Lance Naik Mohammad Sadiq 498
Lance Naik Mohammad Seedick Khan 176
Lance Naik Mohammad Ukbar Khan 154
Lance Naik Mohd, Yusuf Khan 291
Lance Naik Mohd. Baksh 282
Lance Naik Muhammad Din 287
Lance Naik Muhammad Mahfuz 14
Lance Naik Mustaqin 318
Lance Naik Mustkin 297
Lance Naik Nawab Ali 313
Lance Naik Nawais Ali 288
Lance Naik Nazar Hussain 320

Index

Lance Naik Nur Alam 281
Lance Naik Nur Dad 212
Lance Naik Nur Hamed 283
Lance Naik Nur Hussain 498
Lance Naik Nur Mohammad 289
Lance Naik Nur Muhammad 499
Lance Naik Pinnu Khan   282
Lance Naik Puaind Khan 268
Lance Naik Qabala Khan 324
Lance Naik Qadir Beg 286
Lance Naik Rafi-ud-Din 301
Lance Naik Rafi-ud-Din 301
Lance Naik Rafi-ud-Din 301
Lance Naik Rahim 483
Lance Naik Rahim Ali 284
Lance Naik Rahim Khan 295
Lance Naik Raja Khan 314
Lance Naik Rakhim Gul 246
Lance Naik Rakhim Gul 247
Lance Naik Rakkmat Shah 297
Lance Naik Rehman 482
Lance Naik Rehman 483
Lance Naik Roshan Ali 298
Lance Naik Rustam Khan 275
Lance Naik Sabar 483
Lance Naik Sadiq 483
Lance Naik Said Akbar   200
Lance Naik Said Akbar 305
Lance Naik Said Amir 277
Lance Naik Said Asghar
Lance Naik Said Mohammad 280
Lance Naik Said Nur 321
Lance Naik Saida Khan 285
Lance Naik Saif Ali 182
Lance Naik Saif Ali 273
Lance Naik Sajawal Khan 316
Lance Naik Sardi Khan 321
Lance Naik Sarwar 483
Lance Naik Sarwar 486
Lance Naik Sayed Mohammad 292

Index

Lance Naik Shah 485
Lance Naik Shah Nawaz 185
Lance Naik Shah Zada 322
Lance Naik Shaikh Farid 287
Lance Naik Sharaf Ali 319
Lance Naik Sher 213
Lance Naik Sher Ali 303
Lance Naik Sher Khan 201
Lance Naik Sher Mohammad 180
Lance Naik Spin Gul 317
Lance Naik Sukruh Khan 313
Lance Naik Sultan Ahmed 313
Lance Naik Sultan Mahmud 318
Lance Naik Syed Madar 288
Lance Naik Ullah Mohib 498
Lance Naik Walli Dad 312
Lance Naik Walyat Khan 311
Lance Naik Waris Khan 298
Lance Naik Wazir Khan 323
Lance Naik Yaqub 483
Lance Naik Zamal 306
Lance Naik Zaman Ali 287
Lance Naik Zaman Khan 288
Lance Naik Zamir Khan 274
Lance Naik, Rehman 485
Lance Nail Akbar 485
Lance Nail Mohammad 483
Lance-Daffadar Mohibullah 499
Lance-Naik Ghafur Shah 499
Leader Muhammad Iqbal 97
Leading Aircraftman Muhammad Azam Nasir 119
Lieutenant (Dr.) Bashir Ahmad 445
Lieutenant Abrar Hussain 494
Lieutenant Abrar Hussain 494
Lieutenant Adam Khan 373
Lieutenant Ahmed Faruk Khatlani 80
Lieutenant Ahmed Khan 494
Lieutenant Ahmed Munir 81
Lieutenant Ajaib Khan 466
Lieutenant Ameer Mohammad Khan 423

Index

Lieutenant Ata Mohammad 474
Lieutenant Bashir Ahmed 389
Lieutenant Colonel Abdur Rehman 78
Lieutenant Colonel Abdur Rehman 79
Lieutenant Colonel Ghulam Hussain 48
Lieutenant Colonel Ghulam Rasul Raja 73
Lieutenant Colonel Haidar Ali Khan 537
Lieutenant Colonel Haq Nawaz Kayani 104
Lieutenant Colonel Haq Nawaz Kayani 77
Lieutenant Colonel Ihsan Ali Khan 73
Lieutenant Colonel Khalid Nazir 115
Lieutenant Colonel Mahmood Khan Durrani 337
Lieutenant Colonel Mohammad Aslam Khan 343
Lieutenant Colonel Naseerullah Khan Babar 77
Lieutenant Colonel Rasheed Kayani 77
Lieutenant Colonel Sahib Zad Gul 79
Lieutenant Colonel Sahibzada Gul 78
Lieutenant Colonel Tanveer Ahmed Khan 115
Lieutenant Commander Ahmad Tasnim 101
Lieutenant Fazal Karim Mian 479
Lieutenant Fazl Wahid Khan 434
Lieutenant Fazle Rahim Khilji 436
Lieutenant General Abdul Ali Malik 40
Lieutenant General Akhtar Hussain Malik 31
Lieutenant General Masood Aslam 115
Lieutenant General Mohinder Singh Puri 14
Lieutenant General Shah Rafi Alam 75
Lieutenant General Tariq Khan 529
Lieutenant General Ziaur Rahman 50
Lieutenant Hazur Ahmed Khan 359
Lieutenant Hussain Ali 494
Lieutenant Hussain Shah 80
Lieutenant Ifthikar Ahmad Chaudri 465
Lieutenant Kaleem Mahmud 80
Lieutenant Liaqat Saeed Khan Lodi 494
Lieutenant Mohammad Aslam 365
Lieutenant Mohammad Hussain Khan 494
Lieutenant Mohammad Sadiq 494
Lieutenant Mohammad Shamin Ansari 494
Lieutenant Mohammad Yusuf 446

Index

Lieutenant Mohammad Yusuf Khan 436
Lieutenant Mohammad Zarif Khan 466
Lieutenant Saadat Mohammad Akhtar Khan 94
Lieutenant Sadiqullah Khan 436
Lieutenant Said Shah 445
Lieutenant Saiyed Anwar Hasan Rizvi 472
Lieutenant Sajjad Ali Naqvi 494
Lieutenant Sardar Mohammad Afzal Khan 382
Lieutenant Sayed Safdar Ali Khan 412
Lieutenant Syed Ghaffar Mehdi 457
Lieutenant Talibuddin 494
Lieutenant, Sheikh Nazir Ahmed 494
Lt. Col. Ahmed Jan 493
Lt. Col. Ahmed Jan 493
Lt. Col. Syed Mohammad Ishaq 493
Lt. Col. Syed Mohammad Ishaq 493
Lt. Col. Ullah Babar 99
Lt. Colonel Muhammad Akram Raja 49
Lt. General Amir Abdullah Khan Niazi 36
Maharaja Hari Singh 4
Major Abdul Jalil Orakzai 77
Major Abdul Jalil Orakzai 79
Major Abdul Wahab 115
Major Ahmed Khan 493
Major Ali Mohammad Pardiath 493
Major Altaf Qadir 493
Major Ata Ulllah 493
Major Babar Ramzan 113
Major Burki Wajid Ali 493
Major Fakhruddin Mir 493
Major Fayaz Ibrahim 112
Major General Aboobaker Osman Mitha 45
Major General Abrar Hussain 32
Major General Akbar Khan 342
Major General Amir Hamza Khan 102
Major General Amir Hamza Khan Qaisrani Baloch 69
Major General Iftikhar Khan Janjua 70
Major General Mian Ghulam Jilani 529
Major General Mian Hayaud Din 530
Major General Mian Hayauddin 18

Index

Major General Muhammad Jamshed 73
Major General Rahmat Khan 532
Major General Sher Ali Khan 24
Major Ghulam Qadir 380
Major Gul Mawaz Khan 409
Major Haji Mohammad Salamat Ullah 356
Major Hamshad Khan 493
Major Hanif 113
Major Hussain Khan 476
Major Jehangir T Sataravala 433
Major Khadim Hussain Bangash 76
Major Khalid Sohail Sultan 113
Major Khurshid Alam Khan 456
Major Lall Khan 493
Major Malik Aftab Khan 76
Major Malik Munawar Khan Awan 76
Major Mian Hayaud Din 420
Major Mian Hayaud Din 493
Major Mian Raza Shah 78
Major Mian Raza Shah 79
Major Mohammad Abdul Latif Khan 411
Major Mohammad Abdul Latif Khan 493
Major Mohammad Akhtar 100
Major Mohammad Aslam Janjua 77
Major Mohammad Aslam Khan 477
Major Mohammad Attiqar Rahman 421
Major Mohammad Azmatullah Khan 498
Major Mohammad Din 73
Major Mohammad Din 76
Major Mohammad Jamshed 376
Major Mohammad Sadiq Khan 444
Major Mohammad Sher Khan 431
Major Mohammad Zia Ud Din Uppal 78
Major Muhammad Akram 13
Major Muhammad Arshad Hashim 115
Major Muhammad Hanig 115
Major Nawab Khan 493
Major Nazar Hussein 400
Major Qasim 112
Major Raja Aziz Bhatti 9

Index

Major Raja Nadir Pervez Khan 103
Major Rakhman Ghul 432
Major Rana Shabbir Sharif 11
Major Sabir Kamal Meyer 104
Major Saeed Asmat 112
Major Said Ahmad 493
Major Saiyed Naseem Haider Rizvi 78
Major Sardar Ali 407
Major Sarfraz Rabbani 99
Major Sesha Salam 493
Major Shabbir Sharif 103
Major Shabbir Sharif 104
Major Shah Nawaz 79
Major Sheikh Mobaruk Ali 81
Major Sher Ali 497
Major Sohail Sadiq 123
Major Tariq Mahmood 115
Major Tufail Muhammad 8
Major Umar Faroq Rana 123
Major WB Butt 493
Major Wisal Mohammad Khan 403
Major Zafar 123
Major Zia ud Din Ahmed Abbasi 79
Major-General Naseerullah Khan Babar 43
Mansur Khan 173
Marvi Memon 532
Master Warrant Officer Mohammad Ashfaq 120
Master Warrant Officer Mohammad Hafeez 120
Mechanic Rehmat Ullah   308
Mir Sir Ahmad Yar Khan Ahmedzai 502
Mohammad Buksh Khan 145
 Mohammad Khan 162
Mohammad Khan 208
Nai Ghulam Khan 304
Naib Daffadar Assud Khan 151
Naib Ressaidar Sahib Zuma Khan 160
Naib Ressaidar Zoolfeeker Ally 160
Naib Risaldar Ameer Ally Khan 148
Naib Risaldar Azeem Khan 131
Naib Risaldar Jehangir Khan 163

Index

Naib Risaldar Kumuroo Din Khan 157
Naib Risaldar Meer Shamshad Allee 166
Naib Risaldar Meerza Jewon Beg 168
Naib Risaldar Mirza Shadee Beg 166
Naib Risaldar Mohammad Hussain Khan 125
Naib Risaldar Moodookistnah 147
Naib Risaldar Nawab Khan 148
Naib Risaldar Nubbee Buksh Khan 155
Naib Risaldar Shadil Khan 147
Naib Risaldar Shumshodeen 158
Naib Risaldar Sonawar Khan 142
Naib Subedar Aleem Zar 115
Naib Subedar Aqeel Hussain 115
Naib Subedar Ibarat Shah 117
Naib Subedar Muhammad Khaqan 115
Naib Subedar Muhammad Rashid 115
Naib Subedar Nadil Karim 115
Naib Subedar Sher Dullah Khan 115
Naib-Risaldar Feroze Khan 156
Naib-Risaldar Mohammad Buksh Khan 131
Naib-Risaldar Nawab Khan 168
Naik Alla Dad 272
Naik Amir Ali 272
Naik Abbas 280
Naik Abdoola 169
Naik Abdoola Khan 169
Naik Abdul Basith 287
Naik Abdul Karim 292
Naik Abdul Khaliq 315
Naik Abdul Qadir 278
Naik Abdul Razak 314
Naik Abdul Razak 497
Naik Abdul Razak 498
Naik Abdul Rehman 310
Naik Abdulla 320
Naik Abdur Rahman 499
Naik Adam Khan 217
Naik Ahmed 482
Naik Ahmed 486
Naik Ahmed 486

Index

Naik Ahmed Din 296
Naik Ahmed Din 536
Naik Ahmed Khan 152
Naik Ahmed Khan 269
Naik Ahmed Khan 274
Naik Ahmed Khan 295
Naik Ahmed Khan 296
Naik Ajab 482
Naik Ajaib Khan 311
Naik Akbar 484
Naik Alam 485
Naik Alam Shere 172
Naik Ali 481
Naik Ali 481
Naik Ali 482
Naik Ali 482
Naik Ali Akbar 225
Naik Ali Akbar 280
Naik Ali Akbar 312
Naik Ali Nazar 292
Naik Alif Khan 295
Naik Alla Khan 133
Naik Allah 217
Naik Allah Dad 302
Naik Allah Dad Khan 273
Naik Allah Ditta 252
Naik Allah Yar 319
Naik Alwal Khan 285
Naik Amir Dad 290
Naik Amir Hussein 191
Naik Amir Khan 253
Naik An Mir 316
Naik Andaz 482
Naik Anwar Khan 320
Naik Asgar Ali 287
Naik Atta Mohammad 238
Naik Atta Ullah   314
Naik Aurangzeb 482
Naik Awal Khan 305
Naik Aziz 482

Index

Naik Badshah 482
Naik Bag Hussain 267
Naik Bahadur 485
Naik Bahadur Shah 179
Naik Bakhtawar Khan 293
Naik Baksh 482
Naik Bari Sher 286
Naik Baz 484
Naik Baz Khan 318
Naik Bhullan Khan 271
Naik Bhullen Khan 223
Naik Boorhan Khan 129
Naik Bostan Khan 245
Naik Bostan Khan 309
Naik Bostan Khan 320
Naik Burham Ali   289
Naik Buta Khan Ali 193
Naik Dad 483
Naik Dad 483
Naik Dad 485
Naik Dawood Khan 133
Naik Dhunde Khan 297
Naik Dil Sukh 237
Naik Dilwar Khan 312
Naik Din 482
Naik Din 482
Naik Din 483
Naik Din 484
Naik Din Sher 316
Naik Ditta 481
Naik Ditta 482
Naik Diwan Ali 238
Naik Dost Mohammad 310
Naik Dost Mohammad 318
Naik Farman Ali 280
Naik Fateh Khan 298
Naik Fateh Mohammad   312
Naik Fateh Mohammad 300
Naik Fazal Din 333
Naik Fazal Hussein 313

Index

Naik Fazal Hussein 314
Naik Fazal Khan 296
Naik Fazal Khan 314
Naik Fazal Khan 498
Naik Fazl Ahmed 180
Naik Feroz Khan 287
Naik Feroz Khan 287
Naik Feroze Khan 536
Naik Firoze Khan 288
Naik Gauhar Ali 286
Naik Ghasita Khan 299
Naik Ghazi Khan 287
Naik Ghulam Akbar 272
Naik Ghulam Haider 277
Naik Ghulam Haider 497
Naik Ghulam Hassan 221
Naik Ghulam Hassan 536
Naik Ghulam Hussain Khan 276
Naik Ghulam Khan 222
Naik Ghulam Maula Khan 275
Naik Ghulam Qadir 309
Naik Ghulam Qadir 311
Naik Ghulam Qayum 310
Naik Goolam Allee 167
Naik Gul 485
Naik Gul Badshah 281
Naik Gul Mohammad 181
Naik Gul Mohammad 318
Naik Gul Zaman 301
Naik Gul Zaman 301
Naik Gul Zaman 301
Naik Gul, B. 485
Naik Gul484
Naik Gulistan Khan 317
Naik Gulzar Khan 314
Naik Gunga Din 300
Naik Habib Khan 311
Naik Habib Ullah 316
Naik Hagat Ali 268
Naik Haidar Ali Shah 499

Index

Naik Haider Khan 278
Naik Hakim 171
Naik Hakim Ali Khan 283
Naik Haous Khan 167
Naik Hasan Hussain 306
Naik Hashim Allee 167
Naik Hassan 292
Naik Hassan 484
Naik Hayat Mohamand 297
Naik Hazir 173
Naik Hiram Baksh 301
Naik Hiram Baksh 301
Naik Hiram Baksh 301
Naik Hoolas Khan 143
Naik Hubeeboolah Khan 166
Naik Hussain 482
Naik Hussain 483
Naik Hussain 485
Naik Hussaina 301
Naik Hussaina 301
Naik Hussaina 301
Naik Hussien Mohammad 296
Naik Ibrahim 156
Naik Ibrahim 301
Naik Ibrahim 301
Naik Ibrahim 301
Naik Ibrahim156
Naik Ibramim Khan 275
Naik Illah Mohammad 238
Naik Imam Khan 318
Naik Imam Shah 286
Naik Imtiaz Khan 294
Naik Ishar Ullee 152
Naik Jaffar Khan 296
Naik Jahan 484
Naik Jalal Khan 267
Naik Jalal Khan 316
Naik Jalal Khan 281
Naik Jehan Dad 287
Naik Juma 295

Index

Naik Kabai Khan 295
Naik Kala Khan 284
Naik Kamal Khan 254
Naik Karam Ali 287
Naik Karam Dad 290
Naik Karam Ilah 272
Naik Karan Khan 311
Naik Karim Baksh 300
Naik Khadim Khan 152
Naik Khair Din 272
Naik Khairullah 271
Naik Khaista Gul 317
Naik Khan 481
Naik Khan 481
Naik Khan 481
Naik Khan 482
Naik Khan 482
Naik Khan 482
Naik Khan 482
Naik Khan 482
Naik Khan 483
Naik Khan 483
Naik Khan 483
Naik Khan 483
Naik Khan 484
Naik Khan 484
Naik Khan 484
Naik Khan 484
Naik Khan 484
Naik Khan 484
Naik Khan 485
Naik Khan 485
Naik Khan 486
Naik Khan 486
Naik Khan 486
Naik Khan 486
Naik Khan 486
Naik Khan 486
Naik Khan Bahadur 255
Naik Khan Khel 221

Index

Naik Khan Zaman 274
Naik Khan Zaman 314
Naik Khan Zaman 315
Naik Khan, B. 486
Naik Khan, B. 486
Naik Khan, F.
Naik Khan, R. 485
Naik Khel 485
Naik Khial Zada 281
Naik Khoja Khan 286
Naik Khooshial 152
Naik Khushal Khan 255
Naik Lala Khan 306
Naik Laul Homed 133
Naik Mahtab Ali 222
Naik Maksud Ali 314
Naik Malik Khan 223
Naik Malik Shah 296
Naik Manawar Din 315
Naik Mani Khan 315
Naik Mansabdar 485
Naik Maru Khan 275
Naik Maula Baksh 292
Naik Mehdi 485
Naik Mehtab Khan 293
Naik Mian Gul 315
Naik Mihr Din 499
Naik Mir Alam Khan 320
Naik Mir Hassan 316
Naik Mir Said 301
Naik Mir Said 301
Naik Mir Said 301
Naik Mir Shah 323
Naik Mir Zaman 301
Naik Mir Zaman 301
Naik Mir Zaman 301
Naik Mishal Khan 310
Naik Mohammad 481
Naik Mohammad 484
Naik Mohammad 484

Index

Naik Mohammad 485
Naik Mohammad 486
Naik Mohammad 486
Naik Mohammad Abbas 320
Naik Mohammad Akbar 309
Naik Mohammad Akbar 320
Naik Mohammad Alam 267
Naik Mohammad Ali 321
Naik Mohammad Ali Khan 276
Naik Mohammad Azam 317
Naik Mohammad Azam 314
Naik Mohammad Esack Khan 177
Naik Mohammad Fazal 273
Naik Mohammad Fazal 299
Naik Mohammad Hassan 319
Naik Mohammad Hussein 298
Naik Mohammad Hussein 319
Naik Mohammad Khan 273
Naik Mohammad Khan 317
Naik Mohammad Khan 313
Naik Mohammad Nur 300
Naik Mohammad Sharif 498
Naik Mohammad Yakub 310
Naik Mohammad Yaqub 319
Naik Mohd Khan 308
Naik Mohd Mirza 311
Naik Mohd Riaz 310
Naik Mohd Yakub 311
Naik Mowland 152
Naik Mugarrab Khan 319
Naik Mumtaz Ali 312
Naik Munir Khan 264
Naik Munir Khan 498
Naik Munsab Khan 311
Naik Munshi Khan 498
Naik Musharaf Khan 292
Naik Mustaffa Khan 298
Naik Nabi Baksh 268
Naik Nader Ali 270
Naik Najib Khan 298

Index

Naik Nawab Khan 271
Naik Nawab Khan 304
Naik Nehal Khan 154
Naik Nur Badshah 277
Naik Nur Khan 311
Naik Nur Mahi 273
Naik Painda Khan 301
Naik Painda Khan 301
Naik Painda Khan 301
Naik Peer Bux 156
Naik Peer Mahmud 170
Naik Poyudah Khan 152
Naik Puma Khan 183
Naik Qadam Ali 309
Naik Qalander Khan 310
Naik Quadir Buksh 152
Naik Qurban Hussain 315
Naik Rahim Dad 310
Naik Rahim Khan 176
Naik Rahim Khan 230
Naik Rahmat Khan 273
Naik Raj Wali 299
Naik Raja Khan 313
Naik Rajwali 298
Naik Ramzan 484
Naik Rasul 484
Naik Rasul Khan 285
Naik Raz Ali 292
Naik Rehman 482
Naik Rehman 484
Naik Rehmat Khan 320
Naik Roshun 156
Naik Saddar Khan 304
Naik Sadiq 482
Naik Sadiq 484
Naik Sadiq 486
Naik Sadiq 486
Naik Safdar Ali 187
Naik Safirullah 537
Naik Sahib Din 301

Index

Naik Sahib Din 301
Naik Sahib Din 301
Naik Sahib Din 301
Naik Sahib Din 301
Naik Sahib Din 301
Naik Sahib Jan 298
Naik Sahib Shah 280
Naik Saif Ali Janjua 17
Naik Saiyid Hussain 224
Naik Salah Mohammad 272
Naik Samar Din 322
Naik Samundar Khan 283
Naik Sardar Khan 278
Naik Sardar Khan 293
Naik Sardar Khan 310
Naik Sarfaraz 272
Naik Sarwar 305
Naik Sattar Ali 291
Naik Sergun Shah 284
Naik Shah 483
Naik Shah Khan 288
Naik Shah Nawaz Khan 209
Naik Shahamad Khan 329
Naik Shahamad Khan 535
Naik Shahzada 156
Naik Shaick Abdool 154
Naik Shaick Futteh Mohammad 167
Naik Shaick Madar Bux 159
Naik Shaik Abdoola 177
Naik Shaik Alla Deen 145
Naik Shaikh Ramzam 272
Naik Sharaf Din 271
Naik Sharif 482
Naik Sheik Ibrahim 147
Naik Sheikh Abdul Latif 275
Naik Sher Ahmed Khan 300
Naik Sher Ali 313
Naik Sher Ali Khan 321
Naik Sher Baz 185
Naik Sher Mohammad 281

Index

Naik Sher Mohammad 281
Naik Sher Mohammad 292
Naik Sher Mohammad 318
Naik Sher Shah 332
Naik Sheraf Din 311
Naik Shere Ali 144
Naik Sifarsh Khan 318
Naik Sijawal Khan 235
Naik Sikander Khan 315
Naik Sirdar Ali 238
Naik Sohbat Khan 293
Naik Sooklal Dooby 149
Naik Suba Khan 312
Naik Suleman 320
Naik Sultan Ahmed 104
Naik Sultan Ali 289
Naik Sultan Baksh 282
Naik Sultan Khan 267
Naik Sultan Khan 319
Naik Surat Min 323
Naik Surkhru Khan 315
Naik Syad Akhmud 304
Naik Taj Din 272
Naik Taj Mohammad 309
Naik Torsum 297
Naik Ulas Mir 278
Naik Umbrass Khan 283
Naik Wali Dad 291
Naik Wazir Badshah 248
Naik Wazir Khan 296
Naik Wuzeer Beg 152
Naik Yaqub 486
Naik Yaqub 486
Naik Yar 486
Naik Zar Baz 284
Naik Zar Baz 535
Naik Zar Khan 304
Naik Zari Marjan 315
Naik Zarin Khan 283
Naikk Lal Hussain 309

Index

Nail Bahadur Khan 536
Nawab Sir Muhammad Faiz Ali Khan Bahadur 520
Nawab Sir Muhammad Muzammilullah Khan 521
Nawab Sir Shahbaz Khan Bugti 506
Nishan -i- Haider 6
Nishanburder Jaffer Ali 138
Nishanburder Nutteh Khan 127
Noor-un-Nisa Inayat Khan 338
Orderly Abdul Wahab Khan 257
Orderly Mahmud Ali Khan 261
Pilot Officer Rashid Minhas 10
Pioneer Akram Shah 498
Pioneer Zain Abdi 498
Primenister Nawaz Sharif 6
Primenister Zulfikar Ali Bhutto 5
Private Bechee Khan 152
Private Feroz Khan 291
Private Sheikh Hubdar Ali 297
Private Abar 152
Private Abdoola Khan 177
Private Aliff Khan 155
Private Bahadur Allee 152
Private Baj Khan 155
Private Bootcheah 133
Private Busharat Khan 152
Private Chaman Khan 298
Private Edoo Khan 159
Private Elahi Bux 176
Private Fazil Khan 152
Private Fuqroodeen 147
Private Ghosi Khan 297
Private Gomain 153
Private Goolam Mahammad 178
Private Gungadeen 153
Private Hoosain Surwar 133
Private Husn Buksh 152
Private Hussoo Khan 159
Private Hyder Ali Khan 131
Private Iyanah 147
Private Karam Dad Khan 291

Index

Private Khairat Ullee 152
Private Khoda Buksh 152
Private Khoda Bux 159
Private Khodur Bux 153
Private Kurreem Bux 153
Private Lall Mohammad 153
Private Lall Mohammad 176
Private Lateef Khan 133
Private Mahammad Yacoob 169
Private Matta Deen 153
Private Mattadeen 159
Private Meerra Hyder Beg 159
Private Mobaruk Allee 152
Private Mohammad Ali 169
Private Mohammad Ally 147
Private Mohammad Cassim 133
Private Mohammad Hussain 133
Private Muckdoom Buksh 152
Private Muckdoom Buksh 152
Private Mudar Buksh 152
Private Muddath Khan 152
Private Mulluq Ahmed 169
Private Nisar Ullee 152
Private Noor Khan 152
Private Noor Khan 152
Private Peer Buksh 152
Private Quadir Dad Khan 152
Private Ramiah 133
Private Ramiah 133
Private Ramzaun Khan 153
Private Russool Bux, Kullunder 153
Private Russul Khan 176
Private Said Mohammad 177
Private Sana Homed 133
Private Sardar Khan 297
Private Shah Baz Khan 298
Private Shaick 159
Private Shaick 159
Private Shaick Bhoomead 159
Private Shaick Elie Bux 153

Index

Private Shaick Ismail 153
Private Shaick Jahaun 159
Private Shaick Juan Mahmmad 153
Private Shaik Alleebux 155
Private Shaik Ally 133
Private Shaik Budhoo 155
Private Shaik Burray 133
Private Shaik Deenah 133
Private Shaik Emam 133
Private Shaik Homed 133
Private Shaik Lall Mohammad 155
Private Shaik Meeran 133
Private Shaik Modeenah 133
Private Shaik Secunder
Private Shaik Sillar 133
Private Shaik Sooliman 127
Private Shaik Umar 152
Private Sheik Mohdeen 169
Private Shumsheer Khan 152
Private Sirdar Khan 152
Private Sirdar Ullee 152
Private Soobhan Khan 159
Private Suffder Ullee 152
Private Sultan Ahmed 291
Private Sultan Baksh 537
Private Syed Cassin 133
Private Syed Imam 147
Private Syed Silliman 133
Private Syud Mohammad Khan 152
Private Taig Allee 153
Private Toraub Khan 159
Private Ukbar Khan 152
Private Ullee Husn 152
Private Ullee Mohammad 152
Private Uzeem Ooddeen 169
Private Yar Ullee Beg 152
Private Yurseen Khan 152
Q. Master Liakat Ali 269
Recruit Mir Alam Khan 171
Regimentdar Mir Muhiyddin 191

Index

Ressaidar Abdool Ruhman Khan 166
Ressaidar Abdullah Khan 229
Ressaidar Abdullalh Khan 266
Ressaidar Ahmed Khan 136
Ressaidar Allah Oodeen 161
Ressaidar Allau Din Khan 264
Ressaidar Amanut Khan 160
Ressaidar Amir Khan 264
Ressaidar Amir Mohammad Khan 256
Ressaidar Bahadur Khan 228
Ressaidar Bostam Khan 266
Ressaidar Bukshi Ali 162
Ressaidar Fateh Khan 171
Ressaidar Fazal Dad 302
Ressaidar Fazil Khan 166
Ressaidar Ghulam Qadir 302
Ressaidar Hasanmuddin Khan 261
Ressaidar Hassan Shah 498
Ressaidar Huckdad Khan 165
Ressaidar Laurasib Khan 352
Ressaidar Lihaz Gul Khan 209
Ressaidar Major Ahmed Buksh Khan 162
Ressaidar Major Mohammad Hossein Khan 162
Ressaidar Major Mustijab Khan 162
Ressaidar Mansur Khan 173
Ressaidar Meer Mohammad Shah 132
Ressaidar Meera Ahmed Allie Beg 141
Ressaidar Mirza Ellahie Beg 143
Ressaidar Mohammad Amin 180
Ressaidar Mohammad Amin 533
Ressaidar Mohammad shah 301
Ressaidar Mohammad shah 301
Ressaidar Mohammad shah 301
Ressaidar Munsabdar Khan 352
Ressaidar Nizamoodeen Khan 164
Ressaidar Nur Ahmed Khan 208
Ressaidar Salim Khan 170
Ressaidar Shaik Jamal 177
Ressaidar Shamshir Ali Khan 264
Ressaidar Sheik Ahmed Buksh 166

Index

Ressaidar Sher Ali Khan 262
Ressaidar Ushruff Khan 151
Ressaidar Wazir Khan 182
Ressaidar Yakub Khan 265
Ressaidar Zaman Khan 533
Riaz Pirach 532
Rifleman Ali 483
Rifleman Dad 483
Rifleman Fida Hussain 312
Rifleman Gul Sher 296
Rifleman Inayat Ali Khan 312
Rifleman Maula Dad 212
Rifleman Mohammad Yusuf 312
Rifleman Nawab Ali 292
Rifleman Nawab Khan 296
Rifleman Sharif 483
Rirleman Ladu Khan 295
Risaldar Abbas Khan 169
Risaldar Abdul Aziz Khan 260
Risaldar Abdul Razak Khan 363
Risaldar Abdul Satar Khan 264
Risaldar Abdulla Khan 308
Risaldar Abdulla Khan 495
Risaldar Abdulla Khan 495
Risaldar Ahmed Syud Khan 168
Risaldar Ali Haider 319
Risaldar Ali Khan 361
Risaldar Ali Mohsin 305
Risaldar Ali Musa Khan 308
Risaldar Ali Sher 260
Risaldar Allee Woodee Khan 166
Risaldar Alum Khan 166
Risaldar Amir Ali Shah 173
Risaldar Ashak Ali Khan 258
Risaldar Ashraf Ali Khan 302
Risaldar Asul Shah 495
Risaldar Attah Mohammad Khan 151
Risaldar Babur Khan 160
Risaldar Dad Mahammad Khan 169
Risaldar Dadan Khan 302

Index

Risaldar Dhuman Khan 195
Risaldar Dilwar Khan 209
Risaldar Dost Mohammad 195
Risaldar Edoo Khan 306
Risaldar Faiz Mohammad 232
Risaldar Farman Ali 302
Risaldar Farman Ali Khan 302
Risaldar Farzand Ali 261
Risaldar Fazal Elahi 320
Risaldar Feroze Khan 495
Risaldar Feroze Khan 495
Risaldar Futteh Alli Shah 156
Risaldar Futteh Alli Shah 157
Risaldar Fyz Mohammad Khan 167
Risaldar Fyzoollah Khan 148
Risaldar Ghufar Rahman 263
Risaldar Ghulam Hussain 260
Risaldar Ghulam Hussain 474
Risaldar Ghulam Mohammad Khan 262
Risaldar Golaum Mohammed Khan 130
Risaldar Goolam Nabee Khan 168
Risaldar Guli Lal 323
Risaldar Hasham Ali Khan 308
Risaldar Hayat Khan 238
Risaldar Hidayat Ali Khan 264
Risaldar Huckdad Khan 169
Risaldar Ilaudin   305
Risaldar Kale Khan 262
Risaldar Kamaluddin Khan 352
Risaldar Kasim Raza 261
Risaldar Khuda Baksh Khan 196
Risaldar Khurman Khan 151
Risaldar Khurshid Mohammad Khan 256
Risaldar Khurshid Mohammad Khan 260
Risaldar Khwaja Mohammad Khan 266
Risaldar Mahmood Khan Bahar 168
Risaldar Major Ali Musa Khan 495
Risaldar Major Ismail Khan 250
Risaldar Major Mohammad Akbar Khan 228
Risaldar Malik Khan 255

Index

Risaldar Malik Khan Mohammad Khan 190
Risaldar Malik Mohammad Allahdad Khan 250
Risaldar Malik Sultan Khan 259
Risaldar Meer Bunda Allee 149
Risaldar Meer Dilawar Hussain
Risaldar Meer Furzand Ally 160
Risaldar Meer Futteh Khan 145
Risaldar Meer Modood Buksh 167
Risaldar Meer Mohammad 163
Risaldar Mehr Din 495
Risaldar Mir Umjid Ali 160
Risaldar Mohammad Alam Khan 257
Risaldar Mohammad Ali Khan 306
Risaldar Mohammad Amin 238
Risaldar Mohammad Ayaz Khan 164
Risaldar Mohammad Buksh Khan 145
Risaldar Mohammad Hanif 495
Risaldar Mohammad Hayat Khan 264
Risaldar Mohammad Khan 150
Risaldar Mohammad Nur Khan 206
Risaldar Mohammad Reza Khan 156
Risaldar Mohammad Sharif 359
Risaldar Mohammad Wazir Khan 196
Risaldar Moolive Azim Ally 127
Risaldar Mukhtiar Khan 495
Risaldar Munowar Khan 145
Risaldar Nazar Mohammad Khan 361
Risaldar Nazir Mohammad 302
Risaldar Nur Ahmed Khan 350
Risaldar Nur Din 302
Risaldar Qurban Ali 320
Risaldar Rafiq Khan 308
Risaldar Rahim Khan 160
Risaldar Rakhmat Sher Khan 259
Risaldar Roostum Ally Khan 163
Risaldar Sadik Mohammad Khan 207
Risaldar Saif Ali 319
Risaldar Samundar Shah 319
Risaldar Sardar Khan 308
Risaldar Sattar Khan 264

Index

Risaldar Shahzad Mir 499
Risaldar Shaik Ali 131
Risaldar Shaik Hussein Bux 135
Risaldar Shaik Mohammad Khan 168
Risaldar Shaikh Faiz-ud-Din 260
Risaldar Sheik Kurreem 132
Risaldar Shere Mohammad Khan 156
Risaldar Sikandar Khan 495
Risaldar Sirdar Khan 158
Risaldar Sowar Khan 495
Risaldar Wulleeedad Khan 151
Risaldar Yunus Khan 249
Risaldar Yusuf Khan 261
Risaldar Zaidar Khan 266
Risaldar Zaman Khan 179
Risaldar Zardan Khan 495
Risaldar Azam Ali 261
Risaldar Dewan Shah 319
Risaldar Khan Alam Khan 265
Risalder Malik Dad Khan 267
Saddler Mohammad Khan 498
Sahib Sher 284
Said Nakki 303
Salutri Abdullah Khan 264
Salutri Sayyid Ghulam Mahbub
Sapper Abdul Aziz 224
Sapper Abdul Jabbar 273
Sapper Ali 482
 Sapper Art Nawab Khan 236
Sapper Balouch 482
Sapper Baram Muddin 273
Sapper Feroz Khan 274
Sapper Ghulam Aiyuddin 274
Sapper Ghulam Haidar 212
Sapper Gul 482
Sapper Haidar Zaman 272
Sapper Hussain 482
Sapper Ismail 482
Sapper Khan 482
Sapper Khan 482

Index

Sapper Khan Bahadur 273
Sapper Latif 482
Sapper Mahtab Khan 220
Sapper Maula Baksh 203
Sapper Mohammad 309
Sapper Mohammad Sharif 498
Sapper Nawab Khan 238
Sapper Nur Dad 236
Sapper Nur Hussain 271
Sapper Rafiq 482
Sapper Said Ghafar 272
Sapper Said Ullah 498
Sapper Saiyid Abdul Wahab 223
Sapper Shaikh Imam 272
Sapper Sheik Abdul Rahman 202
Sapper Sowar Khan 273
Sapper Syed Abdul Raim 273
Sapper Wali Dad 274
Sapper Bostan 271
Seoy Sheikh Mohammad 279
Seoy Sher Khan 187
Sepoy Arshad Khan 293
Sepoy Ghulam Ali 299
Sepoy Mawiz Khan 283
Sepoy Zawari 278
Sepoy Chota Khan 295
Sepoy Dilbar Shah 291
Sepoy Mehr Mohammad 318
Sepoy Nazir Din 283
Sepoy Abbaz Khan 226
Sepoy Abdoola 161
Sepoy Abdul 485
Sepoy Abdul Basid 288
Sepoy Abdul Ghaffar 294
Sepoy Abdul Ghafur Khan 294
Sepoy Abdul Hasan 292
Sepoy Abdul Hussein 292
Sepoy Abdul Karim 234
Sepoy Abdul Khadar 288
Sepoy Abdul Munaf 167

Index

Sepoy Abdul Nabi 315
Sepoy Abdul Rahim 320
Sepoy Abdula Khan 295
Sepoy Abdulla Khan 184
Sepoy Abdulla Khan 314
Sepoy Abid Ali 317
Sepoy Abkar Khan 285
Sepoy Abul Malik 314
Sepoy Afsar Ali 288
Sepoy Afsar Khan 298
Sepoy Ahmed Ji 299
Sepoy Ahmed Khan 274
Sepoy Ahmed Khan 279
Sepoy Ahmed Khan 296
Sepoy Ain ud Din 304
Sepoy Akbar Khan 172
Sepoy Akbar Khan 311
Sepoy Akram 173
Sepoy Alam Mir 297
Sepoy Ali 483
Sepoy Ali 484
Sepoy Ali 485
Sepoy Ali 485
Sepoy Ali 486
Sepoy Ali 486
Sepoy Ali Dad 287
Sepoy Ali Khan 187
Sepoy Ali Majan 321
Sepoy Ali Mohammad 227
Sepoy Ali Shah Ali 198
Sepoy Ali Zaman 317
Sepoy Allah Dad 282
Sepoy Allah Dad 289
Sepoy Allah Dad 297
Sepoy Allah Ditta 286
Sepoy Allah Ditta 313
Sepoy Allah Ditta Khan 283
Sepoy Allah Ditta Khan 276
Sepoy Allah Khan 179
Sepoy Allah Nur Khan 276

Index

Sepoy Allah Nur Khan 276
Sepoy Allan Ditta 296
Sepoy Almanat Khan 275
Sepoy Alum Beg 314
Sepoy Alum Shah 127
Sepoy Alvaz Khan 284
Sepoy Ameer Khan 156
Sepoy Amir Ali 274
Sepoy Amir Ali 313
Sepoy Amir Ali 314
Sepoy Amir Khan 277
Sepoy Amir Khan 279
Sepoy Amir Khan 304
Sepoy Ashraf 483
Sepoy Ashraf 485
Sepoy Ashraf, M. (33034) 485
Sepoy Ata Mohammad 225
Sepoy Auliya Khan 298
Sepoy Aurangzeb 486
Sepoy Aurangzeb 486
Sepoy Ayam ud din 323
Sepoy Ayub Khan 316
Sepoy Azam Khan 284
Sepoy Babu Khan 276
Sepoy Badshah 483
Sepoy Bahadoor Khan 156
Sepoy Bahadur 284
Sepoy Bahadur Khan 129
Sepoy Bahadur Khan 284
Sepoy Baker Khan 288
Sepoy Bakhmal Jan 115
Sepoy Balghar 324
Sepoy Barkhat Khan 310
Sepoy Bashir 484
Sepoy Baz Gul 130
Sepoy Baz Khan 287
Sepoy Bazid Khan 284
Sepoy Bazm Ali 282
Sepoy Bkukkha Khan 152
Sepoy Boota Khan 298

Index

Sepoy Bostan 152
Sepoy Bostan Khan 288
Sepoy Buctour Khan 143
Sepoy Burhan Ali 214
Sepoy Chaudhri Khan 317
Sepoy Chowdre Khan 280
Sepoy Dad 483
Sepoy Dadum Khan 537
Sepoy Darren Shah 152
Sepoy Dasswandi Khan 311
Sepoy Daulat Khan 200
Sepoy Dheru Khan 283
Sepoy Din 484
Sepoy Din Mohammad 294
Sepoy Ditta 293
Sepoy Diwan Ali Khan 276
Sepoy Dost Mohammad 293
Sepoy Dost Mohammad 498
Sepoy Dullah Khan 279
Sepoy Faiz Ali Khan 306
Sepoy Faiz Mohammad Khan 274
Sepoy Fakeer Shah 166
Sepoy Faqir Ali 238
Sepoy Faqir Khan 323
Sepoy Faqir Mohammad 313
Sepoy Farman Ali 238
Sepoy Farman Ali 282
Sepoy Fateh Ali 280
Sepoy Fateh Mohammad 290
Sepoy Fateh Mohammad 293
Sepoy Fateh Mohammad 297
Sepoy Fateh Mohammad 299
Sepoy Fazal Dad 293
Sepoy Fazal Dad 313
Sepoy Fazal Khan 276
Sepoy Fazal Rahman 310
Sepoy Feroz 215
Sepoy Firoz Khan 288
Sepoy Fuzil Khan 156
Sepoy Gafar Khan 280

Index

Sepoy Gama Khan 282
Sepoy Ghafar Shah 310
Sepoy Ghafur Khan 294
Sepoy Ghazi Khan 315
Sepoy Gheba Khan 215
Sepoy Ghilaf Gul 323
Sepoy Ghose Beg 156
Sepoy Ghulam 234
Sepoy Ghulam Hassan 315
Sepoy Ghulam Hussain 534
Sepoy Ghulam Hussein 295
Sepoy Ghulam Mohammed 488
Sepoy Ghulam Nabi 499
Sepoy Ghulam Rabani 313
Sepoy Ghulam Rasul 319
Sepoy Ghuncha Gul 316
Sepoy Ghunee 167
Sepoy Golab 156
Sepoy Gool Mahmud 170
Sepoy Goolab 156
Sepoy Gour Khan 170
Sepoy Gul 483
Sepoy Gul Amir 317
Sepoy Gul Shere 173
Sepoy Gul Zedah 323
Sepoy Gul, H. 485
Sepoy Gul, S. 485
Sepoy Gulab Khan 276
Sepoy Gulab Khan 283
Sepoy Habib Shah 281
Sepoy Hafiz Ali 537
Sepoy Hafiz Ali 182
Sepoy Haidar Ali 285
Sepoy Haidar Ali 334
Sepoy Haider 486
Sepoy Haider Ali 280
Sepoy Haider Shah 322
Sepoy Haider Shah 322
Sepoy Haji Mohammad 292
Sepoy Hakim 175

Index

Sepoy Hakim Khan 246
Sepoy Hanif Jan 322
Sepoy Hasham Khan 285
Sepoy Hashim Ali Khan 276
Sepoy Hassain 319
Sepoy Hassan Khan 170
Sepoy Havildar Peer Bux 167
Sepoy Hayat 484
Sepoy Hayat Mohammad 277
Sepoy Hukum Dad 319
Sepoy Hullum 156
Sepoy Hummeed 152
Sepoy Hussain 484
Sepoy Hussun 167
Sepoy Hyat 156
Sepoy Ibrahim 280
Sepoy Ibrahim 484
Sepoy Ibrahim Khan 242
Sepoy Imam Din 223
Sepoy Inayat Ali Khan 234
Sepoy Inyat Ali Shah 534
Sepoy Inzat Gul 317
Sepoy Irfanullah 115
Sepoy Isa Khan 279
Sepoy Isa Khan 246
Sepoy Ishmael 483
Sepoy Itbar Khan 311
Sepoy Jafar Khan 223
Sepoy Jahangeer Khan 144
Sepoy Jamadar 297
Sepoy Jhangi Khan 321
Sepoy Jiwan Khan 295
Sepoy Jiwan Khan 279
Sepoy Jiwan Khan Baksh 203
Sepoy Juma Baksh 294
Sepoy Kadir Din 298
Sepoy Kamal Khan 297
Sepoy Karam Ilahi 184
Sepoy Karamat Hussain 316
Sepoy Karim 483

Index

Sepoy Karim 486
Sepoy Karim 486
Sepoy Karim Baksh 276
Sepoy Karim Khan 288
Sepoy Karim Shah 276
Sepoy Kasim Khan 295
Sepoy Kassib 298
Sepoy Khabib 485
Sepoy Khair Ali 321
Sepoy Khair Mohammad 324
Sepoy Khaista Jan 323
Sepoy Khan 483
Sepoy Khan 483
Sepoy Khan 483
Sepoy Khan 484
Sepoy Khan 484
Sepoy Khan 484
Sepoy Khan 484
Sepoy Khan 485
Sepoy Khan 485
Sepoy Khan 485
Sepoy Khan 485
Sepoy Khan 486
Sepoy Khan 486
Sepoy Khan 486
Sepoy Khan Malik 315
Sepoy Khan Zada 311
Sepoy Khan Zaman 216
Sepoy Khan, C. 484
Sepoy Khan, F. 484
Sepoy Khan, L. 486
Sepoy Khan, L. 486
Sepoy Khan, M 485
Sepoy Khan, M. 486
Sepoy Khan, M. 486
Sepoy Khan, P. 484
Sepoy Khan, R. 486
Sepoy Khan, R. 486
Sepoy Khan, S. 486
Sepoy Khan, S. 486

Index

Sepoy Khawas Khan 323
Sepoy Khitab 484
Sepoy Khushi Mohammad 312
Sepoy Kukhoo Khan 156
Sepoy Kurban 234
Sepoy Kurban 534
Sepoy Kurban 292
Sepoy Lakhmir Khan 282
Sepoy Lal Khan 280
Sepoy Lal Khan 285
Sepoy Lal Khan 298
Sepoy Lal Mir 284
Sepoy Lal Sher 298
Sepoy Lall Khan 152
Sepoy Madar Ali 288
Sepoy Madat Ali 285
Sepoy Mahmud 485
Sepoy Mahmud Ali Khan 218
Sepoy Makhamad Rasul 316
Sepoy Makhmad Ali 198
Sepoy Malik 486
Sepoy Malik 486
Sepoy Malik Din 278
Sepoy Manawar Khan 316
Sepoy Manga Khan 290
Sepoy Maroof Shah 175
Sepoy Maskin 322
Sepoy Meer Afzul 144
Sepoy Mehr Din 286
Sepoy Mehr Khan 283
Sepoy Mehr Khan 294
Sepoy Mehrab Gul 298
Sepoy Mehtab Ali 290
Sepoy Mian Afraz Gul 499
Sepoy Mian Khan 193
Sepoy Mian Khan 282
Sepoy Mir Abdullah Jan 305
Sepoy Mir Ahmed 310
Sepoy Mir Bad Shah 283
Sepoy Mir Badshah 284

Index

Sepoy Mir Badshah 318
Sepoy Mir Baz 284
Sepoy Mir Shah Jan 304
Sepoy Mirjan 184
Sepoy Mirza Khan 298
Sepoy Mirzada 283
Sepoy Mohammad 236
Sepoy Mohammad 317
Sepoy Mohammad 484
Sepoy Mohammad 485
Sepoy Mohammad 486
Sepoy Mohammad 486
Sepoy Mohammad Akbar 310
Sepoy Mohammad Ali Khan 276
Sepoy Mohammad Amin 252
Sepoy Mohammad Amin 279
Sepoy Mohammad Ayub Khan 241
Sepoy Mohammad Azam 321
Sepoy Mohammad Bux 144
Sepoy Mohammad Bux 157
Sepoy Mohammad Fazal 287
Sepoy Mohammad Goal 167
Sepoy Mohammad Hussain 294
Sepoy Mohammad Khan 279
Sepoy Mohammad Khan 290
Sepoy Mohammad Khan 290
Sepoy Mohammad Khan 299
Sepoy Mohammad Khan 317
Sepoy Mohammad Niwaz 319
Sepoy Mohammad Nur 321
Sepoy Mohammad Said 313
Sepoy Mohammad Sarwar 74
Sepoy Mohammad Shafi 537
Sepoy Mohammad Shah 277
Sepoy Mohammad Shah 310
Sepoy Mohammad Shuffi 173
Sepoy Mohammad Zaman 226
Sepoy Mohammad Zaman 294
Sepoy Mohammad Zaman 299
Sepoy Mohi Khan 304

Index

Sepoy Mowaz 280
Sepoy Mugli Khan 218
Sepoy Mukhmad Khan 229
Sepoy Mukhrtiara 537
Sepoy Munsab Khan 274
Sepoy Munshi Khan 276
Sepoy Munshi Khan 293
Sepoy Munsib Dar 183
Sepoy Munsoor 152
Sepoy Murad Ali 293
Sepoy Murad Ali Khan 275
Sepoy Mustafa Khan 290
Sepoy Muzaffar Khan 293
Sepoy Nabi Baksh 294
Sepoy Nadir Ali 289
Sepoy Nawab Ali 278
Sepoy Nawab Khan 317
Sepoy Nawaz Ali 321
Sepoy Nazir Din 537
Sepoy Neaz Mohammad 152
Sepoy Nek Amal 535
Sepoy Niamat Khan 276
Sepoy Niaz Mohammad 276
Sepoy Niaz Mohammad 313
Sepoy Nihal Khan 128
Sepoy Nikab Gul 296
Sepoy Niwaz 483
Sepoy Nizam Din 297
Sepoy Nizam Ullee Khan 140
Sepoy Noor Hussen 152
Sepoy Nur 486
Sepoy Nur 486
Sepoy Nur Khan 286
Sepoy Nur Shamal 304
Sepoy Nurudin 282
Sepoy Omeer Khan 156
Sepoy Painda Khan 282
Sepoy Peer Bux 167
Sepoy Pehelwan Shah 320
Sepoy Pir Mohammad 303

Index

Sepoy Qadir Baksh 276
Sepoy Qasim Ali Khan 276
Sepoy Rahim Ali 182
Sepoy Rahim Ali 537
Sepoy Rahim Dad 537
Sepoy Rahim Dad Khan 275
Sepoy Rahim Khan 173
Sepoy Rajiv Khan 203
Sepoy Rakhim Gul 317
Sepoy Rang Baz 313
Sepoy Rangin Khan 255
Sepoy Raz Ali 292
Sepoy Redi Gul 201
Sepoy Rehmat All 321
Sepoy Roshan Khan 280
Sepoy Roshun Khan 140
Sepoy Russool 167
Sepoy Sabdal Khan 291
Sepoy Sabit Ullah 242
Sepoy Sadat Khan 247
Sepoy Saddar Din 319
Sepoy Sadiq Hussein Shah 314
Sepoy Sahadut Khan 141
Sepoy Sahib Din 281
Sepoy Sahib Din 313
Sepoy Sahib Gool 152
Sepoy Sahib Jan 201
Sepoy Sahibadeen 167
Sepoy Said Ahmed 298
Sepoy Said Akbar 313
Sepoy Said Amir 297
Sepoy Said Askar 321
Sepoy Said Kasim 303
Sepoy Said Mohammad 318
Sepoy Said Rehmat 292
Sepoy Saiday Khan 202
Sepoy Sajawal Khan 296
Sepoy Sajawal Shah 310
Sepoy Sajwal 483
Sepoy Sajwal Khan 279

Index

Sepoy Salim Khan 321
Sepoy Sar Amir 200
Sepoy Sardar Din 537
Sepoy Sardar Khan 277
Sepoy Sardar Khan 279
Sepoy Sardar Khan 537
Sepoy Sarwar 483
Sepoy Sarwar Khan 229
Sepoy Sarwar Khan 318
Sepoy Saugar Khan 281
Sepoy Sayyid Bale 294
Sepoy Seemurgh Khan 525
Sepoy Sewaz Khan 181
Sepoy Shah 484
Sepoy Shah Mohammad 299
Sepoy Shahza Khan 296
Sepoy Shahzada 167
Sepoy Shaik Ahmud 129
Sepoy Shaik Phultoo 145
Sepoy Shaikh Imam 288
Sepoy Shaikh Koodrut Ali 141
Sepoy Shaikh Ladie 294
Sepoy Shaikh Umar 293
Sepoy Sheikh Allah Buksh 167
Sepoy Shekh Khoda Bux 140
Sepoy Sher 484
Sepoy Sher Ali 321
Sepoy Sher Ali 499
Sepoy Sher Ali 524
Sepoy Sher Dil 288
Sepoy Sher Khan 280
Sepoy Sher Khan 293
Sepoy Sher Khan 315
Sepoy Sher Khan 321
Sepoy Sher Mohammad 290
Sepoy Sher Mohammad 290
Sepoy Sher Mohammad 284
Sepoy Sher Zaman 314
Sepoy Sher Zarin 238
Sepoy Sirdar Khan 129

Index

Sepoy Sirdar Khan 156
Sepoy Sirdar Khan 499
Sepoy Sohbat Khan 303
Sepoy Sujawal Khan 288
Sepoy Suleiman Khan 203
Sepoy Sultan Baksh 298
Sepoy Sultan Baksh 537
Sepoy Sultan Khan 238
Sepoy Sultan Khan 317
Sepoy Sultan Mohammad
Sepoy Summer Gul 283
Sepoy Syud Mohammad 152
Sepoy Taj Mohammad 255
Sepoy Tawalhe Din 304
Sepoy Tor Baz 311
Sepoy Tor Khan 304
Sepoy Ukhter 167
Sepoy Umar Din 279
Sepoy Umar Gul 305
Sepoy Umar Khan 291
Sepoy Usman Khan 200
Sepoy Walayat Khan 282
Sepoy Waryam Khan 298
Sepoy Yaqub 486
Sepoy Yar Akhmad 278
Sepoy Yusuf Ali 294
Sepoy Zaid Baksh 310
Sepoy Zaid Gul 294
Sepoy Zakim 321
Sepoy Zaman 484
Sepoy Zaman 486
Sepoy Zaman 486
Sepoy Zaman Ullah 304
Sepoy Zarif Khan 202
Sepoy Zarif Khan 324
Serang Abdul Khalaque 498
Sergeant Rehman 485
Shabbir Ahmed 532
Sheikh Inayut Huck 149
Sheikh Mujibur Rahman 5

Index

Signaller Inyatt Ullah 308
Signalman Khan 482
Signalman Mohammad 482
Signalman Mohammad Aslam 309
Sillidar Nuttay Khan 132
Simla 5
Sindh 5
Sir (Fazalbhoy) Currimbhoy Ebrahim 507
Sir Abdul Halim Ghaznavi 508
Sir Abdul Karim Ghaznavi 501
Sir Abdullah Haroon 510
Sir Ahmad Yar Khan Ahmedzai 504
Sir Fazal Ibrahim Rahimtoola 508
Sir Ghulam Hussain Hidayutullah 510
Sir Hajji Nawab Kalb Ali Khan Bahadur 500
Sir Ibrahim Rahimtoola 512
Sir Khan Bahadur Sayyid Sir Fazl Ali 504
Sir Khawaja Nazimuddin 522
Sir Malik Ghulam Muhammad 509
Sir Malik Mohammed Umar Hayat Khan 515
Sir Mian Fazl-i-Husain 511
Sir Mir Turab Ali Khan 500
Sir Mirza Muhammad Ismail 513
Sir Mohammad Yamin Khan 516
Sir Mohammed Saleh Hydari 513
Sir Muhammad Ahmad Said Khan Chhatari 507
Sir Muhammad Akbar Nazar Ali Hydari 512
Sir Muhammad Faiyaz Ali Khan 516
Sir Muhammad Habibullah 508
Sir Muhammad Iqbal 513
Sir Muhammad Mahabat Khanji III Rasul Khanji 521
Sir Muhammad Zafarullah Khan 523
Sir Nawab Khwaja Ahsanullah 504
Sir Nawab Sir Muhammad Ali Beg 501
Sir Nizamat Jung Bahadur 514
Sir Rafiuddin Ahmed 522
Sir Sadiq Muhammad Khan V Abbasi 517
Sir Shah Nawaz Bhutto 506
Sir Sheikh Sir Abdul Qadir 501
Sir Sikandar Hayat Khan 518

Index

Sir Sultan Muhammed Shah, Aga Khan III 502
Sir Syed Ahmad bin Syed Muhammad Muttaqi 519
Sir Syed Shamsul Huda 511
Sir Syed Sultan Ahmed 503
Sir Syed Sultan Ahmed 505
Sir Syed Wazir Hasan 512
Sir Ziauddin Ahmad 503
Sir Ziauddin Ahmad 505
Soobhan Alli 145
Sowar Abdul Shakur Khan 257
Sowar Atta Mohammad 258
Sowar Firoz Khan 257
Sowar Ghafur Ali Khan 257
Sowar Ghulam Khan 257
Sowar Ghulam Mohammad 257
Sowar Ghulam Mohd, Khan 256
Sowar Hashim Khan 257
Sowar Hidayat Khan 259
Sowar Maqbal Ahmed Khan 256
Sowar Mir Badshah 257
Sowar Mohammad Sayyid 261
Sowar Nishan Ali 256
Sowar Ramzan Khan 257
Sowar Shamsudin Khan 257
Sowar Yakub Khan 256
Sowar Abdi Khan 308
Sowar Abdool Rahman 150
 Sowar Abdoola Khan 151
Sowar Abdullah Khan 205
Sowar Abdullah Khan 264
Sowar Aibala Khan 265
Sowar Akbar Khan 261
Sowar Akhtar Khan 127
Sowar Alam Ali Khan 308
Sowar Ali 481
Sowar Ali Mohammad Khan 266
Sowar Alim Khan 308
Sowar Alla Ditta 207
Sowar Allah Dad Khan 536
Sowar Ameer Khan 177

Index

Sowar Amir Khan 260
Sowar Asghar Ali Khan 263
Sowar Aslam Khan 266
Sowar Ayub Khan 303
Sowar Badshah Khan 323
Sowar Bagh Khan 156
Sowar Bahadoor Khan 131
Sowar Bahawaklin Khan 171
Sowar Bhure Khan 308
Sowar Bujjoo Khan 131
Sowar Burma Deen 177
Sowar Dost Mohammad Khan 266
Sowar Dost Mohd. Khan 259
Sowar Dost Mohd. Khan 263
Sowar Dullee Khan 126
Sowar Fakir Khan 265
Sowar Fateh Khan 264
Sowar Fayez Mohammad Khan 154
Sowar Fazal Khan 174
Sowar Firman Khan 264
Sowar Ghazee 150
Sowar Ghazi Khan 160
Sowar Ghiba Khan 259
Sowar Ghoolam Hussein Khan 135
Sowar Ghulam Hussain 261
Sowar Ghulam Hussain 265
Sowar Ghulam Mohammad 262
Sowar Gohur 160
Sowar Golab Khan 160
Sowar Hayat Mohammad 205
Sowar Hazrat Shah 265
Sowar Hidayutullah 173
Sowar Hyat Khan 145
Sowar Ibrahim 235
Sowar Ibrahim 534
Sowar Illahi Bux 126
Sowar Inyut Khan 160
Sowar Ismail Khan 264
Sowar Jhuadah Shah 157
Sowar Kaller Khan 131

Index

Sowar Kambar Ali 265
Sowar Kan Jan Khan 175
Sowar Karam Khan 262
Sowar Kassim Alli 150
Sowar Khan 481
Sowar Khan Mohammad Khan 196
Sowar Kurreem Khan 131
Sowar Kurreemooolah 163
Sowar Kurrum Khan 160
Sowar Lalla Jan 265
Sowar Liakat Hussain 208
Sowar Makan Khan 259
Sowar Mardan Ali 265
Sowar Mazammal Khan 258
Sowar Mazhar Khan 216
Sowar Meer Ijut Ali 160
Sowar Meer Zoolficar Ally 166
Sowar Mir Akbar Khan 258
Sowar Mohammad 481
Sowar Mohammad Afzal 308
Sowar Mohammad Afzul 156
Sowar Mohammad Shah 138
Sowar Mohammad Sharif Khan 259
Sowar Mohammad Umami Khan 160
Sowar Mohammad Yar Khan 262
Sowar Mubarak Shah 303
Sowar Muhaman Hussein 206
Sowar Muhammad Hussain 12
Sowar Munowar Khan 145
Sowar Munsabdar Khan 149
Sowar Myboob Khan 132
Sowar Nadir Khan 260
Sowar Nahar Khan 131
Sowar Nujjo Khan 166
Sowar Nutty Khan 151
Sowar Qasim Ali Khan 264
Sowar Sadulla Khan 264
Sowar Salloo Khan 128
Sowar Sarwar Ali 231
Sowar Sarwar Ali 534

Index

Sowar Sayed Abdul Majid 260
Sowar Sayyad Abdul Majid 534
Sowar Shah Zada 266
Sowar Shahdul Khan 144
Sowar Shahzad Khan 189
Sowar Shaick Abdoola 158
Sowar Shaik Hoossain 177
Sowar Sheik Dowlut 160
Sowar Sheik Ismail 132
Sowar Sheik Rahim-ud-Din 160
Sowar Sheikh Kaim Ali 160
Sowar Sheikh Subsati 160
Sowar Sher Dil 258
Sowar Sher Khan 171
Sowar Sher Mohammad 266
Sowar Shumshoodeen 135
Sowar Sirbuland Khan 177
Sowar Sirdar Khan 499
Sowar Subhan Khan 260
Sowar Suller Khan 131
Sowar Sultan Khan 259
Sowar Sultan Mohammad 226
Sowar Sungur Khan 147
Sowar Suraj Din 261
Sowar Syud Alli 145
Sowar Syud Imam Ali 176
Sowar Talib Hussein 259
Sowar Townkul Khan 132
Sowar Wali Mohammad Khan 264
Sowar Wazir Khan 160
Sowar Yar Khan 263
Sowar Yashin Khan 258
Sowar Zaidulla 172
Sowar Zaighin Shah 265
Sowar Zarif Khan 303
Sowar Zeeaoodeen 173
Squadron Leader Alauddin Ahmed 96
Squadron Leader Aslam Choudhry 109
Squadron Leader Azim Daudpota 84
Squadron Leader Farooq Omer 105

Index

Squadron Leader Ishfaq Hameed 109
Squadron Leader Jamal A. Khan 85
Squadron Leader Javed Afzal Ahmed 106
Squadron Leader Khusro 110
Squadron Leader Mervyn Middlecoat 84
Squadron Leader Mir Abdul Rashid 87
Squadron Leader Muhammad Mahmood Alam 86
Squadron Leader Muniruddin Ahmed 97
Squadron Leader Najeeb A Khan 87
Squadron Leader Peter Christie 109
Squadron Leader Rais A Rafi 85
Squadron Leader Sarfaraz Ahmad Rafique 98
Squadron Leader Sarfaraz Ahmed Rafiqui 57
Squadron Leader Shabbir H Syed 86
Squadron Leader Shuaib Alam Khan 87
Squadron Leader Syed Manzoor Ul Hassan 84
Squadron Leader Syed Sajjad Haider 85
Subedar Abbas Ali 280
Subedar Abbas Khan 270
Subedar Abdar Rehman 314
Subedar Abdool Azees 163
Subedar Abdool Hoosain 134
Subedar Abdoola Khan 144
Subedar Abdul Aziz 307
Subedar Abdul Aziz Khan 238
Subedar Abdul Gafoor 494
Subedar Abdul Ghafar Khan 281
Subedar Abdul Ghani 374
Subedar Abdul Ghani Khan 295
Subedar Abdul Jabar 392
Subedar Abdul Jabbar 310
Subedar Abdul Majid 449
Subedar Abdul Majid Khan 312
Subedar Abdul Salam Siddiqiue 495
Subedar Abdul Sattar 398
Subedar Ahamat Ullah 495
Subedar Ahmed Din 191
Subedar Ahmed Din 291
Subedar Ahmed Khan 151
Subedar Ahmed Khan 255

Index

Subedar Ahmed Khan 274
Subedar Ahmed Khan 286
Subedar Ahmed Khan 315
Subedar Ahmed Khan 495
Subedar Akbar Ali 305
Subedar Akbar Khan 281
Subedar Akbar Khan 281
Subedar Akbar Khan 286
Subedar Akhmed Shah 322
Subedar Alam Khan 238
Subedar Alam Khan 274
Subedar Ali Akbar 285
Subedar Ali Bahadur 272
Subedar Ali Bahadur Khan 275
Subedar Ali Beg 277
Subedar Ali Dad 402
Subedar Ali Dost 292
Subedar Ali Dost 292
Subedar Ali Dost 533
Subedar Ali Mohammad Shah 299
Subedar Ali Shafa 292
Subedar Ali Zaman 480
Subedar Alif Khan 273
Subedar Allah Dad 315
Subedar Allah Dad Khan 296
Subedar Allah Ditta 238
Subedar Allah Ditta 290
Subedar Allah Ditta 316
Subedar Allah Ditta 494
Subedar Allah Jan 320
Subedar Allah Nur 277
Subedar Aman Gul 279
Subedar Amar Ali Khan 293
Subedar Amir Ali 290
Subedar Amir Ali 290
Subedar Amir Khan 317
Subedar Amir Khan Bahadur 353
Subedar Amir Zaman Khan 273
Subedar Anil Gul 274
Subedar Arsla Khan Bahadur 354

Index

Subedar Aseem Khan 139
Subedar Aslam Khan 130
Subedar Aslam Khan 309
Subedar Asmatullah Khan 315
Subedar Atta Mohammad 310
Subedar Atta Mohammad 313
Subedar Atta Mohammad 319
Subedar Atta Mohammad 413
Subedar Attar Khan 206
Subedar Awalnur 238
Subedar Aziz Ullah 235
Subedar Aziz Ullah 276
Subedar Aziz-ud-Din Khan 275
Subedar Badar-ud-din 311
Subedar Badi-ul-Zaman 281
Subedar Badshah 319
Subedar Bagh Ali 273
Subedar Bagh Ali 318
Subedar Bagh Khan 323
Subedar Bahadur Jung 316
Subedar Bahadur Khan 204
Subedar Bahadur Khan 255
Subedar Bahadur Khan 468
Subedar Bahadur Shah 288
Subedar Bahadur Shah 533
Subedar Barkat Shah 316
Subedar Baz Gul 173
Subedar Baz Mohammad 323
Subedar Bhag Ali 280
Subedar Chand Khan 139
Subedar Dabee Deen 146
Subedar Darweza Khan 228
Subedar Daud Beg 289
Subedar Deen Mohammad 154
Subedar Dilwar Ali Khan 313
Subedar Din Mohammad 378
Subedar Dost Mohammad 1292
Subedar Dost Mohammad 205
Subedar Dost Mohammad 316
Subedar Durani Khan 298

Index

Subedar Emam Bux 136
Subedar Eman Khan 168
Subedar Falak Sher 450
Subedar Faqir Hussain 307
Subedar Farman Ali 290
Subedar Fateh Jang 284
Subedar Fateh Khan 273
Subedar Fateh Khan 299
Subedar Fateh Mohammad 243
Subedar Fateh Mohammad 413
Subedar Fateh Mohammad 494
Subedar Fateh Mohammad Khan 293
Subedar Fatteh Khan 369
Subedar Fayez Mohammad Khan 154
Subedar Fazal Din 273
Subedar Fazal Din 494
Subedar Fazal Elahi 494
Subedar Fazal Ellami 494
Subedar Fazal Karim 294
Subedar Fazal Shah 271
Subedar Fazl Shah 271
Subedar Feroz Khan 312
Subedar Fiaz Mohammad Khan 276
Subedar Firoz Khan 281
Subedar Fyz Mohammad Khan 144
Subedar Ghulam Abbas 437
Subedar Ghulam Ali 353
Subedar Ghulam Haidar 181
Subedar Ghulam Hussain 238
Subedar Ghulam Jilani 533
Subedar Ghulam Khan 288
Subedar Ghulam Mohammad 276
Subedar Ghulam Mohammad 314
Subedar Ghulam Mohammad 319
Subedar Ghulam Mohammad Khan 533
Subedar Ghulam Muhiddin 289
Subedar Ghulam Mustafa 243
Subedar Ghulam Rasul 471
Subedar Ghulam Ullah Khan 458
Subedar Ghulam Unis 296

Index

Subedar Ghulam Yasin 417
Subedar Gul Akbar Bahadur 354
Subedar Gul Badshah 306
Subedar Gul Din Khan 247
Subedar Gul Din Khan 253
Subedar Gul Khan 219
Subedar Gul Majid 322
Subedar Gul Wahid 318
Subedar Gul Wahid Khan 494
Subedar Gul Zaman 185
Subedar Gulistan Khan 495
Subedar Gulistan Khan 495
Subedar Habib Khan 277
Subedar Habib Khan 438
Subedar Habib Ullah Khan 281
Subedar Hadjee Khan 165
Subedar Hakim Khan
Subedar Hakim Khan 251
Subedar Hamid Khan 284
Subedar Haq 309
Subedar Hasham Gul Khan 321
Subedar Hashmat Dad Khan 293
Subedar Hassan Ali 314
Subedar Havildar Ramzan Khan 499
Subedar Hayat Khan 275
Subedar Hubbeeb Khan 152
Subedar Hubeeb Khan 143
Subedar Hubeeb Khan 166
Subedar Hukam Dad 533
Subedar Hukmal Khan 317
Subedar Hukum Dad 233
Subedar Hussain Shah 309
Subedar Hussein Shah 288
Subedar Ibrahim Khan 283
Subedar IIam Din 321
Subedar Illahi Baksh 472
Subedar Ilyasdar Khan 291
Subedar Imam Ali 494
Subedar Imam Ali 495
Subedar Imam ud Din Khan 238

Index

Subedar Iqbal Khan 324
Subedar Isa Khan 283
Subedar Ismail Khan 272
Subedar Ismail Khan 535
Subedar Itbar Khan 311
Subedar Jafar Ali 234
Subedar Jahan Dad 371
Subedar Jan Bahadur 323
Subedar Jan Gul 182
Subedar Jan Mohammad 285
Subedar Jan Mohammad 379
Subedar Janas Khan 282
Subedar Jehandad Khan 204
Subedar Jehangir 307
Subedar Jemadar Khan 313
Subedar Jilal Din 287
Subedar Jiwan Khan 355
Subedar Jodh Khan 227
Subedar Juma Khan 172
Subedar Kalandar 255
Subedar Kalandar Khan 455
Subedar Kanwal Khan 494
Subedar Karam Dad 199
Subedar Karam Dad 223
Subedar Karam Din 289
Subedar Karam Din 294
Subedar Karam Khan 281
Subedar Karam Khan 317
Subedar Karam Shah 297
Subedar Karim Khan 375
Subedar Karram Khan 293
Subedar Khan Abdullah 495
Subedar Khan Bahadur 315
Subedar Khan Bahadur Sher Jang 499
Subedar Khan Mohammad Khan 188
Subedar Khan Sahib 303
Subedar Khan Zaman 459
Subedar Khroolla Khan 164
Subedar Khudadad Khan 325
Subedar Kudrat Shah 151

Index

Subedar Kummur Deen 151
Subedar Kwan Khan 304
Subedar Lahir Khan 299
Subedar Lal Khan 189
Subedar Lal Khan 285
Subedar Lal Khan 463
Subedar Lal Zada 321
Subedar Lall Badshah 408
Subedar Latif Khan 287
Subedar Liaquat Hussein 367
Subedar M. Fateh Din 269
Subedar Mada Mir 426
Subedar Mahammad Hosein Khan 151
Subedar Major Abbas Ali 494
Subedar Major Abdul Siddique 494
Subedar Major Ahmed Khan 385
Subedar Major Ahmed Khan 494
Subedar Major Ajab 214
Subedar Major Alam Khan 232
Subedar Major Alam Khan 533
Subedar Major Atta Mohammad 494
Subedar Major Aziz-ur-Rahman 494
Subedar Major Bir Khan 233
Subedar Major Boi Khan 533
Subedar Major Farman Ali 220
Subedar Major Gulmir 217
Subedar Major Haider Rahman 494
Subedar Major Hassan Mohammad 533
Subedar Major Hussain Shah 224
Subedar Major Hyasdar Khan 533
Subedar Major Hyder Khan 178
Subedar Major Karam Ilahi 494
Subedar Major Khan Mohammad, 397
Subedar Major Khitab Gil 533
Subedar Major Khitab Gul 225
Subedar Major Khushi Mohammad 494
Subedar Major Mirza Sakhi Mohammad 494
Subedar Major Mohammad Baksh 220
Subedar Major Mohammad Din 533
Subedar Major Mohammad Feroze 494

Index

Subedar Major Mohammad Khan 494
Subedar Major Mohibullah Khan 533
Subedar Major Mussaik Khan 447
Subedar Major Nasim Khan 215
Subedar Major Nasir Khan 536
Subedar Major Noor Khan 469
Subedar Major Pehlwan Khan 495
Subedar Major Sarbuland 186
Subedar Major Sardar Khan 237
Subedar Major Sher Baz 182
Subedar Major T. Mohammad 495
Subedar Major Walayat Hussain 494
Subedar Makhmad Anwar 254
Subedar Makhmand Azam 202
Subedar Malham Khan 304
Subedar Mamur Khan 387
Subedar Mansabdar Khan 423
Subedar Mansar Ali 291
Subedar Mansur Khan 283
Subedar Maquam Khan 304
Subedar Maula Baksh 311
Subedar Mauz Ali Shah 472
Subedar Mawaz Khan 278
Subedar Meer Jaffir 143
Subedar Mehdi Khan 295
Subedar Mehr Din 272
Subedar Mehr Khan 395
Subedar MIA Qureshi 499
Subedar Mian Khan 527
Subedar Mian Mohammad 319
Subedar Mir Afzal 323
Subedar Mir Akbar 278
Subedar Mir Akhmad 305
Subedar Mir Fazal 300
Subedar Mir Fazal 302
Subedar Mir Most 535
Subedar Mirza Fuzal Beg 151
Subedar Mirza Khan 296
Subedar Misri Khan 410
Subedar Moghal Baz 406

Index

Subedar Mohabbat Khan 322
Subedar Mohammad 242
Subedar Mohammad Abbas 239
Subedar Mohammad Abdul 498
Subedar Mohammad Abdul Aziz 285
Subedar Mohammad Afsar 373
Subedar Mohammad Afsar Khan 395
Subedar Mohammad Afzal 183
Subedar Mohammad Alam 197
Subedar Mohammad Ali 227
Subedar Mohammad Anwar 446
Subedar Mohammad Arbi 187
Subedar Mohammad Atta 255
Subedar Mohammad Azad 341
Subedar Mohammad Aziz 313
Subedar Mohammad Din 494
Subedar Mohammad Din 533
Subedar Mohammad Gul 255
Subedar Mohammad Hassan 305
Subedar Mohammad Hassan 275
Subedar Mohammad Hayat 494
Subedar Mohammad Hayat 495
Subedar Mohammad Ismail 289
Subedar Mohammad Khan 205
Subedar Mohammad Khan 279
Subedar Mohammad Khan 285
Subedar Mohammad Khan 286
Subedar Mohammad Khan 315
Subedar Mohammad Khan 358
Subedar Mohammad Khan 438
Subedar Mohammad Khan 495
Subedar Mohammad Qasim Khan 396
Subedar Mohammad Raheem Khan 167
Subedar Mohammad Razak 416
Subedar Mohammad Sardar 439
Subedar Mohammad Shah 152
Subedar Mohammad Sherif 314
Subedar Mohammad Yaqub 323
Subedar Mohammad Yusaf 380
Subedar Mohammad Yusuf 255

Index

Subedar Mohammad Yusuf 313
Subedar Mohammad Zaman 450
Subedar Mohammad Zaman 459
Subedar Mohd. Baksh 238
Subedar Moossum Allee 15
Subedar Muhammad Israel Khan 75
Subedar Mukurrum Khan 156
Subedar Musa Khan 223
Subedar Musahib Khan 403
Subedar Mushrif Khan 396
Subedar Mustafa Khan 238
Subedar Muzaffar Ahmed 307
Subedar Muzaffar Khan 494
Subedar Muzarab Shah 280
Subedar Najib Ullah Khan 199
Subedar Nathe Khan 273
Subedar Nawab Khan 308
Subedar Nawab Khan 315
Subedar Naz Mohammad 255
Subedar Nazir Khan 536
Subedar Neamut Allie 149
Subedar Nek Amal 202
Subedar Nek Mohammad 314
Subedar Nishan Ali 533
Subedar Noor Mohammad 309
Subedar Now Shere 298
Subedar Nur Akhmed 316
Subedar Nur Khan 252
Subedar Nur Mohammad 314
Subedar Nuzzur Khan 172
Subedar Peer Buccus Khan 155
Subedar Peer Buksh 151
Subedar Peer Bux 153
Subedar Peer Khan 133
Subedar Pehlwan Khan 427
Subedar Pyand Khan 154
Subedar Qalbi Ali 115
Subedar Qudrat Shah 323
Subedar Rahim Baksh 292
Subedar Rahim Khan 189

Index

Subedar Raj Talab 284
Subedar Raj Wali Khan 291
Subedar Raj Wali Khan 401
Subedar Ramzan Khan 494
Subedar Raza Mohammad 313
Subedar Rehmat Khan 252
Subedar Rehmat Zaman 303
Subedar Sabdal Khan 388
Subedar Sada Din 238
Subedar Sadar Din 533
Subedar Safdar Ali 457
Subedar Saghar Khan 385
Subedar Sahib Gul 281
Subedar Sahib-i-Haq 228
Subedar Said Asghar 305
Subedar Said Baz 324
Subedar Saidam Shah 272
Subedar Saif Ali   494
Subedar Saiyed Abdul Ghafur 533
Subedar Sallah Mohammad 295
Subedar Sarbuland 184
Subedar Sardar Khan 238
Subedar Sardar Khan 238
Subedar Sardar Khan 278
Subedar Sardar Khan 304
Subedar Sarfaraz 449
Subedar Sarfaraz Khan 215
Subedar Sarfraz Khan 249
Subedar Sayed Razak 293
Subedar Sayyid Ali 282
Subedar Secunder Khan 155
Subedar Sew Churrun Misser 153
Subedar Seweblurn Misser 169
Subedar Shaadat 322
Subedar Shah Khan 322
Subedar Shahi Beg 451
Subedar Shaick Goolam Ghose 156
Subedar Shaick Ibrahim 166
Subedar Shaik Ali 161
Subedar Shaik Amanut 146

Index

Subedar Shaik Baker Ally 135
Subedar Shaik Daood 146
Subedar Shaik Homed 133
Subedar Shaik Panchcouree 146
Subedar Shaik Sillar 134
Subedar Shaikh Abdulla 355
Subedar Shaikh Mohammad 324
Subedar Shaikh Yasin 293
Subedar Sher Afzal 297
Subedar Sher Afzal 357
Subedar Sher Baz 181
Subedar Sher Baz 273
Subedar Sher Gul 281
Subedar Sher Khan 149
Subedar Sher Khan 290
Subedar Sher Khan 315
Subedar Sher Mohammad 470
Subedar Sher Mohammad Khan 192
Subedar Sher Mohammad Khan 275
Subedar Sher Zaman Khan 286
Subedar Shere 156
Subedar Shumush Khan 152
Subedar Soojub Khan 162
Subedar Soojut Khan 161
Subedar Sowar Khan 245
Subedar Sudderooddeen 167
Subedar Sultan 238
Subedar Sultan Ahmed Bahadur 467
Subedar Sultan Ali 424
Subedar Sultan Ali 425
Subedar Sultan Khan 298
Subedar Sultan Mohammad 414
Subedar Syed Mohammad Shah 533
Subedar Syed Muhammad Shah 115
Subedar Syud Mohammad Khan 167
Subedar Taj Mohammad 415
Subedar Taza Gul 321
Subedar Tika Khan 227
Subedar Tor Khan 304
Subedar Tor Khan 448

Index

Subedar Turra Baz 233
Subedar Umar Khan 238
Subedar Umar Khan 296
Subedar Usman Ghani 390
Subedar Wahid Ali Khan 185
Subedar Walayat Khan 240
Subedar Walayat Khan 378
Subedar Walayat Khan 494
Subedar Wali Dad 366
Subedar Wali Mohammad 292
Subedar Wulayat Shah 323
Subedar Yakub Khan 495
Subedar Yar Mohammad 439
Subedar Zaffar Khan 303
Subedar Zaman Khan 193
Subedar Zaman Khan 201
Subedar Zaman Khan 357
Subedar Zaman Shah 220
Subedar Zargun Shah 283
Subedar Zergun Khan 205
Subedar Zulaf Din 384
Subedar Zulfikar Ali 306
Subedar Zulfikar Ali 498
Subedar Zurreef Khan 153
Subedar-Major Farman Ali 354
Subedar-Major Haider Rehman Khan 447
Sub-Inspector Mohi-ud-Din Ghulam 496
Sudedar Feroz Khan 295
Sudedar Gul Khan 305
Suhail Hameed 532
Sweeper Mehr Din 317
Tashkent 5
The Jehangir Baronetcy 514
Trooper Abdool Razak Khan 166
Trooper Abdul Kurreem Khan 162
Trooper Ahmed Khan 125
Trooper Ali Sher Khan 132
Trooper Alif Khan 141
Trooper Alla Dawd Khan 132
Trooper Allie Khan 165

Index

Trooper Alluf Khan 168
Trooper Aman Khan 137
Trooper Ameer Khan 168
Trooper Bhurmadeen 136
Trooper Budroodeen Khan 162
Trooper Eman Ali Khan 132
Trooper Fyzoollah Khan 168
Trooper Fyzullah Khan 136
Trooper Ghassy Khan 137
Trooper Goolam Gouse Khan 168
Trooper Goolam Rasool 136
Trooper Hussun Khan 168
Trooper Inayat Ali Beg 168
Trooper Jaffer Ali Beg 162
Trooper Jaffer Khan 162
Trooper Lalloo Khan 162
Trooper Meer Ahsan Ali 132
Trooper Meer Hossain Ali 168
Trooper Mehboob Khan 132
Trooper Mohammad Akbar 146
Trooper Mohammad Alli 146
Trooper Mohammad Khan 132
Trooper Mohammad Khan 162
Trooper Mohammad Uzgur 168
Trooper Mukarram Khan 162
Trooper Mytab Khan 162
Trooper Noor Khan 162
Trooper Nubbee Buksh 152
Trooper Nujmodeen Khan 168
Trooper Nussoor Ally 136
Trooper Nutteh Khan 162
Trooper Nutteh Khan 162
Trooper Ruza Beg 168
Trooper Sadoola Khan 162
Trooper Sahadut Ally 168
Trooper Salar Buksh Khan 168
Trooper Shabaz Khan 148
Trooper Shaick Kubeerodeen 162
Trooper Shaick Meeran 162
Trooper Shaick Omar 162

Index

Trooper Shaik Hyat Mahmod 126
Trooper Sheik Chand 132
Trooper Sheik Kurramut Khan 168
Trooper Sheik Mohammad Ali 168
Trooper Sheikh Goolam Nubbi 162
Trooper Sheikh Mohammad 162
Trooper Shere Ali 162
Trooper Suadut Khan 162
Trooper Syud Osman 162
Trooper Ullee Khan 152
Trooper Ullee Khan 152
Trooper Usman Khan 137
Trooper Wherwan Khan 126
Trumpeter Abdul Majid Khan 256
Trumpeter Abdul Sattan Khan 266
Trumpeter Azim Khan 152
Trumpeter Kaim Din 258
Trumpeter Mahub Ally 128
Trumpeter Meah Khan 160
Trumpeter Meer Yad Ally 128
Trumpeter Murad Ali 263
Trumpeter Shah Alum 173
Vice-Admiral Afzal Akram Rahman Khan 62
Vice-Admiral Haji Mohammad Siddiq Choudri 489
Vice-Admiral Syed Mohammad Ahsan 343
Ward Orderly Shahbaz Khan 498
Wing Commander Anwar Shamim 82
Wing Commander Hakimullah 105
Wing Commander M A Sikandar 83
Wing Commander M. G. Tawab 82
Wing Commander Mervyn L Middlecoat 108
Wing Commander Muhammad Ahmed 108
Wing Commander Nazir Latif 83
Wing Commander Salahuddin Zahid Butt 83
Woodie Major Munsabdar Khan 149
Woodie Major Nasrut Jung Khan 168
Woodie-Major Shaik Amir Ali 177
Woody-Major Meer Heidat Ali 138

The Author

Narindar Singh Dhesi was born in 1940 at Eldoret in Kenya, where his father had migrated from the Punjab. He moved to England in 1957 and joined the British Army. After leaving the armed forces in 1964, he worked in the building and construction industry. He is married with four children and living in retirement at Southend on Sea, England. He is the author of seven books on Sikh Soldier, exploring the Sikh Military Traditions. During his research he came cross of the colossal number of gallantry awards made to the Muslim Soldier and decided to record their stories.

The books by Mr. Dhesi are available from the Naval and Military Press. The author can be contacted on: narindardhesi@yahoo.co.uk

www.ingramcontent.com/pod-product-compliance
Lightning Source LLC
Chambersburg PA
CBHW071352300426
44114CB00016B/2034